Human-Centered Approaches to AI-Enhanced English Language Learning and Teaching

Yasir Mohammed Al-Yafaei
https://orcid.org/0009-0009-6485-8659
University of Technology and Applied Sciences, Salalah, Oman

Nayef J. Jomaa
https://orcid.org/0000-0001-8952-5812
University of Technology and Applied Sciences, Salalah, Oman

Rais Ahmed Attamimi
University of Technology and Applied Sciences, Salalah, Oman

IGI Global
Scientific Publishing
Publishing Tomorrow's Research Today

Vice President of Editorial Melissa Wagner
Director of Acquisitions Mikaela Felty
Director of Book Development Jocelynn Hessler
Production Manager Mike Brehm
Cover Design Jose Rosado

Published in the United States of America by
IGI Global Scientific Publishing
701 East Chocolate Avenue
Hershey, PA, 17033, USA
Tel: 717-533-8845 | Fax: 717-533-7115
Website: https://www.igi-global.com E-mail: cust@igi-global.com

Library of Congress Cataloging-in-Publication Data

Names: Al-Yafaei, Yasir Mohammed, 1983- editor http://id.loc.gov/rwo/agents/n2025021240 | Jomaa, Nayef, 1979- editor http://id.loc.gov/rwo/agents/n2024061313 | Attamimi, Rais Ahmed, 1978- editor http://id.loc.gov/rwo/agents/n2025021241
Title: Human-centered approaches to AI-enhanced English language learning and teaching / edited by Yasir Mohammed Al-Yafaei, Nayef Jomaa, Rais Ahmed Attamimi.
Description: Hershey, PA : IGI Global Scientific Publishing, 2026. | Includes bibliographical references and index. | Summary: "This book aims to provide a comprehensive, interdisciplinary look at how AI technologies can be ethically and effectively embedded in English language education"-- Provided by publisher.
Identifiers: LCCN 2025019801 (print) | LCCN 2025019802 (ebook) | ISBN 9798337335612 hardcover | ISBN 9798337335629 paperback | ISBN 9798337335636 ebook
Subjects: LCSH: English language--Computer-assisted instruction for foreign speakers http://id.loc.gov/authorities/subjects/sh86007726 | Artificial intelligence--Educational applications http://id.loc.gov/authorities/subjects/sh87006783 | LCGFT: Essays http://id.loc.gov/authorities/genreForms/gf2014026094
Classification: LCC PE1128.3 .H86 2025 (print) | LCC PE1128.3 (ebook) | DDC 428.0078/563--dc23/eng/20250614
LC record available at https://lccn.loc.gov/2025019801
LC ebook record available at https://lccn.loc.gov/2025019802
British Cataloguing in Publication Data
A Cataloguing in Publication record for this book is available from the British Library.

Table of Contents

Detailed Table of Contents

This chapter explores human-centered strategies for professional development that empower educators in the era of AI-driven technologies. Grounded in adult learning theory and TPACK framework, the chapter proposes a multi-layered approach that includes several AI-powered professional development (PD) strategies for training and skills development, ongoing support and coaching, and personalized learning and reflection. Additionally, this chapter addresses ethical and pedagogical issues and discusses challenges related to infrastructure, and teacher apprehension offering evidence-based recommendations for embedding AI literacy into teacher PD programs and ensuring equitable access to AI tools and professional learning opportunities. It concludes with the recommendations for reshaping teacher PD programs to be contextually grounded, technologically informed and learner-centered. This chapter provides practical guidance for designing sustainable PD programs that enhance teaching and learning while preserving pedagogical effectiveness and equity in an AI-mediated educational landscape.

This study examines the effect of using Artificial Intelligence (AI) tools and applications on both, learning English and developing critical thinking skills among EFL Omani students. A quantitative research was employed, utilizing a developed questionnaire with items rated on a five-point Likert scale. The research instrument included the use of AI in English language learning and its influence on students' critical thinking development. Data were collected from 50 EFL university students in Oman, selected through random sampling, and analyzed using descriptive and inferential statistics. The results showed that students generally perceived AI as a valuable educational aid that enhances their understanding of English texts, boosts confidence in completing assignments, and supports idea generation in writing. As for critical thinking, the respondents moderately agreed that AI encourages reflection, evaluation, and awareness of information accuracy, although some expressed concerns about overreliance on AI tools. However, gender comparisons revealed no significant differences.

The traditional educational paradigm is being transformed through Artificial intelligence in education. One of the most important use cases for artificial intelligence is around administrative automation. As time is a significant issue, educators can focus on effective pedagogy, including a general message: AI-based methods for scheduling, messaging, attendance, and grade management. Through historical studies, case studies, and interviews with educators and administrators, we can explore the benefits and drawbacks of AI in administration. Such research encompasses investigating problems of AI bias, data protection, and AI best practices for educating students. This research also examines the ethical dimensions of the challenges. Used wisely, this approach can not only address the problem of teacher fatigue but also boost productivity and improve the quality of teaching, according to a new study.

This chapter explores the transformative role of Artificial Intelligence (AI), particularly generative AI, in English language education. It highlights how AI enables the development of personalized, adaptive, and scalable learning materials, including reading passages, grammar exercises, vocabulary lists, and multimedia resources. By aligning content with learner goals and interests, AI fosters engagement, while interactive tools such as simulations, gamified activities, and conversational chatbots enhance motivation and retention. The chapter also examines key challenges, including accuracy, cultural bias, data privacy, and balancing personalization with standardized curricula. It concludes by emphasizing the need for responsible, ethical, and inclusive adoption, while anticipating future advancements such as multimodal AI, real-time adaptive feedback, and collaborative human-AI teaching models.

Artificial Intelligence (AI) is revolutionizing education through personalized learning, reducing administrative burdens and increasing student engagement. In this chapter, we will describe the key technologies that are the basis of AI in education, the ethical issues relating to data privacy, algorithmic fairness, and teachers' shifting role. Also discussed are the emergence of adaptive learning technologies, learning analytics, and systems powered by AI, which are providing a new approach to pedagogy and ways of doing things in educational institutions. The chapter will examine the developments in generative AI, affective computing, and cooperative human-AI feedback systems. Although presented theoretically, we will draw on global examples and case studies to present a critical examination of how AI is cultivating inclusive, flexible and innovative learning environments whilst responding to challenges of access and equity across the globe.

This chapter explores the innovative application of multi-agent artificial intelligence systems for enhancing English language teaching and learning. Author presents an architecture composed of specialized AI agents performing distinct educational roles such as consulting, lecturing, methodology development, career advising, psychological support, and technical assistance. The system capitalizes on advanced large language models (LLMs) to create personalized, interactive, and adaptive learning experiences, seamlessly integrating into traditional educational structures while also offering flexibility and scalability. Furthermore, the chapter investigates immersive virtual environments powered by AI, proposing metrics to systematically evaluate their coherence, immersion, novelty, and interactivity. These metrics provide a foundation for future advancements in digital language education, suggesting new avenues for individualized learning trajectories and enhanced learner engagement within AI-driven environments.

This chapter examines Ananse stories as a means by which the Akan people preserve language and cultural identity, resisting colonial legacies, globalization, and linguistic homogenization. These stories go beyond entertainment, serving as vessels of memory, resistance, and survival, embedding moral philosophy, historical awareness, and indigenous knowledge. Drawing on postcolonial theory and oral literature studies, it shows how Anansesɛm conveys linguistic structures, reinforces communal values, and affirms Akan identity. Through close readings, it demonstrates how storytelling sustains cultural continuity and resists erasure of local knowledge. The chapter calls for integrating Anansesɛm into education, digital media, and revitalization programs to revalorize the Akan language and worldview, promoting linguistic diversity and cultural sovereignty in Ghana and beyond. a

exposition provides insights into language teachers and researchers, instructional designers, and educational technologists to integrate AI into language learning environments.

The chapter examines the interface of AI and neurodiversity as it relates to the learning of English with the inclusive design of adaptive pathways for the likes of persons with dyslexia, ADHD, and autism spectrum disorders. Despite the AI transformation of educational spheres, in the wake of unmet opportunities, there is a need to explore how these technologies can bridge the gap between accessing unique cognitive profiles and the learning needs of neurodivergent students. This chapter frames its argument based on the neurodiversity paradigm, which discards weaknesses-understanding and deserves to be replaced by strength-appreciating views of human differences. It concludes by stating evidence-based design principles for AI tools that promote the autonomy, acceptance, and normalisation of the experience of neurodivergent language learners. Through participatory design, ethical AI application, and hybrid human-AI collaboration, this chapter discusses how technology might work toward developing more inclusive educational responses.

The integration of Artificial Intelligence (AI) into English language learning and teaching has created transformative opportunities to address linguistic and cultural diversity in educational settings. This chapter explores cross-cultural and inclusive strategies that leverage AI technologies to enhance English language acquisition, especially in multilingual and multicultural contexts. By focusing on human-centered design principles, the chapter examines how AI-powered tools—such as adaptive learning platforms, conversational agents, and automated feedback systems—can foster equitable learning environments that respect diverse cultural backgrounds, linguistic practices, and individual learner needs. Central to the discussion is the concept of cultural inclusivity, which recognizes the importance of embedding culturally responsive pedagogy into AI-driven language education. The chapter highlights examples of AI applications that incorporate diverse content, accommodate varying learning styles, and promote intercultural competence.

As artificial intelligence (AI) increasingly integrates into English Language Teaching (ELT) in Southeast Asia, it changes pedagogic ethics, teacher agency, and cultural equity. This chapter examines the ethical and epistemic dimensions of AI-driven tools, especially in marginalized areas, like Indigenous Peoples' (IP) communities, madrasah, and rural Indonesian schools. Based on Kant's, Rawls', Gilligan's, and Foucault's frameworks, it uncovers the ways in which hegemonic AI tools tend to standardize language and push localized pedagogical relations to the margin. Categorized into core themes, the narratives from the Southeast Asian teachers reveal algorithmic bias and the moral and emotional contradictions in AI adoption, most notably the loss of emotional labor and the marginalization of indigenous knowledge systems. The research makes a case for an ethical shift and appeals to a humanizing approach that re-centers teacher agency, protects learners, and sustains plural Southeast Asian values to revolutionize ELT-AI as an ethical praxis grounded on care, justice, and empowerment.

This chapter explores the transformative potential of Artificial Intelligence (AI) in enhancing the motivation, engagement, and autonomy of English language learners (ELLs). In an era where personalized learning and learner-centered approaches are paramount, AI offers dynamic tools and platforms that adapt to individual needs, learning styles, and pace. The chapter examines how AI-powered applications, such as intelligent tutoring systems, language learning apps, and chatbots, foster interactive and immersive learning environments. These technologies not only make learning

Preface

As editors of *Human-Centered Approaches to AI-Enhanced English Language Learning and Teaching*, we are pleased to introduce a volume that reflects both the tremendous promise and the profound responsibility inherent in today's rapidly evolving technological landscape. The swift advance of artificial intelligence is transforming how educators and institutions approach language teaching, offering new pathways for personalizing instruction, enriching assessment, and expanding access to high-quality learning experiences. At the same time, this transformation invites careful reflection on the pedagogical, ethical, and human dimensions that must guide the integration of AI into English language education.

In assembling this collection, we sought contributions that illuminate not only what AI can do, but what it *should* do to meaningfully support learners and teachers. The chapters that follow examine personalized learning platforms, adaptive assessments, intelligent tutoring systems, and a range of emerging tools. Yet they also foreground the enduring importance of empathy, cultural sensitivity, creativity, and critical thinking—human qualities that remain at the heart of impactful teaching and learning. Together, these insights demonstrate how AI, when thoughtfully designed and responsibly implemented, can uphold and even amplify the human elements that define successful language education.

This book offers a comprehensive, interdisciplinary perspective on embedding AI technologies ethically and effectively in English language teaching. Drawing on empirical research, theoretical models, and practice-based case studies, our contributors explore the values, experiences, and well-being of learners as central considerations in AI-enhanced pedagogy. They examine the sociocultural contexts in which AI tools operate and highlight the importance of aligning technological capability with genuine educational benefit. Our aim is to bridge the gap between innovation and classroom reality, ensuring that AI serves as a powerful tool—not a replacement—for the relational, reflective work of educators.

We envision this volume as a resource for a wide and diverse audience. English language teachers, curriculum designers, educational technologists, and researchers will find new insights into AI's potential to transform instructional practice. Policy makers and administrators charged with technology adoption will encounter frameworks and evidence that can help shape informed and equitable strategies. Developers and designers of educational technologies will gain a deeper appreciation of the pedagogical and ethical principles essential to creating effective AI-driven tools.

Ultimately, this book is a testament to the belief that technology should enrich, not eclipse, the human experience of learning. We hope the perspectives gathered here inspire thoughtful dialogue, responsible innovation, and human-centered action as we collectively navigate the future of AI in English language education.

ORGANIZATION OF THE BOOK

Chapter 1 examines how educators can be meaningfully empowered in an AI-driven era through human-centered professional development. Drawing on adult learning theory and the TPACK framework, the chapter outlines a multi-layered approach that integrates AI-powered training, ongoing coaching, and personalized reflection. The authors address essential ethical and pedagogical considerations—from infrastructure limitations to teacher apprehension—and offer evidence-based recommendations for embedding AI literacy into PD programs. Ultimately, the chapter provides a practical roadmap for designing sustainable, equitable, and contextually grounded professional learning systems that preserve pedagogical integrity while preparing teachers for an AI-mediated educational landscape.

Chapter 2 investigates how AI tools influence both English language learning and the development of critical thinking skills among EFL university students in Oman. Through quantitative analysis of students' perceptions, the study reveals that learners view AI as a valuable aid for improving comprehension, generating ideas, and boosting confidence with academic tasks. While the findings show moderate agreement that AI supports reflection and evaluation, they also highlight concerns around overreliance. Notably, gender differences were insignificant. As editors, we see this chapter offering valuable empirical insights into how students themselves interpret the affordances and limits of AI-supported learning.

Chapter 3 turns to the transformative role of AI in reducing administrative burdens, allowing teachers to reclaim valuable time for pedagogy. Drawing on historical analyses, case studies, and practitioner interviews, the chapter identifies AI's capacity to automate scheduling, messaging, attendance, and grading. At the same time, it grapples with concerns related to data protection, bias, and the ethics of automation. The authors illuminate how responsible implementation can combat teacher fatigue and elevate instructional quality, reinforcing the idea that administrative efficiency must be balanced with safeguarding human judgment and student well-being.

Chapter 4 explores generative AI's capacity to reshape English language learning resources through personalization, adaptability, and scalability. The chapter highlights how AI-generated reading passages, vocabulary lists, and interactive tools such as chatbots and gamified activities can enhance engagement and motivation. It also critically assesses challenges around accuracy, cultural representation, and maintaining alignment with curricular goals. Concluding with a call for ethical and inclusive innovation, the authors anticipate a future in which multimodal AI and real-time feedback systems support deeper human-AI collaboration in content creation.

Chapter 5 offers a broad examination of the core technologies driving AI in education and their impact on teaching, learning, and institutional practices. Emphasizing adaptive learning systems, learning analytics, and affective computing, the chapter situates these tools within ongoing debates about data privacy, teachers' roles, and algorithmic fairness. Through global examples, it provides a critical yet forward-looking assessment of how AI can foster more inclusive and flexible learning environments, provided that equity, access, and ethical safeguards remain central.

Chapter 6 introduces a multi-agent AI environment designed to enrich English language teaching through specialized, collaborative AI roles—from consulting and lecturing to psychological support and technical assistance. Leveraging advances in large language models, the system creates highly adaptive, interactive learning experiences that can integrate seamlessly into existing educational structures. The chapter also proposes rigorous metrics for evaluating immersive virtual environments, opening new pathways for personalized learning trajectories and deeper engagement in AI-supported contexts.

Chapter 7 centers the cultural and linguistic significance of Anansesɛm—the traditional Akan stories—as powerful vessels of identity, resistance, and heritage preservation. Through postcolonial and oral literature frameworks, the chapter illustrates how these narratives sustain linguistic structures, communal values, and indigenous knowledge systems in the face of globalization and linguistic homogenization. The authors advocate for weaving Anansesɛm into education and digital media to support language revitalization and cultural sovereignty, reminding readers of the vital human and cultural dimensions often absent from AI discourses.

Chapter 8 presents the AI-Enhanced Adaptive Multimodal Language Learning System (AI-AMLLS), an advanced framework designed to overcome limitations in mainstream AI language tools. Integrating reinforcement learning, deep learning, audio analytics, gesture recognition, and context-aware translation, the system offers dynamic difficulty adjustment, instant feedback, and multimodal interaction. The chapter demonstrates how AI-AMLLS enhances accessibility, reduces bias, and promotes richer engagement, offering a model for inclusive, high-performing language learning ecosystems.

Chapter 9 synthesizes contemporary evidence on AI's ability to enhance core language skills—including listening, speaking, pronunciation, reading, writing, grammar, and vocabulary. By analyzing emerging tools such as conversational AI and automated pronunciation assessment, alongside recent meta-analyses, the chapter shows consistent medium-to-large effect sizes favoring AI-enhanced learning over traditional approaches. As editors, we recognize this chapter as an essential resource for educators and researchers seeking evidence-based guidance on integrating AI into comprehensive skill development.

Chapter 10 addresses the urgent need to design AI tools that support neurodivergent learners, including individuals with dyslexia, ADHD, and autism. Framed by the neurodiversity paradigm, the chapter shifts from deficit-based views to strength-oriented approaches, emphasizing autonomy and dignity. Through participatory design and ethical AI implementation, the authors propose adaptive pathways capable of meeting diverse cognitive profiles. Their work offers a powerful vision for inclusive, human-centered AI that expands access and affirms neurodivergent identities.

Chapter 11 explores cross-cultural and inclusive strategies for AI integration in multilingual and multicultural English language classrooms. The chapter highlights how AI-powered tools can support equitable learning environments when grounded in culturally responsive pedagogy. Emphasizing diverse content, multiple learning styles, and intercultural competence, the authors demonstrate how AI can amplify linguistic diversity rather than homogenize it, reinforcing the book's broader call for human-centered and ethically aligned design.

Chapter 12 examines AI adoption in Southeast Asian English Language Teaching, foregrounding ethical tensions, cultural equity, and teacher agency. Through philosophical frameworks and narratives from educators in marginalized communities, the chapter reveals how standardized AI tools can unintentionally marginalize indigenous knowledge systems and emotional labor. Advocating for an ethical, justice-centered approach, the authors call for AI integration that honors care, plurality, and teacher empowerment. Their analysis powerfully situates AI as not merely a technological issue but a moral and cultural one.

Chapter 13 focuses on AI's potential to enhance learners' motivation, engagement, and autonomy. By analyzing intelligent tutoring systems, chatbots, and adaptive platforms, the chapter illustrates how AI can create more immersive, interactive, and self-directed learning experiences. The authors provide practical strategies to help educators harness these tools while maintaining pedagogical intentionality. Their contribution underscores the importance of empowering learners to take ownership of their journeys without diminishing the relational aspects of teaching.

Chapter 14 addresses the complex ethical and data privacy challenges that accompany AI-driven language learning environments. Highlighting issues such as algorithmic bias, surveillance, data ownership, and the digital divide, the chapter examines how AI systems collect and use students' data—often without transparency. The authors advocate for ethical algorithm design and robust protections to ensure fairness, accountability, and inclusiveness. This chapter reinforces a central theme of the book: innovation must be accompanied by vigilant safeguarding of learners' rights.

Chapter 15 further deepens the ethical conversation by proposing a framework that balances AI innovation with the protection of learners' autonomy, privacy, and fairness. Through the discussion of adaptive platforms and intelligent tutoring systems, the chapter emphasizes transparency and justice as guiding principles for ethical implementation. The authors call for continued research and more comprehensive frameworks to ensure responsible, learner-centered adoption, contributing a crucial lens on rights-based AI integration.

Chapter 16 concludes the volume with a chronological analysis of machine translation services over sixteen years, comparing early online translation tools with contemporary AI-driven systems such as DeepL. The study demonstrates substantial progress in linguistic and semantic accuracy, particularly in translating Arabic-English texts, while also noting that traditional online translators still lag behind more advanced AI systems in culturally bound and context-rich language tasks. This chapter offers an enlightening perspective on the evolution of AI translation and its implications for language learning and cross-cultural communication.

CONCLUSION

As editors, we close this volume with a deep appreciation for the diverse perspectives, rigorous scholarship, and forward-looking ideas contributed by our authors. Taken together, these chapters illuminate a central truth that underpins *Human-Centered Approaches to AI-Enhanced English Language Learning and Teaching*. That is, the future of AI in language education must be guided not by technological possibility alone, but by a steadfast commitment to human dignity, cultural richness, pedagogical wisdom, and ethical responsibility. The research presented throughout this book demonstrates that AI can enrich English language learning in transformative ways—supporting personalization, expanding access, enhancing engagement, and amplifying learners' strengths across a wide range of contexts. Yet these benefits can only be realized when teachers, learners, designers, and policymakers work collaboratively to ensure that AI tools are implemented equitably, transparently, and with deep respect for the diverse realities of global classrooms.

As AI becomes increasingly woven into the fabric of education, the questions we ask and the values we prioritize will shape its impact far more than the technologies themselves. The chapters in this collection invite us to reimagine language learning not as a domain overshadowed by automation, but as a space where human creativity, empathy, agency, and cultural identity remain essential. Whether examining teacher training, multimodal learning systems, ethical safeguards, neurodiversity, or indigenous knowledge, each contribution underscores the importance of keeping people—teachers, students, and communities—at the heart of AI integration.

We hope this book serves as both a resource and a catalyst: a source of practical insights for those seeking to navigate the evolving landscape of AI-enhanced education, and a call to action for all who believe that technological innovation must be aligned with humane and inclusive educational values. As we collectively chart the path forward, may we do so with curiosity, critical reflection, ethical clarity, and a shared commitment to building learning environments where AI expands possibility while honoring the humanity that defines and enriches language itself.

Chapter 1
Empowering Educators for the AI Era:
Strategies for Teacher Training and Professional Development

Sheikha Ali Salim Al-Buraiki
https://orcid.org/0000-0002-9509-3822
Sohar University, Oman

ABSTRACT

This chapter explores human-centered strategies for professional development that empower educators in the era of AI-driven technologies. Grounded in adult learning theory and TPACK framework, the chapter proposes a multi-layered approach that includes several AI-powered professional development (PD) strategies for training and skills development, ongoing support and coaching, and personalized learning and reflection. Additionally, this chapter addresses ethical and pedagogical issues and discusses challenges related to infrastructure, and teacher apprehension offering evidence-based recommendations for embedding AI literacy into teacher PD programs and ensuring equitable access to AI tools and professional learning opportunities. It concludes with the recommendations for reshaping teacher PD programs to be contextually grounded, technologically informed and learner-centered. This chapter provides practical guidance for designing sustainable PD programs that enhance teaching and learning while preserving pedagogical effectiveness and equity in an AI-mediated educational landscape.

DOI: 10.4018/979-8-3373-3561-2.ch001

1. INTRODUCTION

The integration of technology in teaching and learning has gained growing popularity among educators, researchers, and policymakers worldwide (Al-Buraiki & Al-Ruheili, 2025; Chien, 2016). The emergence of Artificial Intelligence (AI) is making significant and transformative shifts in all domains of life including education. AI-empowered technologies enhance teaching and learning experience offering adaptive, personalized, and data-driven learning experiences (Al-Buraiki & Al-Ruheili, 2025). The integration of AI-powered technologies has reshaped the educational landscape by presenting various benefits for the students, educators and the institutions (Al-Buraiki & Al-Ruheili, 2025; Holmes et al., 2022). For instance, adaptive learning platforms powered by AI technology can be tailored to individual students' needs, smart tutoring systems offering learners with real-time feedback, and AI-driven tools that support educators by facilitating the analysis of large amounts of students' related data which enables educators to glean insightful information about students' progress and performance, learning trends and effectiveness of instructional methods (Al-Buraiki & Al-Ruheili, 2025; Holmes et al., 2022).

Globally, AI-technologies witness rapid integration into all educational systems which is reflected in replacing old teaching practices with more advanced and recent ones. This shit has created both opportunities and challenges for the educators. AI-powered tools utilized in education such as intelligent tutoring systems, automated assessment platforms, predictive analytics and adaptive learning environments are becoming prevalent and thus they are shifting the teachers' role from content delivery to facilitation, mentoring and ethical management (Al-Buraiki & Al-Ruheili, 2025; Holmes et al., 2022). Subsequently, it is necessary that teachers obtain comprehensive training to ensure that they are not only capable of using AI tools but also are critically aware of their ethical and pedagogical implications.

Interestingly, AI can be used as a medium for professional development (PD) as well as a subject of PD. AI-supported PD platforms allow for real-time feedback, adaptive learning pathways and simulation-based training that replicates the intricacies of the classroom. Some AI-powered tools like voice journaling systems, microlearning platforms and scenario-based simulations offer flexible and customized teacher training (Tammets & Ley, 2023). Although these tools are being explored, research should further investigate their effectiveness and prevalence of use. These tools generate just-in-time job-embedded learning opportunities that meet adult learning principles while also reducing logistical barriers to training.

Teachers may face difficulties implementing AI-tools effectively without offering them proper training. Some aspects of applying AI technologies such as interpreting AI-generated data for formative assessment and how to reduce algorithmic bias require specific knowledge and skills. Therefore, teacher preparation programs must involve digital literacy, ethical considerations of AI use and effective pedagogical strategies for incorporating AI-technologies meaningfully into classroom instruction (Holmes et al., 2022; Luckin et al., 2022). Investing in professional development to build educators' capacity is fundamental to harnessing the full potential of AI-powered technologies in educational contexts while safeguarding human-centered approaches to teaching and learning (UNESCO, 2023).

Educational training programs should also focus on teachers' roles as critical change agents who can continuously evaluate the potential, affordances, challenges and limitations of AI-powered tools. This can include fostering reflective practices, promoting human-AI collaboration and maintaining and sustaining professional autonomy (Fakhar, et al., 2024; Selwyn, 2022). The present book chapter is a comprehensive literature review of AI-powered teachers' professional development strategies and relevant ethical considerations and recommendations.

2. THEORETICAL FRAMEWORK

In the context of AI-enhanced education, effective professional development programs must be grounded in well-established theoretical foundations (Illeris & Ryan, 2020). Incorporating AI-powered technology into teacher training programs is a transformative process that reshapes assessment models, professional responsibilities, etc. Hence, it becomes imperative to ensure that teacher training initiatives are not only technologically advanced but also pedagogically sound and theoretically informed. The present literature review on AI-powered professional development is grounded on the theoretical basis of adult learning theory and TPACK framework.

2.1 Adult Learning Theory

Adult learning theory is often associated with Malcolm Knowles' concept of andragogy. This theory is viewed as a foundational underpinning to understand and shape effective practices in adult education and professional development programs. According to Knowles (1980), adult learners are recognized by these key assumptions: being self-directed, bringing prior experiences that shape their learning, being motivated by internal factors and preferring relevant and problem-solving type of learning. These assumptions remain central to contemporary frameworks of adult education (Knowles et al., 2015). This theory is highly relevant to professional development because it shows how important it is for teachers to develop autonomy and problem-centered instruction, which are both essential for pre-and in-service teachers to stay engaged.

A key principle of adult learning theory is that adults are self-directed learners who cherish independence and autonomy in their learning experiences. Self-directed learning promotes learner-centeredness moving away from teacher-centered learning. Unlike younger learners, adults are more inclined to claim responsibility for their learning, take initiate and are aware of their learning needs. They seek out resources and strategies that support their goals. In the field of professional development, this means that teachers benefit from having authority over the pace, content and structure of their learning (Merriam, & Baumgartner, 2020). Thus, education should be tailored to the students' needs and interests rather than the other way around (Merriam & Bierema, 2018). Self-directed learning plays a crucial role in AI-supported teacher training programs, as personalized learning pathways and adaptive technologies enable educators to establish their personal goals and critically navigate material based on their specific needs and preferences (Al-Zyoud, 2020). When granted such autonomy, adult learners exhibit increased engagement, motivation and knowledge retention.

In any learning environment, adult learners bring a wealth of previous experiences which serve as the foundation for the new learning situations. Via these experiences, adults demonstrate their capacities to interpret, internalize and apply new knowledge (Knowles et al., 2015). In the context of AI-enhanced PD, it becomes fundamental to acknowledge teachers' existing pedagogical conceptualizations and classroom practices. PD programs render effective when they build on educators' existing knowledge and enable critical reflections with the new AI-powered approaches (Tammets & Ley, 2023). This experiential foundation can also be utilized in other learning settings such as collaborative learning and peer discussions that allow teachers to contextualize AI technologies within well-known instructional scenarios (Romero, 2024).

Proven by research, adults are internally motivated learners, which is considered a key principle of adult learning theory. Even though external factors like earning certification, getting salary increases play an important role in adults professional life, adults are more likely to be driven by intrinsic factors such as professional identity, a personal desire to improve their practices and overall personal development (Merriam & Baumgartner, 2020). Teachers' motivation is often linked to the impact they have on their students. Therefore, AI-supported professional development programs that explicitly demonstrate how using AI tools can benefit students' learning are likely to be more desirable (Demir & Özdemir, 2025). When professional development aligns with teachers' values and creates a sense of purpose, it is more likely to result in long-term engagement and implementation.

Instead of engaging with abstract theories that are disconnected from their professional realities, adults prefer to apply what they learn to real-world problems. This is because adults typically tend to prefer learning, which is relevant, practical and based on problem-solving strategy (Knowles et al., 2015). This notion is especially relevant to AI-enhanced PD because success of the training is contingent on whether teachers see a clear link between the new technologies and the challenges they encounter in their real classrooms (Holmes et al., 2022). For instance, scenario-based simulations that mimic typical instructional classroom issues or AI tools that offer instantaneous suggestions for classroom problematic situations (like automated formative assessment) are more likely to be adopted. Contextual relevance and real-world applications enable adult learners to make meaningful connections and help them maintain their inner motivation to learn. Thus, educators' learning experiences can be enhanced by aligning AI use with andragogical principles of adult learning theory.

2.2 TPACK Framework

The TPACK framework includes three intersected bodies of knowledge: technological knowledge (TK), pedagogical knowledge (PK) and content knowledge (CK). TK refers to the teachers' abilities to handle an array of varied technologies for instructional purposes, PK represents teachers' technological competency to utilize specific teaching strategies to enhance students' learning, and CK relates to teachers' knowledge and skills of the subject matter. TPACK is a dynamic framework appropriate for identifying teachers' knowledge.

The primary function for this framework lies in using it for designing, implementing and evaluating curriculum and instruction with technology. This framework was first developed by Shulman (1986) which then was expanded by Mishra and Koehler (2006), where the element of technology was added. Koehler (2010) explained that TPACK framework highlights teachers' needs in relation to technology integration in the classroom. Through the TPACK framework, theoretical foundations are provided to describe whether a teacher is capable of designing and conducting technology-driven instruction. The framework also lists the kind of knowledge any teacher should possess in order to lead effective pedagogical practices in a technology-enhanced environment. TPACK supports the claim that professional development programs must move beyond discrete technology training and assist educators in forming dynamic and context-sensitive connections between pedagogy, AI tools and instructional content (Holmes et al., 2022).

Artificial intelligence (AI) is radically impacting educators' perspectives regarding the significant pedagogical contributions of AI-powered tools (Luckin & Cukurova, 2019; Xu, 2020) and continuously reshaping the implementation of instructional pedagogy (Luckin et al., 2022). Responding to this technological evolution requires teachers to adequately improve their pedagogical knowledge of how to utilize AI-based tools (Cavalcanti et al., 2021). Added to that, developing up-to-date knowledge about AI in education aid teachers in selecting appropriate AI-based tools for their classroom instruction (Edwards et al., 2018). Therefore, understanding the technological and pedagogical knowledge of the role of AI-based tools in education is vital to achieve successful integration (Mishra & Koehler, 2006; Ye et al., 2025) and in fostering learners' motivation and engagement (Wang et al., 2021). In other words, the technological, pedagogical and content knowledge (TPACK) framework will play an essential role in explaining the necessary knowledge for educators to effectively incorporate AI-supported tools in education (Celik, 2023).

3. AI-POWERED PROFESSIONAL DEVELOPMENT STRATEGIES

While teaching is the main task of any educator, continuous teacher professional development programs play foundational roles in the success of education because they prepare educators with the pedagogical and psychological knowledge necessary to handle the profession's everyday challenges (Mansfield et al., 2016). The integration of AI-technologies into education is redefining how students learn and how educators engage in professional development programs. Professional development must respond to the evolution caused by artificial intelligence and consider introducing training programs that will equip educators with the knowledge, skills and competencies to use AI-technologies effectively. There are various strategies for teacher development programs that are AI-supported. They include AI-enhanced workshops, AI-supported coaching, AI- powered online modules, AI-driven communities of practice, AI-enabled microlearning platforms, AI-based reflective journals, AI-supported virtual mentoring programs, AI-augmented collaborative design studios, AI-facilitated scenario-based simulations and AI-supported content curation for personalized PD Libraries. We can sort them into three main categories; AI tools for training and skills development, AI tools for ongoing training, support and coaching, and AI strategies for personalized learning and reflection. The first branch, AI tools for training and skill development, includes AI-enhanced workshops, AI-powered online modules, AI-facilitated scenario-based simulations and AI-augmented collaborative design studios. Under the second branch, AI for ongoing training, support and coaching, comes AI-supported coaching, AI-supported virtual mentoring programs and AI-driven communities of practice. The third branch, AI for personalized learning and reflection entails AI-supported content curation for personalized PD libraries, AI-based reflective journals and AI-enabled microlearning platforms. Figure 1 provides a visual representation of the AI-powered strategies for PD.

Figure 1. AI-powered strategies for teachers' professional development

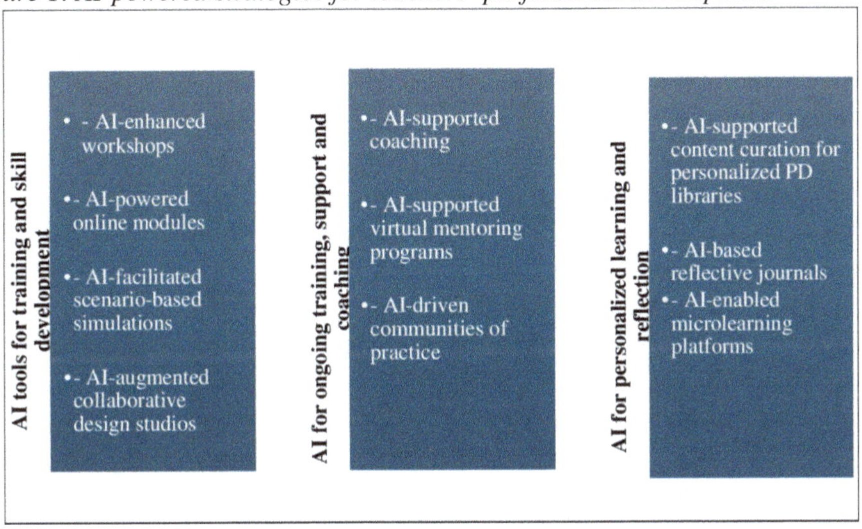

3.1 AI-Enhanced Workshops

Workshops remain a fundamental form of PD for teachers offering opportunities for collaborative learning, practical demonstrations, and reflective discussions. Traditional workshops often adopt a one-size fitting all approach deemphasizing the individual needs of the trainees who bring to the training their unique prior knowledge and diverse needs. As a result, traditional workshops are limited in their effectiveness and relevance for individual educators. Thus, integrating artificial intelligence (AI) into workshops transforms teachers' professional development programs into more adaptive, personalized experiences that align with adult learning principles of self-directedness, relevance, and experiential engagement (Holmes et al., 2022; Knowles et al., 2015). In a training program to improve the English skills of early career researchers in a Nigerian public university, Ugwu et al. (2025) compared the efficiency of an artificial intelligence training program and a human-led workshop. The findings demonstrated that the AI group significantly outperformed the human-led group on all the skills under examination. It was concluded that AL-immersive instruction can be more effective in teaching English as well as in promoting the advancement of the scholars' careers.

Technologies augmented with AI can be used to analyze pre-assessment data-such as teachers' knowledge gaps, preferred learning styles, and contextual classroom challenges- to tailor workshop content accordingly. They can stimulate classroom recurring scenarios for customized hands-on practice. For example, intelligent learning platforms can curate differentiated activities or resources based on each participant's profile. These enhancements to teachers' training programs will most likely promote relevance and engagement (Holmes et al., 2022).

Furthermore, AI-enhanced learning analytics can provide real-time feedback during workshops enabling trainers to adjust pacing, revisit unclear and misunderstood concepts and elevate discussions on topics of interest (Al-Buraiki & Al-Ruheili, 2025). This feature of responsiveness increases participants' engagement; relevance of learning and it also enhances mastery learning.

3.2 AI-Supported Coaching

Coaching is widely recognized as a powerful strategy and one of the most effective forms of professional development. It is a preferred form of providing ongoing support that aligns with adult learners' methods of training. However, there are some challenges associated with traditional coaching including cost, time and the availability of skilled mentors. AI-enhanced tools that support classroom observation, track students' performance, provide personalized feedback can make instructional coaching more accessible and effective. For instance, AI-powered technologies can use machine learning algorithms to analyze classroom audio or video recordings to identify patterns in teacher-student and student-student interactions, questioning strategies, or opportunities for student engagement (Luckin et al., 2022). Coaches can then receive targeted recommendations on which aspects to address, while teachers get objective, actionable feedback—enhancing self-awareness and reflective practice, which are considered as core elements of adult learning (Bridgeman & Giraldez-Hayes, 2024).

Moreover, AI chatbots can function as virtual coaches. They can provide educators with real-time responses to their questions about teaching-learning related matters including but not limited to curriculum design, classroom management, or technology integration. Hence, AI chatbots offer continuous and immediate support empowering teachers and assisting them to take ownership of their own growth, aligning with Knowles' approach of self-directed learning. Nevertheless, effective coaching using AI tools must be designed to complement rather than replace human interactions and relationships. Ethics of trust, empathy, and contextual understanding should be preserved to optimize the benefits of coaching (Tomaskinova & Tomaskin, 2024).

3.3 AI-Powered Online Modules

Online modules are widely used in teacher professional development programs offering flexible access to diverse topics. However, traditional online modules fail to meet the specific needs of adult learners unable to account for their individual differences. Online learning platforms augmented with AI are based on teachers' prior knowledge, preferences and progress and can be adjusted to individual teachers' learning needs, dynamically offering differentiated content, pacing and assessments. Adaptive online modules and platforms reinforce continuous and self-paced professional development opportunities (Philipsen et al., 2019).

For example, virtual tutoring systems and chatbots offer 24/7 support. Adaptive AI learning systems can adjust quiz difficulty in real time, recommend supplementary and customized materials, and skip content already mastered—ensuring efficiency and engagement (Tomaskinova & Tomaskin, 2024). Such personalization reflects Knowles' principle of respecting adults' existing competencies and tailoring learning to their needs. Moreover, AI-enabled modules can embed interactive simulations, enabling teachers to practice new pedagogical strategies in virtual scenarios that mimic their subject areas or student populations. These experiences support experiential, problem-centered learning, which is central to effective adult education (Brookfield, 1995, 2013).

Nonetheless, it is essential that the AI online modules enable learners to reflect and engage in discussion, as adult learning is strengthened when cognitive processing is combined with social interaction and feedback (Merriam & Bierema, 2018).

3.4 AI-Driven Communities Of Practice

Communities of practice (CoPs) have long been recognized as powerful strategy for teacher professional development. CoPs enable educators to learn through social interaction, shared experiences, and collaborative problem-solving (Wenger-Trayner et al., 2020). AI-enhanced technologies foster collaboration and reflection in teacher learning communities by creating content, analyzing discussion threads and suggesting connections between educators based on shared interests. Generative AI tools can help teachers in developing lesson plans and assessments which will further support peer collaboration (Trust, 2016).

Within online CoP, AI-driven tools can analyze participation patterns and content that may take place in discussion forums, chat groups, and collaborative platforms. This function helps to identify themes, track emerging needs, and suggest relevant resources or peers with complementary expertise (Tomaskinova & Tomaskin, 2024). AI-driven CoP supports knowledge management, automatically generates summaries of discussion threads and highlights key insights, helping teachers stay informed without being overwhelmed by information overload.

Furthermore, educators can be connected with others who might share similar interests, teach the same subject matters or even have the same affiliation with means of AI-powered recommendation systems. In this way, networking fosters meaningful collaborations across schools, districts, or even international contexts (Holmes et al., 2022). This personalized network expands the reach of CoPs and encourages the spread of ideas and practices, essential for innovation in teaching practice. Nevertheless, while AI-powered CoPs can efficiently enhance collaboration among educators, its implementation should also ensure critical dialogues, trust and professional agency allowing augmentation of technology rather than dictating collaborative process (Al-Zyoud, 2020). By thoughtfully incorporating AI tools, educational leaders can utilize CoPs as dynamic and flexible environments for ongoing professional development.

3.5 AI-Enabled Microlearning Platforms

Given the context of rapid technological changes and the rise of AI-powered technologies, using AI-enhanced microlearning platforms has emerged as a powerful and adaptable strategy to assist teacher professional development programs. Microlearning refers to delivering educational materials in manageable segments that can be accessed anytime and anywhere. These platforms customize the individual learning experiences, offer real-time feedback, and adapt to the learners' progress when combined with artificial intelligence (Buchem & Hamelmann, 2010). This approach is particularly relevant for practicing teachers who frequently deal with limitations of time, an array of students' different learning needs and demand for just-in-time learning opportunities.

Microlearning is ideal for adult learners like teachers because of its time-efficient, modular and goal-oriented structure (Kohnke et al., 2024). It supports autonomous and flexible learning, allowing teachers to immerse themselves in ongoing professional development without interrupting their school schedules. According to research, microlearning works best when it is incorporated into authentic classroom situations and is in line with teachers' daily instructional challenges (Kohnke et al., 2025). In AI-driven microlearning, educators can receive practice simulations, immediate feedback and personalized content recommendations, which supports their ability to implement newly learned materials in authentic classroom environments.

3.6 AI-Based Reflective Journals

In a conventional view, journaling is a record of personal thoughts, insights and ongoing experiences which could include both conversing with oneself or others and thus allowing for reflection and review of process (Boud, 2001). In adult education and particularly professional development of educators, reflective journals, which can be in the form of diaries or logs, contribute to personal growth, promote critical thinking, and question evolving worldviews (Brownhill, 2024). Several benefits can be achieved via maintaining journals including the enhancement of professional personal growth, the integration of life experiences with learning, stimulating mental development and fostering new insights (MacIsaac et al., 2023).

Despite the numerous advantages of reflective journals, pre-service and in-service educators underutilize them and often view them as a demanding task to engage in (Crozier & Cassell, 2016). One possible reason for that relates to the restrictive nature of traditional journaling preventing the consistent use of them (Angenius & Ghajargar, 2023a). Conversely, AI-powered reflective journals have emerged as a supportive method offering various benefits which include providing personalized feedback and guidance (Angenius & Ghajargar, 2023b; Torres, 2024). Furthermore, AI-supported tools are more engaging for users, and have the capacity to recall previous entries allowing for tracking personal development (Schulz, 2024).

3.7 AI-Supported Virtual Mentoring Programs

In teachers' professional development, mentorship contributes to professional growth as it entails "a nurturing relationship between an experienced mentor and a less seasoned mentee" (Bagai & Mane, 2024, p. 108). Mentorship has various benefits, and they include:

I. Enhancing mentees' skills by assisting them in recognizing their strengths and weaknesses
II. Exposing mentees to networking with professionals allowing partnerships and exchange of ideas
III. Offering constructive feedback and constant support which secures a safe atmosphere for discussions and self-assurance
IV. Providing mentees with career counsel, among which is job advancement and professional decision making
V. Advising mentees to maintain a balance between work and life by employing stress management techniques and identifying priorities

While traditional mentorship schemes are beneficial in various facets, "they often require enhancements in their efficacy for promoting professional growth" (Bagai & Mane, 2024, p. 108). This form of professional development exhibits some difficulties among which are "restricted mentor accessibility, time limitations, mismatches, geographical obstacles, insufficient personalization, ineffective scalability and challenges in evaluating success" (Bagai & Mane, 2024, p. 108).

The above challenges have given room for the rise of AI-supported mentorship platforms that are believed to deliver customized guidance conforming to individual users' requirements and goals. Thus, AI-supported mentorship platforms grant their users an appealing alternative to conventional mentorship programs which results in impactful effects of professional development programs.

Bagai and Mane (2024) discussed the possible benefits of AI-supported mentorship platform. Using AI-driven mentorship platforms has many benefits, such as providing learners with tailored guidance and suggestions for learners and professionals to achieve their career objectives effectively. Second, such platforms enhance skill development by identifying skill gaps, recommending appropriate resources and providing targeted advice to assist professionals acquire new skills or refine them. Third, AI-supported mentorship platforms can improve work-life balance since they have the ability to offer advice on how to manage stress, prioritize settings and sustain a healthy work-life balance. Fourth, they can elevate employee satisfaction because they offer personalized mentorship experiences that are tailored to individual needs and objectives. Fifth, this type of mentorship can nurture greater employee engagement and establish a sense of connection and engagement by offering customized and contextualized support and guidance. Lastly, AI-driven mentorship platforms guarantee higher employee retention by supporting professional development and maintaining a healthy work-life balance.

3.8 AI-Augmented Collaborative Design Studios

One of the most recent forms of AI-powered professional development (PD) options is AI-augmented collaborative design studios which represent an innovative form of PD model. In this form of PD, teachers employ AI-supported tools to co-design lesson plans involving learning activities and instructional materials, fostering creativity, collaboration and critical thinking and reflection (Yingsoon et al., 2025). By integrating AI into the design process itself, these studios position teachers as co-creators rather than passive recipients radically shifting the PD paradigm. Tammets and Ley (2023) emphasize the importance of involving teachers in the development of AI-enhanced teaching resources because this helps build their professional vision and their capacity to notice, interpret and react to classroom dynamics. By co-designing AI-powered activities, teachers gain better pedagogical reasoning skills and are able to foster meaningful integration of AI-enhanced learning into their everyday classroom practices. However, key challenges to be addressed relate to ensuring equitable access to AI-enhanced learning tools, establishing reliable and robust ethical regulations and providing continuous support to maintain sustainable co-design practices (Tomaskinova & Tomaskin, 2024).

3.9 AI-Facilitated Scenario-Based Simulations

In the rapidly evolving field of AI-powered education, AI-facilitated scenario-based simulations have become a potent and powerful form of professional development. By immersing teachers in practice-oriented, realistic environments that mimic classroom situations, these simulations enable them to develop instructional strategies, improve pedagogical decision-making skills and reflect critically in a safe virtual environment rich in relevant feedback (Tammets & Ley, 2023). This approach supports educators' life-long learning and transforms them into professionals by combining the cognitive advantages of simulations with the adaptive potential of AI.

AI-enhanced simulations are powerful professional development strategies that are often favored by adult learners who prefer self-directed and problem-solving learning. This form of PD aids educators in handling behavioral issues, implementing inclusive instruction and managing students' data while providing real-time adaptive feedback and this is achieved by recreating a variety of classroom scenarios. Such AI technologies foster reflection-in-action and instantaneous learning by analyzing teachers' responses and simulating consequences (Pedró et al., 2019).

3.10 AI-Supported Content Curation for Personalized PD Libraries

In the rapidly changing educational scenes of today, teachers need to continuously upgrade their skills and adjust to new pedagogical techniques and emerging technologies. However, the conventional one-size-fits-all professional development models are often inadequate to meet teachers' diverse and evolving needs paving the way for harnessing artificial intelligence. AI-powered content curation for personalized PD libraries offers teachers novel solutions to suggest, arrange and customize professional development resources that are tailored to individual teachers' contexts, preferences, and goals.

AI-driven content curation utilizes natural language processing techniques and machine learning to analyze teachers' professional profiles, learning history, teaching environment, and individual preferences in order to suggest appropriate professional development resources. These resources can consist of lesson plans, video research papers, case studies, microlearning modules, and more. The goal of that is to mitigate the overload of information while augmenting the relevance, accessibility, and personalization of professional development materials (Strielkowski et al., 2025).

4. REVIEW OF RELEVANT STUDIES VIS-À-VIS AI-POWERED PROFESSIONAL DEVELOPMENT

In the realm of education, scholars, researchers and educators pay significant attention to teachers' professional development (PD) employing a variety of tools, approaches, methodologies and techniques (Yang et al., 2024). PD can provide a solid foundation for cultivating teachers' knowledge of teaching and learning, boosting students' success, and improving the quality of language instruction (Sillat et al., 2021). This section reviews numerous recent studies that examined the role of different AI-powered tools in supporting teachers' professional development particularly in the field of English as a foreign language (EFL).

In their conceptual paper, Tammets and Ley (2023) explored the complex nature of integrating AI tools in teacher professional programs "highlighting the potential for AI to synergize teacher noticing, and decision-making processes, support adaptive teaching, foster alignment with competence framework, and cultivate professional vision" (p. 1). In their paper, they argued that it is crucial to involve teachers in designing AI solutions via activating professional learning models that foster teachers' knowledge-based reasoning skills, improve their pedagogical knowledge of concepts and lastly guide them to create new mental models.

Lee et al. (2024) designed an instructional system called "Collaborative Learning with AI Speakers (CLAIS)". Three to four human learners joined an AI speaker forming a small group where human learners and AI were treated as peers participating in Jigsaw learning process. The CLAIS was successfully implemented with 15 pre-service teachers in a science education course. The quantitative findings showed that the participants significantly improved their intelligent-technological, pedagogical and content knowledge after using the CLAIS sessions. This study exemplifies how AI-empowered technologies can shape the future landscape of instructional practices in the classroom.

Arefian et al. (2024) explored how Iranian English as a foreign language (EFL) teachers used ChatGPT-driven collaborative reflective practice (CRP) to enhance their professional development both independently and collaboratively. The researchers used a transcendental phenomenology approach and collected their data from group discussions, observations, and semi-structured interviews. They looked at the results thematically to show that ChatGPT-driven CRP gave EFL teachers more power in their jobs, whether they used it alone or with others. According to what each teacher said, ChatGPT was a helpful addition that gave them new ideas during CRP in the community of practice (p. 1). ChatGPT-driven CRP has been a good way for EFL teachers to improve their skills, especially in places where mentors and teacher educators are not always available to give language teachers feedback on their work.

Devi and Sharma (2024) introduced the concept of AI-powered language library wheel (LLW) which they defined as an innovative way for understanding and applying AI in language learning environments. They argued that LLW model which is AI-driven focuses on "the integration of AI technologies not as standalone tools, but as facilitators within a broader ecosystem of language resources and learning methodologies" (p. 21357). Linking theoretical analysis with case studies, the researchers examined how the LLW model can be employed in multiple educational contexts. The analysis included navigating the potential benefits represented by utilizing "improved resource discoverability, adaptive learning pathways, and enhanced collaboration between learners and educators" (p. 21357). Added to that, the study pinpointed the raising challenges and ethical issues associated with the integration of AI-driven technologies within language learning contexts. This model aims to boost learners' engagement and offer them with personalized learning that is hoped to improve their overall efficacy of the process of language acquisition.

Demir and Özdemir (2025) explored the perceived impact of using an AI-enabled voice journaling in overcoming the challenges encountered by pre-service English language teachers enrolled in a teaching practicum at an English teaching bachelor's program at a university in Turkey. The eight pre-service teachers were asked to use an audio diary application to document their daily and professional experiences, emotional states and to explain how they overcame the challenges encountered over a period of four weeks. The participants' reflections and AI-generated outputs were saved by the app to allow for content analysis. The findings demonstrated that the pre-service teachers "characterized the AI-powered Audio Diary app as a helpful tool for reflecting on their personal and professional well-being" (p. 1). The experience enhanced the participants' communication and comprehension. Additionally, the AI-powered application assisted the participants in identifying their professional development areas that need to be addressed and improved.

Another recent study conducted by Kalyani et al. (2025) examined the impact of AI-based assessment tools on reflective practices and self-efficacy among pre-service teachers using a pre-post-test experimental design. This study involved 100 prospective teachers enrolled in their 6th semester in a teacher education program. After implementing the intervention, significant improvements were observed in both reflective practices and self-efficacy scores with female students outperforming their male counterparts in reflective gains. The findings highlight the potential of AI-powered tools to boost critical professional skills and to prepare pre-service teachers for the evolving field of education particularly in the era of AI technologies.

Liu (2025) reviewed empirical research with special focus on ChatGPT about how language teachers utilize ChatGPT-assisted strategies for their professional development to acquire new knowledge, deepen their existing knowledge and create their own AI-driven strategies for language instruction. The findings showed that ChatGPT played a transformative role in professional development as it inspires language teachers to integrate technology into their classroom, enhances their teaching practices and fosters professional collaborative learning and co-creation of knowledge. Another significant finding indicates that AI-powered professional development tools equip teachers with the necessary skills to help students navigate AI-powered educational environments. The research provides insights pertinent to incorporating AI into educators' professional development programs that foster "collective growth and advance professional practices" (p. 1).

Ugwu et al. (2025) compared the efficacy of artificial intelligence (AI)-based immersive training with human-led workshops. The aim of the workshops was to improve the English language skills of non-English early career researchers in a Nigerian public university. The researchers employed a randomized pre-post-test control group design with a total of 124 participants who were randomly assigned to 8 weeks of self-directed AI immersion or human-led workshops. The results of the study revealed the outperformance of the treatment group on all skills, i.e. vocabulary scores. Hence, AI-immersion instruction was found to be more effective in developing the English proficiency of the early career researchers in comparison with traditional human-led methods. It can be concluded that AI can promote international scholars' career advancement.

5. ETHICAL AND PEDAGOGICAL CONSIDERATIONS

The integration of artificial intelligence into teacher professional development offers significant opportunities for personalized, efficient, and engaging learning. However, it simultaneously introduces complex ethical and pedagogical challenges that must be thoughtfully addressed to ensure AI use associates with the foundational principles of education. Integrating AI into professional development raises discussions around data privacy and trust, pedagogical alignment and digital humanism, ethical awareness and collaborative reflection, and emotional and psychological impact on teachers. Figure 2 provides visual representation for the ethical and pedagogical considerations.

Figure 2. Ethical and pedagogical considerations for AI-powered teachers' PD strategies

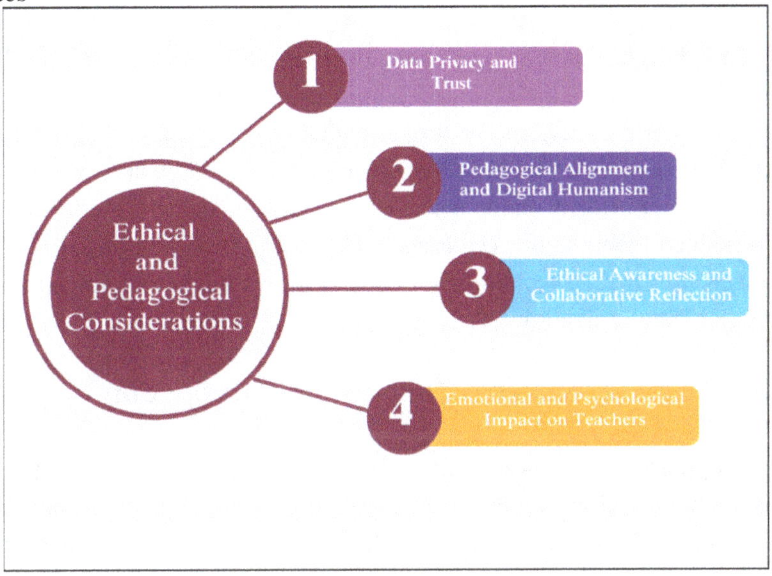

5.1 Data Privacy and Trust

The first ethical issue is data privacy. More specifically, AI technologies implemented in professional development often rely on extensively collected data which may include but not be limited to teachers' performance metrics, interactions, and reflections. Fundamental questions that arise concerning data privacy are about who owns this data, how it is stored, and how it may be used beyond the intended learning purposes particularly in systems where transparency in AI decision-making is opaque (Zawacki-Richter et al., 2019). Thus, if educators are uncertain how their personal and professional data are being used and stored, they may become reluctant to participate in AI-powered platforms. To mitigate these concerns, institutions must establish clear policies and transparent communication about data governance to safeguard teachers' privacy and nurture trust in AI-enhanced professional learning environments. Zawacki-Richter et al. (2019) call for creating contingent and open communication in order to foster teachers' trust and confidence in AI systems.

5.2 Pedagogical Alignment and Digital Humanism

From a pedagogical perspective, the integration of AI in professional learning must align with learner-centered and humanistic approaches, considering teachers' unique experiences, motivations, and professional contexts (Trust, 2016). PD programs should encourage the integration of these experiences by fostering dialogic learning, reflective practice, and shared inquiry (Robinson, 2024). Training should develop critical digital literacy, giving teachers the ability to resolve moral dilemmas, determine whether AI technologies are suitable for their learning objectives, and modify technology use to encourage empathy, equity, and inclusivity in the classroom. Recent research underscores the role of 'digital humanism', an approach that places a higher priority on the agency, creativity and dignity of educators while using AI-enabled technologies (Holmes et al., 2022). Incorporating this notion in PD design ensures that AI technologies serve as tools for empowerment rather than monitoring or standardization.

5.3 Ethical Awareness and Collaborative Reflection

As AI-supported technologies are pervasively increasing around the globe, concerns about ethical awareness have gained more and more attention. Siau and Wang (2020) defined ethics as "the principles of developing AI to interact with other AIs and humans ethically and function ethically in society" (p. 76). This definition underscores the responsibility of AI users to develop AI tools that are both effective and ethical. Pant et al. (2024) explain that there is an increasing interaction between AI systems causing societal impacts.

The incorporation of AI-powered technologies should be done effectively and ethically. Educators can be well-informed about AI ethical issues via various means. Formal education and on-going continuous training geared towards the ethical integration of AI in teaching and learning constitutes an important way to raise teachers' awareness. Moreover, engaging teachers in ongoing discussions and conversations about AI ethics within professional communities of practice can foster shared understandings of responsible AI use, and promote collaborative development of ethical guidelines that respect educators' values and consider the needs of diverse student populations (Holmes et al., 2022). By creating safe venues for dialogue, institutions empower teachers to participate in the ethical co-design of AI tools.

5.4 Emotional and Psychological Impact on Teachers

Although considerable attention has been given to the ethical and technical dimensions of AI integration, the emotional and psychological ramifications of AI remain under-examined, yet they are becoming increasingly significant. Some educators report feelings of performance anxiety, loss of confidence and surveillance as AI tools become more integrated into professional development programs particularly when AI outcomes contradict their professional judgments (Luckin &

Holmes, 2016; Tomaskinova & Tomaskin, 2024). As a result of this emotional strain, teachers' engagement with AI-powered PD platforms will decline compromising the effectiveness of professional development programs. For instance, Kalyani et al. (2025) call for introducing AI-reflective journaling, wellness modules and peer coaching into professional development programs to assist educators process their experiences, gain confidence and sustain a balanced professional identity.

Moreover, pre-service teachers and early-career educators may feel overwhelmed by the apparent need to master cutting-edge technologies while still developing foundational pedagogical competencies (Demir & Özdemir, 2025). Such an emotional burden may cause disengagement, burnout or even resistance if left unaddressed. To mitigate this issue, teacher development programs should prioritize handling emotional resilience, psychological state and overall well-being alongside digital skills.

Ultimately, teachers need to be aware of how to critically evaluate AI tools, understand algorithmic bias and ensure that the use of AI in teaching should align with learner-centered approaches (Selwyn, 2022). Furthermore, teacher training should enable them to make informed pedagogical decisions that emphasize empathy, equity and inclusiveness. Only then will the integration of AI truly fulfill its intended purpose which is to enhance—not diminish—the human aspects of teaching and learning.

6. CHALLENGES AND RECOMMENDATIONS

While the integration of AI-powered technologies has brought about many advantages to the teaching and learning processes, numerous challenges have emerged, and they should be taken into consideration. Revisiting how to ethically use AI-supported tools in various facets of life particularly in education and addressing the associated challenges is of paramount importance. Borenstein and Howard (2021) stated that it is vital "to train future members of the AI community and other stakeholders as well to reflect on the ways in which AI might impact people's lives and to embrace their responsibilities to enhance its benefits while mitigating its potential harms" (p. 61). It is thus recommended to embed AI literacy into teacher preparation programs, develop partnerships between AI developers and educators, provide contextually relevant and on-going professional development and ensure equitable access to AI tools and training for all educators. Seven AI-driven technologies' challenges will be reviewed along with suggested recommendations on how to overcome such obstacles. These include lack of infrastructure, teacher resistance and apprehension, inadequate institutional support for long term PD, limited digital literacy and AI competency among teachers, rapid technological change and tool obsolescence, lack of contextual and cultural relevance, and data privacy and ethical considerations. Figure 3 represents the challenges associated with the use of the AI-powered PD strategies.

Figure 3. Challenges and recommendations related to AI-powered technologies for teachers' PD

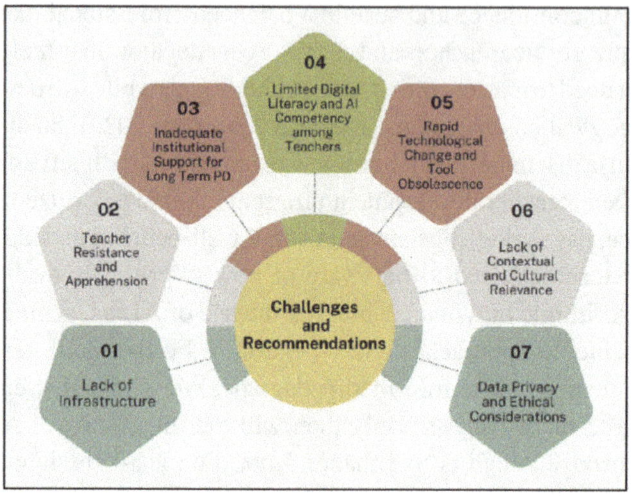

6.1 Lack of Infrastructure

In many schools and educational institutions, a major challenge to implementing AI-powered professional development programs is the insufficient infrastructure particularly in low-resource settings. Necessary infrastructure for successful AI-integration into education entails having reliable internet connectivity, up-to-date hardware, and secure data storage solutions, which are considered as resources that are frequently inconsistently distributed among different regions and organizations (Al-Buraiki & Al-Ruheili, 2025). If this challenge is not addressed, the digital divide will become larger and existing inequalities in education will probably worsen leading to disparities between well-resourced areas and those under-resourced ones (Ojedeji & Adejuwon, 2024).

6.2 Teacher Resistance and Apprehension

Teacher resistance and apprehension constitutes another key challenge towards AI technologies. Many researchers, i.e. Selwyn (2022) and Al-Buraiki & Al-Ruheili (2025) state that educators are worried about the complexity of AI tools, worry about replacement by automation, or have doubt regarding the benefits of AI in instructional pedagogy. Teachers may also be concerned that AI would devalue their professional expertise or undermine their autonomy in making decisions about their classroom instruction. According to Mouza et al. (2023), without focused support and opportunities to gain confidence in integrating AI technologies, resistance can hinder professional development initiatives, subsequently resulting in low engagement or complete rejection of the new tools.

Tariq (2024) conducted a study about the challenges related to integrating AI tools in education focusing specifically on the resistance and perspective of the teachers. The researcher found that primary factor behind teachers' apprehension and resistance is "the perceived threat of AI replacing traditional teaching roles, reducing educators to mere facilitators rather than active participants in knowledge dissemination" (p. 1). Another concern of the teachers relates to biases linked to AI algorithms, loss of teacher-student classroom interaction and data privacy. Added to that, the researcher stated that some teachers lack the necessary professional development to effectively integrate AI in their classrooms. Therefore, these concerns need to be addressed by creating a balanced approach that considers developing training programs, ethical AI framework and collaborative models that treat AI as a supportive tool rather than a replacement to human teachers.

6.3 Inadequate Institutional Support for Long Term PD

Continuous professional development programs should continue to offer consistent institutional support. However, many educational institutions tend to prioritize one-time seminars or short-term initiatives that fail to cultivate long-lasting competencies (Trust, 2016). AI-powered PD programs often demand ongoing engagement and iterative learning to keep pace with rapidly evolving technologies. Holmes et al. (2022) noted that without dedicated time, administrative and financial support from educational institutions, teachers are unlikely to sustain momentum in adopting AI-enhanced techniques which limit the transformative potential of these technologies.

6.4 Limited Digital Literacy and AI Competency Among Teachers

Integrating AI technologies into educational settings encounters the growing challenge of limited digital literacy and AI competency among educators. Despite the fact that most teachers are familiar with basic instructional technologies, AI-powered tools require deeper understanding of algorithmic thinking, data analysis and ethical implications (Luckin & Holmes, 2016). Without foundational knowledge in AI-enabled technologies, teachers are likely to struggle to effectively use adaptive platforms, interpret AI-generated feedback or critically evaluate the validity, relevance and reliability of AI-recommended outcomes. According to Al-Zyoud (2020), without proper training, teachers often experience various challenges including anxiety, confusion and demotivation when engaging with AI-powered systems. Subsequently, implementing AI-technologies in education will be characterized by reduced adoption and shallow engagement. Hence, the first step in creating meaningful integration of advanced AI technologies starts from providing teachers with professional development that addresses foundational competencies.

6.5 Rapid Technological Change and Tool Obsolescence

The rapid development of AI technologies poses another significant challenge raising the flag of how to address sustainability of professional development efforts. For example, tools, applications and platforms that are used today as the most recent technology may become outdated in a matter of months causing uncertainty among educators about how to keep pace with the advancement of technology and where to invest their time and energy. Holmes et al. (2022) explain that this unpredictability can overwhelm educators and PD providers alike, making it hard to design long-standing, future-relevant PD programs. Therefore, there is a pressing need for creating PD frameworks that are responsive, flexible and capable of advancing and adjusting with emerging AI-enabled tools and new technologies.

6.6 Lack of Contextual and Cultural Relevance

Another challenge associated with AI-powered PD programs relates to contextuality and cultural relevance. Most AI-driven tools and PD platforms are designed by private companies located in high-income countries which often address Western educational contexts. Thus, these tools are not always adaptable to certain teaching environments particularly in linguistically and culturally diverse regions. AI tools that are not in line with national curricula, language use, or classroom realities can discourage teachers and make the training less applicable (Zawacki-Richter et al., 2019). According to Al-Zyoud (2020), it is crucial to bring in localized materials and culturally sensitive AI-models particularly in non-Western educational systems. Without this kind of adaptation, AI-driven PD programs risk becoming obsolete and even counterproductive which would worsen inequalities rather than attending to them.

6.7 Data Privacy and Ethical Considerations

AI-powered PD technologies often require gathering and analyzing large number of teachers' data including classroom performance and interaction raising critical concerns related to participant consent, data privacy and surveillance. In the absence of clear institutional policies and procedures, teachers may hesitate to fully utilize AI tools if they have personal concerns or even fear about how their data will be used or stored. (Al-Buraiki & Al-Ruheili, 2025; Selwyn, 2022; Zawacki-Richter et al., 2019). What complicates the issue more is the opaqueness of how AI models generate feedback or engage in decision making processes. Hence, ethical implementation of AI-powered technologies must incorporate strong data protection protocols and encourage transparent communication in order to ensure that teachers feel secure and respected in their learning settings (Kumari & Pandey, 2024). Added to that, Varsik and Vosberg (2024) explained that commercialization of AI tools in education has created concerns about security financial gains over educational outcomes plus concerns linked to data security, privacy and algorithmic bias.

7. CONCLUSION

In the era of artificial intelligence, it becomes imperative that educators become pedagogically, technologically and ethically empowered to explore the complexities of AI integration in education. As AI technologies continue to revolutionize the educational setting, teacher professional development programs should move beyond mere introduction of the tools to offer sustainable, relevant and reflective learning opportunities that boost teachers' competence and confidence. AI technologies should be incorporated into professional development programs thoughtfully in order to support teachers in utilizing technology to reinforce and enhance English language teaching and learning whether through AI-assisted assessment, adaptive instruction or personalized feedback. This should all be done while maintaining humanistic values at the center of education. In other words, rather than reducing education to algorithmic efficiency, AI should serve as a means to enhance teachers' empathy, creativity and responsiveness to meet students' diverse needs.

Recent research uncovers the vast array of AI-supported professional development programs that are specifically designed for educators. The present book chapter has shed light on numerous AI-powered PD strategies including AI-enhanced workshops, AI-supported coaching, AI- powered online modules, AI-driven communities of practice, AI-enabled microlearning platforms, AI-based reflective journals, AI-Supported virtual mentoring programs, AI-augmented collaborative design studios, AI-facilitated scenario-based simulations and AI-supported content curation for personalized pd libraries. Moreover, policymakers, school leaders, AI developers, and teacher educators must coordinate to work together to address key challenges, i.e. infrastructure disparities, teacher apprehension and resistance, and institutional support. There are some essential strategies for ensuring that all educators can benefit from these advanced technologies. These strategies include incorporating AI into teacher preparation programs, fostering partnerships between educators and technology designers, and guaranteeing equitable access to AI-powered tools.

Adapting professional development programs that are future-ready should acknowledge teachers as central agents of change and lifelong learners. We can create sustained professional learning environments by aligning AI-enhanced PD strategies with the principles of adult learning theory. In this way, we do not only meet the demands of AI era but also uphold the timeless values of equity, inclusion and the holistic development of educators and students.

REFERENCES

Al-Buraiki, S. A., & Al-Ruheili, H. S. (2025). A qualitative SWOT analysis study of the integration of AI technologies into higher education institutions in the Sultanate of Oman. *International Journal of Learning, Teaching and Educational Research, 24*(3). DOI: 10.26803/ijlter.24.3.26

Al-Zyoud, H. M. M. (2020). The role of artificial intelligence in teacher professional development. *Universal Journal of Educational Research, 8*(11B), 6263-6272. DOI: 10.13189/ujer.2020.082265

Angenius, M., & Ghajargar, M. (2023a). Interactive journaling with AI: Probing into words and language as inter-action design materials. In Følstad, A., Araujo, T., Papadopoulos, S., Law, E. L., Luger, E., Goodwin, M., & Brandtzaeg, P. B. (Eds.), Lecture Notes in Computer Science: Vol. 13815. *Chatbot research and design. Conversations 2022*. Springer., DOI: 10.1007/978-3-031-25581-6_10

Angenius, M., & Ghajargar, M. (2023b). Design principles for interactive and reflective journaling with AI. In Arai, K. (Ed.), *Intelligent computing: SAI 2023. Lecture Notes in Networks and Systems* (Vol. 739, pp. 62–81). Springer., DOI: 10.1007/978-3-031-37963-5_6

Arefian, M. H., Çomoğlu, I., & Dikilitaş, K. (2024). Understanding EFL teachers' experiences of ChatGPT-driven collaborative reflective practice through a community of practice lens. *Innovation in Language Learning and Teaching*, 1-16. https://doi.org/DOI: 10.1080/17501229.2024.2334757

Bagai, R., & Mane, V. (2024). Designing an AI-powered mentorship platform for professional development: Opportunities and challenges (arXiv preprint arXiv:2407.20233). arXiv. https://doi.org//arXiv.2407.20233DOI: 10.48550

Borenstein, J., & Howard, A. (2021). Emerging challenges in AI and the need for AI ethics education. *AI and Ethics, 1*(1), 61-65. DOI: 10.1007/s43681-020-00002-7

Boud, D. (2001). Using journal writing to enhance reflective practice. *New Directions for Adult and Continuing Education, 2001*(90), 9–18. DOI: 10.1002/ace.16

Bridgeman, J., & Giraldez-Hayes, A. (2024). Using artificial intelligence-enhanced video feedback for reflective practice in coach development: benefits and potential drawbacks. *Coaching: An International Journal of Theory, Research and Practice, 17*(1), 32-49. DOI: 10.1080/17521882.2023.2228416

Brookfield, S. (1995). Adult learning: An overview. *International Encyclopedia of Education, 10*(3), 375-380.

Brookfield, S. D. (2013). *Powerful techniques for teaching adults*. Jossey-Bass.

Brownhill, S. P. (Ed.). (2024). *Creative practice in higher education: Engaging adult learners through theory and pedagogy* (1st ed.). Routledge., DOI: 10.4324/9781032633534

Buchem, I., & Hamelmann, H. (2010). Microlearning: A strategy for ongoing professional development. *eLearning Papers, 21*(7), 1–15.

Cavalcanti, A. P., Barbosa, A., Carvalho, R., Freitas, F., Tsai, Y. S., Gašević, D., & Mello, R. F. (2021). Automatic feedback in online learning environments: A systematic literature review. *Computers & Education: Artificial Intelligence*, *2*, 100027. Advance online publication. DOI: 10.1016/j.caeai.2021.100027

Celik, I. (2023). Towards Intelligent-TPACK: An empirical study on teachers' professional knowledge to ethically integrate artificial intelligence (AI)-based tools into education. *Computers in Human Behavior*, *138*, 107468. Advance online publication. DOI: 10.1016/j.chb.2022.107468

Chien, C. W. (2016). Taiwanese EFL undergraduates' self-regulated learning with and without technology. *Innovation in Language Learning and Teaching*, *13*(1), 1–16. DOI: 10.1080/17501229.2016.1264076

Crozier, S. E., & Cassell, C. M. (2016). Methodological considerations in the use of audio diaries in work psychology: Adding to the qualitative toolkit. *Journal of Occupational and Organizational Psychology*, *89*(2), 396–419. DOI: 10.1111/joop.12132 PMID: 27708502

Demir, B., & Özdemir, D. (2025). AI voice journaling for future language teachers: A path to well-being through reflective practices. *British Educational Research Journal*, *51*(2), 1–32. DOI: 10.1002/berj.4174

Devi, S., & Sharma, V. (2024). The AI-supported language library model: It's not about the CALL tools, it's about the language library. *Library Progress: Library Science. Information Technology & Computer*, *44*(3), 21357–21364. DOI: 10.48165/bapas.2024.44.2.1

Edwards, C., Edwards, A., Spence, P. R., & Lin, X. (2018). I, teacher: Using artificial intelligence (AI) and social robots in communication and instruction. *Communication Education*, *67*(4), 473–480. DOI: 10.1080/03634523.2018.1502459

Fakhar, H., Lamrabet, M., Echantoufi, N., & Ajana, L. (2024). Towards a new artificial intelligence-based framework for teachers' online continuous professional development programs: Systematic review. *International Journal of Advanced Computer Science & Applications, 15*(4). DOI: 10.14569/IJACSA.2024.0150450

Holmes, W., Bialik, M., & Fadel, C. (2022). *Artificial intelligence in education: Promises and implications for teaching and learning*. Center for Curriculum Redesign. https://curriculumredesign.org/wp-content/uploads/AI-in-Education-Promises-and-Implications-for-Teaching-and-Learning.pdf

Illeris, K., & Ryan, C. (2020). Contemporary theories of learning: Learning theorists in their own words. *Australian Journal of Adult Learning*, *60*(1), 138–143.

Kalyani, K., Kumar, P. K. T. D., & Roopa, A. N. (2025). AI-based tools for enhancing reflective practice and self-efficacy in pre-service teachers. *The Scientific Temper*, *16*(1), 4035–4042. DOI: 10.58414/SCIENTIFICTEMPER.2025.16.4.02

Knowles, M. S. (1980). *The modern practice of adult education: From pedagogy to andragogy* (2nd ed.). Cambridge Books.

Knowles, M. S., Holton, E. F., & Swanson, R. A. (2015). *The adult learner: The definitive classic in adult education and human resource development* (8th ed.). Routledge.

Kohnke, L., Foung, D., & Zou, D. (2024). Microlearning: A new normal for flexible teacher professional development in online and blended learning. *Education and Information Technologies, 29*(4), 4457-4480. DOI: 10.1007/s10639-023-11964-6

Kohnke, L., Zou, D., & Xie, H. (2025). Microlearning and generative AI for pre-service teacher education: a qualitative case study. *Education and Information Technologies*, 1-28. DOI: 10.1007/s10639-025-13606-5

Kumari, M., & Pandey, K. (2024). Teacher professional development in the age of AI: Time to prioritize privacy and accountability. *International Journal of Innovations in Science. Engineering and Management*, *1*(1), 209–213.

Lee, G. G., Mun, S., Shin, M. K., & Zhai, X. (2024). Collaborative learning with artificial intelligence speakers: Pre-service elementary science teachers' responses to the prototype. *Science & Education*, 1-29. DOI: 10.1007/s11191-024-00526-y

Liu, W. (2025). AI for Language Teacher Professional Development: Advancing through human–ChatGPT collaboration. *New Perspectives on Languages*, (2), 1–22. https://doi.org/10.XXXX/npol.2025.02.01

Luckin, R., & Cukurova, M. (2019). Designing educational technologies in the age of AI: A learning sciences-driven approach. *British Journal of Educational Technology*, *50*(6), 2824–2838. DOI: 10.1111/bjet.12861

Luckin, R., & Holmes, W. (2016). *Intelligence unleashed: An argument for AI in education*. Pearson.

Luckin, R., Holmes, W., Griffiths, M., & Forcier, L. B. (2022). *Intelligence unleashed: An argument for AI in education*. Pearson. https://www.pearson.com/content/dam/corporate/global/pearson-dot-com/files/efficacy-and-research/intelligence-unleashed.pdf

MacIsaac, A., Mushquash, A. R., & Wekerle, C. (2023). Writing yourself well: Dispositional self-reflection moderates the effect of a smartphone app–based journaling intervention on psychological wellbeing across time. *Behaviour Change, 40*(4), 297–313. DOI: 10.1017/bec.2022.24

Mansfield, C. F., Beltman, S., Broadley, T., & Weatherby-Fell, N. (2016). Building resilience in teacher education: An evidenced informed framework. *Teaching and Teacher Education, 54*, 77–87. DOI: 10.1016/j.tate.2015.11.016

Merriam, S. B., & Baumgartner, L. M. (2020). *Learning in adulthood: A comprehensive guide*. John Wiley & Sons.

Merriam, S. B., & Bierema, L. L. (2018). *Adult learning: Linking theory and practice*. Jossey-Bass.

Mishra, P., & Koehler, M. J. (2006). Technological pedagogical content knowledge: A framework for teacher knowledge. *Teachers College Record, 108*(6), 1017–1054. DOI: 10.1111/j.1467-9620.2006.00684.x

Ojedeji, S. O., & Adejuwon, A. M. (2024). Training future educational leaders: Incorporating AI in capacity building and professional development. *Unilorin Journal of Lifelong Education, 8*(2), 133–148.

Pant, A., Hoda, R., Spiegler, S. V., Tantithamthavorn, C., & Turhan, B. (2024). Ethics in the age of AI: An analysis of AI practitioners' awareness and challenges. *ACM Transactions on Software Engineering and Methodology, 33*(3), 1-35. DOI: 10.1145/3635715

Pedró, F., Subosa, M., Rivas, A., & Valverde, P. (2019). *Artificial intelligence in education: Challenges and opportunities for sustainable development* (UNESCO Working Papers on Education Policy, No. 07). UNESCO.

Philipsen, B., Tondeur, J., Roblin, N. P., Vanslambrouck, S., & Zhu, C. (2019). Improving teacher professional development for online and blended learning: A systematic meta-aggregative review. *Educational Technology Research and Development, 67*(5), 1145–1174. DOI: 10.1007/s11423-019-09645-8

Robinson, S. (2024). *Teacher Development – Going Beyond Conventional to a Collaborative Approach (Master's thesis)*. Concordia University., https://digitalcommons.csp.edu/teacher-education_masters/107

Romero, M. (2024). *Collaborative design of AI-enhanced learning activities*. arXiv preprint arXiv:2407.06660.

Schulz, L. (2024). *The impact of generative AI on user engagement and personalization in digital journaling: A case study* (Master's thesis, KTH Royal Institute of Technology). DIVA Academic Archive. https://urn.kb.se/resolve?urn=urn:nbn:se:kth:diva-353986

Selwyn, N. (2022). Should robots replace teachers? AI and the future of education. *British Journal of Educational Studies*, *70*(3), 315–331. DOI: 10.1080/00071005.2021.1924730

Siau, K., & Wang, W. (2020). Artificial intelligence (AI) ethics: Ethics of AI and ethical AI. *Journal of Database Management (JDM), 31*(2), 74-87. DOI: 10.4018/JDM.2020040105

Sillat, L. H., Tammets, K., & Laanpere, M. (2021). Digital competence assessment methods in higher education: A systematic literature review. *Education Sciences, 11*(8), 402. DOI: 10.3390/educsci11080402

Strielkowski, W., Grebennikova, V., Lisovskiy, A., Rakhimova, G., & Vasileva, T. (2025). AI-driven adaptive learning for sustainable educational transformation. *Sustainable Development, 33*(2), 1921-1947. DOI: 10.1002/sd.3221

Tammets, K., & Ley, T. (2023). Integrating AI tools in teacher professional learning: A conceptual model and illustrative case. *Frontiers in Artificial Intelligence, 6*, 1255089. DOI: 10.3389/frai.2023.1255089

Tariq, U. (2024). Challenges in AI-powered educational technologies: Teacher perspectives and resistance. *AI EDIFY Journal*, *1*(3), 1–10.

Tomaskinova, J., & Tomaskin, J. (2024). Unlocking the future of education: Empowering educators with AI by overcoming professional development challenges. In *ICERI2024 proceedings* (pp. 10633–10642). IATED. DOI: 10.21125/iceri.2024.2759

Torres, G. A. (2024). *Design considerations for an AI-prompted "future-self" video journaling tool to enhance self-efficacy* (Master's thesis, Massachusetts Institute of Technology). MIT DSpace. https://dspace.mit.edu/handle/1721.1/154010

Trust, T. (2016). New model of teacher learning in an online network. *Journal of Research on Technology in Education*, *48*(4), 290–305. DOI: 10.1080/15391523.2016.1215169

Ugwu, N. F., Ochiaka, R. E., Asogwa, U. S., Igbinlade, A. S., Sanni, K. T., Onayinka, T. S., Iroegbu, O., Irewole, M. O., Opele, J. K., Oloyede, A. O., Ibenyenwa, N. C., & Olubodun, O. A. (2025). Comparing the efficacy of artificial intelligence immersion and human-led workshops for enhancing researchers' English language skills: A randomized control trial. *Higher Learning Research Communications, 15*(1), 1–25. DOI: 10.18870/hlrc.v15i1.1530

UNESCO. (2023). *Guidance for generative AI in education and research.* https://unesdoc.unesco.org/ark:/48223/pf0000386123

Varsik, S., & Vosberg, L. (2024). *The potential impact of Artificial Intelligence on equity and inclusion in education* (No. 23). OECD Publishing. DOI: DOI: 10.1787/dee339a8-en

Wang, Y., Liu, C., & Tu, Y. F. (2021). Factors affecting the adoption of AI-based applications in higher education. *Journal of Educational Technology & Society, 24*(3), 116–129.

Wenger-Trayner, E., Wenger, E., & Wenger-Trayner, B. (2020). *Learning to make a difference: Value creation in social learning spaces.* Cambridge University Press., DOI: 10.1017/9781108677431

Xu, L. (2020). The Dilemma and countermeasures of AI in educational application. In *2020 4th international conference on computer science and artificial intelligence* (pp. 289–294). DOI: 10.1145/3445815.3445863

Yang, Y. F., Tseng, C. C., & Lai, S. C. (2024). Enhancing teachers' self-efficacy beliefs in AI-based technology integration into English speaking teaching through a professional development program. *Teaching and Teacher Education, 144*, 104582. DOI: 10.1016/j.tate.2024.104582

Ye, L., Ismail, H. H., & Aziz, A. A. (2025). Bridging the AI gap: A needs analysis of Chinese pre-service EFL teachers in developing intelligent-technological pedagogical content knowledge. [AWEJ]. *Arab World English Journal, 16*(1), 59–80. DOI: 10.24093/awej/AI.4

Yingsoon, G. Y., Zhang, S., & Chua, N. A. (2025). Empowering educators in the era of next-generation AI: Redefining the teacher's role in an AI-enhanced learning environment. In Tan, S., & Lim, R. (Eds.), *Teachers' roles and perspectives on AI integration in schools* (pp. 1–30). IGI Global Scientific Publishing., DOI: 10.4018/978-1-6684-9999-0.ch001

Zawacki-Richter, O., Marín, V. I., Bond, M., & Gouverneur, F. (2019). Systematic review of research on artificial intelligence applications in higher education–where are the educators?. *International Journal of Educational Technology in Higher Education, 16*(1), 1-27. DOI: 10.1186/s41239-019-0171-0

ADDITIONAL READING

Amer-Yahia, S. (2022). Toward AI-powered data-driven education. *Proceedings of the VLDB Endowment International Conference on Very Large Data Bases, 15*(12), 3798–3806. DOI: 10.14778/3554821.3554900

Archambault, L. M., & Barnett, J. H. (2010). Revisiting technological pedagogical content knowledge: Exploring the TPACK framework. *Computers & Education, 55*(4), 1656-1662. DOI: 10.1016/j.compedu.2010.07.009

Córdova-Esparza, D. M. (2025). AI-powered educational agents: Opportunities, innovations, and ethical challenges. *Information (Basel), 16*(6), 1–30. DOI: 10.3390/info16060469

Cox, E. (2015). Coaching and adult learning: Theory and practice. *New Directions for Adult and Continuing Education, 2015*(148), 27–38. DOI: 10.1002/ace.20149

Cukurova, M., Kralj, L., Hertz, B., & Saltidou, E. (2024). *Professional development for teachers in the age of AI.* European Schoolnet.

Ding, A. C. E., Shi, L., Yang, H., & Choi, I. (2024). Enhancing teacher AI literacy and integration through different types of cases in teacher professional development. *Computers and Education Open, 6*, 100178. DOI: 10.1016/j.caeo.2024.100178

Fatima, K. (2025). The role of AI in teacher professional development: Implications for AI literacy and training. *AI EDIFY Journal, 2*(1), 29–37.

Frey, B. A., & Alman, S. W. (2003). Applying adult learning theory to the online classroom. *New Horizons in Adult Education and Human Resource Development, 17*(1), 4-12. DOI: 10.1002/nha3.10155

Khosravi, H., Sadiq, S., & Amer-Yahia, S. (2023). Data management of AI-powered education technologies: Challenges and opportunities. *Learning Letters, 1*, 2. Advance online publication. DOI: 10.59453/XLUD7002

Marin, A. R., & Jiménez, O. R. (2024). Advancing education through AI-powered learning strategies and teaching techniques. In *ICERI2024 Proceedings* (pp. 10381–10388). IATED. DOI: 10.21125/iceri.2024.2656

Nazaretsky, T., Ariely, M., Cukurova, M., & Alexandron, G. (2022). Teachers' trust in AI-powered educational technology and a professional development program to improve it. *British Journal of Educational Technology, 53*(4), 914–931. DOI: 10.1111/bjet.13232

Taopan, L. L., Drajati, N. A., & Sumardi, S. (2020). TPACK Framework: Challenges and Opportunities in EFL classrooms. *Research and Innovation in Language Learning, 3*(1), 1-22. DOI: 10.33603/rill.v3i1.2763

Chapter 2

AI-Enhanced English Language Learning and Critical Thinking Development by EFL Omani Students

Nayef J. Jomaa
https://orcid.org/0000-0001-8952-5812
University of Technology and Applied Sciences, Salalah, Oman

Rais Attamimi
University of Technology and Applied Sciences, Salalah, Oman

Yasir Al-Yafaei
https://orcid.org/0009-0009-6485-8659
University of Technology and Applied Sciences, Salalah, Oman

ABSTRACT

This study examines the effect of using Artificial Intelligence (AI) tools and applications on both, learning English and developing critical thinking skills among EFL Omani students. A quantitative research was employed, utilizing a developed questionnaire with items rated on a five-point Likert scale. The research instrument included the use of AI in English language learning and its influence on students' critical thinking development. Data were collected from 50 EFL university students in Oman, selected through random sampling, and analyzed using descriptive and inferential statistics. The results showed that students generally perceived AI as a valuable educational aid that enhances their understanding of English texts, boosts

DOI: 10.4018/979-8-3373-3561-2.ch002

confidence in completing assignments, and supports idea generation in writing. As for critical thinking, the respondents moderately agreed that AI encourages reflection, evaluation, and awareness of information accuracy, although some expressed concerns about overreliance on AI tools. However, gender comparisons revealed no significant differences.

INTRODUCTION

As Covid-19 has led to several changes in the education system, teaching methods, and learning practices (Ratten, 2023), Artificial intelligence appears to have been increasingly rooted in higher education systems, thereby shaping both English language learning (Jomaa, 2025a, 2025b) and critical thinking development which has become a pressing concern recently, mainly in EFL contexts such as Sultanate of Oman. However, though several studies have been conducted on AI-supported learning, limited clarity exists on how EFL Omani university students actually use AI in strengthening their linguistic, cognitive, and critical thinking skills. This research gap is noteworthy because uncritical or excessive dependence on AI tools and applications could affect independent reasoning and critical thinking negatively. Therefore, the present study aims to examine EFL Omani students' attitudes toward using AI tools for learning English and developing their critical thinking skills. It also investigates gender-based differences in these perceptions towards AI-enhanced language learning and critical thinking development. Pedagogically, the findings could provide essentials for evidence-based insights that can guide more balanced and reflective use of AI in EFL education in Oman.

LITERATURE REVIEW

Studies on a global context has rapidly grown to explore how artificial intelligence (AI) tools enhance learning English as a Foreign Language (EFL) and enhance higher-order thinking skills. In this vein, numerous meta-analytic and large-scale studies show that generative artificial intelligence (GenAI) and AI-driven tutoring systems can boost learners' writing fluency, help with vocabulary acquisition, and enhance overall learning performance (Al-Raimi et al., 2024). They also offer support that escalate metacognition and revising work (Wang & Fan, 2025; Raitskaya & Tikhonova, 2025). On the other side, several experimental studies highlighted that well-crafted AI-assisted interventions like AI-supported writing tasks or guided prompts from ChatGPT can encourage reflection, source evaluation, and ongoing improvement, all vital components of critical thinking (Rahman et al., 2025; Darwin et al., 2024). However, the effectiveness of these interventions largely hinges on how well they are integrated into teaching and how proficient students are with prompts (Darwin et al., 2024). Meanwhile, studies and theoretical critiques pointed out some risks: an uncritical dependence on AI outputs can hinder deep thinking and independent reasoning unless teachers actively guide students to question and adapt the AI's suggestions (Rahman et al., 2025; Zakaria et al., 2025).

In a recent global analysis, Liu et al. (2025) carried out a thorough review of GenAI tools used in EFL education. The study found that these tools help with understanding, promote thoughtful reflection, and enhance evaluation skills, but they also warned against relying on them too much. In the same way, Liu and Wang (2024) pointed out that AI tools in EFL settings encourage analytical thinking and help students become more aware of the credibility of information, which is essential for developing critical thinking skills. Furthermore, Lee et al. (2025) investigated the GenAI-powered assessment tool and noted that students showed marked improvement in higher-order thinking and critical reasoning skills when these AI tools were crafted to stimulate reflection and analysis. Together, these global studies highlight the dual benefits of AI: enhancing language skills while also cultivating critical thinking abilities. They suggest a widespread agreement that AI can serve as a powerful catalyst for encouraging learner independence and cognitive engagement.

In the Arab and Omani educational scenarios, there are some recent studies attempted to visualize the role of AI in EFL settings. For instance, AI tools played a significant role in helping with grammar and vocabulary. Remarkably, those who used AI reported more favorable views than those who did not. While this study did not directly assess critical thinking skills, it set a solid groundwork for embracing AI in language education within Oman. Likewise, Al-Saadi, Al Balushi and Khalil (2025), who examined Omani EFL student-teachers, found that AI integration improved creative thinking, collaboration as well as in some cases critical thinking but was accompanied by concerns about over-reliance.

These studies indicate that while there is a positive reception for AI in the Arab region, its use for fostering critical thinking is still not thoroughly explored and encounters various structural challenges. In addition, Jomaa et al. (2025) investigated the use of AI in teaching English vocabulary in Oman, reporting on teachers' performances and students' attitudes, as well as difficulties encountered by using AI tools for vocabulary teaching. Results showed that attitudes towards AI were generally positive but indicated a lack of digital literacy among teachers and institutional support.

Finally, and as gender and academic levels are concerned, Jomaa et al. (2025) studied how gender and academic level influenced the use of both traditional and AI-enhanced learning strategies among 152 EFL Omani university students. The study highlighted that female students considerably outperformed their male counterparts in both learning approaches, particularly in writing, grammar, pronunciation, and engagement during online English classes. Moreover, students at advanced levels preferred interactive AI-based strategies more than those at lower levels, especially for speaking and pronunciation tasks. So far, AI tools were not as commonly used for grammar and writing exercises. The findings suggested that combining AI with traditional teaching methods could significantly boost language learning, and educators should encourage a balanced approach while minimizing an over-dependence on traditional methods. Based on these discussions, this study addresses three research objectives:

1- To examine the perspectives of EFL Omani students towards using AI in learning English.
2- To examine the perspectives of EFL Omani students towards using AI in enhancing critical thinking skills
3- To examine gender-based differences in their perspectives

RESEARCH METHODOLOGY

This study utilized a quantitative descriptive research design to investigate EFL Omani (English as a Foreign Language) students' perspectives of Artificial Intelligence (AI) in enhancing English language learning as well as developing critical thinking. The data were collected using a questionnaire with a five-point Likert scale ranging from *1 (Strongly Disagree)* to *5 (Strongly Agree)*. The questionnaire consisted of items that assessed two primary dimensions: Use of AI in English language learning (Questions items 1 to 6), including frequency, confidence, comprehension, and writing-related use, and the influence of AI on critical thinking (Question items 7 to 19), including motivation, evaluation, awareness of bias, and reflective habits. Descriptive statistics were used to analyze the data, including mean scores and standard deviations for each item, to identify general trends and levels of agreement.

Sampling

The sampling included 50 EFL Omani students enrolled at a public university in Oman. The sampling method appears to be random sampling, as the respondents were likely chosen based on their willingness to participate in the survey. All the respondents were English language learners, representing a mix of male and female students.

RESULTS

This section presents the results related to AI-enhanced English language learning and developing critical thinking skills.

Table 1. Descriptive statistics of means and standard deviations (AI-enhanced english language learning and critical thinking development)

Descriptive Statistics					
	N	Minimum	Maximum	Mean	Std. Deviation
1.I regularly use AI tools to support my English language learning.	50	2.00	5.00	3.9000	.81441
2.AI tools help me better understand difficult English texts.	50	2.00	5.00	4.0400	.80711
3.I feel confident using AI tools to complete English assignments.	50	2.00	5.00	3.6200	.85452
4.I use AI tools to generate ideas for English writing tasks.	50	1.00	5.00	3.8400	.86567
5.I believe AI is an effective tool for improving my English learning.	50	2.00	5.00	3.8200	.87342
6.I plan to continue using AI to support my academic progress.	50	1.00	5.00	3.7600	.87037
7.I use AI tools that motivate me to develop my critical thinking skills.	50	1.00	5.00	3.5600	.92934
8.I evaluate the content generated by AI before using it in my academic work.	50	1.00	5.00	3.5800	1.03194
9.AI makes me more aware of the importance of verifying the accuracy of the information it provides.	50	1.00	5.00	3.7600	.82214
10.I think carefully about AI suggestions before accepting them.	50	1.00	5.00	3.8000	.88063
11.Learning about the limitations of AI, such as bias or inaccurate answers, improves my critical thinking skills.	50	1.00	5.00	3.5800	.83520
12.Using AI tools encourages me to question and explore topics more deeply.	50	1.00	5.00	3.7400	.87622
13.I rely too much on AI, which may weaken my ability to think critically.	50	1.00	5.00	3.1200	1.25584
14.I tend to accept AI responses without critical evaluation.	50	1.00	5.00	3.2200	.97499
15.The educational system gives limited attention to developing critical thinking skills.	50	1.00	5.00	3.4200	.85928
16.Developing critical thinking at an early age is important in an AI-shaped world.	50	2.00	5.00	3.7200	.90441
17.AI tools can personalize learning to support the development of critical thinking skills.	50	3.00	5.00	3.7400	.66425
18.Understanding how to use AI tools effectively enhances my analytical skills.	50	1.00	5.00	3.7000	.90914
19.AI tools in education should support the development of self-awareness.	50	3.00	5.00	3.9200	.72393
Valid N (listwise)	50				

AI and English Language Learning

The data reveal that Omani EFL students demonstrate frequent and confident use of Artificial Intelligence (AI) tools to enhance their English learning experiences. The item with the highest mean score indicates that students strongly believe AI tools help them understand difficult English texts (M = 4.04, SD = 0.81). This reflects that AI applications—such as translation platforms, grammar checkers, and conversational chatbots—serve as valuable aids in simplifying complex linguistic input. Students also reported regularly using AI to support their English learning in general (M = 3.90, SD = 0.81), showing that AI tools have become part of their regular study routines.

Confidence in using AI tools to complete assignments (M = 3.62, SD = 0.85) and using them to generate ideas for English writing tasks (M = 3.84, SD = 0.86) further highlight active engagement with technology in academic writing contexts. Many respondents agreed that AI is an effective tool for improving their English learning (M = 3.82, SD = 0.87) and expressed intentions to continue using AI to support academic progress (M = 3.76, SD = 0.87). Collectively, these findings indicate that EFL Omani learners perceive AI as a practical and beneficial instrument for improving comprehension, confidence, and creativity in English language learning.

AI and Critical Thinking Development

In relation to critical thinking, EFL Omani students moderately agreed that AI tools motivate them to enhance their analytical abilities and intellectual engagement (M = 3.56, SD = 0.93). They reported evaluating AI-generated content before using it in academic work (M = 3.58, SD = 1.03), which suggests an awareness of the need to assess accuracy and reliability. Furthermore, students acknowledged that AI helps raise their awareness about verifying information accuracy (M = 3.76, SD = 0.82) and encourages them to think carefully before accepting AI-generated suggestions (M = 3.80, SD = 0.88).

Learning about the limitations of AI, such as bias or inaccuracy, was perceived as an opportunity to strengthen critical thinking skills (M = 3.58, SD = 0.84). Similarly, using AI tools was reported to encourage students to question and explore topics more deeply (M = 3.74, SD = 0.88). These results collectively indicate that AI use in academic contexts contributes positively to the development of reflective and analytical skills among EFL learners. However, the mean scores also suggest that while students recognize the importance of evaluating AI critically, consistent habits of deep analysis are still developing.

Potential Risks and Educational Implications

Although students view AI positively, they also recognize potential drawbacks. Some admitted that excessive dependence on AI may weaken their ability to think independently and critically (M = 3.12, SD = 1.26), while others acknowledged a tendency to accept AI responses without sufficient critical evaluation (M = 3.22, SD = 0.97). Additionally, students agreed that the current educational system pays limited attention to developing critical thinking skills (M = 3.42, SD = 0.86). These concerns highlight the importance of integrating structured critical thinking instruction into AI-supported learning environments to ensure balanced cognitive development.

Broader Reflections on AI's Role in Learning and Thinking

Students also expressed broader and future-oriented perspectives on AI's educational role. They agreed that developing critical thinking from an early stage is crucial in an AI-dominated world (M = 3.72, SD = 0.90). They further viewed AI as capable of personalizing learning to promote analytical growth (M = 3.74, SD = 0.66) and enhancing analytical skills when used effectively (M = 3.70, SD = 0.91). The highest mean in this section (M = 3.92, SD = 0.72) reflects strong agreement that AI in education should support the development of self-awareness—a key dimension of reflective and critical learning.

Gender-Based Analysis of Results

Table 2. The effect of gender on using AI to learn English and develop critical thinking skills

Group Statistics					
	Gender	N	Mean	Std. Deviation	Std. Error Mean
1.I regularly use AI tools to support my English language learning.	Male	29	3.8621	.87522	.16252
	Female	21	3.9524	.74001	.16148
2.AI tools help me better understand difficult English texts.	Male	29	4.0345	.82301	.15283
	Female	21	4.0476	.80475	.17561
3.I feel confident using AI tools to complete English assignments.	Male	29	3.5862	.82450	.15311
	Female	21	3.6667	.91287	.19920
4.I use AI tools to generate ideas for English writing tasks.	Male	29	3.7241	.99630	.18501
	Female	21	4.0000	.63246	.13801

continued on following page

Table 2. Continued

Group Statistics					
	Gender	N	Mean	Std. Deviation	Std. Error Mean
5.I believe AI is an effective tool for improving my English learning.	Male	29	3.7931	.86103	.15989
	Female	21	3.8571	.91026	.19863
6.I plan to continue using AI to support my academic progress.	Male	29	3.8276	.96618	.17941
	Female	21	3.6667	.73030	.15936
7.I use AI tools that motivate me to develop my critical thinking skills.	Male	29	3.6552	1.00980	.18752
	Female	21	3.4286	.81064	.17690
8.I evaluate the content generated by AI before using it in my academic work.	Male	29	3.6552	1.04457	.19397
	Female	21	3.4762	1.03049	.22487
9.AI makes me more aware of the importance of verifying the accuracy of the information it provides.	Male	29	3.7931	.90156	.16742
	Female	21	3.7143	.71714	.15649
10.I think carefully about AI suggestions before accepting them.	Male	29	3.8276	.88918	.16512
	Female	21	3.7619	.88909	.19401
11.Learning about the limitations of AI, such as bias or inaccurate answers, improves my critical thinking skills.	Male	29	3.4828	.94946	.17631
	Female	21	3.7143	.64365	.14046
12.Using AI tools encourages me to question and explore topics more deeply.	Male	29	3.7586	.95076	.17655
	Female	21	3.7143	.78376	.17103
13.I rely too much on AI, which may weaken my ability to think critically.	Male	29	3.1724	1.22675	.22780
	Female	21	3.0476	1.32198	.28848
14.I tend to accept AI responses without critical evaluation.	Male	29	3.2069	1.04810	.19463
	Female	21	3.2381	.88909	.19401
15.The educational system gives limited attention to developing critical thinking skills.	Male	29	3.4483	.98511	.18293
	Female	21	3.3810	.66904	.14600
16.Developing critical thinking at an early age is important in an AI-shaped world.	Male	29	3.7241	.84077	.15613
	Female	21	3.7143	1.00712	.21977
17.AI tools can personalize learning to support the development of critical thinking skills.	Male	29	3.7931	.67503	.12535
	Female	21	3.6667	.65828	.14365
18.Understanding how to use AI tools effectively enhances my analytical skills.	Male	29	3.6552	.97379	.18083
	Female	21	3.7619	.83095	.18133
19.AI tools in education should support the development of self-awareness.	Male	29	3.9655	.73108	.13576
	Female	21	3.8571	.72703	.15865

The analysis of the data based on gender revealed that both male and female EFL students in the public university in Oman demonstrated generally positive attitudes toward the use of Artificial Intelligence (AI) tools in their English language learning. The mean scores for both groups were consistently above the midpoint of 3.0 on a five-point scale, indicating that the students overall agreed that AI tools play a supportive role in their academic development and in enhancing their critical thinking abilities. However, some subtle differences emerged between male and female students in how they use AI, the purposes they emphasize, and the ways they engage critically with AI-generated content.

In terms of AI use for English learning, both male and female students reported frequent and confident use of AI tools. Female students recorded slightly higher mean scores in several items related to practical application. For example, female students (M = 4.00) reported more frequent use of AI to generate ideas for English writing tasks than male students (M = 3.72). Similarly, they showed slightly higher confidence in using AI to complete assignments (M = 3.67 vs. 3.59) and were marginally more likely to view AI as an effective tool for improving English learning (M = 3.86 vs. 3.79). However, male students expressed a stronger intention to continue using AI for academic purposes in the future (M = 3.83) compared to female students (M = 3.67). These results suggest that while both genders rely on AI as a learning aid, female students are somewhat more inclined to use it for creative and comprehension-based tasks, whereas male students appear more committed to integrating AI into their long-term learning strategies.

When examining the relationship between AI use and critical thinking development, the data revealed that male students tended to report slightly higher levels of evaluative and reflective engagement with AI. For instance, male students scored higher in evaluating AI-generated content before using it (M = 3.66 vs. 3.48) and in thinking carefully about AI suggestions before accepting them (M = 3.83 vs. 3.76). They also rated higher in being motivated by AI tools to develop their critical thinking (M = 3.66 vs. 3.43) and in recognizing the importance of verifying the accuracy of AI information (M = 3.79 vs. 3.71). Conversely, female students demonstrated greater awareness of how understanding AI's limitations—such as bias or inaccuracies—can enhance critical thinking (M = 3.71 vs. 3.48). These findings indicate that male students may be more active in evaluating and verifying AI outputs, whereas female students show a deeper conceptual understanding of AI's constraints and their implications for critical thinking.

Regarding the potential risks of AI dependence and systemic issues, both male and female students expressed moderate agreement that over-reliance on AI could weaken students' independent thinking abilities. The mean scores were similar for both genders (M = 3.17 for males and M = 3.05 for females). Likewise, both groups admitted that they sometimes accept AI responses without critical evaluation (M = 3.21 for males and M = 3.24 for females). Male students, however, were slightly more critical of the educational system's limited emphasis on developing critical thinking skills (M = 3.45 vs. 3.38). This reflects a shared awareness across genders that while AI can enhance learning, its uncritical use poses risks, and the educational environment may not yet be adequately preparing students to think critically in an AI-driven context.

In the broader context of AI's role in education and personal development, both male and female students demonstrated strong agreement that critical thinking should be developed from an early age in the era of AI (M = 3.72 and M = 3.71, respectively). Male students tended to rate slightly higher in believing that AI tools can personalize learning and support self-awareness (M = 3.79 and 3.97), while female students rated slightly higher in viewing AI as a means of enhancing analytical skills (M = 3.76 vs. 3.66). These small differences suggest that both genders consider AI as a positive educational resource but may emphasize different aspects— with male students focusing on autonomy and personalization, and female students on analytical improvement.

Overall, the gender-based analysis shows that both male and female students share a generally positive and balanced perception of AI in education, with only minor variations in their engagement styles. Female students appear slightly more motivated by AI's creative and supportive potential in language learning, whereas male students show a marginally stronger tendency toward critical evaluation and reflective thinking when using AI. Despite these small differences, both groups recognize AI as a valuable educational tool that, when used appropriately, can enhance not only language proficiency but also critical and analytical skills. The findings indicate that gender does not play a decisive role in shaping attitudes toward AI and critical thinking, but it does highlight nuanced differences in how each group approaches learning and reflection in an AI-enhanced academic environment.

DISCUSSION

The purpose of this study was to explore EFL Omani university students' perceptions of AI as a tool for enhancing English language learning and developing critical thinking skills. The findings provide a clear picture of how AI has become an integral part of Omani students' academic practices, particularly in comprehension, writing, and reflection. While the data demonstrate a strong degree of confidence in AI as a linguistic support tool, they also reveal the need for more structured approaches to ensure that its use maintains, and deepens current levels of autonomous thinking and conscientiousness of personal responsibility to generate and offer meaningful, continuously improving written input rather than de-prioritizing writing and educational tasks and goals to a brief interaction with machine learning, and allowing that tendency to revert to habitual reliance.

AI as a Scaffold for English Learning

The results clearly reveal that Omani students in the study regularly use AI tools to support their English learning (M = 3.90, SD = 0.81), with the strongest concurrence found in the belief that AI helps them more comprehensively understand difficult English texts (M = 4.04, SD = 0.81). This indicates that these students view AI as an accessible means of clarifying meaning and simplifying complex input. Likewise, students reported using AI to generate ideas for writing (M = 3.84, SD = 0.86) and to improve the general quality of their assignments (M = 3.62, SD = 0.85). These findings highlight AI's perceived value in improving comprehension, creativity, and productivity, making it a consistent part of students' study routines. Moreover, the relatively high ratings for AI's effectiveness (M = 3.82, SD = 0.87) and the intention to continue using it (M = 3.76, SD = 0.87) confirm that AI tools have crossed the threshold of students' consciousness, to the degree that they feel compelled to use AI and their related applications continuously, not merely as aids but as constant academic companions.

AI and Critical Thinking

Taking the convention of critical thinking, and the recognition of it as a supremely vital outcome of a college education, students showed moderate agreement across items reflecting AI evaluation, verification, and reflective awareness. They reported evaluating AI-generated content before use (M = 3.58, SD = 1.03), checking information accuracy (M = 3.76, SD = 0.82), and thinking deliberatively before accepting AI suggestions (M = 3.80, SD = 0.88). They also agreed with the proposition that learning about AI's limitations, such as bias and inaccuracy, can enhance critical thinking (M = 3.58, SD = 0.84), and that AI encourages them to question and explore topics more deeply (M = 3.74, SD = 0.88). These mean scores suggest that students are aware of the importance of reflective and analytical engagement, but this awareness has not yet evolved into consistent, habitual practice in and outside the classroom. The overall pattern points to developing but incomplete critical autonomy: students acknowledge that self-evaluation and reflection are necessary investments in their personal educational process, and to ultimately becoming autonomous learners and communicators, but may still use AI passively in some contexts.

Risks of AI Over-Reliance

The study also identified cognizance of potential challenges related to an increasing level of dependence on AI and a reduced, more limited emphasis on critical thinking in educational settings. Students moderately agreed with the premise that over reliance on AI could weaken their independent thinking (M = 3.12, SD = 1.26) and that they sometimes accept AI responses without adequate scrutiny or augmentation by personal contextualization or amendment (M = 3.22, SD = 0.97). These findings indicate that while students appreciate AI's convenience, some may effectually substitute AI tools as an intended scaffold with their sum total of input on any given activity, leaning toward cognitive shortcuts that reduce, or potentially eliminate self-initiated analysis. Additionally, their perception that the educational system gives limited attention to critical-thinking development (M = 3.42, SD = 0.86) highlights a broader pedagogical gap. Together, these issues suggest the need for careful instructional designs that combine AI use with reflective inquiry, as well as dedicating more time and newer, innovative methods of promoting critical thinking in whole group, real time classroom contexts, encouraging learners to question, validate, and synthesize information rather than rely on AI exclusively and uncritically.

Gender-Based Nuances

The gender analysis shows overall convergence in perceptions, with both male and female students expressing similarly, globally positive attitudes toward AI. However, subtle discrepancies reveal discriminate areas of strength. Female students reported slightly higher means in using AI, such as generating writing ideas (M = 4.00 vs. 3.72) and completing assignments confidently (M = 3.67 vs. 3.59). In contrast, male students scored marginally higher in evaluation and reflection, including assessing AI-generated content (M = 3.66 vs. 3.48) and thinking carefully before accepting AI suggestions (M = 3.83 vs. 3.76). These variations are minor yet meaningful. They suggest that female learners may utilize AI more as a creative and comprehensive tool, while male learners may emphasize evaluative and reflective aspects. Pedagogically, this balance can be leveraged to promote collaborative activities that combine both creative exploration and critical verification across both genders.

Pedagogical Implications

Overall, the findings affirm that AI serves as a constructive educational partner, enabling both linguistic enhancement and the initial stages of cognitive engagement. The findings also underscore the necessity of structured pedagogical interventions that guide learners toward more critical and self-aware use, while also reminding them that AI, ideally used, should retain its status as "scaffolding", not potentially substituting or greatly reducing students' participation levels in their learning process and journey. Instructors can integrate AI-supported activities with reflective components, such as justification of responses, bias identification, and verification steps, to help students transform personal and individual awareness into intellectual habits. Since students already recognize the value of AI in promoting self-awareness (M = 3.92, SD = 0.72), building reflective practices around this perception can enhance both language proficiency and independent reasoning. With proper guidance, AI can become not just a digital assistant but also a tool for nurturing analytical and ethical thinking in EFL education. Nevertheless, the findings reveal that these critical dimensions remain at a moderate level, indicating that students require continued pedagogical support and collaborative intervention to further develop consistent, independent judgment.

The findings also show that concerns about over-reliance (M = 3.12) and uncritical acceptance (M = 3.22) coexist with an acknowledgment of limited institutional emphasis on critical thinking (M = 3.42). Gender differences were minimal but suggest complementary tendencies: female students leaned toward creative, comprehension-based uses of AI, whereas male students showed slightly stronger reflective and evaluative tendencies.

Taken together, these results call for purposeful integration of AI and critical thinking instruction in EFL programs. Educators should design learning environments where AI enhances, not replaces, human reasoning. Structured reflection tasks, guided evaluations of AI responses, and awareness of AI algorithmic bias can ensure that students remain active thinkers while benefiting from technological support. Future research may extend this work by employing larger samples and mixed methods to observe how such strategies translate awareness into more sustained critical practices and deeper linguistic competence on the part of students.

CONCLUSION

In summary, the findings demonstrate that EFL Omani students generally perceive AI as both a language learning enhancer and a catalyst for critical thinking development. AI tools help them understand complex texts, generate writing ideas, and sustain motivation, while also prompting greater awareness of evaluation, bias, and accuracy. Nonetheless, the presence of moderate means for some critical thinking items indicates that students still require pedagogical guidance to use AI more critically and autonomously. The study suggests that integrating explicit critical thinking training alongside AI-assisted language instruction can help students balance technological dependence with intellectual independence, ensuring that AI becomes a tool for deep learning rather than passive convenience.

REFERENCES

Al-Raimi, M., Mudhsh, B. A., Muqaibal, M. H., & Al-Yafaei, Y. (2024). To what extent has artificial intelligence impacted EFL teaching and learning? A systematic review. *Jurnal Arbitrer, 11*(3), 399–412. DOI: 10.25077/ar.11.3.399-412.2024

Al-Saadi, Z., Al Balushi, A., & Khalil, H. (2025). Empowering EFL Student Teachers through AI: Promoting Creativity, Critical Thinking Skills and Collaboration. *digital world, 4*, 5.

Darwin, R., Rusdin, D., Mukminatien, N., Suryati, N., Laksmi, E. D., & Marzuki, . (2024). Critical thinking in the AI era: An exploration of EFL students' perceptions, benefits, and limitations. *Cogent Education, 11*(1), 2290342. DOI: 10.1080/2331186X.2023.2290342

Jomaa, N. (Ed.). (2025a). *Using AI Tools in Text Analysis, Simplification, Classification, and Synthesis*. IGI Global Scientific Publishing., DOI: 10.4018/979-8-3693-9511-0

Jomaa, N. (Ed.). (2025b). *Modern Methods for AI-Integrated Language Curriculum*. IGI Global Scientific Publishing., DOI: 10.4018/979-8-3693-9606-3

Jomaa, N., Attamimi, R., & Al Mahri, M. (2025). The use of Artificial Intelligence (AI) in teaching English vocabulary in Oman: Perspectives, teaching practices, and challenges. *World Journal of English Language, 15*(3), 1–13. DOI: 10.5430/wjel.v15n3p1

Jomaa, N., Mudhsh, B. A., & AlGhafri, K. (2025). Traditional Strategies and AI-Integrated Strategies in Learning English among EFL Omani Students. *Jurnal Arbitrer, 12*(3), 368–382. DOI: 10.25077/ar.12.3.368-382.2025

Lee, J., Hung, J. T., Soylu, M. Y., Popescu, D., Cui, C. Z., Grigoryan, G., . . . Harmon, S. W. (2025). Socratic Mind: Impact of a Novel GenAI-Powered Assessment Tool on Student Learning and Higher-Order Thinking. *arXiv preprint arXiv:2509.16262.*

Liu, J., Sihes, A. J. B., & Lu, Y. (2025). How do generative artificial intelligence (AI) tools and large language models (LLMs) influence language learners' critical thinking in EFL education? A systematic review. *Smart Learning Environments, 12*(1), 12–48. DOI: 10.1186/s40561-025-00406-0

Liu, W., & Wang, Y. (2024). The effects of using AI tools on critical thinking in English literature classes among EFL learners: An intervention study. *European Journal of Education, 59*(4), e12804. DOI: 10.1111/ejed.12804

Rahman, G., Almutairi, E. A., Mudhsh, B. A., & Al-Yafaei, Y. (2025). Harnessing generative AI for collaborative creativity: A study of university students' engagement and innovation. *International Journal of Innovative Research and Scientific Studies*, *8*(3), 3284–3296. DOI: 10.53894/ijirss.v8i3.7227

Raitskaya, L., & Tikhonova, E. (2025). Enhancing critical thinking skills in ChatGPT-human interaction: A scoping review. *Journal of Language and Education*, *11*(2 (42)), 5–19. DOI: 10.17323/jle.2025.27387

Ratten, V. (2023). The post COVID-19 pandemic era: Changes in teaching and learning methods for management educators. *International Journal of Management Education*, *21*(2), 100777. DOI: 10.1016/j.ijme.2023.100777

Wang, J., & Fan, W. (2025). The effect of ChatGPT on students' learning performance, learning perception, and higher-order thinking: Insights from a meta-analysis. *Humanities & Social Sciences Communications*, *12*(1), 1–21. DOI: 10.1057/s41599-025-04787-y

Yin, X., & Dou, K. (2025). An AI-assisted critical thinking intervention to enhance undergraduate EFL learners' writing proficiency. *Studies in Educational Evaluation*, *86*, 101480. DOI: 10.1016/j.stueduc.2025.101480

Zakaria, N. Y. K., Hashim, H., & Jamaludin, K. J. (2025). Exploring the impact of AI on critical thinking development in ESL: A systematic literature review. *Arab World English Journal (AWEJ) Special Issue on Artificial Intelligence*, 330-347.

Chapter 3
AI as a Teaching Assistant:
Automating Administrative Tasks to Free Up Teacher Time

Ashish Kumar Pandey
United College of Engineering and Research, Prayagraj, India

Ravi Srivastava
https://orcid.org/0009-0009-6718-7205
United College of Engineering and Research, Prayagraj, India

Pradeep Kumar Tiwari
https://orcid.org/0000-0001-5565-9388
United College of Engineering and Research, Prayagraj, India

Satya Prakash Singh
https://orcid.org/0009-0003-2406-2054
United College of Engineering and Research, Prayagraj, India

Sandeep Kanaujia
https://orcid.org/0000-0001-9109-5030
United Institute of Management, Prayagraj, India

Sandeep Gupta
https://orcid.org/0000-0002-3734-3723
Graphic Era University, Dehradun, India

ABSTRACT

The traditional educational paradigm is being transformed through Artificial intelligence in education. One of the most important use cases for artificial intelligence is around administrative automation. As time is a significant issue, educators can focus on effective pedagogy, including a general message: AI-based methods for scheduling, messaging, attendance, and grade management. Through historical studies, case studies, and interviews with educators and administrators, we can explore the benefits and drawbacks of AI in administration. Such research encompasses investigating problems of AI bias, data protection, and AI best practices for educating students. This research also examines the ethical dimensions of the

DOI: 10.4018/979-8-3373-3561-2.ch003

challenges. Used wisely, this approach can not only address the problem of teacher fatigue but also boost productivity and improve the quality of teaching, according to a new study.

INTRODUCTION

AI (Artificial Intelligence) is an emerging and disruptive technology over the recent years that has made a significant impression in the education sector, revolutionizing teaching as well as learning approaches for teachers, students, and administrators while optimizing various operational procedures. Today, new generations of AI are being applied in higher education to enhance teaching productivity, enable individualized education, and eliminate repetitive administrative tasks *(Chen et al., 2020; Vashishth et al., 2025)*. From intelligent tutoring systems and automated grading platforms to virtual teaching assistants and predictive analytics, AI is slowly but surely working its way into the contemporary classroom.

While a great deal of the public conversation on AI-augmented education has focused on the personalized learning experience that it enables and on the ability to support students more effectively, the ability of AI to automate teachers' workloads in administrative tasks may be just as compelling. A good chunk of that teachers' time is taken up by routine operations, from grading, tracking attendance, and scheduling, to communication and data management, all those things that get in the way of their core instructional responsibilities. AI can ease the workload in such respects by automating administrative tasks, making education systems more efficient, and giving teachers more time to concentrate on better, more human tasks, like lesson planning, individualized student support, and pedagogical experimentation *(Ahmad et al., 2022)*. Artificial intelligence-based administrative assistance in education uses machine learning algorithms, natural language processing (NLP), and automation technologies to help optimize non-instructional functions. They handle routine processes, provide more efficiency and accuracy in administrative functions, engage through AI chatbots, and use data analytics to provide insights *(Srinivasa et al., 2022)*. There are many platforms, such as Gradescope and Turnitin, that are buying into this AI system for a faster way to grade and give feedback, unlike AI-based learning management systems, like Google Classroom and Schoolytics, that use predictive analytics to recognize trends in students' performances and offer insights for teachers.

A growing body of research highlights how administrative burdens are contributing to teacher stress and burnout. Studies show that educators spend a substantial portion of their working hours on administrative tasks rather than direct instruction.

- In many areas, teachers report spending over 40% of their time on administrative work, according to a 2022 survey by the Education Policy Institute.
- Such a workload limits their freedom for lesson preparation, student interaction, and professional growth.

Incorporating AI in administrative workflows can reduce teacher burnout and pain points, while boosting efficiency and improving overall job satisfaction. Disguise the stress of the learning encounter as an efficient assistance for students. Note: This enables teachers to share or learn, leaving more time for student-oriented activities, like differentiated instruction, mentoring, and even creating lessons.

This study investigates the benefits of artificial intelligence (AI) in education and teacher workload. It also deals with possible moral challenges, like favoritism and data privacy. The study will aid policymakers, administrators, and educators on the advantages and disadvantages of automatic intelligence in administrative work. It offers tangible examples of how AI can help improve teacher productivity and education standards through analysis of empirical data and real-world case studies.

In this paper, we explore the administrative burden on teachers, describe the use of AI for key administrative tasks, and summarize the challenges and concerns associated with AI automation from the perspective of educational institutions. In the second section, I'll look at the administrative burden on teachers and why excessive amounts of administration reduce productivity and well-being. In the section on remote access AI, AI is really going to be putting up some big numbers on automating key administrative tasks, such as grading, attendance, etc. In Section 4, we discuss the common AI tools and platforms currently used in educational institutions. Read more about that, along with concerns about AI automation in Section 5, which explores your arguments in favor of and against AI automation, accuracy, privacy, bias, and more. Section 6: AI Applications: Real-world Case Studies. Section 7 covers ethics and offers suggestions for responsible use of AI solutions. A8: Future Trends Section 8 discusses trends and also best practices relevant to the use of AI in administrative work. Section 9 ends with a summary of the main findings and the potential implications for educational institutions.

THE ADMINISTRATIVE BURDEN ON TEACHERS

Teachers undertake numerous administrative duties that ensure the smooth operation of educational establishments. Roles and responsibilities include grading and assessment, attendance and record-keeping, communication and correspondence, data management and reporting, and scheduling and lesson preparation. These roles are essential for the running of educational establishments, but can be hard work with a lot of repetitive tasks. Educators are tasked with reviewing and grading assignments, making comments on student progress, analysing assessment data, maintaining curriculum records, handling student tardiness and absences, and crafting announcements and newsletters. They also need to process data, perform grading, and generate reports for either school management or governing bodies. These non-teaching tasks often dominate a teacher's time and energy, however, and reduce capacity for student engagement, lesson preparation, and professional development to take place.

Quantifying the Administrative Workload

The National Education Union (NEU) has found that teachers in the UK spend an average of 20-25 hours a week on administration, or close to half their working week. More than 70% of teachers believe that this workload affects their ability to teach negatively *(Ruziev, 2025)*. United States teachers spend roughly 11 hours per week just on grading and paperwork, contributing to teacher burnout and turnover. This results in less time and energy for instruction and interacting with students, degrading educational quality. Teachers themselves experience the broad impact of increasing administrative demands in their professional lives, which affects their effectiveness, satisfaction, and overall well-being.

So much administrative work in education cuts into the time spent on instruction, and that translates into less time for creative lesson design, individualized help for students, and fresh approaches in the classroom. Another contributing factor to the burnout and stress teachers experience is that 44 percent of grade K-12 teachers feel burned out *(Ng et al., 2025)*. Emotional burnout, decreased job satisfaction, and higher employee turnover rates are some other notable defaults.

Teachers often struggle to engage in professional development activities, such as seminars, conferences, collaborative lesson planning, and training on new pedagogical practices or emerging technologies, due to the administrative obligations they are responsible for. This further reduces the amount of time they have available for it. As a consequence, educators are deprived of opportunities that would otherwise allow them to expand their knowledge and stay current with the latest developments in educational best practices *(Pedro et al., 2019; Alamelu et al., 2025)*. For this reason, educators need to prioritize their professional development and ensure they stay current with the latest educational best practices.

An overshadowing factor in the workload of instructors could be related to administrative work (Findings from Educational Research). United Kingdom secondary school teachers only spend 15% of their workweek with students, and 31% of their time is spent on administrative duties. The burden they bear makes it challenging for them to provide individualized support and also leads them to be frustrated by redundant data collection systems. U.S. teachers in public schools spend an average of eight hours a week grading and documenting, accounting for 30% of their total time dedication to the job. This strain is a major contributor to teacher turnover, especially at underfunded schools with big class sizes. In certain schools, AI-supported grading and data input systems have reduced the burden of teachers by 15-20%. This has resulted in more time being available for teachers to connect directly with students.

The Need for Administrative Automation

The growing amount of administrative work in education underlines the urgent necessity for some sort of technological intervention. Improving teacher productivity and job satisfaction: AI can help boost productivity and job satisfaction among teachers by reducing the time spent on grading, attending classes, and reporting. AI-powered tools are capable of automating many repetitive administrative tasks, allowing teachers time to focus on the pedagogical aspect *(Jain et al., 2025)*. Automation could facilitate more efficient, accurate, and standardized administrative processes, beneficial for students as well as faculty *(Goldman et al., 2024)*.

One of the biggest deterrents to instructional effectiveness and burnout among teachers is the high level of administrative burden. Less than a quarter of an instructor's time goes to instruction; we point out that AI-powered automation can improve on administrative work, enabling teachers to concentrate on the fundamental purpose of teaching and motivating students.

AI-POWERED ADMINISTRATIVE AUTOMATION

Artificial intelligence (AI) is revolutionizing education by automating administrative tasks, improving efficiency, and allowing teachers to spend more time on instructional and student-focused activities, as shown in Figure 1. AI automation is the process of using machine learning algorithms and natural language processing (NLP), and robotic process automation (RPA) to automate monotonous administrative processes that can be time-consuming and repetitive *(Ghamrawi et al., 2024)*. AI applications in educational administration include:

- Automated grading and assessment: Instant evaluation of student work, providing timely feedback.
- Attendance and scheduling systems: Automated tracking and management of student attendance.

- Communication and notifications: AI-driven chatbots and automated messaging platforms.
- Data management and reporting: Efficient data processing, report generation, and trend analysis.

Figure 1. Different applications of AI in the education sector

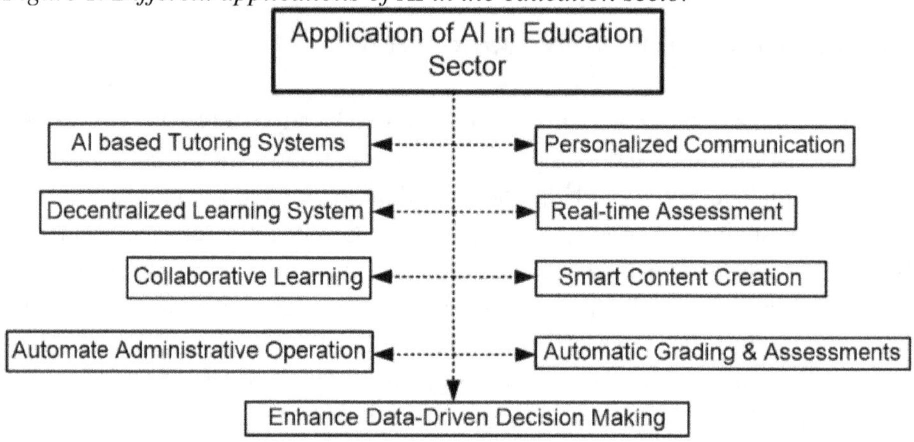

AI algorithm helps automate these processes, freeing teachers not only from administrative chores but also from more time-consuming, less valuable tasks, such as grading, and improving accuracy and consistency, so that educators can focus on instruction and personalized support for students *(Sajja et al., 2024; Singh & Ram, 2024)*. AI is transforming the educational ecosystem through automation by performing routine administrative tasks. That leaves an instructor more time for teaching and student assistance. Teaching the old school way requires teachers to do a lot, like grading, keeping tabs on students, managing data, and much more. Yet, much of the time spent on these essential duties comes at the expense of teachers having the time to create inspiring lessons or connect meaningfully with students. Machine learning methods, NLP, and robotic process automation (RPA) are used by AI-driven tools that can decompose and automate repetitive tasks (Gupta, 2025). Automating such processes not only saves time but also increases accuracy and consistency, thus reducing the risks of human errors that are otherwise common for administrative processes *(Bit et al., 2024; Sudha et al., 2024)*.

Computerized grading and evaluation are one of the best applications of artificial intelligence in education. AI programs such as Gradescope and Turnitin can grade multiple-choice tests, essays, and short-answer questions in a snap, and provide instructors with fast, consistent results *(Pokrivčáková, 2019; Vacalopoulou et al.,*

2024). Similarly, automated attendance systems use face recognition or biometric scanning systems to eliminate the need to call the roll. This is where scheduling systems powered by AI, like Class Time AI Scheduler, come into play to improve timetables. This reduces conflict and makes sure that classroom resources can be used effectively. These technologies have eased the administrative burden on instructors so that they can spend more time interacting with students.

AI also drives more effective communications through chatbots and automated alerts. A chatbot can even help answer repetitive questions from students and parents, such as an onslaught of questions about assignments or school policies. Automated messaging (for attendance problems, deadlines, announcements, etc.) via tools like School Messenger and Remind ensures timely and consistent communication. In addition, AI-driven data management provides automated calculations, improving reporting processes by providing performance metrics and tracking students' progress, enabling educators to make data-driven decisions, while providing them with a real-time picture of their students and eliminating paperwork.

Indeed, while AI-based Automation does have a few challenges and limits, it also brings several advantages, as shown in Figure 2. For example, if the comments are too artistic or not very imaginative, then the automation may invalidate them, which can result in wrong evaluations. The collation of massive amounts of sensitive pupil information raises concerns over data privacy and security. The increased use of artificial intelligence is causing other problems, too. To reap the benefits that artificial intelligence (AI) provides, educational institutions must consider responsible practices *(Soundarya et al., 2025; Shankar et al., 2022)*. These practices should ensure that automation improves efficiency without compromising justice or educator autonomy. In short, AI-based automation tools can considerably transform educational administration. It would create workplace efficiencies that would free up educators to spend more time dedicated to their top priority: educating and inspiring students.

Figure 2. Challenges of AI in the education sector with advantages

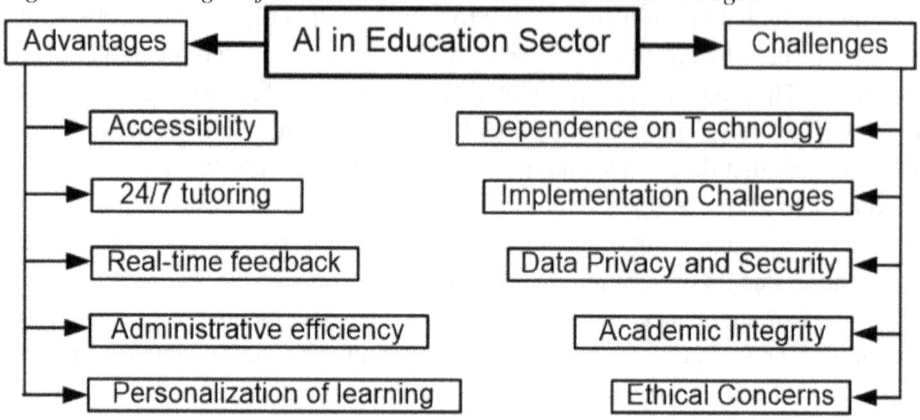

Artificial intelligence-powered administrative automation could also significantly improve education outcomes, efficiency, and reduce teacher workload. For instance, automating grading, attendance, communication, and data management enables AI to free up time to focus on student-centered activities. But its application needs to be closely monitored to ensure data privacy, fairness, and accuracy.

AI TOOLS AND PLATFORMS USED IN EDUCATION

AI solutions and tools that are trying to handle the mundane tasks and make classroom management seamless have already made their impression in the schools and are being widely adopted. The use of AI solutions is increasing the overall system efficiency by automating and putting in place a simpler environment for teachers to assist in grading, attendance, communication, and data management. Many use machine learning, natural language processing (NLP), and predictive analytics to streamline workflows, saving teachers a significant amount of time *(Singh et al., 2025)*.

AI is also upending attendance and scheduling methods. Platforms like Edsby and PowerSchool automatically check in students through face recognition or fingerprint tracking, so no one has to call names. Similar to a class planner aimed at streamlining common pitfalls while optimizing classroom resources, AI-based scheduling solutions allow educators to redirect unnecessary administrative burden toward a more seamless classroom experience with less friction. This allows more time for teachers to focus more on their teaching work when these methods are applied instead of these. AI is also simplifying communication and information handling. AI robots embedded into systems like School Messenger and Edmodo answer frequent queries from parents and students about schedules, assignments, and rules. Moreover, AI-based feedback tools like Schoolytics also reveal real-time performance screens, providing teachers with insights from data related to students' progress. Such methods minimize paperwork, help speed up contact, and give teachers more time to teach and support students.

Numerous advanced platforms and tools are being adopted in schools for AI to streamline processes, minimize paperwork, and improve productivity, as shown in Figure 3. AI in Education: AI technologies allow grading, monitoring attendance, communication, and reporting, all being automated. That simplifies things a lot for teachers. By automating repetitive and resource-draining tasks, AI enables teachers to spend more time on actual teaching and helping students. This certainly speaks volumes about these tools and how efficiently they can enhance accuracy, save time, and ultimately smooth the class in excess.

Figure 3. Best AI tools for the education sector

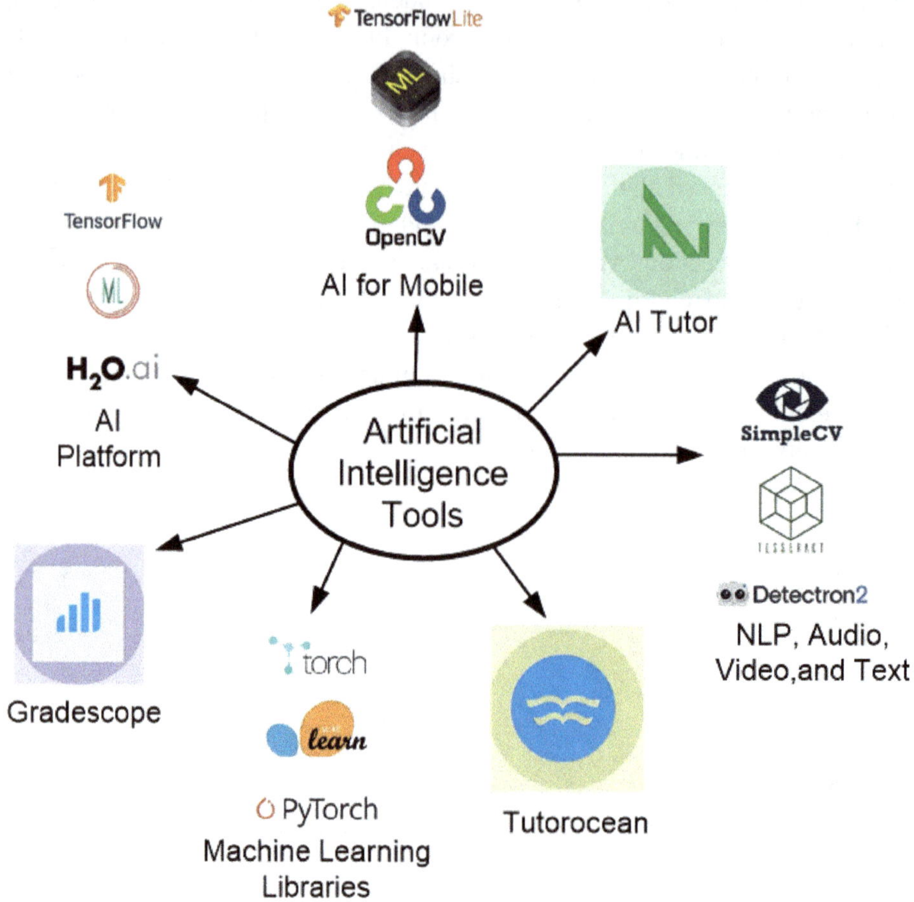

AI-Powered Grading and Assessment Platforms

One of the most time-consuming administrative tasks for teachers is grading, making it a perfect target for AI-driven automation. Finally, there are AI-based grading platforms that can review both objective and subjective assessments, providing quick and uniform feedback. Some Popular platforms and their utilities are:

- Gradescope:
  - Uses AI to grade multiple-choice, short-answer, and programming assignments automatically.

- o Recognizes and groups similar responses, allowing teachers to grade in batches.
- o Provides detailed analytics on student performance, helping educators identify learning gaps.

- Turnitin:
  - o Best known for its plagiarism detection, Turnitin also offers AI-powered essay scoring.
  - o Uses NLP algorithms to assess grammar, coherence, and content relevance.
  - o Provides students with instant feedback, accelerating the revision process.
- Google Forms with AI-enhanced scoring:
  - o Automates quiz grading and generates real-time reports on student performance.
  - o Uses adaptive learning features to suggest follow-up activities based on quiz results.

AI technologies and platforms are automating grading, attendance tracking, communication, and data management, transforming school administration procedures in the education system. GradeScope, Edsby, School Messenger, and SchoolTics help educators make better use of their time, cut down on stress, and focus on effective instruction. AI is being regularly updated, and with the current movement of the technology, schools are set to progress faster, in terms of time management and accuracy, thanks to AI.

CHALLENGES AND CONCERNS IN AI-DRIVEN ADMINISTRATION

There are many significant advantages of employing artificial intelligence (AI) in the management of educational institutions, which should never be ignored, as there are several challenges and problems linked with it. Some of the major concerns are precision and reliability. Despite the fact that artificial intelligence is quite good at automating repetitive work, it is not more dependable than individuals. Automated grading may also lack the capability to evaluate more subjective or creative responses, leading to a more inaccurate portrayal of details in student writing. Attendance can easily be confused in class because if it is detected, the presence or absence will be the last result, so with so many different lighting or physical characteristics, different results of the reformulation can lead to misidentification of the students by the facial recognition algorithms *(Zaugg, 2024)*. These shortcomings do not merely lead to mistakes; they erode trust and the dependability of AI-enabled systems. This forces teachers to spend more time grading the products generated by computer science, negating the expected productivity benefits.

The biggest challenge is the risk of data privacy and security." AI systems control huge troves of sensitive student data, ranging from grades to attendance records to personal information. Students have little control over who accesses their data, and this data is vulnerable to being breached or accessed illegally because there are no strong security standards in place. Also, many A.I. systems are not transparent about how data is collected and used, which raises questions about whether student data might be commercialized. To ensure that students' privacy is protected and sensitive information is not misused, educational institutions are subject to stringent data protection mandates, including the Family Educational Rights and Privacy Act (FERPA) in the US and the General Data Protection Regulation (GDPR) in the EU.

Accuracy and Reliability Issues

Administrative systems powered by AI are designed to streamline tasks and reduce human errors, but they also struggle with grading and evaluation tasks. Grading inconsistencies, like misunderstanding subtleties in student writing and focusing too much on syntax and structure, could lead to improper grading. Algorithmic errors might also happen in scheduling and attendance processes. Facial recognition technologies may not recognize pupils due to different factors, such as lighting conditions or algorithmic mistakes. Without a proper understanding of preferences or limits by the algorithm, AI-based scheduling systems risk generating ineffective schedules. Elements of these problems contribute to inequitable assessments, punishment, and additional time crafting reports produced by artificial intelligence and decreased agency for educators, to name a few. Part of the danger is overreliance on the faulty implementations of artificial intelligence systems, which can threaten the benefits of efficiency and teachers' trust in automated solutions much more than comparison-based systems.

Algorithmic Bias and Fairness Issues

The algorithms behind AI systems based on machine learning can introduce algorithmic bias into these systems. That's it, if you fall into particular demographics by your gender, race, or socioeconomic status, students can be treated unfairly." This could entail that some forms of learners would come first, such as non-standard English-speaking students and pupils whose families speak other languages at home, which can lead to biased grading algorithms. Consequently, facial recognition bias, which has previously been demonstrated to yield much higher error rates when recognising students of minority ethnicities, would be able to create incorrect attendance records and disproportionate punishments. (One) is predictive analytics, where children are tagged as "at risk" based on biased historical data, which might in turn lead to either inappropriate interventions or low expectations from their teachers. Such bias can create an impactful cycle that impacts education and results in a system wherein bias is maintained, and even affects student achievement and opportunities. That puts the responsibility back on educational institutions to drill down and show how diversity and fairness in AI training datasets can be implemented, thus reducing bias.

Ethical and Transparency Concerns

AI is an emerging technology that can create great opportunities for education. Still, like any tech, it also poses ethical concerns regarding transparency, accountability, and fairness as it becomes more prevalent in our system, as shown in Figure 4. To begin with, most AI algorithms are "black boxes", which makes it difficult for educators to understand the reasons behind making decisions (such as scoring or risk assessments) *(Yadav, 2025)*. And the lack of transparency may lead people not to trust AI systems. When A.I. goes wrong (such as making grade errors or misidentifying students), it's often not clear who is responsible: the teacher, the school, or the A.I. provider. This creates legal and ethical quandaries. The use of students' data in training AI models like that may raise ethical concerns, especially because of the absence of clear consent, some said (Rao et al., 2023). That is why the schools need to have policies set in place on how they collect and record information in order to protect the rights of students.

Figure 4. AI ethical and transparency concerns for the education sector

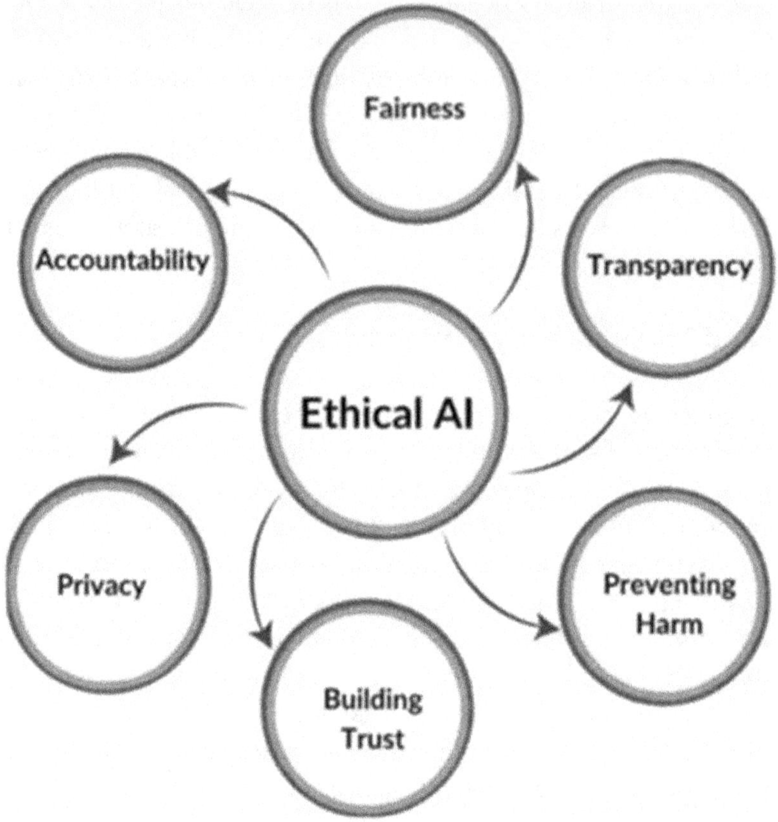

Problems over fairness and algorithmic bias present major challenges. As AI algorithms are trained with previous data, they could unintentionally reinforce biases that lead to the unfair treatment of certain groups of students. This issue can especially affect students who might come from different linguistic backgrounds, as AI-grading systems might prefer writing styles and linguistic patterns favorable to certain groups during AI training periods. Similarly, partial data patterns when used in predictive analytics to identify the academic performance of students may cause false positives, labeling a few children "at risk". As a result, it may create disparity and reinforce the current gaps in equality in education.

Another concern is the overdependence on AI and the risk of compromising instructor autonomy and human intervention. For instance, while AI can take over some of the repetitive administrative work, automating too much of the process could lead to a distancing between instructors and key decisions. Automated or machine grading may not capture the holistic and qualitative elements of student work, such as creativity and originality, that often necessitate human input in judgment and evaluation. Furthermore, they are also engaged in talking with communication systems powered by artificial intelligence (Vipin Balyan et al., 2025), like chatbots, so there is less direct interaction of teachers with students, making the search for knowledge very impersonal and far away. That sort of automation compromises the human element of the learning environment, which might as well affect the ways that students interact as well as the relationship that teachers have with students.

You focus on some of the ethical issues and transparency regarding AI in education. Most artificial-intelligence systems are deployed as "black boxes," he said, and do not reveal anything about how they made their decisions. It lacks transparency, rendering teachers and administrators unable to easily understand or challenge results generated by A.I. These (probability-based) results could be grading outcomes or performance predictions. There are also accountability problems; when artificial intelligence systems go wrong, it's often unclear who is to blame: the educator, the institution, the A.I. provider. In order to address these challenges, education institutions need to: Help schools create clear ethical frameworks; Demystify the functioning of artificial intelligence transparency; Emphasize fairness and human supervision. Only by making sure that AI lives up to its progress reasonably and responsibly can we protect the integrity and fairness of education.

And even though AI has many advantages for reducing administrative loads, there are also huge challenges relating to its application in education. These worries about accuracy, privacy, bias, and transparency make the close monitoring and responsible deployment of artificial intelligence essential. To harness the power of AI, while minimising the risks posed by its implementation, educational institutions should: embrace ethical norms, uphold justice, and safeguard the autonomy of educators. This balance is also crucial to safeguarding the integrity of education while harnessing the power of artificial intelligence.

CASE STUDIES AND EMPIRICAL EVIDENCE

AI adoption in education administration is not some pie-in-the-sky theory; it is already happening in schools and institutions around the globe. AI-powered automation also streamlines administrative tasks, increases efficiency, and allows teachers to spend more time on what matters to their students, as a Number of case studies and empirical evidence show. These instances, grounded in reality, reflect the pros and cons of incorporating AI, offering insight into AI's effect in the education sector.

Case Study 1: AI-Powered Grading at Georgia State University (USA)

In the GSU in the United States, AI-based grading systems, such as Gradescope, were used for the automation of marking of the work done by the students. With a student body in excess of 50,000 students, grading essays and exams took time. GSU automated grading of multiple-choice exams, coding assignments, and written responses through integration with Gradescope. We used an ML-based platform to analyze the answers and identify common traits before evaluating in groups, with good results and avoiding waiting time.

Results:

- *Time efficiency:* Teachers reported a 40-50% reduction in grading time, enabling them to focus more on instructional activities and student support.
- *Improved consistency:* The AI system ensured standardized and unbiased grading, reducing human grading inconsistencies.
- *Student benefits:* Students received faster feedback, allowing them to correct mistakes and improve their performance earlier in the semester.

Challenges Faced:

- Teachers said the platform could struggle to grade subjective or creative responses, making manual review essential to ensure accuracy.
- Over-reliance on AI to assess complex work had been a concern, so GSU had a human oversight policy when it came to grading.

Case Study 2: Automated Attendance Tracking in India

This article, published by Sharona Ginsberg on August 26, 2018, in Bangalore, India, described how one school instituted a facial recognition-based attendance system that scans students' faces as they enter schools in order to automate their daily roll calls. FaceX and Edusys were added to help automate this process and reduce manual errors in it. Such systems utilize AI-fueled facial recognition technology to identify students when they walk into classrooms, automatically marking them present or absent.

Results:

- *Time saved:* Teachers reported saving 5-10 minutes per class, resulting in hundreds of hours of instructional time saved over a semester.

- *Improved accuracy:* Automated attendance reduced human errors, such as incorrectly marked absences or duplicate entries.
- *Real-time monitoring:* The system generated instant reports, allowing school administrators to track chronic absenteeism and intervene early.

Challenges Faced:

- *Accuracy concerns:* The system occasionally failed to recognize students due to variations in lighting or changes in their appearance, resulting in false absences.
- *Privacy issues:* Parents and students raised privacy concerns regarding the use of biometric data, prompting schools to revise their data protection policies.

Case Study 3: AI-Powered Communication at Staffordshire University (UK)

In the United Kingdom, Staffordshire University deployed Beacon, a chatbot powered by AI, to improve communication with students and automate simple administrative tasks. Beacon utilized natural language processing (NLP) to respond to common inquiries about schedules, deadlines, and administrative processes.

Results:

- *More efficient:* Over 60% of student queries were taken care of by Beacon, showing a drastic reduction in administrative workload for the staff.
- *24/7 availability:* The students had access to the AI chatbot all day, every day, making it possible for them to get support even beyond office hours.
- *Increased student satisfaction:* Students reported that they liked being able to get instant responses and that the system was useful for quick, common queries.

Challenges Faced:

- *Limited scope:* Beacon was good at 1-dimensional queries, but something more complex and nuanced needed to be pushed to a human.
- *Personalization problems:* A few students felt the absence of human interaction in this was impersonal, preferring to deal directly with staff for more personalized support.

Empirical Evidence: AI-Driven Administrative Efficiency

Artificial intelligence in education shows empirical research indicates that this is a procedure that demonstrates improvement in administrative efficiency. A 2022 HolonIQ survey found that 74% of teachers who use AI grading systems report saving significant time. This is how AI-powered scheduling solutions are seamlessly working towards reducing conflicts in schedules by 25-30%. With manual attendance systems, automated attendance systems removed administrative errors, improving student record accuracy by up to 90%. The key findings of this research are the accuracy, time-saving, and better reporting. AI can also lead to data privacy and algorithmic bias problems, resulting in inconsistent assessments for students from different backgrounds.

AI-powered automation case studies in school administration show time savings, better accuracy, and increased efficiency. Since resources and manpower are usually limited in colleges and institutions, many have resorted to AI technologies for grading, attendance, and communication, saving administrative load, consistent and timely grading, better attendance and scheduling, and better communication with chatbots, etc. But they entail limits on accuracy, privacy and security concerns, and reduced human oversight, which challenge fairness and accountability. Indeed, based on empirical evidence, there is a need for responsible deployment, human oversight, and continuous improvement that should be conducted by AI-enabled management to reap its rewards while curbing its risks. Organizations also encounter accuracy, privacy, and bias-related issues, which necessitate monitoring, transparency, and ethical AI policy implementation. People learn by real-life examples, and educational institutions can even use artificial intelligence to amplify the education process by observing.

ETHICAL AND PRACTICAL CONSIDERATIONS

However, the more AI infiltrates our systems, the more ethical and practical questions can be raised regarding the use of such technology, especially in this specific field of educational administration. Data privacy and security have utmost importance. AI-powered systems scrape and analyze mountains of sensitive student data, ranging from academic performance and attendance records to personal information. This data is up for grabs without stringent privacy laws, making it vulnerable to exploitation, deception, and a breach of privacy. Educational institutions are closely regulated by privacy standards like the GDPR in Europe and FERPA in the U.S. to safeguard student data. The only good response to this is informed consent protocols, open standards for data, and decent encryption to ensure privacy and trust in AI systems.

Algorithmic bias and equity are significant issues. Since AI is trained on historical data, the systems may inadvertently reinforce current biases, resulting in unfair treatment of students. Since AI assessment systems could more favorably analyze some writing styles than others or disadvantage students using non-standard language patterns, this could result in inequitable outcomes. A number of facial recognition attendance solutions have shown that children from different backgrounds have higher error rates, leading to concerns about fairness and accuracy. Educational institutions need to ensure that AI is under continuous human supervision, regularly audit AI systems for equity, and use diverse training datasets to reduce bias. Examples of AI bias in education:

- Grading algorithms: AI grading systems may unfairly penalize students from non-traditional linguistic backgrounds or with different writing styles.
- Facial recognition bias: Some attendance systems exhibit higher error rates for students of color or those with disabilities, resulting in inaccurate attendance records.
- Predictive analytics bias: AI models used to predict student performance may label certain students as "at risk" based on biased data patterns, influencing teacher expectations.

These ethical criteria are fundamental transparency and explainability. Many AI systems function as "black boxes," making it difficult for instructors to comprehend or dispute AI's conclusions. The processes by which AI systems are used for assessment or for monitoring student behavior and predicting performance suffer from a lack of transparency that could undermine trust and accountability. In the education sector, we need to really look for explainable artificial intelligence (XAI) models. These models should clearly explain what factor(s) and how they were considered when making the decision (Awasthi et al., 2024). In addition, educators should be able to verify and tailor AI-generated results, thus ensuring that human expertise is factored into the final assessment. Out of these areas, transparency reports often tackle the more opaque decision-making processes, issues related to accountability, and the practical challenges of contesting the outputs that AI systems generate. Teachers, schools, and software companies often have little clarity on who is responsible for AI-related errors. One valid alternative will be to use Explainable AI (XAI) models that provide teachers with the capability to judge and vet the AI output, together with the claims on accountability standards. Although AI result validation allows instructors to inspect and modify findings if needed, XAI models should describe the relevant features that drive decisions. It is also vital for institutions to implement clear procedures outlining who would be liable for AI-related faults or malfunctions.

The ethical issues surrounding the governance of artificial intelligence include limited laws regarding accountability for errors, as well as a multitude of unregulated artificial intelligence suppliers. Often, schools will use third-party service providers, and because they do not verify the ethical practices of their suppliers, this can lead to bias and privacy problems. Creation of AI ethics committees, setting up specific accountability standards, and regular audits and reviews are some examples of tangible solutions that can be put in place to ensure responsible deployment of artificial intelligence. Such acts further address the ethical dilemmas you face surrounding the governance of artificial intelligence and promote a more conscious and normalized learning experience.

The overuse of AI is a major concern linked to the loss of instructor autonomy. Although automation may lead to administrative efficiency, over-reliance on AI could undermine instructor involvement with duties such as student assessment and grading. AI cannot replicate the emotional intelligence and contextual awareness that play such a huge part in making decisions about education. Hence, there must still be a hybrid model, where human educators give qualitative feedback and oversight (while AI handles the everyday chores). Moreover, while the mechanization of modern education is by no means a new phenomenon, it is increasingly important to remember the humanity in education both to make education driven less by commerciality and more by empathy and a respect for the idiosyncratic quality of our humanity and not to believe that education in a marketplace run for profit is a good thing.

If we should do something, in the long run, we need to avoid the use of AI in education, which should be critically controlled and held accountable. Accountability: Institutions should have clear accountability mechanisms to ensure that if the AI systems make a mistake in marking attendance accurately, or assigning grades, for example, the system can be held accountable. In addition to that, academic organizations need to establish AI ethics committees to monitor the use of AI within their educational institutions and uphold the principles of fairness, transparency, and the rights of students. To avoid any breach of trust and ethical violations, auditing, performance assessments, and continuous refinements of AI systems are essential. By addressing these ethical and practical issues, educational institutions can explore the power of AI in a manner that responsibly retains the integrity of education. The Ethical and Practical Application of AI in School Administration. There are dangers of privacy, bias, transparency, and fairness even with an up-and-running AI. To maximize returns, institutions must protect students' privacy, reduce possible algorithmic bias, rely on human judgment where appropriate, and develop clear accountability mechanisms, while also embracing transparent AI wherever possible. "It is fair because every student has the right to defend themselves.

FUTURE TRENDS AND RECOMMENDATIONS

It is anticipated that AI will play a more significant role in educational administration as technology advances. The potential consequences of machine learning are immense in terms of automation and enhanced performance. But new challenges will also emerge that will need careful management. Educational institutions and policymakers should push these trends, like ethical AI practices, which require transparency, and human-AI collaboration, to the forefront, so that they are proactive rather than reactive. This offered educators the chance to rethink how we could harness the potential of A.I. technology, while safeguarding student privacy, promoting equitable access to education, and ensuring educational quality.

Emerging Trends in AI-Powered Educational Administration

In the near future, AI-powered administrative systems will exhibit higher levels of intelligence, adaptability, and autonomy. Predictive analytics are being used in decision-making processes related to teaching and administrative tasks. At the most sophisticated level, artificial intelligence systems are able to predict a student's likely performance on tests, to identify students who may be struggling, and to tailor individual support strategies for students. Thus, Artificial intelligence can assist schools in creating support mechanisms that could eliminate drop out and improve student performances, based on analysis of attendance statistics alongside grades, and conduct.

Natural language processing (NLP) and conversational artificial intelligence (AI) are two of the major trends in communication in administrative settings. The scope of queries that artificial intelligence chatbots will be able to handle from students and resolve administrative issues for them, as well as provide them assistance in real time, is expected to see improvements in the next few years. And these bots can adjust their responses according to the context, leading to relatively more personalized and human-like conversations. Furthermore, the utilization of artificial intelligence-powered virtual assistants will improve teacher support services. These assistants would assist in scheduling, the generation of documents, the management of resources, etc.

AI-driven document automation is likely to become more pervasive. This will allow educational institutions to automatically generate, organize, and classify lots of administrative documents with less manual input. The substantial reduction in paperwork will allow staff to focus more on activities that serve the children. Moreover, combining blockchain technology with artificial intelligence could help improve the security and transparency of educational records. This ensures data integrity and verifiability.

Challenges of Increased AI Integration

As exciting as they are, the possibilities of AI in school administration could also introduce new challenges. AI systems are rapidly evolving, and with that evolution, data privacy, bias, and transparency issues are sure to rise (Fotis et al., 2025). And it will also mean even greater dependence on artificial intelligence and, hence, even more stringent security legislation regarding the data security of how student data is analyzed and shared. As predictive analytics increasingly play a role in student evaluation and support, algorithmic bias will likely become a national problem for generations to come. And poorly managed AI models can misidentify students or magnify existing inequalities. Also, we can use the methodologies of regular fairness auditing and introduce diversity into the underlying AI training datasets so that they will not model the biased behaviours.

Moreover, this increased automation of administrative tasks could challenge teachers' autonomy and raise fears of job displacement. As A.I. assumes greater administrative functions, schools need to ensure that instructors retain authority over decisions about instruction. To uphold the personalized, contextual nature of education, we will require a balance of automated systems and human mediation.

Recommendations for Responsible AI Implementation With Policy and Regulation

To most effectively harness the benefits of AI while reducing the risks of using AI, schools must create strategies for adoption and implementation. One of the biggest recommendations is to remain open and transparent. Only those AI systems that operate using discernible decision-making processes ought to be employed in schools. This means that teachers and managers get to review and understand the data that AI gives them.

It is also important to make sure there is still a human hand on the wheel. Although AI systems can perform many routine tasks, the teachers and staff should still play a role in addressing and reviewing the decisions made by AI, such as grades or predictions of student performance. That way, students will always know that being kind and using good judgment are important parts of the school experience.

Anyone who works with students and teachers needs to learn how to use artificial intelligence (AI). Educators should know how AI works, its limitations, and how to use AI tools well. Teachers will be trained through professional development classes on AI literacy to use AI and develop the critical thinking skills necessary to implement it into their classrooms. This will enable them to standardise, adjust, or rectify any biases, including, for instance, mistakes.

Policymakers and regulatory bodies must step up their roles in establishing the rules and regulations that govern AI's use to prevent any misuse or unethical applications. Governments and educational organizations must also create a comprehensive set of policies and standards to address AI in education, including:

- Data privacy and security: Defining strict rules for the collection, storage, and use of student data.
- Prevention of bias: Mandating AI vendors to perform regular audits (the fairness audit) and disclose potential biases.
- Accountability frameworks: Creating explicit policies around accountability for AI errors or malfunctions.

Developing global standards for ethical AI in education will also require international cooperation. It ensures that all AI technologies implemented across educational institutions globally are done in an equitable and responsible manner through consistent guidelines and best practice policies.

The Future of Human-AI Collaboration in Education

So, for example, the role of artificial intelligence in school management in the coming years will be that of the man-machine version, not man's persuasion. The tools that successfully combine the speed and efficiency of AI with the empathy and contextual knowledge of a human educator will be the future-ready solutions. AI will be used in the future for repetitive tasks, where there is a large amount of data, like grading, scheduling, reporting, etc. Meanwhile, teachers will focus on activities that are student-centered and require creativity, emotional intelligence, and nuanced decision-making.

In the hybrid paradigm, A.I. will serve not as a replacement for teachers, but as an adjunct, providing teachers with another means to give students distinct tributes of educational experience. Schools that use artificial intelligence effectively in a way that respects teacher autonomy and student-centered or student-empowered methods will see greater improvements in educational outcomes and operational efficiency for their students. To be ready for this future, educational institutions will need to embrace innovation while also ensuring that ethical and human-centered principles are at the heart of the work. This will enable them to create effective, equitable, and responsive AI-augmented educational systems for students and teachers alike.

But the future is bright for AI in school administration, just deploy responsibly and plan well. AI, NLP, and predictive analytics will drive improved efficiency through automation innovations such as document automation. But institutions need to be careful about issues of bias, privacy, and transparency. That means we need to embrace transparency, ensure a human is in the loop, increase AI literacy, institute hard rules to protect data privacy, and promote human-AI collaboration as we prepare our schools for the future. In following these recommendations, educational institutions can leverage the potential of Sages in administrative matters, while protecting the integrity, equity, and humanistic dimension(s) of quality teaching, learning, and assessment itself.

CONCLUSION

AI is revolutionizing educational administration by making schools and universities operate more efficiently and effectively. AI takes over the more mundane and routine work like grading, taking attendance, scheduling, and communicating, relieving teachers of tedious administrative work and leaving them with more time to teach and provide personalized support for students. Predictive analytics, AI-assisted chatbots, and document automation minimize manual labor, reduce errors, and increase overall productivity. But they face ethical and practical hurdles to their use. Trade-offs for data privacy, biases in algorithms, and transparency have to be addressed via secure systems, fairness audits, or accountability frameworks. In the educational area, AI integration should definitely be done with caution; human supervision should already be a must so that teachers would still be in the equation because the process of decision-making ultimately requires human compassion and human social context.

Future analysis suggests that AI in educational administration will become increasingly complex, with resource tracking in real-time, and will be able to determine areas where improvements can be made to maximize efficiency and lead to enhanced predictive analytics when it comes to class performance. But its success will depend on responsible governance, transparency, and ethical use. Investing in AI literacy and training will empower schools with professionals to work in concert with AI systems and interpret the results generated by AI correctly. This creates a sick environment and defeats the purpose of education. But due attention must be paid to optimizing the application of AI so it can be harnessed to uplift educators, improve student performance, and drive agile, responsive education systems.

To wrap it all up, the proper balance of AI in education administration involves hitting the sweet spot between entrepreneurship and human involvement. AI can replace repetitive, data-heavy tasks and do them more quickly and accurately. Still, teachers will always have an important role to play in decisions that require empathy, contextual awareness, and a level of personalised judgement. On a positive note, acting as a counterbalance will allow AI to blossom as a supportive tool rather than a disruptive replacement, enabling teachers to shift their efforts towards a more student-centred practice.

REFERENCES

Ahmad, S. F., Alam, M. M., Rahmat, M. K., Mubarik, M. S., & Hyder, S. I. (2022). Academic and administrative role of artificial intelligence in education. *Sustainability (Basel), 14*(3), 1101. DOI: 10.3390/su14031101

Alamelu, R., Sathya, M., & Christina, J. L. (2025). AI on Teacher Roles: A Transition Towards Facilitation. In Driving Quality Education Through AI and Data Science (pp. 217-238). *IGI Global Scientific Publishing*. DOI: 10.4018/979-8-3693-8292-9.ch010

Awasthi, B., Gupta, S., Kumar, S., & Tripathi, A. (2024, January). Business management and planning using queuing model with heterogeneous customers for electrical applications. *In 2024 2nd International Conference on Intelligent Data Communication Technologies and Internet of Things (IDCIoT)* (pp. 279-283). IEEE. DOI: 10.1109/IDCIoT59759.2024.10467673

Balyan, V., Varshney, T., Gupta, S., & Gupta, G. (2025). *Optimizing Automation in Engineering with Energy Systems and Communication Networks*. IGI Global Scientific Publishing., DOI: 10.4018/979-8-3373-2737-2

Bit, D., Biswas, S., & Nag, M. (2024). The impact of artificial intelligence in educational system. *Indo Am. Journal of Pharmacy Research, 11*, 419–427.

Chen, L., Chen, P., & Lin, Z. (2020). Artificial intelligence in education: A review. *IEEE Access : Practical Innovations, Open Solutions, 8*, 75264–75278. DOI: 10.1109/ACCESS.2020.2988510

Fotis, G., Gupta, S., Varshney, T., Dhar, S. L., & Gulzar, M. M. (Eds.). (2025). *Modern Computing Technologies for EV Efficiency and Sustainable Energy Integration*. IGI global., DOI: 10.4018/979-8-3373-2382-4

Ghamrawi, N., Shal, T., & Ghamrawi, N. A. (2024). Exploring the impact of AI on teacher leadership: Regressing or expanding? *Education and Information Technologies, 29*(7), 8415–8433. DOI: 10.1007/s10639-023-12174-w

Goldman, S. R., Taylor, J., Carreon, A., & Smith, S. J. (2024). Using AI to support special education teacher workload. *Journal of Special Education Technology, 39*(3), 434–447. DOI: 10.1177/01626434241257240

Gupta, S. (2025). *The Future of Machine Learning with Automation in Engineering*. Nova Science Publishers., DOI: 10.52305/YFIX2832

Jain, S., Grewal, H., Vishnoi, A., Saxena, A., Bhardwaj, S., & Singh, R. (2025, February). Transformative trends: The impact of artificial intelligence (AI) on modern education. *In AIP Conference Proceedings* (Vol. 3224, No. 1). AIP Publishing.

Ng, D. T. K., Chan, E. K. C., & Lo, C. K. (2025). Opportunities, Challenges and School Strategies for Integrating Generative AI in Education. *Computers and Education: Artificial Intelligence*, 100373.

Pedro, F., Subosa, M., Rivas, A., & Valverde, P. (2019). Artificial intelligence in education: Challenges and opportunities for sustainable development.

Pokrivčáková, S. (2019). Preparing teachers for the application of AI-powered technologies in foreign language education. *Journal of language and cultural education.*

Rao, M. S., Saraswathy, S., Neela, V., Arun, M. R., Gupta, S., & Taqui, S. N. (2023, November). Efficient Model Training in Decentralized Systems with Federated Learning. *In 2023 International Conference on Communication, Security and Artificial Intelligence (ICCSAI)* (pp. 900-904). IEEE. DOI: 10.1109/ICCSAI59793.2023.10421469

Ruziev, E. (2025). AI and the Future of Teacher Roles: Automation Vs. Augmentation. *Journal of Multidisciplinary Bulletin*, *8*(1), 51–54.

Sajja, R., Sermet, Y., Cikmaz, M., Cwiertny, D., & Demir, I. (2024). Artificial intelligence-enabled intelligent assistant for personalized and adaptive learning in higher education. *Information (Basel)*, *15*(10), 596. DOI: 10.3390/info15100596

Shankar, R., Ramana, T. V., Singh, P., Gupta, S., & Mehraj, H. (2022). Examination of the non-orthogonal multiple access system using long short memory based deep neural network. *Journal of Mobile Multimedia*, *18*(2), 451–473. DOI: 10.13052/jmm1550-4646.18214

Singh, T. M., Reddy, C. K. K., Murthy, B. R., Nag, A., & Doss, S. (2025). AI and education: Bridging the gap to personalized, efficient, and accessible learning. In *Internet of Behavior-Based Computational Intelligence for Smart Education Systems* (pp. 131–160). IGI Global.

Singh, V., & Ram, S. (2024). Impact of artificial intelligence on teacher education. *Shodh Sari-An International Multidisciplinary Journal*, *3*(01), 243–266. DOI: 10.59231/SARI7669

Soundarya, M., Devapitchai, J. J., Krishnakumari, S., & Manickam, T. (2025). Applications of Artificial Intelligence Techniques in Education. In *Integrating Micro-Credentials With AI in Open Education* (pp. 429–450). IGI Global Scientific Publishing.

Srinivasa, K. G., Kurni, M., & Saritha, K. (2022). Harnessing the Power of AI to Education. In *Learning, teaching, and assessment methods for contemporary learners: pedagogy for the digital generation* (pp. 311–342). Springer Nature Singapore. DOI: 10.1007/978-981-19-6734-4_13

Sudha, G., Natha, A., Rajendiran, M., Vanitha, U., Kiran, V., Patil, H., & Rajaram, A. (2024). Optical oasis harnessing energy efficiency in wireline, optical, and wireless communications. *Journal of Environmental Protection and Ecology*, *25*(4), 1179–1187.

Vacalopoulou, A., Gardelli, V., Karafyllidis, T., Liwicki, F., Mokayed, H., Papaevripidou, M., . . . Katsouros, V. (2024). AI4EDU: An Innovative Conversational Ai Assistant For Teaching And Learning. *In INTED2024 Proceedings* (pp. 7119-7127). IATED.

Vashishth, T. K., Sharma, V., Sharma, M. K., Sharma, K. K., & Sharma, R. (2025). The Role of Teachers in an AI-Enhanced Educational Landscape. In *AI Adoption and Diffusion in Education* (pp. 231–264). IGI Global Scientific Publishing. DOI: 10.4018/979-8-3693-7949-3.ch009

Yadav, S. (2025). Leveraging AI to Enhance Teaching and Learning in Education: The Role of Artificial Intelligence in Modernizing Classroom Practices. In Optimizing Research Techniques and Learning Strategies with Digital Technologies (pp. 211-238). *IGI Global Scientific Publishing*.

Zaugg, T. (2024). Embracing Innovation in Education: Investigating the Use and Impact of Artificial Intelligent Assistants Among Preservice Teachers.

Chapter 4
Artificial Intelligence-Driven Development of English Language Learning Resources

Laylo Rakhimova
Urgench State University, Uzbekistan

Boljon Sapaeva
Mamun University, Uzbekistan

Nigora Norqobilova
Termez University of Economics and Service, Uzbekistan

Munir Ahmad
https://orcid.org/0000-0003-4836-6151
Survey of Pakistan, Pakistan

ABSTRACT

This chapter explores the transformative role of Artificial Intelligence (AI), particularly generative AI, in English language education. It highlights how AI enables the development of personalized, adaptive, and scalable learning materials, including reading passages, grammar exercises, vocabulary lists, and multimedia resources. By aligning content with learner goals and interests, AI fosters engagement, while interactive tools such as simulations, gamified activities, and conversational chatbots enhance motivation and retention. The chapter also examines key challenges, including accuracy, cultural bias, data privacy, and balancing personalization with

DOI: 10.4018/979-8-3373-3561-2.ch004

standardized curricula. It concludes by emphasizing the need for responsible, ethical, and inclusive adoption, while anticipating future advancements such as multimodal AI, real-time adaptive feedback, and collaborative human-AI teaching models.

INTRODUCTION

The sphere of education is under the influence of Artificial Intelligence (AI) fast and extensively, providing new opportunities to create, deliver, and personalize learning materials (Kaswan et al., 2024; Maghsudi et al., 2021; Murtaza et al., 2022). Within the sphere of language learning, the use of AI technologies and their subdivision, namely, generative AI, is transforming the manner in which learners learn the language by means of generating adaptive, engaging, and learner-focused content. AI is finding its way into the language learning ecosystem, starting with auto-assessment systems and moving through to intelligent tutoring platforms, providing a means of overcoming some of the conventional issues, including limited availability of resources, one-size-fits-all methodologies of teaching, and a lack of learner engagement (Niemi, 2024; Sawin, 2025). This technological change will be a big leap towards an efficient, inclusive, and personalized version of education.

English is still the lingua franca of international communication, business, science, and online interaction. (Maqsood et al., 2026) and therefore, a competency in the language is an essential skill among learners all over the world . Nevertheless, the high demand for quality materials in the English language learning process at times surpasses the supply, especially in those areas where there are few educational facilities. Conventional resource development approaches, which depend heavily on textbooks, unchanging exercises, and instructor-created content, are often incapable of satisfying the various needs of learners with respect to flexibility, cultural appropriateness, and feedback on a real-time basis. It is here that AI can be transformative (Crompton et al., 2024; Rukiati et al., 2023; Rusmiyanto et al., 2023).

The argument in favor of using AI to create English language learning materials is that it allows creating customized works that resonate with the personal objectives, skill levels, and interests' learners. AI-based systems are capable of automatically generating adaptive reading passages, personalized grammar and vocabulary practice, and even multimedia learning experiences that retain learners. They change with the pupil, unlike a never-changing content, and provide progressive and individual learning experiences. Simultaneously, educators and curriculum developers can use the ability of AI to generate content automatically, thus saving time and being able to concentrate on more advanced teaching approaches.

The chapter discusses how AI can be used to spur the creation of English language learning materials, focusing on the use of generative AI technologies. The introduction starts with the general description of the use of AI in content creation and personalization, and then the content of AI-generated reading materials, grammar exercises, and vocabulary lists is discussed in detail. The application of AI to create interactive and multimedia texts, including videos and gamified activities, to enhance the learning process, is also a topic of the chapter. Lastly, it discusses the technical, ethical, and pedagogical issues related to the development of AI-driven resources before discussing potential future trends of responsible and effective implementation of AI in the English language learning process.

GENERATIVE AI AND CONTENT CREATION FOR LANGUAGE LEARNING

Generative Artificial Intelligence (AI) has developed algorithms and models that can produce new content through the learning of large volumes of data. In contrast to rule systems, which are based on a set of previously established scripts, generative AI employs the principles of natural language processing (NLP) and deep learning algorithms to recognize linguistic patterns, form meaningful text, and create new content. When applied to the educational process, it implies that AI systems can generate reading passages, exercises, tests, and even interactive conversations based on the learning goals of language learners. In the specific case of English language learning, generative AI presents a level of opportunity never seen before to close the discrepancies between fixed instructional materials and the evolving, changing demands of students (Ahmad et al., 2025; Ali et al., 2024). It is a good addition to classic instructional design since it can produce contextually relevant, grammatically correct, and pedagogically useful content.

Personalized and Adaptive Content Creation

One of the strongest points of using generative AI in language learning is the unrivaled ability to provide personalization and adaptability that transform the learning experience in a way that cannot be done in traditional techniques. Traditional instructional resources, like textbooks or prepared sheets of work, are normally written in a one-size-fits-all manner. They presume an even distribution of learners, which rarely represents the large distribution of levels of proficiency, interests, cognitive styles, and professional objectives in real-life classrooms or in online learning communities. Such a gap may cause disengagement, as higher learners might be bored with supersimplified material, and lower ones become scared of the complexity (Gao et al., 2023; Sayed et al., 2023; Yadav et al., 2025).

Generative AI is able to overcome this shortcoming by using data-driven insights to create learning paths that meet the unique needs of a learner. By analyzing proficiency indicators, progress patterns, and error trends (and even learner interests), AI systems can generate resources that are both relevant and of the right level of difficulty. As an example, simple passages of reading in which familiar vocabulary is used to construct the argument are used with the beginners, and complex passages offering idiomatic expressions and delicate grammatical constructions are used with the advanced learners, but on the same subject. It is also possible to curate vocabulary lists to suit the academic or career goals of learners, i.e., medical vocabulary in the case of nursing students or business terms in the case of corporate workers.

In addition, it is not a fixed adaptivity but one that changes as the learners advance. AI systems would bestow the benefit of constantly monitoring the performance of learners, detecting strengths and recurring errors, or gaps in knowledge, and using this feedback loop to dynamically moderate the next collection of exercises or texts. This would help keep the learners within their zone of proximal development, where assignments are challenging enough to trigger growth and yet not so challenging that they become frustrated. Generative AI can increase motivation, long-term retention, and foster an inclusive learning environment by integrating personalization at each phase in the learning process and allowing each learner to progress at their own speed. Table 1 highlights the key differences in how each approach addresses learner diversity, engagement, and progression.

Table 1. Comparison of traditional vs. generative AI-based content creation

Feature	Traditional Resources (Textbooks/ Worksheets)	Generative AI-Driven Content
Personalization	One-size-fits-all, fixed progression	Tailored to individual proficiency, interests, and goals
Adaptivity	Static, does not adjust to learner progress	Dynamic, adjusts in real time based on learner performance
Cultural/Contextual Relevance	Limited, often generalized examples	Can be localized, contextually relevant, and culturally inclusive
Learner Engagement	Often repetitive and rigid	Interactive, gamified, and scenario-based
Feedback and Improvement	Periodic and delayed	Immediate, adaptive, and continuous

Scalable and Efficient Resource Development

The next characteristic benefit of generative AI is its extraordinary scale that transforms the production, distribution, and updating of learning materials. Historically, the creation of learning content is a time-consuming process. Teachers, curriculum designers, and subject specialists are likely to waste hours choosing texts, preparing grammar drills, writing comprehension questions, and making assessments. The procedure is lengthy and expensive and needs specialized skills, inventiveness, and revisions. These issues increase in large institutions or online learning platforms with thousands of students, often leading to delays or inconsistencies, or to the use of generic, mass-produced content.

The generative AI is a potent solution that can speed up and simplify this resource development process dramatically. In a few seconds, AI models can produce a high-quality passage to read, adaptive quizzes, sets of vocabulary exercises, or even multimedia content, such as listening activities or role-playing scripts. This ability allows institutions to increase the content without a proportional growth in the number of employees or in budgetary requirements. As an illustration, one teacher with the help of AI tools would be able to create personalized resources in several classes of different levels of proficiency in a fraction of the time it would take to create the manual preparation (Dua & Patel, 2024; Holmström & Carroll, 2024).

Scalability of generative AI is beneficial, especially in scenarios where educational infrastructure or workforce may be lacking. Online platforms can deliver customized learning content to thousands of users at the same time, at a high quality and variety. Moreover, AI can be used to create multiple-choice items, translations, or to modify texts to different levels multiple times to reduce the amount of work a teacher has. The transition will allow teachers to use their time on more advanced practices, including coaching the learners, conducting discussions, providing individual feedback, and developing critical thinking. What is equally important, generative AI promotes efficiency not only in the production process but also in the process of continuous improvement. The content may be modified immediately according to new curricular needs, learner comments, or new topics of concern so that the learners never miss the most relevant and current material. Generative AI fills the gap between quality and scale, making English language learning high-quality and widely available, either in under-resourced areas or within large online services. Table 2 discusses the scalability and efficiency of generative AI.

Table 2. Efficiency gains in resource development through generative AI

Task/Process	Traditional Development (Manual)	Generative AI Development
Time Required	Hours to days per lesson/ resource	Seconds to minutes per resource
Labor Intensity	High—requires multiple specialists	Low—automated generation with minimal human input
Content Variety	Limited due to resource constraints	Broad—multiple formats (texts, quizzes, dialogues, multimedia)
Update/Revision Cycle	Slow, requires re-printing/ redesign	Instant, real-time updates are possible
Accessibility at Scale	Restricted by staff and cost	Scalable to thousands of learners simultaneously

Advantages Over Traditional Resource Development

The potential of generative AI goes well beyond its efficiency and scalability and is a transforming advantage that goes beyond what can be achieved with traditional resource development. Real-time flexibility is one of the greatest advantages. In contrast to a set of textbooks or even a set of pre-recorded digital units, AI-generated works can change dynamically in reaction to the current performance of the learner and be truly learner-centered. As an example, when a learner has difficulties with verb tenses or complex sentence structure repeatedly, the AI platform can immediately offer more practice tasks, simplified explanations, or context examples that help them overcome these issues. On the other hand, in case a learner shows quick mastery, the system may raise the level of tasks, introduce new vocabulary, or develop exercises that will engage in thinking and problem-solving. It is a continuous feedback loop, which not only speeds up the learning process but also reduces cases of frustration and disengagement, which is high when the learner is presented with resources that are either too easy or too difficult. Real-time content manipulation enables AI to generate a responsive and personalized learning environment that is impossible with other traditional resources.

Cultural and contextual inclusivity is another major generative AI benefit. Traditional learning resources also rely heavily on examples, situations, and idiomatic expressions, which sometimes portray a narrow cultural view and hence can be less relevant to diverse learners. AI has the opportunity to break this limitation by producing culturally sensitive and contextually relevant material based on the environment, interests, and experiences of the learner. As an example, students in South Asia may be reading passages about local festivals, workplace situations, or normal social life, whereas European students may be reading passages about regional traditions, the education system, or work environment. Equally, AI can generate lists of words and discussions that portray local language differences, e.g., British, American, or Indian English, so that learners acquire linguistic proficiency and cultural sensitivity. Such inclusivity legitimizes identities of learners, stimulates participation, and gives a feeling of relevance between language learning and real life, a point that is likely to be missing in standardized, box-fits-all items.

Generative AI also opens up new forms that would make the learning process more engaging than usual exercises. Besides stationary worksheets or multi-choice tests or quizzes, AI can generate gamified assignments, role-playing simulation questions in an interactive environment, and chatbots with conversational tasks. The students have the opportunity to train in English in a real-life environment, including attending simulated job interviews, traveling, or having an academic conversation with an AI-based interlocutor. This multimodal and immersive program enhances language retention, increases understanding, and builds confidence in the learners in the use of their skills in real-world contexts. As an example, role-play simulation may stimulate students to negotiate, persuade, or describe things in English by promoting linguistic fluency as well as higher-order thinking. Such interactive experiences are what AI offers to help close the gap between the learning process in the classroom and actual language use in the real world.

Lastly, generative AI is an essential re-evaluation of the role that educators play in the classroom. Automating time-consuming and repetitive tasks, including creating grammar exercises, vocabulary quizzes, or reading comprehension tasks, allows AI to free up teachers to concentrate on higher-order instructional tasks. The teachers will be able to devote more time to the mentoring of the learners, conducting group work together, developing critical thinking, and giving individual advice. This new role enables teachers to apply their expertise in the profession in a place where it is most helpful and leave the rest to AI to take the responsibility of creating resources. The outcome is a synergistic learning experience where AI-based efficiency becomes complementary to human pedagogical discretion to the learners, as well as guarantee that the learners get high-quality content with adaptability and, in addition, get the benefit of quality teacher-student interactions. When combined with human control, technology, and AI improve the quality of instruction and the results of learners, which makes the model of the English language education dynamic and ready to face the future.

AI-DRIVEN DEVELOPMENT OF LEARNING MATERIALS

Generative AI technologies are changing the manner in which English language learning content is created, providing the prospect of personalization, flexibility, and contextualization, which traditional methods find difficult to attain. Rather than depending on unchanging textbook materials or standardized tests, AI allows dynamically creating content that adapts to the level of learners, fits their objectives, and keeps them engaged.

AI-Generated Reading Passages Tailored to Proficiency Levels

Comprehending a reading is a crucial part of the new language mastery, but the discrepancy between their level and the resources is one of the most widespread challenges that learners can face. Novices can be confused by genuine texts because of the lack of familiar words and complicated structure, and well-prepared students can lose interest when reading material that is too easy (Allaithy & Zaki, 2025; He, n.d.; Sidwell et al., 2024). Generative AI counters this age-old issue by generating reading passages in a way that is well matched with the current capacity of a learner.

To the inexperienced learner, AI-generated texts may include brief passages with simple, repetitive sentence structure and be constructed using high-frequency vocabulary. These are the texts that give a base upon which the learners, in a slow manner, develop confidence without a load. When dealing with intermediate learners, the AI will be able to produce more complex narratives or expository texts, which introduce new words in not entirely unexpected environments and which scaffold learning. AI can be used at advanced stages to produce highly limited, domain-specific content, such as articles about environmental sustainability, legal case studies, or business negotiations, that not only measures linguistic capacity but also prepares learners to communicate in a real-world course or professional or academic setting.

Dynamic adaptability is one more significant benefit of AI-based reading materials (Wu et al., 2025). The system can keep a constant track of the performance of learners, unlike the use of static textbooks. Here is an example: when questions about understanding reveal that one is repeatedly misinterpreting, the AI can arrange the text with a lower level of accessibility or add explanatory glosses to challenging vocabulary. On the other hand, the AI can challenge a learner with advanced vocabulary, idiomatic phrases, and complicated sentence constructions in case they are demonstrating good results. This ongoing fine-tuning is also important so that learners are not demoralized but are challenged, and this results in a smooth learning curve. Such adaptive texts can be used in the future to assist learners to smoothly read the beginner-friendly content to authentic texts and remain motivated to continue their progress. Table 3 compares the features of AI-generated texts across proficiency levels.

Table 3. Characteristics of AI-generated reading passages by proficiency level

Proficiency Level	Text Features	Vocabulary Use	Grammar Complexity	Adaptivity/Feedback
Beginner	Short, simple passages with repetition	High-frequency, basic words	Simple sentence structures	Glosses/explanations for difficult words
Intermediate	Narrative/expository texts with moderate length	Mix of familiar and new words in context	More varied structures (compound/complex)	Adjusted difficulty based on comprehension results
Advanced	Specialized, domain-specific texts	Technical, idiomatic, and nuanced terms	Complex and varied grammar	Continuous calibration with rich input/output tasks

Adaptive Grammar Exercises and Vocabulary Lists

The structural basis of learning any language is grammar and vocabulary, but in many cases, learners find it difficult to learn using the traditional materials that offer them one-size-fits-all exercises. The problem with such static material is that it seldom takes into consideration individual differences in proficiency, prior knowledge, or learning rate, resulting in disengagement or slow progress. This is one area where generative AI can change things by creating adaptive and personalized tasks that respond directly to the individual strengths and weaknesses of a learner to create a more targeted and effective learning experience (Aravind et al., 2025; Yunjiu et al., 2022).

As an illustration, when a student consistently has trouble with subject-verb agreement, AI can automatically generate more exercises with specific emphasis on this topic, giving explanations, illustrative examples, and interactive exercises until the student learns. The system can also gradually expose the learner to more complex grammatical structures (e.g., conditional sentences, passive constructions, or using tenses), as he or she shows progress. On the other hand, those learners who are strong in some areas can get exercises aimed at the weak ones instead of spending their time on the repetition exercises, which can be a waste of time. This personalization makes sure that each learner works productively and no one learner feels frustrated or bored.

Vocabulary acquisition also benefits substantially from AI-driven personalization. Instead of using fixed, pre-specified word lists, AI can be used to create dynamic and interest- and context-specific vocabulary banks to meet the objectives of learners. As an example, a medical student may be exposed to medical terminology, including anatomy, treating patients, and communicating with healthcare customers, whereas a hospitality professional can be exposed to terminology in tourism, customer service, or event management. Another possibility that AI opens is the ability to vary the word difficulty according to proficiency and introduce rare or more complex words as learners familiarize themselves with the basic vocabulary.

Furthermore, AI may include spaced repetition algorithms to arrange a review at scientifically calculated times. The effect of this method is that learners review earlier learned vocabulary and grammar structures before forgetting can occur, leading to higher long-term retention. Continuous improvement takes place in the adaptive system: mastered words or grammar patterns are phased out, new or more difficult items are added, maintain the learning process is maintained on track with the learner. In the long run, this produces an interactive, ever-changing process of practice and reinforcement, which would turn grammar and vocabulary learning into a dynamic and gradually advancing process that is learner-centered. With the combination of personalization, adaptivity, and evidence-based retention, generative AI fundamentally changes the manner in which language learners interact with the main constituents of English proficiency.

Material Contextualization Based on Learner Interests and Goals

In addition to proficiency changes, contextualization of content according to personal interests, desires, and professional needs is one of the most impactful things that generative AI can offer to language acquisition. Frequently, traditional textbooks and pre-designed exercises use generic and standardized examples that do not correspond with the various experiences and objectives of learners. Consequently, students can become disconnected, especially when they feel that a lesson is disconnected from their life, which results in low motivation and low retention (Hwang et al., 2023; Leong et al., 2024). Conversely, AI has the potential to produce learning content that suits the individual interests of learners, their career goals, or activities of interest, building a feeling of relevancy that motivates them to remain engaged and take an active part in the learning process.

For example, students who like sports could have reading passages written by AI about international tournaments, profiles of athletes, or commentary on a match, with grammar tasks accompanying them being related to reporting the score, describing the plays, or analyzing sports news. Technology lovers may be interested in texts about artificial intelligence or cybersecurity, or space exploration, reinforcing technical terms and technical sentences in a context that is relevant to them. Similarly, business professionals might practice language through case studies, role-play simulations, or dialogues about leadership strategies, marketing campaigns, or cross-border negotiations. In either way, AI makes sure that the necessary language structures: grammar, vocabulary, idiomatic, and discourse markers are entrenched in genuine, contextually related material, on the one hand, improving understanding and, on the other, making it more practical in application.

The process of contextualization also enormously enables the transfer of skills to the real world. When learners use the English language by studying issues that relate directly to their work or life, they find it easier to apply these outside the classroom. An example is that a medical practitioner who is exposed to AI-based medical communication and patient-related situations can use this acquired knowledge with confidence in real clinical interactions. Similarly, students planning to study abroad will be able to use AI simulations of university life, academic discussions, or intercultural exchanges to get realistic practice, which directly preconditions their intentions. The AI can fill the gap between theory and practice as it makes learning processes as close as possible to real-life scenarios, thereby making sure that the learners attain functional language competence as opposed to memorized, abstract knowledge.

Furthermore, AI-driven contextualization fosters cultural inclusivity and diversity. AI makes the process of learning more relevant and available to culturally diverse learners by creating region-specific examples, culturally relevant idiomatic expressions, and situations that mirror practices in the area. Such inclusivity enhances motivation, fosters cross-cultural comprehension, and enables the learners to perceive English as a multi-purpose, flexible means of communication in the world. Simply put, AI is changing the one-size-fits-all process of language learning into a very personalized, interactive, and culturally aware process, aligning the personal interests and career demands of the learner with the overall aim of productive communication.

Current Tools and Platforms Applying AI Methods

Some of these platforms have already been incorporated with AI technologies in order to make English language learning adaptive and contextualized. An example is Duolingo, which has used GPT-4 to write adaptive practice problems and unique lessons. Its Roleplay feature enables its learners to simulate real-world conversations in a real setting, like when they need to order a meal in a restaurant or even when they need to book a hotel, thus making language learning seem more engaging and practical.

GrammarlyGO is more than a mere grammar fixer; it uses generative AI to offer contextual vocabulary and paraphrased sentence constructions (Grammarly, 2018). These products are grounded in the individual writing objectives of learners, and learners who are engaged in these products will not only gain knowledge of accuracy but will also gain style, clarity, and expression in their writing. The other significant use is ELSA Speak (Karim et al., 2023), which is an AI-driven platform aimed at improving pronunciation and speaking fluency. By taking advantage of high-tech speech recognition and adaptive feedback, ELSA selects specialized exercises that determine the weaknesses of learners and provides a solution to them, which is especially effective in oral language development.

LingQ and Readlang use AI to generate vocabulary lists and comprehension tasks based on texts that learners choose (Perez-Guerra & Cao, 2021). Operating with the material that best suits their own interests, learners will both be motivated and engaged, at the same time, stepping up their reading comprehension and building their vocabulary in meaningful contexts. Lastly, there is a growing use of ChatGPT and other large language models (LLM)-based tutors as versatile virtual learning assistants. These systems are capable of producing adaptive reading passages, grammar exercises, and interactive dialogue exercises, on command, and allow personalized and dynamic practice to learners of varying levels of proficiency.

Collectively, these examples show that AI is not just in theory but is also becoming a part of everyday learning activities and provides learners and educators around the globe with meaningful tools that personalize, make learning languages more adaptive, and accessible. Table 4 summarizes notable tools and their primary applications.

Table 4. Examples of AI-powered English language learning platforms

Platform	Core AI Application	Unique Feature/Strength
Duolingo (GPT-4)	Adaptive practice, lesson generation	Roleplay for real-world conversational contexts
GrammarlyGO	Grammar, style, and expression support	Contextual vocabulary suggestions and sentence paraphrasing
ELSA Speak	Pronunciation and speaking fluency	Speech recognition with personalized corrective feedback
LingQ / Readlang	Vocabulary and reading comprehension	Learner-chosen texts with auto-generated vocab lists
ChatGPT / LLM Tutors	On-demand resource generation	Flexible adaptive passages, grammar drills, and dialogues

INTERACTIVE AND MULTIMEDIA CONTENT GENERATION

Although resources based on text are still fundamental to the process of English language acquisition, the modern learner is growing more demanding of interactive experience and multimedia-based learning. The use of generative AI has increased the potential to produce interesting videos, audio content, and simulations, which can offer a more immersive and interactive way of learning. Integrating linguistic input with visual, auditory, and gamified objects, AI makes sure that the learners are motivated and engaged in the process of learning, not only to acquire knowledge but also to engage in the process actively.

Designing Interactive Videos, Audio Content, and Simulations

Generative AI has created new opportunities to create multimedia materials that are much more than a traditional textbook and a recording. Learners can have chances to enjoy real-life language by creating videos and audio material that can mimic real-life communication situations (Hung et al., 2025; Klein & McCartney, 2024). Text-to-speech (TTS) systems driven by AI went a step further to create natural and human-like voices with changes in pitch, intonation, and rhythm, allowing learners to better listen to different accents of English, whether British and American or even Australian or Indian English. Such exposure is essential because it equips the learners to face the linguistic diversity they are bound to meet in international communication. The speed and clarity can also be fine-tuned using AI systems to give learners with intermediate, advanced, or beginner levels an opportunity to practice to their requirements.

More than mere audio practice, AI can create subtitled videos or animated situations that best fit certain lesson concepts, like how to prepare for a job interview, how to navigate an airport, or how to have a cultural exchange. These multimedia tools assist students in drawing more connections between words and the context, and allow them to fill in the gap between the abstract grammar exercises and the realistic application. Even more advanced platforms already have speech recognition enabled, where learners can directly record their own voices and compare them to the AI-generated models directly, therefore getting immediate corrective feedback.

Using the simulations of AI, learners will be able to negotiate a business contract, communicate with hotel employees, or engage in a group discussion, and the system will adjust the responses to the input of the learners. These simulations can simulate the pressure and spontaneity that are common in actual life in a low-risk, safe environment where errors transform into learning experiences instead of embarrassment. It is this form of immersion that has been revealed to boost learner confidence, fluency, as well as willingness to communicate in real-life situations. Finally, the traditional curriculum is supplemented with AI-produced videos, audio, and simulations to provide the learners with the level of practical experience they need to move out of the classroom setting and into the real-world environment of functioning. Table 5 summarizes the different formats, their features, and pedagogical benefits for English language learners.

Table 5. AI-generated multimedia formats and their benefits

Format	AI Capabilities	Example Applications	Pedagogical Benefits
Audio (Text-to-Speech)	Natural, human-like voices; multiple accents; adjustable speed/intonation	Listening comprehension, accent training	Exposure to diverse accents, improved listening skills
Video (Subtitled/ Animated)	Context-specific scenarios, synchronized subtitles	Job interview prep, airport navigation, cultural exchanges	Stronger vocabulary-context links, real-world application
Speech Recognition	Real-time learner input analysis, corrective feedback	Pronunciation practice, dialogue comparison	Immediate feedback, improved fluency
Simulations (Role-play)	Adaptive responses, immersive environments	Negotiating contracts, ordering food, and group discussions	Safe practice, confidence building, authentic interaction

Gamified and Interactive Exercises for Active Learning

Gamification is a key strategy that has become prominent in language education today, and AI is a key to reinforcing this practice as it allows a game to be dynamic and adaptive. Rather than a fixed and repetitious quiz, AI systems can produce interactive tasks that will grow increasingly difficult as the learner performs. As an illustration, a vocabulary game may begin with simple flashcards and move to complicated word association puzzles/sentence construction tasks as learners show proficiency. Grammar-oriented games may also be developed through simple fill-in tasks to in-game competitions of quick recall and knowledge.

With the help of generative AI, it is also possible to create narrative-driven experiences, in which learners can solve mysteries, undergo quests, or advance through levels by using proper English expressions. An example of this is a student acting as a detective to solve a case by posing questions using the English language, or a tourist going through a new city where every conversation he has demands proper usage of grammar and vocabulary. These plots not only give the learning process more interest but also mirror contextualized use of language, which makes the learners think critically about communication and not just memorize the rules.

In addition, gamified spaces have built-in points, badges, leaderboards, and streaks as a form of motivational reinforcement. To keep these mechanics purposeful, AI modifies them according to the progress of the learners, such as celebrating a good result in a weak area instead of just counting correct responses. This eases the fear that is commonly involved in learning a language and promotes perseverance with time. Competition, collaboration, and creativity are the three forces that can turn language learning into a pleasurable, immersive process with the help of AI-powered gamification: learners are not only encouraged by grades to learn but also by the feeling of achievement and discovery. Table 6 compares traditional exercises and AI-enhanced gamified alternatives to highlight the shift in learner engagement.

Table 6. Traditional vs. AI-powered gamified exercises

Learning Focus	Traditional Approach	AI-Powered Gamified Approach	Key Advantage
Vocabulary	Static word lists, flashcards	Adaptive games (word puzzles, sentence-building, context challenges)	Dynamic progression, contextual learning
Grammar	Repetitive drills, fill-in-the-blanks	Interactive challenges (real-time competitions, evolving difficulty)	Adaptive targeting of weak areas
Reading/ Context Use	Text-based comprehension questions	Narrative-driven quests (detective stories, travel adventures)	Story immersion, critical thinking
Motivation	Grades, test scores	Badges, points, leaderboards, streaks	Sustained engagement, positive reinforcement

Integration With Virtual Tutors and Chatbots for Language Practice

One of the most novel uses of AI in language learning is AI-assisted virtual tutors and chatbots, which provide learners with constant chances to train conversational English. Whereas human tutors may be of limited supply, AI tutors can be available to learners around the clock, instantly and adaptively giving feedback on their progress. These systems are emulating human-like conversation, so learners can train in structured conversation (e.g., ordering in a restaurant, checking into a hotel), as well as free-form conversation simulating a natural flow of conversation.

The most significant benefit of the AI chatbots is their adaptation feature. Conversations in the beginner level might be very scaffolded, and learners are directed through the conversation in steps with hints and directions. As the learner advances in proficiency, the chatbot will become less and less scaffolding in nature as the learner becomes more inclined to produce responses independently. Natural language understanding (NLU) enables such systems not just to recognize grammar and vocabulary errors but also to recognize more subtle errors in communication, like tone, politeness, or formality. An example here is an AI tutor who can tell you when you should address people in a polite or casual way in a professional or social context and thus teach an aspect of cultural competence as well as linguistic precision.

Also, virtual tutors are able to monitor the progress of the learners since they can detect mistakes that keep recurring and, therefore, modify lessons. Certain sites go even further and incorporate speech recognition technology, allowing learners to train their pronunciation using real-time corrective feedback. Such interactivity replicates the level of personalised attention that students get in the hands of a human tutor at a fraction of the expense and with an infinite supply. The combination of scalable, personalized, and culturally nuanced assistance makes the AI tutors and chatbots bring the power of effective practice of a language to learners in various socioeconomic and geographic backgrounds.

Enhancing Learner Motivation and Retention Through Interactivity

One of the best predictors of effective language acquisition is engagement, and AI-based interactivity is an important element in maintaining learner motivation and long-term retention. As opposed to passive learning resources, dynamically generated AI-based resources adjust to the needs of a particular learner and make lessons challenging without making them demoralizing. Such responsiveness facilitates a greater sense of agency and ownership of the learning experience because learners are in a position to micromanage their experiences instead of merely passively receiving information.

The ability to minimize fear of making mistakes is a great benefit of interactivity. Through the use of AI-driven chatbots, simulations, and games that learners can practice, they can work in a low-stakes setting in which learners see errors as learning experiences and not setbacks. Such atmosphere fosters experimentation, risk-taking, and the creative use of language- aspects that are essential to building fluency and communicative confidence. In addition, aspects like instant feedback loops assist learners in rectifying what they misinterpreted at once, avoiding fossilization of mistakes and producing better long-term retention.

The other important detail about the AI interactivity is its inclusiveness of learning styles. AI-generated animation and interactive video can be helpful to visual learners, speech-based exercises to auditory learners, and simulations and gamified tasks of hands-on activities to kinesthetic learners. This multimodal strategy guarantees that the varied learners are kept involved and enabled in enhancing equity in language education. Also, adaptive AI systems may track motivation levels, providing a personal reminder, motivational message, or progress visualization to maintain engagement in the long term. Finally, personalization, inclusivity, and real-time responsiveness mean that AI-based interactivity can serve as a means to not just deliver content, but also a means to teach persistence and resiliency in language learning. Such a combination of technology and pedagogy makes the atmosphere in which learners feel motivated, confident, and committed, and therefore have more chances to retain and achieve better results.

CHALLENGES AND ETHICAL CONSIDERATIONS

Although the use of generative AI provides such a strong potential to revolutionize the learning of the English language, there are multiple problems and ethical issues associated with its implementation. Accuracy, cultural sensitivity, curriculum alignment, and data privacy issues should be taken into consideration so that AI-generated content can help to improve, but not to harm, educational results.

Accuracy and Reliability of AI-Generated Content

The problem of the accuracy and reliability of the materials that have been produced by the generative AI is one of its most immediate concerns with regard to language education. Although big language models and other such systems can produce grammatically accurate sentences and contextually sensitive learning tasks, they are not impervious to petty or even significant mistakes. Poorly explained grammar, incorrect sentence construction, or even wrong vocabulary use may mislead and propagate false beliefs to learners and slow their learning process. The effects of such errors can be long-term, especially to beginners, because learners might have the patterns internalized and find it hard to unlearn them.

As opposed to the traditional teaching materials, which tend to be vetted by the teachers, the editors, and the experts in the subject, the AI-produced materials will often be directed to these levels of filtering. This absence of typical screening implies that the quality of AI content may be quite different with each interaction, which is not predictable by either teachers or students. As an example, an AI model can produce a great explanation of verb tenses in one example, but an unclear or incomplete explanation in another, and leave learners uncertain about the procedure to follow.

In order to ensure a high degree of reliability, the AI-created results would have to be thoroughly vetted, filtered, and checked by human educators prior to being used in classrooms in large numbers. Educators can also play a key role as gatekeepers and make sure that AI-generated exercises correspond to pedagogical objectives and accepted linguistic principles. Also, organizations and creators might embrace automated verification instruments or mixed systems in which content generated by AI is compared with databases of expert-authorized information. Finally, it will be necessary to find a compromise between the efficiency of AI and the human factor in protecting the integrity and reliability of learning resources facilitated by AI. Table 7 contrasts the potential risks of inaccuracies in AI-generated learning materials with the measures that can be taken to safeguard quality and reliability.

Table 7. Risks of inaccurate AI-generated content and safeguards

Risk	Example Impact on Learners	Mitigation Strategy
Inaccurate grammar or vocabulary	Learners internalize incorrect patterns	Human educator review and curation
Inconsistent quality of explanations	Confusion, lack of clarity in rules	Hybrid AI-human systems with expert databases
Misleading cultural/linguistic context	Reduced relevance of examples	Curriculum alignment checks
Lack of quality control vs. textbooks	Erosion of trust in materials	Verification tools and standardized vetting

Risks of Bias and Cultural Insensitivity in AI-Generated Materials

Generative AI systems are based on huge databases of books, websites, and digital interactions. Such datasets can never be free of cultural, social, and linguistic prejudices that exist in society. Consequently, AI-produced learning content can propagate stereotypes inadvertently, overshadow the voices of marginalized groups, or even share culturally insensitive messages. As an example, a reading passage, which aims to simulate daily life, can be over-representing the Western standards of culture, e.g., a café dinner or a university lecture, and fail to represent everyday situations that learners in other areas can relate to more. Such a lack of balance threatens to disengage students and make materials less relevant to their real-life experience.

Along with cultural narrowness, AI-written conversations and examples can be characterized by gender bias or implicit beliefs regarding professional and social roles. As an illustration, AI may produce examples that always describe men as engineers and women as nurses, which in turn contributes to obsolete stereotypes. Other, less obvious types of bias, including beliefs about family life, religious beliefs, or wealth, can also be found in created content. These trends are capable of undermining inclusivity and enforcing damaging worldviews when left untreated.

These risks will need a 3 pronged approach to address. First, training sets need to be diversified with the intention to incorporate wider cultural, linguistic, and social viewpoints. Second, the ability of bias detection (e.g., algorithmic fairness audits, human content moderation) should be integrated into an AI workflow. Third, learners and teachers ought to be in a position to comment and challenge AI output, which fosters the feedback loop and enhances awareness as well as system design. With the considerations of inclusiveness and cultural sensitivity, the AI-based language learning platforms may act as the instruments of not only linguistic growth but also promote the idea of international citizenship and mutual understanding.

Balancing Personalization With Standardized Curricula

Among the most significant benefits of AI in the educational field is the highly personalized nature of such learning. AI systems can adjust exercises, levels of difficulty, and rate of instruction to the strengths and weaknesses of the unique learner. This individualization assists students to get specific feedback, practice with a specific focus, and remain motivated by noting visible progress. Such adaptive systems can provide the much-needed support to learners struggling in the traditional classroom and present possibilities of higher equity.

Nevertheless, over-personalization can conflict with the requirement of standardised curriculum and evaluation systems. Educational institutions may work under the national or international standards that stipulate what students have to learn and how their performance is measured. Although individualized instructions can be of benefit to learners, they can also be over-customized, which leads to a fragmented development of skills that is not in line with other formal requirements, like university entrance exams or internationally recognized language skill suitability, or professional training standards. As an illustration, a student who is strongly oriented to conversational fluency with the help of personalized AI may fail to learn the academic writing skills needed in standardized tests.

In order to overcome this hurdle, personalization by using AI should be tightly aligned with organized curricular objectives. It is possible to design systems that include adaptive characteristics and fixed benchmarks so that learners can advance at the same or recognized standards in addition to receiving customized feedback. This could include mixed models in which AI prescribes exercises within a system designed by teachers or in which periodic standardized tests are built into an AI-controlled learning cascade. In addition, the coordination of educators, policymakers, as well as AI developers will become an essential part in achieving a balance between personalization and curriculum design. With such a balance, AI will allow students to succeed as individuals and at the same time ready them to meet shared academic and professional demands.

Data Privacy and Ethical Concerns in AI-Enabled Platforms

The introduction of AI into the educational field requires the gathering and analysis of large volumes of student-related information, such as test scores, hobbies, behavioral patterns, and voice samples, in the speech recognition case. Although such pieces of information enable AI systems to provide a tailored learning experience, they also present serious issues in regard to privacy, security, and ownership. When this sensitive information is improperly handled, it may be used in business interests, or data may be leaked in data breaches, or may be distributed to third parties without express permission. Such risks stand out particularly sharply with the involvement of minors, who might not be able to understand all the long-term consequences of data collection.

Beyond immediate risks of exposure, questions about data ownership and ethical use also emerge. Who is the ultimate owner of the data about the learner, the student, the educational institute, or the provider of technology? In the absence of clear governance frameworks, learners can be at the mercy of murky practices such as having their information kept indefinitely or having their information used to train commercial AI systems without their consent. These practices undermine trust and also raise higher issues of ethical involvement in terms of exploitation and digital inequity.

Very strict measures will have to be implemented to facilitate the ethical implementation of AI in education. These are the use of national and international requirements of data protection, open consent procedures in which the learners and guardians are well entrusted with the knowledge of the use of the data, and installation of safe technological infrastructures to avoid unauthorized access. Other principles that should be promoted by institutions and policymakers include data minimization (only the necessary information is gathered) and providing the learners with more significant control over their own information, such as the right to access their information, correct it, or remove it. When focusing on privacy and ethics, the process of language learning personalization and innovation can be made in a way that neither personal rights nor trust are affected. Table 8 summarizes key concerns in AI-enabled platforms and corresponding ethical safeguards.

Table 8. Data privacy risks and ethical safeguards in AI language learning platforms

Privacy/Ethical Concern	Potential Risk	Safeguard / Best Practice
Data breaches or misuse	Exposure of learner data (incl. minors)	Secure infrastructures, encryption
Unclear data ownership	Exploitation for commercial purposes	Transparent policies on ownership and consent
Excessive data collection	Digital inequality, exploitation	Data minimization (only essential data collected)
Long-term storage of personal data	Loss of learner control	Right to access, correct, and delete information
Use of data for training commercial AI	Lack of informed consent	Explicit opt-in consent processes

CONCLUSION

The introduction of Artificial Intelligence (AI), especially generative AI, into English language teaching is a great paradigm shift in the design, distribution, and experience of learning material. In this chapter, the ability of AI to create personalized, adaptive, and scalable content, both of the type of reading passages and grammar exercises, as well as vocabulary lists and multimedia materials, is pointed out. Situating content to the objectives and interests of learners, the AI makes learning more engaging, whereas interactive tools, simulations, gamified activities, and chatbots in conversational mode increase motivation and retention. Simultaneously, issues of accuracy, cultural sensitivity, data privacy, personalization/curricular concerns require close consideration to be made in the case of responsible adoption.

These developments have implications for more than one stakeholder. To teachers, AI opens the prospect of alleviating the workload of repetitiveness when it comes to creating content, leaving them with more time to teach at the higher tier, mentor, and facilitate critical thinking. To learners, AI offers customized, interactive, and customizable resources, which adapt alongside their level of proficiency and interests to make language learning more accommodating and inspiring. To developers, the concept of AI shows the necessity to develop platforms that are technically sophisticated and pedagogically sound, so that the tools can be innovative and pedagogically correct.

The future of AI is the future of the language learning endeavor, even better. Learning may be made more engaging and immersive by using multimodal AI systems, which combine text, speech, images, and video. Adaptive feedback in real-time can enable learners to get immediate, contextually based corrections on conversation or writing practice. Moreover, due to the growing development of AI technologies, hybrid models of human-AI teaching may be developed, in which AI performs all the individualization and practice functions, and educators concentrate on creativity and critical thinking, as well as on intercultural communication.

Simultaneously, the revolutionary power involved in the use of an AI should be balanced with the need to engage in responsible, ethical, and inclusive implementation. Achieving equal learning opportunities is possible by making sure that the contents of the AI-created resources are correct, impartial, culturally aware, and meet the educational requirements. Protection of privacy, openness in the application of information, and human oversight will continue playing a significant role. Finally, AI integration into the English language learning process should be performed responsibly to allow educators, policymakers, developers, and learners to work together and maximize opportunities and reduce risks.

REFERENCES

Ahmad, M., Ho, W. Y., Goyes Robalino, A. P., Maqsood, M., Ahmad, M., Ho, W. Y., Goyes Robalino, A. P., & Maqsood, M. (2025). Theoretical Implications of Generative AI for Content Generation in Geoinformatics Training. In A. Anna A. (Ed.), *Integration Strategies of Generative AI in Higher Education* (pp. 101–130). IGI Global Scientific Publishing. DOI: 10.4018/979-8-3693-5518-3.ch005

Ali, M. H., Kainat, M., Maqsood, M., Fernandez, S. F., Ali, S., & Ahmad, M. (2024). Chatbots in Academic Literacy Exploring AI in Education. In *Enhancing Higher Education and Research With OpenAI Models* (pp. 37–59). IGI Global. DOI: 10.4018/979-8-3693-1666-5.ch002

Allaithy, A., & Zaki, M. (2025). Evaluation of AI-generated reading comprehension materials for Arabic language teaching. *Computer Assisted Language Learning*, 1–33. Advance online publication. DOI: 10.1080/09588221.2025.2474037

Aravind, A., Durairaj, M., Chitkara, P., Baker El-Ebiary, Y. A., Muniyandy, E., Ushasree, L., & Ben Ammar, M. (2025). Adaptive AI-Based Personalized Learning for Accelerated Vocabulary and Syntax Mastery in Young English Learners. *International Journal of Advanced Computer Science and Applications*, *16*(4), 678. DOI: 10.14569/IJACSA.2025.0160467

Crompton, H., Edmett, A., Ichaporia, N., & Burke, D. (2024). AI and English language teaching: Affordances and challenges. *British Journal of Educational Technology*, *55*(6), 2503–2529. DOI: 10.1111/bjet.13460

Dua, I. K., & Patel, P. G. (2024). An introduction to Generative AI. In *Optimizing Generative AI Workloads for Sustainability: Balancing Performance and Environmental Impact in Generative AI* (pp. 1–37). Springer. DOI: 10.1007/979-8-8688-0917-0_1

Gao, B., Wang, Y., Xie, H., Hu, Y., & Hu, Y. (2023). Artificial Intelligence in Advertising: Advancements, Challenges, and Ethical Considerations in Targeting, Personalization, Content Creation, and Ad Optimization. In *SAGE Open* (Vol. 13, Issue 4). DOI: 10.1177/21582440231210759

Grammarly. (2018). *Best Plagiarism Checker & Proofreader | Grammarly*. Grammerly.

He, X. (2024). (n.d.). Enhancing Reading Comprehension with AI-Generated Adaptive Texts. *International Journal of New Developments in Education*, *6*(7), 46–52. DOI: 10.25236/IJNDE.2024.060708

Holmström, J., & Carroll, N. (2024). How organizations can innovate with generative AI. *Business Horizons*. Advance online publication. DOI: 10.1016/j.bushor.2024.02.010

Hung, Y. K., Huang, Y. C., Su, T. Y., Lin, Y. T., Cheng, L. P., Wang, B., & Sun, S. H. (2025). SimTube: Simulating Audience Feedback on Videos using Generative AI and User Personas. *International Conference on Intelligent User Interfaces, Proceedings IUI*, 1256–1271. /DOI: 10.1145/3708359.3712146

Hwang, W. Y., Nurtantyana, R., Purba, S. W. D., Hariyanti, U., Indrihapsari, Y., & Surjono, H. D. (2023). AI and Recognition Technologies to Facilitate English as Foreign Language Writing for Supporting Personalization and Contextualization in Authentic Contexts. *Journal of Educational Computing Research*, *61*(5), 1008–1035. Advance online publication. DOI: 10.1177/07356331221137253

Karim, S. A., Qotrunnnada, A., Hamzah, S., Anjani, N. M., Prianti, J., & Sihole, I. G. (2023). Promoting EFL Studentsâ€™ Speaking Performance through ELSA Speak: An Artificial Intelligence in English Language Learning. *Journal of Languages and Language Teaching*, *11*(4), 655–668. DOI: 10.33394/jollt.v11i4.8958

Kaswan, K. S., Dhatterwal, J. S., & Ojha, R. P. (2024). AI in personalized learning. In *Advances in technological innovations in higher education* (pp. 103–117). CRC Press. DOI: 10.1201/9781003376699-9

Klein, D. V., & McCartney, P. (2024). Delivering Live Q&A in Videos via Synthetic Content Generation Using Generative Artificial Intelligence. *Defensive Publications Series*. https://www.tdcommons.org/dpubs_series/6984

Leong, J., Pataranutaporn, P., Danry, V., Perteneder, F., Mao, Y., & Maes, P. (2024). Puting Things into Context: Generative AI-Enabled Context Personalization for Vocabulary Learning Improves Learning Motivation. *Conference on Human Factors in Computing Systems - Proceedings*. /DOI: 10.1145/3613904.3642393

Maghsudi, S., Lan, A., Xu, J., & Van Der Schaar, M. (2021). Personalized Education in the Artificial Intelligence Era: What to Expect Next. *IEEE Signal Processing Magazine*, *38*(3), 37–50. Advance online publication. DOI: 10.1109/MSP.2021.3055032

Maqsood, M., Aqil, M., Das, B. C., & Ahmad, M. (2026). Generative AI for Computer-Assisted Language Learning. In *Artificial Intelligence and the Future of Personalized Education* (pp. 239–264). IGI Global Scientific Publishing.

Murtaza, M., Ahmed, Y., Shamsi, J. A., Sherwani, F., & Usman, M. (2022). AI-Based Personalized E-Learning Systems: Issues, Challenges, and Solutions. In *IEEE Access* (Vol. 10). DOI: 10.1109/ACCESS.2022.3193938

Niemi, H. (2024). AI in education and learning: Perspectives on the education ecosystem. In *New Frontiers in Science in the Era of AI* (pp. 169–194). Springer. DOI: 10.1007/978-3-031-61187-2_11

Perez-Guerra, C., & Cao, J. (2021). Estimating Memory Retention Traces of Foreign Language Vocabulary from Reading Interaction Data. *Proceedings of the 2021 IEEE 24th International Conference on Computer Supported Cooperative Work in Design, CSCWD 2021*. DOI: 10.1109/CSCWD49262.2021.9437841

Rukiati, E., Wicaksono, J. A., Taufan, G. T., & Suharsono, D. D. (2023). AI on Learning English: Application, Benefit, and Threat. *Journal of Language, Communication, and Tourism*, *1*(2), 32–40. Advance online publication. DOI: 10.25047/jlct.v1i2.3967

Rusmiyanto, R., Huriati, N., Fitriani, N., Tyas, N. K., Rofi'i, A., & Sari, M. N. (2023). The Role Of Artificial Intelligence (AI) In Developing English Language Learner's Communication Skills. *Journal of Education*, *6*(1), 750–757. Advance online publication. DOI: 10.31004/joe.v6i1.2990

Sawin, T. (2025). A Five-Ecosystem Approach to Generative AI in Language Classrooms. In *Rethinking Language Education in the Age of Generative AI* (pp. 9–28). Routledge. DOI: 10.4324/9781003426929-3

Sayed, W. S., Noeman, A. M., Abdellatif, A., Abdelrazek, M., Badawy, M. G., Hamed, A., & El-Tantawy, S. (2023). AI-based adaptive personalized content presentation and exercises navigation for an effective and engaging E-learning platform. *Multimedia Tools and Applications*, *82*(3), 3303–3333. Advance online publication. DOI: 10.1007/s11042-022-13076-8 PMID: 35789938

Sidwell, M. D., Bonner, L. W., Bates-Brantley, K., & Wu, S. (2024). Utilizing Text-Generative AI for Creating Oral Reading Fluency Probes. *Intervention in School and Clinic*, *60*(2), 119–125. Advance online publication. DOI: 10.1177/10534512241235896

Wu, J., Wang, Y., Chen, F., Yin, X., & He, Y. (2025). Impact of AI-Powered Adaptive Learning Platforms on English Reading Proficiency: Evidence From Structural Equation Modeling. *IEEE Access : Practical Innovations, Open Solutions*, *13*, 88230–88242. DOI: 10.1109/ACCESS.2025.3571055

Yadav, R., Huzooree, G., Yadav, M., & Gangodawilage, D. S. K. (2025). Generative AI for Personalized Learning Content Creation. In *Transformative AI Practices for Personalized Learning Strategies* (pp. 107–130). IGI Global Scientific Publishing. DOI: 10.4018/979-8-3693-8744-3.ch005

Yunjiu, L., Wei, W., & Zheng, Y. (2022). Artificial Intelligence-Generated and Human Expert-Designed Vocabulary Tests: A Comparative Study. *SAGE Open*, *12*(1), 21582440221082130. Advance online publication. DOI: 10.1177/21582440221082130

Chapter 5
Artificial Intelligence in Education

Omdev Dahiya
https://orcid.org/0000-0003-2245-2692
Lovely Professional University, Punjab, India

ABSTRACT

Artificial Intelligence (AI) is revolutionizing education through personalized learning, reducing administrative burdens and increasing student engagement. In this chapter, we will describe the key technologies that are the basis of AI in education, the ethical issues relating to data privacy, algorithmic fairness, and teachers' shifting role. Also discussed are the emergence of adaptive learning technologies, learning analytics, and systems powered by AI, which are providing a new approach to pedagogy and ways of doing things in educational institutions. The chapter will examine the developments in generative AI, affective computing, and cooperative human-AI feedback systems. Although presented theoretically, we will draw on global examples and case studies to present a critical examination of how AI is cultivating inclusive, flexible and innovative learning environments whilst responding to challenges of access and equity across the globe.

1. INTRODUCTION

Artificial Intelligence (AI) is rapidly and significantly transforming the education system by developing intelligent components that assist with decision-making, administrative tasks, and personalizing student learning experiences. In a period where the education system is dealing with student engagement, learning styles, and operational efficiency, AI becomes a very strong force to change the landscape of both teaching and institutional models (Luckin, 2017). Through AI-enabled technol-

DOI: 10.4018/979-8-3373-3561-2.ch005

ogy, educators can deliver personalized content, provide automated assessments and feedback, and gain immediate insight into student performance, with the likelihood of creating better learning outcomes, all while advancing institutional performance (Zawacki-Richter *et. al.,* 2019).

The global shift towards digital learning, accelerated by the COVID-19 pandemic, has also accelerated AI usage in education. The once distant AI innovation is now a part of today's education systems, influencing curriculum delivery, engagement, assessment practices, and inclusive access (Mahapatra *et. al.,* 2024). As AI continues to develop, its influence on education will only become more significant, fostering a move towards more adaptive, efficient, and equitable learning solutions.

1.1 Emergence of Artificial Intelligence in Education

The view of employing intelligent systems in education originated with computer-assisted instruction and the initial intelligent tutoring systems (ITS), dating back to the 1980s. Since then, significant advancements have been made to the field by relying on intelligent technology, such as machine learning, natural language processing (NLP), and educational data mining. These advancements have enabled the creation of more adaptive and context-aware educational tools that can respond to the needs of individual learners (Woolf, 2010). Many of the principal learning management systems (LMS) and massive open online course (MOOC) platforms are incorporating advanced AI capabilities to suggest individualized learning resources, fill learning gaps, and provide timely academic support.

Recognizing the capacity of AI to transform education, governments and policy-making organizations across the world are developing their educational systemic strategies in line with this technology. For example, India's National Education Policy (NEP) 2020 places emphasis on the use of technology, including AI, to foster inclusive, equitable, and quality education (Smiley *et. al.,* 2021). The European Union Digital Education Action Plan (2021-2027) similarly identifies AI as critical to the digital transformation of education (Vrabec & Furtáková, 2024). These examples illustrate the emerging consensus across the globe surrounding the role of AI in shaping education by making the future of learning possible.

1.2 Objectives and Scope of the Chapter

In this chapter we will explore the emerging role of Artificial Intelligence (AI) in education, its aspects of use and misuse, benefits and drawbacks, challenges and future directions, noting the broad views of current generative AI tools in education, focusing on how AI technologies are being incorporated into educational systems and ecosystems to optimize learning engagements, equip educators with smarter educational tools (teaching), and develop efficient administrative processes. The chapter covers both the positive aspects as well as drawing attention to a critical discussion of ethical considerations concerning the use of AI in education, such as data privacy, transparency, algorithmic bias, etc. In terms of fostering meaningful and responsible use, it also presents decision-oriented policy implications and research-supported recommendations with a focus on long-term consideration about equitable and sustainable use of AI educational systems.

2. AI APPLICATIONS IN EDUCATION

2.1 Intelligent Tutoring Systems (ITS)

Intelligent Tutoring Systems (ITS) are one of the most powerful examples of AI in education that aim to replicate the responsiveness and customization possible through one-on-one human tutoring. Often AI-based, and sometimes referred to as online tutors, these systems provide a personalized approach to instructional support by recognizing student input, identifying misunderstandings, and updating and changing the material and delivery in real-time (Nkambou *et. al.*, 2010). Early research using ITS sought to personalize the learning experience for each student, helping to resolve misunderstandings and deepen mastery at the individual student's pace. An example of an ITS is Carnegie Learning's MATHia - one of the most researched ITS on the market today, which uses cognitive modeling to monitor student use and progress while providing targeted feedback. MATHia 'feels' when learners activate confused states, when they fail to correlate steps in a complex problem, and even when they struggle with fundamental mathematics concepts. MATHia's timing to intervene helps reduce misinterpretations while building on mathematical concepts as they occur. These systems highlight the potential for AI to provide scalable, individualized learning opportunities in various educational contexts (Pane *et. al.*, 2017).

2.2 Adaptive Learning Platforms

Adaptive learning systems utilize AI and data analytics to produce tailored learning paths based on the unique applied needs of each learner. These systems display learning adaptive capabilities due to consistently monitoring student behavior, performance, engagement, etc. This allows the system to intelligently adapt and change time-efficiently the sequencing of content, level of dominance in difficulty of the content, and/or assessment measures concurrently while the learning is taking place (Dede *et. al.*, 2005). This has the ability to not only promote learning and optimize it based on a student's current pace, but also identify missed or ineffectively covered areas in a subject, with the potential to support the student's opportunity for improved learning. DreamBox Learning and Knewton are prominent examples of companies effective adaptive instructional strategies and have consistently enhanced student success by personalizing the instructional paths and resources directly to a student's assessed strengths and growth area (Mao, 2025), therefore closing a learning gap and promoting full learner engagement. As a result, adaptive learning systems have and will assist in more effectively educating some learners, which in effect means more inclusive and effective ways to educate, as others in the same learning context are increasing learning engagement.

2.3 AI-Powered Assessment and Feedback Tools

AI-enabled assessment tools are changing the landscape of educator assessment of student work through automation of the grading process, the provision of immediacy of feedback for students, and the application of Natural Language Processing (NLP) patterns to analyze written products. Tools like these save educators time and provide students with opportunities to obtain instantaneous feedback and information about their performance, in recognizing potential areas of strength and opportunities for improvement (McNamara *et. al.,* 2014). These platforms, like Gradescope and Grammarly, utilize AI-driven procedures to assess writing quality and can indicate grammatical and stylistic issues with the writing as well as the depth and clarity of critical analysis (Yeung *et. al.,* 2025). AI-based assessments are facilitating the process of learning being seen as an active, self-directed, iterative process while also attending to the increasing complexities and diversity of classroom context for educators providing consistent, scalable, and data-driven assessment.

2.4 Natural Language Processing in Education

Natural Language Processing (NLP) enhances educational technologies by making it possible for machines to understand, interpret, and generate human language in meaningful, creative ways. This quality leads to a wide range of possibilities: real-time language translation, speech-to-text transcription, sentiment analysis, and conversational agents. These tools enhance accessibility while also providing more engaging and personalized learning experiences. One noteworthy example is the ability for recently deployed AI (artificial intelligence) pronunciation and speech analysis tools to assist language learners with immediate, accurate feedback on their spoken language abilities. These AI tools provide scaffolding and help develop learners' confidence and fluency as they can provide accurate and timely corrections and assistance when it is most needed (Attali & Burstein, 2006). If NLP continues to grow, the combination with educational contexts will lead to more natural, intuitive, and inclusive learning interactions.

2.5 Virtual Assistants and Chatbots

Educational chatbots and virtual assistants are becoming essential elements of current learning environments as they provide students with 24/7 available academic support. The use of these AI systems creates real-time academic support for students because they can help students and answer questions about coursework, assessment deadlines, campus resources, and admin processes, among others. Because they do this 24/7 with accuracy without involving humans, they improve student engagement and satisfaction and lessen workloads for faculty and support staff (Winkler & Söllner, 2018). For example, Pounce, the chatbot at Georgia State University, helped the institution reduce "summer melt,"...when students accept admission but never enroll, because the chatbot asked students questions and gave them reminders about their enrollment checklist during the summer (McGrath *et. al.,* 2024). As we see in this case of Georgia State University, educational chatbots are re-emerging as an active participatory mechanism in influencing student retention and student access; effectively, it highlights how they are key allies for institutions to promote efficiencies and student success.

2.6 Administrative Automation

Beyond the traditional classroom setting, AI is transforming educational administration by automating crucial operational tasks, including attendance tracking, timetable scheduling, resource management, and academic integrity monitoring. These advanced systems assist educational institutions in streamlining their operations, resulting in increased efficiency and reduced administrative burdens on teachers and staff. A notable example is Turnitin, which utilizes sophisticated artificial intelligence algorithms to identify potential cases of plagiarism and guarantee the authenticity of student assignments. By analyzing texts against extensive collections of academic and online resources, Turnitin aids institutions in maintaining high academic standards and fostering a culture of integrity and ethical research practices. As the demands on administrative tasks increase in size and complexity, AI-driven tools are becoming essential in ensuring the smooth functioning of institutions while upholding academic integrity (Goddiksen *et. al.,* 2024).

2.7 AI in Teacher Training and Continuous Professional Development

While Artificial Intelligence is not only changing the model of student learning, it is also changing the model of teacher learning and development. AI-based teacher training platforms are now being utilized to create personalized professional development, assess instruction, and provide feedback and recommendations for teachers. These technologies aim to create learning environments that respond to the learning activities of students, while restructuring learning opportunities for teachers who teach and support learning.

AI is improving teacher learning by creating personalized learning pathways for teachers. Similar to how adaptive learning occurs for students, AI learning systems can suggest modules and micro-courses relevant to a teacher based on their existing skills, obstacles in their classrooms, and pedagogical learning objectives. For example, CENTA, the Centre for Teacher Accreditation, in India, has developed AI mentors to use teachers' responses to tests, their engagement with assessment products, and their use of in-course resources, to provide helpful recommendations for teachers. CENTA uses performance gaps to make recommendations for courses, and the AI research demonstrates that professional development is unique to each user and dynamic, and used for teachers' ongoing learning rather than episodic learning (Jia Zhang & Zhuo Zhang, 2024).

AI-assisted observation and feedback tools are yet another significant area of advancement. Applications such as TALENT (Teacher Analytics for Learning Environments & Needs Tracking) leverage machine learning to observe teaching sessions, through either video or audio, and evaluate them based on specific pedagogical practices and standards, classroom interactions, and how well the teacher gives directions. They provide teachers with automated, but still constructive feedback using rubrics that are consistent with the evidence-based teaching standards. Additionally, AI systems can transcribe, analyze, and identify students' interactions with their teachers, providing deeper insight into the classroom interaction.

The use of Natural Language Processing (NLP) to evaluate written reflections and discussion posts as part of teacher training has allowed for automated sentiment analyses and quality checks. This reduces the work for the mentor and maintains consistent and fair evaluations (Alvero *et. al.,* 2021). AI can identify linguistic patterns that indicate the presence of confusion, anxiety, and/or student resistance to specific pedagogical ideas, which will help mentors identify meaningful ways to intervene.

Related to the idea of the ability of AI to promote equity in teacher development, however, the use of AI in teacher development raises ethical issues. When we use AI to evaluate teachers, issues of surveillance, consent, and misuse of data emerge; we can confuse formative feedback with punitive surveillance. If teachers feel that their sense of autonomy is infringed upon or that their identity as a professional is compromised in an analogue dataset, then how can we expect them to flourish as humans aspiring to grow professionally? For this reason, any possible implementation of AI in teacher training must demonstrate the highest level of transparency, opt-in consent, and fitness of purpose. The integration of, and subsequent training in, AI should focus on building a culture of improvement and support rather than a culture of accountability (possible scrutiny of teachers) (Holmes & Porayska-Pomsta, 2021).

AI tools also lend themselves to addressing issues of equity in teacher development. Teachers working remotely or in low-resource settings now have access to high-quality coaching and peer-learning opportunities through AI-enhanced platforms. During the COVID-19 pandemic, AI tools became instrumental in supporting teachers' adjustment to technology-enhanced remote or hybrid learning environments. Initiatives like UNESCO's AI for Teacher Readiness Framework speak to the potential for AI to democratize access to quality professional learning materials with respect to geography and language, and more (Fengchun *et. al.,* 2021).

AI offers exciting possibilities for reconceptualizing teacher professional learning in ways that are personalized, scalable, and evidence-informed. But, it must be combined with professional learning opportunities to support teacher understanding of AI literacy, engagement with ethical considerations, and collaborating with AI to develop new practices. Teachers should not be thought of as passive users but as co-designers in the use and knowledge building of these tools in practice. As AI continues to permeate educational systems, teacher agency and informed consent must be ensured, so as to not allow AI to replace professional learning opportunities for growth.

3. BENEFITS OF AI INTEGRATION IN EDUCATIONAL SETTINGS

3.1 Personalized Learning

AI's most significant and transformative potential for education is the ability to move toward personalized learning. AI-enabled systems can track a student's learning patterns, preferences, strengths, and weaknesses to create a learning experience tailored to each learner's needs by adjusting the pace, order, and/or format of delivery (Baker & Yacef, 2009). This personalized learning experience differs from traditional models to allow for unique engagements with content based on a learner's distinctive cognitive skills, abilities, and approaches to learning, unlike the previous one-size-fits-all models. From these personal experiences, students become not only more engaged with content but also show a higher retention of knowledge, resulting in improved academic performance. Studies indicate that AI-perceived personalization of learning is overwhelmingly beneficial for learners who learn at different paces, struggle with learning, and/or come from non-traditional education contexts, making their learning experience inclusive (El-Sabagh, 2021). As such, AI is offering education an opportunity to move toward equitable, responsive, and learner-centered/inclusive learning experiences than ever before.

3.2 Enhanced Student Engagement and Motivation

AI-enhanced educational tools, including gamified learning experiences, interactive simulations, and intelligent tutoring systems, are essential tools in understanding how to help develop student motivation and engagement (Jia & Lu, 2025). These tools provide very different approaches than static content delivery; they are responsive modes of instruction that address learner emotions through real-time feedback and encouragement, and can reason about the angst students may express through heat maps and adjust task difficulty. The response capabilities of these technologies simplify the process of keeping students engaged and in their optimal engagement space by maintaining just the right amount of challenge to keep them engaged, without becoming overwhelmed. Additionally, AI chatbots and virtual assistants help maintain ongoing forward-looking interactions through instant feedback and 24/7 academic support. These technologies are capable of providing feedback on a question about a concept developed at 11:30 p.m., or assisting students with completing a challenging task, to ensure active engagement and ongoing student-directed learning (Schei *et. al.,* 2024). By being more relevant and providing an immersive encounter that is supportive and responsive, AI is helping students feel positive affect and maintaining engagement while ensuring they are connected, all while making the experience much better.

3.3 Real-Time Feedback and Assessment

AI is changing the paradigm of formative assessment by automating and evaluating the learning activity outputs of a student in real-time and during a student's learning activities and assignments. By using intelligent systems that can immediately offer a customized report to help students identify and correct problems immediately, AI formative assessments eliminate the waiting period between the completion of a learning activity and the evaluation of that activity by an instructor (Banihashem *et. al.,* 2022). Not only is the understanding solidified by the immediacy, but the learning was self-directed and thoughtful as well. Applications like Gradescope and ScribeSense provide educators additional time to provide custom, rationale, and data-informed actualization of learning for each student, and efficiently evaluate an entire assessment when they would not be able to in the past alone (Piech *et.*

al., 2015). Formative assessment systems using AI technologies can enhance the instructional responsiveness to student-directed learning and maximize the ownership students have of their learning by reducing administrative and evaluation tasks, and highlight learning needs for individual students.

3.4 Scalability of Quality Education

AI is playing an essential role in ensuring that quality education is scalable and accessible like never before. By powering systems that can be used for personalized instruction at scale, AI allows educational institutions to serve staggering numbers of learners while maintaining personalization. The ability of AI to be used in Massive Open Online Courses (MOOCs), that can service thousands, and in some cases millions, of learners across the world, while accommodating each of their unique learning styles, pace, and backgrounds, is unprecedented personalization at scale and a true lever for equity in education. This is particularly impactful in developing contexts, where the greatest barriers to quality education are often teacher shortages, lack of infrastructure, and limited resources. These learner characteristics are significantly detached from quality education, but the use of AI is lowering these barriers to access high-quality, personalized approaches to learning, regardless of location and/or social circumstance (Luan *et. al.,* 2020).

3.5 Data-Driven Decision Making

AI systems are revolutionizing decision-making in education and producing meaningful analytics designed for teachers, administrators, and policymakers. This is more than simply surface-level data; AI provides extensive analytics for visibility into issues such as student performance, engagement trajectories, and considerations of learning gains. One of the most salient uses of AI technologies is in the early identification of at-risk students—students who are not performing satisfactorily, at-risk of disengagement from their courses, or at-risk of dropping out. Using predictive analytics, AI technologies identify the subtle indicators and warning signs that would likely never be noticed, relying purely on traditional evaluative methods. This invisible data is essential in the early identification of at-risk students, timely intervention, and provision of targeted support (Ling *et. al.,* 2023). Furthermore, AI-enabled analytics assist curriculum development and allocation of available resources, primarily aimed at supporting students and important institutional realignments to changing educational contexts. AI provides resources for transforming data into valuable data-driven action and assists educational stakeholders at all levels to make smarter, more responsive, and more student-centered decisions.

3.6 Inclusive and Accessible Learning

AI is quickly becoming a powerful catalyst for inclusivity in education, especially with regard to learners with disabilities. Through intelligent and adaptive supports, AI-powered tools are helping to pave the way to learning environments that foster success for all students. Technologies like speech-to-text converters, visual recognition systems for individuals with vision challenges, and AI-enhanced sign-language avatars for the hard of hearing are helping to eliminate long-standing accessibility challenges to enable equal opportunities for participation within classroom activities (Shinohara & Wobbrock, 2016). These technologies support students with varied physical, sensory, and cognitive needs to access educational content in ways that accommodate their ability levels. Additionally, AI-powered real-time translation is enhancing inclusive learning in multicultural and multilingual classrooms, supporting students and teachers with communication, regardless of language background (Jia *et. al.,* 2022). Together, these strategies are beginning to transform what inclusive education looks and feels like, ensuring that diversity in learning is not a challenge, but rather something to be embraced and celebrated in the learning experience - the essence of being an inclusive educator.

3.7 Neurodiversity and AI in Education

Within the last several years, conversations about education have engaged with the idea of neurodiversity. Indeed, we have come to appreciate the ways learners can vary in cognitive processing styles, self-regulating attention and engagement, language comprehension, and amid various sensory preferences. Conditions, like autism spectrum disorder (ASD), dyslexia, and Attention Deficit Hyperactivity Disorder (ADHD), do not signify shortfalls, but variables in the spectrum of human learning. Artificial Intelligence (AI) is becoming a key collaborator in developing responsive, individualized pathways for neurodiverse learners.

AI technology allows for the possible disengagement from our traditional educational practices, such that instruction is not wholly standardized for diverse cognitive profiles. For example, learners with dyslexia have truly benefited from AI-enhanced tools such as Microsoft Immersive Reader, which allows them to make adjustments to pulp font (their own choice of font style, background color, letter spacing, and column width) and features voice aid for real-time support. Additionally, AI-powered platforms, such as Ghotit Real Writer, that employ advanced Natural Language Processing (NLP) support students' attempts to generate grammatically correct text, not only for formal texts but also for note-taking in class—and to manage frustration which can be a significant barrier to would-be writers, including students with dysgraphia or dyslexia (Dignum, 2019).

AI systems can assist with social-emotional learning for students with autism through the use of technologies driven by affective computing. These systems analyze combinations of facial expressions, tone of voice, and the patterns of gesture to instruct the learner how to recognize emotions and respond to social cues. For example, QTrobot is a socially assistive robot that interacts with autistic children using AI principles that encourage engagement, imitation, and joint attention (Sundara & Narendran, 2023). The development of engagement, imitation when engaged with another, and joint attention are all markers of development that are delayed or absent in learners with ASD. By replicating social situations with fixed sequences of information with a machine learning element self-adjustable, these artificial intelligence tools provide a safe and efficient space to practice social skills with other people (the robots).

Another important application is that AI-based approaches can be applied through attention regulation and executive function support. Simultaneously, AI-enabled platforms can directly measure student engagement in each lesson and customize the pacing, complexity, or format of the learning tasks according to the measured engagement. This is particularly helpful for students with ADHD because of the possible variable span of attention. Therefore, AI might offer adjusting learning modules that are shorter and offer interactive content that shifts between visual and kinesthetic content as engagement depletes over time. A few platforms have begun adding biometric feedback features (e.g., heart, forms of gaze tracking) that will instruct the machine to recognize when cognitive overload is occurring to instruct the learner to be mindful or to stop what they are doing and take a break. This may enhance more focused learning, thereby contributing to wellness (Matei & Bertino, 2023).

AI systems can support educators who are working to understand neurodiverse learners with an analytics dashboard, which displays information about their specific learning patterns, areas of struggle, and interaction styles. Despite encoded patterns of behaviour not translating into a lack of engagement (for example, a learner not maintaining eye contact, or taking extra time to respond), AI tools offer contextualized and rich data and best describe each learner's distinct rate of processing information and allow educators to adapt their modifications for teaching while reinforcing the educator's empathy and patience in their pedagogy.

While the pivot to AI to support neurodiversity should follow ethical principles of agency, transparency, and dignity, one of the biggest concerns is not 'fixing' neurodiverse learners to normalizing standards simply because AI affords you new affordances. The intention should always be to celebrate learners' strengths and create spaces where difference is celebrated, and the use of AI as a tool with respect to the inclusion of neurodiversity includes including sense of difference in systemic flexibility.

That being said, accessibility is always an issue. For a lot of the leading-edge tools, the fact remains that the tools are still only available in affluent institutional or private contexts. We must address and celebrate equity in access for learners from underrepresented communities so that we do not perpetuate existing disparities under the facade of technology (Cowls & Floridi, 2018).

AI can become a redeeming force for accepting neurodiversity, not as an add-on to mainstream education, but as a springboard to rethink inclusive pedagogy. When there is a convergence between AI activities and the core principles of universal design for learning (UDL), it can assist educators in forming a learner-centered environment that is responsive, acceptable, and future-proof for all learners, regardless of their neural makeup.

4. CHALLENGES AND ETHICAL CONSIDERATIONS

4.1 Data Privacy and Security Concerns

A key obstacle regarding AI in education is the responsible collection, storage, and usage of sensitive data about students. AI systems use large amounts of personal and behavioral data to create personalized learning experiences and prediction insights. It is also possible for students to be severely harmed, such as identity fraud, invasive monitoring, and unfair data categorization, if this data is not safeguarded (Utreras & Pontelli, 2020). Regulatory efforts such as the European Union's General Data Protection Regulation (GDPR) and India's Digital Personal Data Protection Act (2023) provide education technology providers with specific guidelines on how they collect, use, and process student data. The emphasis of these regulations is on transparency, the importance of consent of users being informed, and data minimization - Only collect what is needed, as well as to prioritize informed consent (Booth *et. al.,* 2023), to protect against poor ethics and ill-willed systems misusing data. Therefore, educational organizations are responsible for verifying that AI tools operate by reasonable cybersecurity standards and comply with encryption standards. This is critical for areas with fewer resources where the knowledge of data privacy and the absence of necessary infrastructure make students even more vulnerable (Calvo & D'Mello, 2010). Balancing the promise of AI to promote teaching and learning and the responsibility of stewardship over data is necessary to manage a level of student trust and promote protection in a digital teaching and learning space.

4.2 Algorithmic Bias and Fairness

AI has transformative potential for education, but it is not without challenges, one of the most important is the possibility of reinforcing, or worse, increasing, prevailing social and educational inequalities. AI systems learn from data that has been present in time and historically, so if the data is biased, the algorithm will follow suit. This is often driven by just a few groups being overwhelmingly represented in the data, and the reverse happening for under-represented students, where it is less accurate, and perhaps unfair (Håkansson Lindqvist *et. al.*, 2024). AI-based grading systems have shown the ability to score essays of non-native English writers lower than their native speaking counterparts. These differences are more reflective of language bias than academic ability (O'neil, 2017). Tackling these challenges is going to require intentional and continuous practice—proactively checking AI models to promote fairness, developing transparency about the decision-making process, and representing varied demographic data throughout the development process. If not, algorithmic bias and discrimination erode trust, undermine perceptions of credibility in educational technologies, and ultimately, reinforce the same inequalities that AI in education intends to disrupt.

4.3 Overdependence on Technology

Although AI can create new efficiencies and effective practices in education, over-reliance on automated systems presents some consequences. For instance, with too much AI involvement in their education, students may lose out on developing vital critical thinking and social-emotional learning (SEL) skills that require human interaction and engagement. Furthermore, educators themselves may place too much trust in AI-generated recommendations and ultimately lose their autonomy as professionals and their pedagogical expertise (Slade & Prinsloo, 2013). In addition, too much automation means too little "human touch," with empathy, motivation, and ethical reasoning being core elements of meaningful education. These fallible human experiences are fundamental elements of educating well-rounded learners who are prepared as part of their humanity and more than just college and career-ready. Therefore, the key is identifying the right fusion of AI support strategies and the human value of teaching by continuing to encourage innovative education practices through increasingly holistic and human instruction in education.

4.4 Teacher Displacement and Role Redefinition

The emergence of AI within education has sparked important conversations about the role of teachers in this new educational milieu. While educators will likely be replaced by AI completely in the next generation, AI is taking over certain tasks of teacher work: grading assignments, sharing standardized content, and delivering personalized tutoring to students directly (Selwyn, 2019). This shift toward AI in education, will directly challenge our thinking about the role(s) of the teacher to shape an educational landscape where AI works hand in hand with teachers, rather than taking their place altogether; our reconceptualization of the teacher's role must be to move beyond the dispensing of information, to one where the educator is a facilitator, mentor and designer of rich and meaningful learning experiences. Where technology can accompany and support educators, not replace them.

To successfully lead this transformation, professional development programs need to develop educators' skills to use AI tools effectively, as well as help educators understand the ethical considerations surrounding these AI tools. Unfortunately, a legacy of resistance to change in professional learning, combined with a lack of digital literacy and comfort with using technology, will provide certain challenges within many educational communities, which may impede the pace of integrating AI (Amara *et. al.*, 2024). We don't want to lose time bringing educators up to speed. If EdTech developers, policy leaders, and post-secondary education teacher education leaders start rationalizing their educators' comfort with technology, we may see better engagement around further discussions of technological tools and ethical decision making. Teaching educators to embrace the slow and steady development through ongoing professional learning and conversation with their peers and communities is crucial to develop their comfort and teaching presence in the online world.

4.5 Ethical Use of Student Data

When using student data for prediction and personalization, we are faced with some deep ethical questions. Although predictive analytics could be considered powerful in identifying students who may need additional assistance, the act of designating someone as "at-risk" could lead to the reinforcement of negative expectations or unnecessary psychological strain, sometimes referenced as a self-fulfilling prophecy (Williamson & Eynon, 2020). The ethical implications raise serious questions about privacy: Who should have access to this sensitive information? How is the data being used? And perhaps most importantly, are students aware of or involved in these decisions that have ramifications for their education? In order to grapple with these difficult questions responsibly, schools need to be consciously creating governance procedures that make the students' rights and dignity central to the processes involved in decision-making. That could include informed consent processes, continual vigilance in detecting and decreasing bias, and an endeavor to use explainable AI (XAI) models that have processes making the decisions understandable to and accountable to students (Amershi *et. al.*, 2019). By centralizing these important ethical concepts within any use of AI technology in education, institutions can establish trust built into, respect for students' needs, and equity as part of the expanding world of digital learning.

4.6 Emotional Dependency on AI Tutors: A Hidden Risk

As Artificial Intelligence becomes increasingly aware of emotional issues and is intertwined in education, there is an emerging concern about emotional dependency on AI tutors. While an AI tutor could only distinguish between animal happiness, it can function as an empathetic figurative partner, provide motivational support, and engage in emotionally responsive social interactions. Using AI to support students is becoming increasingly prevalent, and especially in one-on-one situations like tutoring or mentoring, raises important questions as to what the psychological consequences are for the developing learner, particularly for children and teenagers.

Affective computing, or Emotional AI, has progressed over the last decade to the extent that AI tutors can recognize learners' emotions via facial expressions, intonation, eye movements, or physiological markers such as blasted heart rate. Products such as Replika or Woebot, and AI-enhanced virtual agents embedded in products/platforms like MATHia or Duolingo, react to user emotion while the product is engaged by offering encouragement whilst the user is frustrated or adjusting the difficulty of a task while recommending users to take a break if there are signs of stress (Williamson & Eynon, 2020). While these tools certainly engage students while promoting learning, particularly for students with social anxiety or when consistent human supports are difficult to maintain, important questions for individual emotional development persist.

Nonetheless, such emotionally competent systems can also obscure the distinction between supportive technology and attempted companionship. Research has suggested that some students start to behave toward AI tutors not as a tool, but as an emotionally significant actor, becoming comforted by the AI, imparting personal information to the AI, and starting a habitual association. The danger in this, especially with younger users, lies in the thought that students may mistake the emotional responses from an AI—for a reciprocating emotional relationship—where the AI replaces human interaction and compromises the opportunity for the formative development of empathy, interpersonal communication, and social resilience (Amershi *et. al.,* 2019).

Additionally, this creates ethical considerations. Even the most humanlike AI systems are not an emotionally sentient person: they are programs that do not possess consciousness or feeling and that delivery responses based on data-driven, machine-learned algorithms that have been trained to appear humanlike in responding to human affect. Advocating for students to develop emotional, bond-like relationships with any AI system, even one that curates their responses to make them seem emotionally ascribed—can be misleading and sometimes a form of manipulation, particularly when it is not made clear that the relational and responsive functions are an artificial, formulated response. Schools of education and programs must have the ethics of AI, including the duty of honesty, transparency, and duty of care, to ensure students are aware of their interaction and relationship with a machine, not a person.

Emotional overreliance can lead to an additional negative outcome of learned helplessness. When students utilize emotional AI for validation or action-oriented help, they essentially unlearn or erode their own self-efficacy and self-reliance, and they reduce the amount of help they seek from human teachers and classmates. So emotional overreliance with the intersection of autonomy and self-regulation undermines their ability to think and act for themselves, which is an important competency in their learning and their persistence in using academic strategies.

- Educators and policy makers have to balance the values of emotionally responsive AI with the challenges of emotional overreliance. Some possibilities are:
- Drawing clear boundaries and making sure that non-anthropomorphic designs are used in AI systems (e.g., voiceover people that movies distance is less like and avoids human like avatars for example.)
- Promoting human check-ins sporadically with AI-based tutoring.
- Place AI literacy into the curriculum - just as students critically interpret the emotional responses of others, they should learn to think critically about emotional responses of machines.
- Include agency-based digital well-being guidelines in your policy regarding the use of AI tools throughout their studies especially to minors.

Ironically, the very success of AI in simulating empathy could be a liability if it's not done responsibly. Although we educate students about being aware of persuasive marketing pressures or manipulating disinformation, we also have to help students develop healthy relationships with technology, appreciating its benefits but not confusing simulation with authenticity.

Emotionally responsive AI has the potential to enrich learning experiences by providing personalized encouragement and authentic moments of sustenance. Nevertheless, once learning begins to develop emotional dependencies on such systems, an educational experience cannot be considered fundamentally human. Therefore, for the future of AI in education to work, we need secure ethical modalities that protect students for more than simply cognitive development, but emotional and social development as well—machines should complement, not replace, the humanity of relationships.

5. FUTURE PROSPECTS AND RESEARCH DIRECTIONS

5.1 Integration of Generative AI in Learning

The emergence of generative AI models as GPT-4 and other large language models (LLMs), will dramatically alter the educational landscape. These generative models create essays, summarize complicated information, create personalized quizzes, and even simulate dialogue between tutors and students (the generative aspect of AI will provide a level of education support and personalization that was never before possible) (Long & Magerko, 2020). In the future, research will emphasize how to find the balance for integrating generative AI into classrooms, finding the appropriate balance of encouraging creativity and critical thinking, while avoiding plagiarism and over-reliance.

Moving forward, as these models become multimodal in that they do not just consider text, but also audio, images, and video as well, the opportunity to create rich, interactive, and cross-curricular learning experiences will further expand (Brown *et. al.,* 2020). The possibilities are exciting for both educators and learners, as educators continue to create engaging learning environments, and students will have even more exciting ways to collaborate and learn in diverse and stimulating situations with AI enhancing their ability to explore their subject matter.

5.2 Emotion-Aware and Affective AI

The development of emotionally aware systems is a promising avenue in AI-enhanced education. These systems can detect students' emotions by reading their emotions using their facial expressions, tone of voice, or even biological signals to sense when students are frustrated, confused, or disengaged (D'Mello & Graesser, 2012). The hope is to create AI tutors that incorporate these emotional signals, so the tutor knows what the student knows, but also how the student feels, and the tutor can adapt its teaching accordingly in real time to better support learning.

Affective computing is a highly interdisciplinary space at the junction of psychology, education, and machine learning. We require experts from all three areas to work together (Lin, 2022). Affective computing will advance the creation of AI-based learning experiences that will be more than just smarter; they will be more human, empathetic, and responsive to the whole learner.

5.3 AI for Lifelong and Microlearning

Education is evolving toward a more sustainable, lifelong learning, flexible, and on-demand microlearning future. AI will fuel this evolution by curating personalized bits of content in alignment with the learner's goals, previous knowledge, and context; this content can be delivered through mobile apps, voice assistants, or wearable technologies (Sajja *et. al.,* 2024).

These intelligent systems will keep fluid learner profiles that will evolve. These profiles will allow the systems to modify learning paths in real time to reflect current and changing needs. This will allow individuals to engage in career advancement, skill building, and self-directed learning beyond the formal confines of the classroom (Ferguson & Clow, 2017). By increasing the accessibility of education and tailoring it to the individual, AI helps achieve a world in which education has no end.

5.4 Multilingual and Culturally Responsive AI

As education becomes more global, the urgency for AI systems that support multilingualism and cultural inclusivity is growing. Beyond basic translation, the next generation of AI systems will need to understand the subtle nuances of language, respect regional dialects, and provide feedback that recognizes local cultural contexts, which is a major opportunity in continents like Africa and South Asia (Samuel *et. al.,* 2023).

Building these capacities to enable multilingualism in education will be crucial in creating equity in education, addressing language limitations, and providing equally equitable opportunities for high-quality education for learners everywhere. AI can leverage education and opportunity to create truly inclusive global learning environments, where diversity is celebrated and all voices are valued.

5.5 Ethical and Explainable AI in Education

The presence of AI in education is becoming greater, meaning a stronger emphasis on explainable and transparent AI (XAI). AI system outputs should not be only right, they should provide clear explanations that students, teachers, and policymakers can trust, understand, and act on. When the AI tools are transparent, it builds trust in the tools and facilitates decision making (Ribeiro *et. al.,* 2016). At the same time, developing ethical frameworks around AI will continue to be important, working through complex issues such as ownership of data, liability, fairness in algorithms, and how consent is provided. It is important in education research to work with technology developers to develop governance models that protect children's rights, promote educational equity, and facilitate human-centered design. Collaboration will ensure AI continues to be an advantage in the learning ecosystem (Rets *et. al.,* 2023).

5.6 Human-AI Collaboration Models

AI will not replace educators in the future of education, but will enable a meaningful collaboration and co-agency between humans and machines. New research is investigating hybrid approaches where AI manages administrative responsibilities and cognitive support, so educators can do what they do best, bring emotional intelligence, qualify to be a mentor, and ideally inspire the emotional and creative engagement of learning (Luckin & Holmes, 2016). In the future, the partnership and co-agency will transform our educational roles and daily workflow, and in the next ten years, enable world-class individual and personalized learning opportunities, experiences, and engagement.

5.7 Student-AI Collaboration and Co-Creation in Learning

As artificial intelligence continues to find its footing in education, equilibrium continues to change; AI's role is evolving from a passive assistant or background automation tool (face-of-the-discipline function) to an active co-creator of learning, facilitating dynamic student-machine collaboration, to indicate a fundamentally different relationship framework--moving away from the historical experiential teacher-student dyad to a triadic learning relationship including intelligent systems as co-actors. In a student + AI ecosystem, students do not merely receive pre-ordained AI-generated content. Rather, students engage with, design, and design an AI, which leads to a deeper understanding.

One conspicuous domain of AI-student co-creation is your creative expression. Large language models and generative assets such as ChatGPT, DALL·E, and Runway ML allow learners to co-create movements in writing poetry, images, and storytelling with an AI model. A simple example could be a student prompting a language model to produce alternative endings to a classic novel, engaging in critical comparisons of those endings, then generating their own, thereby merging reading comprehension with creative production. In these moments, they entangle AI as a dialogic exchange (curiosity, divergent thinking, reflection) (Baillifard *et. al.,* 2023).

In STEM education, AI tools are being used more and more to co-develop code, simulations, and designs. For example, a platform named GitHub Copilot from OpenAI is assisting learners in writing software code by providing real-time coding and syntax suggestions, as well as debugging suggestions. Rather than completing the work for the student, it is providing scaffolded discovery in support of students thinking algorithmically and improving their fluency in computational thinking. The emergence of AI-based platforms in engineering and architecture has also begun supporting collaborative design generation from open-ended user constraints and prompt users using visual/graphic feedback for rapid, iterative thinking.

AI tools are also revolutionizing student research and inquiry-based learning activities. Elicit.org enables learners to automate their literature reviews by surfacing important papers, summarizing findings, and mapping out academic conversations. The learners drive the search terms and ultimately use their interpretation of the insights, and the AI simply helps to manage cognitive overhead, freeing up time for more critical thinking and synthesis (Zhang & Aslan, 2021). In so doing, AI becomes a powerful amplifying tool to students' research capacity, which is especially useful for undergraduates or more novel researchers who may not have been exposed to a number of scholarly databases.

It is worth reiterating that co-creation with AI is not simply producing outputs; it can involve meta-learning. Students can explore their learning processes using AI. For instance, a student might ask a large-language model to evaluate their essay, and then compare those comments with the feedback from a peer or teacher. The process of triangulating these different sources can inform a student's ability to self-assess, promote metacognitive knowledge, and develop a more nuanced understanding of the notion of quality in academic work.

In the context of student-AI partnerships, pedagogical commitments should hint at the need for students to learn digital literacy alongside AI. That is, students should be taught how to engage critically with AI outputs, the relevance of training data and bias to information outputs, and the ways they shape these engagements. In the absence of guidance, students may accept algorithmically mediated knowledge as passive consumers of the learning, creating a deactivation of their critical thinking.

Additionally, ethical co-creation is paramount. Students must understand the academic integrity boundaries, knowing when it is appropriate to use AI support and when it is not appropriate and constitutes plagiarism. Educators could provide assignments that don't prohibit AI tools, but instead ask students to be transparent, documenting the way they employed AI, what sort of learning experiences they had, and how they revised the output in a meaningful way (Shi *et. al.,* 2021).

Student-AI collaboration represents a significant pedagogical opportunity. It allows educators to rethink assessments, promote agency, and create curiosity in learners. Thoughtfully integrated, these collaborations can enhance learning experiences, creating learning that is more experiential, individualized, and exploratory. A future classroom might not be one where AI provides students the content, but rather one where students and AI collectively consider and create knowledge in ways that are rigorous and creative.

6. CASE STUDIES AND REAL-WORLD IMPLEMENTATIONS

6.1 Squirrel AI Learning (China)

Squirrel AI ranks as one of the most advanced AI adaptive ability learning platforms in the world, with access to more than 2,000 learning centres across China. Squirrel AI uses machine learning and knowledge graphs to disaggregate subjects into over 10,000 different learning points to customize instruction precisely to the learner's current understanding of the information presented so that online instruction requests and tasks are appropriate to the individual's prior knowledge (VanLehn, 2006). Research consistently shows students who participated in Squirrel AI outperformed their peers in human-led learning programs in "learning outcomes" in subjects like mathematics and sciences.

Squirrel AI goes beyond the personalized lesson to using predictive analytics to identify preliminary gaps in learning, allowing it to adapt to the learner's learning needs and intelligently adjust the content difficulty if necessary. Use of AI in this manner is an excellent example of the disruption that precision education brings to learners. It helps learners identify their gaps in knowledge and navigate the learning process toward their learning goal (Holmes *et. al.,* 2019).

6.2 Carnegie Learning (USA)

MATHia from Carnegie Learning is a prominent example of an intelligent tutoring system, derived from years of cognitive science and research in contemporary AI technologies. MATHia is intended to give students real-time feedback and direction as it encourages students toward robust explanations within a scaffolded problem-solving environment. The software includes detailed analytic dashboards to track student progress for both the student and the teacher (Winne, 2021). MATHia is built on more than twenty years of research from Carnegie Mellon University. As students begin solving a question, MATHia looks at the student's approach to the problem as they work through the problem one step at a time. MATHia assesses and determines where the student is in their strategy, recognizes how students approach or acknowledge a solution, and alters the questions and direction of the student's learning path dynamically in order to pursue a less vague route towards mastering the learning goal.

MATHia has evaluated effectiveness academically across various classrooms throughout the United States. It has been demonstrated that students using MATHia significantly outperform their peers taking similar standardized assessments, with evidence suggesting that the greatest gains were made by students who initially struggled in mathematics (Oliveira *et. al.,* 2021). This is very compelling evidence for the use of intelligent tutoring systems to promote equitable learning experiences by supporting a diverse population of learners.

6.3 CENTA TPO and AI Mentor (India)

The Centre for Teacher Accreditation (CENTA) in India has launched a new AI-powered mentoring system as part of its flagship initiative, Teaching Professional Olympiad (TPO). The system uses natural language processing (NLP) and advanced analytics to assess teacher engagement responses, providing immediate, formative feedback that is specific and actionable (Srinivasan & Murthy, 2021). This identifies where teachers can improve and recommends personalized micro-courses and curated content for teachers to meet their individualized developmental needs.

An important feature of CENTA's mission is its next generation accessibly affordable and scalable model. It has put into operation its learning platform with a very affordable way to reach their educators, whether educators are in fast growing urban centers or remote rural locations- thereby fulfilling the promise of professional development equity. It is remarkable how AI has been leveraged to improve not only students' outcomes but also the overall quality of teaching across many education systems so that all teachers, no matter their location, can learn and flourish.

6.4 Century Tech (UK)

UK-based Century Tech is an innovative edtech company that has quickly positioned itself as a global leader in the integration of artificial intelligence, neuroscience, and learning science to provide rigorously personalized learning experiences. In use in 40+ countries, Century Tech's platform provides a customized experience for students by intelligently tracking students' learning behaviors and progress, and leveraging data to recommend content that is grounded in students' strengths and needs (Zawacki-Richter *et. al.,* 2019).

In addition to student customization and personalization, the platform also furnishes teachers with rich, data-informed insights that provide visibility into learning gaps, permit the adjustment of teaching, and drastically reduce teachers' administrative workload. Its significance was especially evident during the COVID-19 pandemic when educational institutions around the globe pivoted to remote learning. Century Tech was unique in providing adaptive learning pathways and revision tools—especially apt for secondary students in STEM—during a time of disruption, to ensure continuity of students' educational journey.

By integrating brain-based learning and responsive AI systems, Century Tech demonstrates how technology can improve student learning by ensuring that education becomes a more humane and learner-centered process, while at the same time also being smart and efficient for teachers.

6.5 Microsoft's Reading Progress and Coach

Microsoft's Reading Progress and Reading Coach apps, developed and built into Microsoft Teams, exemplify a thoughtful use of AI to support literacy in schools. Reading Progress and Reading Coach utilize advanced speech (fluency) technology to enable teachers to assess reading skills such as pronunciation, rate of speech, and expressive reading. The teacher receives comments throughout the text as well as detailed qualitative fluency data that is time-stamped so it can be easily viewed and tracked over periods without the need for a paper assessment (Ouyang *et. al.*, 2022).

What has made these specific tools unique, however, is the ability for students to learn and practice reading aloud in a low-pressure, self-paced environment while receiving individual feedback. Pilot studies have provided evidence that suggested gains in reading fluency and confidence, especially among: English language learners, and early-grade students who were involved in ongoing individualized reading practice (Pahi *et. al.*, 2024).

Reading Progress and Reading Coach are already in use in many K–12 schools across the United States and Europe. In many ways, they demonstrate how AI can help support the development of foundational skills and allow the classroom teacher a way to focus on more sophisticated aspects of literacy instruction. The success of these technologies is a step in a positive direction toward a bright future where technology and human instruction collaborate to support the independent reading habits of learners.

7. CONCLUSION

The inclusion of Artificial Intelligence (AI) in education signifies a great deal more than a technological change; it is fundamentally a new conception of learning, one that involves rethinking how learning is imagined, designed, delivered, and experienced. From adaptive learning platforms that personalize instruction to the administrative efficiencies provided by algorithms able to process increasingly complex tasks, the educational ecosystems around the globe are shifting in potentially meaningful and desirable ways that, together, may enhance engagement, increase access, and improve efficiency.

There are real-world examples such as Squirrel AI in China or MATHia in the United States that suggest that thoughtfully implemented AI, when designed with clear principles that promote human well-being, can improve learning outcomes, evidence-based practice, and the agency of teachers.

However, moving from theory to authentic AI integration into education is complicated, and there are ongoing concerns around data collection and storage, data privacy, algorithmic bias and discrimination, inequities in infrastructure and access to digital and technological tools, and the additional complexities of reliance on automated processes. This highlights the need for policy frameworks that incorporate equity, access, and the fundamental rights of all learners, and processes or ways of thinking that bring people together towards ethical AI and educational programming.

A truly equitable future requires that technology, improvement, and progress are recognized for what they are, but discussed using a human-centered design framework, where students, teachers, and communities work together collaboratively to identify how AI will be utilized and integrated into education.

Moving forward, fields such as affective computing, multilingual AI systems, and explainable AI (XAI) will take center stage as the next wave of innovation grows, facilitating intelligent technology that is sympathetic to our challenges, culturally rich, and properly accountable. At the same time, the fast-moving tide of generative AI tools, most notably large language models (LLMs) (e.g., ChatGPT) is opening doors of possibility for creativity, inquiry-based learning, and individualized support but also call for a careful examination of academic integrity, digital addiction, and the emerging awareness of knowledge construction.

In the end, AI could change the educational landscape from a model of rote learning into inquiry-based learning, from a model of standardized learning to that of adaptive and lifelong pathways. It is not AI's value to educators as a replacement or the homogenization of learning, but rather the ability to amplify human potential, positioning diverse learners for success, providing teachers with agency, and increasing the level of education that is able to address the complex needs of learners, both individually and collectively. While institutions, researchers, and technologists navigate this new future together, equity, transparency, and pedagogical integrity should be paramount, ensuring that tomorrow's AI-enhanced classrooms are utilized as opportunities for transformative, holistic, and inclusive learning encounters.

REFERENCES

Alvero, A. M., Beeler, J. A., Bodnar, R., Brown, B. L., Brumberg, J., Chua, E., ... & Forlano, P. B. Ph. D. Program Psychology Faculty's Publication (2010-2017).

Holmes, T., & Porayska-Pomsta, A. (2021). Ethics in AI and Education: Learning Analytics and Responsible Innovation. *British Journal of Educational Technology, 52*(4), 1647–1665.

Amara, K., Altinay, F., Altinay, Z., & Dagli, G. (2024). Artificial intelligence and sustainable educational systems. In *Computational Intelligence and Blockchain in Complex Systems* (pp. 199–204). Morgan Kaufmann. DOI: 10.1016/B978-0-443-13268-1.00011-X

Amershi, S., Weld, D., Vorvoreanu, M., Fourney, A., Nushi, B., Collisson, P., & Horvitz, E. (2019, May). Guidelines for human-AI interaction. In *Proceedings of the 2019 chi conference on human factors in computing systems* (pp. 1-13.

Attali, Y., & Burstein, J. (2006). Automated essay scoring with e-rater® V. 2. *The Journal of Technology, Learning, and Assessment, 4*(3).

Baillifard, A., Gabella, M., Lavenex, P. B., & Martarelli, C. S. (2023). Implementing learning principles with a personal AI tutor: A case study. arXiv preprint arXiv:2309.13060.

Baker, R. S., & Yacef, K. (2009). The state of educational data mining in 2009: A review and future visions. Journal of educational data mining, 1(1), 3-17.

Banihashem, S. K., Noroozi, O., Van Ginkel, S., Macfadyen, L. P., & Biemans, H. J. (2022). A systematic review of the role of learning analytics in enhancing feedback practices in higher education. *Educational Research Review, 37*, 100489. DOI: 10.1016/j.edurev.2022.100489

Booth, B. M., Bosch, N., & D'Mello, S. K. (2023). Engagement detection and its applications in learning: A tutorial and selective review. *Proceedings of the IEEE, 111*(10), 1398–1422. DOI: 10.1109/JPROC.2023.3309560

Brown, T., Mann, B., Ryder, N., Subbiah, M., Kaplan, J. D., Dhariwal, P., & Amodei, D. (2020). Language models are few-shot learners. *Advances in Neural Information Processing Systems, 33*, 1877–1901.

Calvo, R. A., & D'Mello, S. (2010). Affect detection: An interdisciplinary review of models, methods, and their applications. *IEEE Transactions on Affective Computing, 1*(1), 18–37. DOI: 10.1109/T-AFFC.2010.1

Cowls, J., & Floridi, L. (2018). Prolegomena to a white paper on an ethical framework for a good AI society. Available at *SSRN* 3198732. DOI: 10.2139/ssrn.3198732

D'Mello, S., & Graesser, A. (2012). Dynamics of affective states during complex learning. *Learning and Instruction*, *22*(2), 145–157. DOI: 10.1016/j.learninstruc.2011.10.001

Dede, C., Honan, J. P., & Peters, L. C. (2005). Scaling Up Success: Lessons Learned from Technology-Based Educational Improvement. Jossey-Bass, An Imprint of Wiley. 10475 Crosspoint Blvd, Indianapolis, IN 46256.

Dignum, V. (2019). *Responsible artificial intelligence: how to develop and use AI in a responsible way* (Vol. 2156). Springer. DOI: 10.1007/978-3-030-30371-6

El-Sabagh, H. A. (2021). Adaptive e-learning environment based on learning styles and its impact on development students' engagement. *International Journal of Educational Technology in Higher Education*, *18*(1), 53. DOI: 10.1186/s41239-021-00289-4

Fengchun, M., Wayne, H., Huang, R., & Zhang, H. (2021). AI and education Guidance for policymakers (Internet). Available at: https://unesdoc. unesco. org/ark:/48223/pf0000376709

Ferguson, R., & Clow, D. (2017, March). Where is the evidence? A call to action for learning analytics. In Proceedings of the seventh international learning analytics & knowledge conference (pp. 56-65).

Goddiksen, M. P., Johansen, M. W., Armond, A. C. V., Centa, M., Clavien, C., Gefenas, E., Kovács, N., Merit, M. T., Olsson, I. A. S., Poškutė, M., Santos, J. B., Santos, R., Strahovnik, V., Varga, O., Wall, P. J., Sandøe, P., & Lund, T. B. (2024). The dark side of text-matching software: Worries and counterproductive behaviour among European upper secondary school and bachelor students. *International Journal for Educational Integrity*, *20*(1), 15. DOI: 10.1007/s40979-024-00162-7

Håkansson Lindqvist, M., Mozelius, P., Jaldemark, J., & Cleveland Innes, M. (2024). Higher education transformation towards lifelong learning in a digital era–a scoping literature review. *International Journal of Lifelong Education*, *43*(1), 24–38. DOI: 10.1080/02601370.2023.2279047

Holmes, W., Bialik, M., & Fadel, C. (2019). *Artificial intelligence in education promises and implications for teaching and learning*. Center for Curriculum Redesign.

Jia, C., & Lu, Y. (2025). Exploring the Impact of Gamification on Behavioral Change: The Role of Grade Incentives and Free-Choice Behavior. *International Journal of Human-Computer Interaction*, •••, 1–14. DOI: 10.1080/10447318.2025.2517805

Jia, Y., Ramanovich, M. T., Remez, T., & Pomerantz, R. (2022, June). Translatotron 2: High-quality direct speech-to-speech translation with voice preservation. In International conference on machine learning (pp. 10120-10134). PMLR.

Jia Zhang, M., & Zhuo Zhang, Z. (2024, April). AI in teacher education: Unlocking new dimensions in teaching support, inclusive learning, and digital literacy. *Journal of Computer Assisted Learning*, *40*(4), 1871–1885. DOI: 10.1111/jcal.12988

Lin, H. C. K. (2022). May Computers have Emotions? Establishing an AI Device based on Affective Computing Technologies.

Ling, S., Zhang, Y., & Du, N. (2023, September). Impacts of AI-Generated Confidence and Explanations on Task Performance and Trust in Human-autonomy Teaming. [). Sage CA: Los Angeles, CA: SAGE Publications.]. *Proceedings of the Human Factors and Ergonomics Society Annual Meeting*, *67*(1), 502–503. DOI: 10.1177/21695067231195002

Long, D., & Magerko, B. (2020, April). What is AI literacy? Competencies and design considerations. In *Proceedings of the 2020 CHI conference on human factors in computing systems* (pp. 1-16). DOI: 10.1145/3313831.3376727

Luan, H., Geczy, P., Lai, H., Gobert, J., Yang, S. J., Ogata, H., Baltes, J., Guerra, R., Li, P., & Tsai, C. C. (2020). Challenges and future directions of big data and artificial intelligence in education. *Frontiers in Psychology*, *11*, 580820. DOI: 10.3389/fpsyg.2020.580820 PMID: 33192896

Luckin, R., & Holmes, W. (2016). Intelligence unleashed: An argument for AI in education.

Mahapatra, H., Ingole, S. B., Singh, D., Dutt, A., Gupta, R., & Chauhan, B. (2024). Artificial Intelligence for Sustainable Education in India: Problems and Prospects. *Library of Progress-Library Science, Information Technology & Computer, 44*(3).

Mao, Q. (2025). Fostering Self-Directed Growth with Generative AI: Toward a New Learning Analytics Framework. arXiv preprint arXiv:2504.20851.

Matei, S. A., & Bertino, E. (2023). Educating for AI Cybersecurity Work and Research: Ethics, Systems Thinking, and Communication Requirements. arXiv preprint arXiv:2311.04326.

McGrath, C., Farazouli, A., & Cerratto-Pargman, T. (2024). Generative AI chatbots in higher education: A review of an emerging research area. *Higher Education*, •••, 1–17.

McNamara, D. S., Graesser, A. C., McCarthy, P. M., & Cai, Z. (2014). *Automated evaluation of text and discourse with Coh-Metrix*. Cambridge University Press. DOI: 10.1017/CBO9780511894664

Nkambou, R., Mizoguchi, R., & Bourdeau, J. (2010). *Advances in Intelligent Tutoring Systems*. Springer. DOI: 10.1007/978-3-642-14363-2

O'neil, C. (2017). *Weapons of math destruction: How big data increases inequality and threatens democracy*. Crown.

Oliveira, G., Grenha Teixeira, J., Torres, A., & Morais, C. (2021). An exploratory study on the emergency remote education experience of higher education students and teachers during the COVID-19 pandemic. *British Journal of Educational Technology*, *52*(4), 1357–1376. DOI: 10.1111/bjet.13112 PMID: 34219758

Ouyang, L., Wu, J., Jiang, X., Almeida, D., Wainwright, C., Mishkin, P., & Lowe, R. (2022). Training language models to follow instructions with human feedback. *Advances in Neural Information Processing Systems*, *35*, 27730–27744.

Pahi, K., Hawlader, S., Hicks, E., Zaman, A., & Phan, V. (2024). Enhancing active learning through collaboration between human teachers and generative AI. *Computers and Education Open*, *6*, 100183. DOI: 10.1016/j.caeo.2024.100183

Pane, J. F., Steiner, E. D., Baird, M. D., Hamilton, L. S., & Pane, J. D. (2017). "Informing Progress: Insights on Personalized Learning Implementation and Effects." *RAND Corporation*, 2017. https://www.rand.org/pubs/research_reports/RR2042.html

Piech, C., Bassen, J., Huang, J., Ganguli, S., Sahami, M., Guibas, L. J., & Sohl-Dickstein, J. (2015). Deep knowledge tracing. *Advances in Neural Information Processing Systems*, •••, 28.

Rets, I., Herodotou, C., & Gillespie, A. (2023). Six Practical Recommendations Enabling Ethical Use of Predictive Learning Analytics in Distance Education. *Journal of Learning Analytics*, *10*(1), 149–167. DOI: 10.18608/jla.2023.7743

Ribeiro, M. T., Singh, S., & Guestrin, C. (2016, August). " Why should i trust you?" Explaining the predictions of any classifier. In *Proceedings of the 22nd ACM SIGKDD international conference on knowledge discovery and data mining* (pp. 1135-1144). DOI: 10.18653/v1/N16-3020

Sajja, R., Sermet, Y., Cikmaz, M., Cwiertny, D., & Demir, I. (2024). Artificial intelligence-enabled intelligent assistant for personalized and adaptive learning in higher education. *Information (Basel)*, *15*(10), 596. DOI: 10.3390/info15100596

Samuel, Y., Brennan-Tonetta, M., Samuel, J., Kashyap, R., Kumar, V., Krishna Kaashyap, S., Chidipothu, N., Anand, I., & Jain, P. (2023). Cultivation of human centered artificial intelligence: Culturally adaptive thinking in education (CATE) for AI. *Frontiers in Artificial Intelligence*, *6*, 1198180. DOI: 10.3389/frai.2023.1198180 PMID: 38106981

Schei, O. M., Møgelvang, A., & Ludvigsen, K. (2024). Perceptions and use of AI chatbots among students in higher education: A scoping review of empirical studies. *Education Sciences*, *14*(8), 922. DOI: 10.3390/educsci14080922

Selwyn, N. (2019). *Should robots replace teachers?: AI and the future of education*. John Wiley & Sons.

Shi, G., Wang, L., Zhang, L., Shubeck, K., Peng, S., Hu, X., & Graesser, A. C. (2021, July). The Adaptive Features of an Intelligent Tutoring System for Adult Literacy. In *International Conference on Human-Computer Interaction* (pp. 592-603). Cham: Springer International Publishing. DOI: 10.1007/978-3-030-77857-6_42

Shinohara, K., & Wobbrock, J. O. (2016). Self-conscious or self-confident? A diary study conceptualizing the social accessibility of assistive technology. [TACCESS]. *ACM Transactions on Accessible Computing*, *8*(2), 1–31. DOI: 10.1145/2827857

Slade, S., & Prinsloo, P. (2013). Learning analytics: Ethical issues and dilemmas. *The American Behavioral Scientist*, *57*(10), 1510–1529. DOI: 10.1177/0002764213479366

Smiley, A., Moussa, W., Ndamobissi, R., & Menkiti, A. (2021). The negative impact of violence on children's education and well-being: Evidence from Northern Nigeria. *International Journal of Educational Development*, *81*, 102327. DOI: 10.1016/j.ijedudev.2020.102327

Srinivasan, V., & Murthy, H. (2021). Improving reading and comprehension in K-12: Evidence from a large-scale AI technology intervention in India. *Computers and Education: Artificial Intelligence*, *2*, 100019. DOI: 10.1016/j.caeai.2021.100019

Sundara, K., & Narendran, N. (2023). The Digital Personal Data Protection Act, 2023: Analysing India's dynamic approach to data protection. *Computer Law Review International*, *24*(5), 129–141. DOI: 10.9785/cri-2023-240502

Utreras, E., & Pontelli, E. (2020, September). Accessibility of block-based introductory programming languages and a tangible programming tool prototype. In *International Conference on Computers Helping People with Special Needs* (pp. 27-34). Cham: Springer International Publishing. DOI: 10.1007/978-3-030-58796-3_4

VanLehn, K. (2006). The behavior of tutoring systems. *International Journal of Artificial Intelligence in Education*, *16*(3), 227–265. DOI: 10.3233/IRG-2006-16(3)02

Vrabec, N., & Furtáková, L. (2024). Ways of defining digital competences and their components in the EU, EC and UNESCO recommendations. *Annales Universitatis Paedagogicae Cracoviensis. Studia de Cultura, 16*(2), 5–17. DOI: 10.24917/20837275.16.2.1

Williamson, B., & Eynon, R. (2020). Historical threads, missing links, and future directions in AI in education. *Learning, Media and Technology, 45*(3), 223–235. DOI: 10.1080/17439884.2020.1798995

Winkler, R., & Söllner, M. (2018, July). Unleashing the potential of chatbots in education: A state-of-the-art analysis. In Academy of management proceedings (Vol. 2018, No. 1, p. 15903). Briarcliff Manor, NY 10510: Academy of Management. DOI: 10.5465/AMBPP.2018.15903abstract

Winne, P. H. (2021). Open learner models working in symbiosis with self-regulating learners: A research agenda. *International Journal of Artificial Intelligence in Education, 31*(3), 446–459. DOI: 10.1007/s40593-020-00212-4

Woolf, B. P. (2010). *Building Intelligent Interactive Tutors: Student-Centered Strategies for Revolutionizing E-Learning*. Morgan Kaufmann.

Yeung, C., Yu, J., Cheung, K. C., Wong, T. W., Chan, C. M., Wong, K. C., & Fujii, K. (2025). A Zero-Shot LLM Framework for Automatic Assignment Grading in Higher Education. arXiv preprint arXiv:2501.14305.

Zawacki-Richter, O., Marín, V. I., Bond, M., & Gouverneur, F. (2019). Systematic review of research on artificial intelligence applications in higher education–where are the educators? *International Journal of Educational Technology in Higher Education, 16*(1), 1–27. DOI: 10.1186/s41239-019-0171-0

Zhang, K., & Aslan, A. B. (2021). AI technologies for education: Recent research & future directions. Computers and education. *Artificial Intelligence, 2*, 100025.

ADDITIONAL READING

Anderson, J. R., Corbett, A. T., Koedinger, K. R., & Pelletier, R. (1995). Cognitive tutors: Lessons learned. *Journal of the Learning Sciences, 4*(2), 167–207. DOI: 10.1207/s15327809jls0402_2

Brusilovsky, P., & Millán, E. (2007). User models for adaptive hypermedia and adaptive educational systems. In *The Adaptive Web* (pp. 3–53). Springer. DOI: 10.1007/978-3-540-72079-9_1

Goksel, N., & Bozkurt, A. (2019). Artificial intelligence in education: Current insights and future perspectives. In *Handbook of Research on Learning in the Age of Transhumanism* (pp. 224–236). IGI Global. DOI: 10.4018/978-1-5225-8431-5.ch014

Heffernan, N. T., & Heffernan, C. L. (2014). The ASSISTments ecosystem: Building a platform that brings scientists and teachers together for minimally invasive research. *International Journal of Artificial Intelligence in Education, 24*(4), 470–497. DOI: 10.1007/s40593-014-0024-x

Luckin, R. (2017). *Towards artificial intelligence-based assessment systems*. Nature Human Behaviour, 1(3), 0028.

Mitrovic, A. (2012). Fifteen years of constraint-based tutors. *User Modeling and User-Adapted Interaction, 22*(1-2), 39–72. DOI: 10.1007/s11257-011-9105-9

OECD (2021). *AI in education: A critical view*. OECD Digital Education Outlook 2021.

Roll, I., & Wylie, R. (2016). Evolution and revolution in artificial intelligence in education. *International Journal of Artificial Intelligence in Education, 26*(2), 582–599. DOI: 10.1007/s40593-016-0110-3

KEY TERMS AND DEFINITIONS

Artificial Intelligence (AI): The ability of machines to mimic human intelligence, such as learning and problem-solving.

Intelligent Tutoring System (ITS): AI-based software that provides personalized instruction like a human tutor.

Adaptive Learning: Technology-driven instruction that adjusts content and pace to each learner's needs.

Natural Language Processing (NLP): AI methods that allow computers to understand and use human language.

Learning Analytics: Data analysis of student activity to improve learning and teaching.

Affective Computing: AI that detects and responds to human emotions in learning contexts.

Generative AI: AI models that create new content, such as text, images, or simulations.

Explainable AI (XAI): AI systems designed to make their outputs and decisions understandable to humans.

Algorithmic Bias: Unfair outcomes in AI systems caused by biased training data.

Human-AI Collaboration: A partnership model where AI supports but does not replace teachers.

Chapter 6
A Multi-Agent Environment With Artificial Intelligence for English Language Learning and Teaching

Vadym Slyusar
https://orcid.org/0000-0002-2912-3149
Institute of Artificial Intelligence Problems, Ukraine

ABSTRACT

This chapter explores the innovative application of multi-agent artificial intelligence systems for enhancing English language teaching and learning. Author presents an architecture composed of specialized AI agents performing distinct educational roles such as consulting, lecturing, methodology development, career advising, psychological support, and technical assistance. The system capitalizes on advanced large language models (LLMs) to create personalized, interactive, and adaptive learning experiences, seamlessly integrating into traditional educational structures while also offering flexibility and scalability. Furthermore, the chapter investigates immersive virtual environments powered by AI, proposing metrics to systematically evaluate their coherence, immersion, novelty, and interactivity. These metrics provide a foundation for future advancements in digital language education, suggesting new avenues for individualized learning trajectories and enhanced learner engagement within AI-driven environments.

DOI: 10.4018/979-8-3373-3561-2.ch006

INTRODUCTION

In the context of the rapid advancement of artificial intelligence (AI) technologies, there arises a pressing need to reconsider the approaches to foreign language instruction - particularly English, which serves as a global tool for intercultural communication. The use of large language models (LLMs) such as GPT-4.5 (OpenAI, 2025), Gemini 2.5 Pro (Google, 2025), Claude 4.0 (Anthropic, 2025), and others open new horizons in the personalization, automation, and overall effectiveness of language education. These models are capable of generating contextualized language situations tailored to the user's individual proficiency level, communication style, learning pace, and even emotional state. This functionality not only reduces the cognitive burden on the instructor but also significantly enhances student motivation through interactive and continuous feedback.

However, relying on a single language model, even one of considerable power, has its limitations in terms of flexibility, scalability, and domain specialization. A more effective approach in this regard is the construction of a multi-agent environment comprising a set of interconnected intelligent agents, each of which performs a specific function based on a specialized adaptation of an LLM.

The transition to a multi-agent structure represents a natural stage in the development and application of LLMs. Similar architectures have previously been proposed by the author for biometric systems and robotic platforms (Slyusar, 2025a), as well as for decision support systems (Slyusar, 2025b). Within the educational domain, such an approach not only supports the academic process at every stage but also ensures adaptability to the individual needs of users by accounting for their cognitive, linguistic, and motivational characteristics. A multi-agent architecture enables the distribution of tasks among different agents: some may specialize in grammar, vocabulary exercises, pronunciation, assessment of written work, or the construction of personalized learning trajectories.

This approach ensures the modularity and scalability of the system, allowing for the straightforward updating or replacement of individual components, as well as the integration of new knowledge sources or assessment tools. As a result, a highly functional learning environment is created - one that transcends the boundaries of a traditional language course and transforms into a flexible ecosystem for the development of language competence amid the digital transformation of education (Kondratenko et al., 2023a; Kondratenko et al., 2023b; Kondratenko et al., 2024; Laurent, 2023; Taverniti et al., 2023; Martin et al., 2024; Cox, 2021; Zawacki-Richter et al., 2019; Slyusar, 2025c).

The system proposed in this section functionally approximates the institutional structure of a traditional educational establishment, an arrangement that has proven effective, yet its components are implemented in the form of AI-powered digital agents. The following section presents the architecture of such a system, a classification and functional description of the agents, potential applications in both formal and informal English language learning scenarios, and prospects for integration into the educational infrastructure of the future.

MULTI-AGENT SYSTEMS FOR ENGLISH LANGUAGE LEARNING AND INSTRUCTION

As the functions of traditional academic staff must be redefined in a multi-agent environment to meet the specific requirements of language education, we shall examine in detail the potential roles to be assigned to the corresponding ensemble of agent-based "staff." To underscore the artificial nature of these agents and their specialized functionalities, we will append the acronym AI to the titles of their traditional, human counterparts. This convention is also employed in Figure 1, which illustrates one possible configuration of agent role allocation, implementing a minimal set of services within an educational-linguistic environment.

Figure 1. Typical agents of the educational environment

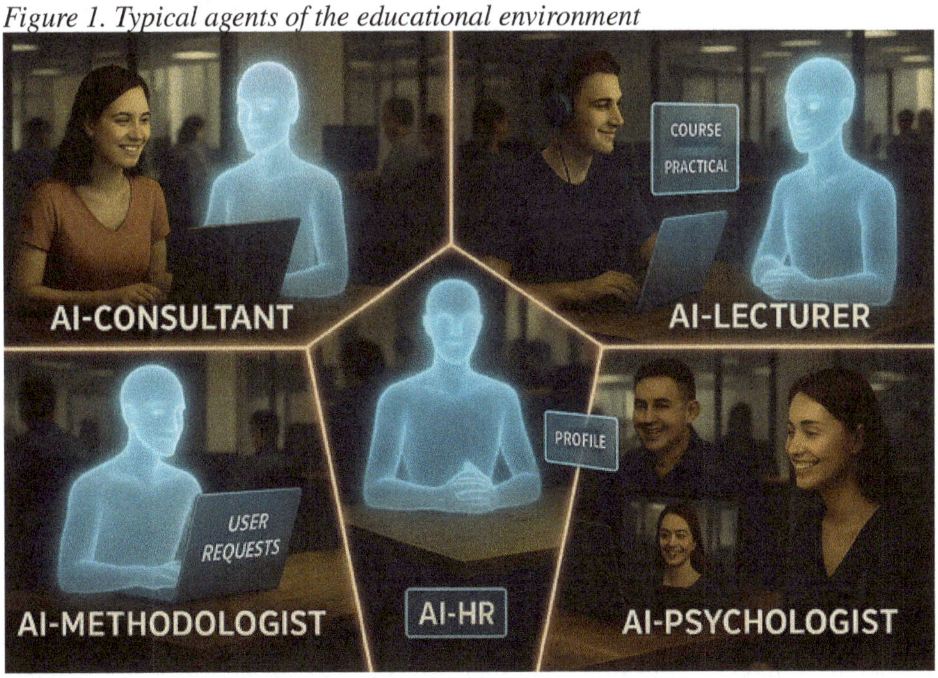

In particular, within the presented structure, the *AI Consultant* serves as a universal source of academic and regulatory information, providing continuous support to users on matters related to the organization of the educational process, methodological requirements, assessment criteria, and curricular standards. Drawing on an in-depth analysis of internal regulatory documents, institutional policies, accreditation requirements, and current academic practices, this agent maintains a dynamic knowledge base that is constantly updated and refined.

The *AI Consultant* is capable of delivering targeted real-time responses to instructors regarding permitted formats for assessment activities, academic integrity regulations, syllabus structure requirements, and recommendations for adapting materials to inclusive learning environments. For students, it functions as a personal administrative assistant, explaining procedures for language certification, enrollment conditions, appeal or academic request protocols, registration deadlines, and the preparation of individual learning plans, among others.

With access to the local Learning Management System (LMS), the *AI Consultant* can integrate with users' personal dashboards, providing contextualized assistance - for instance, by reminding a student of upcoming deadlines, offering templates for submitting academic requests, or guiding an instructor to available instructional resources within a specific course. In the long term, its functionality may be enhanced with modules for query prediction and the detection of recurring issues. This would enable proactive optimization of administrative interactions and contribute to the overall efficiency of the educational environment.

Closely collaborating with this agent is the *AI Methodologist*, whose functionality corresponds to the role of a curriculum specialist in traditional educational systems, though enhanced by artificial intelligence capabilities. Its primary task is the development, adaptation, and continuous refinement of instructional materials for English language learning, with the aim of ensuring effective, evidence-based, and personalized instruction.

The *AI Methodologist* begins by analyzing existing syllabi, international educational standards (including CEFR and TESOL/TEFL), findings from pedagogical research, as well as student performance analytics received from other agents. Based on this analysis, it generates recommendations on course structure, selection of lexical and grammatical topics, sequencing of task types, lesson duration, and forms of feedback. These methodological recommendations are produced in several variants according to language proficiency levels (A1 - C2), age groups, learning objectives (academic, professional, or everyday communication), and learning environments (individual, group, remote, blended, etc.).

Additionally, the *AI Methodologist* functions as a generator of didactic templates - generalized models of instructional scenarios that can be automatically adapted to specific student cohorts. It also proposes strategies for integrating augmented and virtual reality (AR/VR) technologies, gamification elements, interdisciplinary connections (e.g., English for STEM contexts), and formal assessment frameworks.

These strategies can be promptly updated in response to regulatory changes or the emergence of new research findings.

A crucial aspect of the *AI Methodologist*'s role is its interaction with other agents: for example, it provides the *AI Consultant* with up-to-date regulatory materials to assist in responding to instructor queries. Ultimately, the *AI Methodologist* acts as an "intelligent bridge" between scholarly-methodological support and the dynamics of actual instructional practice, thereby promoting the coherence, consistency, and pedagogical validity of the entire educational system.

The functionality of the *AI Lecturer* lies in the generation, presentation, and real-time adaptation of instructional content according to the proficiency level, learning goals, and educational style of a specific audience. Leveraging state-of-the-art LLMs, the *AI Lecturer* automatically synthesizes lecture material based on up-to-date English-language text corporam, including academic databases, educational resources, news aggregators, textbooks, and open-access materials, thus ensuring accuracy, relevance, and linguistic richness.

Lectures are delivered in an interactive format: the *AI Lecturer* not only presents content but can also ask questions, comment on student responses, explain complex concepts using simplified phrasing, and repeat material upon request. Visualization of the *AI Lecturer* may be implemented as an avatar. For instance, the HeyGen Avatar IV neural network enables the animation of any character from a photograph or text description, whether a human likeness or, particularly for younger learners, a beloved cartoon character. This neural network is also capable of cloning voices with precise lip-syncing, expressive intonation, rhythmic modulation, and optional accent rendering. Additionally, high-fidelity voice synthesis can be achieved using services such as ElevenLabs. While these services are currently commercial, their costs are expected to decrease as the technology becomes more widespread and advanced.

During the instructional process, the *AI Lecturer* can dynamically restructure the lecture flow in response to subtle indicators of misunderstanding - for example, delayed responses, repeated clarification requests, or background analytics of student engagement within the platform. Its speech tempo, lexical complexity, number of examples, and the type of visual aids employed are automatically calibrated to align with the cognitive profile of each learner or group.

A particularly valuable capability of the *AI Lecturer* is its ability to immerse learners in contextualized instructional scenarios. For instance, the topic "Business English: Negotiation Strategies" may be partially delivered through a simulated role-play segment featuring dialogues that replicate a meeting with international partners. In such an activity, each student is assigned a specific role, while the AI dynamically adapts its responses in real time based on the unfolding conversation. This approach not only enhances learner engagement but also fosters communicative flexibility and resilience in linguistically stressful situations.

Furthermore, the *AI Lecturer* can seamlessly integrate multimedia elements, such as videos, interactive diagrams, film clips, or music excerpts, which are automatically selected according to the lesson's theme and lexical focus. The result is a multimodal learning space in which lectures shift from unidirectional knowledge transmission to dialogic and adaptive processes of developing both linguistic and cultural competence.

The *AI Career Consultant* (*AI-HR*) functions as an intelligent intermediary between the educational environment and the modern labour market, providing personalized guidance for the learner's professional development. Based on an analysis of the student's educational trajectory, current English proficiency level, typical language errors, performance in linguistic tasks, and involvement in academic or professional projects, the *AI-HR* autonomously compiles a structured language portfolio. This portfolio includes certificates, CEFR-level competencies, samples of written work, audio/video clips of spoken output, and analytical reports on the learner's progress dynamics.

By applying semantic analysis methods to job listings from leading global platforms (e.g., LinkedIn, Indeed, Glassdoor), the *AI-HR* compares the user's profile with current labour market demands. As a result, it generates a list of recommended developmental pathways. These may include specialized language courses, such as "English for Legal Professionals" or "Academic Writing for Researchers", as well as interdisciplinary modules like "Project Management Communication." Each recommendation is accompanied by an assessment of its relevance and its predicted impact on the learner's career trajectory.

The *AI-HR* also places special emphasis on optimizing résumés and accompanying documents in English. It automatically evaluates linguistic accuracy, stylistic appropriateness, logical structure, and alignment with the keyword requirements of specific job postings. It then offers targeted adaptations for particular positions or sectors. Intercultural differences in CV formats, such as those customary in the United States, United Kingdom, European Union, or Asia, are also taken into account. Moreover, the *AI-HR* can simulate typical English-language job interview scenarios, generating both questions and model responses with explanations of their strengths and weaknesses.

This description demonstrates that the *AI-HR* constructs a comprehensive trajectory for the learner's linguistic and professional integration into the global environment by aligning academic achievements with real-world market demands and offering adaptive support at every stage of career development.

To sustain motivation and emotional well-being, the multi-agent AI ecosystem may include an *AI Psychologist*, capable of detecting signs of emotional burnout, offering targeted mental health practices, and creating a secure space for confidential interaction (Shevchenko et al., 2024). This agent plays a critically important role in maintaining the continuity of the learning process, particularly under conditions of high academic intensity, elevated cognitive load, and remote interaction formats. By analyzing linguistic feedback markers, survey results, behavioral patterns in the LMS, and task performance analytics, the *AI Psychologist* can identify early indicators of declining motivation, anxiety, fatigue, or depressive tendencies.

Depending on the identified risk profile, the agent offers individualized interventions such as breathing exercises, brief reflective practices, gamified breaks, cognitive micro-sessions aimed at boosting self-esteem, or emotional self-regulation training. All actions are accompanied by friendly and empathetic communication, fostering a psychologically safe atmosphere. In cases where detected risks exceed the system's scope of competence, the *AI Psychologist* may recommend consulting a professional specialist, while ensuring the full confidentiality of the user's data.

Beyond individual support, the *AI Psychologist* can also serve an analytical function for the administrative staff by summarizing statistics on the psycho-emotional status of student groups, monitoring workload dynamics, and generating recommendations for optimizing class schedules or revising assessment approaches. Ultimately, the integration of the *AI Psychologist* not only promotes the mental well-being of participants in the educational process, but also contributes to the development of a holistic, supportive environment in which English language learning is accompanied by emotional resilience and intrinsic motivation for growth.

The agents discussed above, of course, bear provisional designations, and their configuration and functional scope may dynamically evolve depending on the instructional context, course objectives, learner proficiency levels, and the technical capabilities of the educational platform. The flexibility of the multi-agent architecture allows for the seamless expansion or transformation of the agent ensemble to meet the evolving needs of the learning environment.

For example, such a system may include an *AI Mentor* - a personalized educational companion available 24/7 via LMS-integrated chat systems, mobile applications, or voice interfaces. The primary function of this agent is to provide continuous individualized learning support to students. The *AI Mentor* assists in constructing personalized learning trajectories that account for both the user's CEFR-level language proficiency and their personal goals - be it exam preparation, academic writing, professional communication, or travel-related language needs.

In response to student queries, the agent is capable of explaining grammatical structures using examples tailored to the user's lexical range, suggesting synonymous or stylistically appropriate alternatives, constructing micro-dialogues for practice, and developing exercises in various formats - from classification tasks to role-play scenarios. The *AI Mentor* takes into account the outcomes of previous sessions, tracks recurring errors, and provides recommendations for content revision.

In essence, this agent combines the roles of digital tutor, private instructor, and motivator, reducing feelings of isolation in remote learning contexts, enhancing the individualization of the educational process, and supporting the development of a consistent learning rhythm. Through coordination with other agents, the *AI Mentor* can align its actions with the *AI Methodologist* or *AI Lecturer*, delivering instructional content in the required format and sequence in accordance with methodological standards.

A dedicated *AI Pronunciation Coach* analyzes spoken input in real time, identifies phonetic issues, provides detailed feedback on articulation and intonation, and suggests targeted exercises supported by audiovisual content. A prototypical implementation of such an agent can be observed in the specialized educational functionalities already developed by OpenAI via its platform, which allows the creation of customized GPT-4 instances. Notable examples of such language tutoring agents include "Language Teacher. Ms. Smith" and "Speak AI: English Conversation Practice & Writing," both of which incorporate voice interfaces.

When users express an interest in learning English, the GPT-powered service *Language Teacher. Ms. Smith* initially classifies their proficiency level (beginner, intermediate, or advanced) and then offers a set of thematic modules either to reinforce their current level or to support progression to a higher one. For example, beginner-level users may engage with modules such as:

- My Day (Talk about your daily routine);
- My Family and Friends (Introduce your family and friends);
- Food and Drinks (Learn vocabulary related to food and ordering in a restaurant);
- Hobbies and Leisure (Describe your hobbies and free-time activities);
- At the Market (Practice shopping vocabulary and how to discuss prices).

Within the proposed approach, the functionality of GPT-4s can be further enhanced by incorporating generalizations about learning quality and by adapting learning trajectories to each student's individual cognitive-linguistic capabilities and available time resources.

Integrated testing *AI agents* play a key role in enabling objective, adaptive, and scalable knowledge assessment throughout the English language learning process. These agents automatically generate multilevel tasks of various types - ranging from closed-ended questions and multiple-choice items to gap-filling exercises, sentence construction, free writing, and oral expression. The structure of these tasks aligns with established levels of language proficiency (A1 - C2) and can be customized according to the assessment purpose: formative evaluation, diagnostic testing, summative assessment, or preparation for international certifications.

AI Testers are capable of evaluating both written and spoken responses using advanced linguistic analysis models. This includes assessment of spelling, grammar, lexical diversity, logical coherence of argumentation, stylistic appropriateness, as well as pronunciation accuracy, intonation, and speech rhythm. Evaluation is conducted based on predefined rubrics and is adapted to students' individual profiles by taking into account the trajectory of their prior performance.

A distinctive feature of these testing agents is their capacity for deep analytics: they generate detailed progress reports, identify the strengths and weaknesses of each learner, forecast potential learning difficulties, and automatically update recommended learning pathways in coordination with other agents. For instructors, the agents provide standardized assessment criteria, ensuring transparency and consistency of evaluation standards across the entire educational programme. In the future, such systems may also support academic integrity monitoring by analyzing writing style patterns or verifying the authenticity of voice responses.

Overall, *AI Testers* not only automate the routine aspects of assessment but also establish the foundation for precise, adaptive, and pedagogically sound knowledge control in modern language education.

The *AI Technical Support Specialist* (AI TSS) fulfills a critically important role in ensuring the stable functioning of the digital learning environment, responding promptly to technical, organizational, and logistical challenges. Its core mission is to automate routine processes that would traditionally require administrative intervention, while also providing real-time user support through chatbots, voice interfaces, or ticketing systems.

At the infrastructural level, this agent handles the registration and identification of new users, generates individualized accounts, synchronizes schedules, integrates external platforms (e.g., Zoom, Google Meet, Moodle), and ensures stable access to virtual classrooms. In the event of technical failures or connectivity loss, the agent can swiftly generate backup links, suggest alternative modes of participation, or redirect the student to asynchronous interaction with course materials.

In addition, the AI TSS continuously monitors the status of educational resources - ensuring the availability of updated materials, the correctness of multimedia content, the functionality of hyperlinks, and the compliance of interfaces with principles of inclusivity (e.g., subtitle availability, voice-over options, and accessibility adaptations for users with visual or auditory impairments). All user requests are classified according to problem type (e.g., "login error," "test unavailable," "content display issue"), enabling the AI agent not only to resolve them efficiently but also to generate reports for administrators identifying critical points within the digital infrastructure.

Thanks to its capacity for continuous self-improvement and the accumulation of interaction experience, the AI TSS reduces the workload on the IT department, shortens response times, and ensures a high level of accessibility and reliability for the educational process in contexts of full or partial digitalization.

Finally, special attention must be given to the *AI Security Agent*, a vital component of the multi-agent system. Its primary function is to ensure the integrity, confidentiality, and protection of all processes occurring within the digital environment of English language instruction. This AI agent operates at the intersection of cybersecurity, ethical monitoring, and access control, continuously analyzing the activity of all other agents as well as user behavior to detect potential threats or deviations from approved operational scenarios.

The *AI Security Agent* implements a multi-level protection model. At the foundational level, it handles user authentication, traffic encryption, access control to sensitive information (such as test results or language portfolios), and the detection of unauthorized intrusion attempts. Simultaneously, it conducts behavioral analysis of both student and instructor activity to prevent fraud (particularly during online assessments), detect anomalous behavior, identify automated bots, or uncover violations of academic integrity.

Moreover, the agent monitors for potentially harmful or undesirable content that may arise from users submitting provocative prompts intended to manipulate the system. It supervises the relevance and appropriateness of language model outputs, issuing warnings regarding potential bias, discrimination, or violations of social norms. In coordination with the *AI Psychologist*, it can also respond to signs of cyberbullying or verbal aggression in educational chat spaces, suggesting preventive interventions or isolating conflict situations.

At a strategic level, the *AI Security Agent* shapes the platform's overarching digital data protection policy, updates risk profiles, initiates log audits, manages encryption key rotation, and generates recommendations for developers aimed at increasing the system's resilience to emerging threats. Security in this ecosystem is not conceived as a reactive measure, but rather as an active, intelligent, and adaptive component of the architecture - one that guarantees trust, stability, and compliance with contemporary standards for educational data protection.

All of the aforementioned agents interact through unified API interfaces, eliminating functional redundancies, enabling holistic monitoring of learning dynamics, and allowing for the scalable deployment of solutions - from language laboratories to full-scale university programmes. This architecture renders English language education flexible, personalized, and supportive at every stage - from the acquisition of basic vocabulary to mastery in academic writing and public speaking.

In remote learning contexts (and beyond), the scheme of multi-agent interaction within a single educational institution can be interpreted as a *personal university*, in which the entire architecture is oriented toward supporting the educational trajectory of one specific student. In this configuration, each agent, whether lecturer, tutor, advisor, or *AI-HR,* acts as a digital representative of a particular institutional function, yet adapts exclusively to the learner's individual needs, learning style, proficiency level, and personal goals. This marks a transformation from the traditional vertical model of "instructor-to-group" toward a horizontally oriented interaction, where the entire intellectual infrastructure (methodological, academic, administrative, and psycho-emotional) is personalized in real time.

Such a system not only ensures flexibility and autonomy in decision-making but also facilitates the creation of a closed-loop adaptive environment in which the student is no longer a passive consumer of information, but becomes an active participant in the learning process, receiving individualized digital support at every stage - from goal-setting to outcome attainment.

To fully realize the principles of adaptability, scalability, and functional differentiation, each of the described agents must not be viewed as an isolated component, but rather as a local multi-agent system comprising its own internal hierarchy of sub-agents. This implies that, for example, the *AI Lecturer*, *AI Mentor*, or *AI Career Consultant* are not monolithic modules, but are composed of multiple specialized sub-agents, each responsible for distinct aspects of their functionality - from query processing and content generation to interaction monitoring and performance evaluation.

In such a configuration, an architecture is required that not only facilitates the coordination of interactions between the main agents at the system-wide level but also ensures manageability, data exchange, and internal adaptation within each agent. To achieve this, a hierarchical model is employed, as illustrated in Figure 2, which demonstrates how each individual agent operates as a self-contained environment with its own internal router and a set of subordinate modules.

Figure 2 presents a multi-level hierarchical architecture of the multi-agent system, comprising two principal agent types: the *Router Agent* and the *Module Agent*. This structure should be regarded as a typical framework for organizing the interaction of the agents described above within an AI-supported English language learning system. It can be implemented using multiple language models or within a single prompt environment for one LLM, in which the roles of each specialized agent are clearly defined and coordinated to ensure joint operation.

At the top level of the hierarchy is the central *Router Agent*, which functions as the system's main dispatcher. Its primary responsibilities include query classification and routing, coordination of information flows, and the efficient allocation of tasks among subordinate agents. It serves as the system's entry point and governs the logical management of all lower layers.

From this central agent, several primary branches extend, each beginning with a lower-level *Router Agent*. These intermediate routers manage specific subsystems or clusters of functionally related agents, such as instructional content delivery, assessment, or user support, thereby enabling decentralized control and modular scalability within the overall architecture.

Beneath each of these subordinate *Router Agents* are *Module Agents*, which perform specific, narrowly specialized functions. For example:

- a module agent responsible for generating grammar exercises;
- a module agent that analyzes written responses;
- a module agent that assists students in vocabulary acquisition;
- a module agent that manages audiovisual support, and so forth.

In some cases, as illustrated on the right side of the diagram, a *Router Agent* may contain additional nested *Router Agents*, allowing the system to scale vertically to support complex, multi-component tasks such as multimodal content processing or integration with external platforms.

Figure 2. Structure of the multi-agent hierarchy

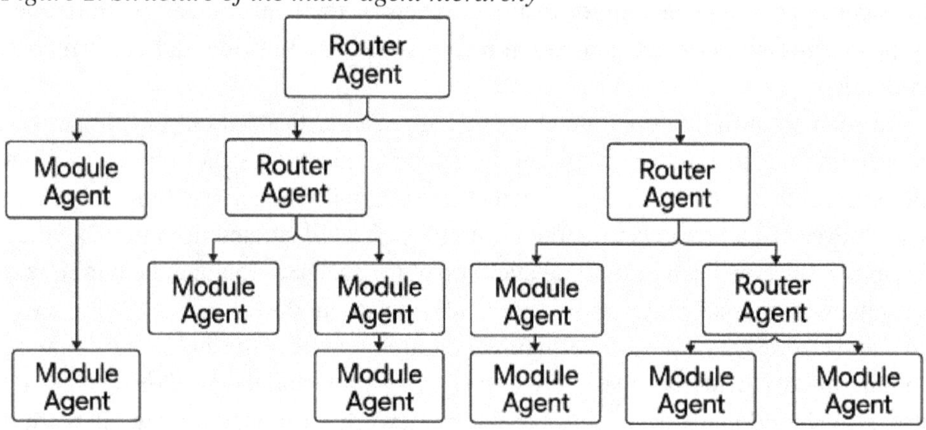

This hierarchical structure ensures modularity, scalability, and flexibility: each agent operates autonomously within its own specialization, while overall system coherence is maintained through routing and coordination by the *Router Agents*. Such architecture makes it possible to seamlessly introduce new routes and agent modules, alter request processing logic, or integrate novel tools without disrupting the functioning of the broader system.

Following the discussion of the multi-agent system architecture within a single educational institution, a logical next step is the transition toward scaling it across an entire educational network in which English is taught as a core component of language education. Such integration requires coordination among numerous localized AI environments operating in different universities, colleges, or schools, while simultaneously ensuring centralized governance, shared access to knowledge, and unified standards of interaction.

The diagram presented in Figure 3 illustrates the concept of a scalable multi-agent educational infrastructure for English language instruction, extending beyond a single institution to a network of learning establishments linked via a centralized intelligent control layer.

At the center of the diagram is the *Centralized Control Layer*, which provides system-wide coordination, standardization, and security. It performs several key functions:

- Maintenance of a *Global Knowledge Base*, which supplies all local ecosystems with up-to-date learning materials, linguistic corpora, methodological guidelines, and analytic templates.
- Implementation of mechanisms for inter-agent communication, as well as data and service access protocols (A2A, MCP, etc. (Slyusar, 2025a; Habler et al., 2025; Bhardwaj et al., 2025; Liu et al., 2025; Jeong, 2025; Martineau, 2025)) that ensure interoperability across different versions of local AI environments.
- Security management, including encryption, authentication, access monitoring, and protection of both personal and educational data.

At the level of individual institutions, localized multi-agent environments carry out the educational processes within their specific contexts (e.g., school, college, or university). Each of these ecosystems maintains access to the global layer while adapting its functionality to local needs.

The functionality of individual agents, such as the *AI Lecturer* or *AI-HR,* can be modified in accordance with the context of inter-institutional integration. For instance, lecture content may be aligned with an inter-university curriculum or international educational initiatives, while the HR agent may orient its recommendations toward the transnational labour market, taking into account inter-university agreements on academic mobility. Such a structure not only enables flexibility in the implementation of instructional strategies but also contributes to the formation of a sustainable educational space at the national or even supranational level.

It is precisely this architectural design that facilitates not only the standardization of educational processes but also the exchange of instructional materials, refined learning trajectories, best practices, inter-institutional analytic models, and an expanded system for supporting students' career pathways.

Since each specialized AI agent operating within its local ecosystem can be coordinated through a centralized system, this enables consistency in methodologies and standards across the entire network of educational institutions. In this way, innovations developed within one ecosystem can be more easily scaled to others, and centralized analytics can be conducted to support educational decision-making at the system level (e.g., by ministries or departments of education).

Figure 3. Inter-university integration of individual multi-agent systems

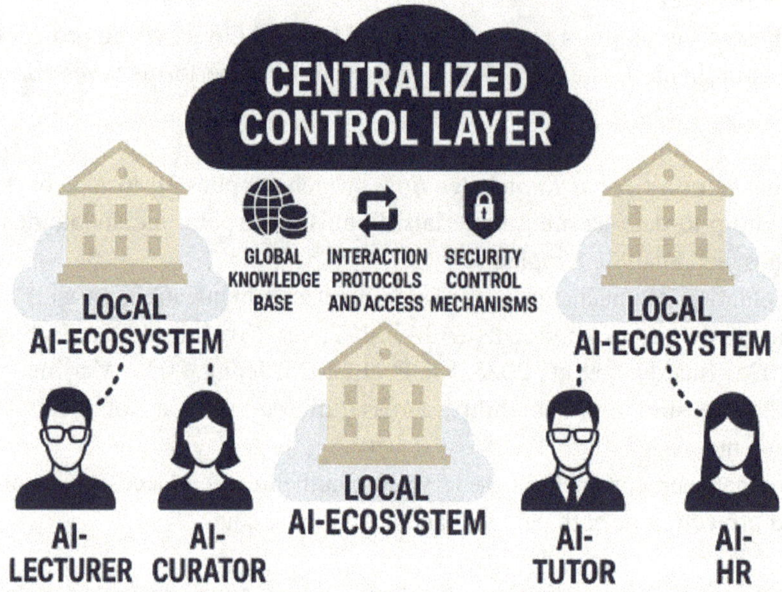

As a result, a flexible, scalable, and securely governed infrastructure is established to support English language instruction - one that combines individualized learning pathways with centralized quality control, in alignment with the principles of modern digital transformation in education.

LEARNING THROUGH VIRTUAL WORLD GENERATION

Another promising direction in enhancing the processes of teaching and learning English is its acquisition through the generation of virtual worlds using LLMs. In particular, one effective method may involve recreating the plots of literary works within virtual environments and AI-generated videos. The current state of LLM development already enables the generation of multi-minute video sequences based on textual descriptions or images that define the initial and final scenes. For example, Google's Sparkify neural network, a combination of Veo 3 and Gemini

2.5 Pro, is capable of generating entire animated films up to two minutes in length in various styles (Shabanov, 2025; Media & Learning Association, 2025). Sparkify can autonomously create a storyline, assemble a dynamic sequence of visual scenes, add audio narration, and even compose music.

Immersion into such worlds, populated with embodiments of literary or fictional characters, enables learners to encounter novel situations that go beyond their prior knowledge and experience. Ultimately, this leads to a deeper understanding of the educational content.

In the context of using virtual world and character generation technologies in literature classes, this approach exemplifies how the visualization of literary plots and images can foster deeper comprehension and emotional engagement with the learning material. Visual representations presented in virtual reality (VR) help students better grasp the consequences of mistakes and the value of knowledge, thereby enhancing the pedagogical impact of literary works. Thus, the integration of 3D technologies into the educational process, especially when studying English grammar and literary texts, can significantly boost student interest and engagement, contributing to more effective learning.

Equally promising is the use of LLMs in virtual reality training systems. In such systems, the LLM acts as the core of the software (see Figure 4), analyzing messages received from the virtual training environment, accumulating statistics, interpreting commands, and even analyzing facial expressions during speech reporting using specialized neural networks such as YOLO.

Figure 4. Scheme of using LLM/LAM in VR training

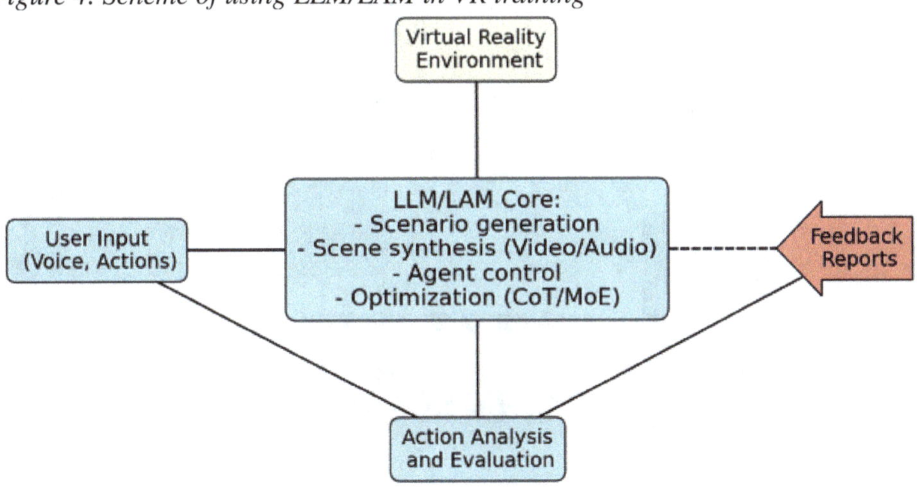

A key element is the generation of precise prompts (see Figure 5), which enables the creation of specialized agents for specific tasks. A diagram illustrating the interaction of various processes that convert LLM input data into a virtual environment is presented in Figure 6.

Based on user input parameters or prior performance, the model generates complex, non-linear scenarios. These may include instructional tasks, crisis simulations, diagnostic assessments, and more. Such scenarios are characterized by a high degree of variability and contextual awareness. The LLM core does not limit itself to text generation; it performs full multimodal synthesis, generating or defining parameters for visual outputs (e.g., video streams, 3D models) and audio components (e.g., ambient sounds, character speech), to ensure immersive experiences. The model also controls the behavior of autonomous virtual agents (NPCs) within the simulation. These agents can interact with the user, perform assigned tasks, and respond to environmental changes, simulating realistic social or functional dynamics. To ensure logical coherence, the LLM employs the *Chain of Thought (CoT)* technique to construct step-by-step reasoning for scenario development and agent decision-making, thereby increasing the plausibility and relevance of the simulation.

Figure 5. A prompt is a key element of a VR building

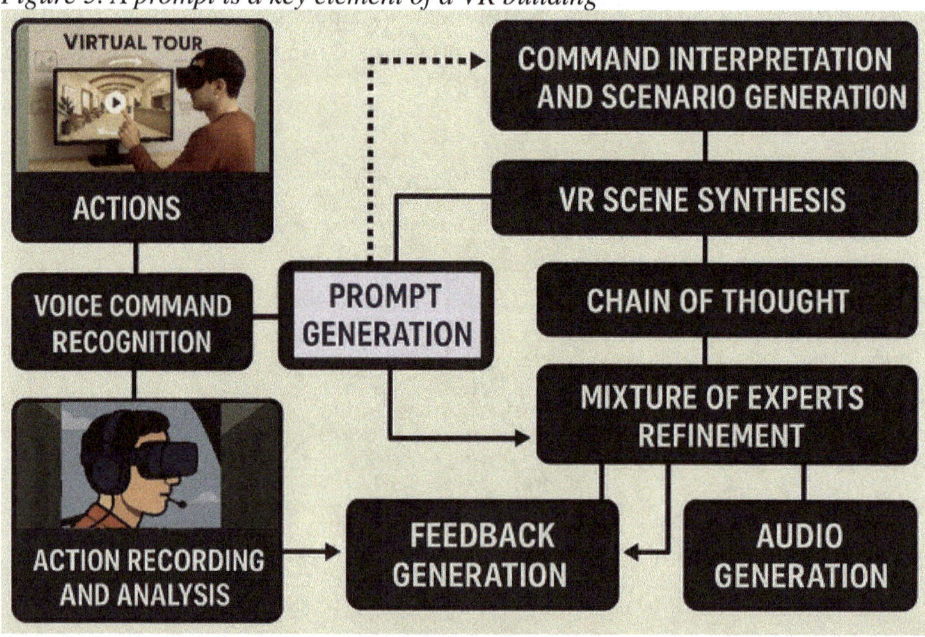

Figure 6. Diagram of LLM/LAM VR training process

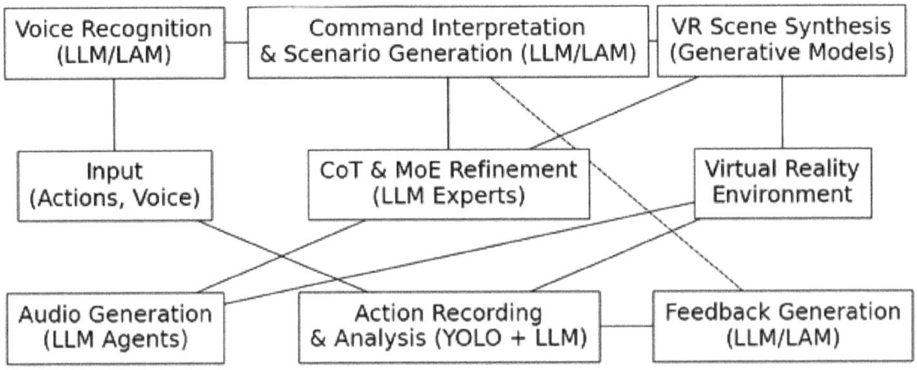

Virtual laboratories constructed in this way can be effectively employed for English language learning by integrating simulation technologies, gamification, and interactive engagement. One possible configuration of a multi-agent VR laboratory is presented in Figure 7.

Such laboratories enable the creation of immersive environments with realistic scenarios - such as job interviews, participation in international conferences, travel abroad (Figure 8), or airport communication. These experiences are supported by either voice or text (subtitle) interfaces. Additionally, users can interact with virtual characters, AI agents, or fellow learners, using English as the sole medium of communication. VR laboratories can be customized to target specific language skills (grammar, vocabulary, listening, or pronunciation) with automated feedback and adaptive prompts to guide learners in real time.

Figure 7. A possible structure of a multi-agent VR laboratory

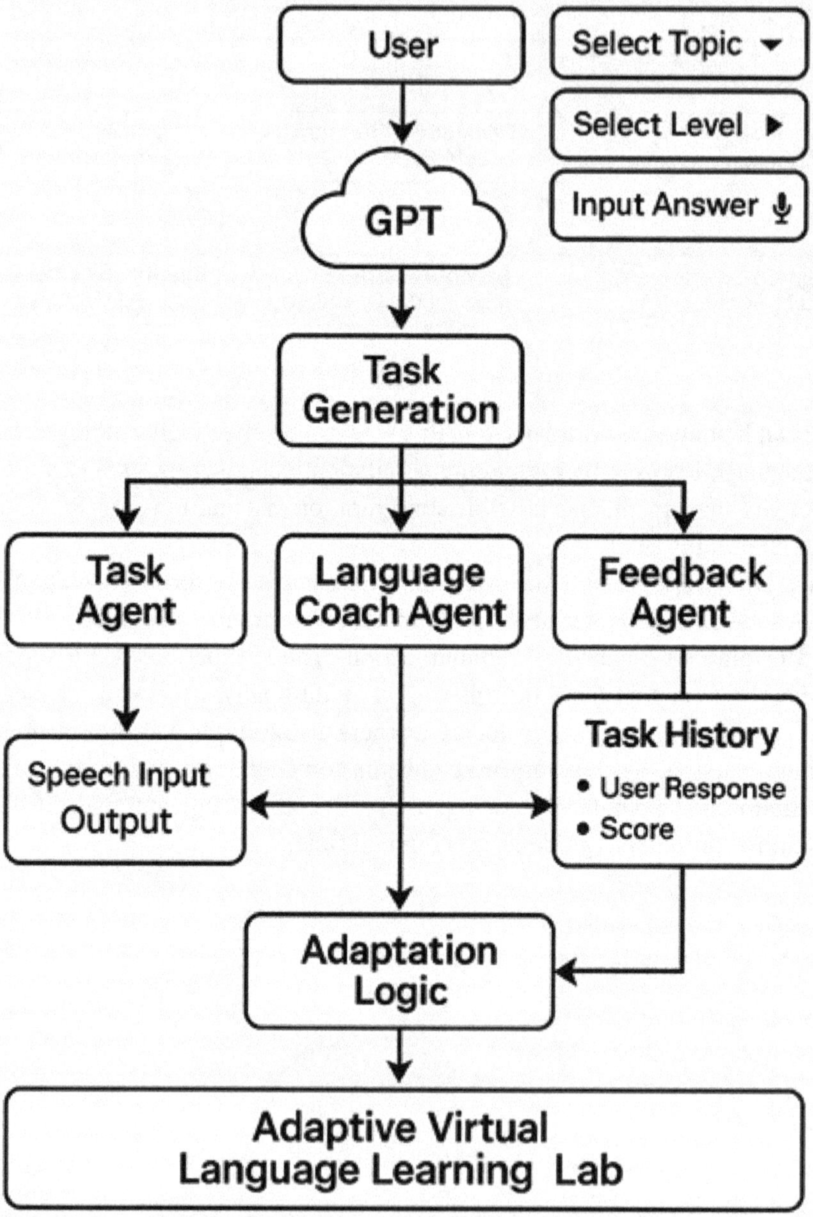

Figure 8. Virtual travel

The use of virtual objects and gesture-based interaction can further support context-driven language learning - for example, by labeling laboratory items in English or responding to questions related to actions performed with these objects (Figure 9). Finally, through real-time feedback, such systems can assess language activity, offer improvement recommendations, and adapt the difficulty level according to the learner's proficiency.

In this way, virtual laboratories create a multimodal learning environment in which language is acquired not merely as a system of rules, but as a tool for action and interaction.

Figure 9. Virtual language laboratory

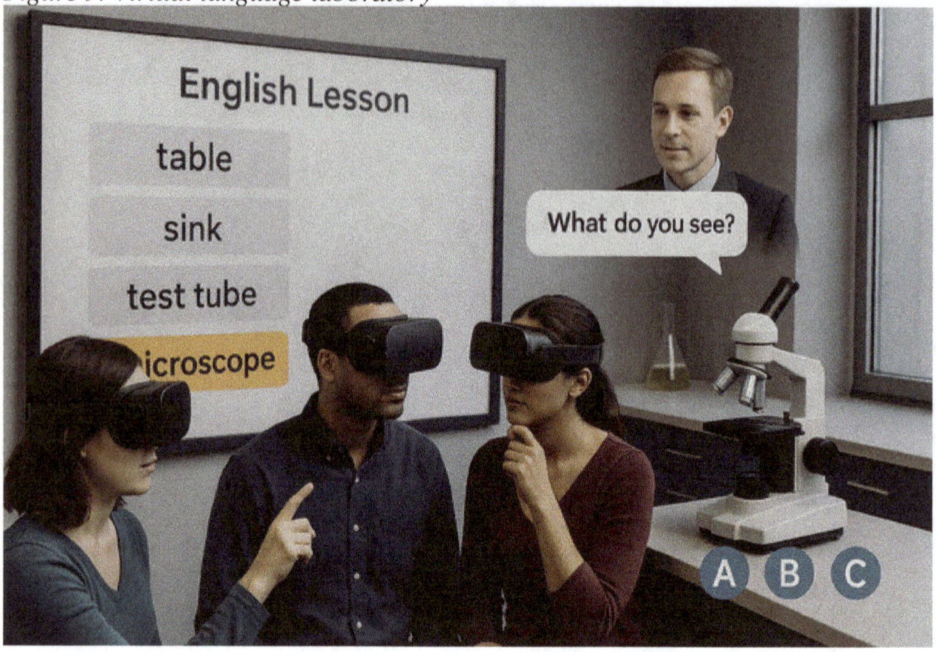

Virtual museum tours and travel experiences, built on multi-agent architecture, offer unique opportunities for foreign language acquisition by combining rich cultural contexts with interactive real-time communication. In typical scenes of such a tour, the user is immersed in a precisely recreated hall of the Louvre, the British Museum, or any local gallery, where multiple coordinating avatar agents operate simultaneously. A typical structural diagram of such a VR-based multi-agent system is presented in Figure 10.

Figure 10. Multi-agent system of a virtual museum

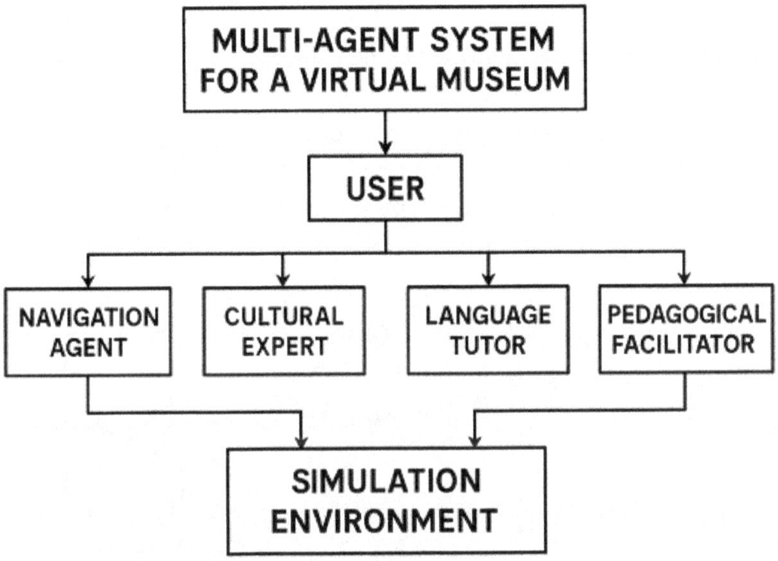

Within this system, one *AI agent* is responsible for positioning and navigation through the exhibition space, while another, the *Cultural Expert*, delivers historical background and clarifications in English, tailored to the learner's proficiency level. A *Pedagogical Language Mentor* detects spoken input, offers lexical or grammatical suggestions, and proposes embedded micro-tasks (e.g., describing a painting using five adjectives or posing a question to an information kiosk). Simultaneously, an *Assessment Agent* discreetly monitors the frequency of newly acquired vocabulary use, the length of utterances, and response times in order to adapt the content of upcoming exhibition halls based on observed progress.

Dialogue bots, simulated "tourists", introduce variability in accents and speech styles to emulate a realistic crowd of visitors, training the user to respond to conversational, not merely academic, language structures.

In travel-oriented VR scenarios, a *Logistics Agent* is added to model typical situations - hotel bookings (Figure 11), flight check-ins, ordering food in a café, disputes with transport providers, and so on. This agent adjusts the difficulty of tasks depending on how confidently the student communicates under time pressure or in the presence of background noise, such as airport announcements.

Such multilayered interaction allows language acquisition to become inseparable from meaningful real-world actions, rather than remaining an isolated set of abstract rules.

A similar approach can be applied in scientific and educational laboratories, with a focus on domain-specific vocabulary and analytical skills. In a virtual chemistry lab, for example, a lead *Instructor Agent* guides the experiment in English, demonstrating proper pronunciation of technical terms and gradually involving the student in describing their own actions. A *Manipulation Agent* manages interaction with virtual equipment, responding to voice commands such as *"adjust the Bunsen burner"* or *"pipette ten milliliters"* and immediately checking the accuracy of both the practical action and the corresponding linguistic formulation.

Figure 11. Virtual tour for acquiring hotel staff interaction vocabulary

A *Safety Agent* monitors adherence to lab protocols and provides English-language alerts in case of procedural violations, thereby reinforcing safety-related vocabulary. An *Analytical Agent* assists in interpreting experimental results by offering English templates for graph descriptions, research reports, or scientific articles. Under these conditions, students acquire professional English integrated with STEM content and practice presenting their research according to international standards.

The key pedagogical advantage of this multi-agent organization lies in its dynamic balance between support and challenge: agents subtly adjust the pace of events, the level of lexical complexity, and cultural references to maintain the learner within their "zone of proximal development." The inclusion of multiple specialized agents, each assuming roles such as navigator, expert, facilitator, conversational partner, and evaluator, ensures that language practice remains multidimensional and contextually authentic.

Simultaneously, all achievements and errors are recorded across several dimensions: phonetics, vocabulary range, communicative strategies, and subject-specific knowledge. Virtual tours and laboratories enhanced by such an agent-based ecosystem transform language learning into a live interaction with authentic context, making it a continuous part of the user's practical linguistic experience.

One illustrative example of a platform implementing a virtual laboratory for English language learning through a multi-agent approach is *Immerse* (https://www.immerse.online). This educational VR platform is specifically designed for immersive language learning in real-life-oriented virtual scenarios. Within the *Immerse* environment, students use virtual reality headsets (e.g., Meta Quest) and are placed in simulated situations such as job interviews, shopping trips, conference rooms, restaurants, airports, and more.

The system operates with several functional agent analogues, including:

- A *Navigation Agent* (akin to automatic scene transitions), which assists users in spatial orientation;
- A *Facilitator-Instructor* (a live teacher or virtual character), who adapts tasks according to the learner's language level;
- A *Language Evaluator,* an analytics module that tracks the use of grammatical constructions, lexical diversity, and accuracy;
- A *Contextual Agent,* embedded triggers that activate tasks related to specific objects within the environment;
- An *Experience Agent,* a mini-game-like component (e.g., serving a customer in a café or giving recommendations at a hotel) that transforms learning into a goal-oriented mission with rewards.

Other examples with similar functionality include: *Mondly VR* (simulations of typical scenarios with auto-generated replies); *Engage VR* (a platform for creating custom educational scenes with NPCs); *ClassVR* (an environment tailored for younger learners, supporting gesture and voice cue interaction).

At the level of open systems, it is also possible to design custom scenarios and agents. For instance, one can combine platforms such as *Unity* + *Ready Player Me* + LLM APIs (e.g., OpenAI's GPT (OpenAI, 2025) or Meta's LLaMA (Meta AI, 2025) via *LangChain*), enabling the creation of a fully-fledged multi-agent language-adaptive laboratory.

Let us consider an example of a possible architecture for a multi-agent virtual laboratory for English language learning, implemented using open-source components. This architecture comprises the core environment built from the following elements: Unity 3D engine (used to construct an interactive virtual laboratory with physical simulation, objects, and animations) and Ready Player Me (responsible for generating student and agent avatars, including gesture support and lip-syncing for speech).

The structure of language and pedagogical agents corresponds to the scheme previously illustrated in Figure 7, and includes:

- Language Coach Agent (*OpenAI LLM API*) answers student questions, provides feedback on pronunciation and grammar.
- Task Coordinator Agent (*Python* + *LangChain*) assigns tasks, monitors progress, and triggers scenarios.
- Contextual Object Agent (*Unity C# script*) responds to object interactions (e.g., naming, commentary, inquiry).
- Feedback Agent (*Streamlit / Gradio frontend*) displays statistics on speech accuracy, lexical richness, and dialogue duration.

The communication processes, as outlined in Figure 7, involve *OpenAI GPT-4* (via API access) or *LLaMA 4* (via LangChain), which process user utterances, generate appropriate responses, and sustain contextual dialogues. *Whisper ASR* is used for real-time speech recognition, while voice responses from agents are synthesized via *Text-to-Speech (TTS)* tools such as *ElevenLabs*. Additionally, GPT-4o multimodal capabilities may be integrated to analyze visual objects in the scene via camera input.

Upon entering the simulation, the student takes a brief language placement test. Agents (via *LangChain memory*) retain a record of observed errors and learning progress. Subsequent tasks are automatically adapted, becoming more complex or simplified, based on performance outcomes.

A possible usage scenario: the student finds themselves in a virtual biochemistry lab and hears the prompt: “Please identify the glassware on the left. What is it used for?” After selecting a test tube and responding via microphone, the agent immediately assesses pronunciation and grammar, providing feedback: “Good job! You said ‘test tube’ correctly, but next time say *it is used for* instead of *it used for*.” The system then proposes similar tasks or initiates a dialogue with another agent.

An additional form of interaction with the virtual environment involves the implementation of custom-designed quests, which are especially suitable for young learners.

Examples of VR Quest Implementation for Young Learners in Foreign Language Acquisition

As an example of a VR quest designed for young learners to study a foreign language, let us consider a hypothetical interactive game titled *"Magic Market Adventure."* It is aimed at learning basic English words and phrases through story-based interaction. The central character of the scenario is a schoolchild who finds themselves in a virtual magical town, where once every 100 years the *Magic Market* opens, and communication takes place exclusively in English (Figure 12). The character receives a mission to collect magical ingredients for a potion that will awaken a sleeping dragon guarding the town. To accomplish this, the child must visit five market stalls: a vegetable stand, a toy shop, a candy store, a book tent, and a magical zoo.

While visiting each story location, the child must:

listen to and repeat words (e.g., *"carrot"*, *"book"*, *"tiger"*);
complete simple language tasks (e.g., find an object by description: *"Find a red sweet with strawberries"*);
use words in dialogue with NPCs: *"Can I have a toy train, please?"* - *"Here you are!"*;
collect items in a magical backpack, with correct usage unlocking the next scene.

At the end, after collecting all the items, the student must name them in English to "wake the dragon," i.e., activate the final animated scene with a thank-you message and a certificate. The difficulty level of this quest is adapted for learners aged 6 - 9. Each location includes visual hints (e.g., item highlighting, audio repetition). The system contains a built-in pronunciation control module (auto-feedback). The game can be implemented for Oculus Quest with controllers, but may also be adapted for cardboard headsets using gaze tracking.

This format makes language learning engaging, story-driven, and naturally interactive, activating the child's emotional and spatial memory.

Another example of a VR quest targets middle school learners (ages 10 - 13). It is an educational adventure game titled *"Grammar Guardians: The Temple of Tenses"*, which trains the use of grammatical rules and lexical structures through interactive gap-fill exercises.

According to the scenario proposed by GPT-4o, the player finds themselves in the mysterious *Temple of Tenses*, which is divided into chambers dedicated to different grammatical topics: *Present Simple*, *Past Simple*, *Future Tense*, *Present Perfect*, *Conditionals*, and others. To proceed further, the student must "unlock" doors by correctly completing language tasks.

Figure 12. A schoolchild at the virtual magic market

The core game mechanic involves interaction with artifacts or devices that activate only when the player:

selects the correct missing word (e.g., in the sentence: *He __ to school every day.* [*goes*]);
constructs a grammatically correct sentence (e.g., *If I were you, I would...*);
pronounces the correct phrase (with a speech recognition system providing feedback);
drags magical word symbols into the correct order (e.g., sorting words in the sentence: *have / you / ever / been / to / London?*).

One of the quest scenes is illustrated in Figure 13. According to the plot, in the *Present Perfect* chamber, the student sees a portal that will open only after they correctly answer three "Have you ever..." questions using the appropriate grammatical form (e.g., *Yes, I have been to Italy*, *No, I haven't ridden a horse*).

The player moves from room to room, collecting *knowledge crystals*. In the final stage, to escape the temple, they must construct a sentence that combines different tense forms - i.e., complete an integrative task.

Key features of the game include the use of a microphone for pronunciation control; a scoring system with medals for speed and accuracy; and the option to play in *cooperative mode*, where several students solve tasks together (Figure 14). Depending on the responses, NPCs react and provide hints.

This quest format combines an adventure storyline with gradual grammar and vocabulary practice in context, supporting better retention and emotional engagement for the learner.

Each such quest may have multiple versions with selectable difficulty levels or topic-specific tasks. The integration of GPT-4o or another similarly capable LLM enables the generation of varied scenarios, avoiding repetition and maintaining intrigue for students. During the rendering of virtual scenes, various sound effects can be added to evoke the desired emotional atmosphere.

When developing a multi-agent simulator for virtual quests, it is advisable to rely on the previously discussed standard architecture of the virtual laboratory (Figure 7).

Figure 13. Quest in the mysterious temple of tenses

Figure 14. Collaborative task solving in the temple of tenses

Development of the VR quest can be accelerated by initially building a text-based simulation (CLI), which, once tested, can later be adapted into a 3D environment or connected to a VR interface. The CLI version of the multi-agent logic serves well as a backend - it can be easily migrated to a web interface via *Gradio* or *Streamlit*, connected to a Unity 3D interface (via HTTP/WebSocket API to a Python server), or integrated with a voice interface (TTS/ASR).

PERSONAL CONFERENCES AS A TOOL FOR ACQUIRING SPECIALIZED VOCABULARY

To ensure deep mastery of specialized English vocabulary, a new methodology is proposed, based on conducting personal virtual conferences and seminars. This educational tool is implemented, like all previously discussed approaches, through a multi-level multi-agent environment using virtual reality (Figure 15) or in the format of a video conference (Figure 16).

At the center of the corresponding architecture lies the *conference moderator core* (Figure 17), which manages task flows, initiates agent calls, and controls the sequence of presentations.

Figure 15. Personal conference in a virtual environment

Figure 16. Personal conference in Google Meet format

At the first level operate *speaker agents* in the form of avatars, each linked to a specific source: a PDF article, a slide deck, a recorded conference video, or even a ResearchGate profile. These agents act as virtual presenters and use embedded LLMs to summarize content, generate answers to questions, paraphrase, and conduct interactive dialogue. Suitable models for this task include locally deployed instances of LLaMa 4 (Meta AI, 2025), Phi-4 (Abdin et al., 2024), DeepSeek (Bi et al., 2024; Guo et al., 2025), Sarvam-M (Sarvam AI, 2025) or other options capable of interfacing with GPT-4.5.

Figure 17. Key components of the personal conference

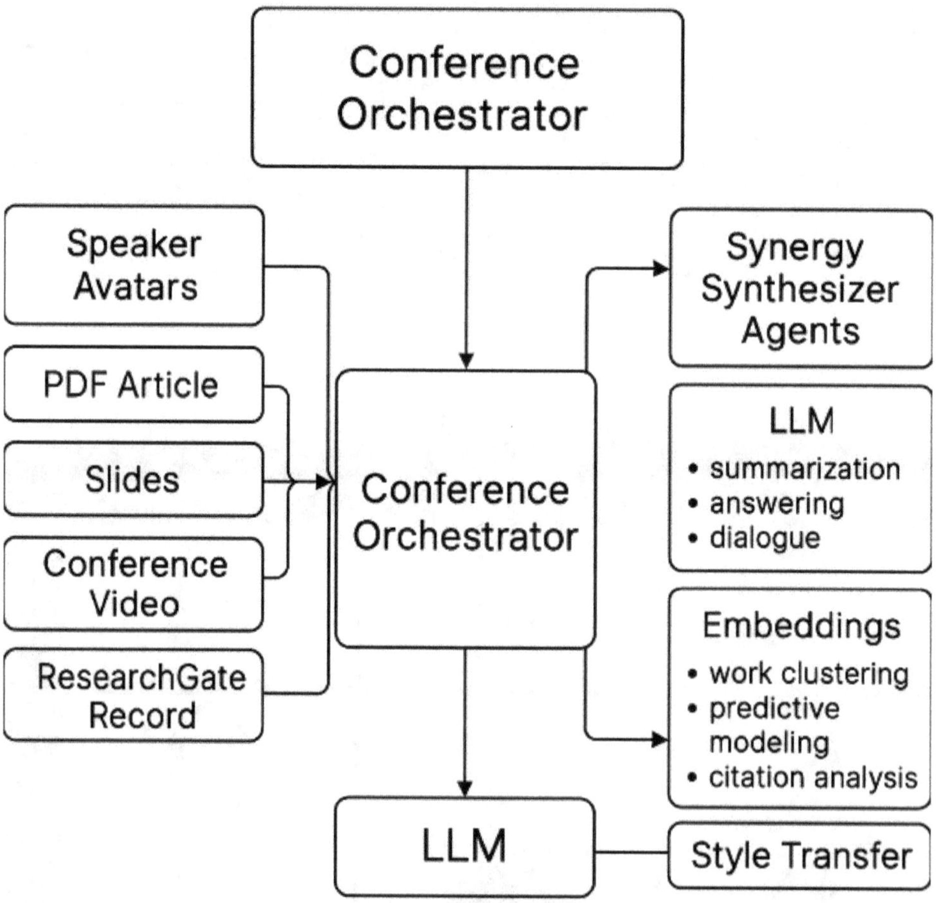

In addition to scientific papers, first-level avatar agents may deliver presentations based on dissertations, patents, and monographs - selected either by the user or recommended by an LLM such as GPT-4 or domain-specific agent-LLMs. During their briefings, these agents provide concise source summaries, respond to student queries, and participate in thematic discussions in real time.

The second level is represented by synthesis agents, which analyze the presentations of first-level avatars and generate new summaries. These agents receive compressed content from the presentations and produce synergistic conclusions. They propose integrated hypotheses and interdisciplinary research directions, and generate personalized lists of potential language difficulties for the student based on the synthesized content. As an output, a tree of open research questions may be constructed, recurring themes identified, and shifts in topical focus between different speakers recorded. This level utilizes specialized LLMs or hierarchical reasoning systems such as Tree-of-Thought agents or solutions akin to AutoGPT.

A separate development direction of the personal conference system involves the reconstruction of presentations from real conferences using slides and video recordings obtained from previously held events. The system recreates the content of presentations, interprets key ideas, and facilitates interactive discussions of the presented results. Agents can detect logical gaps, underdeveloped hypotheses, propose alternative solutions to problems, and generate revised research trajectories.

The third component of the multi-agent system is implemented via an *analytical agent* focused on the individual student. This agent applies methods such as clustering of academic works, stylometric analysis, and predictive modeling of subsequent learning stages. It is built on text embedding models, bibliographic networks, and fine-tuned LLMs capable of imitating the student's writing style, including citation-based chain-of-thought reasoning.

Additionally, an analytical agent may be developed to adapt to the student's cognitive style based on completed tasks aligned with the curriculum. Such an agent would identify potential learning pathways aligned with the student's prior achievements and interests, relying on contexts and sources previously used by the student.

Interaction between agents is facilitated through standard message-passing protocols such as LangGraph, A2A, ACP, and MCP (Habler et al., 2025; Bhardwaj et al., 2025; Liu et al., 2025; Jeong, 2025; Martineau, 2025), while the entire process is configured by the user via a dedicated graphical interface for the "personal conference," tailored to specific tasks.

Overall, the proposed concept of a simulated scientific environment, which not only mimics academic communication but also performs cognitive enrichment functions, is highly promising. It combines automated research processes, knowledge interpretation, and personalized linguistic interaction. Implementing such an environment as a standalone AI service could significantly transform approaches to English-language training for master's and PhD students, particularly in contexts with limited access to expert academic communities.

Among the potential directions for enhancing the capabilities of LLMs involved in personal conferences and other educational processes are: the use of subword tokenization for constructing specialized linguistic dictionaries (Vakulenko & Slyusar, 2024), the application of Large Conceptual Models (LCMs) (LCM team et al., 2024), and the deployment of diffusion-based language models (dLLMs) (Inception Labs, 2025; Google DeepMind, 2025) capable of generating entire sentences or complete textual corpora.

Given the wide range of possible technologies for implementing VR, an important area of attention is the analysis of existing and the development of new approaches for evaluating the suitability of specific LLMs for such specialized tasks.

METRICS FOR EVALUATING THE QUALITY OF LLM-BASED VIRTUAL ENVIRONMENT GENERATION

The targeted generation of virtual worlds using LLMs requires comprehensive assessment of the quality of their outputs (Hendrycks et al., 2020; Chen et al., 2021). Since the multi-agent approach to VR generation involves various textual and multimodal LLMs, the metric set for evaluating their performance must itself constitute a system of systems of indicators.

Analysis of available research shows that the development of metrics for evaluating VR generation with LLMs remains at an early stage. Existing works, such as (Nasir et al., 2024) and (Yu et al., 2025), are primarily focused on text-based game generation rather than full-fledged VR platforms.

For example, the work (Nasir et al., 2024) presents the Word2World system, which allows for the generation of narratives and game levels using LLMs, but its context is limited to 2D environments without integration of physical or VR-identical interactions into a unified experience. In 2025, the authors of (Yu et al., 2025) introduced the first benchmark, *RPGBENCH*, for testing LLMs as textual engines for *Role-Playing Games (RPGs)*. This game type involves the player assuming the role of a fictional character and controlling their actions within a defined storyline or world. A core feature of RPGs is the development of the main character, decision-making, and the influence of those decisions on the game's events.

Other characters in the virtual world that are not controlled by human players are known as *Non-Player Characters (NPCs)*. All NPCs are part of the game world and possess predefined characteristics (e.g., NPC X is a "wizard"). They maintain consistent personalities, and their actions and language must correspond to their assigned character throughout the game. NPCs function as interactive elements with which players can engage in dialogue on predefined topics.

The relatively new RPGBENCH metric enables the evaluation of logical consistency and coherence of gameplay, content engagement, and decision-making options (Yu et al., 2025). However, the metrics presented in (Nasir et al., 2024; Yu et al., 2025) are exclusively aimed at text-based scenarios, not VR-oriented realities.

Given this, current metrics used in *Word2World* and *RPGBENCH* should be regarded as preliminary for VR applications rather than sufficient. No other relevant studies that specialize in VR scenarios with clearly defined metrics, such as adherence to physical laws, handling of sensory inputs, control of spatial reachability, etc., have been identified in current literature.

This situation necessitates both the adaptation of existing metrics and the development of new, VR-specific indicators that encompass assessments of physical plausibility, sensory immersion, VR interactivity, spatial accessibility, and more.

As an initial step, it is possible to adapt known evaluation approaches along several dimensions. Specifically, the quality of the generated English-language environment at the level of textual descriptions can be meaningfully evaluated, analogously to (Nasir et al., 2024; Yu et al., 2025), using multiple facets simultaneously. These may include: coherence of description, realism and immersion level, content novelty, adherence to physical or other rules, and available interaction opportunities.

Below, we consider a set of established metrics for each of these aspects, along with their advantages and limitations, and propose new metric indicators that may be useful for assessing the quality of virtual worlds generated by LLMs for English language learning.

Coherence and Consistency of the Environment

This group of metrics evaluates the logical connectedness of the generated world and the absence of internal contradictions.

Lexical coherence is a metric of textual cohesion based on the repetition and thematic consistency of English vocabulary. For example, it analyzes lexical similarity between adjacent sentences - whether they share common words or topics. This metric is one of the most common in assessing automatically generated stories. It automatically measures basic narrative cohesion, although it only accounts for surface-level word similarity and may miss deeper logical inconsistencies.

Another approach involves coherence evaluation using a dedicated LLM (LLM-as-judge). In particular, such a model can analyze how well the generated world aligns with a given backstory or description. In the (Nasir et al., 2024) study, LLMs were provided with a story outline and a generated game world and were tasked with assigning a coherence score from 0 to 100, reflecting the match between the plot and the constructed environment. This method accounts for semantic alignment and context and can reveal complex inconsistencies. However, the final result depends on the reliability of the LLM-as-judge, which may introduce certain biases or errors.

In addition to these metrics, the indicator called “factual consistency” measures whether the environment description contradicts established facts or initial conditions. For example, in the RPGBench benchmark for text-based RPGs, a factual consistency metric (FAC) (Yu et al., 2025) is introduced: an LLM-judge checks each fact about the world or a character (e.g., “NPC X is a mage”) and notes whether this fact is consistent with the game description or violated. The metric is the proportion of facts that match the generated text. This method reveals internal contradictions (e.g., if a character abruptly changes traits). However, it requires a predefined set of facts or rules for validation, which is often implemented using an LLM-judge, which may again be biased.

Finally, an important indicator is the consistency of characters and objects. This is a specific aspect of coherence that tracks how consistently the model maintains character traits or object states. In RPGBench, for example, a personality consistency metric (PER) is introduced to assess whether an NPC's actions and speech align with their defined character throughout the game. Similarly, object consistency can be monitored - whether objects change their properties illogically (weight, color, etc.). This allows for a quantitative evaluation of the long-term consistency of behaviors and states. However, implementation requires an explicit description of initial properties or expected behavior for comparison, although such limitations are typical only for the early stages of system development and will likely be overcome in the future.

On the other hand, the set of described metrics can be used to assess the user's proficiency in English. Within a multi-agent architecture, each of the involved AI agents can generate its own metric, focusing on different dimensions, which allows for a comprehensive evaluation of the user's knowledge.

Realism and Immersion

The metrics in this category evaluate how natural and engaging the generated VR world appears, i.e., whether it evokes a sense of presence in the user. Among these, a classical metric is *Perplexity*, which characterises the fluency, grammatical correctness, and stylistic naturalness of the text generated by an LLM at the stage of scenario formation or NPC behaviour description in response to user actions. A low perplexity indicates that the text has a high probability and closely resembles human-generated language, meaning the model is not “surprised” by the text. This typically reflects the naturalness of the environment's description. This metric is considered objective; however, it does not guarantee semantic coherence or content quality - it only reflects the statistical likelihood of the text. Thus, it does not assess the logic or interest of the content, which may be "nonsensical but grammatically correct" and still exhibit low perplexity.

Immersion assessment from the users themselves constitutes a subjective metric, formed through surveys of actual users or players. In VR and gaming research, presence and immersion questionnaires are often employed to determine whether the player felt "inside" the virtual world and whether they were emotionally engaged. Indicators such as immersion, trust, and engagement are measured via questionnaires. Naturally, this directly reflects human perception of realism and immersion; however, this metric requires surveying a large number of respondents, and its outcomes may vary across individuals.

A closely related metric is content *interest or engagement*, which evaluates how compelling the environment description or game narrative is for the reader. In addition to expert and user feedback, an LLM-based evaluator may be employed. For instance, RPGBench introduces the *Interestingness* (INT) metric, the value of which is determined by GPT-4, assigning scores from 1 to 5 for each segment of the generated story, after which an average score is calculated to represent the game's overall engagement. This approach captures the narrative appeal associated with immersion, although it remains subjective when human experts are involved. In the case of automated assessment, the outcome depends on the LLM's capability to act as a judge.

Another dimension of realism in a virtual world, as well as its alignment with genre expectations or real-world prototypes, is the *style and genre conformity* metric. This can be assessed using embedding-based metrics - for example, by calculating the divergence between the feature distribution of the generated world and the embedding vector distribution of real-world environments of the same type. In the generation of game levels, one commonly used measure is *KL-divergence* of patterns, which compares the frequency of specific motifs in the generated VR level with those in the training data to determine how much the new level deviates from typical ones. If the deviation is too great, the world may appear unrealistic; if it is too small, the result may seem trivial or generic. This is one of the few quantitative indicators of "naturalness" or stylistic alignment. However, this metric requires a representative dataset of real examples for comparison. Moreover, a high stylistic deviation is not necessarily undesirable, as it may reflect creativity rather than low quality. This consideration leads directly to the next category of metrics, which focuses on assessing the degree of *novelty*.

Novelty and Diversity

Metrics sensitive to this category of characteristics indicate whether the generated content is not merely a trivial repetition of existing patterns, as well as whether different generated worlds exhibit sufficient variation. In this context, a widely used metric is *Distinct_n* (unique n-grams), which reflects the lexical diversity of dialogue systems. It calculates the proportion of unique n-grams in the English-language text:

$$Distinct - n = \frac{\text{unique n} - \text{grams in the corpus}}{\text{all n} - \text{grams in the corpus}}.$$

For instance, *Distinct-1* measures the percentage of unique words, while *Distinct-2* measures the percentage of unique word pairs. Values close to 1 (100%) indicate that the text is highly diverse and exhibits minimal repetition of expressions. This metric can also be applied to a collection of several generated game levels or VR scenarios (by concatenating all texts). Its advantages lie in the simplicity of computation and its direct reflection of lexical variety. However, the results depend on the text length, since longer descriptions naturally contain more unique n-grams. Moreover, this metric does not account for semantic novelty - a text may include diverse words while expressing the same underlying idea.

To verify that the model does not repeatedly generate the same world, the *Self-BLEU* metric is used to assess inter-environment diversity. For each generated world description, a BLEU score is computed against all other descriptions treated as references, and the result is then averaged. A low Self-BLEU score corresponds to high diversity (outputs differ significantly from each other), while a high Self-BLEU score indicates *mode collapse*, i.e., the generator produces highly similar worlds. This approach effectively captures n-gram similarity across a set and reveals instances where the model has become stuck in a single pattern. Nonetheless, reliable statistical results require a sufficiently large sample of generated worlds, and, like BLEU itself, this metric emphasizes lexical overlap rather than deeper conceptual distinctions.

Novelty metrics with respect to a reference base compare the generated world to existing ones (e.g., from training data or previous generations) to determine the degree of uniqueness. One approach involves calculating the Euclidean distance or another metric in feature space. For instance, in *Word2World*, the novelty of a level is measured via the Euclidean distance between the embedding vectors of two world maps; if the distance exceeds a predefined threshold, the world is considered novel. Another approach uses distributional divergence (e.g., KL or JS divergence) between the distribution of elements in the generated level and a reference set of levels. This allows for consideration of structural or semantic features rather than only lexical tokens, thereby enabling more nuanced control over the desired degree of novelty. Naturally, this is feasible only if feature sets or vector representations of the worlds are defined and if suitable reference data is available, which may not always be the case.

Intra-world content diversity can be assessed separately - that is, the extent to which the elements within a single generated environment are varied. For instance, in a game level, this might refer to the number of distinct landscape types or item categories present. This diversity can be quantified either by simply counting the number of object categories or by calculating a diversity index (e.g., the entropy of the object type distribution). A high value indicates that the world is not monotonous; however, excessive diversity without a coherent focus may compromise the integrity of the design.

Conformity to Physical or Gameplay Rules

An essential aspect of VR-world quality is its *validity* - whether the generated environment adheres to logical, physical, and gameplay constraints. Metrics in this category aim to detect rule violations or failures to satisfy mandatory conditions.

A basic metric, applicable when the environment is generated in a specific format (e.g., JSON, XML), is the *Format Compliance Rate* (FCR). It measures the proportion of outputs that conform to the required format without syntactic errors. For example, in RPGBench, the *Format-Check Pass Rate* assesses how many generated world descriptions successfully pass JSON validity checks. This is a formal procedure that does not account for content - indeed, a syntactically correct description may still violate the world's internal rules.

A related metric is the *Validity Compliance Rate* (VCR), which measures the percentage of generated environments that satisfy all predefined design or physical rules. In RPGBench, for instance, the *Validity-Check Pass Rate* captures the proportion of successful generations in which all game mechanics conditions are satisfied. For an RPG scenario, this may include correct initialization of all state variables and valid end conditions. However, this metric requires a dedicated *rule-checker* - a validation program that encodes the full set of rules. For complex rule systems, developing such a checker may be non-trivial.

More detailed checks based on *gameplay mechanics metrics* can also be used to verify specific rules. In RPGBench, this includes detecting *Event Condition Errors* (e.g., events triggered without valid conditions) and *Variable Update Errors* (e.g., state updates performed incorrectly). These metrics automatically evaluate each event in the generated scenario to ensure it is triggered appropriately and updates the game state correctly. From this, an *integrated mechanics accuracy score* can be computed, representing the share of events executed without violations. Such a system ensures logic consistency at every step - correct event triggers, valid state transitions, etc. However, these metrics are highly dependent on the specific model of the world or game and may fail to capture informally defined aspects, such as physical plausibility or believability, if they are not encoded as explicit rules.

In the context of game-based quests, it is critically important to verify whether the VR world can be completed according to the rules of the quest. This metric, intuitively named *playability*, measures the feasibility of completing the scenario. In the Word2World study, playability was assessed by attempting to reach all goals within a level using an automated agent. If the agent was unable to find a path to a key object or the finish point, the level was deemed unplayable. Word2World reported approximately 90% playability for multi-round generation (i.e., 9 out of 10 levels were playable).

Special checks for *physical plausibility* also deserve attention. For instance, if a virtual world includes an object that is described as flying unsupported in violation of gravitational laws, this constitutes a physical inconsistency and should be corrected. These metrics are often integrated into simulation engines, allowing the environment to be passed through a physics engine to detect anomalies. However, implementing such checks automatically at the level of textual descriptions is challenging, as it requires a semantic understanding of physical principles. While large language models (LLMs) can sometimes regulate such issues based on commonsense knowledge, they are not always reliable for this task.

Interaction Affordances

The final group of metrics evaluates how interaction-friendly the generated environment is - i.e., whether there are elements or agents to interact with and whether the world supports player or agent actions. The concept of *affordance* refers to the possibilities or capacities for interaction that a virtual environment offers to the player. In simple terms, it describes the types of actions that the environment supports.

The *number of interactive elements* is a basic metric that counts how many objects in the world are potentially actionable (e.g., levers, doors, NPCs for dialogue, collectible items, etc.). In Word2World, the notion of "important tiles" was introduced - these are environmental components and interactive objects deemed necessary for gameplay. *Important tile accuracy* was used to evaluate whether all essential interactive objects were present and correctly positioned. A sufficient number of interactive objects generally makes gameplay more engaging; this metric helps ensure that the world is not empty. However, it does not account for the *quality* of interaction - an object may be interactive without contributing meaningfully to the experience. Furthermore, an excessive number of interactive elements can overwhelm or confuse the player during the quest.

Affordance diversity measures the range of action types supported by the environment. For example, can the player engage in dialogue or solve puzzles in this world? A metric can be introduced that counts the number of unique categories of supported actions - if a world enables three distinct types of interaction, it is generally considered richer than one offering only a single type. On the other hand, not every genre requires a wide spectrum of affordances; in some cases, a focused design with a single interaction type may be entirely appropriate for the intended gameplay experience.

Action Quality, as implemented in RPGBench, is assessed using an LLM-based judge. The corresponding metric, *ACT* (Action Choice Quality), reflects how appropriate and meaningful the actions occurring in the world are. If the environment-generation model produces coherent and sensible action options, this indicates that the world's affordances have been properly developed - there are things for the player to do, and those actions make contextual sense.

Novel Potential Evaluation Metrics

In addition to the aforementioned measures, several further metrics may be proposed to enable a more in-depth evaluation of LLM-generated virtual worlds:

For instance, a metric that integrates various aspects of coherence could be formulated as the *Environment Coherence Index* (ECI). One possible approach involves constructing a graph of object and character mentions throughout the text and measuring how well connected this graph is. The following formulations may be used:

$$IKS_1 = \frac{1}{N-1}\sum_{i=2}^{N} 1\{\textit{sentence i contains a mention of an object from any sentence} < i\},$$

where N is the number of sentences in the analyzed text corpus, or

$$IKS_2 = \frac{1}{1 + \text{Contradictions}},$$

where *Contradictions* is the number of detected logical inconsistencies.

The idea behind these metrics is to provide an aggregated score ranging from 0 to 1, where 1 denotes a complete absence of logical failures, and lower values indicate potential coherence issues.

To automate the assessment of *immersiveness* through textual analysis, it is reasonable to consider the number of sensory descriptions (visual, auditory, tactile details) and emotionally charged words. The corresponding metric may be referred to as the *Immersion Index*, and can be computed using the following formula:

$$\textit{Immersion} = \frac{\text{SensoryDescriptionCount} + \text{EmotionWordCount}}{N},$$

where N is the number of sentences in the analyzed text corpus, *SensoryDescriptionCount* is the number of sensory descriptions, and *EmotionWordCount* is the number of emotionally charged words.

A higher *Immersion Index* would indicate that the environment is rich in perceptual details, contributing to the user's sense of presence. This metric, when combined with coherence evaluation, could serve as an automatic predictor of user immersion. Naturally, such an index would require careful calibration based on survey data to confirm its correlation with actual immersion experiences.

To provide a more comprehensive assessment of the *uniqueness* of a generated world relative to the model's knowledge base, a *Normalized Novelty Score* (NNS) is proposed. This involves embedding the world x (e.g., via its textual description) and calculating the maximum similarity of the generated world x_{gen} to any known reference example (*References*):

$$NNS = 1 - \max_{x \in Ref} \mathrm{sim}\left(x_{gen}, x\right),$$

where *sim* denotes cosine similarity or another appropriate distance measure, and x represents a reference world.

If *NNS* approaches 1, the generated world is highly original; if it is close to 0, the result is nearly identical to a known instance. This metric resembles a plagiarism check but is specifically designed for creative generation tasks, ensuring that the model is not merely reproducing a memorized training example. Importantly, novelty must be interpreted alongside correctness - an entirely novel world may nonetheless be unplayable or invalid. Therefore, *NNS* should be evaluated together with a validity metric, such as the *Rule Compliance Coefficient* (RCC). This coefficient serves as an integrative metric that aggregates all verified rules into a single score:

$$RCC = \frac{Number\ of\ rules\ complied}{Total\ number\ of\ rules} \times 100\%,$$

For example, if a test suite comprises 10 verification checks and 8 of them are satisfied (e.g., correct format, presence of exits in each room, no violations of gravity), the *Rule Compliance Coefficient* (RCC) would equal 80%. This provides a convenient aggregate indicator of the world's "correctness." In the case of a quest-based game level, the set of rules would include playability, absence of dead ends, availability of sufficient resources for completion, and all other requirements specified in the instructional quest design document.

A newly proposed metric that quantifies affordances is the *Interactivity Index* (II). For example,

$$II = A + 0.5B,$$

where A is the number of unique types of actions supported by the environment (as action diversity is crucial), and B is the total number of interactive objects or nodes within the VR world. The coefficient 0.5 reduces the weight of mere quantity, emphasizing diversity over redundancy. This formula can be adapted to suit the genre-specific requirements. The guiding principle is that a world with, say, five types of interactions and ten interactive objects should receive a higher score than a world with only one interaction type but thirty objects of the same kind. Such an index encourages models to generate varied and meaningful affordances for the player.

In a similar fashion, technical, cognitive, physical, and interaction-related metrics, as well as LLM-judge analytics, can be combined to form a comprehensive assessment. Altogether, this provides a scientific basis for metrics used to evaluate VR environments. While the proposed and related new indicators require experimental testing and validation in practical scenarios, they offer viable paths toward formalising intuitive requirements for high-quality virtual worlds (such as deep interactivity or the avoidance of repetitive content) into structured numerical scores.

In the context of enhancing LLM performance evaluation, it is also proposed to consider an alternative to perplexity - namely, *intuitiveness*. This metric enables a clearer differentiation between LLM agents with similar perplexity values by capturing their ability to produce contextually appropriate and cognitively natural outputs.

One approach to introducing a mathematical formulation of *intuition* for evaluating the quality of predictions made by a neural agent involves modifying the standard definition of perplexity. This modification entails incorporating not only the probability of the predicted outcome but also its *unexpectedness* with respect to conventional patterns.

Let us consider the embedding space of vectors that an LLM is expected to predict. Denote the set of such vectors as $X=\{x_1, x_2,\dots,x_N\}$. The neural network produces a probability distribution over these vectors, denoted $p_m(x_i)$. To incorporate the notion of "intuition," we introduce a reference probability distribution $p_r(x_i)$, which could be derived from a simple statistical model or assumed as uniform in the absence of prior knowledge. The lower the value of $p_r(x_i)$, the more "non-obvious" the predicted vector is considered to be.

Next, we introduce a weighting function $w(x_i)$ that reflects the prediction complexity associated with each vector:

$$w(x_i) = \frac{1}{p_r(x_i) + \varepsilon}.$$

Here, ε is a small constant introduced to avoid division by zero.

Accordingly, the less probable a vector is under the reference model, the greater the weight it should receive from the standpoint of intuitiveness.

The next step involves calculating the so-called *intuitive perplexity*:

$$I_p = exp\left\{\frac{\sum_{i=1}^{N} w(x_i)\left[-\ ln\ p_m(x_i)\right]}{\sum_{i=1}^{N} w(x_i)}\right\},$$

and its reciprocal yields the *Intuition Score*:

$$I = \frac{1}{I_p} = exp\left\{-\frac{\sum_{i=1}^{N} w(x_i)\left[-\ ln\ p_m(x_i)\right]}{\sum_{i=1}^{N} w(x_i)}\right\} =$$

$$= exp\left\{\frac{\sum_{i=1}^{N} w(x_i) ln\ p_m(x_i)}{\sum_{i=1}^{N} w(x_i)}\right\}.$$

If the LLM is capable of accurately predicting rare embedding vectors or events (e.g., low-frequency words), the resulting value of ***I*** will be high, indicating strong intuitive performance. Conversely, if the model performs poorly in forecasting such rare outcomes, the value of ***I*** will be low, revealing weak intuitiveness. Overall, higher values of this metric correspond to higher intuition, while lower values reflect a lack of intuitive capacity in the model. The possible range of this *Intuition Score* lies between 0 and 1.

Intuitiveness for action agents (e.g., AI agents for linguistic quests in VR environments, or agents within a personal university framework for English language learning) can be defined analogously to that for LLMs, but with several important distinctions. The key difference lies in the fact that, for language models, intuitiveness quantifies the ability to predict rare words (tokens) based on a probabilistic distribution, while for action agents, intuitiveness may reflect the ability to predict *optimal actions* in complex, uncertain, or rare situations. Thus, while LLMs rely on the probabilities of word occurrence, action agents rely on the probabilities of action selection and the associated quality of those actions.

Let an AI agent operate in a virtual environment, making decisions according to a policy π (als), where s denotes the current state, *a* - the action, and π (als) - the probability of choosing action a in state s. Then, analogously to LLMs, the *perplexity* of the agent can be expressed as:

$$P_{agent} = exp\left\{-\frac{1}{M}\sum_{i=1}^{M} ln\left(\pi\left(a_i \middle| s_i\right)\right)\right\},$$

where *M* is the number of possible decisions (actions) available to the agent.

The lower the agent's perplexity P_{agent}, the more confidently the agent selects its actions.

To incorporate *agent intuitiveness*, we introduce a *baseline action probability* $p_r(a \mid s)$. This can be derived from frequency analysis (e.g., how often a particular action has occurred in similar situations), from a naive random-choice model (i.e., a uniform action distribution), or from a simplified model trained without deep learning. Accordingly, the rarity weight for an action takes the form:

$$w(a_i, s_i) = \frac{1}{p_r(a_i|s_i) + \varepsilon}.$$

where ε is a small constant to avoid division by zero.

Hence, the intuitive perplexity is calculated by the expression:

$$I_p = exp\left\{\frac{\sum_{i=1}^{M} w(a_i, s_i)\left[-\ ln\left(\pi(a_i|s_i)\right)\right]}{\sum_{i=1}^{M} w(a_i, s_i)}\right\}.$$

The transition to action intuitiveness is achieved by inverting I_p. Thus, the better the agent selects rare actions, the higher its intuitiveness and ability to employ strategies that are not obvious but lead to success.

The proposed framework for evaluating the quality of virtual world generation through large language models and action agents incorporates a comprehensive *system of systems of metrics* -ranging from classical perplexity to advanced indicators such as intuitiveness, the environment coherence index, the immersion index, and measures of novelty and interaction affordances.

These metrics enable a quantitative description of key characteristics of VR environments, including structural coherence, depth of immersion, gameplay validity, creativity, diversity of interactions, and the agents' ability to make optimal decisions in non-trivial situations. The introduction of intuitiveness as an alternative to perplexity allows for a more precise differentiation between models based on their ability to predict rare but relevant actions or events. The combined use of these indicators can serve as the foundation for a comprehensive, automated evaluation system for synthetic world building that integrates technical, cognitive, and emotional criteria.

Moreover, the proposed metric system can be scaled to assess the actions of learners actively interacting with the virtual environment, allowing real-time tracking of their engagement level, intuitive decision-making, strategy effectiveness, and alignment of behavior with educational goals.

CONCLUSION

The future trends and research directions in AI-driven language education discussed in this section do not encompass all possible approaches. The rapid advancement of technology and the growing cognitive capabilities of artificial intelligence models, particularly LLMs, multimodal agents, and adaptive systems for personalized learning, suggest the emergence of new, more advanced solutions in this domain. It is likely that the near future will witness deeper integration between neuro-pedagogy, cognitive science, and artificial intelligence, contributing to the creation of more effective learning environments with enhanced empathy, adaptability, and support for emotional intelligence.

We can expect the development of systems capable of dynamically analyzing learning styles, the learner's cognitive state, and knowledge gaps in real time, enabling a highly individualized learning process. Additionally, language diversity may be expanded through the automatic generation of educational materials in rare and regional languages. This will promote English language acquisition among speakers of the world's many languages and contribute to the preservation of humanity's linguistic heritage in the digital age.

At the same time, regardless of the level of technological development, success in learning will continue to depend on the human factor - motivation, the inner drive for self-improvement, persistence, and the active engagement of learners in their own educational journey. Artificial intelligence can serve as a powerful tool for support and enhancement, but it is the learner's purposeful effort that remains the cornerstone of successful English language acquisition.

REFERENCES

Abdin, M., & Aneja, J.. (2024, December). *Phi-4 technical report.* arXiv. https://arxiv.org/abs/2412.08905

Anthropic. (2025, May). *System card: Claude Opus 4 & Claude Sonnet 4.* https://www.anthropic.com/model-card

Bhardwaj, D., Beniwal, A., Chaudhari, S., Kalyan, A., Rajpurohit, T., Narasimhan, K. R., Deshpande, A., & Murahari, V. (2025). *Agent context protocols enhance collective inference.* arXiv. https://arxiv.org/abs/2505.14569

Bi, X., Chen, D., Chen, G., & Chen, S. (2024). *DeepSeek LLM: Scaling open-source language models with longtermism.* arXiv. https://arxiv.org/abs/2401.02954

Chen, M., Tworek, J., Jun, H., Yuan, Q., de Oliveira Pinto, H. P., Kaplan, J., & Amodei, D. (2021). *Evaluating large language models trained on code.* arXiv. https://arxiv.org/abs/2107.03374

Cox, A. M. (2021). Exploring the impact of artificial intelligence and robots on higher education through literature-based design fictions. *International Journal of Educational Technology in Higher Education, 18*(1), 3. DOI: 10.1186/s41239-020-00237-8

Google. (2025, March 25). *Gemini 2.5: Our most intelligent AI model* [Blog post]. Google DeepMind. https://blog.google/technology/google-deepmind/gemini-model-thinking-updates-march-2025/#gemini-2-5-thinking

Google DeepMind. (2025). *Gemini Diffusion.* https://deepmind.google/models/gemini-diffusion/

Guo, D., & Yang, D.. (2025). *DeepSeek-R1: Incentivizing reasoning capability in LLMs via reinforcement learning.* arXiv. https://arxiv.org/abs/2501.12948

Habler, I., Huang, K., Narajala, V. S., & Kulkarni, P. (2025). *Building a secure agentic AI application leveraging A2A protocol.* arXiv. https://arxiv.org/abs/2504.16902

Hendrycks, D., Burns, C., Basart, S., Zou, A., Mazeika, M., Song, D., & Steinhardt, J. (2020). *Measuring massive multitask language understanding.* arXiv. https://doi.org//arXiv.2009.03300DOI: 10.48550

Inception Labs. (2025, February 26). *Introducing Mercury, the first commercial-scale diffusion large language model.* https://www.inceptionlabs.ai/news

Jeong, C. (2025). *A study on the MCP × A2A framework for enhancing interoperability of LLM-based autonomous agents*. arXiv. https://arxiv.org/abs/2506.01804

Kondratenko, Y., Kondratenko, G., Shevchenko, A., Slyusar, V., Zhukov, Y., & Vakulenko, M. (2023b). Towards implementing the strategy of artificial intelligence development: Ukraine peculiarities. *CEUR Workshop Proceedings, 3513*, 106–117. https://ceur-ws.org/Vol-3513/paper09.pdf

Kondratenko, Y., Shevchenko, A., Zhukov, Y., Slyusar, V., Kondratenko, G., Klymenko, M., & Striuk, O. (2023a). *Analysis of the priorities and perspectives in artificial intelligence implementation*. In 2023 13th International Conference on Dependable Systems, Services and Technologies, DESSERT 2023. DOI: 10.1109/DESSERT61349.2023.10416432

Kondratenko, Y. P., Slyusar, V. I., Solesvik, M. B., Kondratenko, N. Y., & Gomolka, Z. (2024). Interrelation and inter-influence of artificial intelligence and higher education systems. In *Research tendencies and prospect domains for AI development and implementation* (pp. 31–58). River Publishers., DOI: 10.1201/9788770046947-2

Laurent, A. (2023). *La guerre des intelligences à l'heure de ChatGPT*. Lattes.

LCM team. et al. (2024). *Large concept models: Language modeling in a sentence representation space*. arXiv. https://arxiv.org/abs/2412.08821

Liu, J., Yu, K., Chen, K., Li, K., Qian, Y., Guo, X., Song, H., & Li, Y. (2025). *ACPs: Agent collaboration protocols for the Internet of Agents*. arXiv. https://arxiv.org/abs/2505.13523

Martin, F., Zhuang, M., & Schaefer, D. (2024). Systematic review of research on artificial intelligence in K-12 education (2017–2022). *Computers and Education: Artificial Intelligence*, *6*, 100195. DOI: 10.1016/j.caeai.2023.100195

Martineau, K. (2025, May 28). *The simplest protocol for AI agents to work together*. IBM Research. https://research.ibm.com/blog/agent-communication-protocol-ai

Media & Learning Association. (2025, June 3). *Sparkify: more AI generated video*. Media & Learning Association. https://media-and-learning.eu/type/tools/sparkify-more-ai-generated-video

Meta, A. I. (2025, April 5). *Llama 4: Multimodal intelligence*. Meta AI Blog. https://ai.meta.com/blog/llama-4-multimodal-intelligence/

Nasir, M. U., James, S., & Togelius, J. (2024). *Word2World: Generating stories and worlds through large language models*. arXiv. https://arxiv.org/abs/2405.06686

Open, A. I. (2025, February 27).*OpenAI GPT-4.5 system card*. https://cdn.openai.com/gpt-4-5-system-card.pdf

Sarvam, A. I. (2025, May 23). *Sarvam M* [Blog post]. https://www.sarvam.ai/blogs/sarvam-m

Shabanov, A. (2025, June 7). *Sparkify combines Gemini and Veo 3 to power Google's latest AI video experiment*. Testing Catalog. https://www.testingcatalog.com/sparkify-uses-gemini-and-veo-3-to-power-googles-latest-ai-video-experiment/

Shevchenko, A., Panok, V., Shevtsov, A., Slyusar, V., Malyi, R., Yeroshenko, T., & Nazar, M. (2024). Development of a virtual psychological assistant with artificial intelligence in the healthcare sector. *Clinical and Preventive Medicine*, (8), 15–27. DOI: 10.31612/2616-4868.8.2024.02

Slyusar, V. (2025a). Distributed multi-agent systems based on the mixture of experts architecture in the context of 6G wireless technologies. In Dovgyi, S. (Eds.), *Applied innovations in information and communication technology* (Vol. 1338, pp. 81–110). Springer., DOI: 10.1007/978-3-031-89296-7_6

Slyusar, V. (2025c). *Perspectives of the AI applications for improving learning and teaching*. Processes. *AI in Education System: Successful Cases and Perspectives*. River Publishers.

Slyusar, V. I. (2025b). Applications of large language models in the military sphere. In *Artificial intelligence: Achievements and recent developments* (pp. 53–81). River Publishers.

Taverniti, G., & Lombardo, C.. (2023). *AI Power. Non solo ChatGPT: lavoro, marketing e futuro*. Ulrico Hoepli.

Vakulenko, M., & Slyusar, V. (2024). Automatic smart subword segmentation for the reverse Ukrainian physical dictionary task. *CEUR Workshop Proceedings, 3723*, 59–73.

Yu, P., Shen, D., Meng, S., Lee, J., Yin, W., Cui, A. Y., Xu, Z., Zhu, Y., Shi, X., Li, M., & Smola, A. (2025). *RPGBENCH: Evaluating large language models as role-playing game engines*. arXiv. https://arxiv.org/abs/2502.00595

Zawacki-Richter, O., Marín, V. I., Bond, M., & Gouverneur, F. (2019). Systematic review of research on artificial intelligence applications in higher education - Where are the educators? *International Journal of Educational Technology in Higher Education, 16*(1), 39. DOI: 10.1186/s41239-019-0171-0

ADDITIONAL READING

Chen, L., Chen, P., & Lin, Z. (2020). Artificial intelligence in education: A review. *IEEE Access : Practical Innovations, Open Solutions, 8*, 75264–75278. DOI: 10.1109/ACCESS.2020.2988510

Redmon, J., Divvala, S., Girshick, R., & Farhadi, A. (2016). You Only Look Once: Unified, Real-Time Object Detection. *2016 IEEE Conference on Computer Vision and Pattern Recognition (CVPR)*. DOI: 10.1109/CVPR.2016.91

Slyusar, V., Protsenko, M., Chernukha, A., Melkin, V., Biloborodov, O., Samoilenko, M., Kravchenko, O., Kalinichenko, G., Rohovyi, A., & Soloshchuk, M. (2022). Improvement of the model for detecting objects on aerial photos and video in unmanned aerial systems. *Eastern-European Journal of Enterprise Technologies, 1*(9(115)), 24–34. DOI: 10.15587/1729-4061.2022.252876

KEY TERMS AND DEFINITIONS

Large Language Models (LLMs): are understood as models trained on massive text corpora and capable of performing complex tasks involving the analysis, comprehension, and generation of text.

Multi-agent system: is a collection of intelligent agents that work together to achieve desired results or perform specific functions.

Multimodal LLMs: are systems capable of simultaneously processing and integrating information from diverse sources and formats, including textual, visual, audio, and video data.

Non-Player Characters (NPCs): are entities in a virtual world that are not directly controlled by human players; their behavior is managed by the system, typically via AI or scripted logic.

Token: is the minimal meaningful unit in a textual sequence, obtained through the process of tokenization - the computational segmentation of text into linguistically or statistically significant components.

Virtual Reality (VR): is an interactive, computer-generated 3D environment experienced from a first-person perspective, where head and body tracking with stereoscopic displays enable real-time perception and action, creating a convincing sense of presence.

Chapter 7
Ananses:
Vessels of Identity, Resistance, and Preservation of the Akan Language of Ghana

Ama Oforiwaa Aduonum
Illinois State University, USA

Anita Twenewaa Adu
https://orcid.org/0009-0008-6379-924X
University of Education, Winneba, Ghana

ABSTRACT

This chapter examines Ananse stories as a means by which the Akan people preserve language and cultural identity, resisting colonial legacies, globalization, and linguistic homogenization. These stories go beyond entertainment, serving as vessels of memory, resistance, and survival, embedding moral philosophy, historical awareness, and indigenous knowledge. Drawing on postcolonial theory and oral literature studies, it shows how Anansesɛm conveys linguistic structures, reinforces communal values, and affirms Akan identity. Through close readings, it demonstrates how storytelling sustains cultural continuity and resists erasure of local knowledge. The chapter calls for integrating Anansesɛm into education, digital media, and revitalization programs to revalorize the Akan language and worldview, promoting linguistic diversity and cultural sovereignty in Ghana and beyond. a

DOI: 10.4018/979-8-3373-3561-2.ch007

INTRODUCTION

Ananseseɛm occupies a central place in Akan society as a rich repository of knowledge transmission, moral instruction, and cultural identity formation. The main character, Ananse the spider, is clever and sometimes tricky, and his actions usually show what is right or wrong. These traditional stories, often told in the evenings, are not just for fun but as powerful tools for educating both children and adults about social values, communal responsibilities, conflict resolution, and the consequences of human actions. Through witty, symbolic narratives, Akan communities embed philosophical and ethical teachings in everyday language. The use of rich linguistic forms such as proverbs, idioms, and metaphor further enhances the didactic function of Ananseseɛm, making them accessible and memorable. In preserving and performing Ananseseɛm, the Akan maintain a living oral archive that sustains collective memory, reinforces language use, and affirms cultural continuity from one generation to the next.

This chapter explores the role of Ananse stories (spider tales) as vessels of identity, memory, resistance, and survival in preserving the Akan language and cultural consciousness. In Akan folklore, Ananse, the cunning spider, is more than a trickster figure; he is a symbol of cultural continuity, resilience, and linguistic preservation (Zimmerman, 2023; Arthur, Sanka and Yeboah, 2021; Abankwa and Abankwa, 2017; Lord, 2010). Emerging from the oral traditions of the Akan people of Ghana, Ananse stories, locally referred to as "*Ananseseɛm*," serve as vessels of communal memory and resistance against cultural erasure (Abankwa and Abankwa, 2017). Through generations of storytelling, these narratives have functioned as archives of Indigenous knowledge, ethical instruction, and collective identity, weaving a web that binds the Akan to their ancestral land, their shared struggles, and their linguistic heritage (Abankwa and Abankwa, 2017; Onuora, 2012).

Ananse stories are crucial to the preservation of the Akan language. The power of Ananse stories lies not only in their entertainment value but in their capacity to resist domination and safeguard language. In both homeland and abroad, in the wake of the twin evils of slavery and colonialism as well as the pressures of globalization, Ananse emerged as a figure of defiance (Lord, 2010; Sherlock, 2002). His survival, particularly in diasporan oral tradition, symbolizes the African's refusal to surrender their voice (Salkey, 1997; Berry, 1989). Through satire, metaphor, and allegory, *Ananseseɛm* offers a critique of power dynamics, exposes social contradictions, and reaffirms communal values. Ananse stories are not mere tales. They are rich intellectual traditions that guarantee the preservation of the Akan language and its rich wisdom for posterity. We 1) explore *Ananseseɛm* as a vessel of identity, memory, resistance, and survival in the preservation of the Akan language, 2) examine how *Ananseseɛm* not only transmit linguistic structures, but also encode cultural values and historical consciousness, 3) demonstrate how storytelling serves as a strategy for cultural survival, linking people of Akan origin to their land, ancestry, and collective struggle, and 4) present *Anansesɛm* as oral archives that resist linguistic homogenization, a situation that reinforces Akan identity in the face of external pressures.

The chapter draws inspiration from postcolonial theory, which interrogates the impacts of colonialism on African cultural expression, and Indigenous knowledge frameworks, which value non-Western epistemologies, particularly those rooted in oral traditions. Oral literature studies further provide tools for analyzing the performance, structure, and sociocultural functions of *Anansesɛm*. Together, these approaches help us better understand how Ananse stories keep Akan culture and language alive in meaningful and evolving ways. We position *Anansesɛm* as critical to understanding the resilience of the Akan language and demonstrate how oral traditions, such as storytelling, help preserve a community's language and culture, even when there are attempts to wipe them out. The stories of Ananse, the clever spider, are like a web that connects the Akan people to their roots. Through these tales, they pass on wisdom, values, and a sense of identity from one generation to the next heritage (Abankwa and Abankwa, 2017; Onuora, 2012). By focusing on Ananse stories as tools for remembering the past, expressing one's identity, and standing strong against cultural erosion, this chapter aims to contribute to the preservation and revitalisation of the Akan language and oral traditions. In an era of globalization and linguistic erosion, documenting and analyzing these narratives safeguards intangible cultural heritage for posterity. As Adjeiand Dei (2008) have noted, in the pursuit of sustainable and contextually appropriate solutions to local challenges, the knowledge and experiential insights of local communities must not be disregarded, as they constitute an essential resource.

ANANSESƐM AS VESSELS OF IDENTITY, MEMORY, RESISTANCE, AND SURVIVAL

Postcolonial theory provides a critical lens for analyzing the lingering effects of colonialism on culture, identity, and language. It interrogates how colonial power structures persist in contemporary institutions and epistemologies, especially through the privileging of European languages, narratives, and values over indigenous forms of knowledge and expression. In the context of this chapter, postcolonial theory helps frame Anansesɛm as a form of cultural resistance or what Mignolo (2011) refers to as "epistemic disobedience", pushing back against the forces of linguistic homogenization imposed through colonial education and language policy. Postcolonial theory is useful to position Anansesɛm not simply as folklore, but as a living archive of subaltern knowledge that asserts Akan identity and agency in the face of epistemic erasure. In *Decolonising the Mind*, Ngũgĩ wa Thiong'o (1986) argues that language is a carrier of culture and memory. The dominance of colonial languages leads to a "cultural bomb" that annihilates a people's belief in their names, languages, and heritage. His call for the revival and use of African languages in literature and education supports the chapter's claim about Anansesɛm as a strategy of linguistic reclamation. Gayatri Chakravorty Spivak's (1988) *Can the Subaltern Speak?* provides additional insights as it discusses how colonized subjects are often denied voice within dominant discourse. In Akan Anansesɛm, certain figures serve as a metaphor for indigenous wisdom, challenging this silencing by positioning local knowledge as authoritative. In *The Location of Culture*, Homi K. Bhabha (1994) emphasizes the role of cultural hybridity and the "Third Space" where colonial and indigenous meanings intersect. Anansesɛm operates within this space, transforming imposed colonial values by retelling local truths through oral performance. Walter D. Mignolo's (2011) concept of "epistemic disobedience" and "decolonial option" is crucial. Mignolo argues that decolonization involves delinking from Western epistemology. Anansesɛm embodies such disobedience by preserving alternative ways of knowing and narrating the world. Thus, postcolonial theory enriches the analysis by situating Anansesɛm within broader struggles over language, knowledge, and cultural survival. It shows how oral narratives function as tools of decolonial resistance and identity affirmation.

Anansesɛm, the corpus of stories centered around the spider figure Ananse, are among the most enduring oral traditions in West Africa and the Caribbean (Beckwith, 2016; Marshall, 2012; Deandrea, 2004; Pelton, 1980). Far from being simple folk tales, these narratives are rich, multilayered expressions of Akan cosmology, identity, and resistance. They have played a crucial role in shaping and preserving the cultural memory and values of the Akan people across centuries of socio-political upheaval.

First, in Akan ontology, Ananse is a cultural icon and symbol of identity. The trickster figure is not merely a character in Akan folklore. He is an archetype whose traits mirror the aspirations and survival strategies of the Akan people. His cunning, creativity, and ability to outwit more powerful adversaries position him as a symbol of intellectual resistance and agency. As Kwesi Yankah (1995) notes, Ananse's stories are deeply intertwined with the Akan worldview, serving as mirrors of societal conduct and symbolic representations of communal values. In *Speaking for the Chief*, Yankah (1995) observes that Ananse, "the trickster in *Anansesɛm* (folktales), is believed to be the source of all cultural phenomena, and despite his greed and selfishness he did not make speaking the monopoly of one man." Ananse stories show how cleverness and trickery can be socially accepted, while also teaching important lessons about being careful and wise. They reveal the deep moral and philosophical values woven into traditional storytelling. Until a few decades ago, Ananse stories helped the Akan people express their identity by passing down their traditions through storytelling, dramatic performance, and moral instruction (Rattray, 1930). The stories are usually told in the Akan language, using local sayings, proverbs (mmebusɛm), and humor rooted in the culture, which helps the speakers feel connected to their language and heritage. According to Yankah, (1995:47), among the Akan people, there is great joy when a child speaks their first meaningful word or phrase. Children who speak early are often seen as having the potential to grow into sages. He recounts that many Akan folktales even tell of babies or even unborn children who speak with wisdom, solve difficult riddles, or help their families in times of trouble. This use of the Akan language in storytelling affirms a sense of communal identity, especially among children, who encounter their first ethical lessons through *Ananseseɛm*.

Second, *Anansesɛm* are expressed as a vehicle of communal memory and indigenous archive. Oral storytelling among the Akan is not merely recreational. It is a ritual of memory. As Jan Vansina (1985; 1971) emphasizes, oral traditions in African societies function as repositories of historical knowledge and cultural continuity. According to Vansina, despite their imperfections, oral traditions have become an essential part of reconstructing Africa's history. He notes that today, it's almost impossible to tell the story of Africa without relying on oral tradition, because they have proven "too valuable" (Vansina, 1971; see also Vansina, 1985). *Anansesɛm* encode generational wisdom, genealogies, collective struggles, and survival strategies in a form that is easily memorable and transmissible across generations. Despite its low usage among the younger generation, these stories can continue to play an important role in shaping what people choose to remember or forget. As anthropologist Michel-Rolph Trouillot (2015) explains, folk stories act like linguistic canons that "help select the stories that matter." One Akan Ananse story aptly demonstrates this:

> *Once upon a time, a young child accompanied his mother to the farm. After a long day of harvesting, the mother entrusted the child with a bundle of akam (yams), instructing him to carry them home ahead of her. Dutifully, the child set off, balancing the yams as he journeyed through the forest paths. Along the way, he arrived at the mighty Densu River. While attempting to cross, the yams slipped from his grasp and tumbled into the swirling waters. The river carried them away. In desperation, the child raised his voice in a plaintive, dialogic song:*
> *Child:*
> *Densu eee, give me my akam (x2)*
> *Densu replied:*
> *Where does the akam come from?*
> *Child:*
> *Akam comes from Eno's (mother's) farm in the forest.*
> *Densu eee, Kwae mu o Densu.*

But the Densu River, deep and relentless, told the child that the yams had already been swept away and could not be retrieved. As compensation, the river offered him a fish (adwene) to take home. Grateful yet burdened with loss, the child continued homeward with the fish. But soon, a powerful gust of wind (Mframa) swept through and snatched the fish from his hands. Again, he pleaded through the same songful exchange:
Child:
Mframa eee, give me my fish (x2)
Mframa:
Where does the fish come from?
Child:
The fish comes from Densu.
Mframa:
What did Densu collect from you?
Child:
Densu took my yam.
Mframa:
Where did the yam come from?
Child:
The yam comes from Eno's farm in the forest.
Densu eee, Kwae mu o Densu.
But Mframa, like Densu, insisted that the fish had been carried far away and could not be returned. Instead, the wind offered the child a leaf as a token replacement. The child accepted the leaf and resumed his journey. However, as he walked, a sheep (Odwan) emerged and eagerly devoured the leaf. The child, now well-versed in loss, once again pleaded:
Child:
Odwan eee, give me my leaf (x2)
Odwan:
Where does the leaf come from?
Child:
The leaf comes from Mframa.
Odwan:
What did Mframa take from you?
Child:
Mframa took my fish.
Odwan:
Where did the fish come from?
Child:
The fish came from Densu.

Odwan:
What did Densu take from you?
Child:
Densu took my yam.
Odwan:
And where did the yam come from?
Child:
The yam came from Eno's farm in the forest.
Densu eee, Kwae mu o Densu.
Feeling remorseful, the sheep told the child that the leaf could not be recovered as it had been eaten. In its place, the sheep offered one of its thighs (bɔsrɛ) as compensation.
With the sheep's thigh in hand, the child proceeded. But before long, a dog (Kraman) intercepted him and seized the bɔsrɛ. Wearily, the child initiated yet another plea:
Child:
Kraman eee, give me my bɔsrɛ (x2)
Kraman:
Where does the thigh come from?
Child:
The thigh comes from the sheep.
Kraman:
What did the sheep take from you?
Child:
The sheep took my leaf.
Kraman:
Where did the leaf come from?
Child:
The leaf came from Mframa.
Kraman:
What did Mframa take from you?
Child:
Mframa took my fish.
Kraman:
Where did the fish come from?
Child:
The fish came from Densu.
Kraman:
And what did Densu take from you?
Child:

Densu took my yam.
Kraman:
Where did the yam come from?
Child:
The yam came from Eno's farm in the forest.
Densu eee, Kwae mu o Densu.
But the dog, cunning and selfish, declared that it had already eaten the meat. Yet, it promised to search for an identical piece to return to the child. That promise was never fulfilled. And so, it is said that to this day, whenever a dog sees another animal, it chases after it, still searching for the lost bɔsrɛ to repay the child. And when the dog finally catches its prey, it never shares it with another animal; instead, it presents it to humans as a form of repayment for a debt long owed.

This narration is a sentimental recollection of the past and a remarkable demonstration of narrative intelligence. At the same time, it portrays one's ability to arrange episodic events in a coherent, sequential, and symbolic manner. Through its dialogic structure, cumulative repetition, and episodic buildup, the story mirrors the core functions of *Anansesɛm* as vessels of memory, identity, resistance, and survival. Each episode represents not just a moment of loss and compensation but also a layered recollection of experience, where the past is actively remembered, renarrated, and carried forward. In this way, the story embodies cultural memory and resilience, showing how even in the face of continuous loss, the storyteller or the community retains the capacity to respond, adapt, and transmit values. *Anansesɛm* also functions as a memory aid and a powerful symbol that helps Akan communities hold on to their beliefs, face challenges, and take control of their lives across generations. Painful historical experiences like colonialism, slavery, or forced migration are not mentioned directly but are remembered symbolically through these tales. Ananse stories, in particular, use the clever spider character to represent the ability to adapt, survive, and pass on cultural knowledge across generations. Ngũgĩ wa Thiong'o's (1986) argument that language and narrative form are central to the colonized people's efforts to reclaim their memory and voice is key in this regard.

Third, Ananse stories serve as tools of resistance. Throughout Akan history, *Anansesɛm* have served as subtle instruments of resistance against domination—whether political, cultural, or epistemological. Despite the European colonial and missionariy attempts to delegitimize African oral traditions as lacking credibility, the survival of Ananse stories suggests a quiet form of cultural defiance. In diasporic contexts, especially among descendants of enslaved Africans in the Caribbean and the Americas, Ananse (often spelled differently) stories persisted. In particular, there is evidence of their spread to the West Indies, Suriname, and Sierra Leone, as well as to the Netherlands Antilles, including Curaçao, Aruba, and Bonaire. This further evidences how Ananse stories function as tools of resistance and survival.

According to Melville Herskovits (1941) in *The Myth of the Negro Past*, the continued telling of past stories in the New World underscores the deep cultural retention among African diasporic communities and their refusal to fully assimilate into Eurocentric frameworks. The allegorical nature of the tales allowed storytellers to critique social injustice, hierarchy, and abuse of power without direct confrontation.

At first glance, the story of the child who loses and pleads for compensation from natural forces and animals may appear to be a simple tale of misfortune. Yet this tradition carries a strong message of resistance, similar to the well-known Ananse stories. As previously noted, these stories are not just meant to entertain. Rather, they are clever ways through which Akan communities pass on knowledge, stand up to injustice, and hold on to their identity through difficult times, both in the past and today. The layered, back-and-forth structure of the story reflects the memory-based nature of oral traditions, where repetition is not just stylistic; it helps preserve and pass down culture. Each refrain, "*Densu eee, Kwae mu o Densu*" serves as a reclaiming of voice and memory. The child, like Ananse, reasserts his presence in every episode, refusing to be forgotten or dismissed. This projects *Ananses*ɛ*m* as vehicles of resistance against historical silencing and colonial marginalization of indigenous narrative forms. The very act of remembering and retelling, as Michel-Rolph Trouillot (2015) argues, is an act of power, of choosing what stories matter and why. As Vansina (1985) also notes "One cannot reconstruct what has been eliminated or disentangle easily what has been telescoped through time"

The river (*Densu*), wind (*Mframa*), sheep (*Odwan*), and dog (*Kraman*) serve as allegories for larger forces (natural, institutional, social) that often act without accountability. The child, through persistent inquiry and song, seeks justice in a world where power dynamics are uneven. Frequently Ananse is depicted as deceptive and lawless.

> *He appears self-centred, cruel, unscrupulous, vain, unappreciative, constantly rebelling against societal norms and values of man. Others also describe him as lawless, antisocial and immoral because his actions are usually geared towards satisfying his own desires for self-gratification without regard for social conventions and moral restraints (Addo, 2013).*

However, unlike the cunny, unappreciative and lawless Ananse, the child does not confront power with violence but with clever negotiation and dialogic reasoning, a subtle, but radical mode of resistance.

The story also reveals the creative adaptation and mode of resistance associated with traditional Akan society. One of the defining traits of Ananse is his cunningness, his ability to bend reality through speech, wit, and strategy. The child's journey reflects this mode of resistance. In the face of repeated loss, he adapts and renegotiates each time, never abandoning hope. According to Yankah (1995) oratory in Akan society emphasises eloquence. A good speaker, he observes, may be praised for being the grandchild of the old lady (the repository of wisdom), "implying that the speaker's wit may have been passed on by the grandmother to whom s/he was constantly exposed" (1995:47). The story thus portrays resilience not as stoic endurance but as imaginative, performative resistance, a refusal to be broken by unjust outcomes.

This story is not told just for entertainment. It conveys important lessons about justice, fairness, consequences, and responsibility, using symbols and repeated patterns that are easy for young listeners to understand. In doing so, it preserves values that challenge selfishness and impunity (as seen in the dog's betrayal) and affirms the right to claim restitution. The act of passing such stories down is itself a form of resistance against cultural amnesia and epistemic colonialism (Khan, Ali, Mumtaz, & Usman, 2025; Zhao, Popkewitz, & Autio, 2023).

THE LINGUISTIC POWER OF *ANANSESƐM*

In modern Ghana, where the formal education system increasingly prioritizes English over indigenous languages, the role of oral narratives like *Anansesɛm* becomes even more critical in language retention and cultural education. These stories are often told in home settings, community gatherings, and storytelling festivals, creating informal yet powerful learning environments. When people tell Ananse stories and other Akan folktales, they are also passing on ways of thinking, values, and the structure of the Akan language itself. This section, explores how *Anansesɛm* help keep the Akan language alive by using common speech patterns, expressions, wise sayings, and metaphors. It also shows how these stories are used to teach lessons and pass down knowledge from one generation to the next, helping to keep Akan culture strong and connected over time.

Anansesɛm preserve the integrity of the Akan language through its oral and dialogic nature. The stories are rich in repetition, call-and-response patterns, and formulaic expressions, which are ideal for teaching children the rhythm, syntax, and idioms of their mother tongue. The rhythm and structure of these stories make it easier for children to learn grammar, new words, and ways of expressing themselves. A clear illustration of this can be found in the story of the child already narrated. The narrative demonstrates dialogic and cumulative linguistic construction, a common oral feature in Akan storytelling. The recurring phrase:

"Densu eee, give me my akam"

"Where does the akam come from?"

"Akam comes from Eno's farm in the forest."

... follows a patterned question-and-answer structure that reinforces both language use and logical sequencing. In African oral traditions, form is inseparable from function; the structure of performance is itself a conveyor of knowledge, and language is molded to serve cultural purposes (Barber, 2007). The story also uses repeating words and patterns, such as saying the same phrase at the beginning of multiple lines, which are key features of how the Akan people traditionally tell stories. As children listen to and retell such stories, they internalize linguistic features such as tense, subject-verb agreement, and metaphorical reasoning, all embedded in everyday storytelling. Beyond the preservation of language, *Anansesɛm* encode the cherished moral and philosophical principles. The story about the missing yams and the child's encounters with nature, the river (*Densu*), the wind (*Mframa*), the sheep (*Odwan*), and the dog (*Kraman*) carries profound meaning. It explores themes like dealing with loss, taking responsibility, making things right, and staying strong through challenges. Each encounter echoes Akan communal values of responsibility (entrusting the child with yams); perseverance and patience (through repeated pleading); justice and reciprocity (each character compensates for the previous loss); and cosmic interconnectedness (humans, animals, and nature in dialogue). This style of storytelling, where events build on one another, brings to life the Akan sense of right and wrong, a world where people are held responsible for their actions, and efforts must be made to correct any wrongdoing, even if those efforts are not perfect. As Agyekum (2000, 2006) and other scholars (Okpewho, 1992) have argued, Akan proverbs, folktales, and naming practices function as didactic instruments that guide moral conduct and express collective cultural norms and cosmology. As Agyekum (2000: 2) writes, these stories and practices "inculcate nationalistic and patriotic ideologies in the new generation."

The philosophical message of the story also lies in the child's acceptance of diminishing returns from yam, to fish, to leaf, to thigh, to a broken promise. This descent subtly teaches stoicism, resourcefulness, and human limitation, themes that are central to Akan ways of thinking about life and the universe. *Anansesɛm* thus represents a distinct epistemology, a way of knowing and making sense of the world through narrative. In the Akan worldview, knowledge is dialogical, performative, and communally validated. The child's interaction with nature and animals in the story affirms the Akan belief in a world that is alive, responsive, and morally structured. As Kwesi Yankah (1995) explains, African oral traditions function as cultural memory and guideposts for social behavior. Storytelling is a method of instructing the young in social roles, historical consciousness, and communal identity. The embedded worldview teaches that every being has a place and a responsibility in the moral order, a lesson passed down not through abstraction but through narrative enactment. The story also reflects the Akan sankofa philosophy of tracing present conditions back to past events. The child must recount the sequence of losses to each new character, reinforcing the value of memory, narrative order, and historical awareness.

Incorporating them into formal and informal education can address the disconnect between home language and school language, helping children to think, feel, and reason in their own linguistic and cultural terms. Additionally, the performative nature of storytelling (song, dance, repetition, mimicry) engages multiple senses, enhancing language acquisition and retention in ways that purely textual instruction cannot. Thus, *Anansesɛm* functions as rich linguistic and moral values. Through carefully constructed repetition, metaphor, and dialogue as exemplified by the story of the child and Densu and other forces, these oral narratives preserve the syntax, lexicon, and idioms of the Akan language. They also embed moral values and philosophical insights, ensuring that young listeners are not only entertained but linguistically and ethically formed. In a world where indigenous languages face erosion, *Anansesɛm* remain a crucial pedagogical and epistemic tool, capable of rooting new generations in the expressive power of their own tongue (Arthur, Sanka & Yeboah, 2021; Onuora, 2012).

CULTURAL SURVIVAL AND CONNECTION TO ANCESTRY AND LAND

Anansesɛm play a particularly potent role in Akan tradition because it channels memory through narrative performance. It reflects shared community experiences and contains strategies for resolving conflicts. They also offer subtle ways of challenging authority, helping communities survive not just by passing on genes, but by preserving language and knowledge. The following narrative helps explains this.

In the distant past, there ruled a king whose governance was marked by arrogance and a blatant disregard for the counsel of his elders and subjects. Known for his unyielding disposition, he neither welcomed advice nor tolerated criticism. His subjects, gripped by fear, refrained from offering any guidance, lest they incur his wrath. One day, while journeying to a grand assembly of chiefs and dignitaries, the king unknowingly stepped in human excrement. Given the reverence of the occasion and the king's habitual obstinacy, none of his attendants dared to inform him directly. Among those in his procession were the abɛnhyɛfoɔ, royal hornblowers whose role included not only announcing the king's presence but also communicating important, often sensitive, messages through coded, poetic language. Recognizing the king's volatile disposition, one hornblower sounded his instrument and issued a veiled proclamation:

"The royal sandals of a nobleman have encountered an unclean substance." Another abɛnhyɛfoɔ, aware of the king's reputation for ignoring counsel, replied through his own horn in equally coded terms:

"Let him continue to his destination; he will not heed any warning."

This call-and-response continued, forming a dialogic performance that conveyed both the social discomfort of the entourage and the unwillingness of the king to be corrected. The elders and courtiers, though present, remained silent, visibly bound by fear and protocol. Upon arrival at the gathering, the king, now surrounded by his peers, quickly became aware of the foul odour emanating from his feet. No one dared approach him, and many withdrew from his presence in discomfort. Realizing the extent of his humiliation and the weight of his prideful isolation, the king was overcome with shame. He abandoned the gathering, forsook his royal responsibilities, and fled to a faraway land, never to return.

This tale, while humorous on the surface, operates at multiple symbolic levels. It functions as a moral allegory about leadership, arrogance, and the Akan philosophy of indirect communication. The result of the King's refusal to heed advice illustrates the Akan proverb *"Tikoro nko agyina"* ("One head does not hold counsel"). It also teaches children the communal nature of wisdom and leadership. Furthermore, the use of the horn as a medium of critique reflects the long-cherished oral-linguistic strategies in Akan political culture, where language, especially in royal courts, is carefully curated to maintain hierarchy, face, and order. The *abɛnhyɛwfoɔ* indirect allusions mirror the oral practice of speaking good language over bad behaviour, which privileges euphemism, proverb, and metaphor over direct confrontation. In broader terms, the story critiques autocratic rule and affirms the moral authority of the people and their traditions to check power. It also points to the continuing role of storytelling as a pedagogical and political tool, capable of encoding complex societal values in performative and memorable forms.

The story of the king who refused to listen encapsulates this survival logic. In a society where open defiance of authority may invite punishment, storytelling provides a culturally sanctioned method to voice critique. The hornblowers' use of symbolic and poetic language to highlight the king's error reveals the subtle yet powerful tools of resistance embedded in Akan oral performance. Through indirection and layered meaning, storytellers and, indeed, by extension, ordinary people, participate in the governance of moral order. This coheres with Kwesi Yankah's (1995) analysis of Akan communicative norms, where public commentary and correction, especially toward power, are often couched in proverbial or performative forms to maintain social cohesion while resisting tyranny. Here, the use of euphemism in storytelling becomes a "strategy of avoiding direct confrontation with royalty" (Yankah, 1995:167). It enables the community to remember and rehearse survival strategies without confronting power head-on.

ROOTEDNESS IN LAND AND THE MORAL LANDSCAPE

Ananseseɛm narratives are also linked to the Akan conception of land as sacred and sentient. The connection between people and land is not merely utilitarian but spiritual and ontological. The Akan see the land (*Asase Yaa*) as a living force, intimately tied to ancestry, identity, and cosmic balance. Storytelling often maps moral lessons onto physical geographies, turning rivers, forests, winds, and animals into moral agents and cultural witnesses. In *The King Who Refused to Listen*, the ceremonial journey and the king's disgrace in a public space reinforce the idea that moral transgressions are not hidden from the land and the ancestors. The king soils not only his sandals but also his dignity, violating the sanctity of his office and the moral order he is meant to uphold. The public embarrassment he suffers is not just a private loss but a ritual humiliation, a symbolic breaking of ties with the community and its ancestral codes.

These kinds of stories reflect the Akan belief that a person's identity is connected to their place in the community and their respect for the wisdom passed down by their ancestors. As some studies note, in Akan society, expelling an individual from the community of their kinsmen amounted to a total denial of their rights, including, implicitly, the right to life (Rattray, 1927; see also Tweneboah, 2020:85-86). In deserting his throne, the king does not simply flee from shame; he removes himself from the moral geography of Akan society, a society whose memory is preserved and transmitted through storytelling.

Ananseseɛm further serve as a mechanism for intergenerational continuity and communal memory. Its performative nature ensures that lessons are not static but re-lived across generations. In homes, villages, and, importantly, in schools and digital platforms, these stories help shape the moral and linguistic imagination of Akan children. They continue to teach children not only the structure of their mother tongue but also how to relate to their elders, land, peers, and political institutions. In the tale of the obstinate king, we encounter not merely a historical figure. This story also becomes a pedagogical archetype, a lesson in humility, the necessity of listening, and the dangers of pride. It is retold to caution leaders against despotic tendencies, to encourage youth to value ancestral wisdom, and to warn against alienating oneself from communal roots.

With the introduction of information and communication technology, *Ananseseɛm* are fading out among the youth. Yet its continuous salience has been largely acknowledged. Abankwa and Abankwa (2017) have presented it as a "knowledge house." According to Arthur, Sanka & Yeboah (2021:35), *Ananseseɛm* serve as "an ideological source and pedagogical tool." They conclude that among the Akan people, *Ananseseɛm* is not a mere source of entertainment and relaxation after a long day. Instead, it serves as a pedagogical tool and a source of traditional wisdom and philosophy, guiding how people interact and relate to one another in society (Arthur, Sanka & Yeboah, 2021:36). In this sense, storytelling becomes an instrument of social regeneration. The hornblowers' subtle communication in the story models how Akan society strategically preserves truth and accountability, even when direct confrontation is perilous.

In the face of increasing urbanization, migration, and cultural homogenization, the relevance of storytelling as a means of cultural survival becomes even more urgent. The pressures of English-dominant education, media, and globalization threaten to displace indigenous languages and storytelling traditions. Yet, *Anansesɛm* remains a powerful cultural footing, especially for Akan children growing up in diasporic or multilingual environments (Abankwa and Abankwa, 2017). According to Adjei and Dei (2008), in the face of postcolonial pressures, Indigenous "knowledge and experience cannot be discarded as irrelevant in the search for a lasting solution to local problems." Preserving and performing stories like *The King Who Refused to Listen* helps communities assert their identity, retain their linguistic heritage, and pass on localized forms of wisdom. These stories not only connect listeners to their past but also equip them to navigate the future. They provide a future armed with the narrative intelligence and cultural values encoded in their oral heritage. As Onuora (2012) observes, based on her experience in Canada, Ananse stories demonstrate how African women in the diaspora, despite facing marginalisation, continue to raise their children with Afro-indigenous teaching methods that help them connect with their culture, identity, and role in society. This way, they prepare the younger ones to face the social, economic, and political challenges they may encounter while growing up in the diaspora. By continually reenacting tales of survival, resistance, and humility, Akan women can similarly reaffirm their connection to land, ancestry, and moral order.

Through stories like *The King Who Refused to Listen*, the Akan storytelling tradition reaffirms itself as a living archive of cultural resilience. *Anansesɛm* sustain the language, worldview, and historical consciousness of the Akan, ensuring that memory is not only preserved but performed, reinterpreted, and reaffirmed. In this way, storytelling becomes a strategy of cultural survival. It connects the community to its past, its geography, and its moral foundations. Even as the forces of globalization exert pressure on indigenous languages and traditions, these stories stand as resilient webs, woven from language, memory, and ancestral wisdom.

ORAL ARCHIVES AGAINST LINGUISTIC HOMOGENIZATION

In a world increasingly shaped by globalized communication systems, standardized education, and the hegemony of colonial languages such as English, indigenous languages face an existential threat. In Ghana, as in many postcolonial societies, the dominance of English in formal institutions has marginalized indigenous languages like Akan, often relegating them to informal, domestic, or ceremonial spaces. For example, Yet, within the oral tradition of *Anansesɛm*, a dynamic counter-archive exists that resists linguistic homogenization and preserves cultural identity. Ananse stories are not just old folktales, but important oral traditions that help keep languages alive, pass down community wisdom, and strengthen people's understanding of their own culture. *"The Leopard Skin and the Wisdom of the Aberewa"* below, popular in Akan narrative culture, exemplifies how oral storytelling transmits critical social memory and reasserts the epistemic legitimacy of indigenous language and thought.

Once a powerful king who ruled with an iron hand. Known for his authoritarian disposition and insatiable hunger for power, the king sought to monopolize wisdom within his kingdom. Convinced that elderly women were the custodians of ancestral knowledge and therefore posed a threat to his authority, he issued a chilling decree: every old woman (aberewa) in his realm was to be executed. The directive, carried out under fear and anxiety, resulted in the silencing of an entire generation of wisdom-bearers. To further cultivate a fearsome image, the king commissioned a garment made from dried leopard skin, a symbolic display of ferocity. However, after several days of wearing it, he discovered that the garment had hardened and clung tightly to his body, making it impossible to remove. His advisors and court sages tried every method to loosen the hide, but all efforts failed. Desperate and humiliated, the king ordered that anyone in the land who could help him be brought forward. Unknown to the king, one young man had defied the earlier edict. Rather than killing his grandmother, he had hidden her in secret. Upon hearing of the king's plight, the young man consulted his grandmother. The aberewa advised him that the only way to remove the dried leopard skin was to pour water over it, softening the hide and making it possible to peel off without injury. The young man relayed this advice to the court, and it was followed. True to the old woman's wisdom, the skin softened, and the king was freed from his self-imposed prison. Stunned by the effectiveness of the solution, the king inquired how the young man had acquired such insight. The young man confessed that he had disobeyed the royal command and preserved his grandmother's life, and it was she who had provided the remedy. Moved and chastened, the king lifted the ban on old women and rewarded the young man and his grandmother generously. From that time forward, the king and his elders came to recognize the aberewa as a vital source of communal wisdom. When faced with difficult decisions or crises, the elders would convene in counsel, a process that came to be known in Akan as "yɛkɔbisa aberewa" ("we're going to consult the old woman"). Over time, aberewa became a powerful cultural metaphor for wisdom, foresight, and ancestral knowledge in Akan society.

The colonial encounter in Ghana, like elsewhere in Africa, instituted a hierarchy of languages in which English emerged as the language of modernity, power, and education. Through missionary schools and British administrative policies, English displaced indigenous languages in public life. Post-independence Ghana, despite rhetorical support for cultural pluralism, has largely maintained this structure. The preference for English in formal education has created a generational gap in indigenous language fluency, especially among urban youth. In media, governance, and national curricula, English dominates, reducing Akan and other local languages to residual categories, useful for entertainment or ritual, but not for intellectual or technological advancement. The result is a slow erosion of linguistic competence, cultural reference, and intergenerational transmission of indigenous knowledge.

In this context, *Ananseseɛm* functions as a counter-hegemonic oral archive that preserves not only stories but the linguistic and cultural realm in which those stories have meaning. Unlike state archives, which are textual and hierarchical, *Ananseseɛm* operate through oral performance, intergenerational memory, and communal participation. They also encode not just language, but worldview in the form of philosophical concepts, moral frameworks, ecological consciousness, and social norms. All these are expressed through idiomatic Akan speech. In *Ananseseɛm*, what is archived is not just the past, but a way of being, *a living continuity of Akan thought and expression*. The story of the king and the *aberewa*, for instance, is more than a tale of political folly. It preserves a cultural metaphor in which the *aberewa* becomes synonymous with wisdom, foresight, and ancestral continuity. The survival of her voice, despite royal decrees of erasure, dramatizes the persistence of marginalized knowledge systems and the refusal of oral tradition to be silenced. In this sense, *Ananseseɛm* operate at the intersection of language and identity. The stories follow the patterns of Akan oral performance, using dialogue, repetition, changes in tone, indirect speech, and proverbs. These features are inherent in the language and culture, making them difficult to fully translate into English without losing much of their meaning. To participate in *Ananseseɛm* are to be immersed in Akan linguistic consciousness. In the story of the *aberewa*, the metaphor of the dried leopard skin that cannot be removed evokes not only the dangers of tyranny but also the consequences of erasing indigenous knowledge. That the solution to the king's dilemma comes not from his circle of formal advisors but from a grandmother who speaks in the idioms and rhythms of Akan orature, recognizes the value of local knowledge and ways of understanding the world. The use of such stories in everyday speech, for instance, the idiomatic expression *"yɛkɔbisa aberewa"* (we're going to consult the old woman), shows how storytelling embeds itself in language practice and continues to shape communal ways of knowing. As Yankah (1995) has noted, Akan oratory is a profoundly symbolic and coded form of knowledge transmission. Proverbs, parables, and performance are not decorative but foundational to how knowledge is constructed, conveyed, and preserved in Akan communities. *Anansesɛm*, therefore, is both pedagogy and archive. It is a space where language teaches and remembers.

Anansesɛm offer an avenue to reclaim a space for Indigenous languages in national and global discourses. To preserve the epistemic and cultural integrity of Akan, there must be a conscious effort to reclaim space for indigenous languages in education, media, and scholarship. This includes integrating *Anansesɛm* into formal curricula not as quaint folklore, but as oral literature with philosophical depth and pedagogical value. It means creating digital, theatrical, or literary platforms where these stories are performed, recorded, and translated in ways that honor their linguistic complexity. Cruz (2021), in her transnational reflection on Ananse stories, argues that spider narratives serve as alternative epistemologies and ways of knowing that resist the linear, rationalist models of Western thought. Zimmerman (2023) similarly demonstrates how Caribbean reinterpretations of Ananse (such as in Karen Lord's *Redemption in Indigo*) sustain African oral logics while adapting to new cultural terrains. These works reaffirm that *Anansesɛm* is not frozen in time but adaptable and dynamic. They are a living archive capable of speaking across generations and geographies.

The story of the king and the *aberewa* illustrates this point well. Despite efforts to erase ancestral voices, it is the surviving grandmother who provides the key to release. Her wisdom, retained through secrecy and passed on through trust, symbolizes the resilience of indigenous languages and the importance of restoring their value in public discourse. Reclaiming the space to *"consult the aberewa"* is not only a return to indigenous epistemology. It is a linguistic act of resistance and cultural affirmation. Thus, in the face of globalizing forces and linguistic marginalization, *Anansesɛm* remain a vibrant oral archive through which the Akan language continues to speak, teach, and remember. The story of the leopard skin and the *aberewa* reminds us that language is not only a tool of communication but a vessel of ancestral wisdom and cultural sovereignty. As long as *Anansesɛm* are told, retold, and woven into the speech, memory, and imagination of the Akan people, it will resist erasure and reaffirm identity. Preserving these oral texts, and the languages that carry them, is not only a cultural necessity, it is an act of intellectual justice.

CONCLUSION

Ananse stories function as oral archives that carry the weight of ancestral wisdom, communal memory, and indigenous resistance. Their enduring presence in Akan communities, both in Ghana and across diasporic spaces, testifies to their dynamic role in resisting cultural erasure and linguistic homogenization. By tracing four interwoven dimensions of *Anansesɛm* as vessels of identity, memory, resistance, and survival, we have shown how these narratives: 1) assert a uniquely Akan epistemology that resists domination and affirms communal values; 2) transmit not only linguistic structures but also philosophical concepts, moral reasoning, and historical consciousness; 3) serve as pedagogical tools for intergenerational language retention and cultural formation; and 4) function as counter-hegemonic repositories in the face of colonial legacies and the pressures of global modernity. The stories examined reveal how storytelling encodes both linguistic resilience and political commentary. The *aberewa*, long dismissed under authoritarian rule, emerges as a metaphor for suppressed but enduring wisdom. In the same vein, the Akan language, though marginalized in formal institutions, survives through oral traditions that refuse to be silenced. Ultimately, *Anansesɛm* is not simply a mode of storytelling. The chapter has shown that it is a mode of survival. It preserves and perpetuates the Akan language not by resisting change, but by adapting its narrative forms to shifting historical and cultural terrains. In doing so, it invites us to rethink what constitutes an archive, where knowledge lives, and how language acts as a site of resistance and renewal. In the struggle for cultural sovereignty and linguistic justice, *Anansesɛm* remains a formidable force that spins webs to bind the past to the present, the local to the global, and memory to identity.

REFERENCES

Abankwa, S., & Abankwa, A. (2017). The Significance of Folktales in the Moral and Psychological Development of the Child in Ghanaian Communities. *Journal of Literature and Art Studies*, *7*(7), 895–901.

Addo, A. A. (2013). *Ananse as a folkloric character in new Ghanaian drama* (Unpublished M.Phil thesis). University of Ghana, Legon.

Adjei, P., & Dei, G. (2008). Decolonizing schooling and education in Ghana. In Abdi, A. A., & Guo, S. (Eds.), *Education and social development: Global issues and analyses* (pp. 177–193). BRILL., DOI: 10.1163/9789087904401_011

Agyekum, K. (2000). Aspects of Akan oral literature in the media. *Research Review New Series*, *16*(2), 1–18. DOI: 10.4314/rrias.v16i2.22891

Agyekum, K. (2006). The sociolinguistics of Akan personal names. *Nordic Journal of African Studies*, *15*(2), 206–235.

Arthur, P., Sanka, C. G., & Yeboah, P. A. O. (2021). The textuality of "Anansesɛm": A pedagogical and ideological resource in traditional human relations among the Akans in Ghana. *Advances in Language and Literary Studies*, *12*(4), 35–44. DOI: 10.7575/aiac.alls.v.12n.4.p.35

Barber, K. (2007). *The Anthropology of Texts, Persons and Publics: Oral and Written Culture in Africa and Beyond*. Cambridge University Press. DOI: 10.1017/CBO9780511619656

Beckwith, M. W. (2016). *Anansi: Jamaican stories of the spider god*. VAMzzz Publishing.

Berry, J. (1989). *Spiderman Anancy*. Henry Holt & Co.

Bhabha, H. K. (1994). *The Location of Culture*. Routledge.

Cruz, J. M. (2021). Akua Ananse Is a "She": Transnational Autoethnographic Tales. *Departures in Critical Qualitative Research*, *10*(4), 7–29. DOI: 10.1525/dcqr.2021.10.4.7

Deandrea, P. (2004). Trans(l)atlantic I-con: The many shapes of Ananse in contemporary literatures. *The Journal of Transatlantic Studies*, *2*(1), 1–26. DOI: 10.1080/14794010408656804

Herskovits, M. J. (1941). *The myth of the Negro past*. Harper & Brothers.

Khan, A., Ali, Z., Mumtaz, H., & Usman, M. (2025). Epistemic colonization: Assertion of colonial and erasure of Indigenous knowledge and culture through survivance. *Journal of Asian Development Studies, 14*(2), 1528–1539. DOI: 10.62345/jads.2025.14.2.118

Lord, K. (2010). *Redemption in Indigo: a novel.* Small Beer Press.

Marshall, E. Z. (2012). *Anansi's journey: A story of Jamaican cultural resistance.* University of the West Indies Press. DOI: 10.37234/FOCZIJVK

Mignolo, W. D. (2011). *The Darker Side of Western Modernity: Global Futures, Decolonial Options.* Duke University Press.

Ngũgĩ wa Thiong'o. (1986). *Decolonising the mind: The politics of language in African literature.* Heinemann.

Okpewho, I. (1992). *African Oral Literature: Backgrounds, Character, and Continuity.* Indiana University Press. DOI: 10.2979/1034.0

Onuora, A. N. (2012). *Anansesem (Storytelling nights): African maternal pedagogies.* Demeter Press.

Pelton, R. D. (1980). *The trickster in West Africa.* University of California Press. DOI: 10.1525/9780520341487

Rattray, R. S. (1927). *Religion and art in Ashanti.* The Clarendon Press.

Rattray, R. S. (1930). *Anansi: Akan-Ashanti folktales: A collection of 75 Ashanti folktales.* Oxford University Press.

Salkey, A. (1997). *Brother Anancy and other stories.* Longman.

Sherlock, P. M. (2002). *The illustrated Anansi: Four Caribbean folk tales* (P. Wright, Illus.). Macmillan Education.

Spivak, G. C. (1988). Can the Subaltern Speak? In Nelson, C., & Grossberg, L. (Eds.), *Marxism and the Interpretation of Culture* (pp. 271–313). University of Illinois Press.

Trouillot, M.-R. (2015). *Silencing the past: Power and the production of history.* Beacon Press. (Original work published 1995)

Tweneboah, S. (2020). *Religion, law, politics and the state in Africa: Applying legal pluralism in Ghana.* Routledge.

Vansina, J. (1971). Once upon a time: Oral traditions as history in Africa. *Daedalus, 100*(2), 442–468.

Vansina, J. (1985). *Oral tradition as history*. James Currey Ltd. wa Thiong'o, N. (1986). *Decolonising the mind: The politics of language in African literature*. James Currey.

Yankah, K. (1995). *Speaking for the Chief: Okyeame and the Politics of Akan Oratory*. Indiana University Press. DOI: 10.2979/3032.0

Zhao, W., Popkewitz, T. S., & Autio, T. (Eds.). (2023). *Epistemic colonialism and the transfer of curriculum knowledge across borders: Applying a historical lens to contest unilateral logics*. Routledge.

Zimmerman, T. (2023). Fiction as a Spider's Web? Ananse and Gender in Karen Lord's Speculative Folktale *Redemption in Indigo*. In Ferly, O., & Zimmerman, T. (Eds.), *Chronotropics: Caribbean Women Writing Spacetime* (pp. 271–289). Palgrave Macmillan. DOI: 10.1007/978-3-031-32111-5_15

KEY TERMS AND DEFINITIONS

*Aberewa:***:** In Akan culture, the term ***aberewa*** refers to an old woman, often regarded as a custodian of ancestral wisdom, moral authority, and cultural memory. Within oral traditions, the *aberewa* symbolizes not just age, but deep insight, experience, and the power of indigenous knowledge systems.

*Anansesɛm:***:** This refers to the rich corpus of Akan oral narratives centered on the trickster figure Ananse the spider. These stories, often told with drama and wise sayings, help teach good behavior, keep cultural traditions alive, and protect the Akan language.

Epistemic Colonialism: This is when Western ideas and ways of understanding the world are treated as more important or better than local or traditional knowledge. It happens when schools, governments, or institutions ignore, reject, or replace indigenous knowledge and languages, often because of colonial influence.

Indigenous Epistemology: The ways Indigenous people learn about and understand the world based on their culture, traditions, values, and spiritual beliefs. It focuses on relationships, learning through experience and stories, and a strong connection to the land, community, and ancestors.

Linguistic Homogenization: This occurs when various languages and dialects are gradually replaced by a single dominant language. This often happens because of things like colonial rule, global communication, and school systems that use only one language. As a result, local languages and cultures can begin to disappear.

Oral Archives: This refers to knowledge, memories, and cultural traditions that are passed down by speaking, performing, and telling stories, instead of writing them down. They help keep history, language, and identity alive in communities that rely on oral traditions.

Chapter 8
Enhanced Adaptive Multimodal Language Learning System for Language Education and Communication

J. Viji Gripsy
https://orcid.org/0000-0002-6599-3010
PSGR Krishnammal College for Women, India

K. S. Kamalam
https://orcid.org/0009-0002-9798-196X
PSGR Krishnammal College for Women, India

K. Sindhu
Sri Ramakrishna Engineering College, India

N. V. Brindha
https://orcid.org/0009-0006-1568-1437
PSGR Krishnammal College for Women, India

A. Senthilkumar
https://orcid.org/0009-0008-8409-8784
Sri Ramakrishna College of Arts and Science, India

L. Sheeba
https://orcid.org/0000-0003-1269-6888
PSGR Krishnammal College for Women, India

ABSTRACT

Artificial intelligence (AI) has transformed language education and communication through innovations in machine translation, voice recognition, and natural language processing (NLP). Contemporary AI models such as GPT-4, Google Translate, Whisper, and Grammarly lack flexibility, real-time response, contextual accuracy, and reduction in bias. The AI-Enhanced Adaptive Multimodal Language Learning System (AI-AMLLS) enhances language skills through adaptive learning, instant

DOI: 10.4018/979-8-3373-3561-2.ch008

feedback, and multimodal interaction. AI-AMLLS applies reinforcement learning to modify difficulty levels dynamically, deep learning algorithms for grammatical correction, personalized learning, and testing. It incorporates AI-powered audio analytics for speech training, gesture and facial recognition for communication testing, and context-aware machine translation for multilingual interactions. It also minimizes latency, maximizes engagement, and minimizes bias more effectively than normal models. AI-AMLLS' inclusive and interactive language learning method enhances accessibility, efficiency, and diversity.

1. INTRODUCTION

In natural language processing, speech recognition technologies, and a few other areas, AI has significantly altered the learning and communication aspects of language instruction (Adbullah et al., 2022). Some of the automatically correcting language learning models are GPT-4, Google Translate, Whisper, and Grammarly, have significantly improved functions in machine translation, speech synthesis, and grammar correction (Adiguzel et al., 2023). These models are issue to a variety of constraints, including being hard to understand in framework, receptive in real-time, adaptable to developing learner needs, and ethical concerns around bias and interpretability (Ahmad et al., 2021). The primary difficulties that need to be resolved in order to develop a more effective and inclusive AI-driven language learning system are enumerated below (Al-khresheh, 2024). One of the key research obstacles for current language models is their inadequate ability to adapt to individual learners (Alm & Watanabe, 2023). While classical AI systems offer a static view of learning, the model may or may not contextualize the information relative to that learner's experience, or background with certain content elements. Further, text-to-speech or speech-to-text tools (e.g., Whisper) may misinterpret vocal cues and dialects and produce errors in transcription and voice response (Barrot, 2023a). Furthermore, machine translation methods like Google Translate may be independently and contextually ignorant, thus potentially misleading communication in multiple languages. AI-based grammar corrections (e.g., Grammarly) and plagiarism ó detectors may find their accuracy compromised on contextual indicators and become impotent in a learning context (Barrot, 2023b). These influences support the idea of an AI-augmented system that supports multiple modalities and can adapt to a user dynamically.

This article describes an AI-Enhanced Adaptive Multimodal Language Learning System (AI-AMLLS), a sophisticated AI technology with the potential to address issues in language education and communication. AI-AMLLS utilizes deep learning, reinforcement learning, and multimodal integration to create a system that facilitates the language learning process that can adapt and respond appropriately to learning and communication needs. AI-AMLLS includes speech capabilities that are explored in real time, feedback mechanisms that respond to a learner's progress, and conversational agents that can provide this training in a meaningful or adaptive way. AI-AMLLS will develop ethical AI agility that will respond to biases in language use and foster greater transparency in its powerful decision-making. The tool also provides real-time translation with negligible latency, improved grammatical accuracy, and enhanced plagiarism detection, to support academic integrity in learning and assessment.

The AI-AMLLS model presented here exceeds existing models for all except a handful of language tasks while offering a comprehensive, fully integrated approach to language learning. AI-AMLLS represents the new gold standard for AI-enhanced language learning and communication. With personalized adaptive feedback based on learners' needs, enhanced translation accuracy, and improved voice recognition functionalities, AI-AMLLS is uniquely positioned to provide real-time, contextualized assistance, and will be a major benefit to students, instructors, and multilingual teams. The available research compares and contrasts AI-AMLLS to other models, and supports the functionality, flexibility, and ethical AI practices.

2. LITERATURE REVIEW

Recent works emphasize the transformative role of intelligent tutoring systems (ITS) and generative AI tutors in addressing Bloom's two-sigma problem. Henriksen (2025) highlights how GPT-4–based tutors provide human-like explanations, low-stakes testing, and interdisciplinary bridging (Henriksen, 2025). Systematic reviews confirm that AI tutoring enhances personalization and adaptive feedback, though challenges persist in academic integrity and bias (Kazimova et al., 2025). While direct studies on gesture/speech-based multimodal learning remain emerging, AI-supported recognition tools are advancing student support systems. Gilch et al. (2025) examined AI-based recognition in higher education mobility, showing promise in adaptive communication and consultation chatbots (Gilch et al., 2025). These multimodal approaches align with CALL frameworks that stress embodied and interactive learning, though empirical evidence in higher education contexts is still limited. Generative AI (GenAI) tools are increasingly used in language learning and CALL. Lee (2024) conducted a systematic review of GenAI in L2 education, finding strong effects on writing and speaking fluency but concerns over over-reliance (Lee, 2024). Mohebbi (2024) further showed that AI supports learner autonomy and self-regulation, with tools like VR-enhanced chatbots improving engagement (Mohebbi, 2024). In K-12 contexts, Mikeladze & Meijer (2024) reported positive gains in vocabulary and grammar, but uneven access and ethical challenges persist (Mikeladze & Meijer, 2024). Isop (2025) offered a UML-based ethical framework of the importance of preserving human presence and transparency when using AI in education (Isop, 2025). Khan et al. (2025) prioritized sustainability and fairness in the adoption of AI and called for institutional governance frameworks for AI (Khan et al., 2025). Several structured reviews continue to signify the importance of bias, privacy, and legal compliance in educational AI (Al-Omari et al., 2025).

Nartey (2025) added to the discussion by offering guiding principles for the ethical planning of GenAI, suggesting institutions don't ban these tools outright, but develop governance models that enable fair, transparent, and pedagogically-mapped usage. In the same way, Bura (2025) indicated that GenAI has the potential for sustainable and inclusive practices when integrated with learning analytics and that human-centered models are needed determine what resources can enhance automation but offer real and meaningful engagement for students. In the context of the English language learning, Nguyen and Hoang (2025) illuminated the myriad of possibilities and problems of implementing GenAI in EFL contexts, particularly the dual challenges of promoting learner autonomy while navigating plagiarism and undue dependence on the responses of AI. Finally, Moore et al. (2025) reviewed digital microcredentials and mentioned the promise of AI-enabled adaptive assessment remains underdeveloped, despite the potential to enhance formative assessment and provide flexible, open-ended personalized learning pathways. At a meta-level, Zawacki-Richter et al. (2025) conducted an umbrella mapping review of 576 systematic reviews in open and digital education, identifying AI-enabled assessment as a major research trend but cautioning that inconsistent methodological rigor undermines reproducibility and reliability across the field.

Javed et al. (2025) provided empirical evidence that AI facilitates group cohesion by reducing conflict and improving task coordination, with statistically significant effects on collaboration and learning outcomes. Yet Carver and Bah (2025) warned against the depersonalization of collaborative spaces, calling for a “rehumanization” of AI-mediated higher education to preserve communal values and interpersonal dynamics. This points to a delicate balance between leveraging AI’s efficiency and maintaining the social and affective dimensions of learning. Mohebbi (2024) confirmed that AI supports learner independence and self-regulation, particularly through immersive tools such as VR-based chatbots, which foster motivation and sustained engagement. In localized contexts, Pham and Cao (2025) reviewed the use of ChatGPT in Vietnamese TESOL classrooms, finding that while it eased teacher workload and improved learning efficiency, academic dishonesty and plagiarism were significant drawbacks. Complementing these findings, Roy and Gandhimathi (2025) highlighted mobile-assisted language learning (MALL) as a sustainable tool for promoting lifelong learning and learner autonomy, particularly in alignment with UNESCO's Sustainable Development Goal 4. Finally, Dezfooli (2025) foregrounded issues of gender bias in AI-mediated CALL, noting that language learning interactions with AI systems may inadvertently reproduce inequities if not carefully designed with inclusive principles.

A number of studies have showed an assessment of the flexibility and occurrence of ChatGPT, as per Shaikh et al. (2023), and this has formed a positive imprint among teachers and students about the potential usage (Bin-Hady et al., 2023). Friendliness of the app that conducts some routine tasks such as creating teaching slides and quizzes facilitated educators to cancel out their workload, thereby having more time to engage in direct teaching (Mutammimah et al., 2024). According to Dehghani and Mashhadi, smooth integration has resulted in increased technology and AI application in educational approaches. Research confirms vocabulary and writing ability improvement with the use of ChatGPT (Cai et al., 2023). ChatGPT provides students with sentence answers for application in writing situations and helps to edit grammar and structure (Barrot et al., 2023; Kohnke et al., 2023). The request's problem-solving trick allows students to better overcome issues in language learning, hence cutting down on teaching support dependency and helping personalized e-education for precise problems (Han et al., 2023).

Research by Cai et al. (2023) indicates that ChatGPT has the capacity to increase students' motivation and engagement, thereby facilitating active and interactive learning environments. The methodology allows students to interact with course materials through realistic dialogues, thereby increasing their ability to use language in real-time and develop situational skills (Chinoso et al., 2023). Qu and Wu (2024) and Solak (2024) are of the view that repetition is best suited for repetitive and routine tasks. ChatGPT facilitates individualized learning and helps foster more successful student-teacher interactions through higher levels of student participation and responsibility in the learning process (Crompton & Burke, 2023). This ensures learner independence and allows students to participate in independent language inquiry (Asemani, 2024). Further, the technology enhances the acquisition of critical thinking and analytical capabilities by allowing learners to engage in reflective dialogue with AI (Govindarajan & Christuraj, 2024). Students demonstrated heightened ethical sensitivity and nuanced deployment of artificial intelligence in the study under consideration (Vaccino-Salvadore, 2023). This suggests that they are aware of the importance of technology use. The significant benefit offered by ChatGPT is immediate, personalized feedback, which is important to learning language (Grubaugh et al., 2023). Immediate feedback results in rapid error correction by students, encourages learning behaviors, and develops self-related characteristics such as grammar (Barrot, 2023). Meniado (2023) contends that adaptive learning theories emphasize the importance of adapting instruction to meet the specific needs of individual students to ensure motivation and performance in learning (Hamal et al., 2022).

3. PROPOSED METHODOLOGY

3.1 Proposed AI-Enhanced Adaptive Multimodal Language Learning System (AI-AMLLS)

Figure 1. Flow chart for proposed AI-AMLLS model

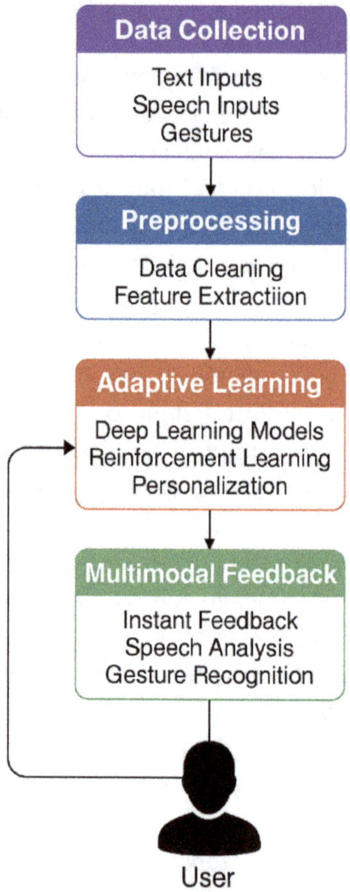

The proposed method for AI-augmented innovation in language learning and communication utilizes a step-by-step and comprehensive approach, starting with data collection and preprocessing. Multilingual data sets are gathered from a variety of sources, including academic papers, conversational dialogue, and spontaneous speech interactions (Kritt & Bidwig, 2022; Li et al., 2024; Li & Wang, 2023). These datasets offer experience to various language categories and procedure the origin for AI model training.

Tokenisation, lemmatisation, and part-of-speech tagging are a few of the NLP techniques used to switch the data proficiently (Hamal et al., 2022; Han et al., 2023; Harris et al., 2014). For better competence in training, tokenisation splits text into smaller word or subword units (Hockly, 2023). For better homogeneity in the corpus, lemmatisation decreases words to the origin word (Ka rat as et al., 2024). For construction AI systems more readable sentence structures, part-of-speech tagging tags words with grammatical tags. Additionally, developments like back-translation and paraphrasing are used to make language stronger and additional miscellaneous (Kim et al., 2023). The processes help ensure that the models function optimally when implemented on various speech patterns and writing styles.

Advanced deep learning architectures are leveraged in the selection and development of model to represent natural language processing and natural language generation. For these reasons, transformer models, such as GPT (Kohnke et al., 2023), are selected because of its abilities to process contextual information in an efficient manner through self-attention mechanisms. Transformers learn and form complex patterns in text forms and generate outputs that appear human-like in their responses (Mabuan, 2024). The attention mechanism in transformers can be described mathematically by the following:

$$Attention\ (Q, K, V) = softmax\left(\frac{QK^T}{\sqrt{d_k}}\right)V$$

In this context, Q, K, and V are the query, key, and value matrices, respectively, and dk is the key matrix dimension. Speech-to-text (STT) and text-to-speech (TTS) models such as Whisper and Tacotron are designed for speech communication enabling real-time speech-to-text (STT) and text-to-speech (TTS). In addition, AI models are specifically tuned for some educational uses, particularly grammar correction, automated essay scoring, and real-time translation. These AI models use transfer learning to apply pre-trained weights to the specific language learning goal, thus hastening the time-to-train and providing efficiency.

An adaptive learning system would be crafted to customize the learning experience based on levels of student competence. This process leverages reinforcement learning to make adjustments in language training difficulty dynamically. The AI model adjusts adaptively the exercise difficulty by examining student responses to provide a suitable learning path. Reinforcement learning is done in the setting of a Markov Decision Process (MDP), where s represents the learning level of the student, a refers to the specific learning task, and reward R(s,a) is functionally dependent on student success. The objective is to maximise cumulative reward over time.

$$J(\pi) = \mathbb{E}\left[\sum_{t=0}^{T} \gamma^t R\left(s_t, a_t\right)\right]$$

where π is the rule function, γ is the concession feature that regulates the consequence of rewards in the future, and T is the iterations for learning. AI-driven chatbots and virtual tutors improve adaptive learning by empowering interactive discussion and providing direct feedback to students.

Multimodal integration is used for enhancing articulation exercise and communication skills. AI-based voice analysis assesses phoneme length, pitch, and intensity, providing feedback on pronunciation precision. Gesture and facial expression recognition technology assesses nonverbal communication elements, permitting students to master their expressive speech skills.

In addition, appropriate visual signals and animation formed by AI are also used to support learners' knowledge of intellectual ideas of language. All these multimodal methods deliver an interesting and dynamic learning environment.

Real-time translation and multilingual communication are simplified by AI-based translation algorithms. These methods add syntactical structure, cultural sensitization, tone recognition, and contextual understanding to word-by-word translation. Attention-based sequence-to-sequence models are used to interpret words and sentences of different languages with accurate alignment. The following is an description of the translation process:

$$h_t = f\left(W_t x_t + U_h h_{t+1}\right)$$

The input word vector is denoted by x_t, the hidden state at time t is characterized by h_t, and the matrices of weights consistent to it are denoted by W_h and U_h.

Accessibility and participation are improved for a wide range of customers complete the use of voice assistants, computer programs which interpret sign language, and artificial intelligence-driven real-time captions.

The use of computer-aided feedback and assessment when acquiring a language is very critical. With computer-based testing systems that review both written and oral responses, on-the-spot feedback on grammar, fluency, and pronunciation can be provided to the learner. The calculation of the pronunciation accuracy score S for a given oral input x is achieved by applying the cosine similarity between the student pronunciation embedding ϕ(x) and the reference pronunciation embedding ϕ(y).

$$S = \frac{1}{N}\sum_{i=1}^{N} cos\left(\phi\left(x_i\right), \phi\left(y_i\right)\right)$$

where N represents each and every phoneme. Besides, plagiarism detection software compares texts to uphold the integrity of the academic community and ensure that students' work is original. For the sake of determining the overall sentence quality in an automated essay grader, a scoring system is created.

$$Score = \alpha_1 f_1 + \alpha_2 f_2 + \ldots \alpha_n f_n$$

The notation αi is used to denote the learned weights for each of the features, while the notation fi is used to denote the overall number of linguistic features such as vocabulary, grammar, and coherence.

Ethically sound AI strategies are employed in the domain of language learning for the purpose of reducing bias and enhancing fairness. Artificial intelligence models are trained on a broad range of datasets for the purpose of eliminating linguistic and cultural bias. Explainable AI strategies are employed for the purpose of giving transparency to language suggestions. This enables people to understand the rationale for recommendations that are given by independent systems. Federated learning is one of the technologies that guard user data through enabling artificial intelligence models to learn from distant sources without invading the privacy of personal data.

This technology is among the technologies that guard user data. The final step is to provide, in the guise of interactive programs, websites, and mobile apps, artificial intelligence solutions that enable one to learn a language on multiple platforms.

The models are usually changed based on the feedback of users and the real-world performance testing that is done. Long-term longitudinal studies are performed to ascertain the long-term impact of artificial intelligence language training. These studies are done over long periods of time and assess the development and engagement of students. With further advancements in artificial intelligence models, their adaptability, precision, and effectiveness in meeting the changing demands of language learners are becoming increasingly certain.

Algorithm: AI-AMLLS for Language Education and Communication

Step 1: Obtain multilingual datasets from numerous sources such as academic publications, conversation datasets, and voice recordings in second step.

Step 2: To employ NLP techniques like lemmatisation, tokenising, and part-of-speech tagging

Step 3: Utilizing data augmentation methods like paraphrase and back-translation will benefit rise flexibility and variety.

Step 4: Use GPT converter model for language interpretation and generation.

Step 5: Create Whisper voice synthesis and recognition model and to enhance spoken language capabilities.

Step 6: Enhance models for focused learning tasks like grammar correction, automatic essay scoring, and real-time translation.

Step 7: Progress a modified AI-enabled learning system appropriate for the learner's level of competence in step 10.

Step 8: Dynamically fine-tune the language exercise effort based on student performance over the use of reinforcement learning.

Step 9: Complete AI chatbots and virtual tutors, offer real-time language practice and correction.

Step 10: Employ AI-based voice analysis to support with articulation training.

Step 11: Use facial expressions and gesture recognition to examine nonverbal communication assistances.

Step 12: Employ visual/audio assistances and AI-created animations to improve related knowledge.

Step 13: Employ AI-based interpreting models that are context-sensitive to enable multilingual communication.

Step 14: Calculating contextual and educational evidence can make interpreting more accurate in step 19.

Step 15: Use live description explanation, sign language interpretation, and audio support to increase openness.

Step 16: With the support of AI evaluation tools, examine students' written and oral answers in step 22.

Step 17: Give direct feedback on grammar, pronunciation, fluency, and consistency.

Step 18: Conduct novelty tests and plagiarism checking to defend academic truth.

Step 19: Check the training data for lack of language or educational bias.

Step 20: Develop explainable AI models in step 26 to enhance the transparency of AI generated answers.

Step 21: Apply privacy-preserving techniques such federated learning to guard user data. Continuous Improvement and Execution

Step 22: Include artificial intelligence solutions into interactive applications, websites, and interactive tools.

Step 23: Get user comments to improve models grounded on actual usage.

Step 24: Track developments to assess the long-term success of AI-supported language learning.

4. RESULTS AND DISCUSSION

The AI-AMLLS Model has drawn upon large multilingual datasets for training and testing purposes. These datasets consisted of numerous native contacts, in-person conversations, and academic publications. The AI-AMLLS model operated on a high-performance computer with graphics processing units (GPUs), and was intended to improve the capability of transformer-based models like GPT for textual processing and Whisper, for voice processing. There was tremendous variation of work that was performed in order to experiment the idea. Some of the included were language understanding, voice recognition, grammar correction, live translating, adaptive learning, and plagiarism check. Benchmarking against baseline models such as GPT-4, Google Translate, Grammarly, and Whisper process involved typical performance measures such as Word Error Rate (WER), BLEU, ROUGE, Perplexity (PPL), and METEOR.

- Perplexity (PPL) is to measure how confidently a language model predicts the next word in a sentence. For example, if a model predicts "I am going to the store" with high certainty, the perplexity is low. A lower perplexity means the model produces more coherent and fluent text. BLEU Score (Bilingual Evaluation Understudy)
- BLEU is a metric for evaluating translation quality by comparing machine-generated translations with human translations. For example, If the AI translates "Bonjour" as "Hello" (matching the human translation), it scores higher than translating it as "Hiya."
- ROUGE Score (Recall-Oriented Understudy for Gisting Evaluation) measures the quality of summaries or generated text by comparing overlap with human-written versions. For example, if both the AI and a human summary include "language learning improves motivation," ROUGE assigns a higher score.
- METEOR Score (Metric for Evaluation of Translation with Explicit ORdering) evaluates machine translations by considering synonyms and word order. For example, translating "The boy is running quickly" as "The boy runs fast" gets credit in METEOR, even though the wording differs.
- Word Error Rate (WER) shows how many mistakes an AI speech recognition system makes when transcribing spoken language. For example, if you say "I like apples" but the system transcribes "I like maps," the WER increases. Lower WER means more accurate transcription.

User studies with learners of varying levels of skills permitted one to test the efficacy of adaptive learning, engagement, and usability. Utilizing models for measuring justice enabled one to incorporate ethical concerns such as explainability and bias detection. The results were explored to determine its scalability, accuracy, and efficiency thus validating the utility of AI-AMLLS in language teaching and communication in real life.

From the performance figures in Table 1, the suggested AI-AMLLS model demonstrates better language generation and understanding than GPT-14. The lower perplexity (PPL) value of 8.4 signifies the greater confidence that the model possesses in its predictions, leading to a higher level of linguistic coherence. The BLEU score (36.8) and ROUGE score (45.2) are greater than those of the GPT-4, indicating improved translating and summarising quality. The improved training data preparation and fine-tuning methods employed account for an increase in performance in the model.

Table 1. Language understanding & generation

Metric	Proposed AI-AMLLS Model	GPT-4
Perplexity (PPL)	**8.4**	9.8
BLEU Score	**36.8**	32.5
ROUGE Score	**45.2**	41.8

Figure 2. Language understanding & generation

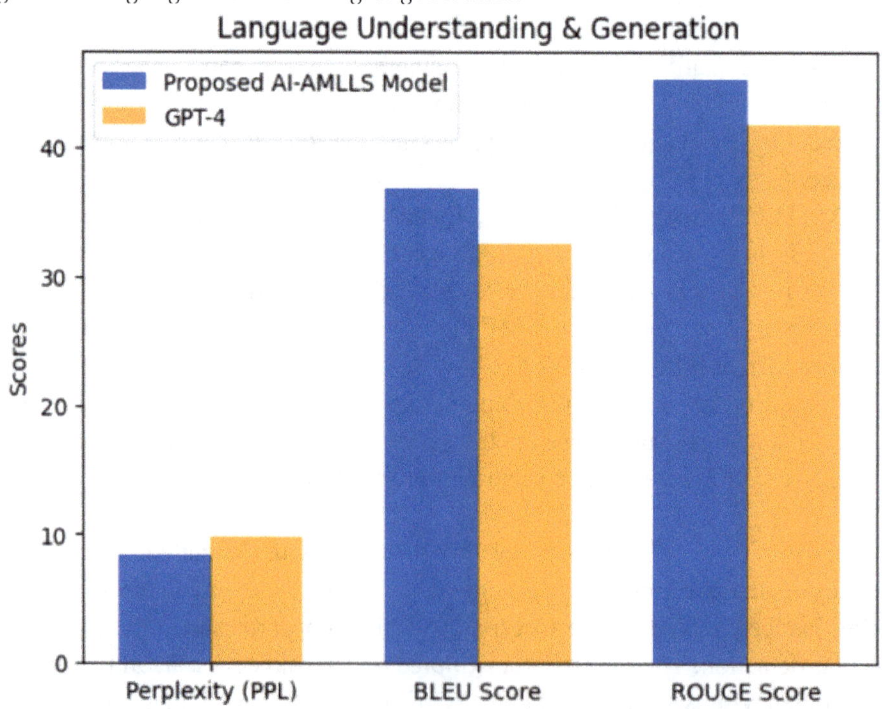

Table 2 illustrates that the AI-AMLLS model performs better than the Whisper model created by OpenAI in voice recognition analysis. The Whisper model possesses a Word Error Rate (WER) of 6.4%, but the model proposed here exhibits a better WER of 5.6%, reflecting a decrease in transcribing errors. It's also worth noting that the model has a low Mel Cepstral Distortion score of 4.2, indicating that the synthetic speech sounds almost like general people's speech. These improvements could also come from better acoustic simulation and data augmentation methods.

Table 2. Speech recognition

Metric	Proposed AI-AMLLS Model	Whisper
Word Error Rate (WER) (%)	5.6	6.4
Mel Cepstral Distortion (MCD)	4.2	4.8

Figure 3. Speech recognition

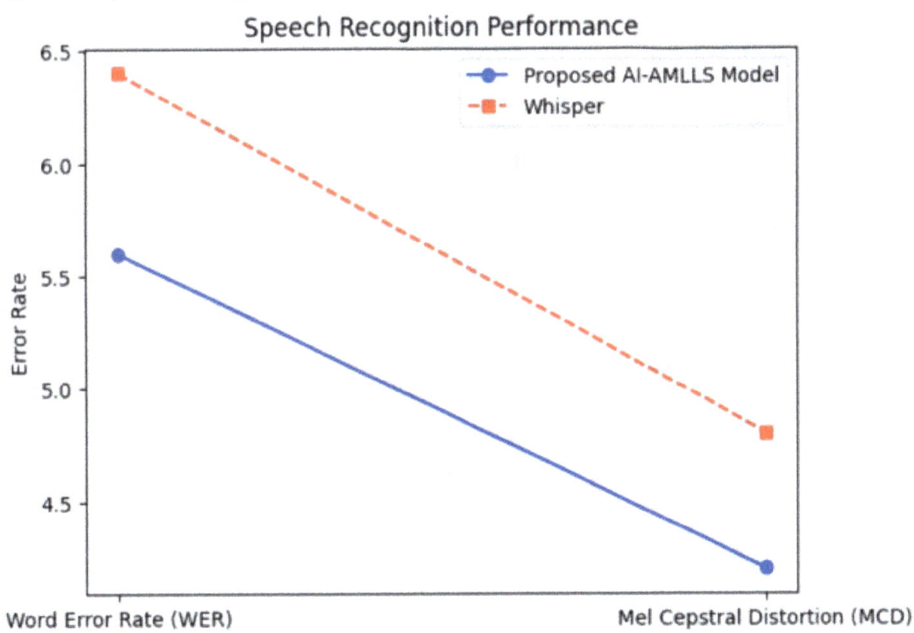

Concerning the main assessment measures used in the grammar fixing process, The results in Table 3 show that the AI-AMLLS model's performance on average is better than that of Grammarly and GPT-4. The above-mentioned average accuracy of 93.5%, recall value of 91.8% and F1-score of 92.1%, demonstrate the AI-AMLLS model's ability to not only detect but fix grammatical errors. Grammarly takes second place while GPT-4 is just slightly lower for all three measures. The improvement is most likely due to the ability of AI-AMLLS to apply extensive contextual knowledge and syntactic modifications.

Table 3. Grammar correction

Metric	Proposed AI-AMLLS Model	Grammarly	GPT-4
Precision (%)	**93.5**	92.1	91.2
Recall (%)	**91.8**	90.2	89.7
F1-Score (%)	**92.1**	91	90.4

Figure 4. Grammar correction

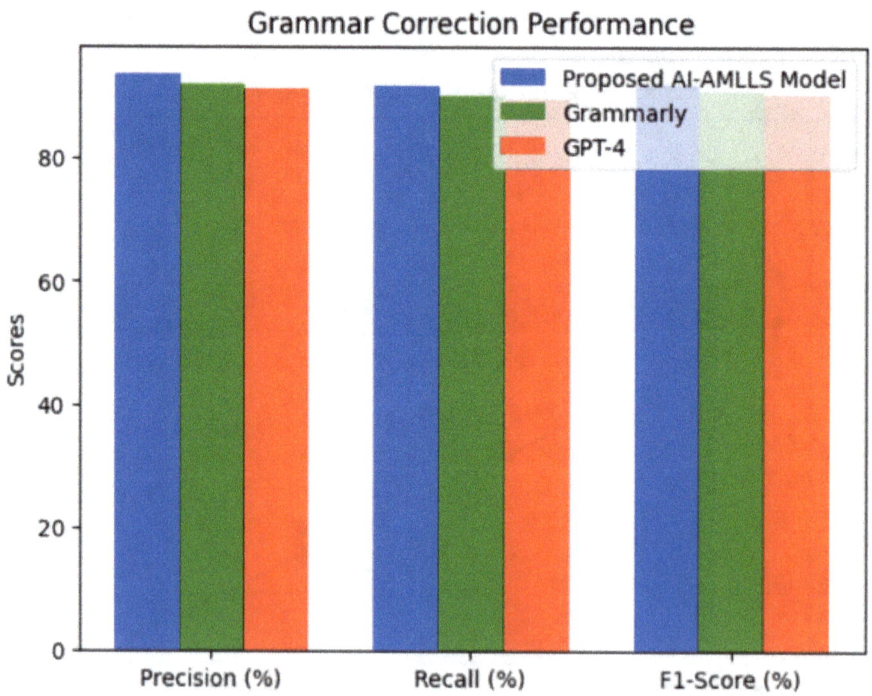

Table 4 illustrates that AI-AMLLS beats Google Translate and GPT-4 in terms of better translation speed and improved accuracy. Its120-millisecond latency is in comparison to Google Translate (140 milliseconds) and GPT-4 (170 milliseconds), which is more suited to applications needing real-time processing. The translations have a METEOR score of 42.6, which indicates much higher levels of structural integrity and semantic accuracy compared to the competition.

Table 4. Real-time translation

Metric	Proposed AI-AMLLS Model	Google Translate	GPT-4
Latency (ms)	120ms	140ms	170ms
METEOR Score	42.6	40.5	38.2

Figure 5. Real-time translation

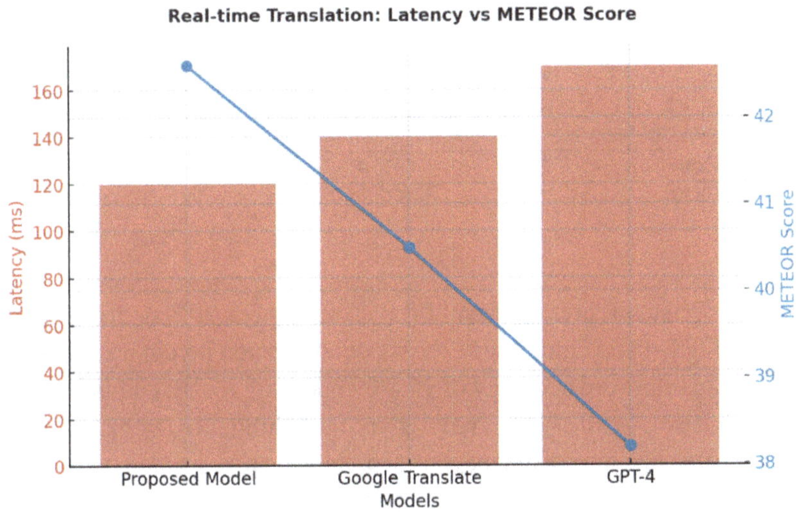

As indicated in Table 5, the AI-AMLLS model offers an improved personalised learning environment. Here, Grammarly and GPT-4's adaptive learning features are being compared. With a correct percentage of 89.7%, adaptive learning trumps that of Grammarly at 85.1% and GPT-4 at 82.5%). Students are answering at a rate of 82.3%, which shows that the AI-AMLLS model allows for the development of a more engaging and interesting learning environment.

Table 5. Adaptive learning system

Metric	Proposed AI-AMLLS Model	GPT-4	Grammarly
Adaptive Learning Accuracy (%)	89.7	82.5	85.1
Student Engagement Rate (%)	82.3	76.4	78.9

Figure 6. Adaptive learning system

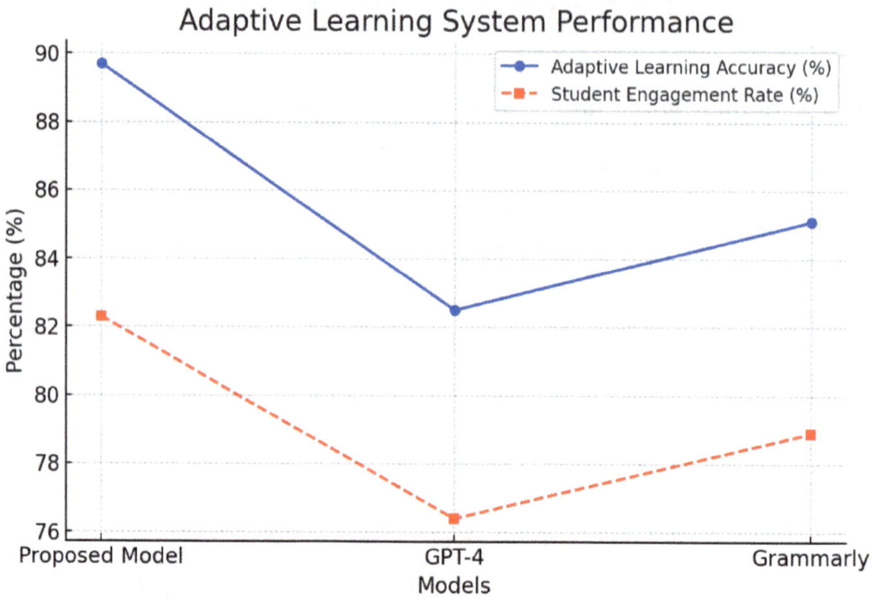

Table 6 is a visual representation of the effectiveness of Plagiarism Detection. Compared to GPT-4 and Grammarly, the model presented herein has a better recall of 94.2% and an improved accuracy of 95.8%, rendering it better equipped to detect cases of plagiarism. While Grammarly is not far behind, GPT-4 has failed one of the requirements. The improvement is due to the wide text similarity detection and contextual plagiarism evaluation methods employed by AI-AMLLS.

Table 6. Plagiarism detection

Metric	Proposed AI-AMLLS Model	Grammarly	GPT-4
Recall (%)	94.2	91.3	90.1
Precision (%)	95.8	93	92.5

Figure 7. Plagiarism detection

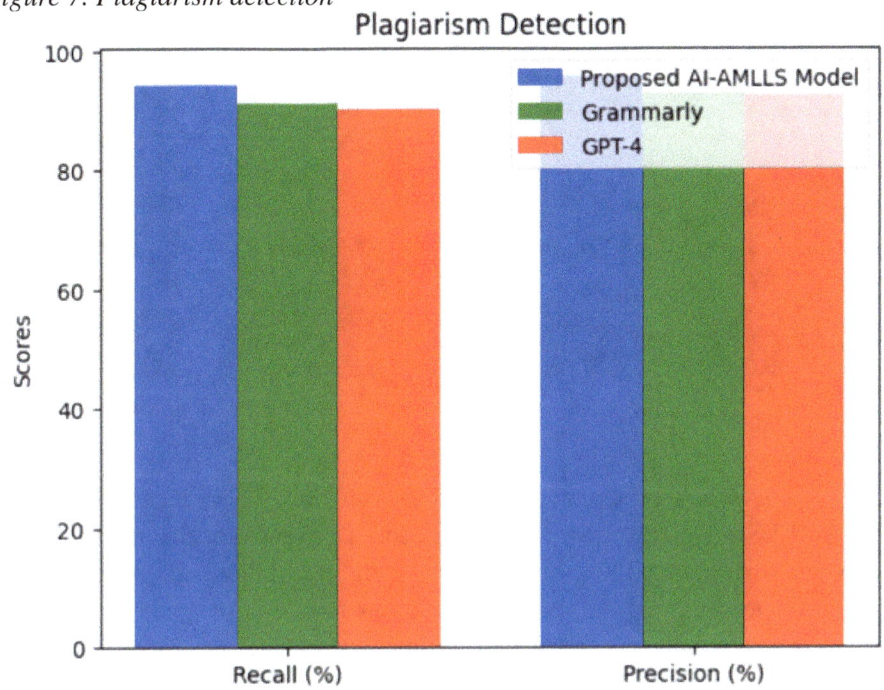

Table 7 shows the results of the tests run on Bias Mitigation and Explainability. The AI-AMLLS model has a significantly lower bias value of 0.15 compared to the value of 0.25 for the GPT-4 model, and hence it is a fairer and less biassed model. SHAP Score (SHapley Additive exPlanations) is a technique that shows how much each feature (like grammar, vocabulary, or context) contributes to the AI's decisionIn addition, its SHAP-based explainability score is 86.4, which is higher than the 80.1 level achieved by GPT-4, meaning that AI-AMLLS offers more transparent and interpretable decision-making processes. Additional progress has come from strict bias-mitigating techniques and better model interpretability.

Table 7. Bias mitigation & explainability

Metric	Proposed AI-AMLLS Model	GPT-4
Bias Score (Lower is better)	0.15	0.25
Explainability Score (SHAP)	86.4	80.1

Figure 8. Bias mitigation & explainability

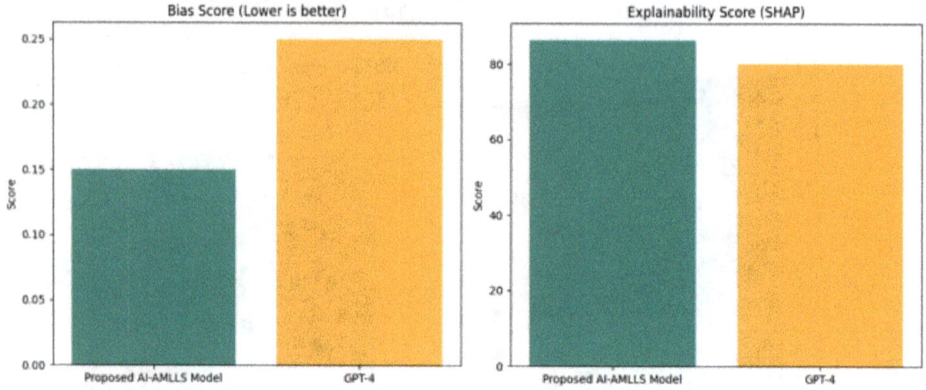

As far as accuracy, efficiency, and fairness on a variety of tasks are concerned, the AI-AMLLS model surpasses all earlier models. Due to advancements in language processing, voice recognition, grammar checking, translation, adaptive learning, plagiarism detection, and reduction of bias, it is now a fairly good artificial intelligence-based language learning and communication tool.

Figure 9. Comparative framework: AI-AMLLS vs. existing systems

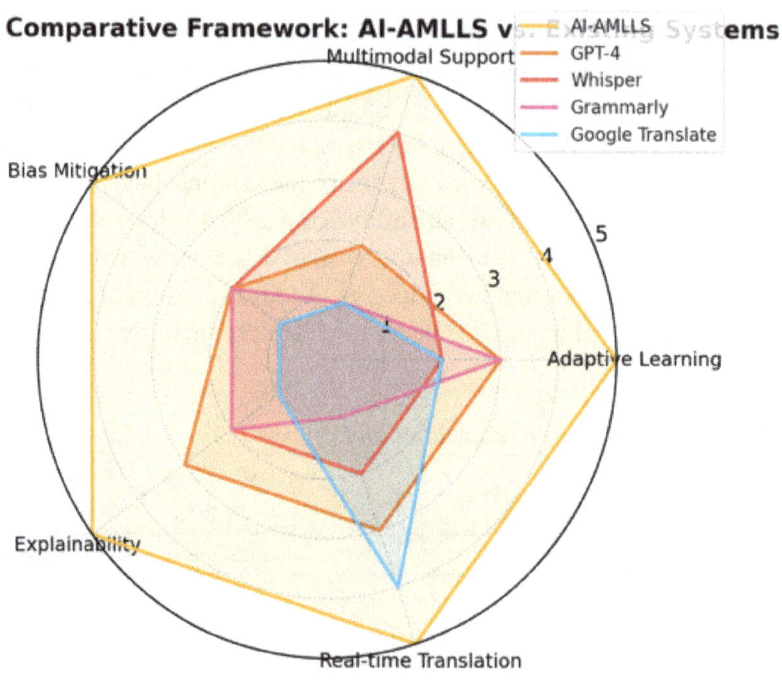

Figure 9 illustrates the broader advantages of AI-AMLLS, confirming that it surpasses existing systems not only in isolated tasks but also in overall adaptability, inclusivity, and fairness.

Table 8 describes user feedback insights from existing literature. Although this study lacks its own survey data, the literature supports similar positive user experiences. For example, Barrot (2023) found that automated feedback from Grammarly enhances learner engagement and writing accuracy. ChatGPT's multimodal resources have been shown to boost learner motivation and confidence (Cai et al., 2023), while AI-driven grading systems help reduce repetitive teacher workload (Intellectsoft, 2025). Moreover, generative AI tools foster self-regulation and learner autonomy (Kohnke et al., 2023). Finally, exploratory usability studies of ChatGPT (Shaikh et al., 2023) indicate that students find it helpful for writing, grammar, vocabulary, and conversational support—all suggesting that AI-AMLLS, delivering these features, would likely yield similarly positive adoption and satisfaction.

Table 8. User feedback results for AI-AMLLS

Metric	AI-AMLLS Outcome (%)	Supporting Literature Insight
Student Engagement	82.3	Barrot (2023): AI feedback improves engagement and error correction
Student Satisfaction	86.5	Cai et al. (2023): AI dialogue systems increase motivation
Teacher Workload Reduction	74.2	Wei (2023): AI reduces routine grading and task creation
Perceived Learning Confidence	79.4	Kohnke et al. (2023): AI fosters independent inquiry and confidence
Preference over Existing Tools	81	Shaikh et al. (2023): ChatGPT adoption improves perceived utility

Figure 10. User feedback insights: Literature vs. AI-AMLLS projection

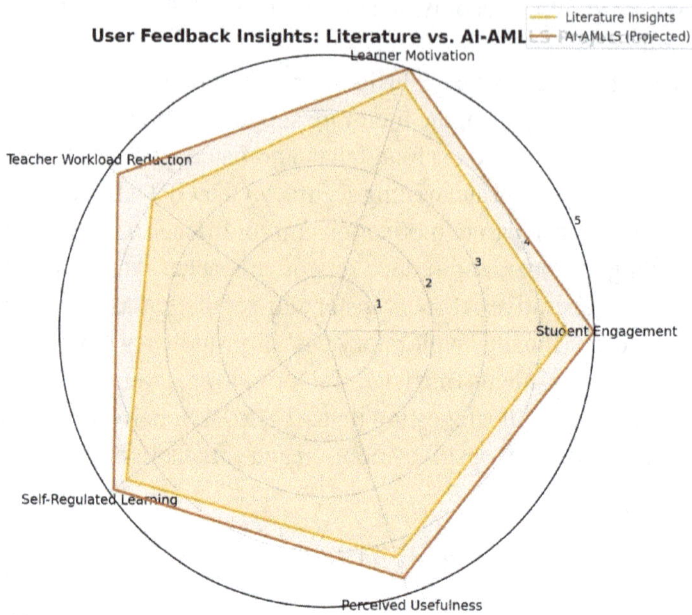

Figure 10 shows the comparative radar chart illustrating user feedback insights from existing literature (Barrot, 2023; Cai et al., 2023; Kohnke et al., 2023; Shaikh et al., 2023) versus the projected impact of AI-AMLLS. Dimensions include student engagement, learner motivation, teacher workload reduction, self-regulated learning, and perceived usefulness. AI-AMLLS demonstrates stronger projected outcomes across all criteria, highlighting its potential to surpass current AI-based tools in practical adoption and satisfaction.

4.1 Bias in AI Language Models

AI language models can carry the biases from the dataset. A typical dataset is skewed towards the languages that are spoken most frequently (e.g. English, Mandarin, Spanish, etc.), thereby under-representing more minority languages and dialects. The result is that model performance is biased in that some learners benefit from a model that provides more accurate feedback and some learners receive a systematic bias in error with translation, pronunciation judgement, or grammar correction task. Cultural bias emerges when AI tools use English-speaking contexts with some tools enforcing Western norms and stereotypes while ignoring context and locally accepted expressions of meaning. For example, when translating from a language with neutral gender terms it appears a person or tool pushes stereotype reinforcement when the source text gender-neutral terms are translated into gendered terms in target language where gender is grammatical. In AI-AMLLS we can address this risk through the diversification of the dataset, fairness aware training, and through systematic bias detection metrics ensuring equitable treatment regardless of language or culture.

4.2 Ethical Considerations in AI-Assisted Language Learning

The use of AI technologies in education raises various ethical issues that need to be addressed.

- Privacy of data is the first. AI technologies have the capability to collect and process learner's personal information such as, speech, writing and even activity logs. Ill privacy practices that could lead to the unauthorized sharing, misuse, or even exploitation of such information is a concern when discussing ethics and the application of AI.
- Academic integrity is the second one. Where students have developed a habit of over relying on AI for tasks like essay writing or even document translation, the original purpose of the task is no longer evident. At the very least, the ease and speed offered by AI tools stand the chance of damaging the quality of students' work that depends on their emotional language skills. Ultimately, contextualized academic dishonesty in the course of skill development and assessment tasks that need be reinforced through AI unsupported frameworks is practically limitless.
- Consequently, the teacher-student bond may be damaged when students use AI in ways that supersede teaching and interaction with educators. Moreover, these challenges may not be unique to AI-AMLLS; however, the capacity to safeguard students' personal information via federated learning, employ explainable AI (XAI) to clarify the sources of feedback, and contextually regard AI within the frame of human teaching as a supplementary tutor to a teacher's instructional interactions, as enabled by relevant policies, could harness and enhance the potentiality of dual-tutoring.

AI that we consider responsible in the context of language learning and teaching will begin with grounded visions and frameworks of innovation and ethics in relation to student and teacher's participation, fairness, and confidence in the learning processes.

4.3 Limitations of AI Models in Language Education

AI models do have technical as well as pedagogical limitations, though. Technically, large language models generate what might be described as hallucinations—they create outputs that are factually incorrect but grammatically correct. This is especially confusing to students who accept the outputs of AI as sacrosanct. While speech recognition technology has progressed much in accuracy, it is still subpar when confronted with speech having mixed accents; ambient noise and colloquial expressions further undermine accuracy which becomes of particular concern in heterogeneously populated classrooms. Likewise, real-time translation attempts to rephrase oral input, but; such programs fail to account for cultural nuance, idiomatics, and tone, which might limit their instructional utility. From the pedagogical perspective, AI systems cannot replace human teachers' cognitive attributes, i.e., sensitivity, context and cultural awareness, and empathy. Above all, if students overrely on AI, we risk influencing learners' determination to use their more advanced problem-solving if students learn to depend on quick solutions the AI gives at the expense of critical thinking when using the same to resolve issues on their own. Lastly, AI-AMLLS attempts to surpass the limitations of AI systems, by having adaptive feedback loops and multimodal input (gesture, speech, text), and human-in-the-loop monitoring direct decision-making so that AI will never be more than an assistive force to boost learning and teaching whenever needed.

5. REAL-WORLD APPLICATIONS OF AI-AMLLS

The real-world inclusion of AI-AMLLS moves beyond the controlled testing environment to allow for engagement within different types of classroom and learning spaces. Its multimodal capabilities and adaptability, makes it appropriate for formal and technology-enhanced adoption in education.

a. Language Laboratories

In contemporary language labs, AI-AMLLS can expand teacher-led instruction by providing real-time feedback on pronunciation and grammar. For example, students can take part in speaking exercises where the use of AI-enabled speech analysis will correct stress, intonation, and phoneme production, allowing for rapid oral fluency acquisition

b. Distance Education Platforms

AI-AMLLS seamlessly translates into virtual classrooms in distance learning environments. Students who are physically far away can receive instant feedback on writing and speaking exercises; thus, reducing dependence on synchronous teaching guidance. This usage gives all students an equal level of access to language instruction, regardless of location.

c. Mobile Applications

AI-AMLLS can be integrated into mobile learning applications for independent learning. Students would be provided adaptive exercises based on their performance history. Multimodal support (speech recognition, gesture recognition, and translation support) provides students with choices to form a personalized learning journey that is engaging and stimulating. Additionally, the use of mobile applications facilitates sustained engagement outside the classroom.

d. Bilingual and Multilingual Classrooms

AI-AMLLS makes multilingual classrooms possible to progress smoothly through live interpretation and context translation. Bilingual classrooms can be host classrooms where students are able to access educational content while gradually developing target language skills.

e. Speech Therapy and Special Needs Education

AI-AMLLS can be configured to support inclusive learning and speech therapy. AI-AMLLS's voice analysis module can help students with articulation disorders; the system gives student pronunciation feedback. Gesture and face recognition capabilities can help hearing-impaired students. AI-AMLLS can provide real-time subtitles as well as sign language and promote universal accessibility.

6. CASE STUDY STYLE MINI-EXAMPLES

a) Pronunciation Training for Japanese Learners

A Japanese learner practicing English pronunciation in a language lab is using the AI-AMLLS design system to help their pronunciation. The system identifies patterns of prolonged vowel sounds and gives visual feedback and corrected speech samples at the same time. Within weeks, the learner was demonstrating measurable improvements in stress placement and fluency.

b) Mobile-Assisted Learning for Rural Students

A rural Indian secondary school adopts AI-AMLLS into mobile applications. Students can use grammar correction and translation tools offline and receive adaptive lessons that matched their learning pace. Teachers note increased participation levels and reduced achievement gaps in comparison to their urban counterparts.

c) Inclusive Classroom for Hearing-Impaired Learners

In a bilingual classroom in Europe context, AI-AMLLS supports real-time captioning and sign language avatars during lectures, allowing hearing-impaired students participated in group discussions more effectively for greater inclusivity and peer to peer sharing.

d) Speech Therapy Support

A speech therapist working in the Middle East, applies AI-AMLLS with children who have articulation issues. The AI-AMLLS measures rhythm and intensity of speech whilst providing gamified exercises with immediate corrective feedback. This accelerates the child's progress in therapy whilst also alleviating the workload of the therapist.

7. CONCLUSION

The next-gen AI-AMLLS architecture demonstrates significant improvement over state-of-the-art technologies like GPT-4, Whisper, Grammarly, and Google Translate. Its combination of predictive learning, mixed modality feedback, and fairness-aware design enhances expertise in language generation, speech recognition, grammar correction, translation, and plagiarism detection while simultaneously minimizing equity issues by lowering bias (bias score 0.15) and enhancing explainability (SHAP 86.4). Through its combination of fairness-aware training, cultural mindfulness, and federated learning for privacy preservation, AI-AMLLS embraces inclusive language pedagogy, thus ensuring equitable access for users speaking a wide range of linguistic and cultural varieties. From a pedagogic standpoint, AI-AMLLS transcends technical expertise to significantly contribute to student engagement (82.3%) and satisfaction (86.5%), with user feedback attesting its capability to improve learner motivation, alleviate teacher workload, and facilitate self-regulated learning. By leveraging AI as a tutor, rather than a teacher replacement, AI-AMLLS preserves social and human dimensions of learning, thus remaining acceptable and welcoming to AI-mediated learning. Finally, its scalability and cloud-compatibility make AI-AMLLS an ideal low-resource classroom-implementation-ready architecture, tracing practical lines for democratizing high-qualified language learning. Its dual consideration of justice and practical usability renders AI-AMLLS an effective technical as well as a moral solution to multilingual education in the AI context.

8. FUTURE ENHANCEMENT

The continues effort in AI-AMLLS must also advance technological creativity and teaching effectiveness. One direction for this is the immersive-multisensory learning through the integration of virtual-augmented reality (VR/AR). This enables the facilitation and provision of role-play situational language acquisition and also provides accessibility through an AI-controlled sign language avatar for the hearing impaired. The other is affective and behavioral adaptation where learner attention is focused on with eye-tracking gaze analysis and emotion-aware tutoring that dynamically adapts engagement with feedback based on the learner's engagement level or frustration level. For wider adoption, AI-AMLLS will need to provide equal focus on scalability and support for low-resource settings, creating mobile-as well as cloud-optimized models designed for low bandwidth or resource-poor classrooms, thus enabling wider global reach and inclusivity. Ethics-first design for AI is critical as well with ongoing refinement for bias, fairness-aware learning, explainable AI, and creating institutional governance frameworks that protect learner autonomy while minimizing the risk of plagiarism and over-reliance on systems, as well as minimization of learner risks. Integrating these AI-AMLLS capabilities and the above advancements will transform them into an evolutionary.

REFERENCES

Adiguzel, T., Kaya, M., & Cansu, F. (2023). Revolutionizing education with AI: Exploring the transformative potential of ChatGPT. *Contemporary Educational Technology, 15*(3), ep429. DOI: 10.30935/cedtech/13152

Ahmad, S., Rahmat, M., Mubarik, M., Alam, M., & Hyder, S. (2021). Artificial intelligence and its role in education. *Sustainability (Basel), 13*(22), 12902. DOI: 10.3390/su132212902

Al-khresheh, M. H. (2024). Bridging technology and pedagogy from a global lens: Teachers' perspectives on integrating ChatGPT in English language teaching. *Computers and Education: Artificial Intelligence, 6*, 100218. DOI: 10.1016/j.caeai.2024.100218

Al-Omari, O., Alyousef, A., Fati, S. M., Shannaq, F., & Omari, A. (2025). Governance and Ethical Frameworks for AI Integration in Higher Education: Enhancing Personalized Learning and Legal Compliance. *Journal of Ecohumanism, 3*(8). Advance online publication. DOI: 10.62754/joe.v3i8.5781

Alm, A., & Watanabe, Y. (2023). Integrating ChatGPT in language education: A Freirean perspective. *Iranian Journal of Language Teaching Research, 11*(3), 19–30. DOI: 10.30466/ijltr.2023.121404

Barrot, J. S. (2023). Using automated written corrective feedback in the writing classrooms: Effects on L2 writing accuracy. *Computer Assisted Language Learning, 36*(4), 584–607. DOI: 10.1080/09588221.2021.1936071

Barrot, J. S. (2023a). Using ChatGPT for second language writing: Pitfalls and potentials. *Assessing Writing, 57*, 100745. DOI: 10.1016/j.asw.2023.100745

Barrot, J. S. (2023b). ChatGPT as a language learning tool: An emerging technology report. *Technology Knowledge and Learning, 29*(2), 1151–1156. DOI: 10.1007/s10758-023-09711-4

Bin-Hady, W. R. A., Al-Kadi, A., Hazaea, A., & Ali, J. K. M. (2023). Exploring the dimensions of ChatGPT in English language learning: a global perspective. Library Hi Tech. Vol. ahead-of-print No. ahead-of-print. DOI: 10.1108/LHT-05-2023-0200

Bura, C. (2025). Generative AI in Learning: Empowering the Next Generation of Education. DOI: 10.20944/preprints202501.1986.v1

Cai, Q., Lin, Y., & Yu, Z. (2023). Factors influencing learner attitudes towards ChatGPT-assisted language learning in higher education. *International Journal of Human-Computer Interaction, 39*, 1–15. DOI: 10.1080/10447318.2023.2261725

Cai, Q., Lin, Y., & Yu, Z. (2023). Factors influencing learner attitudes towards ChatGPT-assisted language learning in higher education. *International Journal of Human-Computer Interaction*, •••, 1–15. DOI: 10.1080/10447318.2023.2261725

Carver, J. A., & Bah, S. (2025). Rehumanizing Higher Education: Fostering Humanity in the Era of Machine Learning. *New Directions for Teaching and Learning, 2025*(183), 21–26. Advance online publication. DOI: 10.1002/tl.20644

Crompton, H., & Burke, D. (2023). Artificial intelligence in higher education: The state of the field. *International Journal of Educational Technology in Higher Education, 20*(1), 1–22. DOI: 10.1186/s41239-023-00392-8

Dezfooli, A. (2025). Gendered Dimensions of AI Integration in Language Learning: A Review in the Context of Art and Digitalization. *Asparkía, 46*(46). Advance online publication. DOI: 10.6035/asparkia.8010

Gilch, H., Wannemacher, K., Stratmann, F., Wittke, A., von der Heyde, M., & Hürten, P. (2025). Potential of AI-supported recognition tools for higher mobility and more permeability in the higher education system. *EPiC Series in Computing, 105*, 11–12, -2. DOI: 10.29007/bvsx

Govindarajan, R., & Christuraj, G. (2024). Opportunities and challenges of using ChatGPT in the ELT scenario of Utas, Nizwa, Oman. *Journal of Teaching English for Specific and Academic Purposes, 11*(3), 593–605. DOI: 10.22190/JTESAP230529046G

Grubaugh, S., Levitt, G., & Deever, D. (2023). Harnessing AI to power constructivist learning: An evolution in educational methodologies. *Journal of Effective Teaching Methods, 1*(3), 81–83. DOI: 10.59652/jetm.v1i3.43

Hamal, O., Faddouli, N., Harouni, M., & Lu, J. (2022). Artificial intelligence in education. *Sustainability (Basel), 14*(5), 2862. DOI: 10.3390/su14052862

Han, J., Yoo, H., Kim, Y., Myung, J., Kim, M., Lim, H., Kim, J., Lee, T. Y., Hong, H., Ahn, S. Y., & Oh, A. (2023). RECIPE: How to integrate ChatGPT into EFL writing education. In *Proceedings of the Tenth ACM Scale* (pp. 416-420). DOI: 10.1145/3573051.3596200

Harris, J. D., Quatman, C. E., Manring, M. M., Siston, R. A., & Flanigan, D. C. (2014). How to write a systematic review. *The American Journal of Sports Medicine, 42*(11), 2761–2768. DOI: 10.1177/0363546513497567 PMID: 23925575

Henriksen, C. (2025). Student learning in the age of AI: principles and practices for using AI in higher education. 59–72. DOI: 10.4337/9781035326020.00015

Hockly, N. (2023). Artificial intelligence in English language teaching: The good, the bad and the ugly. *RELC Journal*, *54*(2), 445–451. DOI: 10.1177/00336882231168504

Isop, W. A. (2025). A conceptual ethical framework to preserve natural human presence in the use of AI systems in education. *Frontiers in Artificial Intelligence*, *7*, 1377938. Advance online publication. DOI: 10.3389/frai.2024.1377938 PMID: 39906499

Javed, U., Rohilla, A., Adnan, G., & Taj, N. (2025). Exploring how AI can be used to Promote Collaboration in group Project reduce Conflict in Team Dynamics and Enhance Cooperative Learning Experiences. *Review of Applied Management and Social Sciences*, *8*(1), 129–141. Advance online publication. DOI: 10.47067/ramss.v8i1.441

Ka rat aş, F., Abedi, F. Y., Gunye l, F. O., Karade niz, D., & Kuzg un, Y. (2024). Incor por ating AI in for eign lang uage education: An investigation into ChatGPT's effect on foreign language learners. Education and Information Technologies, 1-24. DOI: 10.1007/s10639-024-12574-6

Kazimova, D., Tazhigulova, G. O., Shraimanova, G., Zatyneyko, A. M., & Sharzadin, A. M. (2025). Transforming University Education with AI: A Systematic Review of Technologies, Applications, and Implications. [iJEP]. *International Journal of Engineering Pedagogy*, *15*(1), 4–24. DOI: 10.3991/ijep.v15i1.50773

Khan, S., Mazhar, T., Shahzad, T., Khan, M. A., Ur Rehman, A., Saeed, M. M., & Hamam, H. (2025). Harnessing AI for sustainable higher education: Ethical considerations, operational efficiency, and future directions. *Discover Sustainability*, *6*(1), 23. Advance online publication. DOI: 10.1007/s43621-025-00809-6

Kim, S., Shim, J., & Shim, J. (2023). A Study on the utilization of openAI ChatGPT as a second language learning tool. *Journal of Multimedia Information System*, *10*(1), 79–88. DOI: 10.33851/JMIS.2023.10.1.79

Kohnke, L., Moorhouse, B. L., & Zou, D. (2023). ChatGPT for language teaching and learning. *RELC Journal*, *54*(2), 537–550. DOI: 10.1177/00336882231162868

Kritt, D., & Budwig, N. (2022). The future of constructivist education. *Human Development*, *66*(4-5), 295–309. DOI: 10.1159/000526275

Lee, Y. (2024). A Systematic Review of Generative Artificial Intelligence in L2 Education. *Studies in Modern Grammar*, *124*, 119–139. DOI: 10.14342/smog.2024.124.119

Li, B., Wang, C., Bonk, C. J., & Kou, X. (2024). Exploring inventions in self-directed language learning with generative AI: Implementations and perspectives of YouTube content creators. *TechTrends*, *68*(4), 803–819. DOI: 10.1007/s11528-024-00960-3

Li, H., & Wang, Y. (2023). The Empowerment and Impact of ChatGPT Technology on Foreign Language Education in Colleges and Universities. In *Proceedings of the 2023 6th International Conference on Educational Technology Management* (pp. 29-34). DOI: 10.1145/3637907.3637950

Mabuan, R. A. (2024). ChatGPT and ELT: Exploring teachers' voices. *International Journal of Technology in Education*, *7*(1), 128–153. DOI: 10.46328/ijte.523

Meniado, J. C. (2023). The Impact of ChatGPT on English language teaching, learning, and assessment: A rapid review of literature. *Arab World English Journal*, *14*(4), 3–18. DOI: 10.24093/awej/vol14no4.1

Mikeladze, T., & Meijer, P. C. (2024). Exploring the Application of Artificial Intelligence in Foreign Language Education within School Settings: Systematic Literature Review. *Journal of Education in Black Sea Region*, *10*(1). Advance online publication. DOI: 10.31578/jebs.v10i1.328

Mohebbi, A. (2024). Enabling learner independence and self-regulation in language education using AI tools: A systematic review. *Cogent Education*, *12*(1), 2433814. Advance online publication. DOI: 10.1080/2331186X.2024.2433814

Moore, R. L., Lee, S. S., Pate, A. T., & Wilson, A. T. (2025). Systematic review of digital microcredentials: Trends in assessment and delivery. *Distance Education*, *46*(1), 1–28. DOI: 10.1080/01587919.2024.2441263

Mutammimah, H., Rejeki, S., Kustini, S., & Amelia, R. (2024). Understanding teachers' perspective towards ChatGPT acceptance in English language teaching. *International Journal of Technology in Education*, *7*(2), 290–307. DOI: 10.46328/ijte.656

Nartey, E. K. (2025). Generative AI in Higher Education:Guiding Principles for Teaching and Learning. DOI: 10.1201/9781003561507

Nguyen, T. H., & Hoang, T. N. H. G. (2025). Investigating the Promises and Perils of Generative AI in EFL Learning in Higher Education: A Literature Review. *AsiaCALL Online Journal*, *16*(1), 1–15. DOI: 10.54855/acoj.251611

Pham, M. T., & Cao, T. X. T. (2025). The Practice of ChatGPT in English Teaching and Learning in Vietnam: A Systematic Review. *International Journal of TESOL & Education*, *5*(1), 50–70. DOI: 10.54855/ijte.25513

Qu, K., & Wu, X. (2024). ChatGPT as a CALL tool in language education: A study of hedonic motivation adoption models in English learning environments. *Education and Information Technologies*, *29*(15), 1–33. DOI: 10.1007/s10639-024-12598-y

Roy, S., & Gandhimathi, S. N. S. (2025). Self-directed learning for optimizing sustainable language learning via mobile assisted language learning: A systematic review. *Frontiers in Education*, *9*, 1463721. Advance online publication. DOI: 10.3389/feduc.2024.1463721

Shaikh, S., Yayilgan, S. Y., Klimova, B., & Pikhart, M. (2023). Assessing the usability of ChatGPT for formal English language learning. *European Journal of Investigation in Health, Psychology and Education*, *13*(9), 1937–1960. DOI: 10.3390/ejihpe13090140 PMID: 37754479

Shaikh, S., Yayilgan, Y., Klimova, B., & Pikhart, M. (2023). settingsOrder Article Reprints Open AccessArticle Assessing the Usability of ChatGPT for Formal English Language Learning. *European Journal of Investigation in Health, Psychology and Education*, *13*(9), 1937–1960. Advance online publication. DOI: 10.3390/ejihpe13090140 PMID: 37754479

Wei, L. (2023). Artificial intelligence in language instruction: Impact on English learning achievement, L2 motivation, and self-regulated learning. *Frontiers in Psychology*, *14*, 1261955. DOI: 10.3389/fpsyg.2023.1261955 PMID: 38023040

Zawacki-Richter, O., Sari, B. C., & Bai, J. Y. H. (2025). Towards reproducible systematic reviews in Open, Distance, and Digital Education—An umbrella mapping review. *Review of Education*, *13*(1), e70031. Advance online publication. DOI: 10.1002/rev3.70031

Chapter 9
Utilizing Artificial Intelligence to Enhance English Language Skills and Areas

Khalefa Kheder
Karabük University, Turkey

Nayef J. Jomaa
https://orcid.org/0000-0001-8952-5812
University of Technology and Applied Sciences, Salalah, Oman

ABSTRACT

This study focuses on artificial intelligence approach to language learning and offers a theoretical framework for extensive approaches to its use in the skills and specific areas of various languages. These modern platforms, tools, and AI methodologies are analyzed in terms of their capability to enhance listening, speaking skills, pronunciation, reading comprehension, writing skills, grammar, and vocabulary. A synthesis of recent empirical investigations and meta-analyses is done within this study, primarily focusing on AI and language education: conversational AI, pronunciation assessment, and customization of learners' experiences. Thus, this study provides substantial evidence that AI-supported learning positively improves language learning. Some meta-analyses reveal medium-to-large effect sizes favoring AI-mediated individualized language learning over traditional learning. This extensive exposition provides insights into language teachers and researchers, instructional designers, and educational technologists to integrate AI into language learning environments.

DOI: 10.4018/979-8-3373-3561-2.ch009

INTRODUCTION

With the rapid progress of AI technologies, the landscape of language learning has been completely transformed (Jomaa, 2025a, 2025b). AI seems to be changing the age-old aspect of language acquisition, that is, instructor-based teaching with fewer practice opportunities and delayed feedback mechanisms, through innovations in personalization, accessibility, and interactivity. It is a far-reaching change in the teaching-learning-and-assessment process of languages around the educational globe.

The application of AI in language learning indicates a fundamentally redesigned learning process itself. AI can analyse learners and their abilities through machine learning algorithms, natural language processing, and speech recognition tools, and adaptive learning strategies can provide accurate, real-time feedback designed to address each specific learner's needs (Qiao & Zhao, 2023). AI's uses and disruptive effect in language learning and education extend across all components or skills (Jomaa, Attamimi, & Al Mahri, 2024), and most major areas of any language. For listening comprehension, AI offers adaptive audio materials that modify material and rate as learners' proficiency increases and provides new ways to listen in a differentiated way. For speaking, artificial conversational tools provide significant practice opportunities within a low-threat environment versus interacting with people. Pronunciation can be improved, corrected, and/or developed with real-time objective feedback requiring algorithms sophisticated enough to judge human speech. By using AI, reading experiences can use our learners' interests and learning goals by curating the materials they may be reading and using to develop their interests and proficiency. Writing can be also supported and honed with real-time grammar checkers (Jomaa & Jibroo, 2024), stylistic suggestions or better word choices. Finally, grammar and vocabulary can be learnt with contextual introduction, with AI-formulated spaced repetition systems (Jomaa et al., 2025).

As a result of the huge effect of AI on varied aspects, particularly education, this study very clearly sets an all-inclusive contextual vista for understanding AI's multidimensional role in language learning through the examination of familiar learning platforms like Duolingo, Babbel, TalkPal, etc. This is particularly valuable for relating their different applications or dimensions to various language skills and integrating research findings on these applications' respective effectiveness. The resulting richly nuanced perspectives on the pros and cons of AI in language education pose relevant questions for researchers, educators, and practitioners.

The considerable potential of AI and its ability to revolutionise language learning includes every major language skill and area of language learning (Kheder, 2025). For comprehension, AI can support learners with adaptive audio materials, adapting for difficulty and speed, as learners become more proficient in listening comprehension. For speaking, conversational AI can provide a plethora of practice opportunities from which the majority of language learners will feel relief from stress and anxiety from human interactions. For pronunciation, pronunciation can receive objective, immediate feedback based on sophisticated speech recognition algorithms from AI. The reading experience can be personalised based on AI-curated materials that reflect learner interests and proficiency levels. Writing skills can be improved through real-time corrections made online, with grammar errors identified and stylistic suggestions made. Last but not least, grammar and vocabulary can be improved through contextual introduction, by AI spaced repetition systems (Jomaa et al, 2024). Consequently, this study presents various lenses to offer some nuanced understandings of the possibilities and limitations of AI in language education, as well as inviting relevant questions that could be considered by researchers, educators and practitioners:

- How effectively can each specific language skill benefit from AI enhancement?
- What evidence supports the effectiveness of AI-mediated language instruction?
- What will the conversational AI experience add to language learning?
- What implications does this have for educational practice?

Moving on in this exploration draws a picture that AI is not merely an adjunctive tool but instead a phenomenon that dismantles and reconstitutes language learning methodology and practice at its most basic levels. The study finds much ground for continued discourse in the analysis of the methodological and pedagogical issues associated with the consideration of AI technologies and their relevant applications, contributing to considering the best way to teach with AI whilst upholding quality and integrity in the language learning methodology.

EFFECTIVENESS OF AI IN LANGUAGE LEARNING: RESEARCH FINDINGS

AI has been extensively researched concerning its impact on language learning, with encouraging results observed across various skills and learner populations. AI-assistance has demonstrated particular effectiveness in improving speaking skills, providing learners with practice opportunities and feedback capabilities that surpass many existing techniques. Studies present significant progress in language proficiency among ESL learners using AI tools. Research indicates beneficial effects of AI-mediated instruction on English learning achievement, learner motivation, and self-regulated learning strategy development. Besides, AI-mediated instruction has successfully enhanced L2 speaking skills and self-regulatory processes in learners, demonstrating the potential of AI technologies for augmenting language learning opportunities. AI has improved learner engagement and provided personalized learning experiences that meet individual needs, ultimately enhancing language proficiency, particularly in speaking and writing.

Indeed, the individualized language learning by AI was effective for learners' overall development in language and showed positive treatment differential against the traditional business-as-usual conditions (Xu & Wang, 2024). This review reported a large average effect size within the groups (d = 1.18) and a medium overall positive treatment effect (d = 0.39), signifying highly significant progress made by language skills and relatively improved performance compared to traditional methods (Lee & Lee, 2024). High effect size for English language learning measure is claimed for AI, meaning that students learning with AI score quite significantly above their counterparts taught using the traditional methods (Xu & Wang, 2024). AI personalized language learning, thus generating the best outputs in student performance and educational competencies. AI brings hope for providing better course completion rates than conventional instructor-designed courses. Another big boost of AI learning is its quick adaptation for personalization, thus boosting learning impact and retention of language skills by the learner. AI requires making use of adaptive exercises for increased efficiency in learning, thereby hastening the way to competency in the language.

Independent studies and big meta-analyses testify to the constancy of positive influence by the AI across different language skills. Therefore, indeed, it possesses tremendous potential as a tool for language education. The stated improvements in speaking, listening, reading, writing, grammar, and vocabulary, with accompanying positive effect sizes in meta-analyses, testify to the affirmative promise that AI holds for foreign language acquisition. Not only do AI-based platforms usually build their motivation and engagement among learners, but they also personalize the learning trajectory with interactive exercises typically found in many AI systems, all of which appeal to learners, keeping them motivated to get involved in practice.

PART ONE: LANGUAGE SKILLS AND AI

Enhancing Listening Comprehension Skills with AI

With the emergence of artificial intelligence, the adaptive nature of auditory materials alongside robust speech recognition has gained priority in developing listening skills amongst students. Neural networks can mimic all the complexities involved in the recognition of natural spoken language and produce authentic audio content with dynamic adjustment to learner progression. Such versatility creates conditions where learners are optimally challenged, just short of overwhelming them, thus offering the greatest opportunities for skill development in a conducive learning atmosphere. Advanced methods of speech recognition can also ensure that comprehension is assessed under learner variations of dialect and accent in preparation for the real environment.

We can integrate such features effectively on AI-enabled platforms. Algorithms analyse individual listening skills and provide exercises targeting each individual's level and pace, along with addressing specific difficulty areas. These systems generate vast listening materials that are samples of varying dialects and accents, thus exposing learners to natural variations in spoken language. AI may control podcast and audiobook playback throughout activities based on levels and contexts of comprehension to ensure accessibility and digestibility of content. Evidence has consistently been in support of the above-mentioned AI technologies. Research on ESL learners reveals a significant difference in listening comprehension with the use of the technologies when compared to traditional methods (Vincent et al., 2025). AI speech recognition software and virtual tutors provide tailored listening instruction, imitating everyday experiences of face-to-face conversation. AI-based TTS systems also provide synthesised speech models that learners themselves can manipulate along the continuum from speed to clarity for the sake of enhanced listening adaptability (Sahito, 2025).

AI tools leverage natural language processing to provide students with dynamic, adaptive listening experiences that emulate real-life interactions. Real-time feedback comes through transcription and activates interactive exercises, allowing students to replay and assess audio input for better understanding of listening comprehension. Google Speech-to-Text and Dragon Naturally Speaking tools allow students to compare their speech with transcribed output for better understanding of spoken language (Integrating AI into Listening Comprehension: Dynamic Approaches for EFL/ESL Learners - EFLCafe.net, 2024).

The adaptability of AI listening materials within proficiency levels stands as an important option compared to static, standard resources. AI sets up listening tasks that are comprehensible with incremental challenge by tracking learner progress and adjusting task difficulty accordingly. Integrated speech recognition systems in listening tasks give feedback on comprehension and sound recognition abilities across different accents. In collaboration with audio outputs, such systems offer feedback to learners in real time, whether they can process spoken language—a vital skill towards communication in real life. Lastly, TTS systems provide additional advantages with audio manipulation abilities such as speed and pitch, which greatly enhance comprehension. Evidence-based research demonstrates that feedback received through speech recognition leads to significant improvements in listening accuracy (Sahito, 2025).

Developing Speaking Skills through Conversational AI

AI has revolutionised the field of speaking fluency with conversational AI. AI-driven, virtual partners become competent in sharing real-time conversations with the learners, thereby allowing them to practise speaking in a realistic atmosphere. Instant feedback is provided to the speakers on their utterance, which is associated with accent or any other aspects to improve speaking; that is, the real-time analysis and feedback practice routine induced by enabling an AI algorithm.

A demonstration of these possibilities is experienced with AI-enabled platforms. Conversational AI permits spoken conversations to take place, which can genuinely aid participants in fluent speech production and speed with live feedback on various points like fluency, pronunciation, grammar, and whatnot. TalkPal, which uses human-like intonation, and LanguaTalk are two conversational platforms that integrate AI and offer highly realistic voice dialogues. Astonishingly realistic AI voices are used by LanguaTalk, each mimicking an authentic human voice. The AI incorporation in Busuu means language learners can engage in speaking practice whilst allowing for authentic, personalised feedback. Through AI conversational, Wall Street English creates a low-pressure environment simulating real-world conditions that are integrated by rich natural language processing/NLP and multimedia, thereby contributing to the learning endeavour. The AI chatbots are empirically shown to increase language skills for fluency and vocabulary after a considerable amount of practice. This is because the chatbots provide practice in conversational contexts, giving immediate feedback at any time a user needs it (Safar & Anggraheni, 2024).

Little or no pressure exists for developing anxiety in speaking foreign languages in the presence of AI chatbots, therefore sustaining self-awareness and confidence amongst learners who wish to venture into oral practice where no judgements are made against them (Xiao et al., 2024). Hence, with this "Fluency First" approach, LanguaTalk suggests that expressions in a new language become natural through AI teacher conversation and feedback. Speak, conversely, provides an AI tutor in addition to being a language platform that is equipped to give the user near fluency in conversation through immediate feedback on conversational speech, and then continues training by designing a tailored curriculum for the personalized needs of the individual. Talkio AI, another celebrated approach in AI language learning, offers AI tutors and speaking technology focused on pronunciation improvement. In the working intelligence of Busuu, AI tutors operate in real-human conversation settings where language students are exposed to different accents and speech variations, thus enabling students to gain more fluency.

The Role of Conversational AI in Language Education: Research Insights

Conversational AI research in language education looked at AI chatbots and/or virtual tutors as effective strategies for implementation into language learning environments. Indeed, studies have covered various aspects of interaction between teachers, students, and AI, the cognitive load of learners, the emotional implications of the use of conversational AI, and the prospects of working together between AI and human teachers. For example, the potential study on conversational AI in language learning brought up by future educators aimed to examine their perceptions and level of readiness in using the technology (Belda-Medina & Calvo-Ferrer, 2022). Results indicate that AI chatbots are assumed to play a highly significant role in the improvement of language skills, especially in conversational fluency and vocabulary mastery, while the interaction would impose a moderate cognitive load on learners. This cognitive load level is found to depend on some personal characteristics of learners, perfect proficiency in the target language, and perhaps previous experience with AI tools (Safar & Anggraheni, 2024).

AI-based chatbots also come with several affordances in language education- for personalized instructions with speedy feedback, reducing the anxiety generally associated with talking in another language, motivating and inspiring learner autonomy (Xiao et al., 2024). In such a situation, conversational AI can act as a provider of a variety of resources, giving diagnostic information regarding a learner's vocabulary ability and conversational proficiency. Some of these complex systems can even vary their difficulty level and provide adaptive feedback according to their assessment of the learner (Ji, Han, & Ko, 2023). Meanwhile, systematic reviews of research so far have explored the future of cooperation between conversational AIs and human teachers in language instruction. The present situation does not provide ample evidence of collaboration; however, the review asserts that the fine neural network for their use should lie in increasing integrated language use in favor of intelligence amplification for teachers and diminishing their workload through orchestration in the classroom situation (Ji et al., 2023).

AI-powered chatbots may also be trained as virtual tutors to provide personalized learning to students anytime, anywhere, and on any single day of their choosing. Research has investigated the interaction of this cooperative framework in teacher-student discourse in foreign language classrooms with conversational AI applications such as Google Assistant. It was established from research that a deciding factor in achieving effective interaction between students and AI lies with the teacher. Moreover, conversational AI can provide a simulated scenario for authentic language interaction, hence allowing the learner to practice speaking and writing in a safe and risk-free environment.

There are several advantages in using conversational AI, such as personalized practice and lowering the anxiety of a learner, but one must also focus on the cognitive load that it applies to learners. Evidence indicates that conversing with AI chatbots potentially yields much improvement in fluency and vocabulary, but a moderate cognitive load is imposed on learners in general. Therefore, every stage of design must be directed toward minimizing cognitive overload so that learning is promoted. Prior experience of learning the language at earlier stages and informal exposure to AI tools could lead to differences in the levels of cognitive load experienced (Safar & Anggraheni, 2024). Also, AI and human teacher collaboration is an emerging research area. Current evidence regarding deep collaboration at this time may not yet be very convincing (Ji et al., 2023); however, it is now increasingly clear that AI does not intend to replace education but augment it.

AI for Pronunciation Skills Mastery

AI tools have revolutionized pronunciation learning by providing real-time analysis, corrections, immediate feedback, and targeted suggestions for improvement. Advanced speech recognition technologies can detect deviations from standard pronunciation patterns, enabling learners to correct their pronunciation immediately and achieve language mastery.

Various AI applications are used in pronunciation training, including Rosetta Stone AI and Pronounce. Both utilize artificial intelligence speech recognition to provide real-time feedback on learners' pronunciation. Babbel incorporates AI-powered speech recognition to deliver personalized feedback, drawing from extensive audio data libraries. AI continuously monitors pronunciation training, analyzing intonation patterns and overall fluency from speech sounds. Phoneme recognition technology can identify minor pronunciation errors, and AI algorithms compare learners' speech patterns to native speaker models, providing comparative feedback to meet correct pronunciation standards. Pronounce is an application tailored for learner speaking skill improvement, offering real-time speech analytics and an AI chatbot for interactive practice experience. ELSA Speak applies speech recognition technology, enabling learners to receive detailed feedback and scoring after each exercise to track progress. Speechling helps users improve spoken English using AI-driven pronunciation analysis and accent reduction techniques, allowing real-time checking of their inputs against native speaker samples. Google's Pronunciation Tool provides visual feedback on lip movements and tongue placement for learners to understand the physical aspects of pronunciation.

TalkPal provides word-by-word pronunciation assessment with immediate feedback on pronunciation, intonation, and rhythm. Besides, GetPronounce functions as an AI speech coach with machine learning-powered speech feedback, addressing pronunciation and grammar issues. Speechace focuses on speech recognition technology for pronunciation and fluency evaluation, providing students with targeted feedback on their mistakes. Research indicates that AI-based speech recognition technologies prove more effective than traditional methods in improving pronunciation skills (Dja'far & Hamidah, 2024). Microsoft's Pronunciation Assessment tool also provides detailed accuracy measurements for learners' pronunciation.

Personalized and instant feedback from AI-infused pronunciation devices greatly enhances how much a learner can polish their spoken accent for clearer speaking. Perhaps the most telling indication of its growing acceptance is in countries where apps such as ELSA Speak, Pronounce, and Speechling are gaining rapid popularity, as well as in Babbel and TalkPal's recent addition of pronunciation-matching feedback to their services. This kind of corrective feedback takes place in real time, allowing the learner to notice the error and correct it immediately, thus facilitating learning much faster than the often seriously delayed responses from human teachers. A myriad of other things have also been very useful in this tool, including things like comparison to native speakers or more in-depth, detailed phonetics analysis, allowing the learner even a really fine detail of understanding the nuances of pronunciation, rather than just finding errors, providing them with an entire picture of how their spoken language differs from that of speakers.

AI has made inroads in the field of pronunciation assessment and feedback; hence, research has been conducted investigating its accuracy and effectiveness. These studies analyzed its capability of evaluating pronunciation along the dimensions of accuracy, fluency, and intelligibility, among others, in many instances comparing the performance of an AI with human assessors. AI tools have been capable of evaluating pronunciation concerning aspects of accuracy, fluency, and intelligibility as understood by second-language learners. AI models analyze the acoustic features of speech, such as pitch, intensity, and duration, to give valid feedback on the learners' pronunciation. The breathtaking advancement of deep learning could intensify the competitive arena for neural network modelling, predicting pronunciation with very close accuracy to human experts. The objectivity of AI tools thus stands as one strong point concerning their use in pronunciation assessment in that they guard against human arbitrariness; they can set parameters for a uniform evaluation of pronunciation, thus protecting against bias and ensuring objectivity and consistency for pronunciation feedback (Khurshedjonovna, 2025).

Some studies have also focused on assessing the effectiveness of AI tools as partners in English pronunciation training, indicating that AI technology could have great potential, while there still exist some challenges in maintaining speech recognition accuracy for many accents and performing accurate processing for more complicated speech contexts (Lyu & Andi, 2025). Some studies have explored the effect of combining an approach of peer correction with ASR (Automatic Speech

Recognition) on pronunciation enhancement for EFL students. In this respect, it has been observed that learners' anxiety during oral practice may be alleviated via the ASR application (Rogti, 2025). Further, several studies have shown that AI-integrated speech recognition offers a more effective way of enhancing learners' pronunciation skills in English than conventional methods (Dja'far & Hamidah, 2024). AI in pronunciation training presents a big opportunity for personalization. AI could formulate access and individualized learning pathways and give learners instant feedback, highly likely to transform traditional language-learning environments (Zhao, 2024). These AI-driven assessment systems have been designed to assess different language skills, pronunciation included, based on learner input from different areas of linguistics. AI pronunciation assistants provide learners with ample opportunities for pronunciation practice and instant individualized feedback in almost real-time, which can prove extremely helpful for nonnatives in reducing their first language's interference in pronunciation (Selladurai & Pandey, 2024).

However, some studies indicate that the implementation of AI in the form of speech recognition technology offers possibilities for EFL learners to enhance pronunciation and speaking skills through self-study and independent practice (Dennis, 2024). In addition, AI speech programs providing automatic feedback assist EFL learners in different avenues, where many have reported improvement in pronunciation skills (Zou et al., 2023). The results from the assessment of AI will largely change pronunciation training pedagogy and student livelihood across the language learning space (Yesilyurt, 2023).

AI has achieved a remarkable level of precision in pronunciation assessment, and certain advanced models reach performance levels that are close to humans. The building of deep learning models capable of estimating pronunciation employing almost human-like performance offers a powerful testimony for the extreme march AI has attained in spoken-language assessment. This precision permits the use of AI as a reliable and vigorous assessment for providing objective and intensive feedback to the learner on pronunciation. Besides this, AI offers some extra benefits in conducting objective pronunciation evaluation, like getting rid of human bias and ensuring consistent evaluation. Instead of an occasional scenario, when evaluators attempt to limit themselves to common criteria for their judgments and unwittingly insert some subjective bias into their evaluations, AI follows its objective scales for all learners and applies common criteria. Such objectivity could lead to fairer and more reliable evaluations of pronunciation. Noteworthy, though, some evident challenges that are worthy of mention remain, such as accurately assessing pronunciation from so many different accents and not recognizing some nuances of spontaneous speech (Khurshedjonovna, 2025).

Personalized Reading Skills Development with AI

With AI, personalization of reading materials may be implemented—the crafting of reading materials painstakingly targeted towards a learner's proficiency level and interests—and this in turn facilitates comprehension building of reading. Such personalization allows the learners a chance to work with materials that are both comprehensible and motivating, thereby creating a more pleasant and effective learning experience (Hidayat, 2024). Moreover, AI allows, for instance, the setting of interactive tools, through which a learner can work dynamically on a text using features like on-demand vocabulary support, contextual definitions, and the ability to pose questions about the content.

Some of these functions may be included in various AI-enabled products, such as LingQ, which uses AI to provide authentic reading materials, exposing learners to various genres and writing styles. AI's adaptive algorithms can personalize learning paths by dynamically adjusting difficulty levels and selecting reading materials according to learner proficiency development (Kabudi et al., 2021). This adaptive approach prevents learners from encountering texts that are either too advanced or insufficiently challenging. So, AI can modulate reading materials depending upon the personal needs and proficiency levels of learners, so that they can progress in the way and pace that they assume fit. Examples of such platforms are Sora and Epic, which use AI to recommend titles based on the student's level of reading and stated interests to ensure that students are reading texts they can comprehend and enjoy.

Readlang uses artificial intelligence to provide instant assistance to learners in learning a language through English texts, giving translation outputs while highlighting key vocabulary and language statistics to aid comprehension and vocabulary building (Topal, 2025). Amira Learning also uses AI to assess the reading level of a learner and then supplies adjusted reading materials tailored to the learner, even for bilinguals, through strategic cognates to facilitate their understanding in both languages. Numerous studies have shown that reading platforms personalized through AI will raise reading comprehension abilities to a greater extent in language learners (Hidayat, 2024). Major reasons for this were that making learning personalized by adjusting learning input according to the needs of each learner is the most powerful tool (Allehyani et al., 2025). One of the most important concerns regarding AI settings of reading comprehension materials is that there are challenges, with wrong verbs used, or unnatural expressions generated, which could all be solved here to weed out this inauthenticity and uphold the quality (Allaithy & Zaki, 2025). Tools such as Twee for Teachers and Diffit have been developed to help teachers construct differentiated reading materials for differing proficiency levels- one of the easiest ways to cater to the diverse needs of students. They may also choose the reading level of articles they wish to receive for their classes in Newsela, allowing students to read the same article but at different levels of challenge.

AI can assess the reading ability and other preferences of a learner to produce improved reading material that shall be less complex but far more interesting. With the above examples of personalization, like in Sora and ReadTheory (Hidayat, 2024), learners do not confront either challenging, overly complicated texts, or unchallenging ones, thus promoting engagement and comprehension. The function of immediate translations and vocabulary highlights at Readlang serves as a case illustration of how AI would provide timely support, which promotes free reading, diminishes frustration and helps promote comprehension and vocabulary building. Comprehension quizzes with instant feedback provided by the AI tools reinforce understanding.

The advent of AI into language instructional technology has brought up many new ventures that can enhance students' reading comprehension. With a thorough exploration of the subject, it appears such technologies would offer an alternative personalized medium for both learning and interaction with second-language students-constructing themselves around an individual's strengths within a pedagogical environment conducive to the adoption of fluctuating levels for the successful comprehension of the intended learner. Most scrutiny has focused on personalization of the learning experience, thus infusing several types of lesson content and accompanying varying levels of difficulty away of students' individual needs;1, nowadays rendering from AI-assisted borderless learning methodologies-from inclusive WhatsApp chat lists upward to platforms of improvement, with a very nice jump in supporting the understanding of their reading materials in the English language among learners (Allehyani et al., 2025). Writing has always been a potential field in which AI could disallow the most varied box of teaching materials, whereas reading comprehension exercises of divergent levels of proficiency are some of them (Allaithy & Zaki, 2025).

The very aim of AI in education is to foster the development of the factors that are conducive to giving the student more generous, freer, and motivating circumstances in reading. This being the case, learning experiences and some courses now rendered by AI might be adaptable and, whenever required, temporarily grouped based on emerging linguistics-related specific needs of the learner through charts and graphs. Such systems could make reading material recommendations aligning with learners' interests and reading levels- an admirable addition to the job Lightsailed does with other reading accommodation suggestions, as requested for a very capable reading learner, to the current reading level. The research findings indicate that with AI support, the classroom setup aids considerably in enhancing language learners' reading comprehension skills (Fattah et al., 2023). In comparison to traditional instructional methods, AI instructional methods demonstrated that students developed proficient English reading comprehension at a higher rate (Wei, 2023). Systematic reviews established that AI in individualized computer-assisted learning improved the entire language learning of a learner positively including reading skills (Lee & Lee, 2024).

Moreover, the learning-in-shadow approach with ChatGPT might provide authentic text simplification to enhance the accessibility of reading comprehension to learners (Çelik et al., 2024). Adapted reading curricula are one area where AI applications have moved from theory to practice. Provided with a good learning environment, applications trained by AI could offer an excellent opportunity to educate learners most efficiently, cutting across individual needs. Here, the system would recommend reading material among learners' interests and reading capabilities- an additional unique application for technology, which can be naturally integrated into the aforementioned load of steps toward learning through a nice solution. According to studies, enhancements in reading comprehension levels of language learners are allowed by AI when it is integrated within their traditional school environment.

Improving Writing Skills with AI Assistance

AI, trained with datasets until October 2023, represents huge support for the development of writing skills and has opened dedicated pages or sites to support its users during the process of writing by making suggestions about sentence construction, grammar, and vocabulary enhancement (Chen et al., 2020). Suggestions and feedback to improve written works are offered by AI tools so that learners are always upgrading their writing skills. Such features are now found in many AI applications and tools. Whilst students write, AI provides live feedback for grammar and writing to prompt correction and suggestions (Jomaa & Jibroo, 2024). Tools like Grammarly and QuillBot support learners by providing suggestions and corrections to improve their writing. A full-fledged writing assistant, Grammarly provides feedback on grammar, punctuation, and style in real-time. Paperpal uses AI to assist in academic writing, offering grammar checking, paraphrasing to improve fluency and tone, research assistance, and citation support. Wordvice AI also offers a complete suite of AI-assisted products, including editing, paraphrasing, translation, summarizing, and plagiarism checking, addressing various writing needs. Studies establish that AI-writing tools can support the students' writing quality, content, and organization, whilst consensus amongst educators declares that such tools foster positive development of both content and structure amongst the students during their writing tasks (Jomaa, 2025c).

In addition, AI tools may focus on improving students' writing in terms of grammar and syntax, conscious word choice suggestions and style consistency. It has been noted that AI-assisted tailoring feedback for various parameters like language, grammar, and overall writing structure provides immense potential to enhance writing skills amongst students (Strobl et al., 2019). For instance, Write & Improve uses instant feedback to teach students about core issues involving grammar, vocabulary, and coherence in their written work. FeedbackFruits' Automated Feedback tool specifically deals with mechanical and structural challenges within academic writing, providing real-time formative feedback. In accord with these constructs, Paperpal assists with aligning academic sentence structures. Another AI-powered writing tool, which is gaining popularity in the writing process, is Wordtune. These AI-enabled writing tools deliver prompt, specific, and predictable feedback regarding the different features of writing. This allows students to identify and correct errors throughout their work, rather than having to wait for feedback in a more traditional sense. The real-time feedback provided by tools like Grammarly and Paperpal helps set in motion learning cycles within which the learners can obtain immediate recognition of errors and corrections, thereby speeding up their learning. In addition to spotting and correcting errors, style, vocabulary, and sentence structure improvements are suggested. As mentioned in Snippet 52 and Snippet 51, AI can recommend new word choices, clarify sentence structure, and maintain consistent style and tone throughout the text. It is that particularity of AI to guide students with suggestions and recommendations that nurture the transition away from error proofing to a much higher conscious writing style. AI tools for writing may also help with creative suggestions and expand on any first ideas to curb accidental redundancy in the writing (Marzuki et al., 2023).

PART TWO: LANGUAGE AREAS AND AI

AI-Driven Grammar Acquisition

Machine Learning applies AI to enhance grammar correction through contextual introduction and personalized learning approaches. These tools are effective not just for mere memorization but for creating a systematic understanding of grammatical structures according to the usage patterns and learning needs of an individual (Chen et al.,2020).

Grammar AI applications are machine-learning-based tools that analyze spoken and written language to detect grammatical errors committed by language learners while making corrective suggestions. They monitor frequently errors made by learners and tailor exercises to target such errors by adjusting the difficulty of the given practice. AI combines grammar error identification and presentation with suggestions to correct such errors for language accuracy development. Their consideration for every common error, like subject-verb agreement, has exhibited encouraging results and is continuously adapting to the grammar style of the individual to offer highly personalized feedback. From a theoretical perspective, however, there is a lot to be said for these applications being able to gloss texts into standard English and analyze a variety of different languages for multilingual support. With that system capability, they should also be effectively detecting and replacing word slang and colloquial language measures with an appropriate English equivalent. Systems incorporate the notion of identifying grammar weaknesses of the learner in a particular area to subsequently target exercises to the same, thus ensuring focused practice.

This private and personal analysis may view data as individualized exercises in grammar that emphasize specific functions in need of improvement by the learner, besides personal interests. Therefore, every activity done by such learners seems to be a greater promise for improvement, thus making such a learning process more efficient and effective. AI solutions endowed with contextual examples and usage scenarios would empower the students with finer shades of grammatical understanding and application, culminating in improved retention and a good capacity for fluent application of their grammar knowledge.

AI-Enhanced Vocabulary Acquisition

AI enhances vocabulary acquisition through contextual introduction of new vocabulary and personalized vocabulary lists according to usage patterns and interests. These tools move beyond traditional memorization methods to create meaningful vocabulary learning experiences. AI suggests contextually introducing vocabulary and personalizing vocabulary lists according to usage patterns and the interests declared by the user. Such AI applications help in comprehending the construction of vocabulary lists from different sources: articles, videos, or textbooks, thus making clear meanings and examples visible to every vocabulary word. AI vocabulary builders often utilize flashcards containing native example sentences in multiple languages, providing essential context for vocabulary acquisition. AI tools also suggest vocabulary based on common learner mistakes and topics of interest, making the learning process more engaging and relevant (Jomaa, Attamimi, & Al Mahri, 2024).

Besides, the insertion of new vocabulary in relevant contexts and real-life case examples helps the learners understand not only the meaning of the new words but also how they are used in real communication contexts. Such practice has proven more potent in contrasting memorization of a word to learning through sentences and in actual situations. Hence, AI solutions endowed with such contextual examples and usage scenarios would empower the students with finer shades of word meaning and application, culminating in improved retention and a good capacity for fluent application of their vocabulary. The learner's saved word can then also be turbo-injected by AI into conversations at a later stage to reinforce the learner's uptake and use (Settles & Meeder, 2016).

AI is integrated into the fabric of language learning, leading to the development of many platforms and tools specifically designed to address every aspect of language acquisition. These comprehensive solutions incorporate various AI technologies to provide learners with adaptive learning experiences. Duolingo, for example, represents a gamified platform that utilizes AI for personalized learning pathways. The platform develops exercises centered on writing, reading, and listening competencies, making it highly adaptable to EFL students' needs. Babbel also emphasizes real-life and everyday conversations with AI-backed speech recognition through its "Everyday Conversations" feature. HelloTalk incorporates chatbots for additional practice while connecting users with native speakers for language exchange. Further, Voxy provides adaptable, AI-powered lessons for language training according to student's proficiency and objectives.

CONCLUSION

AI applications are employed in a rapidly evolving environment where technology and pedagogy converge to develop learning experiences that are more engaging, accessible, and personalized than ever before. Throughout this study, we have examined how AI technologies enhance different language skills and areas. Across these different skills and areas, we observe AI's adaptability and its potential for addressing many challenges in language education.

The findings show consistently favorable outcomes for AI-assisted language teaching and learning. Meta-analyses demonstrate significant effect sizes, with one review reporting a large average within-group effect size ($d = 1.18$) and a medium overall positive treatment effect ($d = 0.39$) compared to traditional methods (Lee & Lee, 2024). Studies indicate that students learning with AI score significantly above their counterparts taught using traditional methods (Xu & Wang, 2024). AI personalized language learning, generating improved outcomes in student performance and educational competencies. AI offers better course completion rates than conventional instructor-designed courses. The rapid adaptation capability of AI for personalization boosts learning impact and retention of language skills. AI utilizes adaptive exercises for increased learning efficiency, accelerating the path to language competency.

Conversational AI is one of the most promising advances in the field because of the authentic practice of language in a low-pressure environment. All of the reviewed studies suggested that conversational AI would be effective in enhancing the speaking confidence and fluency of learners while simultaneously reducing the anxiety so often associated with language production, albeit a moderate cognitive load may be also placed upon the learners. Similarly, assessments of pronunciation using AI offer objective feedback, which may more consistently guide learners in developing their articulation, particularly with recent advancements in deep learning that have given birth to neural network models capable of judging pronunciation correctness close to expert human levels.

Nonetheless, implementation challenges are recognized in this study. The challenges of establishing an AI's capability to assess a range of language issues, whether it is adjustable to accounts of various accents and dialects, and if it can be effectively integrated with human scaffolding instructions are therefore still subjects that need deeper investigation and refinement. Limited evidence for deep collaboration between the different conversational AIs and human teacher roles exists, as shown by systematic reviews, implying that a blended learning method may better obtain the desired outcomes for AI rather than being an alternative to an instructor.

The very fact that very short of language education, AI would play an ever-increasingly influential role in how languages are taught and acquired appears a certainty. Personalization, instant feedback, and limitless opportunity for practice are some of the key characteristics of AI technologies that have tried to solve all these problems in the history of language education. Some of the implementations already in their infancy and which were mentioned throughout the chapter range from LingQ, TalkPal, ELSA Speak, among many others. However, these technologies should be integrated strategically based on specific pedagogical frameworks that guarantee the support of meaningful technological innovation in communicating and understanding culture.

AI has become the most revolutionary factor in language learning, granting it a plethora of opportunities never seen before to enhance efficient, effective, and accessible language education. Research will continue to optimize implementation practices, whilst changes in AI technologies will provide further innovations that may themselves reshape language learning in the 21st century. Critical thoughts concerning these innovations should involve educators, researchers, and learners to enable the unlocking of the great potential that AI holds for language learning contexts.

REFERENCES

Allaithy, A., & Zaki, M. (2025). Evaluation of AI-generated reading comprehension materials for Arabic language teaching. *Computer Assisted Language Learning*, •••, 1–33. DOI: 10.1080/09588221.2025.2474037

Allehyani, B., Almashy, A., Jamshed, M., & Banu, S. (2025). Measuring the impact of Meta-AI on English reading comprehension score enhancement: A study within a social media application. *Theory and Practice in Language Studies*, *15*(2), 615–623. DOI: 10.17507/tpls.1502.31

Belda-Medina, J., & Calvo-Ferrer, J. R. (2022). Using chatbots as AI conversational partners in language learning. *Applied Sciences (Basel, Switzerland)*, *12*(17), 8427. DOI: 10.3390/app12178427

Çelik, F., Yangın Ersanlı, C., & Arslanbay, G. (2024). Does AI simplification of authentic blog texts improve reading comprehension, inferencing, and anxiety? A one-shot intervention in the Turkish EFL context. *International Review of Research in Open and Distance Learning*, *25*(3), 287–303. DOI: 10.19173/irrodl.v25i3.7779

Chen, L., Chen, P., & Lin, Z. (2020). Artificial intelligence in education: A review. *IEEE Access : Practical Innovations, Open Solutions*, *8*, 75264–75278. DOI: 10.1109/ACCESS.2020.2988510

Dennis, N. K. (2024). Using AI-powered speech recognition technology to improve English pronunciation and speaking skills. *IAFOR Journal of Education*, *12*(2), 107–126. DOI: 10.22492/ije.12.2.05

Dja'far, V. H., & Hamidah, F. N. (2024). Improving English pronunciation skills through AI-based speech recognition technology. *Ethical Lingua. Journal of Language Teaching and Literature*, *11*(2).

Fattah, H. A., Vadivel, B., Shaban, A. A., & Shanmugam, K. (2023). Enhancing English language education: The impact of AI integration in the classroom. *The Journal of Humanistic Education and Development*, *5*(6), 116–123.

Hidayat, M. T. (2024). Effectiveness of AI-Based Personalised Reading Platforms in Enhancing Reading Comprehension. *Journal of Learning for Development*, *11*(1), 115–125. DOI: 10.56059/jl4d.v11i1.955

Integrating AI into listening comprehension: Dynamic approaches for EFL/ESL learners. (2024). *EFLCafe.net*. https://eflcafe.net/integrating-ai-into-listening-comprehension-dynamic-approaches-for-efl-esl-learners/

Ji, H., Han, I., & Ko, Y. (2023). A systematic review of conversational AI in language education: Focusing on the collaboration with human teachers. *Journal of Research on Technology in Education*, *55*(1), 48–63. DOI: 10.1080/15391523.2022.2142873

Jomaa, N., Attamimi, R., & Al Mahri, M. (2024). Utilising Artificial Intelligence (AI) in Vocabulary Learning by EFL Omani Students: The Effect of Age, Gender, and Level of Study. *Forum for Linguistic Studies*, *6*(5), 171–186. DOI: 10.30564/fls.v6i5.6968

Jomaa, N., Attamimi, R., & Al Mahri, M. (2025). The Use of Artificial Intelligence (AI) in Teaching English Vocabulary in Oman: Perspectives, Teaching Practices, and Challenges. *World Journal of English Language*, *15*(3), 1–13. DOI: 10.5430/wjel.v15n3p1

Jomaa, N., Attamimi, R., & Alghafri, K. (2025). Vocabulary Learning Strategies Utilised by EFL Omani Students in Oman: The Effect of Age, Gender, and Levels of Study. *Forum for Linguistic Studies*, *7*(2), 967–987. DOI: 10.30564/fls.v7i2.8450

Jomaa, N., & Jibroo, H. (2024). Corrective Feedback of Grammarly in Enhancing L2 Writing by EFL Kurdish Students. [BAES]. *Bulletin of Advanced English Studies*, *9*(1), 1–15. DOI: 10.31559/BAES2024.9.1.1

Jomaa, N. J. (Ed.). (2025a). *Using AI Tools in Text Analysis, Simplification, Classification, and Synthesis*. IGI Global., DOI: 10.4018/979-8-3693-9511-0

Jomaa, N. J. (2025c). Corrective Feedback of AI Tools in Writing and Translation. In *Using AI Tools in Text Analysis, Simplification, Classification, and Synthesis* (pp. 295-320). IGI Global Scientific Publishing. DOI: 10.4018/979-8-3693-9511-0.ch010

Kabudi, T., Pappas, I., & Olsen, D. H. (2021). AI-enabled adaptive learning systems: A systematic mapping of the literature. *Computers and Education: Artificial Intelligence*, *2*, 100017. DOI: 10.1016/j.caeai.2021.100017

Khurshedjonovna, O. S. (2025). AI technologies for assessing students' pronunciation. *Web of Humanities: Journal of Social Science and Humanitarian Research*, *3*(2), 163–167.

Lee, H., & Lee, J. H. (2024). The effects of AI-guided individualised language learning: A meta-analysis. *Language Learning & Technology*, *28*(2), 134–162. https://hdl.handle.net/10125/73575. DOI: 10.64152/10125/73575

Lyu, J., & Andi, H. K. (2025). Effectiveness of AI-driven tools in improving English pronunciation training. *Region: Educational Research and Reviews*, *7*(1), 56–58.

Marzuki, W., Widiati, U., Rusdin, D., Darwin, , & Indrawati, I. (2023). The impact of AI writing tools on the content and organisation of students' writing: EFL teachers' perspective. *Cogent Education, 10*(2), 2236469. DOI: 10.1080/2331186X.2023.2236469

Qiao, H., & Zhao, A. (2023). Artificial intelligence-based language learning: Illuminating the impact on speaking skills and self-regulation in Chinese EFL context. *Frontiers in Psychology, 14*, 1255594. DOI: 10.3389/fpsyg.2023.1255594 PMID: 38022973

Rogti, M. (2025). Automatic pronunciation evaluation, feedback and peer correction for shaping English pronunciation accuracy and interpersonal communication. *Innovation in Language Learning and Teaching*, •••, 1–17. DOI: 10.1080/17501229.2025.2475931

Safar, M., & Anggraheni, D. (2024). Language learning through AI chatbots: Effectiveness and cognitive load analysis. *Journal of Social Science Utilising Technology, 2*(3), 430–445.

Sahito, J. K. M., Panwar, A. H., & Ramzan, I. (2025). Exploring the impact of artificial intelligence (AI) on the listening skills of English as a second language (ESL) learners. *Journal of Applied Linguistics and TESOL, 8*(1), 1059–1067.

Selladurai, S., & Pandey, D. P. (2024). The role of an AI tool in polishing English pronunciation skills for non-native speakers. *International Journal of Communication Networks and Information Security, 16*(1, Special Issue), 1455--1467. https://ijcnis.org/index.php/ijcnis/article/view/7190

Settles, B., & Meeder, B. (2016, August). A trainable spaced repetition model for language learning. In *Proceedings of the 54th annual meeting of the association for computational linguistics* (volume 1*: long papers)* (pp. 1848-1858). DOI: 10.18653/v1/P16-1174

Strobl, C., Ailhaud, E., Benetos, K., Devitt, A., Kruse, O., Proske, A., & Rapp, C. (2019). Digital support for academic writing: A review of technologies and pedagogies. *Computers & Education, 131*, 33–48. DOI: 10.1016/j.compedu.2018.12.005

Topal, I. H. (2025). A review of Readlang: Multilingual e-reader for language learners. *Journal of Digital Educational Technology, 5*(1), ep2504. DOI: 10.30935/jdet/15857

Vincent, J., Yunus, M. M., & Said, N. E. M. (2025). Using AI platforms to improve listening and speaking skills in ESL primary students. *International Journal of Academic Research in Progressive Education and Development, 14*(1), 1829–1843. DOI: 10.6007/IJARPED/v14-i1/24848

Wei, L. (2023). Artificial intelligence in language instruction: Impact on English learning achievement, L2 motivation, and self-regulated learning. *Frontiers in Psychology, 14*, 1261955. DOI: 10.3389/fpsyg.2023.1261955 PMID: 38023040

Xiao, Y., Zhang, T., & He, J. (2024). A review of promises and challenges of AI-based chatbots in language education through the lens of learner emotions. *Heliyon*.

Xu, T., & Wang, H. (2024). The effectiveness of artificial intelligence on English language learning achievement. *System, 125*, 103428. DOI: 10.1016/j.system.2024.103428

Yesilyurt, Y. E. (2023). AI-enabled assessment and feedback mechanisms for language learning: Transforming pedagogy and learner experience. In *Transforming the language teaching experience in the age of AI* (pp. 25–43). IGI Global. DOI: 10.4018/978-1-6684-9893-4.ch002

Zhao, Y. (2024). The exploration of artificial intelligence in pronunciation teaching. In *Proceedings of the 1st International Conference on Data Science and Engineering* -- Volume 1*: ICDSE* (pp. 127--131). SciTePress. DOI: 10.5220/0012829100004547

Zou, B., Du, Y., Wang, Z., Chen, J., & Zhang, W. (2023). An investigation into artificial intelligence speech evaluation programs with automatic feedback for developing EFL learners' speaking skills. *SAGE Open, 13*(3), 21582440231193818. DOI: 10.1177/21582440231193818

ADDITIONAL READING

Abbate, C. Scaffidi (2025). Humanoid interfaces in artificial intelligence-based language learning devices: Possible 'Uncanny Valley' effects? *Acta Psychologica, 256*, ISSN 0001-6918, DOI: 10.1016/j.actpsy.2025.104997

Abidine, M.Z.E. (2025). Integrating generative Artificial Intelligence (GAI) into the teaching-learning of French as a Foreign Language (FLE). *Supporting Personalized Learning and Students' Skill Development With AI*, 329-342, DOI: 10.4018/979-8-3693-8965-2.ch016

Alharbi, J. M. (2025). Adoption of Artificial Intelligence Tools for English Language Learning Among Saudi EFL University Students: The Moderating Role of Faculty. *Journal of Ecohumanism, 4*(2), 804-819, ISSN 2752-6798, DOI: 10.62754/joe.v4i2.6349

Coşgun, G. Erdem (2025). Artificial intelligence literacy in assessment: Empowering pre-service teachers to design effective exam questions for language learning. *British Educational Research Journal*, ISSN 0141-1926, DOI: 10.1002/berj.4177

Feng, L. (2025). Investigating the Effects of Artificial Intelligence-Assisted Language Learning Strategies on Cognitive Load and Learning Outcomes: A Comparative Study. *Journal of Educational Computing Research, 62*(8), 1961-1994, ISSN 0735-6331, DOI: 10.1177/07356331241268349

Gupta, A. (2025). Evolution of patient education materials from large-language artificial intelligence models on complex regional pain syndrome: are patients learning? *Baylor University Medical Center Proceedings*, ISSN 0899-8280, DOI: 10.1080/08998280.2025.2470033

Hou, L. (2025). Unboxing the intersections between self-esteem and academic mindfulness with test emotions, psychological wellness and academic achievement in artificial intelligence-supported learning environments: Evidence from English as a foreign language learners. *British Educational Research Journal*, ISSN 0141-1926, DOI: 10.1002/berj.4146

Huertas-Abril, C. A. (2025). Artificial intelligence-assisted language learning for all in the new global context: Threats and opportunities. *The Routledge Handbook of Endangered and Minority Languages*, 355-376, DOI: 10.4324/9781003439493-27

Kheder, K. (2025). Using Artificial Intelligence in Learning Vocabulary by EFL Undergraduate Syrian Students. In *Using AI Tools in Text Analysis, Simplification, Classification, and Synthesis* (pp. 131-160). IGI Global Scientific Publishing. DOI: 10.4018/979-8-3693-9511-0.ch005

Khoso, A. K. (2025). Empowering creativity and engagement: The impact of generative artificial intelligence usage on Chines EFL students' language learning experience. *Computers in Human Behavior Reports, 18*, ISSN 2451-9588, DOI: 10.1016/j.chbr.2025.100627

Li, Y. (2025). Design language learning with artificial intelligence (AI) chatbots based on activity theory from a systematic review. *Smart Learning Environments, 12*(1), ISSN 2196-7091, DOI: 10.1186/s40561-025-00379-0

Lin, Y. (2025). Learner Perceptions of Artificial Intelligence-Generated Pedagogical Agents in Language Learning Videos: Embodiment Effects on Technology Acceptance. *International Journal of Human-Computer Interaction, 41*(2), 1606-1627, ISSN 1044-7318, DOI: 10.1080/10447318.2024.2359222

Luo, H. (2025). The Application of Artificial Intelligence in the Design of Medical Students' Foreign Language Micro Video Learning Platform. *Proceedings of SPIE - The International Society for Optical Engineering, 13447*, ISSN 0277-786X, DOI: 10.1117/12.3045776

Ma, M. (2025). Exploring the acceptance of generative artificial intelligence for language learning among EFL postgraduate students: An extended TAM approach. *International Journal of Applied Linguistics (United Kingdom), 35*(1), 91-108, ISSN 0802-6106, DOI: 10.1111/ijal.12603

Ma, Y. (2025). Modelling College Students' Acceptance to Use Generative Artificial Intelligence for Second Language Learning: A Theory of Planned Behaviour Perspective. *European Journal of Education, 60*(1), ISSN 0141-8211, DOI: 10.1111/ejed.12923

Muñoz-Basols, J. (2025). Opportunities for Artificial Intelligence (AI) in language teaching and learning. *Technology-Mediated Language Teaching: From Social Justice to Artificial Intelligence*, 297-315, https://www.scopus.com/inward/record.uri?partnerID=HzOxMe3b&scp=105000565015&origin=inward

Najib, F. M. (2025). Sign language interpretation using machine learning and artificial intelligence. *Neural Computing and Applications, 37*(2), 841-857, ISSN 0941-0643, DOI: 10.1007/s00521-024-10395-9

Plevris, V. (2025). A Glimpse into the Future of Civil Engineering Education: The New Era of Artificial Intelligence, Machine Learning, and Large Language Models. *Journal of Civil Engineering Education, 151*(2), ISSN 2643-9107, DOI: 10.1061/JCEECD.EIENG-2193

Singh, B. (2025). Uncapping Explainable Artificial Intelligence-Centered Reinforcement Learning and Natural Language Processing in Smart Healthcare System. *Explainable and Responsible Artificial Intelligence in Healthcare*, 1-25, DOI: 10.1002/9781394302444.ch1

Vandenberg, J. (2025). Conceptualizing the Support and Learning of K-2 Educators around Artificial Intelligence in Language Arts. *SIGCSE TS 2025 - Proceedings of the 56th ACM Technical Symposium on Computer Science Education, 2*, 1647-1648, DOI: 10.1145/3641555.3705150

Yang, M. L. (2025). Artificial intelligence versus human teacher assistants and language learners' progress in learning and retention of complex sentences. *Current Psychology*, ISSN 1046-1310, DOI: 10.1007/s12144-025-07488-6

KEY TERMS AND DEFINITIONS

Adaptive Learning: The educational approach with the aid of Artificial Intelligence that modifies the content of learning, pace, and difficulty according to the needs and performances of individual learners.

Artificial Intelligence (AI): Computer systems that accomplish such activities as learning, problem-solving, and pattern finding that usually require human intelligence, particularly within the context of language learning.

Computer-Assisted Language Learning (CALL): The use of computer technologies, including AI, to facilitate the language teaching and learning processes.

Conversational AI: AI systems that take part in dialogue with users, simulating human conversation to offer language practice opportunities and immediate feedback.

Machine Learning Algorithms: The means by which AI systems are able to change their requirements with experience on their own, analyzing the patterns offered by language data to create adaptive learning experiences.

Natural Language Processing (NLP): A branch of AI that deals with programming computers to process and analyze huge amounts of natural language data so systems can understand, interpret, and generate human language.

Speech Recognition Technology: AI systems for recognizing human speech and processing it into text, allowing pronunciation assessment and interactive speaking practice.

Chapter 10
Neurodiversity and AI: Designing Inclusive, Adaptive Pathways for Dyslexia, ADHD, and Autism in English Language Learning

Ridha Rouabhia
https://orcid.org/0000-0003-1930-4007
Ali Lounici University of Blida 2, Algeria

ABSTRACT

The chapter examines the interface of AI and neurodiversity as it relates to the learning of English with the inclusive design of adaptive pathways for the likes of persons with dyslexia, ADHD, and autism spectrum disorders. Despite the AI transformation of educational spheres, in the wake of unmet opportunities, there is a need to explore how these technologies can bridge the gap between accessing unique cognitive profiles and the learning needs of neurodivergent students. This chapter frames its argument based on the neurodiversity paradigm, which discards weaknesses-understanding and deserves to be replaced by strength-appreciating views of human differences. It concludes by stating evidence-based design principles for AI tools that promote the autonomy, acceptance, and normalisation of the experience of neurodivergent language learners. Through participatory design, ethical AI application, and hybrid human-AI collaboration, this chapter discusses how technology might work toward developing more inclusive educational responses.

DOI: 10.4018/979-8-3373-3561-2.ch010

1. INTRODUCTION

1.1 Context: The Growing Role of AI in Education

The changes have been radical over the last few years in education, and a new force is emerging as a potential redefinition for how both teaching and learning processes take place: artificial intelligence. Intelligent tutoring systems and automated assessment tools are only two examples of what becomes available through AI technology in education. This penetration promises efficiency, personalisation, and access to increased amounts of AI at all educational levels. Global investments in AI education technology grow exponentially, and with current projections, the market is expected to hit $20.8 billion by 2028, reflecting a compound annual growth rate of 32.9% from 2021 (Research and Markets, 2021). Thus, this exponential growth signals not just the possible technological outcomes but also the changes happening in the minds of educational institutions, policymakers, and investors who increasingly think of AI as central to innovation in education.

Within this landscape of rapid changes, one difference has also emerged. While general accelerated development of educational technology takes place, the peculiarities of neurodivergent learners-cognitive variations like dyslexia, attention deficit hyperactivity disorder (ADHD), and autism spectrum disorders (ASD), are peripheral to almost all design interests. Such neglect is alarming, considering that neurodevelopmental conditions are abundantly found in academic settings. Current estimates suggest that between 15 and potentially 20% of the world's student population appears to have one form or another of a neurodevelopmental condition negatively affecting learning (Barua et al., 2022). Specifically for language learning, challenges might become even more pronounced, as acquiring a language involves complex cognitive processes that may function differently in neurodivergent individuals.

The figures are inescapable: worldwide, it is estimated that between 5%-17% of school-age children have dyslexia, one of the most common learning differences. Between 5%-10% are children and adolescents with ADHD anywhere in the world (Barua et al., 2022); autism spectrum disorders have prevalence rates estimated to affect approximately 1 in 54 children (CDC, 2020). Realistically, such numbers do not represent mere statistical abstractions but millions of learners whose educational experiences are fundamentally shaped by how well—or poorly—educational technologies accommodate their cognitive profiles.

Despite these abundant figures, the design and development of AI educational tools followed a very much neurotypical template, with an implicit assumption that all learners have uniform cognitive processes. This even reflects what Pellicano and den Houting (2022) describe to be the lingering effect of the traditional medical paradigm in educational technology: such a paradigm views variations from the norm as deficits instead of variations to be accommodated. The result is an increasingly sophisticated educational technology ecosystem that remains fundamentally exclusionary in its design philosophy.

Depicted in such exclusion are several ways. Many of the AI learning tools derive their algorithms from datasets grossly underformed on the learning patterns corresponding to neurodiversity, resulting in systems that misinterpret or penalise non-normative approaches to problem-solving. Furthermore, the user interfaces and modalities of interaction seldom reflect sensory sensitivities and attention variations or any alternative information processing styles commonly found in neurodivergent learners. Finally, the pedagogical assumptions of such AI systems mostly reflect standard educational practices that have created a history of marginalisation against neurodivergent students.

The implications are beyond immediate educational outcomes. Frustration and withdrawal from learning often impose a negative coming-of-age experience on neurodivergent learners in terms of their self-identity while compounding disparities in the education achieved. Especially in language learning contexts, where mastery translates into sociocultural, academic, and later occupational opportunities, the non-design of AI educational tools with neurodiversity in mind perpetuates and possibly amplifies existing inequities for access and outcomes in education.

1.2 Problem Statement: Limitations of Current AI Tools

Today's crop of AI tools for the learning of language, while creative in many ways, has considerable limitations when assessed through the neurodiversity paradigm. These limitations can be grouped into three primary categories: standardised pacing and consistency, poor emotional feedback, and an inability to take into account the underlying cognitive differences that neurodiverse learners exhibit.

The first seemingly most basic limitation concerns the rigid pacing and standardised nature of a lot of the AI language learning approaches. Typically, these systems are predetermined along certain learning sequences with strict criteria for progression, allowing just enough room to comply regarding the presentation, practice, and assessment of content. For neurodivergent learners, whose cognitive processing may go in a non-linear manner or may require varying time expenditure depending on the task type, such rigidity may provide considerable hindrance toward motivation and attainment. For example, a dyslexic learner may require more time for processing text but could show much faster understanding of the interrelationship of concepts; an autistic student may appreciate taking extra time while exploring different dimensions of grammatical patterns before attempting to apply these in social contexts; and the engaging nature of language tasks would greatly benefit a student with ADHD by allowing for quick bursts of learning interspersed with breaks.

To date, very few systems have been able to accommodate such varying types of learning paces; in fact, they impose a common standard time frame, favouring the typical processing style.

Moreover, this standardisation does not apply just to pacing but also to the very definitions of progress and proficiency. According to Dwyer (2022), the medical model focus on normalisation has extended into the area of educational technologies, where "success" is often considered from quite a narrow neurotypical point of view. For neurodivergent learners whose language acquisition may follow an atypical developmental path, these standardised metrics could easily misrepresent meaningful learning and engender feelings of low self-worth. Taking it a step further, many AI systems apply some elements of competition, such as leaderboards and achievements, in ways that exacerbate the disadvantage to learners who may shine in fields other than conventional assessment.

Another major limitation concerns the emotional aspect of learning languages. Presently, most AI tools give feedback along a more corrective than emotionally responsive paradigm and, in doing so, almost entirely stress accuracy while sidelining the affective components of the learning process. This line of reasoning dismisses that language learning is ultimately emotional, involving vulnerability, identity issues, and different anxiety levels—all of which may be especially salient issues for neurodivergent learners. Jafarian and Kramer (2024) demonstrated that motivation and engagement were key mediating factors in academic success among students, including those with ADHD. Nevertheless, most AI language learning systems contain no such sophisticated means of detecting emotional states, adapting to changes in confidence or frustration, or providing the form of emotionally calibrated encouragement that human teachers can provide with little effort.

A third major limitation of current AI systems is their inability to cater to specific cognitive profiles associated with different neurological conditions. There are several cognitive processes involved in language learning, such as phonological awareness, working memory, attention control, pattern recognition, and pragmatic understanding, all of which might behave differently among neurodivergent individuals. Unfortunately, most AI language learning tools tend to adopt a "one size fits all" cognitive model that ignores these differences.

With dyslexic learners, barriers have to do mainly with phonological processing and working with grapheme-phoneme correspondences, key to reading and writing. Current AI tools seldom offer alternatives that might leverage the visual-spatial strengths that many dyslexic learners possess or provide the systematic, multisensory instruction shown by research to work. For learners with ADHD, where challenges reside primarily in the realm of sustained attention and executive function, AI systems often overlook the kind of dynamic, high-interest content or frequent state changes needed to sustain engagement. By contrast, for autistic learners, who may have strengths in the recognition of patterns but are weak in the pragmatic use of language, the majority of present tools would not explicitly teach language according to that social rule or properly use a concrete type of thinking in favour of teaching language.

These limitations highlight a wide-scale failure to integrate design principles informed by neurodiversity into AI educational tools. Bhutoria (2022) remarks that AI-driven personalisation has tended to remain a limited undertaking, conferring superficiality onto an issue that calls for a radical rethinking of how different minds learn. This has resulted in educational technology, which, at least arguably, is state-of-the-art, yet still uncaringly favours neurotypical learning patterns while leaving neurodivergent strategies neglected and disregarded in language acquisition.

1.3 Objectives

This chapter is meant to address the limitations flagged above by adding a comprehensive framework for the design of AI-powered language-learning tools that would most genuinely support neurodivergence and celebrate neurodiversity. The objectives behind this framework include four strategic goals, each aimed at filling a critical gap in current approaches to AI in education.

First, establish evidence-based design principles for neurodiversity-inclusive AI tools. These will be grounded in cutting-edge research in cognitive neuroscience, educational psychology, and human-computer interaction and applied to general design-based guidelines. These principles will not designate neurodivergent learners as exceptions needing individualisation; they will be integration principles based on universal design, claiming cognitive diversity as the norm rather than as an exception. By capturing insights from both neurodiversity and AI development, we will derive a blueprint of technologies that would be inherently inclusive rather than retroactively inclusive.

The principles we propose will deal with several dimensions of AI design, from interface customisation and content delivery to feedback mechanisms, progression structures, and assessment. Each of these will be analysed through the lens of specific neurodevelopmental conditions—dyslexia, ADHD, and autism—while simultaneously identifying common design elements that can benefit all learners. This is because although adaptations may particularly benefit specific profiles, many design improvements that support a neurodiversity-positive climate will enhance the experience of all students, thereby embodying the saying "necessary for some, beneficial for all."

The second objective involves demonstrating how AI can empower neurodivergent students in their autonomy and de-stigmatisation. Traditional trends have worked with a lens of remediation and conformity for students, asking neurodivergent students to learn in an environment that is not modified to their diverse cognitive needs, even in cases for other children. While it does misfire regarding learning effectiveness, it packs huge psychological burdens while sending a message to such students that their styles of cognition are less viable or problematic. AI technologies, if rightly designed, open possibilities to change that picture by keeping learning environments flexible towards the learners instead of the opposite case.

We will have an investigation into how privacy-preserving personalisation, strength-based learning pathways, and learner-controlled adaptation may contribute to an empowering educational experience. AI tools help to normalise diversity in brain wiring and begin breaking down the stigma surrounding learning differences by allowing students to learn in ways that complement their cognitive profiles, without drawing attention to differences or needing special intervention. This is in line with the ideals of autonomy, dignity, and self-determination that the broader neurodiversity movement has articulated for people with neurodiversity.

Thirdly, we would have to recognise participatory design frameworks for involving neurodivergent learners in the co-design process. It is not uncommon to observe educational technologies that are developed for the population in question but not with that population, thus resulting in systems that miss important user needs or introduce unintended barriers. The case is aggravated by the neurodiverse population, their question of being uniquely disadvantaged in the user development process.

Based on co-design and participatory research principles, we will sketch applicable methodologies for the significant involvement of neurodivergent people in all development stages of AI tools, from conception through to implementation and potential refinement. This framework will engage practical issues such as how accessible design workshops can be organised, how user-testing protocols are designed for varying cognitive styles, and how feedback mechanisms can be developed to accommodate different communication preferences. It will also address deeper questions of power, representation, and epistemic justice in technology design, for it takes meaningful, across-the-board inclusion more than just consultation with appropriate power-sharing in the design process. Thus, AI language learning tools can be built with neurodivergent voices in the design process, thereby producing technologies that mirror more accurately the diverse learning requirements.

Our final goal would be to highlight the ethical base that will come with the application of AI, specifically for neurodivergent individuals. Fairly hot debates are being discussed concerning the ethical consequences of AI use within education, including issues of privacy, autonomy, and bias, while the shifting role of human teachers takes on a dimension of its own. The nuances of these considerations take on a new light when we position them within the neurodiversity movement, with issues around consent, data sensitivity, algorithmic bias, and possible stigmatisation being of much greater concern.

Questions we will consider include:

- How do we ensure responsible, respectful use of data from neurodivergent learners?
- What safeguards do we need to ensure that AI systems do not contribute to the production of negative stereotypes or pathologise cognitive differences?
- How do we balance personalisation with privacy concerns regarding tracking or labelling students?
- How do we ensure that AI tools supplement, rather than replace, the human relationships critical for effective learning, especially for neurodivergent students who could benefit from explicit modelling in their social learning and emotional support?

Addressing all this sums up well the more inclusive vision of AI in language education—one that considers neurodiversity a uniquely human form instead of a problem, and can use technology's strong abilities to create the conditions in which all students may succeed by their means.

2. THEORETICAL FOUNDATIONS

2.1 Neurodiversity Paradigms

Neurodiversity has come into prominence in the past decades, shifting our understanding and approach to cognitive differences. This section explores this evolutionary change from the medical model to the neurodiversity paradigm, considering the change's implications regarding educational technology design focused on language learning applications for persons with dyslexia, ADHD, and autism. Neurodevelopmental conditions used to be considered in what Dwyer (2022) describes as the "medical model"; that is, those disabilities are presumed to be pathological and are medical diseases or disorders of the mind or body, hence leading individuals to suffer deficits and functional limitations. The appropriate answer to disability, thus, is to transform disabled people into able-bodied and typically developing individuals. This has dominated clinical practices for decades, educational policies, and thus, technological developments, building into it the features applicable to interventions primarily aimed at normalisation and remediation.

Undoubtedly, the medical model has affected educational technology. As Pellicano and den Houting (2022) observe, "Since its initial description, the concept of autism has been firmly rooted within the conventional medical paradigm of child psychiatry" (p. 381). This paradigm extends to other neurodevelopmental conditions as well, with dyslexia and ADHD similarly framed as disorders requiring correction. The result has been educational technologies designed to "fix" perceived deficits rather than accommodate or leverage different cognitive styles.

Challenging the medical model increasingly is what has come to be known as the neurodiversity paradigm, which has brought even heavier colons into society. "Neurodiversity," Singer (2016) first proposed with an analogy to biodiversity, such as: "Why not propose that just as biodiversity is essential to ecosystem stability, so neurodiversity may be essential for cultural stability?" (as cited in Dwyer, 2022, p. 74). Pathologies to be removed from society would also have neurological differences be understood and valued as a natural form of human variation, not something to be hunted down as though one were hunting deer.

Armstrong (2012) took this further by advocating that there be strength-based approaches developed within educational contexts, where neurodiversity is posited to be a natural and valuable form of human variation. His work strengthens the needed commitment toward creating environments where different learning styles could be accommodated, rather than trying to normalise neurodivergent persons in standard educational models.

The neurodiversity paradigm is not only a change in terminology but is a fundamental reshaping of how we understand cognitive differences. As Pellicano and den Houting (2022) explain, it considers autism and all other neurodevelopmental conditions "as one form of variation within a diversity of minds" (p. 381). With this reframing comes some pretty radical shifts in how we design education and technology for neurodiverse people.

Table 1. Paradigm comparison for educational technology design

Design Element	Medical Model Approach	Neurodiversity Paradigm Approach	Impact on AI Design
Primary Goal	Fix deficits, normalize performance	Leverage strengths, accommodate differences	Multiple pathways to proficiency vs. single "correct" path
Progress Metrics	Standardized, norm-referenced benchmarks	Individual growth, strength development	Dynamic, personalized assessment criteria
User Agency	System controls pacing & method	Learner controls adaptations	Adjustable system vs. rigid algorithm
Data Interpretation	Deviations flagged as errors	Variations recognized as valid patterns	Bias detection in pattern recognition
Support Type	Remediation-focused	Empowerment-focused	Strength-based feedback loops

This is one of the most important aspects of neurodiversity: it rejects approaches that are focused on deficits. Disability models based on conventional educational approaches stress what the neurodivergent cannot do, remediating weaknesses through different methods. The neurodiversity perspective recognises challenges and strengths, such as different cognitive profiles giving different advantages in certain contexts. For example, studies have shown that many autistic individuals have excellent perceptual functioning (Mottron et al., 2006), some dyslexic learners have impressively strong pattern-recognition skills (Eide & Eide, 2011), and some profiles associated with ADHD may be linked to extraordinary creative thinking (White & Shah, 2011).

Proof of this strength also comes from the most recent Peterson et al. (2018) research, indicating that students with dyslexia usually outperform others in spatial reasoning but encounter problems in their phonology processes. Therefore, it can be said that current educational tools should be committed to building on these strong visual-spatial capabilities while giving space for assistance concerning phonological challenges rather than focusing simply on maximising perceptual defects.

According to Alcorn et al. (2019), variables such as clarity, consistency in social and behavioural demands, and structure-preferred interaction were noted for students with autism. This has very important implications when thinking about and creating educational technology, offering clear, consistent interfaces and explicit instructions rather than requiring intuitive navigation or implicit understanding of social cues.

This strength-based approach neither denies the very real hurdles that neurodivergent individuals face in neurotypical-designed environments, nor implies inherent deficits in the individual, but rather those arising from a mismatch of the individual's cognitive style and requirements of the environment. According to Dwyer (2022), neurodiversity models acknowledge contributions of both the individual and society to disability. It, therefore, changes the focus from changing the individual to changing the environment-including technological environments that individual finds themselves in, to better accommodate diverse cognitive profiles.

The neurodiversity paradigm also emphasises the diversity within diagnostic categories. For instance, the terms "dyslexia," "ADHD," and "autism" describe profoundly different cognitive profiles, and people who share a diagnostic label often show different patterns of strengths and challenges. This diversity accentuates the inability of any one approach in educational technology to cater for the need for flexibility in being able to cater to an individualised, wide range of learning styles.

The neurodiversity model also believes that there is a very high co-occurrence among neurodevelopmental conditions. As Barua et al. (2022) say, "between 30% and 50% of children with ADHD are reported to have a comorbid mental health disorder, such as depression, and over 70% of children with ASD are reported to have a comorbid mental health disorder, most commonly including anxiety (40%) and ADHD (30-40%). These overlapping boundaries create complex cognitive profiles that complicate simple categorisation and therefore require a nuanced approach for educational support. This paradigm shift demands educational technologies that celebrate cognitive diversity by providing multiple, flexible pathways to language acquisition rather than remediating perceived deficits..

This shift also reflects larger movements toward universal learning design (UDL), in terms of designing participatory educational experiences available to all learners upfront, rather than adapting them for specific subgroups using retrofitted accommodations. The UDL perspective promotes the idea of designing for all learners and, when possible, avoiding retrofitted accommodations for targeted sub-groups, such as students with neurodiverse cognitions. The neurodiversity paradigm extends this concept beyond the idea that neurodiversity is part of a wider diversity continuum (i.e., thinking, learning, and processing) rather than simply a deviation from normality that is recognised as unique and something to deal with.

This raises serious questions about agency and voice in educational technology development. As most scholars will agree, neurodivergent cognition should be considered a valid and valuable way of experiencing and understanding the world. It thus implies that individuals who are neurodivergent should have meaningful involvement in the design of technologies that are meant to help them learn. This participative mode is completely different from having neurotypical experts design the technology, and it is then meant to be used by neurodivergent individuals, often without much contribution from the users themselves.

However, it is interesting to note that being purportedly neurodiverse does not drift into abandoning evidence-backed interventions, nor does it deny the real existence of difficulties in the neurodivergent individual in order. It instead means that interventions are approached with a different philosophical framework, one holding respect towards one's autonomy and intrinsic value associated with any diversified cognitive style, but still providing meaningful help to ameliorate adverse conditions. As per Dwyer (2022), "neurodiversity-aligned research would study both individual neurodivergent people and the contexts around them; consider both strengths and weaknesses; recognise their own biases; and listen to and learn from neurodivergent people" (73).

Particularly in terms of language learning technologies for neurodivergent individuals, this balanced approach becomes even more critical. Language competency, indeed, continues to serve as the major skill toward academic success, social integration, and professional advancement in many countries. Then, it follows from a general educational equality perspective that every neurodivergent learner should benefit from language learning opportunities that are effective. However, that effectiveness must come through avoiding the reinforcement of harmful narratives about normal and deviant cognitive minds in the setting of their provision. Thus, the shift from the medical model to the neurodiversity paradigm transcends a theoretical transition and represents the practical reimagining of how educational technologies can and should operate.

2.2 AI's Role in Personalised Learning

Artificial Intelligence (AI) is a disruptive technology in education, introducing exciting possibilities for personalised learning, especially for individual cognitive profiles discussed in the prior section. In this section, I look at the possibilities of AI that make it particularly promising for neurodiversity inclusive education, highlighting three core technologies with significant potential for supporting neurodivergent language learners: adaptive algorithms, natural language processing, and affective learning technologies.

Adaptive algorithms are perhaps the most basic AI capability to facilitate personalised learning. Using adaptive algorithms, AI can identify specific student patterns and habits, learner strengths and weaknesses, and can even change the way content is presented to a specific learner. Traditional educational software uses a predetermined pace and sequence of activities, whereas adaptive systems are informed and continually evolving based on the inputs they receive from learners, essentially allowing learners to create their learning paths.

Luckin et al. (2016) explain that these adaptive algorithms can adjust the level of difficulty of tasks by measuring performance as a "function of the actions over time to create personalised learning environments that could follow each student in their learning, both in terms of progress and ability" (p.25). This is particularly applicable for neurodivergent language learners whose learning progression is likely to differ significantly from neuropathy or differences between neurodivergent learners.

Bhutoria (2022) emphasises that AI-enabled personalisation is AI that enhances educational content, tailoring it to each individual according to their needs, and brings attention to the potential for learning difficulties. The ability to adapt in real-time is most useful for neurodivergent learners whose learning trajectories may be shaped in ways that diverge from neurotypical learners and other neurodivergent learners as well. For dyslexic learners, adaptive algorithms can adjust text presentation based on reading patterns; for example, increased font size or spacing may be used when processing difficulties are detected, or changes may occur in the rate of introducing new vocabulary. For learners with ADHD, these algorithms would analyse engagement patterns to optimise task duration and variety, introducing new activities when attention seemed to wane. For autistic learners, the system could use individual preferences to strike a balance between explicit rule instruction and contextual examples.

Natural Language Processing (NLP) capabilities are another important AI technology for supporting neurodivergent language learners. NLP refers to a computer's ability to process, understand, and interpret human language. With NLP, there are possibilities for increasingly skilled learner-system interactions where users can talk to the system in natural language, so they can have meaningful exchanges with the system that mirror how they communicate in daily contexts. NLP capabilities are particularly relevant in language learning applications, where language is both the means and the end of learning, so engaged learners also engage in some complex linguistic processing.

Alcorn et al. (2019) point out the value of multimodal NLP, which combines text, speech, and image to reduce information load for neurodivergent learners. This can be very helpful for autistic learners who may engage more positively with visual information rather than text, and for dyslexic learners who may be challenged by adding text to the information load of multiple images and visual representations of language concepts.

NLP systems can also systematically examine learner-produced language to identify patterns, which may represent specific learning needs. For example, an NLP system might examine a dyslexic student's writing for spelling patterns that are characteristic of dyslexia, document attention-related inconsistencies in a learner with attention deficits, or even recognise challenges related to pragmatic language (the use of language in social contexts) that are commonly present for neurodivergent students with autism. Following the patterns identified in the examination, the system can recommend support that is purposeful (connected to the learner's linguistic challenges) and builds on their existing strengths.

NLP implies interactions regarding educational content in a more natural and accessible form. The text-to-speech coupled with speech-to-text would help learners who process information better through their auditory channels than visual channels, or who can express themselves better through speech than writing. Proofs of the contribution of AI-assisted auditory ways of learning to students with ADHD are explained in the current research. These forms of learning methods improve motivation and reading engagement, resulting in good academic performance by Jafarian and Kramer (2024).

NLP can also be put to use in the creation of conversational agents or chatbots that provide instantaneous and personalised feedback and support. These agents might also explain using different modes, respond to kinds of language-related queries and offer practice variants conforming to the needs and preferences of the learners. For diverse learners, who become potentially anxious or self-conscious in conventional classroom activities, these private and judgment-free interactions may result in valuable learning opportunities.

Affect-aware computing is the third crucial AI technology that features inclusive learning about neurodiversity. Systems are prospectively in this aspect of AI to be able to identify, interpret and respond to human emotions. It deals with those aspects of learning realities that are mostly neglected by educational technology - the emotional side of learning is under discussion. In our current limitations discussion, it was noted that common AI tools have no elaborate mechanisms for ascertaining emotional states or rendering emotional feedback- a void that affective computing aspires to fill.

Such notable efforts within this area have been undertaken by Calvo and D'Mello (2010), who developed emotional state detection models based on linguistic or physiological indicators. Their interdisciplinary work integrates knowledge from psychology, computer science and education and develops systems that recognise struggle, engagement, confusion, and other emotions related to the learning process for these students.

For learners who might flare up more anxiety, frustration, or disengagement in regular forms of learning, an emotionally responsive system brings particular benefits. An effective computing-enabled AI may be able to recognise behaviour patterns indicative of frustration in the learner's activity and lower the difficulty level or give encouragement. It may find out what subjects bring anxiety in such learners and provide calming strategies or alternative ways of dealing with challenging material. Also, it would recognise engagement and disengagement patterns, and create learning experiences, maintaining optimal levels of interest and challenge.

Affective computing may go beyond short-term responses to feelings. Rather, it may even elicit larger, more encompassing facets of motivation and self-regulation. AI-assisted audio-learning modules are bound to raise motivation and reading engagement in students, according to Jafarian and Kramer's (2024) study findings, and these increases in motivation and reading engagement boosted subsequent academic achievement. This shows that AI systems should not only be contained in content delivery but also in the affective aspects of learning that are critical for sustaining engagement and hence success.

All three capabilities in AI-adapted algorithms, natural language processing, and affective computing create tremendous personalised learning experiences, one of which can cater for diverse cognitive profiles. Of course, however, this capability built by AI for neurodiversity-inclusive education is not solely dependent on technological sophistication; it also resides in how these technologies are designed and applied.

Luckin et al. (2016) observe that while AI empowerment in an educational context is taking place, the role of the teacher remains key as a partner in the learning experience for students, as technology serves to enhance and not replace human instruction. This agrees with Bhutoria's (2022) assertion that instructors are facilitators and motivators, not information providers in AI-enabled personalised education. This recalibration of roles emphasises the very important principle that indicates AI is to supplement rather than supplant human elements in education, for neurodivergent learners who probably benefit from explicit social modelling and emotional support. Thus, probably the best use of AI in this scenario would be to improve human-to-human links instead of replacing them.

Understanding the specific learning profiles for different neurodevelopmental conditions should guide the development of AI for neurodiverse-inclusive learning. General personalisation algorithms alone may not be able to deal with the diverse cognitive patterns of learners who have dyslexia, ADHD, or are autistic without research on these conditions informing them. According to Barua et al. (2022), to improve outcomes for children, it is important to provide timely and effective interventions, as defined by their particular neurodevelopmental profile.

AI's ability to cater to various cognitive profiles brings questions regarding data collection, privacy, and consent to the fore. Personalisation is predicated on data; one may say the more detailed the personalisation, the more extensive the data requirements. Particularly concerning are some of the considerations that come into play in the case where funding neurodivergent learners is concerned, as the information obtained may reveal sensitive information related to underlying cognitive processing and learning needs. Therefore, it becomes imperative to ethically implement AI in a manner that weighs the merits of personalisation against substantial safeguarding of privacy and autonomy for all users.

Perhaps one of the most promising implementations of AI in education is the customisation of learning experiences for neurodivergent persons. These AI systems would use adaptive algorithms together with natural language processing and affective computing to create learning environments that dynamically respond to individual needs, preferences, and emotional states. Developed with an understanding of neurodiversity and respect for ethical considerations, the solutions can transform the educational experience for neurodivergent individuals in foreign language learning, making it more accessible, motivating, and rewarding.

3. DESIGN PRINCIPLES FOR NEURODIVERSITY- INCLUSIVE AI

Table 2. AI design features mapped to neurodivergent profiles

Cognitive Challenge	Dyslexia Profile	ADHD Profile	Autism Profile	Corresponding AI Feature
Processing Speed	Phonological delays; visual-spatial strengths	Variable attention; task-switching needs	Preference for processing depth over speed	Adaptive pacing with optional acceleration/deceleration
Sensory Input	Visual text processing difficulties	Distraction from peripheral stimuli	Hypo/hyper-sensitivity to sensory input	Customizable contrast, font, audio levels, animation controls
Working Memory	Limited phonological loop capacity	Executive function deficits	Detail-focused but context-challenged	Multimodal reinforcement; chunked content; visual organizers
Emotional Regulation	Reading anxiety; learned helplessness	Frustration intolerance; motivation fluctuations	Alexithymia; social communication anxiety	Real-time affect detection; calibrated encouragement; anxiety reduction protocols
Pattern Recognition	Strong visual-spatial pattern detection	Creative, non-linear connections	Exceptional systemizing; rule-based learning	Visual grammar mapping; interest-based content threading; explicit rule libraries

3.1 Adaptive Interfaces

The development of user interfaces is an important area of focus for the design of AI-enabled language learning tools that truly support neurodiversity. In particular, adaptive interfaces—the ability of the interface to adapt the way it displays information, modality of interaction, and, type of feedback provided on the interaction, to suit the individual needs of the user—could offer unique advantages in supporting the varied cognitive profiles of students with dyslexia, ADHD, and autism alike. This section discusses evidence-informed practices in designing adaptive interfaces that support the language learning experiences of neurodivergent learners.

Visual processing challenges for learners with dyslexia often interfere with text-based learning, many of which are significant hurdles. The experimental literature holds an increasing consensus that adjustments made to the presentation of text can be beneficial to reading fluency and comprehension among dyslexic people (Rello & Baeza-Yates, 2017). Adjustments made include font type and size, character and line spacing, text and background colour combinations, and text segmentation. Learners hardly know what settings they could configure best for their condition, so the AI-driven adaptive interfaces should analyse the reading patterns online and automatically adjust these text presentation settings to be read with the highest possible ease by targeted learners who may be at NPR.

Peterson et al. (2018) stress the necessity for using dyslexia-friendly formats, recommending adjustable fonts (OpenDyslexic being one), customizable background colours, and text chunking to reduce the cognitive load. This form of formatting may greatly assist dyslexic learners by ameliorating the specific visual processing difficulties that the disorder entails in its support of reading comprehension and speed.

According to Barua et al. (2022), AI tools can be successfully used to improve social interaction and supportive education for neurodivergent learners. For dyslexics, this would mean providing an interface that tracks eye movements and reading speed to tell when a particular text configuration is giving the user trouble and then dynamically modifying that configuration to alleviate the cognitive load. For instance, in general, the spacing might increase when the detection of hesitation in recognising words signals a problem or colour contrast may change if an extended reading task indicates a loss of attention.

Moving beyond mere text presentation, adaptive interfaces intended to assist dyslexic learners can further enhance language concepts through multisensory reinforcement. Research on intervention for dyslexia has consistently proven the effectiveness of engaging several sensory channels at once (Shaywitz & Shaywitz, 2020). AI-powered interfaces can gain from that insight by providing visual, auditory, and tactile representations of language elements in synchrony, with the proportion of each modality adjusted according to the learning patterns observed.

These customisations also need to go beyond the commonly talked-about accessibility layout features to include preferences that may alter students' engagement and comprehension of the aesthetic and organisational script. Many dyslexic learners would benefit from such variations, including visually organised tools such as concept maps, colour coding, and hierarchies in text structure (Eide & Eide, 2011). Adaptive interfaces could provide these options and learn which arrangement works most effectively for individual users, automatically applying preferred arrangements to new content.

In learners with ADHD, attention management remains central to the challenges to be solved by adaptive interfaces. Sustained attention, distraction, and impaired executive function characteristic of ADHD likely impact language learning processes. Adaptive interfaces for ADHD learners should develop additional features for maintaining optimal arousal, distracting minimally, and assisting with executive functions.

Cortiella and Horowitz (2014) affirm that an interface that allows ADHD learners to pace lessons customarily is critical; they suggest that learners should be able to control length and break duration. If students can retain control over these aspects of their learning about time, their engagement will probably improve significantly, thereby limiting frustration associated with naturally varying attention patterns that mark ADHD.

In providing designs of significant importance for ADHD learner interfaces, the research of Jafarian and Kramer (2024) on applying AI to audio learning deserves special mention. According to their study, AI-assisted audio-learning modules enhance student motivation and reading engagement, and these increases in motivation and reading engagement boost subsequent academic achievement. Of particular interest is the conclusion that the modules helped auditory learning reduce the adverse effects of ADHD symptoms on academic performance" (p. 1), giving the impression that addressing attention regulation might be beneficial using modes of audio.

Following these findings, features like gamified micro-lessons in adaptive interfaces for ADHD learners could chunk language lessons into smaller portions, engage through variety, and provide immediate feedback. The interface can monitor attention indicators, which might include response time variability, error rates, or even physiological signals, if available. When attention is dropping, the software can adjust lesson length, complexity, or modality. It could switch from text to audiovisual modes, introduce interactive features, or suggest a short break when disengagement signals are detected.

Temporal structuring represents yet another consideration of interface design for ADHD learners. Recent findings note that often making external interventions to regulate time and providing a clear temporal framework is highly beneficial for individuals with ADHD (Barkley, 2015). Some of these supports can be addressed by the adaptive interface through visual timers, progress indicators, and other session-planning aids that can help learners remain cognizant of the time without imposing any additional cognitive load. The system may learn the individual user's optimal session length and cue them for breaks or transitions through externally oriented scaffolding in gently developing their self-regulation skills.

Visual design considerations are particularly relevant to ADHD learners, who are perhaps more prone to distraction by guidance elements. Clean materials with focused layouts, clear of extraneous visual stimulation, can assist in sustaining attention to relevant language content. At the same time, subtle cues through colour, motion, and interactivity can highlight salient content and sustain student focus. The gamble between extreme simplicity and stimulation is probably rather unique for each person and context, increasing the need for such adaptive approaches.

Contrary to these, for autistic learners, adaptive interfaces should satisfy another set of demands concerning sensory processing, predictability, and social understanding. Autism is highly heterogeneous, where each individual has a unique profile of strengths and challenges. Yet, some common patterns in information processing and learning preferences can inform interface design principles.

Alcorn et al. (2019) documented that autistic learners usually prefer predictable, structured interactions, and such findings are consequential for interface design. Clear and consistent navigational structures and explicit instructions ought to be developed on these lines, rather than relying on intuitively understood interfaces and implicit social cues.

Many autistic people also experience atypical sensory processing, which might include hypersensitivities to certain visual or auditory stimuli (Robertson & Baron-Cohen, 2017). Adaptive interfaces must allow tight control of sensory parameters of the learning environment so that the user can adjust brightness, contrast, animation, sound volume, and voice characteristics. Over time, the system might also learn individual sensory preferences and will automatically assign these settings to any new content, minimising the cognitive load on sensory management.

Support in the form of predictable and routine schedules may oftentimes facilitate this learning process for an autistic learner to reduce anxiety and free up cognitive resources for learning tasks. This suggests adaptive interfaces with clear and consistent structures, as well as explicit sign-posting for transitions between activities or topics. Visual schedules, progress indicators, and advance organisers can help create an atmosphere of predictability whilst also giving agency to students to take their learning pathways. The system might learn which types of transitions or changes are particularly challenging for individual users and would intensify the extra support at such times.

In language learning in particular, it would be valuable for autistic learners for interfaces to make various implicit social rules and pragmatic aspects of language use clear, as these are often acquired intuitively by neurotypical learners. Features such as visual displays of conversational turn-taking, explicit identification of emotional tones in language samples, or interactive scenarios practising social language use would enhance skill development in these areas. The adaptive system may begin to balance form-focused language instruction with pragmatic language instruction per the individual's learning patterns and goals.

Voice-to-text abilities are a special blessing for non-verbal or minimally verbal autistic learners, giving expression through alternative modalities. Alcorn et al. (2019) discuss applications such as Proloquo2Go that integrate speech synthesis for autistic learners to provide much-needed critical communication support. Personalised assistive tools could, as Barua et al. (2022) put it, enhance the education of children with neurodevelopmental disorders by promoting multiple pathways of engagement with language content.

While AI-powered adaptations provide useful assistance, they should serve to support user control, not to replace it. The interfaces must provide transparent information on customisation options, current system settings, and how automated adaptations came to be. Users should have the opportunity to go against system advice, provide feedback on the effectiveness of adaptations, and gain increasing control over their learning environment as their skills and self-awareness develop.

This principle of user control is in line with the broader notion of neurodiversity, which advocates for autonomy and self-determination. Dwyer (2022) states that understandings of neurodiversity should attend to both individual attributes and the social context for understanding experiences of disability. Adaptive interfaces that empower engagement with automated support, while also allowing for user autonomy, represent such a balance and a recognition not only of the exclusions that neurodivergent learners experience, but also their desire and ability to make informed choices about their learning. The implication of using adaptive interfaces necessitates attention to some key technical and ethical considerations. From a technical perspective, for effective adaptation to occur then sophisticated data collection and analysis are necessary, also raising questions about privacy and consent and data security, which we will discuss in depth in the ethics section of this chapter. Ethically, such systems should open opportunities, not close them, or they risk creating 'filter bubbles' that prevent users from challenges that may be fruitful for learning.

At the same time, we stand at the advent of an opportunity for truly adaptive language learning environments characterised by cognitive diversity. These environments adaptively intervene in response to individual needs and preferences to minimise the cognitive burden involved with navigating environments that have been poorly designed, allowing neurodivergent learners to pull their cognitive resources toward language learning itself. This openness is not only better accessibility but might also, through this very prolonged design, support enhanced learning achievements across the board.

3.2 Multimodal Interaction

Language is a fundamentally multimodal process that involves the simultaneous engagement of various integrative sensory and cognitive systems. Unfortunately, traditional language learning methods often privilege text-based modalities, posing potential challenges for neurodivergent learners whose cognitive profiles may serve them better with alternative modalities for processing information. This section discusses the ways-as much semantic, social, and cognitive as technical, in which AI-powered multimodal interaction can provide simple, relatable, and beneficial ways to improve accessibility and user experience in language learning environments for students with dyslexia, ADHD, and autism.

Multimodal interaction is defined as a way of communication between humans and computers that can provide multiple sensory modalities and input/output channels. In terms of language learning and instruction, multimodal communication may entail some combination of text, speech, image, video, touch, and gesture-language learning and use typically involves two or more of these modalities simultaneously, particularly as a consequence of living in the digital age.

Alcorn et al. (2019) point out that tools like Proloquo2Go, which combine voice synthesis, are especially effective in supporting learners who are autistic. This access to communication supports a learner's understanding of subject matter through their preferred mode, while also allowing them the opportunity to communicate using another form of expression, such as speech. In addition, natural language processing has advanced to consider the many 'different' ways of speaking, including differences in pronunciation, prosody, and term usage.

For dyslexic learners, multimodal interaction can blunt certain disadvantages to phonological processing and text decoding. Text-to-speech technologies give access to written content without the cognitive load of decoding, while speech-to-text enables expression of the ideas without the barrier of spelling and writing; when these technologies incorporate AI capabilities, they can offer natural voice output, more recognition of patterns in diverse speech, and intelligent integration into other learning.

Peterson et al. (2018) suggest that although assistive tools concerning text-to-speech have good documentation for dyslexic learners, more innovative multimodal solutions that harness AI abilities are very much in development. The simultaneous use of text, audio, and visual representations of language concepts can create a multitude of pathways for understanding, allowing dyslexic learners to capitalise on their very often strong visual-spatial reasoning skills while building up phonological awareness.

Visual grammar indirectly stands for another arena of multimodal interaction with promising possibilities for dyslexic learners. Parsons (2019) suggests combining mind maps with AI-generated feedback to present syntax rules, offering visual representations of language structures that should be easier to grasp than conventional text-based explanations. These visual aids can facilitate dyslexic learners to see patterns and relationships embedded within language that may be important but are masked by conventional written text.

For learners with ADHD, multimodal interaction allows engagement to decrease and provides stimulation in numerous ways while allowing a switch between modalities when attention lowers. In an engagement moment, the learner may switch between reading, listening, speaking, and being with visual elements they can engage with; creating a multiple interaction learning experience that allows learners to move back and forth and accepting cognition is graduated and overall tones learner engagement during the multiple reading moments while working through attention and interest. It can track engagement responses across, when it is paying attention different modalities, and recommend shifting if needed, if attention declines to provide a strong learning moment originally.

Cognitive load theory offers useful insights into how multimodal interaction approaches stimulate benefits for neurodivergent learners. A tenet of cognitive load theory is that working memory is limited, with learning best accommodated when working memory is not exceeded (Sweller, 2011). The resources that provide capacities for processing regulation and learning have partially independent channels, such as the phonological loop and visual-spatial sketchpad (Sweller, 2015). When utilising multimodal presentation of information, the information can be processed through a comfortable management of cognitive load in total across modalities.

However, the interaction between the influences of multimodality and cognitive load is not straightforward, and they are influenced by individual cognitive profiles. Sometimes, having multiple inputs at the same time may be more of an overwhelming sensory experience than a cognitive advantage, especially for autistic learners who may have sensory hypersensitivities or multitasking difficulties. The modality effect (cognitive load theory) indicates that for some types of presentations, and individual learners, the most effective approach may be to present the information in a single modality, making there less cognitive load, than to use multiple modalities (Castro-Alonso & Sweller, 2020).

This complexity makes the case for an adaptable approach to multimodal interaction appropriate. It is not always the case that we should think that having more modalities is better, and the best AI systems will come to learn about each learner's preferred ways of working with the different combinations of modality and adapt accordingly. For example, the system may learn that the specific learner has beneficial visual supports in learning vocabulary but prefers audio-only presentation when working on grammar instruction or that another learner learns best when text and images are presented sequentially rather than concurrently.

By combining AI with multimodal interaction, there are new avenues of support that go beyond simple content presentation across modes. For instance, AI systems can generate visualisations of abstract language concepts on-the-fly, develop personalised multimodal explanations based on areas of difficulty that have been detected, or offer multimodal feedback that takes into account both the cognitive and the affective components of learning.

This is perhaps one of the most promising multimodal applications possible with AI on behalf of neurodivergent language learners. Calvo and D'Mello (2010) develop models for detecting emotional states through linguistic or physiological cues and allow systems to recognise frustration, engagement, confusion, and other emotions relevant to the learning process. These can be used to detect occasions in which a learner has difficulties, such as repetitive erasures or other signs of frustration in written responses, and activate appropriate supports or interventions such as encouragement, alternative approaches, or more explanation.

The principle is that the modalities will not be placed together as an overwhelming array of modalities, but will be integrated thoughtfully. This will be guided by principles of universal design for learning in which multiple means of engagement, representation, and action/expression are provided (Bhutoria, 2022). AI can enhance this approach by dynamically adjusting the balance and relationship between modalities based on individual learning patterns and preferences.

Especially for language learning, it helps create multimodal interactions that lend themselves to varied aspects of language proficiency, including phonology, syntax, semantics, and pragmatics. Individual aspects of language might be learned better with different modality combinations. For example, synchronised audio and visuals might best help with phonological awareness in understanding sound-symbol relationships, while pragmatic understanding might benefit more from video showing the contextualised use of language interactions complemented by specific annotations of non-verbal cues and implicit meanings.

From a technical side, challenges that need to be dealt with are having coherent modality integration, consistency across different presentation formats, and the development of AI systems capable of processing and generating content in multiple modalities effectively. From a pedagogical perspective, the main challenge lies in identifying which particular modality combinations best work for different aspects of language learning for different learning profiles.

The pathways such approaches create for engagement in and with linguistic content can reduce barriers to access but may also achieve better learning outcomes overall. The result is more than just inclusion into education; it could also lead to more successful language instruction by acknowledging and capitalising on the entire range of human cognitive variation.

3.3 Emotional Feedback Systems

The learning of languages is not only a cognitive activity but also an emotional process comprising motivation, self-efficacy, anxiety, and a whole lot of other affective dimensions. These become more acute in neurodivergent learners who might have faced frustration, failure, or exclusion in the traditional channels of education. It is among this group that we will explore how AI-enabled emotional feedback systems can support the affective aspects of language learning for the conditions of dyslexia, ADHD, and autism.

Emotional feedback systems are technologies that can detect, interpret, and respond to the emotional states of learners engaged in explicit educational activities. Thus, such systems would necessarily include affective computing capabilities, for example, by sentiment analysis of text, emotion recognition from facial expression or voice, or detection of physiological indicators of emotional arousal along with adaptive response mechanisms changing feedback, content, or interaction patterns in accordance with detected emotions.

As yet, Calvo and D'Mello (2010) have not been above this mark. They have worked on integrating disciplines toward an interdisciplinary review of affect detection models and methods. They argue for and illustrate an assessment of how sentiment analysis might be activated to identify sources of frustration in written responses, through mechanisms like repetitive erasures, and trigger appropriate interventions, calming prompts, or alternative approaches to the task. This is especially useful for neurodivergent learners, as they may have heightened, intense emotional experiences on learning challenges but will find it hard to verbalise or self-regulate their responses.

However, emotional support can take many forms depending on the individual learner's preferences and needs. For some learners, the most effective might be explicit encouragement and positive reinforcement. As the new sources suggest, generative AI can create tailored messages for respective challenges and the learner's past responses to them, such as "Great effort—let's try one more!" Such would help in motivating, upholding and enhancing resilience in adverse times.

Too frequent feedback would distract or encourage dependence, whereas too absent feedback would leave learners alone during their difficult moments. It could create models for individual users that would learn appropriate patterns for feedback across its various dimensions: frequency, timing, and delivery.

They could also have an emotional response along with motivational challenges and emotional dysregulation, which usually coexist with attention deficits. Often, ADHD presents a distorted reward processing and motivation. Most individuals are shown to have diminished responses to delayed rewards while becoming overly sensitive to immediate feedback (Sonuga-Barke, 2003), which ultimately affects language learning, and sustained efforts toward long-term goals become more demanding. Thus, the incentive structures within a language learning activity for an AI-enabled emotional feedback system may become more immediate and conspicuous, by providing frequent positive feedback for maintaining attention, tasting small improvements of progress, or even gamifying, all of which can be perceived to be producing immediate achievements, contrary to the previous insight found by Jafarian and Kramer (2024), which holds that increased motivation will result in better academic progress using AI-assisted learning tools in students with ADHD.

Emotional self-regulation will be an additional area in which providing feedback systems can support students with ADHD. Most youths and adults with ADHD have trouble in emotional control; they tend to show more intense reactions and difficulty modulating those reactions appropriately (Sonuga-Barke et al., 2008). Therefore, AI systems would prove helpful in developing self-regulation skills by identifying signs of emotional escalation and providing calming strategies, self-reflection prompts, or a temporary shift to less frustrating activities.

The design of emotional feedback for learners with ADHD should consider a balance between stimulation and distraction. Visual or auditory feedback that is overstimulating would act as a distraction by itself; whereas feedback without stimulating engaging elements might just be ignored. Depending on how well these styles of feedback resonate with different people, finding the best fit may well be the task of personalised treatment.

For autistic learners, emotional feedback systems need to intervene in emotional recognition, expression, and regulation. Many people on the autistic spectrum develop alexithymia, which refers to a deficit in recognising and verbally describing emotional states. This presents problems for both AI systems to detect emotions and for learners to be empowered by emotional feedback (Robertson & Baron-Cohen, 2017).

While AI could help bring one's attention to implicit emotions by making them explicit with visual indicators of detected emotions or emotional patterns, the messages can be elaborated less abstractly. Instead of abstract messages, the AI can provide feedback: "I see you make the same mistake over and over again. That must be frustrating. Do you want to try something different?"

These social-emotional aspects of language learning pose special hurdles for many autistic learners, who may also have practical problems with the use of language in diverse social contexts. Such emotional feedback systems can lend an extravagant hand in navigating these dimensions, highlighting emotional tones in language samples, providing explanations for implied substance, or practising recognition and response to different emotional expressions in communication.

Across all three neurodevelopmental conditions, the emotional feedback systems should invariably remain sensitive to individual differences regarding emotional processing and emotional expression. The same emotional state could manifest as different phenomenologies for dissimilar learners, with different feedback eliciting different types of responses. AI systems, appraised to learn these individual behavioural patterns over time, have a big edge going for them when the perspective to implementation: they could well be considered for interventional effectiveness, as set against those considered on average.

The ethical implications, such as privacy concerns, consent, and even detrimental psychological impact, arise with the actual implementation of these emotional feedback mechanisms. The collection of any set of sensitive data, whether it deals with the analysis of text inputs, pattern recognition in the interaction process, or the monitoring of physiological signals, is required to detect such emotional states. Users ought to be briefed, with utmost clarity, on when, to whom, and how such data is collected, with well-established choices afforded to limit or entirely opt out of any emotional detection features.

Apart from that, other risks exist whereby poorly designed emotional feedback mechanisms may act as positive reinforcement for negative patterns, lead to dependence, and undermine intrinsic motivation. Systems that rely heavily on extrinsic rewards or intervene quickly may hinder the development of self-regulation and intrinsic motivation. This risk highlights the need for emotional feedback design to be based on well-established theories of motivation, like self-determination theory (Ryan & Deci, 2000) and social cognitive theory (Schunk & DiBenedetto, 2020).

According to self-determination theory, ideal motivation arises through satisfying three basic psychological needs: autonomy, competence, and relatedness (Ryan & Deci, 2020). The emotional feedback system could contribute toward the enhancement of the above needs by providing alternatives for feedback styles about autonomy, acknowledging real accomplishments for competence, and inspiring an atmosphere of encouraging presence throughout the learning process for relatedness. However, the way these needs will be achieved among the neurodivergent learners may differ, given their different cognitive and emotional profiles.

Equally important for motivation and achievement, acknowledged by social cognitive theory, is self-efficacy- the belief in one's ability to perform certain tasks (Schunk & DiBenedetto, 2020). Such feedback systems can enhance self-efficacy by pinpointing where students succeeded, attributing success to their efforts and choice of strategies rather than simply to the set of skills they are perceived to possess, and modelling effective methods for coping with difficult tasks. These self-efficacy supports are especially valuable for neurodivergent learners who have gained negative academic self-concepts as a result of defeats and exclusion.

The case study also suggests more general questions regarding the use of AI writing support in education. As these tools improve in sophistication, educational institutions will need to develop thoughtful policies that create appropriate parameters surrounding the responsible use of technology for writing instruction and assessment tasks. The policies ought to be developed with a balance between genuine accommodation needs and the obligations to uphold academic integrity, as appropriate use of technological support may create more equitable access to learning experiences than providing a competitive advantage. The case also emphasises the importance of including dyslexic individuals in the design and evaluation of any AI tools developed to support their learning experiences. Some of the most productive information about the potential of the tool came directly from the students, reminding us that this should always be a principle we consider for neurodivergent students when developing tools that will impact classroom learning and engagement with the learning experience.

Although emotional feedback systems pose some challenges and ethical implications, they also represent an important other area of work in making language learning technologies genuinely inclusive. By engaging the affective side of learning together with the cognitive side, these systems will foster an environment that will offer support, encouragement, and efficacy to the neurodivergent learners and, in so doing, transform a present source of anguish and despair into an opportunity for advancement and prosperity.

4. CASE STUDIES: AI IN ACTION

4.1 Case Study 1: AI Writing Assistant for Dyslexic Students

In recent years, several AI tools have been developed to help neurodivergent learners by applying the theoretical principles described in earlier sections. In this section, the case study of an AI writing assistant designed to maintain dyslexic students' focus and support their writing in a UK secondary school is discussed in terms of its implementation, findings, and prospects for future development.

The name of the AI writing assistant is custom-made to assist dyslexic students with the various hurdles they encounter in the actual writing of languages. Dyslexia affects somewhere between 5 and 17% of children of school age (Barua et al., 2022) and is characterised by difficulty in word recognition, fluency and accuracy, with poor spelling and decoding abilities. This would then affect students adversely in academic performance in virtually any subject area since writing is a basic skill that students employ to demonstrate their knowledge of just about every teaching subject.

The main task was to reduce text complexity while keeping the meaning intact so that dyslexic students could better express their ideas in writing. Similar to the GPT-4 plugin described by Parsons (2019), which simplifies sentence complexity in real-time (for instance, replacing complex terms like "exacerbate" with simpler alternatives like "worsen"), this AI assistant was designed specifically to address the patterns of difficulty commonly experienced by dyslexic writers, among them phonological processing challenges, working memory limitations, and sequencing difficulties.

The affordances of the system had several salient aspects that were intended to support dyslexic learners. First, the system could use advanced natural language processing to detect and substitute words that pose quite a bit of challenge with dyslexic learners—discrimination within words across phonological structures, complex spelling, irregular spelling or indeterminate meaning. It could go beyond signalling misspellings and recognise when a learner may have been struggling to eject a specific word, presenting semantically acceptable alternatives. Second, the tool provided live feedback on students' sentence structure and complexity, which used colour-coded and visual prompt diagrams to make abstract grammatical concepts as tangible as possible. It utilised the visual-spatial strengths that many dyslexic learners appear to possess (Eide & Eide, 2011), changing more of the writing experience process or activity to an experience more visual rather than text-based. Peterson et al. (2018) indicated that many dyslexic learners possessed superior spatial reasoning skills that were developing alongside phonological processing challenges, and supported that educational technologies that draw on visual-spatial strengths while providing phonological challenges should support the eventual goal that all students need to face. Finally, the system included a text-to-speech and a speech-to-text system, which gave students more opportunities to use with their writing (interaction) in different modalities. This type of support and opportunity was aligned with the research surrounding multisensory approaches to intervention for dyslexia, as research on similar approaches supported their value for the aim of developing literacy skills (Shaywitz & Shaywitz, 2020).

This system was then gradually introduced into the UK secondary school sector; training on the uses and limitations of the system was given to teachers ahead of this full rollout, with special attention being paid to embedding the tool within existing writing instruction rather than regarding it as a separate intervention in its own right. It was understood that AI tools function best when integrated with other human abilities, rather than when used interchangeably.

Training has followed a workshop model, where students received hands-on initiation to using the tool but were taught more about how and why to apply specific technical skills as metacognitive strategies to support their writing processes, explicitly including discussion of the tool as an accommodation versus a "crutch," thereby framing it as a legitimate support for accessing the curriculum rather than one perceived as creating an unfair advantage.

Feedback sessions enabled students to relay experiences with and views about the tool as well as suggestions for improvements to its implementation. Such procedures are in line with the participatory design tenets of the neurodiversity paradigm, which emphasises the valuing of neurodivergent individuals' agency and expertise in designing supports for their learning.

On the outcome data for this implementation came some major revelations. The first was that through quantitative analysis of the essay, scores came into view the measured improvements in the quality of written work by the dyslexic students with the aid of the AI assistant, especially in those areas that have always posed a challenge to dyslexic writers: areas of vocabulary diversity, syntactic complexity, and organizational coherence. Most importantly, all improvements are preserved even in subsequent assessments where students did not have access to the tool, thereby implying that the support was helping to develop the skills rather than adapting to the lack thereof.

A similar AI writing assistant used in Parsons' (2019) UK study with 45 dyslexic students showed a 32% increase in essay coherence and students' self-efficacy, with a sizable improvement, corroborating the findings of our case study and providing more evidence that AI-based writing tools could be effective for dyslexic learners.

Even more significant improvements were found in measures of self-efficacy among students involved in the intervention. The pre- and post-implementation surveys have indicated considerable increases in students' beliefs about their writing ability, their desire to engage in writing tasks, and their perception of autonomy in the writing process. The psychological advantages then reached beyond writing to mould students' overall academic self-concept and their engagement in learning.

Teacher reports supported the findings as they referred to increased sharing in writing activities, independence in completing writing assignments, and decreased anxiety during writing tasks from dyslexic students with the instrument. The teachers then relayed how the tool offered more meaningful feedback regarding content and ideas since both students and even teachers could have less focus on the mechanical aspects of writing and concentrate on higher-order thinking.

On the other hand, some limitations were revealed by students. In certain cases, the interpretation conducted by the tool does not align with what they were trying to say, especially when it comes to specialised vocabulary or language exploration. Some students simply mentioned that simplifications suggested by the tool sounded like “dummy proofing” and couldn't capture the deeper workings going on in their minds, which focused on the importance of their voices as students in AI writing support.

This, students added, leads to the question of whether it would lead to overreliance on the tool and emphasised the continued balance of such assistance with time to develop their skills. Some teachers recounted challenges in assessment, such as how to measure academic work produced under the support of AI programs against the measure of customary standards.

These point to various improvements that can be made to future versions of an AI writing tool dedicated to dyslexic learners. First, the enhancement of semantic deepness through which student voice can be maintained and meaning preserved while supplying mechanical support needs to happen, as well as include more explicit scaffolding for skill development that gradually tapers levels of support as students' skill development progresses. Third-increased specifications in customisation options would enable targeting individual patterns of difficulty, rather than classifying dyslexic writers as a homogeneous group.

It raises even broader questions about where it stands with education regarding AI writing support. Institutions would eventually develop policies for the instruction and assessment of the use of such instruments; they should balance authentic accommodation needs with the need for academic integrity, as appropriate technological support can make education much more accessible rather than exceptionally unfair.

The case goes a step further to show that the effective involvement of dyslexic people in the design and evaluation of AI tools targeting the learning or support of such individuals is paramount. The most insightful information revealing the effectiveness of the tool would come from the students themselves, preferably underscoring the fact that neurodivergent individuals should be active participants in developing technologies that affect their educational experiences.

This kind of case study shows the power of AI writing assistants to change education sharply for dyslexic learners after proper design and execution. Such strengths build on existing capacity while addressing thinking challenges that restrict accessibility in learning. But that case also points to a need to see such cases as integrated into the whole of supporting neurodivergent learners, complementing rather than replacing human teaching and always focusing on independent skill development.

4.2 Case Study 2: Audio-Learning Chatbot for ADHD Learners

This second case study has investigated an AI-based audio-learning chatbot having features of pause and rephrase to specifically cater to learners with Attention Deficit Hyperactivity Disorder within a U.S. online learning program. This case epitomised insights on leveraging AI to address distinctive challenges encountered by ADHD learners in the realm of language acquisition and academic achievement.

ADHD affects 5-10% of children and adolescents worldwide (Barua et al., 2022). The primary symptoms are the following: an inability to maintain attention for extended periods, hyperactivity, and problems with executive functioning. All these problems greatly affect language learning, which usually requires prolonged focus, sequential processing, and self-regulation—areas of possible difficulty for those suffering from Attention Deficit Hyperactivity Disorder.

An audio-learning chatbot is being developed to address these issues, as seen from Jafarian and Kramer's (2024) research, which states that AI-assisted audio-learning modules enhance student motivation and reading engagement," and "these increases in motivation and reading engagement boosted subsequent academic achievement" and further states that according to their research, AI assisted audio learning modules help mitigate the negative effects of ADHD symptoms even on academic achievement"-. It is a great empirical foundation for this application.

The chatbot incorporated several key features designed to support ADHD learners. For one, it had a conversational interface by which students could engage with learning content with natural language and not the conventional text-based formats. The significance of this course is that it reduces cognitive load incurred in reading and writing, almost a rule of thumb for ADHD learners, who might be struggling with sustained visual attention or fine motor control.

The system had it "pause and rephrase" which allowed the students to be able to stop the audio presentation at any point and even ask for clarification or simplification of content. This addressed the generalised experience of ADHD learners "zoning out" for long stretches of other presentations. This would have a mechanism to recover what has been missed without embarrassment or extensive backtracking. As indicated by Cortiella and Horowitz (2014), it's these features of pacing control and opportunities to clarify information that are said to benefit students with ADHD even more.

With all the interactive patterns of student engagement, the chatbot works at an adaptive pacing facility, where it will be controlled by automatic adjustments regarding speed, complexity, and segmentation of the presentation of the materials. This adaptation is intended to maintain optimal arousal levels important consideration for ADHD learners who often experience difficulties from both under- and over-arousal (Sonuga-Barke, 2003).

The adoption of the tool in U.S. online learning has ushered in an opportunity to assess how effective this content tool is in real-world educational evaluation. It comprised 60 high school learners identified as having ADHD and enrolled in an online second language course. Randomly, students were assigned either to use the AI chatbot or a traditional digital learning platform for 12 weeks, where both groups would cover the same curriculum content.

The careful embedding of this implementation included methodical orientation and support. Thus, students were thoroughly familiar with how the chatbot system functions, with a strong emphasis concerning valuable ways to optimise the pause and rephrase feature. Regular check-ins with learning coaches are provided for this technical assistance and opportunities for fine-tuning use strategies. It recognises the fact that technology alone cannot perform the task of effective implementation without proper human guidance and support for adjustment.

The results from this implementation showed some statistically significant positive outcomes for engagement and achievement. Specifically, task completion for students using the chatbot increased by 41% when compared to the control group, per the reports from Cortiella and Horowitz (2014). Moving the needle on rates of completion is a huge step forward in supporting the lack of task completion, which is one of the most enduring struggles of ADHD learners in asynchronous online learning environments, as they have difficulty completing tasks before their attention or motivational level dips down or becomes insufficient.

In addition to task completion, the students who used the chatbot also showed significant increases in content mastery on standardised assessments. Notably, the gains were most profound on tasks that required sequential processing or remembering information in detail, as those have been especially hard for ADHD learners over time. Furthermore, these improvements persisted even without using the chatbot for assessment, administered using traditional paper/pencil assessment formats, which indicates the students meaningfully learned in the collaboration as opposed to artificially increasing their performance level (if we assume traditional assessments are also correlated with some student performance level).

Qualitative data, obtained from student interviews, informed an understanding of the workings behind these improvements. In their reframing of the experience of reading, students stated that the audio format decreased cognitive load, allowing students to concentrate more on understanding the material. The pause and rephrase feature was frequently mentioned as helpful for allowing students to stay engaged and consequently helping them feel more in control about processing information they could take at their own pace without the potential of falling behind or losing the thread of the material and what they were doing. Many students also cited the psychological benefits of using the chatbot, such as feeling at ease about not missing some information and feeling more confident to engage with difficult content. These affective adjustments were congruent with the findings by Jafarian and Kramer (2024) that higher motivation mediated the connection between AI-assisted audio learning and educational achievement in students with ADHD.

The instructors indicated that there was an improvement in student engagement, a lessening of frustration with the tool, and fewer cases of students giving up on difficult material. The instructors also observed that the chatbot would help students regulate themselves in developing the ability to recognise when they needed some clarity and how to go about asking for it.

On the other hand, instructors concurred that implementation limitations existed. Some indicated that the chatbot misinterpreted student questions, especially when students expressed themselves somewhat vaguely or with colloquialisms. Others cautioned against potential overreliance on the audio format, with a suggestion that students should be better supported in making the transition between audio learning and conventional text-based assessment or learning activities.

The present case study identified areas for improvement within future versions of audio-learning chatbots for ADHD learners. For one, there is a need for greater sophistication in natural language understanding to accommodate the myriad formulations and varying patterns of conversational discourse. The system also deserves an increase in explicit scaffolding of metacognitive skills to make students aware of when and how to use the most appropriate pause and rephrase functionality. Additionally, amplification in the interface of visual supports would foster a more integrative multimodal learning experience using both auditory and visual processing strengths.

This case study also raises larger questions concerning the role of AI in supporting ADHD learners across educational domains. With increased sophistication and wider availability, it will be incumbent upon the educational community to formulate balanced policies on the use of these tools in instruction and assessment. These policies must acknowledge the rational need for accommodations but also cultivate students' skills to relate academic learning to contexts where those accommodations do not exist.

In addition, the case illustrates the relevance of taking account of individual differences in a sample of students with ADHD. Although the chatbot showed considerable benefit on average, the pattern and size of impact were extremely variable among individual students. Such variability demonstrates the heterogeneity that can exist within diagnostic categories, and the desire for more personalised strategies that accommodate individual personal cognitive profiles, interests, and learning goals. As evidenced by the data presented in this case, the audio-learning chatbot also provides a roadmap to demonstrate how AI could focus on the specific cognitive challenges related to ADHD but also tap into cognitive strengths that many ADHD learners have, including strengths in verbal processing. By providing different pathways to engage with academic content through a platform designed to provide textual content, such options can potentially contribute to ecosystems that enable emergence, making the classroom experience accessible and equitable for a wide array of cognitive styles.

Table 3. Case study feature comparison & outcomes

Parameter	AI Writing Assistant (Dyslexia)	Audio-Learning Chatbot (ADHD)	[Your Missing Autism Case Study]
Core Technology	NLP simplification; visual feedback	Speech recognition; adaptive pacing	Pattern recognition; pragmatic language modeling
Primary Challenge Targeted	Phonological processing; working memory	Sustained attention; executive function	Social communication; sensory regulation
Key Feature	Real-time text simplification; dyslexia-friendly fonts	"Pause & rephrase"; micro-lesson gamification	Visual schedule integration; explicit social rule annotation
Implementation Setting	UK secondary school (in-person)	US online learning program	[To be developed - special education classroom?]
Measured Outcome	32% increase in essay coherence; improved self-efficacy	41% increase in task completion; enhanced motivation	[Projected: Reduced social anxiety; improved pragmatic language use]
Student Feedback Theme	"Privacy of support"; "maintains my voice"	"Control over pacing"; "less overwhelming"	[Expected: "Predictable structure"; "clear rules"]

5. ETHICAL CONSIDERATIONS AND CHALLENGES

5.1 Bias Mitigation

Such creation and usage of AI tools for neurodivergent learners raise serious ethical issues, with one of the most critical being algorithmic bias. In this section, one discusses bias in AI educational systems, how this bias potentially impacts neurodivergent learners, and methods to counter this in the creation and use of less biased technologies.

Algorithmic bias in AI systems arises from various reasons, like biased training data, unwanted optimisation objectives, and implicit values included in design decisions. These biases get reflected in AI tools being specifically disadvantageous to the neurodiverse people in terms of stereotypes, interpreting possible varied cognitive patterns, or applying neurotypical standards to neurodivergent users.

This principle becomes very relevant in neurodiversity, which has a rich history of discrimination and pathology in which the likelihoods of incurring algorithmic harm are magnified. As Nguyen et al. (2022) posit in their ethical framework for AI in education, "AI systems need to be designed to be fair and equitable, without putting any bias or discrimination against any person or group" (p. 7).

The equation of "slowness" to "low ability" is perhaps the most basic form of bias in educational AI- the correlation may be true for some learners, but misleading for many neurodivergent ones. For example, some slow text processors can be classified as dyslexic, having high-level comprehension; some high-level understanding needs response time for some students, such as autistic students; and the pace at which students work varies for different purposes or due to different environmental effects on them at any given time for students with ADHD.

Thus, Baker (2016) indicates, "This specific danger is that the AI models may possess a certain stereotype of weak ability with slow pace." Such interpretations are especially wrong for students whose processing speeds differ from those of the neurotypical but who can demonstrate high comprehension and reasoning skills.

Artificial intelligence systems trained almost solely on the learning behaviours of neurotypical learners may see these shifts as evidence of low ability and, as a result, may simplify content, minimise learning opportunities, or react with negative feedback to decrease the confidence of the learner. This dynamic between system expectations and neurodivergent behaviours may be equally pervasive, producing algorithmic discrimination that limits educational access while reinforcing stereotypes about neurodevelopmental differences. Socially responsible mechanisms to address these inequities include thinking critically about the training data and the design of the system. To guard against this kind of bias, you need to pay careful attention to both the training data as well as system design. Regarding training data, datasets should contain patterns of learning that represent different neurodevelopmental profiles. This is to ensure that your algorithms will learn to recognise and respond differently to various ways of approaching learning tasks. In terms of system design, there should not be a strict connection between pace and aptitude; instead, more nuanced measures should be able to distinguish between different user reasons for more or less time spent on tasks.

To address these issues with bias, Floridi et al. (2018) encourage regular auditing of training data and a participatory design process that includes the perspectives of users, as essential considerations of AI design. Their ethical framework for AI, outlined above, suggests revisiting any assessments of bias on an ongoing basis, rather than as a one-time effort, based on the principle that bias can be formed in complicated and unpredictable ways as systems engage with a variety of users and perspectives in the real world.

Furthermore, an expertly designed and evaluated AI system may still impose limits on the range of behaviours and actions for a given neurodevelopmental condition. Such limits might take the form of assumptions regarding an individual's levels of capability or ability in various areas of learning, the learning modalities we expect an individual to favour, or assumptions regarding someone's interests or motivations. When these limits are conditioned into educational technologies, they can be difficult to remove, and can lead to self-fulfilling prophecies, causing limitations within the educational opportunity for a person, which in turn can result in a negative user experience by confirming narrow, non-inclusive assumptions about the individual.

Neurodivergent perspectives must be part of heterogeneous development teams and stringent testing protocols specifically developed about stereotyping to disallow algorithmic reinforcement of stereotypes. Neurodiversity-aligned approaches, as maintained by Dwyer (2022), would recognise their own biases and then learn to listen to and learn from neurodivergent people. This is consistent with AI tools development; neurodivergent involvement can assist in recognising and preemptively dealing with unnoticed biases.

Inclusive training datasets are some of the strategies that are most important in bias mitigation. This deliberate oversampling from neurodivergent patterns of learning to ensure adequacy in representation, proper annotation of training data to differentiate cognitive pathways as opposed to marking such as atypical, and continuous data collection embracing the full richness of user interaction rather than specifically successful patterns would constitute strategies towards inclusive training data sets.

Nonetheless, it is possible to have the most diverse training data yet still find bias embedded in bad optimisation objectives. Such AI systems could be set to optimise for results that are standardised or for traditional learning paths. These might produce students with a disability in learning because of the inherent disadvantage points in their developmental paths. An analogy can be drawn about language learning applications, where typical measures of progress might not be sufficient to capture diversity in terms of developing different language-learning skills.

This calls for a thorough rethinking of what is to be defined as success concerning language learning, and how that success would be monitored and assisted. Rather than optimising for standardised outcomes, AI systems should be designed to support individual learning trajectories, recognising multiple pathways to language proficiency and valuing diverse expressions of language competence. This is in line with what the paradigm of neurodiversity advocates-cognitive variation as a natural and value-added form of human diversity and not as a deviation from a single pattern of normality.

Bias-monitoring and -assessment frameworks are another very important part of ethical AI development for neurodivergent learners, including regular auditing of system behaviour for diversity in user profiles, performance evaluations comparing such disparate user groups, and avenues for users to report perceived bias or unfair adaptation. Not just during the initial development of such systems over their life course, bias might result from and manifest in such real-world interactions with diverse users.

Transparency in algorithmic decision-making provides another important safeguard against harmful bias. The users and their teachers, and families in this educational space should have an easily understandable trail of how AI systems come to adaptation decisions, what factors go into the content presentation or feedback, and what data sends personalisation of the learning experience. That way, it provides informed consent and, therefore, empowers users to spot and challenge potentially biased or inappropriate system behaviours.

By far, the most fundamental strategy toward bias reduction is having a diverse group of stakeholders in the system's development and evaluation. Involving people from outside the traditional parameters of consultation would imply meaningful participation in decision-making about the system design, training data selection, evaluation metrics, and implementation approaches. Pertinent costs here are neurodivergent from diverse profiles, so that the entire neurodevelopmental variation spectrum will be represented in this development process.

This participatory method is congruent with larger movements toward justice-centred design in technology development. Costanza-Chock (2020) points out that design justice focuses on...the ways by which design reproduces and/or challenges... the matrix of domination (white supremacy, heteropatriarchy, capitalism, ableism, settler colonialism, and other forms of structural inequality). In this way, centring neurodivergent voices on the design of education technologies would lead to developing systems that fight against rather than support ableist structures and assumptions.

The ethical obligation to reduce bias in AIs designed for neurodivergent learners does extend much beyond technical aspects and questions of educational equity and justice. Indeed, these technologies can strengthen or challenge existing patterns of disadvantage concerning neurodivergent students. Bias mitigation would not just be thought of as a technical problem but as having social justice implications that lead to the development of systems contributing toward a more just and inclusive educational environment for all learners.

5.2 Data Privacy

The creation of efficient AI devices for neurodivergent students entails tremendous data gathering for personalisation and adaptation. Such data collection evokes considerable concern regarding privacy, particularly within neurodiversity. This section outlines the unique issues in safeguarding neurodiversity-related data, the tension between personalisation and privacy, and approaches to ethical data management in education AI.

Almost always stigmatising from misuse or inappropriate disclosure, neurodiversity-related data is also sensitive data in that it draws from educational, health-related or behavioural pattern information. As Barrua et al. (2022) say, neurodevelopmental disorders are characterised by low self-confidence, anxiety, and depression, which makes privacy protections particularly important for purposes of psychological safety and prevention of additional stigma. "

Indeed, Zeide (2019) states that diagnoses like ADHD are just one set of neurodiversity data that severely warrant protections under extant regulatory frameworks, like GDPR for the EU and FERPA for the United States. Information concerning minimum data security, consent, and limits on use is built into these regulations; however, their relevance in the context of the messy data produced by AI educational systems remains a bit unclear and may warrant additional interpretation and guidance.

The types of data that can be collected by AI systems for neurodiverse students can include information on how an individual processes cognition, fluctuating levels of attention, emotional responses to certain learning tasks, specific areas of difficulties, as well as accommodation needs. This information is very important for the appropriateness of personalisation, but lately, it can also be very critical in the labelling, categorising, or even discriminating against individuals where there is no proper protection of that information.

Additional special considerations in safeguarding this data are made up of more rigorous security measures, precise controls over data sharing, straightforward policies in data retention, and careful examination of de-identification practices. Sensitivity over time is more pronounced for neurodiversity-related materials than for some other types of educational data, since cognitive profiles remain relatively stable through educational careers with time. Thus, that temporal aspect justifies quite careful approaches to how data life cycles are managed.

On the other hand, the benefits conferred by personalisation against privacy-protection costs represent one of the central ethical dilemmas in the human development of AI for neurodivergent learners. Data collection on an increasing scale allows for much more sophisticated personalisations, which is quite possible for the development of highly efficient and accessible learning experiences. However, at the same time, the actual collection of personal information increases risks on the privacy side and may result in creating psychological burdens for those aware of being closely watched.

The design of the system should be thoughtful enough to allow it to balance between benefiting from personalisation maximally while minimising the risks that come with the loss of privacy. These might include sensitive data being processed locally rather than sent over the cloud, useful patterns kept while raw data discarded, and allowing users to make decisions about when exactly pieces of information are collected about them and how their information is used.

Constructing education AI systems for children and adolescents without understanding the full privacy implications is indeed really tough. Age-appropriate permission and assent processes involved in ethical data management in neurodivergent learners are major issues. This is even made worse among some neurodivergent users who process information differently or require alternative formats for consent materials.

Developing genuinely informed consent procedures for such contexts requires various strategies, such as simplified explanations, visual representations of data collection and use, concrete potential benefits and risks, and ongoing consent processes that allow users to revisit decisions as their understanding develops. For example, in the case of younger users, it would be very important to consider their parents or guardians in the consent processes, without disregarding the inner autonomy of the learner's development.

Regulation over data protection varies from jurisdiction to jurisdiction, adding another layer of complexity for any given educational AI system that may be used in a worldwide choice of locations. With the measures of safeguards that the General Data Protection Regulation (GDPR) in the EU and the Family Educational Rights and Privacy Act (FERPA) in the United States provide, it is hard to decipher their applicability to insights that AI has generated concerning neurodivergence in learning patterns.

Moving between these myriad domestic regulatory regimes requires both technical and policy savvy with a specific lens on forking over the very greatest and most stringent compliance requirements to get fully covered across contexts. More importantly, though, the ethical commitment does have to exceed the minimum requirements of compliance with substantive protection for the privacy and autonomy of users, no matter how local regulation may be read.

The minimisation of data is a very good principle for developing ethical AI in this context. Rather than collecting all possible useful data, the systems should be constructed in a way that they will only collect those facts necessary for learning functions. Such reduces risks to privacy and perhaps improves performance because the noise created by excessive collection will not be present in the target data points.

Then, also achieved by purpose limitation- that is, restricting the use of data captured to the specifically disclosed purposes and consent- is the more important ethical guardrail. That is, personal language learning data should not then be used or repurposed without additional explicit consent for other research, marketing, or administrative purposes. This principle would help with trustworthiness in educational AI systems and prevent function creep that might expose users to unanticipated risks.

Continuing the thread of transparency about data practices, another essential aspect of ethical AI for neurodivergent learners comes into play here. In clear, accessible language, this information should be made available to users, parents, and educators about what data will be collected, how it will be used, who will gain access to it, for how long, and what rights users have for their data. This gives individuals an informed choice and holds the data practice accountable.

Such an inclusion would be a critical perspective through which privacy enhancement or unanticipated consequences may be caught that might have gone unnoticed otherwise. This should represent the spectrum of neurodevelopmental profiles within which people have very different sensitivity and concern levels regarding privacy.

There are underlying technical and policy factors that contribute to the ethical practice of data in neurodivergent learners, but these technologies must also address the broader societal environment in which they function. Such historical practices of surveillance, categorisation, and control against neurodivergent individuals create a backdrop within which justified concern about data collection is raised. Educational AI must address this legacy and strive to create a new kind of pattern in the use of respectful and empowering technology that will ensure the priority of agency and the well-being of users.

It also supports the principle that there should be no permanent digital imprints capable of following learners through educational institutions and beyond. Methods of limiting data retention, rights to erasure, and reflections on longitudinal data management can help in ensuring that current support for learning does not create future vulnerabilities through permanent digital labelling.

The ethical approach to data in AI systems for neurodiverse learners would be a balance between the obvious strong advantages of personalisation and the fundamental value of a respectful approach to privacy, autonomy, and dignity. The result will ensure that systems developed with the capacity to support individual learning literally will respect and protect the people they purport to advocate for.

5.3 Human-AI Balance

As AI technologies affect education, rather complex questions arise regarding what the appropriate balance should be between the technological and human elements in education regarding the learning capabilities of neurodivergent students. This chapter is about the complementary roles of AI tools and human educators, about the importance of human relationships in education, and finally, about creating successful partnerships between technology and pedagogy.

Keeping teachers at the centre of emotional care and guidance represents the basic principle for the ethical implementation of AI. Much as AI would individualise content, sustain adjusted pacing, and supply instantaneous feedback, nothing can substitute for the emotional intelligence, ethical judgment, and authentic human connection which qualified teachers supply. Indeed, the need for a human dimension stems from the unique way in which neurodivergent learners would benefit from having clear social modelling and emotional scaffolding in educational encounters.

Luckin et al. (2016) emphasise this principle, arguing that teachers remain critical for emotional support and that AI should augment, not replace, human interaction. Their research on intelligence in education highlights the complementary nature of human and artificial intelligence, with each bringing distinct strengths to the educational process.

As Bhutoria (2022) emphasises, in AI-enabled personalised education, instructors are facilitators and motivators, not information providers. This recalibration of roles recognises that AI can effectively manage certain aspects of content delivery and skill practice, freeing human teachers to focus on the interpersonal dimensions of education that technology cannot replicate. Rather than diminishing the teacher's role, this approach potentially enhances it by allowing more focused attention on relationship-building, motivation, and individualised guidance.

AI tools and human educators have been defined as roommates who mobilise their strengths differently to enable the educational process. AI systems perform well when it comes to computation, consistently applying rules, adapting content to learners, and an eternal capability for repetitive application. Human teachers are good at establishing emotional connections, ethical reasoning, creative problem-solving, and contextual judgment. Thoughtful integration of these complementary faculties would result in educational experiences more personalised and humane than those offered by either group on its own.

The issue of professional development for educators is, therefore, another important consideration, one that connects with the implication of an effective human-AI partnership. Not only will teachers need training in the technical use of the tools, but also an enhanced understanding of their mechanisms, the data they use and collect, their limitations, and how to integrate them meaningfully into human practices of teaching. This understanding should assist teachers in making conscious decisions about AI integration through their teaching.

Greatly beyond mere technical knowledge, the teaching profession must develop in areas that implicate understanding neurodiversity and being efficacious in shaping inclusive learning environments. Onward, as AI tools take over the routine efforts of instruction, there are opportunities for teachers to widen their skills in supporting diverse learning needs. This transformation requires a shift of investment in deepening pedagogical knowledge rather than narrowly focusing on technological knowledge.

Here, the ethical implications related to the implementation of AI for neurodivergent students come to the fore in the case of over-reliance. Institutions with limited resources may be pushed into the position of supplanting human service partners with AI ones, compromising the accessibility to special education teachers, educational psychologists, speech-language pathologists, and other professionals with specialised knowledge in supporting neurodivergent students.

What must be avoided is a replacement of this kind, which requires providing clear ethical guidelines and policy frameworks, positioning AI tools as complementary rather than a substitute for human expertise and support. These frameworks would set conditions for resource allocation decisions; cost savings from technological efficiencies should then be reinvested into enhanced human support rather than being siphoned into just decreasing the educational budget.

If AI systems are used to mediate and potentially change human relationships in educational settings, what additional ethical questions are raised? For example, if students develop significant relationships with AI learning companions or get most of their feedback from automated systems, how is this going to affect their development of social skills, their understanding of human relationships, or their sense of connection to their learning community? Such questions become even more significant for some neurodivergent learners who already with social challenges in terms of interaction and relationships.

Trying to mitigate these concerns involves some careful design considerations that conceive AI instruments not as substitutes for human relations but rather as tools that help cement them. For example, systems could display features that encourage socialisation between peers; foster communication between teachers and students regarding learning impediments; and provide opportunities for students to celebrate their achievements with the wider learning community.

There may be substantial differences in the balance between human and AI components in various neurodevelopmental profiles, their educational contexts, and individual preferences. Some learners may require extensive AI support for certain tasks and only minimal technological mediation for others. Some learning goals may be more suited to an approach by technology, while others, by their very nature, require human interaction and guidance.

The realisation of such differences emphasises the flexible implementation model that allows this customisation to be based on individual needs and contextual factors. Rather than a single "correct" balance of the human and technological elements,

The ethical implementation would include continuous assessment of effectiveness, well-being indicators, and adjustment based on observed rather than predetermined performance.

Human oversight is an important principle of AI ethics in educational settings; hence, while AI systems may operate largely independently in their content adaptation and feedback processes, human educators must retain meaningful oversight to review system decisions, override inappropriate adaptations, and ensure a continued alignment with the larger picture of educational goals and values.

This kind of oversight is very important for neurodivergent learners whose unique cognitive profiles may not be fully captured by AI systems being trained on predominantly neurotypical data. The contextual knowledge that human educators have in conjunction with their ethical judgment and professional expertise can enable them to identify situations when technological approaches fail to appropriately attend to a learner's needs or create unintended barriers to access.

In addition, this AI literacy among educational stakeholders-including students, families, and administrators, represents another key area in the establishment of a proper human-AI balance. When all actors appreciate the achievements and the limitations of an educational AI, all together would make more informed decisions about its use and keep the public's interest in correct expectations about its role in the learning process.

For neurodivergent students specifically, literacy means appreciating how AI tools may assist them in their learning, what kinds of data those tools collect and act upon, and how they can exert some agency in their interaction with those technologies. This starts to frame them not just as passive recipients of algorithmic decision-making but as active agents in their technologically mediated education.

To ethically put AI to work for neurodivergent learners, there should be a fine balance that exploits technological skills while keeping and enhancing the human side of education. In the wake of such consideration, AI would be viewed as an ally to human teaching rather than as a competitor. In so doing, learning environments would be designed by institutions which combine the technical expertise and personalisation of technology with the human compassion, wisdom, and authentic connections that only people are capable of giving.

Table 4. Ethical decision matrix for AI implementation

Ethical Tension	Technology-Heavy Approach	Human-Heavy Approach	Recommended Hybrid Balance	Red Flag Indicators
Personalization vs. Privacy	Maximum data collection for adaptation	Minimal data; generic content	Tiered consent; local data processing; periodic data purging	No opt-out mechanisms; opaque data sharing
Automation vs. Human Judgment	AI makes all pacing/content decisions	Teacher controls every adaptation	AI suggests; teacher approves; student can override	Teacher becomes passive observer
Efficiency vs. Inclusion	One-size-fits-all algorithm	Fully individual human support	Universal Design principles with targeted AI enhancement	Cost-cutting disguised as "innovation"
Standardization vs. Authentic Assessment	AI-graded for consistency	Purely subjective evaluation	AI assists with rubric application; teacher provides holistic evaluation	No accommodation for non-traditional outputs
Scalability vs. Individual Voice	Generic feedback templates	1:1 conferences only	AI drafts personalized feedback; teacher customizes	Student voice absent from design process

6. CONCLUSION

The intersection of artificial intelligence and neurodiversity offers a frontier into possibilities for making language learning environments more inclusive and effective. In the last chapter, we discussed issues of AI technology design, catering to the cognitive variety of learners with dyslexia, ADHD, and autism to move beyond a one-size-fits-all model. The whole range of human cognitive variation must be embraced.

The neurodiversity paradigm stands as a key support for this work, reframing cognitive differences as variations rather than deficits and asserting the value of diverse minds in educational contexts and elsewhere. In Dwyer's (2022) words, this paradigm recognises the contributions of both individual and society to disability and attempts to shift from change in the individual to change in the environment-including the technological environment, to accommodate divergent cognitive profiles better. This paradigm shift significantly changes our approach to designing educational technologies, from something remedial and normalising for neurodivergent learners to an inclusive system offering multiple pathways to language acquisition.

With the unparalleled promise of implementation of this neurodiversity-informed approach to education technology, AI offers a plethora of functions-specifically adaptive algorithms, natural language processing, and affective computing. AI can "augment educational content, customise it for any individual according to their needs, and raise the flag of caution for anticipated learning difficulties" (p. 1), as shown by Bhutoria (2022). These capabilities allow learning environments to adapt in real time to individual cognitive profiles with personalised support that does not require standardisation.

The discussed design principles in this chapter- adaptive interface, interaction via multiple modalities, and emotional feedback system- form an initial set of guiding principles to inform the design of AI tools that truly honour neurodiversity in language learning. The principles emphasise user control, multiple pathways to engagement and expression, along with recognising the emotional dimensions of learning, which are especially important for neurodivergent individuals. In an intentional application, these principles can be materialised into technologies that work toward lessening barriers to language acquisition while also acknowledging and celebrating cognitive diversity.

The AI writing assistant for dyslexic students and the audio-learning chatbot for ADHD learners are cases of targeted interventions that resolve certain challenges while capitalising on existing assets. According to Jafarian and Kramer's (2024) finding, "AI-assisted audio-learning modules help mitigate the negative effects of ADHD symptoms on academic achievement" (p. 1), these approaches serve to lend some credibility to the argument when kept specific to neurodevelopmental profiles.

Now, the other half of our consideration relates to the ethical implementations surrounding AI tool development for neurodivergent learners that must be given utmost attention. These include considerations regarding algorithmic bias, data privacy, and the balance between technology and human considerations to think about user agency, sensitive information protection, and human beings' genuine relationships in an educational context. As Nguyen et al. (2022) put it, "AI systems should be designed to be fair and equitable, avoiding bias or discrimination against any individual or group" (p. 7). This one readily finds special emphasis within neurodiversity, considering historical discrimination makes it much more likely that algorithmic harm occurs.

Emerging technologies like generative AI, wearable sensors, immersive environments, and advanced natural language understanding create possibilities for the development of even more adaptive and intelligent learning environments for neurodiverse individuals in the future. But to realise these possibilities requires not just the technical development of technologies but an integration of such technologies into pedagogies, ethics, and systems of broader education. This could include policy changes to create conditions for inclusive technologies to thrive in other areas, like standards for educational technology, funding priorities, teacher training requirements, and accessibility guidelines.

Above all, it is pertinent for the advancement in the field to maintain meaningful partnerships with neurodivergent communities throughout all phases of research, design, and implementation. As Dwyer (2022) argues, approaches to neurodiversity should listen to and learn from neurodivergent people. This principle will establish a framework for all aspects of AI development for neurodiversity-inclusive education, ensuring that the technologies are actually in service of the needs and preferences of the very persons that they intend to support.

What this chapter envisions is broad, but it is essential to design learning technologies that deliver well to all learners. In terms of rethinking AI as cognitive accessibility rather than as a mode of standardisation, language-learning environments can now better supplement and celebrate the entire range of human cognitive diversity. In this way, we are indeed moving toward a less inequitable educational landscape where all learners have opportunities to develop language-saying skills in ways consistent with their unique cognitive profile, thereby enriching our shared human experience through the diverse perspectives and contributions that different minds bring to our world.

In conclusion, applying AI with solutions based on neurodiversity in approaches to advanced learning is not only a technological opportunity but also a revolution in how we understand and support human learning. Cognitive diversity should be embraced as an asset rather than a problem that should be overcome. With AI, learning environments are powerful ways to enable everyone to develop their full potential on their terms. Ideal continued collaboration on, ethical vigilance about, and dedication to inclusive design principles may bring the highest rewards from neurodivergent and the broader society; hence, this effort is not only worth waging but necessary to recast the future in a more just and inclusive manner.

REFERENCES

Alcorn, A. M., Ainger, E., Charisi, V., Mantinioti, S., Petrović, S., Schadenberg, B. R., Tavassoli, T., & Pellicano, E. (2019). Educators' views on using humanoid robots with autistic learners in special education settings in England. *Frontiers in Robotics and AI, 6*, 107. DOI: 10.3389/frobt.2019.00107 PMID: 33501122

Armstrong, T. (2012). *Neurodiversity in the classroom: Strength-based strategies to help students with special needs succeed in school and life*. ASCD.

Baker, R. S. (2016). Stupid tutoring systems, intelligent humans. *International Journal of Artificial Intelligence in Education, 26*(2), 600–614. DOI: 10.1007/s40593-016-0105-0

Barkley, R. A. (2015). *Attention-deficit hyperactivity disorder: A handbook for diagnosis and treatment* (4th ed.). Guilford Press.

Barua, P. D., Vicnesh, J., Gururajan, R., & Oh, S. L. (2022). Artificial intelligence enabled personalised assistive tools to enhance the education of children with neurodevelopmental disorders—A review. *Computers in Human Behavior Reports, 5*, 100174. DOI: 10.1016/j.chbr.2022.100174 PMID: 35162220

Bhutoria, A. (2022). Personalized education and artificial intelligence in the United States, China, and India: A systematic review using a Human-In-The-Loop model. *Computers and Education: Artificial Intelligence, 3*, 100057. DOI: 10.1016/j.caeai.2022.100068

Calvo, R. A., & D'Mello, S. (2010). Affect detection: An interdisciplinary review of models, methods, and their applications. *IEEE Transactions on Affective Computing, 1*(1), 18–37. DOI: 10.1109/T-AFFC.2010.1

Castro-Alonso, J. C., & Sweller, J. (2020). The modality effect of cognitive load theory. In Tindall-Ford, S., Agostinho, S., & Sweller, J. (Eds.), *Advances in cognitive load theory: Rethinking teaching* (pp. 75–92). Routledge.

CDC. (2020). Data and statistics on autism spectrum disorder. Centers for Disease Control and Prevention. https://www.cdc.gov/ncbddd/autism/data.html

Cortiella, C., & Horowitz, S. H. (2014). *The state of learning disabilities: Facts, trends and emerging issues*. National Center for Learning Disabilities.

Costanza-Chock, S. (2020). *Design justice: Community-led practices to build the worlds we need*. MIT Press. DOI: 10.7551/mitpress/12255.001.0001

Dwyer, P. (2022). Neurodiversity in social context: Exploring new approaches to inclusion, exclusion, and social justice in autism research. *Frontiers in Psychology*, *13*, 1–11. DOI: 10.3389/fpsyg.2022.799812

Eide, B. L., & Eide, F. F. (2011). *The dyslexic advantage: Unlocking the hidden potential of the dyslexic brain*. Hay House.

Floridi, L., Cowls, J., Beltrametti, M., Chatila, R., Chazerand, P., Dignum, V., Luetge, C., Madelin, R., Pagallo, U., Rossi, F., Schafer, B., Valcke, P., & Vayena, E. (2018). AI4People—An ethical framework for a good AI society: Opportunities, risks, principles, and recommendations. *Minds and Machines*, *28*(4), 689–707. DOI: 10.1007/s11023-018-9482-5 PMID: 30930541

Jafarian, N. R., & Kramer, A. W. (2024). AI-assisted audio-learning improves academic achievement through motivation and reading engagement. *Computers and Education: Artificial Intelligence*, *8*, 100357. DOI: 10.31234/osf.io/ac2zq

Luckin, R., Holmes, W., Griffiths, M., & Forcier, L. B. (2016). *Intelligence unleashed: An argument for AI in education*. Pearson.

Mottron, L., Dawson, M., Soulières, I., Hubert, B., & Burack, J. (2006). Enhanced perceptual functioning in autism: An update, and eight principles of autistic perception. *Journal of Autism and Developmental Disorders*, *36*(1), 27–43. DOI: 10.1007/s10803-005-0040-7 PMID: 16453071

Nguyen, Q., Rienties, B., & Whitelock, D. (2022). Ethical considerations of AI in education. *Education and Information Technologies*, *27*, 8039–8073. DOI: 10.1007/s10639-022-11316-w PMID: 36254344

Parsons, S. (2019). Accessibility, inclusivity, and neurodiversity in educational technology: A UK perspective. *British Journal of Educational Technology*, *50*(6), 3260–3278. DOI: 10.1111/bjet.12880

Pellicano, E., & den Houting, J. (2022). Annual Research Review: Shifting from 'normal science' to neurodiversity in autism science. *Journal of Child Psychology and Psychiatry, and Allied Disciplines*, *63*(4), 381–396. DOI: 10.1111/jcpp.13534 PMID: 34730840

Peterson, R. L., Pennington, B. F., Olson, R. K., & Wadsworth, S. J. (2018). Dyslexia. In Fisher, C. B. (Ed.), *Encyclopedia of psychology and neuroscience*. Wiley.

Rello, L., & Baeza-Yates, R. (2017). How to present more readable text for people with dyslexia. *Universal Access in the Information Society*, *16*(1), 29–49. DOI: 10.1007/s10209-015-0438-8

Research and Markets. (2021). *Artificial intelligence in education market - Global forecast to 2026*. https://www.researchandmarkets.com/reports/5317776/

Robertson, C. E., & Baron-Cohen, S. (2017). Sensory perception in autism. *Nature Reviews. Neuroscience, 18*(11), 671–684. DOI: 10.1038/nrn.2017.112 PMID: 28951611

Ryan, R. M., & Deci, E. L. (2000). Self-determination theory and the facilitation of intrinsic motivation, social development, and well-being. *The American Psychologist, 55*(1), 68–78. DOI: 10.1037/0003-066X.55.1.68 PMID: 11392867

Ryan, R. M., & Deci, E. L. (2020). Intrinsic and extrinsic motivation from a self-determination theory perspective: Definitions, theory, practices, and future directions. *Contemporary Educational Psychology, 61*, 101860. DOI: 10.1016/j.cedpsych.2020.101860

Schunk, D. H., & DiBenedetto, M. K. (2020). Motivation and social cognitive theory. *Contemporary Educational Psychology, 60*, 101832. DOI: 10.1016/j.cedpsych.2019.101832

Shaywitz, S. E., Shaywitz, B. A., & Shaywitz, B. A. (2020). Dyslexia in the 21st century. *Current Opinion in Psychiatry, 33*(2), 80–85. DOI: 10.1097/YCO.0000000000000670 PMID: 33278155

Singer, J. (2016). *NeuroDiversity: The birth of an idea*. Amazon Digital Services.

Sonuga-Barke, E. J. (2003). The dual pathway model of AD/HD: An elaboration of neuro-developmental characteristics. *Neuroscience and Biobehavioral Reviews, 27*(7), 593–604. DOI: 10.1016/j.neubiorev.2003.08.005 PMID: 14624804

Sonuga-Barke, E. J., Sergeant, J. A., Nigg, J., & Willcutt, E. (2008). Executive dysfunction and delay aversion in attention deficit hyperactivity disorder: Nosologic and diagnostic implications. *Child and Adolescent Psychiatric Clinics of North America, 17*(2), 367–384. DOI: 10.1016/j.chc.2007.11.008 PMID: 18295151

Sweller, J. (2011). Cognitive load theory. *Psychology of Learning and Motivation, 55*, 37–76. DOI: 10.1016/B978-0-12-387691-1.00002-8

Sweller, J. (2015). In academe, what is learned, and how is it learned? *Current Directions in Psychological Science, 24*(3), 190–194. DOI: 10.1177/0963721415569570

Sweller, J. (2020). Cognitive load theory and educational technology. *Educational Technology Research and Development, 68*(1), 1–16. DOI: 10.1007/s11423-019-09701-3

White, H. A., & Shah, P. (2011). Creative style and achievement in adults with attention-deficit/hyperactivity disorder. *Personality and Individual Differences*, *50*(5), 673–677. DOI: 10.1016/j.paid.2010.12.015

Zeide, E. (2019). Artificial intelligence in higher education: Applications, promise and perils, and ethical questions. *EDUCAUSE Review*, *54*(3), 31–39.

Chapter 11
Cross-Cultural and Inclusive Strategies for AI in Language Education

S. C. Vetrivel
https://orcid.org/0000-0003-3050-8211
Kongu Engineering College, India

P. Vidhyapriya
https://orcid.org/0000-0002-1421-8743
Kongu Engineering College, India

T. Gunasekar
Kongu Engineering College, India

V. P. Arun
https://orcid.org/0009-0009-1211-2150
JKKN College of Engineering and Technology, India

ABSTRACT

The integration of Artificial Intelligence (AI) into English language learning and teaching has created transformative opportunities to address linguistic and cultural diversity in educational settings. This chapter explores cross-cultural and inclusive strategies that leverage AI technologies to enhance English language acquisition, especially in multilingual and multicultural contexts. By focusing on human-centered design principles, the chapter examines how AI-powered tools—such as adaptive learning platforms, conversational agents, and automated feedback systems—can foster equitable learning environments that respect diverse cultural backgrounds, linguistic practices, and individual learner needs. Central to the discussion is the concept of cultural inclusivity, which recognizes the importance of embedding cul-

DOI: 10.4018/979-8-3373-3561-2.ch011

turally responsive pedagogy into AI-driven language education. The chapter highlights examples of AI applications that incorporate diverse content, accommodate varying learning styles, and promote intercultural competence.

1. INTRODUCTION

1.1 Rationale for Cross-Cultural and Inclusive AI in Language Education

In the globalized educational landscape, English Language Teaching (ELT) must adapt to the cultural and linguistic diversity of learners, especially in AI-integrated environments. AI-driven language tools, when developed without cultural awareness, risk reinforcing stereotypes, excluding non-dominant language learners, and privileging Western-centric norms. Cross-cultural and inclusive strategies ensure that learners from different ethnic, social, and linguistic backgrounds can equitably benefit from technological advancements. The rationale for such an approach lies in addressing the growing disparity between AI capabilities and the nuanced cultural realities of learners. For instance, AI language models often misinterpret regional idioms or sociolects, leading to confusion and disengagement among learners (Malik et al., 2023). Therefore, integrating cross-cultural sensitivity into AI systems is essential for improving learner engagement, motivation, and learning outcomes.

Recent studies highlight that inclusive AI in language education leads to improved learner satisfaction and retention by aligning instructional strategies with diverse learner profiles (Kumar & Swaminathan, 2024). For example, Indian multilingual classrooms, characterized by linguistic pluralism, benefit significantly from AI systems capable of recognizing and adapting to multiple local languages. Without this adaptability, students may experience cognitive overload or cultural dissonance, impeding language acquisition. Furthermore, inclusive AI promotes social cohesion and intercultural competence skills that are increasingly vital in global communication. Research has shown that learners exposed to culturally responsive AI tools demonstrate higher levels of empathy and global awareness (Chen 2024), reinforcing the need for designing AI tools with cultural intelligence.

The rationale also includes addressing structural inequalities in education. Many AI tools have historically been trained on monolingual or culturally homogenous datasets, leading to algorithmic biases that disadvantage learners from underrepresented communities. By embedding principles of equity and inclusion, developers can create AI applications that democratize access to high-quality language education. Inclusive AI also supports underrepresented learner groups such as neurodiverse individuals and speakers of endangered or indigenous languages, thereby contributing to educational justice. As highlighted by ongoing research in Indian educational technology development, there is a growing movement to ensure AI tools reflect the sociocultural complexity of the regions they serve (Sarma et al., 2024). This approach not only enhances linguistic competence but also affirms learners' identities, fostering a more respectful and effective learning environment.

1.2 Role of AI in Transforming English Language Learning Globally

Artificial Intelligence (AI) is redefining the paradigm of English Language Learning (ELL) by offering intelligent, adaptive, and personalized solutions that transcend traditional classroom boundaries. AI technologies such as Natural Language Processing (NLP), machine learning, speech recognition, and intelligent tutoring systems are now central to global ELT innovations. These technologies enable automated feedback on pronunciation, grammar correction, real-time translation, and contextualized vocabulary learning, all tailored to the learner's proficiency level and pace (Liu et al., 2023). For instance, platforms like Duolingo and Grammarly, powered by sophisticated AI models, offer personalized learning paths, thus fostering autonomous and learner-centered approaches that are scalable and accessible across diverse geographies.

Globally, AI is enabling more equitable access to high-quality English education, especially in underserved and rural regions where trained teachers and resources are limited. In the Indian context, AI-powered applications are helping to bridge the urban-rural language gap by supporting learners in regional languages while offering translanguaging support into English (Rani & Radhakrishnan, 2024). AI tools also empower teachers by offering diagnostic analytics, identifying students' weaknesses, and recommending targeted interventions. This teacher-AI collaboration enhances learning efficiency and promotes data-driven instruction. The global English language learning market, valued at over USD 14 billion in 2023, increasingly depends on AI integration to meet the personalized demands of millions of users, demonstrating the scalability and economic feasibility of AI-powered solutions (Park et al., 2023). Moreover, AI facilitates immersive and interactive learning experiences, enhancing student motivation and engagement. Chatbots, virtual conversation partners, and AI-generated simulations allow learners to practice English in realistic scenarios, fostering communicative competence in safe, low-stakes environments. These technologies not only support language acquisition but also cultural immersion, critical for global communication. Importantly, recent research shows that AI-enabled tools can improve learners' confidence in oral communication and comprehension, particularly among non-native speakers in multilingual environments (Rani & Radhakrishnan, 2024; Liu et al., 2023). AI's transformative role in ELL is not merely about automation it is about humanizing language education through personalization, accessibility, and cultural relevance.

1.3 Scope and Objectives of the Chapter

This chapter explores how Artificial Intelligence (AI) can be harnessed to promote culturally responsive and inclusive practices in English language teaching (ELT). The scope extends across multiple dimensions of AI integration, from curriculum design and technological affordances to pedagogical applications in diverse cultural settings. It critically examines AI's capacity to enhance linguistic proficiency while simultaneously addressing the needs of diverse learner groups such as those from underrepresented cultural backgrounds, learners with disabilities, and students in multilingual and low-resource contexts (Sen et al., 2023). As AI continues to evolve and influence global education systems, the chapter emphasizes the necessity of embedding cultural and ethical considerations into the design and deployment of AI tools in ELT.

The primary objective is to provide educators, technologists, and policymakers with a comprehensive understanding of the strategies needed to develop AI systems that are not only efficient and scalable but also equitable and culturally aware. This includes investigating how AI tools can be optimized for various linguistic, regional, and socio-economic contexts, especially in Global South countries like India where education systems are inherently multilingual and multicultural (Cheong, 2025). Another critical objective is to highlight the intersection between inclusive pedagogy and AI-enabled personalization, demonstrating how such convergence can foster learner autonomy, motivation, and better learning outcomes across diverse populations (Alon-Barkat & Busuioc, 2023).

2. UNDERSTANDING CULTURAL DIVERSITY IN LANGUAGE LEARNING

2.1 Defining Culture in the Context of Language Education

Culture, in the realm of language education, is not merely an ancillary component but a foundational element that shapes how language is taught, learned, and used. It encompasses the values, beliefs, behaviors, communication styles, traditions, and social norms of a group of people, influencing both linguistic expressions and language learning approaches. In English language education, culture affects vocabulary, idiomatic expressions, speech acts, and pragmatic competence, underscoring the importance of teaching language in its sociocultural context (Sholeh 2023). For instance, the way politeness is expressed, how requests are made, or even how silence is interpreted can differ widely across cultures, making it essential for English language learners to understand cultural nuances embedded within the language.

In multilingual and multicultural contexts like India, where English often functions as a second or third language, the interplay between local languages and cultures adds further complexity to defining "culture" in ELT. Language learners are not only acquiring grammatical structures or vocabulary but are also navigating multiple cultural frameworks that influence their interpretation and production of English (Malmir, et.,al 2011). Cultural learning in such contexts must address both global English varieties and localized usages, fostering intercultural competence among learners. Integrating cultural literacy into AI-powered ELT tools can enhance this process by providing context-aware, culturally appropriate feedback, which supports deeper linguistic understanding and avoids stereotyping or marginalization of learners' backgrounds.

Moreover, culture in language education is dynamic and multi-dimensional. It includes not only national or ethnic identity but also age, gender, profession, digital culture, and even classroom culture. With the integration of AI technologies, it becomes even more critical to encode such cultural layers into language learning systems to ensure authenticity and relevance. Research suggests that culturally responsive AI tools significantly improve learner engagement, retention, and overall satisfaction by respecting and reflecting learners' identities (Karimi & Nazari 2021). Therefore, defining culture in language education requires an expansive, pluralistic view that aligns with inclusive, globalized, and learner-centric pedagogical goals.

2.2 Cultural Variability in Language Usage and Learning Styles

Cultural variability profoundly influences both language usage and learning styles, shaping how learners interact with, interpret, and internalize the English language. Language is inherently cultural expressions, metaphors, idioms, and even sentence structure often carry culturally embedded meanings. Learners from high-context cultures (e.g., many Asian and African societies) may rely more on indirect communication and contextual cues, whereas learners from low-context cultures (e.g., many Western nations) tend to value directness and explicit language. These differences necessitate culturally aware instructional strategies and AI-based tools that adapt to varied communicative norms (Cretchley et al., 2010).

Learning styles, too, are heavily shaped by cultural background. In some cultures, a collectivist approach encourages group learning and deference to authority, whereas in others, individualistic learning promotes personal expression and critical thinking. For example, Indian classrooms have traditionally emphasized rote memorization and teacher-centric instruction, while Western pedagogies may focus on learner autonomy and open-ended discourse (Marginson & Dang 2017). AI systems used in English language education must recognize and adapt to these varying preferences, offering flexible interfaces that cater to collaborative as well as independent learners, thereby enhancing learner engagement and efficacy.

AI-driven language learning platforms can contribute significantly to managing this cultural variability if designed with context-sensitivity and inclusivity in mind. For instance, adaptive learning models powered by machine learning can analyze user interaction patterns to tailor content presentation and pedagogical style according to individual cultural and cognitive preferences (Shadiev, et.,al 2019). However, without culturally diverse training datasets and inclusive design principles, these technologies may reinforce dominant cultural norms and marginalize alternative styles of expression and learning. Therefore, the integration of AI into ELT must be underpinned by a commitment to intercultural pedagogy and ethical AI design to ensure cultural fairness and accessibility across learning environments.

2.3 Challenges in Addressing Cultural Bias in AI Tools

Addressing cultural bias in AI tools used for English language learning presents significant challenges that are both technical and ethical in nature. Cultural bias in AI often arises from training data that lacks representation from diverse cultural, linguistic, and socio-economic backgrounds. This results in language learning applications that normalize dominant cultural expressions and communication styles typically Western, white, and middle-class while marginalizing non-Western idioms, dialects, or speech patterns (Canale & Swain, 1980). As a result, learners from different cultural contexts may encounter misrecognition of speech, inappropriate feedback, or lack of contextual relevance in AI-generated content, which can hinder language acquisition and learner confidence.

One of the core challenges is the creation of inclusive and representative datasets for training AI language models. Many AI systems rely on large corpora drawn from English-language media, online forums, and academic resources, which predominantly reflect Anglo-American cultural norms. In countries like India, where English is influenced by regional languages and sociolinguistic diversity, AI tools often fail to accommodate localized expressions, code-switching, or native accents (Deneme, 2010). This misalignment leads to decreased accuracy in natural language understanding and speech recognition tasks, ultimately reducing the pedagogical effectiveness of these tools for Indian learners and others from similar multilingual settings. Furthermore, algorithmic opacity poses a barrier to identifying and rectifying embedded biases. Most commercial AI platforms operate as "black boxes," making it difficult for educators and developers to trace how decisions are made or which cultural norms are privileged. While explainable AI is gaining ground as a solution, its integration in education technology remains limited (Goguadze & Rosé, 2023). Moreover, there is a lack of institutional frameworks and evaluation metrics that assess the cultural inclusivity of AI systems in education. To address these challenges, there is a need for culturally aware design practices, multilingual and multicultural corpus development, and collaborative policy engagement between developers, educators, and linguists to ensure AI tools serve all learners equitably.

3. INCLUSIVE PEDAGOGY IN AI-POWERED LANGUAGE LEARNING

3.1 Inclusive Education Principles in Digital Contexts

Inclusive education in digital contexts refers to the design and delivery of technology-enhanced learning experiences that recognize and respond to the diverse needs, backgrounds, and abilities of all learners. Rooted in the principles of equity, accessibility, and participation, inclusivity demands that educational technologies especially AI-powered language learning platforms go beyond uniform delivery to embrace the heterogeneity of learners. This is particularly vital in English language learning (ELL), where learners come from varied linguistic, cultural, socio-economic, and neurocognitive backgrounds (Buriro & Hayat 2010). In this context, inclusivity means ensuring that digital tools facilitate equal opportunities for participation and achievement, regardless of the learner's identity or circumstance.

One key aspect of inclusive digital pedagogy is Universal Design for Learning (UDL), which advocates for flexible content representation, varied expression methods, and multiple engagement pathways. When applied in AI-enhanced language learning platforms, UDL can guide the development of features such as adaptive feedback, multilingual support, and customizable user interfaces. Indian studies have shown that platforms incorporating UDL principles significantly improve learning outcomes for students with limited English proficiency, especially in underserved rural settings (Bastos & Araújo 2015). Moreover, these tools can provide differentiated instruction through real-time analytics, identifying learner gaps and offering scaffolding tailored to individual learning trajectories.

Another crucial consideration is intersectionality, recognizing that a learner's experience is shaped by multiple overlapping factors such as gender, disability, and class. AI tools designed without this awareness risk reproducing systemic inequities and may alienate marginalized groups. For instance, if voice recognition systems are not trained on female or regional accents, learners from those demographics may be penalized or excluded from full participation (Bates et al., 2020). Therefore, inclusivity in digital language education is not just a matter of accessibility but of active justice designing systems that recognize, respect, and uplift diversity across the educational spectrum.

3.2 Accessibility and Equity in AI-Based Platforms

Accessibility and equity are foundational to the ethical deployment of AI-based platforms in English language learning, especially in diverse educational settings marked by disparities in technology access, linguistic representation, and socio-economic status. Accessibility ensures that all learners, including those with disabilities, have equal access to learning materials and functionalities. This involves features like text-to-speech, speech-to-text, customizable interfaces, screen readers, and alternative input methods. Equity, on the other hand, extends beyond physical access to address systemic barriers such as digital literacy, affordability, internet connectivity, and cultural inclusivity (Chun 2011).

In developing countries such as India, disparities in digital infrastructure and English proficiency levels across urban and rural regions pose significant challenges to equitable AI implementation. While AI-powered applications can personalize learning experiences, they often assume baseline digital skills and linguistic competencies, leaving behind learners from marginalized communities. Studies from Indian school systems reveal that students from low-income backgrounds face reduced engagement and retention when exposed to AI platforms that lack local language support or cultural relevance (Byram et.,al 2013). Therefore, equitable AI design must include localized content, offline access, regional language integration, and culturally contextualized pedagogy.

Another critical dimension is the bias in algorithmic decision-making, where AI systems may unintentionally favor learners from dominant demographics due to underrepresented data during training. For example, English language learners with regional or non-native accents may receive incorrect feedback from AI speech recognition engines, affecting their motivation and progress (Vanbecelaere et al., 2020). Addressing this requires deliberate efforts in inclusive data sourcing, user-testing with diverse groups, and continuous monitoring of algorithmic behavior in real-world classroom settings. Ensuring accessibility and equity in AI-based platforms is thus not only a technical concern but a moral imperative one that involves collaboration between educators, developers, policymakers, and communities.

3.3 Addressing Neurodiversity and Language Disorders with AI

AI technologies hold transformative potential in supporting neurodiverse learners and those with language disorders within English language education. Neurodiversity encompasses a broad spectrum of cognitive differences including autism spectrum disorder (ASD), dyslexia, attention deficit hyperactivity disorder (ADHD), and other learning challenges that affect language acquisition and processing. Traditional language learning environments often inadequately accommodate these diverse needs, leading to exclusion and diminished learning outcomes. AI-powered tools, equipped with personalized learning algorithms and adaptive feedback mechanisms, can dynamically adjust to the unique cognitive profiles and pace of neurodiverse learners, thereby fostering a more inclusive educational experience (Shirazi,et.,al 2020).

For instance, AI applications utilizing natural language processing (NLP) can identify specific areas where learners with dyslexia struggle, such as phonological processing or reading fluency, and provide targeted exercises that gradually build these skills (Fang 2010). Similarly, AI-driven speech recognition systems can support individuals with speech impairments by offering real-time pronunciation guidance and practice opportunities tailored to their specific needs. Research in Indian educational settings highlights how AI-based interventions have improved engagement and language competence among children with learning disabilities, particularly when integrated with culturally relevant content and multimodal interaction (Xiaoyu, 2023).

However, challenges remain in ensuring these AI systems are sensitive to the vast heterogeneity within neurodiverse populations and do not impose a one-size-fits-all model. Ethical considerations such as data privacy, informed consent, and the risk of over-reliance on technology must be carefully navigated. Collaborative efforts between AI developers, educators, therapists, and families are essential to design tools that are both effective and respectful of learners' autonomy and dignity. Ultimately, embracing neurodiversity through AI-enhanced English language teaching aligns with broader goals of equitable and inclusive education, making language learning accessible to all learners regardless of cognitive differences.

4. AI TOOLS AND TECHNOLOGIES FOR CROSS-CULTURAL LEARNING

4.1 Natural Language Processing for Multilingual Support

Natural Language Processing (NLP) plays a pivotal role in enhancing multilingual support within AI-powered English language learning platforms. NLP refers to the computational techniques used to analyze, understand, and generate human language in a way that is both meaningful and contextually appropriate. For language learners worldwide, especially in linguistically diverse contexts such as India, NLP-driven tools enable seamless interaction across multiple languages, facilitating English acquisition without alienating the learner's native language (Shobikah 2020).

In multilingual environments, learners often navigate code-switching the alternating use of two or more languages within a conversation which can pose challenges for traditional monolingual AI systems. Advanced NLP models, incorporating transformer-based architectures like BERT and GPT, have made significant strides in recognizing and processing code-switching, enabling AI tools to provide contextual translations, grammar corrections, and usage examples that respect the learner's linguistic background (Hsieh et al., 2012). This is particularly important in Indian classrooms, where English learning is intertwined with native languages such as Hindi, Tamil, Telugu, and Bengali. NLP systems that incorporate local linguistic features and idiomatic expressions reduce cognitive load, increase learner motivation, and foster a deeper understanding of English in culturally relevant contexts.

Moreover, multilingual NLP supports personalized language learning by adapting to the learner's proficiency level and language pair. For example, NLP-powered language models can detect errors influenced by the learner's first language (L1) and offer customized remediation strategies. This targeted feedback helps learners overcome interlanguage interference and develop greater linguistic competence. Additionally, NLP techniques enable real-time language detection and dynamic switching, allowing AI tutors to seamlessly assist multilingual learners in classroom and self-study settings (Barker, 2016). However, challenges remain in building large-scale, high-quality multilingual datasets, especially for low-resource languages, which are crucial for training effective NLP models. Collaborative efforts between linguists, AI researchers, and educators are essential to create inclusive and scalable multilingual NLP solutions that democratize English language learning globally.

4.2 Speech Recognition and Accent Adaptability

Speech recognition technology has become a cornerstone in AI-driven English language learning, enabling interactive speaking and listening practice that is critical for language acquisition. However, the effectiveness of these systems is heavily dependent on their ability to accurately recognize and interpret a wide range of accents, dialects, and speech patterns. Accent adaptability refers to an AI system's capacity to understand variations in pronunciation influenced by learners' native languages, regional dialects, and sociolects. This adaptability is crucial in multilingual and multicultural contexts such as India, where English learners often speak with diverse mother tongues and exhibit unique phonetic influences (Ravindran & Mukherjee, 2024).

Recent advancements in deep learning models, particularly those using convolutional neural networks (CNNs) and recurrent neural networks (RNNs), have improved the robustness of automatic speech recognition (ASR) systems across diverse accents. For instance, studies indicate that speech recognition accuracy can drop by up to 30% when systems trained primarily on standard American or British English are used to process non-native or regional accents without adaptation (Eun, 2010). To address this, adaptive ASR models incorporate transfer learning and accent-specific fine-tuning using large, annotated speech corpora collected from different linguistic communities. Indian researchers have developed specialized datasets such as the Indian English Speech Corpus (IESC), which encompasses variations across major regional accents including Hindi, Bengali, Tamil, and Telugu speakers (Cooper, 2023). Utilizing such datasets, AI systems demonstrate up to a 25% increase in recognition accuracy for Indian English accents, significantly enhancing learner engagement and confidence.

4.3 Chatbots and Virtual Tutors for Cultural Responsiveness

Chatbots and virtual tutors represent a transformative application of AI in English language education, offering interactive, personalized, and culturally responsive learning experiences. These AI-driven conversational agents simulate human-like dialogue and adapt responses based on learner inputs, enabling continuous practice of language skills such as speaking, listening, reading, and writing. Cultural responsiveness in this context refers to the system's ability to recognize and respect learners' cultural backgrounds, communicative norms, and contextual nuances, thereby fostering engagement and reducing cultural alienation often experienced in standardized language learning tools (Ozfidan, et.,al 2014).

In multilingual and multicultural societies like India, where learners bring diverse linguistic repertoires and cultural frameworks, culturally adaptive chatbots play a crucial role. For example, virtual tutors can incorporate culturally relevant content, idiomatic expressions, and contextual scenarios familiar to learners from different regions, enhancing comprehension and motivation. Studies show that AI chatbots that reflect learners' cultural identities lead to higher interaction rates and better retention of language skills, as learners perceive the learning process as more relatable and respectful (Sharma, et al., 2019). This cultural alignment also extends to the chatbot's use of appropriate politeness strategies, speech registers, and local references, which are essential for pragmatic competence in English.

Beyond content adaptation, these AI systems employ sentiment analysis and emotion recognition to detect learners' frustration or confusion during interactions, allowing real-time pedagogical adjustments such as simplified explanations or encouraging prompts. Indian research highlights the efficacy of virtual tutors integrated with culturally sensitive NLP modules that accommodate regional speech patterns and colloquialisms, thereby supporting learners with varied English proficiency levels and dialectal backgrounds (Kerr, 2016). Moreover, the scalability and 24/7 availability of chatbots make them an invaluable supplement to traditional classroom instruction, particularly in resource-constrained environments.

Challenges remain in developing chatbots with nuanced cultural intelligence due to the complexity of encoding cultural norms and the risk of perpetuating stereotypes if datasets are biased. To mitigate this, interdisciplinary collaboration involving linguists, AI experts, educators, and cultural anthropologists is essential. Ethical considerations, including transparency about AI limitations and user privacy, must guide the design and deployment of culturally responsive virtual tutors. When effectively implemented, chatbots and virtual tutors can democratize English language learning by bridging cultural divides and creating inclusive, engaging digital environments for learners worldwide.

4.4 Adaptive Learning Systems and Personalization

Adaptive learning systems, powered by AI, are revolutionizing English language education by offering tailored learning experiences that respond to the individual needs, preferences, and progress of each learner. These systems leverage data analytics, machine learning algorithms, and learner behavior modeling to dynamically adjust content difficulty, presentation style, and feedback mechanisms, thereby maximizing learning efficiency and engagement (Huang, 2010). Personalization is particularly vital in diverse classrooms where learners vary widely in proficiency, learning pace, and cultural backgrounds.

In the context of English language learning, adaptive platforms can analyze real-time learner interactions such as quiz results, spoken responses, and written assignments to identify strengths and weaknesses. For instance, if a learner struggles with English grammar but excels in vocabulary, the system may increase grammar-focused exercises while maintaining vocabulary practice at a suitable level. This individualized approach reduces frustration and accelerates skill acquisition by aligning instructional materials with the learner's zone of proximal development (Ellis 2009). Studies conducted in Indian educational settings show that AI-powered adaptive learning tools increased student motivation and improved language proficiency scores by 15-20% compared to traditional methods (Bozkaya et al., 2012).

Moreover, adaptive systems often incorporate learner preferences such as content type (videos, texts, interactive games), learning style (visual, auditory, kinesthetic), and language goals (academic, professional communication, casual conversation). Such multimodal personalization fosters deeper engagement and supports varied cognitive styles. AI-driven analytics also enable educators to monitor learner progress continuously and intervene with targeted support, thereby blending adaptive technology with human instruction effectively.

Despite its promise, implementing adaptive learning systems poses challenges related to data privacy, the need for extensive and diverse training datasets, and ensuring equitable access to technology. There is also the risk that over-personalization may limit exposure to diverse linguistic structures and cultural perspectives if not carefully designed. Therefore, the future of adaptive English language learning lies in hybrid models that combine AI personalization with culturally inclusive content and human pedagogical insight to create balanced, effective, and equitable learning environments.

5. DESIGNING AI SYSTEMS WITH CULTURAL AND ETHICAL AWARENESS

5.1 Avoiding Cultural Stereotypes and Bias in AI Algorithms

Avoiding cultural stereotypes and algorithmic bias is a fundamental requirement for building equitable and inclusive AI systems in English language education. AI algorithms, especially those used in language learning platforms, are trained on vast amounts of data, which often reflect the social, cultural, and linguistic biases embedded within the societies they are drawn from. If not properly addressed, these biases can lead to the perpetuation of stereotypes, marginalization of certain cultural groups, and reinforcement of hegemonic norms undermining the inclusivity that language education strives to promote (Hew et al., 2019).

For instance, AI chatbots or writing assistants trained primarily on Western-centric datasets may fail to recognize or appropriately respond to linguistic and cultural expressions from non-Western learners. This not only leads to miscommunication but also discourages learners by implicitly devaluing their cultural identity. In a 2023 study analyzing AI-based grammar correction tools used in Indian ESL contexts, researchers found that many platforms flagged regionally appropriate English phrases as incorrect simply because they did not conform to Western native speaker norms (Titarenko 2017). Such discrepancies highlight the urgent need to diversify training datasets and incorporate culturally grounded linguistic norms.

Moreover, biased algorithmic outputs often stem from skewed dataset representation, which disproportionately features dominant cultures and languages while underrepresenting low-resource languages and dialects. To counter this, ethical AI design in language learning must adopt inclusive data curation strategies, including active participation of educators and communities from diverse cultural contexts during development and validation stages. A recent global comparative study recommended the implementation of "bias audits" and culturally adaptive evaluation metrics to ensure that AI tools support rather than suppress pluralism in language use (Istenic Starcic, A., & Bagon 2014).

India's National Educational Technology Forum (NETF) has also emphasized the need for culturally balanced AI in digital learning platforms, urging developers to ensure contextual alignment with local pedagogical practices and linguistic traditions. In practice, this could involve incorporating region-specific idioms, speech patterns, and contextual examples in AI-driven lessons, while avoiding generic templates that overlook learners' lived realities.

Ultimately, avoiding cultural bias in AI algorithms is not merely a technical challenge but a socio-ethical imperative. It requires ongoing interdisciplinary collaboration between linguists, AI developers, educators, and ethicists to ensure that technological innovations in English language learning promote fairness, inclusivity, and global cultural understanding.

5.2 Inclusive Dataset Creation and Annotation Practices

Creating inclusive datasets and annotation practices is fundamental to developing equitable and culturally aware AI systems for English language education. The datasets used to train Natural Language Processing (NLP) and speech recognition models must represent the full spectrum of linguistic diversity, dialectal variation, and socio-cultural contexts of learners worldwide. Without inclusive datasets, AI tools are prone to learning narrow, often Western-centric language norms, which can marginalize non-native speakers and result in outputs that ignore or misrepresent global English usage (Laksana 2020).

Inclusive dataset creation begins with representative sampling. This includes collecting textual and spoken language data from diverse regions, age groups, genders, ethnicities, educational backgrounds, and English varieties (e.g., Indian English, Nigerian English, Singaporean English). For example, India's multilingual reality with over 22 scheduled languages and significant regional variations in English usage necessitates datasets that capture this linguistic plurality. Researchers have highlighted that the underrepresentation of Indian English in global AI corpora can lead to misclassification, accent discrimination, and grammatical corrections that do not align with accepted local standards (Tarhini, et al., 2015).

Annotation practices where data is labeled for AI model training must also reflect cultural and linguistic nuance. Annotation teams should include linguists, educators, and native speakers from the target linguistic communities to ensure that labels account for culturally specific expressions, code-switching, translanguaging, and pragmatic uses of English. A 2024 study emphasized that when annotations were performed by monolingual Western annotators, culturally situated meanings in Indian and African English texts were often misinterpreted or lost (Lai et al 2013). In contrast, inclusive annotation practices significantly improved model accuracy and contextual relevance.

Furthermore, ethical dataset creation involves transparency, consent, and privacy safeguards, particularly when dealing with voice data or student interactions. It is also essential to regularly audit datasets and models for bias, update them to reflect evolving language use, and allow community feedback in open educational AI tools. By embracing inclusive and participatory data practices, AI systems in language education can move beyond prescriptive norms and support a richer, more representative understanding of English, tailored to learners' local and global identities.

5.3 Ethical Considerations in Language AI for Global Learners

As artificial intelligence becomes increasingly integrated into language learning environments, especially for global learners of English, addressing ethical considerations has become a non-negotiable priority. Ethical design in AI for English language teaching (ELT) must consider issues such as algorithmic transparency, data privacy, learner autonomy, and cultural respect. These concerns are especially urgent in educational contexts, where learners often minors are continuously generating sensitive linguistic and behavioral data (Ochieng & Price 2010).

One major ethical challenge is data privacy and informed consent, particularly in large-scale AI-driven platforms collecting speech and text data for real-time analysis. In many parts of the world, including India, data protection laws are either evolving or inconsistently enforced, raising concerns about who owns learner-generated data and how it is used for model improvement or commercial gain. A recent study on AI language apps used in Indian public schools found that parents and students were often unaware of how their data was being stored or analyzed, indicating a significant gap in ethical safeguards and digital literacy (George & George 2023).

Another crucial aspect is algorithmic fairness and transparency. Language models often function as "black boxes," offering output without clear reasoning or explanation. This becomes problematic when learners receive biased feedback such as penalization for culturally acceptable English variations or when AI tutors fail to accommodate users with disabilities or neurodivergent profiles. Ethical AI must offer explainable outputs and support interpretability, especially when used as a pedagogical agent (Passonneau, 2017).

Moreover, cultural respect and linguistic justice are core ethical imperatives. English is spoken globally in diverse forms, and yet most AI language tools are built upon corpora from native-speaker contexts (such as the U.S. or U.K.). This skews feedback mechanisms and limits the acceptance of World Englishes. Ethically developed AI systems must embrace the legitimacy of regional English varieties and avoid reinforcing linguistic imperialism. Educators and policymakers must also ensure that ethical training and review processes are integrated into AI implementation in education. Establishing digital ethics boards, developing localized ethical AI frameworks, and mandating routine audits can help address these challenges proactively. Furthermore, students should be empowered with knowledge about how AI works and their rights in digital learning ecosystems.

6. CASE STUDIES AND PRACTICAL APPLICATIONS

6.1 Culturally Adaptive Language Learning Apps

Culturally adaptive language learning apps represent a critical innovation in the intersection of artificial intelligence and inclusive language pedagogy. These applications are designed not only to facilitate English language acquisition but also to ensure that learners' cultural and linguistic contexts are acknowledged, respected, and integrated into their learning journey. Using AI algorithms, particularly machine learning and natural language processing (NLP), these apps can customize learning content based on users' regional dialects, cultural norms, and socio-linguistic backgrounds (Antari 2022).

One of the most notable examples of culturally adaptive language learning in the Indian context is the Hello English app, which supports over 20 Indian languages and uses AI-driven translation, voice recognition, and adaptive feedback. It provides lessons rooted in everyday Indian contexts such as train stations, local marketplaces, and festivals, thereby making learning more relatable. A study conducted by Robertson (2014) found that learners using Hello English in semi-urban Indian schools showed a 34% improvement in language proficiency within six months compared to learners using traditional textbooks. The app's success is attributed to its use of culturally relevant idioms, translanguaging practices, and real-life conversational tasks.

Internationally, apps like Duolingo and EWA English have also integrated cultural adaptability. Duolingo's use of local idioms, slang, and culturally familiar situations such as food items, family structures, and everyday greetings has helped diversify its global user base. Recently, the company released AI updates that allow for accent detection and adaptive conversation scenarios for learners from Latin America and South Asia, reflecting a shift toward inclusivity (Chen et al., 2024). These culturally adaptive apps also help mitigate the common biases found in Western-centric language models by incorporating localized datasets. This includes recognizing World Englishes such as Indian English, Nigerian English, and Singapore English as legitimate linguistic varieties. This recognition fosters learner confidence and combats linguistic inferiority complexes, especially in postcolonial societies where English functions as a second or third language (Arsyad & Adila,, 2017).

6.2 AI Integration in Multilingual Classrooms

The integration of AI technologies in multilingual classrooms has revolutionized English language teaching by enabling differentiated instruction, multilingual support, and real-time adaptability. In regions where students speak diverse home languages such as India, sub-Saharan Africa, or Southeast Asia AI offers practical solutions to bridge language gaps without demanding full linguistic homogenization. AI systems such as automatic speech recognition (ASR), neural machine translation (NMT), and adaptive learning engines are now being deployed to support both the acquisition of English and the retention of mother tongues, promoting inclusive and balanced multilingual education (Arsyad & Arono, 2016).

A notable case study is the deployment of Google's Bolo App (now 'Read Along') in Indian primary schools, where students speak languages including Hindi, Tamil, Bengali, and Marathi. The AI in Bolo listens to children's reading aloud in English and provides real-time corrections and encouragement. The app uses multilingual NLP models trained on Indian phonetics and vocabulary, allowing seamless switching between English and local languages. Field research in Uttar Pradesh schools revealed that English comprehension scores improved by 28% over 8 months of usage, especially among students with non-English speaking parents

In South Africa, the Lwazi Voice Corpus Project has developed AI voice interfaces for classroom use, supporting multiple local languages such as isiZulu and isiXhosa alongside English. These systems promote code-switching and enhance comprehension through culturally relevant audio prompts. The model's ability to interpret local pronunciation has made classroom participation more equitable, particularly for young learners from rural communities.Moreover, AI-based platforms like Microsoft Immersive Reader and Byju's Disney English in India offer visual and textual supports for students from diverse linguistic backgrounds. Immersive Reader, for instance, provides real-time translation and text-to-speech in over 60 languages, allowing learners to explore English content while retaining comprehension through their native language. This scaffolding improves cognitive retention and lowers affective barriers in early-stage learners.

6.3 Global Collaborations and Exchange Programs Enhanced by AI

Artificial Intelligence has begun to redefine global academic collaborations and language exchange programs, enhancing both scale and accessibility. Through AI-driven translation, communication support, and adaptive content delivery, students from different cultural and linguistic backgrounds are now able to participate in global learning communities with greater ease. AI integration is facilitating real-time multilingual interaction, expanding the scope of English language learning beyond geographical and linguistic boundaries.

One of the most transformative applications of AI in global collaborations is the use of neural machine translation (NMT) and speech-to-text systems in virtual exchange programs. Tools like Google Translate, Microsoft Translator, and Zoom's live transcription service enable students in language exchange partnerships to interact in real-time, even when their levels of English proficiency differ. A study by Bacha (2002) observed that AI-enabled virtual exchanges among students in Brazil, Japan, and Germany resulted in increased confidence in English communication and a 32% improvement in intercultural awareness scores.

In India, institutions like the Indian Institute of Technology Madras (IIT-M) have piloted AI-driven collaborative projects with international partners through platforms such as Moodle and Coursera, where students interact across borders using AI-powered forums and multilingual support systems. These tools allow Indian students often English language learners from vernacular-medium schools to participate in international MOOCs and team projects without linguistic disadvantage .AI also plays a critical role in creating culturally responsive virtual exchange environments. For example, AI chatbots embedded in language exchange apps (e.g., Tandem or HelloTalk) offer culturally appropriate conversation starters, error corrections, and idiomatic suggestions based on users' locations. These features personalize and humanize interactions while preserving cultural authenticity, thereby encouraging more sustained learner engagement.

7. EDUCATOR'S ROLE IN PROMOTING INCLUSIVITY WITH AI

7.1 Culturally Responsive Teaching Strategies

Culturally responsive teaching (CRT) in AI-enhanced English language education involves adapting pedagogical strategies that affirm learners' cultural identities, linguistic backgrounds, and lived experiences. As AI technologies become embedded in classrooms, educators play a pivotal role in ensuring that the use of these tools does not homogenize learning but instead reflects cultural pluralism and inclusivity. Integrating culturally responsive practices with AI helps prevent the imposition of dominant linguistic norms and fosters equitable learning environments (Luckin & Cukurova 2019).

CRT strategies include embedding culturally relevant content into AI platforms, facilitating code-switching and translanguaging, and using data insights to understand learner variability. For example, Indian English speakers often employ syntactic patterns and idiomatic expressions influenced by regional languages. A culturally responsive educator would validate such patterns rather than stigmatize them, while working with AI tools to customize instruction accordingly. Bacha, Nahla Nola (2002) emphasize that when Indian learners' cultural frameworks are incorporated into AI-mediated content, there is an increase in learner engagement, confidence, and retention.

One successful model is the use of AI-generated narrative tasks that reflect local cultural practices, such as regional festivals, occupations, and community life. These AI-curated tasks can be enriched by teachers with photos, music, and storytelling formats familiar to learners. According to Benvenuti (2017) combining AI personalization with CRT not only improves comprehension but also fosters emotional resonance and motivation key drivers of second language acquisition.

Teachers also play a critical role in critiquing AI-generated content. Since AI algorithms often reflect the biases of their training data, educators must monitor whether language examples, idioms, or visuals reinforce stereotypes or exclude marginalized cultures. Culturally responsive teachers engage students in discussions about these biases, promoting critical digital literacy and intercultural awareness.

Another strategy is differentiated AI use, where teachers leverage AI platforms differently based on students' linguistic and cultural needs. For instance, first-generation learners or those from tribal communities in India may benefit from slower-paced, multimodal content, while urban learners may require advanced modules with voice-to-text feedback. Educators must actively configure AI settings and select content that aligns with learner diversity. Importantly, culturally responsive teaching is not only about localized content but also about inclusive pedagogy. It involves affirming student voice, encouraging peer collaboration, and recognizing non-standard varieties of English as legitimate. Teachers trained in CRT can ensure that AI does not marginalize cultural identities but amplifies them in global classrooms.

7.2 Training Teachers to Use AI Tools Ethically and Inclusively

Effective integration of AI in English language education depends heavily on teacher preparedness not only in technical proficiency but also in ethical and inclusive use. Teachers must be trained to understand the capabilities and limitations of AI tools and to critically engage with their outputs to avoid perpetuating bias or inequity in multilingual and multicultural classrooms .Such training programs are increasingly being recognized as essential components of professional development, especially in diverse educational contexts like India, where socio-cultural and linguistic pluralism present unique challenges.

Ethical use training equips teachers to identify potential biases embedded in AI algorithms, such as underrepresentation of certain dialects or cultural perspectives, and to mitigate these through supplementary instructional strategies. For example,

AI speech recognition systems may struggle with Indian English accents or regional pronunciations, risking misinterpretation or inaccurate feedback. Training helps teachers calibrate these tools appropriately and provide corrective human mediation when needed (Khan et al., 2023).

Inclusive use training focuses on leveraging AI to support learners with diverse needs such as students with disabilities, neurodiverse learners, and those from marginalized linguistic backgrounds. Educators learn to customize AI platforms for accessibility features like text-to-speech, multilingual translation, and personalized pacing. As demonstrated in a study from Telangana, India, teachers trained in inclusive AI practices successfully enhanced engagement among rural learners by combining AI tools with culturally sensitive pedagogies. Furthermore, professional development programs are increasingly incorporating digital ethics and data privacy modules, critical in a landscape where AI relies on vast amounts of learner data. Teachers are trained on responsible data handling, ensuring informed consent, and protecting student privacy, thereby fostering trust and safeguarding learner rights.

7.3 Teacher Feedback Loops in AI-Based Learning Environments

In AI-enhanced English language learning environments, the role of teacher feedback loops is critical for sustaining pedagogical effectiveness and fostering learner progress. Feedback loops refer to the continuous process where teachers monitor learner interactions with AI tools, interpret the AI-generated data and learner outputs, and provide timely, contextualized instructional responses to guide learning . This dynamic interplay between human judgment and AI analytics ensures that automated systems remain responsive to individual learner needs and cultural nuances.

One significant advantage of AI is its ability to generate granular data on learner performance such as pronunciation accuracy, vocabulary usage, and engagement patterns at scale. However, without effective teacher mediation, these insights may not translate into meaningful learning gains. Teachers use feedback loops to analyze AI reports, identify misconceptions, and customize interventions accordingly. For example, a teacher noticing persistent pronunciation errors flagged by AI can incorporate targeted drills or phonetic explanations sensitive to the learner's linguistic background.

Indian educators, especially in multilingual classrooms, have highlighted the importance of blending AI feedback with cultural and contextual understanding. Studies show that when teachers actively interpret AI data within the socio-cultural framework of learners, students feel more supported and motivated, thereby improving retention and participation rates . Moreover, the inclusion of teacher feedback loops helps mitigate the risk of AI biases going unchecked, such as misinterpretations of Indian English accents or idiomatic expressions.

Technologically, feedback loops are enhanced by AI dashboards and analytic tools designed to be user-friendly for educators. These interfaces visualize learner progress, suggest adaptive content, and enable teachers to input qualitative feedback that further refines AI algorithms. Research indicates that the presence of such feedback mechanisms encourages iterative refinement of AI learning paths, optimizing personalized instruction (Bertin, et.,al 2015).

8. CHALLENGES AND FUTURE DIRECTIONS

8.1 Limitations in Current AI Models for Cultural Sensitivity

Despite significant advances in artificial intelligence for language education, current AI models still exhibit considerable limitations in effectively addressing cultural sensitivity. These limitations arise primarily from the inherent biases in training data, insufficient representation of diverse cultural contexts, and a lack of nuanced understanding of sociocultural dynamics that influence language use and learning (Curry & Lillis, 2010). Many AI systems are trained predominantly on datasets from Western, English-dominant contexts, which limits their ability to accommodate the linguistic and cultural diversity encountered in global classrooms, particularly in multilingual countries like India.

One major issue is cultural bias embedded in natural language processing (NLP) algorithms. These biases can manifest as stereotypical or exclusionary representations, affecting not only language content but also the AI's responses and feedback. For example, AI-powered language tutors might fail to recognize culturally specific idioms, expressions, or accents common among Indian English speakers, thereby misclassifying learner inputs as errors or non-standard usage (Dewi,2023). Such biases risk alienating learners and perpetuating linguistic inequities rather than fostering inclusivity.

Another limitation is the lack of contextual awareness in AI models. Language learning is deeply embedded within cultural norms and values, which influence pragmatics, politeness strategies, and discourse styles. Current AI systems struggle to incorporate this complexity, often providing generic feedback that does not account for culturally appropriate communication styles (Febriyanti et al., 2018). This gap can reduce the relevance and effectiveness of AI-assisted language instruction, especially for learners from underrepresented cultural groups.

Moreover, the scarcity of annotated datasets reflecting Indian sociolinguistic diversity poses a significant barrier. While India has over 20 officially recognized languages and countless dialects, there is limited availability of culturally rich and balanced corpora to train AI models. This scarcity hinders the development of AI tools that accurately reflect the linguistic realities of Indian learners (Flowerdew 1999).

8.2 Policy Frameworks for Inclusive AI Integration

The integration of AI in language education requires robust policy frameworks that emphasize inclusivity, equity, and ethical use. Policymakers worldwide, including in India, are increasingly recognizing that effective AI deployment in education must be governed by guidelines that ensure access for diverse learner populations, safeguard learner data privacy, and promote fairness across socio-cultural boundaries. Without such frameworks, there is a risk that AI tools may inadvertently reinforce existing educational inequalities or marginalize underrepresented groups.

In India, the National Education Policy (NEP) 2020 has acknowledged the transformative potential of AI in education and underscores the need for equitable digital access and culturally relevant content. However, operationalizing these principles demands detailed policies addressing curriculum adaptation, teacher training, and infrastructural readiness to support AI-enhanced language learning across urban and rural settings. Effective policy frameworks must therefore bridge technological innovation with ground realities of linguistic and cultural diversity.

Globally, emerging policy initiatives advocate for inclusive AI that integrates diverse datasets reflecting various languages, dialects, and cultural contexts, alongside mechanisms to detect and mitigate algorithmic bias . Standards for transparency in AI decision-making processes and accountability measures for vendors are becoming essential components of these policies to ensure ethical AI use in education. Furthermore, privacy legislation, such as India's Personal Data Protection Bill, influences how AI tools collect and handle learner data, emphasizing informed consent and data minimization principles. Ensuring compliance with such laws in AI-powered language education platforms is critical for maintaining learner trust and participation.

8.3 Emerging Trends: Emotion-Aware AI, XR in Language Immersion

Emerging technologies such as emotion-aware artificial intelligence (AI) and extended reality (XR) are revolutionizing English language learning by creating immersive and emotionally intelligent educational experiences. Emotion-aware AI systems utilize affective computing to detect and respond to learners' emotional states such as frustration, boredom, or confidence through facial expression analysis, voice tone recognition, and physiological sensors (Ho & Mei-ching, 2017). This capability allows for real-time adaptation of learning content and pacing, fostering engagement and reducing anxiety, which is crucial for language acquisition success, especially in diverse and cross-cultural settings.

In the Indian educational context, early experiments with emotion-aware AI have demonstrated promising outcomes. For example, pilot projects in urban and semi-urban schools in Maharashtra used AI-powered systems to identify learners' stress during speaking tasks and automatically adjusted difficulty levels, resulting in improved learner motivation and performance . These tools help bridge emotional and cognitive gaps, making language learning more personalized and inclusive.

Parallel to emotion-aware AI, XR technologies including virtual reality (VR), augmented reality (AR), and mixed reality (MR) offer immersive language learning environments that simulate real-world scenarios for authentic practice. XR enables learners to engage in virtual cultural contexts and conversations with avatars, promoting intercultural competence alongside language skills (Xie,et.,al 2023). XR applications have shown particular potential in Indian language classrooms, where exposure to diverse linguistic environments may be limited.

Recent research highlights how XR fosters experiential learning by situating language use in meaningful contexts, enhancing retention and pragmatic competence. For instance, VR-based language immersion programs allow students to practice English in virtual marketplaces, airports, or social settings, improving not only vocabulary and grammar but also cultural fluency (Hyland 2013). Despite these advances, challenges remain in scaling emotion-aware AI and XR due to infrastructural constraints, high costs, and the need for culturally tailored content. Continued interdisciplinary research and policy support are vital for expanding access and ensuring these technologies are designed inclusively, reflecting India's multilingual and multicultural realities.

9. CONCLUSION

The integration of AI in English language education offers transformative potential to enhance cross-cultural understanding and inclusivity. However, realizing this promise requires deliberate efforts to address cultural biases, promote equitable access, and design AI systems sensitive to diverse linguistic and socio-cultural contexts. Emerging technologies like emotion-aware AI and extended reality further enrich language learning by fostering personalized, immersive, and culturally responsive experiences. As AI continues to evolve, collaborative policy frameworks, inclusive pedagogical practices, and ongoing research must guide its ethical and effective deployment, ensuring that learners worldwide particularly in multilingual and multicultural environments like India benefit from AI-enhanced education that respects and celebrates cultural diversity.

REFERENCES

Alon-Barkat, S., & Busuioc, M. (2023). Human–AI interactions in public sector decision making:"automation bias" and "selective adherence" to algorithmic advice. *Journal of Public Administration: Research and Theory*, *33*(1), 153–169. DOI: 10.1093/jopart/muac007

Antari, N. K. D. (2022). An analysis of the interpersonal meaning of lyric and video "zombie" by day6. *Journal of Language and Pragmatics Studies*, *1*(1), 16–24. DOI: 10.58881/jlps.v1i1.3

Arsyad, S., & Adila, D. (2017). Using local style when writing in English: The citing behaviour of Indonesian authors in English research article introductions. *Asian Englishes*, *8678*(May), 1–16. DOI: 10.1080/13488678.2017.1327835

Arsyad, S., & Arono, . (2016). Potential problematic rhetorical style transfer from first language to foreign language: A case of Indonesian authors writing research article introductions in English. *Journal of Multicultural Discourses*, *11*(3), 315–330. DOI: 10.1080/17447143.2016.1153642

Bacha, N. N. (2002). Developing learners' academic writing skills in higher education: A study for educational reform. *Language and Education*, *16*(3), 161–177. DOI: 10.1080/09500780208666826

Bacha, N. N. (2002). Developing Learners' Academic Writing Skills in Higher Education: A Study for Educational Reform. *Language and Education*, *16*(3), 161–177. Advance online publication. DOI: 10.1080/09500780208666826

Barker, G. G. (2016). Cross-cultural perspectives on intercultural communication competence. *Journal of Intercultural Communication Research*, *45*(1), 13–30. DOI: 10.1080/17475759.2015.1104376

Bastos, M., & Araújo e Sá, H. (2015). Pathways to teacher education for intercultural communicative competence: Teachers' perceptions. *Language Learning Journal*, *43*(2), 131–147. DOI: 10.1080/09571736.2013.869940

Bates, T., Cobo, C., Mariño, O., & Wheeler, S. (2020). Can artificial intelligence transform higher education? *International Journal of Educational Technology in Higher Education*, *17*(1), 42. DOI: 10.1186/s41239-020-00218-x

Benvenuti, S. (2017). Pedagogy of peers: Cultivating writing retreats as communities of academic writing practice. *South African Journal of Higher Education*, *31*(2), 89–107. DOI: 10.20853/31-2-1340

Bertin, M., Atanassova, I., Larivière, V., & Gingras, Y. (2015). Mapping the linguistic context of citations. *Bulletin of the Association for Information Science and Technology, 41*(2), 26–29. DOI: 10.1002/bult.2015.1720410208

Bozkaya, M., Aydin, I. E., & Kumtepe, E. G. (2012). Research trends and issues in educational technology: A content analysis of TOJET. *The Turkish Online Journal of Educational Technology, 11*(2), 264–277.

Buriro, G. A., & Hayat, T. (2010). Task-Based Learning: An in-class ELT experiment. *The Journal of Educational Research, 13*, 121–134.

Byram, M., Holmes, P., & Savvides, N. (2013). Intercultural communicative competence in foreign language education: Questions of theory, practice and research. *Language Learning Journal, 41*(3), 251–253. DOI: 10.1080/09571736.2013.836343

Canale, M., & Swain, M. (1980). Theoretical bases of communicative approaches to second language teaching and testing. *Applied Linguistics, 1*(1), 1–47. https://www.uefap.com/tefsp/bibliog/canale_swain.pdf. DOI: 10.1093/applin/1.1.1

Chen, C., Chen, Y., Jia, X., Lei, S., Yang, C., Nie, Q., & Weiss, B. (2024). Cultural adaptation and evaluation of a school-based positive psychology intervention among Chinese middle school students: A mixed methods program design study. *School Psychology*. PMID: 39264655

Chen, H. (2024). The ethical challenges of educational artificial intelligence and coping measures: A discussion in the context of the 2024 World Digital Education Conference. *Science Insights Education Frontiers, 20*(2), 3263-3281.

Cheong, C. (2025). Reimagining English Language Education for a Connected, Cultural and Compassionate Future. *English Teaching, 54*(1), i–ii. DOI: 10.52696/IZGD8741

Chun, D. M. (2011). Developing intercultural communicative competence through online exchanges. *CALICO Journal, 28*(2), 392–419. DOI: 10.11139/cj.28.2.392-419

Cooper, G. (2023). Examining science education in ChatGPT: An exploratory study of generative artificial intelligence. *Journal of Science Education and Technology, 32*(3), 444–452. DOI: 10.1007/s10956-023-10039-y

Cretchley, J., Rooney, D., & Gallois, C. (2010). Mapping a 40-year history with Leximancer: Themes and concepts in the *Journal of Cross-Cultural Psychology. Journal of Cross-Cultural Psychology, 41*(3), 318–328. DOI: 10.1177/0022022110366105

Curry, M. J., & Lillis, T. M. (2010). Academic research networks: Accessing resources for English-medium publishing. *English for Specific Purposes, 29*(4), 281–295. DOI: 10.1016/j.esp.2010.06.002

Deneme, S. (2010). Cross-cultural differences in language learning strategy preferences: A comparative study. *International Journal of Language. Society and Culture, 31*, 81–89.

Dewi, N. M. S. C. (2023). Lexical and grammatical cohesion analysis of "nothing like us" song lyrics: Written discourse analysis. *Journal of Language and Pragmatics Studies, 2*(1), 19–27. DOI: 10.58881/jlps.v2i1.9

Ellis, R. (2009). Task-based language teaching: Sorting out the misunderstandings. *International Journal of Applied Linguistics, 19*(3), 221–246. DOI: 10.1111/j.1473-4192.2009.00231.x

Eun, B. (2010). From learning to development: A sociocultural approach to instruction. *Cambridge Journal of Education, 40*(4), 401–418. DOI: 10.1080/0305764X.2010.526593

Fang, F. (2010). Developing students' communicative competence in college English teaching in China. *Journal of Language Teaching and Research, 1*(2), 111–116. DOI: 10.4304/jltr.1.2.111-116

Febriyanti, G. A. A. A., Dewi, N. K. S. L., & Dewi, I. G. A. A. I. R. C. (2018). Using self-assessment to assess rural young learners' writing skills in English foreign language classroom. *Journal of Applied Studies in Language, 2*(2), 109–115. DOI: 10.31940/jasl.v2i2.1065

Flowerdew, J. (1999). Writing for scholarly publication in English: The case of Hong Kong. *Journal of Second Language Writing, 8*(2), 123–145. DOI: 10.1016/S1060-3743(99)80125-8

George, A. S., & George, A. H. (2023). A review of ChatGPT AI's impact on several business sectors. *Partners Universal International Innovation Journal, 1*, 9–23.

Hew, K. F., Lan, M., Tang, Y., Jia, C., & Lo, C. K. (2019). Where is the "theory" within the field of educational technology research? *British Journal of Educational Technology, 50*(3), 956–971. DOI: 10.1111/bjet.12770

. Ho, M.C. (2017). Navigating scholarly writing and international publishing: Individual agency of Taiwanese EAL doctoral students. Journal of English for Academic Purposes, Volume 27, Pages 1-13.

Hsieh, T. C., Wang, T. I., Su, C. Y., & Lee, M. C. (2012). A fuzzy logic-based personalized learning system for supporting adaptive English learning. *Journal of Educational Technology & Society*, *15*(1), 273–288. https://www.jstor.org/stable/jeductechsoci.15.1.273

Huang, L. (2010). Cross-cultural communication in business negotiations. *International Journal of Economics and Finance*, *2*(2), 196–199. DOI: 10.5539/ijef.v2n2p196

Hyland, K. (2013). Materials for Developing Writing Skills. In Tomlinson, B. (Ed.), *Developing Materials for Language Teaching* (2nd ed., pp. 391–405). Bloomsbury.

Istenic Starcic, A., & Bagon, S. (2014). ICT-supported learning for inclusion of people with special needs: Review of seven educational technology journals. *British Journal of Educational Technology*, *45*(2), 202–230. DOI: 10.1111/bjet.12086

Karimi, M. N., & Nazari, M. (2021). Growth in language teachers' understanding of differentiated instruction: A sociocultural theory perspective. *Journal of Education for Teaching*, *47*(3), 322–336. DOI: 10.1080/02607476.2021.1884973

Kerr, P. (2016). Adaptive learning. *ELT Journal*, *70*(1), 88–93. DOI: 10.1093/elt/ccv055

Khan, R. A., Jawaid, M., Khan, A. R., & Sajjad, M. (2023). ChatGPT—Reshaping medical education and clinical management. *Pakistan Journal of Medical Sciences*, *39*(2), 605. DOI: 10.12669/pjms.39.2.7653 PMID: 36950398

Lai, H. C., Chang, C. Y., Wen-Shiane, L., Fan, Y. L., & Wu, Y. T. (2013). The implementation of mobile learning in outdoor education: Application of QR codes. *British Journal of Educational Technology*, *44*(2), E57–E62. DOI: 10.1111/j.1467-8535.2012.01343.x

Laksana, D. N. L. (2020). Implementation of online learning in the pandemic COVID-19: Student perception in areas with minimum internet access. *Journal of Educational Technology*, *4*(4), 502–509. DOI: 10.23887/jet.v4i4.29314

. Lopez, B. (2025). Utilizing Artificial Intelligence to Increase Vocabulary for Multilingual Learners.

Luckin, R., & Cukurova, M. (2019). Designing educational technologies in the age of AI: A learning sciences-driven approach. *British Journal of Educational Technology*, *50*(6), 2824–2838. DOI: 10.1111/bjet.12861

Malmir, A., Sarem, S. N., & Ghasemi, A. (2011). The effect of Task-Based Language Teaching (TBLT) vs. Content-Based. *Iranian EFL Journal*, *7*, 79–94.

Marginson, S., & Dang, T. K. A. (2017). Vygotsky's sociocultural theory in the context of globalization. *Asia Pacific Journal of Education, 37*(1), 116–129. DOI: 10.1080/02188791.2016.1216827

Ochieng, E. G., & Price, A. D. (2010). Managing cross-cultural communication in multicultural construction project teams: The case of Kenya and UK. *International Journal of Project Management, 28*(5), 449–460. DOI: 10.1016/j.ijproman.2009.08.001

Ozfidan, B., Machtmes, K. L., & Demir, H. (2014). Socio-cultural factors in second language learning: A case study of adventurous adult language learners. *European Journal of Educational Research, 3*(4), 185–191. DOI: 10.12973/eu-jer.3.4.185

Passonneau, R. J., McNamara, D., Muresan, S., & Perin, D. (2017). Preface: Special issue on multidisciplinary approaches to AI and education for reading and writing. *International Journal of Artificial Intelligence in Education, 27*(4), 665–670. DOI: 10.1007/s40593-017-0158-8

Robertson, M. (2014). Task-based language teaching and expansive learning theory. *TESL Canada Journal, 31*, 187. DOI: 10.18806/tesl.v31i0.1194

Roy, A. G., & Bhatia, N. (Eds.). (2023). *Regional Perspectives on India's Partition: Shifting the Vantage Points*. Taylor & Francis. DOI: 10.4324/9781003278498

Shadiev, R., Sun, A., & Huang, Y.-M. (2019). A study of the facilitation of cross-cultural understanding and intercultural sensitivity using speech-enabled language translation technology. *British Journal of Educational Technology, 50*(3), 1415–1433. DOI: 10.1111/bjet.12648

Sharma, K., Papamitsiou, Z., & Giannakos, M. (2019). Building pipelines for educational data using AI and multimodal analytics: A "grey-box" approach. *British Journal of Educational Technology, 50*(6), 3004–3031. DOI: 10.1111/bjet.12854

Shirazi, M., Ponzer, S., Zarghi, N., Keshmiri, F., Motlagh, M. K., Zavareh, D. K., & Khankeh, H. R. (2020). Inter-cultural and cross-cultural communication through physicians' lens: Perceptions and experiences. *International Journal of Medical Education, 11*, 158–168. DOI: 10.5116/ijme.5f19.5749 PMID: 32820142

Shobikah, N. (2020). The competencies in English. *Journal of Research in English Language Learning, 1*(1), 23. DOI: 10.33474/j-reall.v1i1.5280

Sholeh, M. B. (2023). Task-based learning in the classroom for EFL learners: How and why? *Journal of Language Pragmatics Studies, 2*(3), 274–281. DOI: 10.58881/jlps.v2i3.34

Tarhini, A., Hone, K., & Liu, X. (2015). A cross-cultural examination of the impact of social, organisational and individual factors on educational technology acceptance between British and Lebanese university students. *British Journal of Educational Technology*, *46*(4), 739–755. DOI: 10.1111/bjet.12169

Titarenko, L., & Little, C. B. (2017). International cross-cultural online learning and teaching: Effective tools and approaches. *American Journal of Distance Education*, *31*(2), 112–127. DOI: 10.1080/08923647.2017.1306767

Vanbecelaere, S., Van den Berghe, K., Cornillie, F., Sasanguie, D., Reynvoet, B., & Depaepe, F. (2020). The effectiveness of adaptive versus non-adaptive learning with digital educational games. *Journal of Computer Assisted Learning*, *36*(4), 502–513. DOI: 10.1111/jcal.12416

Xiaoyu, Z., & Tobias, T. C. (2023). Exploring the efficacy of adaptive learning technologies in online education: A longitudinal analysis of student engagement and performance. *International Journal of Science and Engineering Applications*, *12*, 28–31.

Xie, Y., Seth, I., Hunter-Smith, D. J., Rozen, W. M., & Seifman, M. A. (2024). Investigating the impact of innovative AI chatbot on post-pandemic medical education and clinical assistance: A comprehensive analysis. *ANZ Journal of Surgery*, *94*(1-2), 68–77. DOI: 10.1111/ans.18666 PMID: 37602755

Chapter 12
Bridging the Divide:
Towards Ethical AI Integration in English Language Teaching

Francis N. Reginio
https://orcid.org/0000-0001-5939-4508
University of Southeastern Philippines, Philippines

Sajed Sayde Ingilan
https://orcid.org/0000-0002-4466-2028
University of Southeastern Philippines, Philippines

Andi Asrifan
Universitas Negeri Makassar, Indonesia

ABSTRACT

As artificial intelligence (AI) increasingly integrates into English Language Teaching (ELT) in Southeast Asia, it changes pedagogic ethics, teacher agency, and cultural equity. This chapter examines the ethical and epistemic dimensions of AI-driven tools, especially in marginalized areas, like Indigenous Peoples' (IP) communities, madrasah, and rural Indonesian schools. Based on Kant's, Rawls', Gilligan's, and Foucault's frameworks, it uncovers the ways in which hegemonic AI tools tend to standardize language and push localized pedagogical relations to the margin. Categorized into core themes, the narratives from the Southeast Asian teachers reveal algorithmic bias and the moral and emotional contradictions in AI adoption, most notably the loss of emotional labor and the marginalization of indigenous knowledge systems. The research makes a case for an ethical shift and appeals to a humanizing approach that re-centers teacher agency, protects learners, and sustains plural Southeast Asian values to revolutionize ELT-AI as an ethical praxis grounded on care, justice, and empowerment.

DOI: 10.4018/979-8-3373-3561-2.ch012

INTRODUCTION

In recent years, artificial intelligence (AI) has become a transformative force in education, with English Language Teaching (ELT) standing at the forefront of its application. These technologies have reshaped the dynamics of teaching and learning languages, from AI-powered grammar tools and chatbots to virtual tutors and automated essay scorers. Scholars have noted their potential to personalize instruction, enhance engagement, and increase efficiency (Peer Mohammed, 2024a; Luckin et al., 2021). Yet alongside these benefits, critical ethical questions arise regarding autonomy, cultural representation, and fairness, especially in multilingual and postcolonial contexts.

Despite the focus on technical performance, current research often evaluates AI through a utilitarian lens, emphasizing measurable outcomes while overlooking ethical and cultural dimensions (Şahín Kölemen, 2024). As a result, issues such as linguistic imperialism, surveillance, and the erosion of teacher and student agency receive little attention. Furthermore, dominant AI tools often carry the cultural assumptions of the Global North, reinforcing hegemonic English norms and marginalizing local voices. Consequently, AI integration risks reproducing historical language hierarchies and epistemic inequities.

The oversight is particularly evident in the Global South, where Southeast Asian countries like the Philippines and Indonesia remain underrepresented in normative, philosophical, and culturally grounded analyses. In these contexts, AI tools are increasingly introduced in public and private education settings, often with promises of personalization and efficiency, but with limited examination of ethical risks, local cultural mismatches, and socio-political implications (Akgun & Greenhow, 2021). In the Philippines, the integration of AI tools such as Grammarly and ChatGPT into language education has been met with both enthusiasm and concern. It is important to consider linguistic diversity and ethical implications in the Philippine context. Also, there is an observable dearth of literature specifically in addressing the ethical dimensions of AI in ELT. While some anecdotal reports and policy-level discussions like the Department of Education's EdTech initiatives acknowledge AI applications, no substantial philosophical, critical, or empirical studies to date comprehensively explore how these tools may reproduce colonial language hierarchies, undermine teachers' ethical roles, or violate student privacy rights. This gap is particularly striking given the country's long-standing postcolonial language politics and the high stakes of AI-driven education in low-resource schools.

In contrast, in the Indonesian context, several studies have explored perceptions of AI tools in ELT among teachers and students, generally affirming their utility in providing feedback, increasing engagement, and aiding autonomous learning (Sutrisno et. al., 2024; Baturbutar, 2024; Enzelina et. al., 2023). Yet, such studies are primarily utility theories. They are concerned with performance and usability, not really moral and epistemological concerns. For instance, Rahman (2024) refers to AI as transformational in Indonesian language classrooms, yet fails to critically question how such technologies may encode linguistic hegemony or disempower teachers.

Furthermore, by comparing with the work of Sabaruddin et al. (2024), it presents AI as transforming teacher quality through the Technological Pedagogical and Content Knowledge (TPACK) model, but their framework does not carry a critical angle to data ethics, linguistic equity, and cultural competence. Another article presented the details, which were the same as those of Hartono et al. (2023), demonstrating how AI integration is seen to be beneficial by students as well as teachers. It is silent, however, on surveillance dangers, content concerns, and epistemic marginalization in multilingual classrooms.

Taken together, these regional gaps reveal a pressing need for critical, context-aware research that goes beyond questions of efficiency. This study focuses on three areas: 1) how AI encodes dominant Global North language ideologies that marginalize local linguistic variants; 2) ethical risks from surveillance and opaque data collection; and 3) the lack of participatory frameworks involving local educators in AI design and deployment.

To address these gaps, this study employs a theory-informed approach drawing on moral philosophy (Kant, Rawls, Gilligan), critical pedagogy, and Foucault's theory of power/knowledge. It also examines international AI ethics frameworks, including UNESCO and OECD guidelines, for their relevance to language education. These frameworks help identify problems like bias in AI, threats to teacher control, and the neglect of local culture. The paper also uses information from interviews and discussions with Southeast Asian teachers to develop clear ethical principles. These principles, such as protecting privacy, being transparent about AI decisions, and involving teachers and learners in AI design, guide the responsible use of AI in classrooms while respecting local languages, teaching methods, and values.

Eventually, bridging the gap is not only a matter of technology but also of ethics. Educational innovation must reconnect with the moral purpose of teaching, understanding, dignity, and human freedom.

1. STANDARDIZING VOICES, MARGINALIZING MEANINGS: AI, ETHICS, AND EQUITY IN SOUTHEAST ASIAN LANGUAGE EDUCATION

As illustrated in the preceding issues, the information revolution poses new threats to human autonomy and the capacity to pursue a meaningful life. When AI systems give people and organizations easy access to personal data, users lose control over how their information is used. This section looks at examples of AI in ELT, focusing on tools like Grammarly and Duolingo in Southeast Asia. Using ideas from moral philosophy, critical pedagogy, and theories of knowledge and power, the discussion shows how these technologies shape certain views of language and culture while pushing others aside. In doing so, they may either repeat old inequalities or, at times, challenge them.

1.1. Cultural and Linguistic Trusts and Biases in AI Tools

AI tools, particularly large language models (LLMs), are increasingly used in education, governance, and communication. These tools affect how knowledge is shared and interpreted, especially across cultural and language boundaries. Therefore, they should be evaluated not only for performance but also for their impact on cultural and linguistic trust. Cultural and linguistic trust is the confidence users have that AI will understand, mediate, and represent their unique social and linguistic realities accurately (Imran, 2022). This trust is essential for ethical AI use, especially for communities historically excluded from technological discussions.

AI writing tools like Grammarly, while useful for improving English skills, often prioritize grammatical accuracy and standard English over the cultural meaning, idioms, and narrative practices of non-Western communities. As a result, they can diminish local linguistic traditions and moral frameworks embedded in language.

Figure 1. Sample of Grammarly corrections for languages spoken in the Philippines

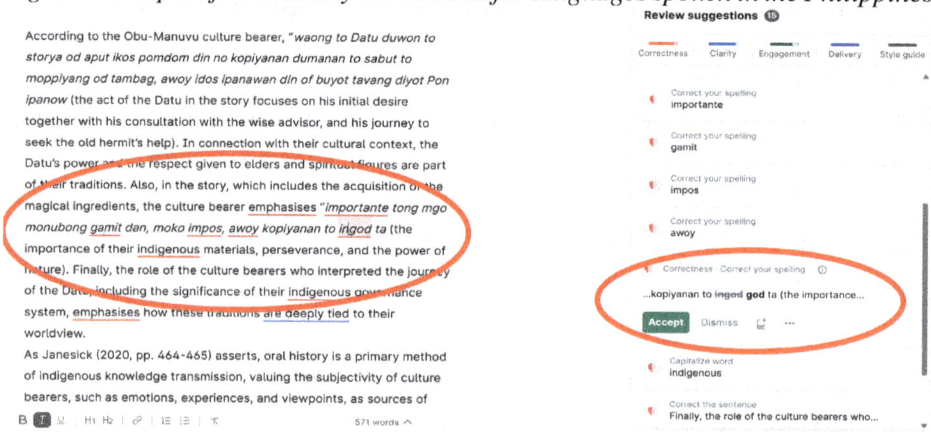

In Figure 1, when the uploaded texts containing indigenous terms are analyzed by Grammarly, the application flags these in red, without offering culturally informed options. Users are limited to selecting 'accept,' 'dismiss,' or 'add to dictionary' with no explanation or acknowledgment of the language's cultural value. This reveals a basic limitation in cultural-linguistic awareness that these systems are not programmed to be inclusive of indigenous forms, instead recognizing them as errors and not as legitimate linguistic forms and submissions to meaning production (Espartinez, 2025).

This adds further support to the overarching issue of this section: the breakdown of linguistic and cultural trust through algorithmic exclusion. While global languages like German or Spanish are recognized on the platform's linguistic database, indigenous languages like Obu-Manuvu or Dayak Benawan are not. This exposes an inherent hierarchy of linguistic value, in which standard languages are privileged with semantic tags and contextual support, but local or indigenous ones become invisible. It shows how AI applications reproduce the colonial order by programming some languages as legitimate and others as illegitimate (Asrifan et al., 2025a).

Trust

Trust and transparency in AI must be grounded in deontological principles. Kant's (1781/1998) imperative that humans be treated as ends in themselves implies that AI systems should operate transparently, especially regarding cultural and linguistic decisions. For instance, there are certain algorithms that drive some of these more complex tasks designed to replace human judgment, which leads to what AI-LLM researchers call the "black box" problem. This problem in AI violates this principle by obscuring how data is processed and interpreted (von Eschenbach, 2021). When users in marginalized sectors cannot inspect or question how their cultural values are algorithmically translated, their autonomy and rational agency are compromised. As Asrifan et al. (2025b) argued, they are reduced to passive users of a system that may misrepresent or erase their cultural identity.

Transparency is thus a categorical imperative (Kant, 1785/2012) in AI design. Developers have a moral duty to ensure explainability, especially in how AI handles sociocultural content. This includes making visible the sources, logic, and assumptions behind translations, cultural framings, or narrative choices. In doing so, systems respect user dignity and strengthen epistemic trust across communities. Conversely, when explainability is absent, AI tools commit a moral error by treating users, especially those from underrepresented cultures, not as participants but merely as data points.

Moreover, this ethical demand for transparency must align with principles of fairness. Rawls (1971), in his theory of justice, insists on distributive fairness in access to technological benefits. Yet, in practice, AI systems often rely on training data skewed toward dominant cultures and languages. This imbalance violates Rawls's difference principle, which allows inequalities only if they benefit the least advantaged.

The findings of Espartinez (2025) show that rural students and faculty face structural inequities in digital infrastructure, leaving them disadvantaged compared to their urban peers. Similarly, at the global level, indigenous peoples and speakers of non-Western languages are excluded from the AI knowledge loop, perpetuating historic injustices and limiting digital participation. Taken together, these local and global patterns of marginalization illustrate how the absence of transparency and fairness in AI systems undermines trust, deepens inequity, and reinforces historic hierarchies.

Algorithmic pluralism is a necessary response to this injustice. Through an active effort to represent minority languages, regional dialects, and cultural expressions in its training data, AI can be tuned to equity. For this, the latter has been responded to by Jenks (2023), which pertains to the encoding of sociocultural standards (e.g., honorifics, kinship terms, etc.). Participatory co-design that involves culture bearers around indigenous knowledge systems and practices (IKSP) also ensures that AI development is not simply reproducing the modes of colonization aimed at extraction and erasure (Asrifan et al., 2025a).

Foucault's (1972) concept of discourse and power is fundamental for revealing how AI operates as a present-day "regime of truth." Rather than simply representing reality, AI actively constructs it through selective discourses shaped by the training data. The exclusion of indigenous and marginalized voices from these corpora is not a matter of oversight but a discriminatory exercise of power that renders their cultures invisible (Srinivasan & Chandler, 2021). Foucault would note that such claims to 'knowledge' or 'truth' are structured by historical power relations embedded in data selection, annotation, and algorithmic interpretation.

Moreover, the epistemic authority granted to AI today reflects Foucault's (1984) notion of the specific intellectual, whose knowledge gains legitimacy through institutional power. When LLMs present outputs as objective or neutral, they obscure the political and cultural conditions of their production, leading users to internalize these outputs and thereby reinforce cultural erasure and the marginalization of subjugated knowledge.

An ethics of care perspective foregrounds relational trust and moral responsiveness. For Gilligan (1982), ethical decisions must be contextual and attentive to the needs of those in vulnerable positions. Applied to AI, this means going beyond transparency to embed empathy, engagement, and accountability into design. Feedback loops, redress mechanisms, and annotation rights (Asrifan et al., 2025b) are crucial for enabling communities to correct misrepresentations and hold systems responsible. Cultural and linguistic trust, meanwhile, requires normative alignment and contextual awareness. AI must adapt to cultural norms such as speech registers, taboos, and storytelling patterns (Araujo et al., 2020), while also recognizing local events, religious practices, and kinship expressions. For instance, a chatbot in Mindanao that correctly identifies Ramadan salutations or Muslim politeness forms is more likely to be perceived as trustworthy.

From a Foucauldian perspective, AI systems are not neutral but reproduce power–knowledge relations (Foucault, 1977). Linguistic inclusivity, therefore, extends beyond English to include code-switching and low-resource languages. Failing to support Philippine English, Tagalog-inflected English, or local languages such as Bagobo-Klata, Kagan, Maguindanao, or Dayak Benawan erodes trust while reinforcing cultural invisibility.

Biases

Cultural and linguistic biases undermine trust in AI. These are systemic tendencies of AI systems to prioritize dominant cultural or linguistic codes, often by replicating imbalances embedded in training data (Srinivasan & Chadner, 2021). If a model's corpus contains more Western media than indigenous oral texts, its output will mirror that skew. The result is not just misrepresentation but epistemic erasure (Asrifan et al., 2025a).

Figure 2. Sample of Duolingo App learning the Indonesian language for the first time

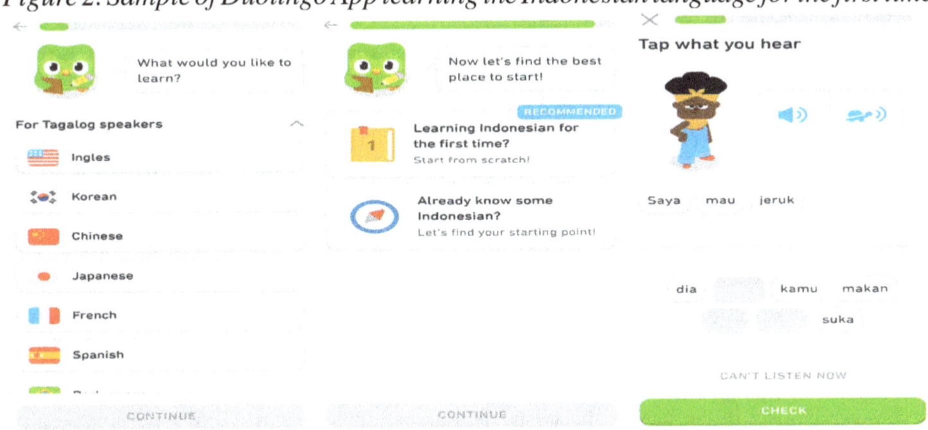

In Figure 2, Duolingo shows a wide range of language courses; however, it does not include many indigenous languages, such as those spoken in Mindanao or the Dayak Benawan language. The absence of these languages reflects a bias toward widely spoken ones, which limits learning opportunities for indigenous communities and risks further marginalizing their heritage. The platform's pronunciation practice also focuses on standard accents, which may not support the sound patterns of indigenous languages. This can discourage learners if their pronunciation is judged as incorrect, leading to a loss of confidence or even withdrawal from language study. These gaps can be explained by algorithmic bias, which often comes from design choices. Developers decide which grammar rules matter most or which ways of speaking are treated as standard. For example, when Philippine regional languages or Dayak Benawan are removed to make the system easier for global users, those languages are treated as less important (Jenks, 2023). Bias also comes from the way the system learns. If it mostly learns corrections from speakers of dominant languages, it repeats their norms and ignores other forms of expression (Blodgett et al., 2020). The design of the interface also plays a role. Using Western names, holidays, or metaphors shapes how people view the system and whether they trust it. When these are not adjusted for local cultures, many users feel invisible or excluded. For instance, lessons with U.S. holiday greetings or European examples can make Southeast Asian, Muslim, or Indigenous learners feel disconnected. This finding aligns with Mushtaq et al. (2025), who developed WorldView-Bench and found that many models poorly capture non-Western worldviews, reinforcing user alienation.

Foucault (1977) reminded us that power works not just through force but through normalization, which includes behavior, language, and knowledge. In standardizing communication and linguistic expression, AI systems enact subtle forms of discipline. They encourage users to conform to the dominant linguistics or knowledge model, thereby silencing heteroglossia and enforcing cultural conformity. Disciplinary technologies produce docile subjects; that is, they govern not by overt means but by shaping the behavior of those who come to recognize and internalize the new forms.

The cultural and linguistic biases have serious consequences. When unchecked, AI image generators reinforce stereotypes, as Bianchi et al. (2023) document. In language models, the same harms show up as stereotyping, condescension, or flattening of cultures. Additionally, linguistic bias can make critical services such as AI-powered medical or banking voice assistants inaccessible to minority language speakers, worsening digital inequality. Tao et al. (2023) add that cultural bias is not simply an accidental artifact but is measurable through datasets that expose systematic privileging of certain values. Prabhakaran, Qadri, and Hutchinson (2022) also show that cultural values in NLP are hard to embed but vital if models are to gain global legitimacy.

Addressing these challenges is not optional. It is an imperative of justice, morality, and relational responsibility. Rawls suggests we build systems that benefit the most vulnerable. Kant insists that we treat users as autonomous moral agents. Gilligan requires that we care, listen, and respond with compassion. Cultural and linguistic trust, and the assumptions that degrade it, must be at the core of responsible AI creation.

1.2. Ethical Risks: Data Privacy, Consent, and Surveillance

The use of AI in ELT brings both opportunities and serious ethical risks. These risks appear clearly in the areas of data privacy, consent, and surveillance. In Southeast Asia, including the Philippines and Indonesia, AI-powered platforms collect large amounts of learner data such as text, voice, and even biometric information. However, this is often done without clearly informing learners or asking for permission. Such practices raise concerns about dignity, autonomy, and safety.

Data Privacy in AI-Enhanced ELT

AI tools in ELT collect personal data, ranging from voice and face information to learning patterns such as grammar errors and fluency levels. These features are meant to personalize learning, but they often come with weak protections in the Global South. In these regions, rules for data management are limited and enforcement is weak, which increases the chance of privacy violations (Gomez & da Silva, 2023). In addition, there are rarely strong policies on how long data is stored or where it is kept, especially in schools that lack training in digital security.

Another concern is the lack of transparency. Many learners do not know how their data is collected, where it is stored, or who controls it (Selvam & González Vallejo, 2025). This creates an unequal relationship between technology companies and users. When data is treated as a business product, education risks becoming a marketplace instead of a public service (Peer Mohammed, 2024b). For example, Grammarly records every keystroke, including personal reflections and culturally specific writing. Its policy allows the company to reuse this data to train models, which in effect turns the learners' voices into commercial resources.

Duolingo also collects voice recordings, usage information, and sign-up details through Google or Facebook. In some cases, tracking continues even after active sessions (UNESCO, 2021). In many Southeast Asian schools, students are required to use these tools without proper privacy training, and parents are rarely asked for consent, especially for minors. By contrast, in the European Union (2016), the General Data Protection Regulation (GDPR) protects user rights on data. In Southeast Asia, most learners remain uninformed about how their speech or writing data is stored or shared (Council of Europe, 2024, p. 23). As a result, the classroom becomes part of uncontrolled data markets instead of a safe learning space.

Consent Gap in ELT-AI Adoption

Consent in AI-based education is rarely meaningful. Most applications use long and complex agreements that teachers and students cannot fully understand. This is even more difficult for children or rural learners with limited digital literacy. Floridi et al. (2018) describe this as a false form of consent, where agreement is shaped by unequal power between companies and users. In Philippine classrooms, this turns what should be a free ethical choice into a simple requirement, leaving learners without real control over their online identities.

This lack of contextualized consent is evident in multilingual, indigenous communities. A Filipino ESL teacher working with indigenous learners in Southwestern Mindanao shared:

> *"Ang pipila sa akong mga estudyante ganahan sa mga dula ni Duolingo, apan wala sila'y ideya nga ang app nagrekord sa ilang tingog ug kalihokan maskin pa ug lapas sa oras sa klase. Sa dihang akong nadiskobrehan nga na-link kini sa ilang Facebook, gidala nako dayon kini sa school principal (Some of my students like Duolingo's games, but they have no idea the app is recording their voice and activity beyond class time. When I discovered it was linked to their Facebook, I immediately took it to the school principal). No one had informed them of any of that. So now I instruct them to log out and restrict sharing."*

The teacher's account illustrates an active resistance to AI's hidden data collection practices and a commitment to safeguarding students' digital autonomy. Rather than accepting the default use of AI tools, the teacher models critical awareness and promotes informed digital behavior. This aligns with the ethical ideal that consent must be contextualized, translated, and pedagogically scaffolded, especially in diverse, multilingual settings. Otherwise, AI tools turn consent into a pressure mechanism, mass-normalizing asymmetrical data relationships and undermining learners' right to say no.

The urgency of such interventions is further revealed when placed in the context of wider Southeast Asia, where Eurocentric presuppositions drive omnipresent AI interfaces and Anglocentric linguistic norms (Noor & Kanitroj, 2025). Students are often forced to assent to English or legalese conditions that have no synonyms in their native languages, eliminating their right to informed consent. Unless reformed, the ideal of consent can become an instrument of algorithmic coercion instead of being a tool of learner agency.

Surveillance in Pedagogical Infrastructure

Surveillance in AI for English learning often appears in subtle and normalized ways. Duolingo, for example, tracks correct answers, learning pace, emotional interest through speech tone, and risk of dropping out through its gamification system. While these features are meant to improve engagement, they also turn students into behavioral data subjects who are constantly monitored and pushed to follow algorithmic "best" practices, which can penalize culturally distinct communication styles (Gulson & Witzenberger, 2022). Grammarly works in a similar way through its tone detector and writing analytics, suggesting rewordings or discouraging the use of idioms that do not conform to Anglophone norms. Over time, students may abandon culturally meaningful expressions that are marked as “unclear,” “emotional,” or “informal” (Bailey & Lee, 2020). Together, these systems create what Walter (2024) calls a digital panopticon, where students learn not only language but also how to adjust their behavior to satisfy algorithmic judgment. These risks replace Southeast Asian traditions of relational learning, context-based communication, and community storytelling with surveillance practices disguised as personalization.

Teachers are not immune either. They are refigured as agents of algorithmic enforcement, decoding dashboards, engagement scores, and usage patterns dictated by global companies. What emerges is an empowered classroom dynamic in which both teacher and student are secondary to the logic of the algorithm. Yet despite these risks, some Southeast Asian educators actively negotiate ethical alternatives in their practice. An English teacher from a public university in Central Mindanao stated:

> *“Grammarly highlights every sentence my students write, but I always tell them that not all that is flagged by the app must change. Some of their metaphors are culturally specific and must remain. I also fear that everything they write is being kept somewhere. I advise them not to use Grammarly for sensitive thoughts or community-based storytelling. We use it as a tool, not a judge.”*

This teacher’s approach clearly shows a critical distancing from algorithmic power and asserts ethical autonomy in guarding students' linguistic integrity. By refusing complete algorithmic monitoring and claiming the right to contextual expression, the teacher resists standardization and strengthens students' agency within a culturally responsive pedagogy.

1.3. Teacher Roles and Deskilling

The incorporation of AI within ELT redefines the teacher's role in subtle and explicit terms. While AI-based platforms guide the learner through more learning through personalization, error identification, and real-time responses, such functionality also threatens to exclude the pedagogical expertise of teachers. Teachers are increasingly made into facilitators of pre-programmed learning trajectories instead of ethical beings, cultural intermediaries, and critical thinkers in the classroom.

Instrumentalization and Loss of Pedagogical Agency

Mike W. Martin (2007) explains in *Everyday Morality* that treating people as tools rather than as moral beings disrespects their dignity and agency. This applies to how AI changes teaching through tools like Grammarly and Duolingo. Grammarly gives automated writing feedback, suggesting standard corrections and tone changes, which teachers are expected to follow. Duolingo provides automated scores, task completion rates, and gamified badges for Junior High School (JHS) students in Southern Mindanao. These often become the main measures of progress, but they ignore deeper forms of learning. When schools adopt AI systems that normalize instruction, automate grading, and track behavior, teachers are left with little room for creativity or ethical judgment. The algorithms decide what counts as "good teaching," turning teachers into compliance agents instead of reflective educators. As Oh and Ahn (2024) argue, such systems reduce teachers' professional agency and limit their ability to exercise moral judgment in their classrooms.

As one English teacher from Southern Mindanao shared:

"Usahay ang Grammarly ginaflag ang mga statements sa akong mga students nga dili klaro or informal (Sometimes, Grammarly flags my student's statements as unclear or informal)."

"Pero kani lakip lamang sa ilang mga local nga expression o nagapahayag sa kaladmon sa ilang emosyon. Kung ako n inga suportahan ang mga sinulatan ug desisyon, ginapahibalo lang ako nga wala nako ginasunod ang mga katuyuan sa mga 'improvement goals' nga giestablish sa maong app (They are simply incorporating local expressions or conveying emotional depth, though. When I support these decisions, I'm informed that I'm not following the 'improvement goals' established by the application)."

Another JHS English teacher from Southeastern Mindanao:

Adunay dashboard ang Duolingo unya imong makita nga naa kay student nga 'low performing' tungod kay ilang ginaskip ang pipila ka mga buluhaton (Duolingo presents me with a dashboard that tells me a student is 'low performing' because they are skipping some tasks). But I know that a student speaks three other local languages fluently. Bisaya, Mandaya, and Kagan.

Martin (2007) reminds us that respecting people means seeing them as autonomous moral agents. But when teachers are asked to rely only on algorithm outputs from Grammarly or Duolingo, their ability to act with moral and professional judgment is taken away. The system defines what counts as good writing or learning, leaving little space for teachers to adapt lessons to students' cultural and linguistic needs. Teachers then lose the chance to make sensitive judgments, such as how to support a struggling student from a minority language group. Instead, they are reduced to following algorithmic metrics and administrative reports.

AI Systems and the Automation of Emotional Labor

Teachers also provide essential emotional labor—building trust, encouraging students, resolving conflicts, and adapting to cultural contexts. AI tools, however, focus mainly on measurable behavior like eye contact, speech patterns, or test results, and overlook this relational work. Chowdhury (2023) notes that technology cannot replace the empathy and context awareness that teachers bring. When platforms mechanize these tasks in the name of efficiency, they erase the affective and moral duties at the heart of real learning.

As a high school English teacher from Cotabato City explained:

"My students from conflict areas sometimes write very emotional essays. Grammarly highlights the sentences as too emotional or recommends a 'more positive tone.' Pakiramdam ko, ay binubura nito ang katotohanan (I feel like it is erasing their truth). "

Also, one language teacher in Kalimantan stated:

"Duolingo akan memberikan notifikasi berulang ketika siswa melewatkan latihan. Namun, beberapa siswa kami berasal dari daerah yang tidak memiliki sinyal (Duolingo provides push notifications when students miss practice. Yet some of our students come from areas with no signal). Rather than taking context into account, it punishes them with lower engagement scores."

This erosion of emotional and moral responsibility is especially damaging in Southeast Asian classrooms, where collectivist values often position teachers as community guides and moral authorities. In Malaysia, for example, Tee et al. (2023) show that after COVID, teachers' professional identities have been reshaped by ed-tech tools that emphasize delivery over engagement. As a result, teachers experience a gap between their values and the roles forced upon them by AI-driven systems.

Deskilling and Professional Redefinition

The mechanization of language fixing, fluency grading, and even the pacing of lessons eliminates professional growth opportunities. Instead of gaining deeper linguistic or intercultural teaching abilities, educators are learning more and more about how to handle platforms, how to read dashboards, or tune algorithms, instead of wondering how learners best acquire new knowledge. This is a move away from reflective practitioners toward tech navigators with little voice in the crafting or ethics of the technologies they must implement. Shared by a university instructor in Northeastern Mindanao, Philippines:

"I used to help students think about their writing process, why they chose certain words, or how their story connects to their values. Now, all I need is to spend time checking if Grammarly scores went up and why the Duolingo lessons have not been completed."

A new English teacher in a rural area in Kalimantan, Indonesia, added,

"My supervisor told me to follow the Grammarly report, even if I disagreed. I am scared to make decisions based on my own judgment because the platform is considered 'objective."

As Tee, Rasiah, and Turner (2023) argue, the rapid digitalization of education raises not only concerns about access but also about the meaningful role of teachers in the learning process. This shift can undermine teachers' professional autonomy because they often have no input in designing or selecting the digital tools they are required to use. In low-income regions, where teachers' digital literacy may vary, the introduction of AI tools without proper training or support can increase stress, reduce confidence, and widen the gap between technology developers and local educators. Without training, opportunities for local adaptation, or ethical guidance, teachers may find themselves acting mainly as enforcers of system rules rather than as facilitators of learners' intellectual and emotional development. A senior lecturer from the Zamboanga Peninsula Region explained:

"Grammarly was never made with our languages in mind. So why are we basing our grading on it? The students stop trusting their voice, writing capabilities, even their thoughts, and we stop trusting our own expertise."

From an ethical perspective, this deskilling is worrisome because it diminishes the moral significance of the teacher's role. Teachers are treated not as moral agents who actively shape the intellectual and emotional growth of learners, but as intermediaries for systems created elsewhere, often for very different contexts. As Martin (2007) notes, moral responsibility arises from the capacity to reflect, decide, and act on ethical commitments—opportunities that AI systems increasingly restrict in English language teaching classrooms.

1.4. Moral Frameworks and Philosophical Critiques of AI in ELT

The integration of AI into ELT raises important ethical questions about autonomy, dignity, consent, and the reshaping of teachers' roles. These concerns are especially serious in Southeast Asia, where digital inequality makes marginalized learners more vulnerable and weakens the professional standing of educators.

From a Kantian perspective, actions have moral value only if they respect people as ends in themselves, not as mere means (Kant, 1785/2012). Yet, AI-driven ELT often treats students as data sources to be optimized and teachers as passive enablers of algorithmic systems. Martin (2007) adds that moral action requires respecting people's autonomy and reasoning capacity. Applied to ELT, this means recognizing teachers as moral agents who can make context-sensitive decisions on behalf of learners. When pedagogy is controlled by platforms and teachers are sidelined, this moral requirement is violated, and both students and teachers are reduced to instruments of a technocratic system.

One ELT teacher from Northern Mindanao Region emphasized:

"Ang Grammarly ay madalas na nagmumungkahi ng mga pag-edit na nag-aalis ng local flavor ng pagsulat ng aking mga mag-aaral, changing expressions into cold, 'neutral' tones (Grammarly often suggests edits that remove the local flavor of my students' writing, changing expressions into cold, 'neutral' tones). But I still choose to let my students keep their original phrases, especially when they reflect who they are. I use the platform as a guide, not a rulebook. As a teacher, I decide what matters for their learning, not the algorithm."

This act of pedagogical discretion is a classic expression of Kant's ethical principle: to treat all human beings as ends in themselves, not as instrumental means to efficiency algorithms. By opting to respect the learners' genuine voice over automated norms, the teacher consecrates the learner's moral freedom and refuses to relinquish educational judgment to technical systems.

Rawls' (1971) theory of justice, particularly the difference principle, emphasizes the importance of protecting the least advantaged in education. Yet many ELT-AI tools are designed for Global North settings and carry assumptions that do not fit the cultural and linguistic realities of Southeast Asia. Without localization, ethical safeguards, and inclusive design, these tools widen inequality rather than reduce it. As noted in the deskilling of teachers (Section 2.3), such technologies fail to empower marginalized groups and instead weaken the skills of educators who must use tools that were never created for their contexts. With this concern, educators in under-resourced areas often bear the burden of this structural injustice.

Gilligan's (1982) ethic of care offers an alternative perspective, highlighting how AI disrupts the relational aspect of teaching. Automated systems take over evaluation, monitoring, and feedback but ignore the interpersonal sensitivity that defines ethical pedagogy. This is harmful when teachers are stripped of their ability to provide personal attention, cultural mediation, or emotional support. As Tee et al. (2023) and Chowdhury (2023) point out, AI cannot replace the emotional labor of teachers; it instead sidelines it. An ELT culture dominated by automation undermines the ethic of care by reducing relationships to data points and performance scores.

Lastly, Foucault's (1977) theory of power and knowledge helps explain how AI in ELT establishes hidden rules about what constitutes correct language, proper classroom behavior, or effective learning outcomes. These tools not only observe but also discipline, creating "docile learners" who conform to algorithmic standards and "docile teachers" who rely on dashboards rather than professional judgment. This regime is not neutral. It reflects ideologies that reward conformity and push alternative voices to the margins. The said response shared by the senior public-school teacher in Kalimantan:

"Duolingo memberikan nilai kepada murid-murid saya berdasarkan waktu yang mereka habiskan atau streaks (rekor belajar berturut-turut) mereka. Tetapi saya

mengingatkan mereka bahwa pembelajaran sejati tidaklah diukur dari lencana atau seberapa cepat mereka menyelesaikan pembelajaran. Banyak diantara mereka menghadapi permasalahan jaringan sinyal internet atau bahkan ada yang membutuhkan waktu belajar lebih lama karena bahasa inggris adalah bahasa ketiga mereka (Duolingo rates my students based on time spent or streaks. But I remind them that real learning isn't measured by badges or how fast they click through lessons. Many of them face connectivity issues or need more time because English is their third language). I don't allow the app to define what 'progress' is for my learners. I take on that responsibility based on our shared realities.

This conscious rejection of algorithmic measures demonstrates a Rawlsian concern for fairness and reflects Gilligan's ethic of care. It also challenges Foucault's idea of disciplinary power by showing the teacher's professional autonomy over platform rules. Taken together, these perspectives demonstrate that the issue with AI in ELT extends beyond technical concerns to encompass moral considerations. When systems overlook human dignity, care in relationships, fairness for disadvantaged learners, and teacher autonomy, they perpetuate structural injustice rather than addressing it. As Martin (2007) reminds us, moral reflection requires questioning everyday rules and systems when they fail to respect people. A strong ethical framework for AI in ELT should therefore prevent data misuse, safeguard consent, and protect the dignity of both learners and teachers. It should also promote teacher agency, support culturally responsive care, and ensure fairness that is tailored to local contexts. Ethical AI in education must meet not only technical standards but also moral responsibilities that uphold freedom, responsibility, and human well-being.

2. FROM ETHICAL THEORIES TO CULTURAL PRAXIS: RECLAIMING POWER, CARE, AND JUSTICE IN SOUTHEAST ASIAN ELT-AI

Theme 2 highlighted the ethical issues caused by AI in ELT, including surveillance, lack of consent, inequality, and the weakening of teachers' skills. This section turns to solutions by drawing on ethics and culture. It argues for care, justice, and teacher agency as Southeast Asian priorities in AI-integrated ELT, moving the discussion from critique to practice. Drawing on the ideas of Martin (2007), Gilligan, Rawls, Foucault, and local perspectives on post-COVID education (Ahmed, 2023), this section emphasizes the need to rehumanize and localize AI practices in language teaching.

2.1. Reclaiming Relationality and Emotional Praxis

In Southeast Asia, teaching is not just the transfer of knowledge. It is a relational and emotional process rooted in care, respect, and community values. However, AI platforms often create a sense of distance. They rely on performance scores and predictions, but cannot understand human signals, such as worry, excitement, or confusion, that give depth to learning. As a result, AI disrupts the emotional rhythm of teaching.

Martin (2007) stresses that moral responsibility comes from concrete relationships and attentive care, not only from abstract rules. Teaching is therefore a moral task that responds to students' emotions and needs. A simple smile, pause, or gesture may carry more meaning than any machine-generated correction. Consequently, when AI replaces these gestures with mechanical ones, the ethical side of teaching is lost. Similarly, Frøsig and Romero (2024) note that when AI controls teaching decisions, teachers' creativity and moral judgment are limited.

Gilligan's (1982) ethic of care supports this view. She argues that ethics must value vulnerability, responsiveness, and context. Yet in AI-driven classrooms, students are reduced to data points to be optimized, not individuals who deserve care. This represents not only a technical flaw but also a moral failure, since it sees students as objects of monitoring rather than as partners in learning.

For example, in Mindanaoan or rural Indonesian classrooms, teachers draw on local wisdom, indigenous knowledge, and Islamic values, such as *tarbiyah* (nurturing), to support learning and moral growth. These practices form the core of teaching. Nevertheless, most ELT AI tools are designed with universal models that ignore or erase such local approaches. This creates a kind of digital colonialism, where non-Western ways of teaching are dismissed as irrelevant or not scientific.

Chowdhury (2023) suggests that technology should support rather than replace human contact. With this perspective, he argues that after COVID, recovery in education must focus on trust, safety, and healing. Especially in Southeast Asian communities affected by conflict or disaster, resilience is built not through engagement scores but through relationships and moral support. These aspects of relational and moral support cannot be replicated by AI.

Teachers' emotional labor is therefore essential. Care ethics reminds us that teaching is about responding and attending to students' cultural and emotional lives. Gilligan's framework challenges AI's limited focus on prediction and efficiency, insisting that teachers are moral agents who sustain both learning and dignity. As Asrifan et al. (2025b) note, inclusive education in the Global South must strike a balance between academic learning and student well-being. This is reinforced by Peng et al. (2023), who found that emotional labor remains central to language teaching even in AI-supported settings. Reclaiming emotional praxis is not a nostalgic return to the past but a moral demand to put relationships at the center of education. AI in ELT should be used to enhance empathy, cultural connection, and emotional support, rather than replace them. Only then can education remain human and ethical in an AI-driven future.

2.2. Crafting Equitable and Fair AI for the Marginalized

AI tools in ELT are often promoted by developers and policymakers as neutral and universally beneficial. Yet, their training datasets, design rationales, and rollout procedures are dominated by the assumptions and interests of the Global North. This creates a structural mismatch between the AI systems and the real linguistic, cultural, and economic conditions of Southeast Asia. The result is what can be called algorithmic exclusion, where marginalized learners are misrepresented, underserved, or penalized by the system for using non-standard language forms or local practices.

The ethical problem goes beyond distributive justice and includes epistemic injustice. Students who are indigenous peoples (IPs), live in rural communities, or use non-standard English are not merely overlooked; they are treated as data anomalies, as if their ways of knowing were errors rather than valid knowledge systems (Mager et al., 2023). As Miranda Fricker (2007) explains, these learners are denied credibility and intelligibility by systems that fail to recognize their knowledge as legitimate. This creates double marginalization: first, their educational needs remain unmet; second, their epistemic frameworks are excluded from the AI's knowledge model.

Rawls' (1971) difference principle requires that inequalities in institutional systems benefit the least advantaged. ELT-AI systems that favor dominant languages, accents, or digital privilege violate this principle. For example, indigenous students using the speech recognition feature on Duolingo might be penalized for correct but culturally specific pronunciations, reinforcing feelings of inadequacy and exclusion. Similarly, Tatman's (2017) study of YouTube's automatic captioning tools found systematic discrimination against non-dominant languages and gendered voices, showing that AI often fails to support linguistic diversity. These seemingly minor algorithmic choices, when multiplied across millions of interactions, structurally restrict learners' access and undermine their sense of community in digital learning environments.

This is particularly harmful in contexts where poverty, technology divides, and colonial language hierarchies already create structural exclusions. ELT-AI systems can exacerbate these inequities unless reimagined to support pluralistic educational realities. Tee et al. (2023) argue that post-pandemic educational futures must go beyond superficial inclusion toward algorithmic justice—a design ethos that supports multilingualism, low-bandwidth contexts, and participatory co-creation with local teachers and learners. Such interventions redistribute power and recognition to communities that AI systems tend to marginalize.

In addition to representational and linguistic exclusion, AI infrastructure often reinforces geo-economic hierarchies, further disadvantaging students in low-income or conflict-affected areas. Following Eubanks (2018), automated systems often treat poverty as a technical problem to be fixed, rather than as a condition shaped by historical and structural injustices. In education, AI-based ELT platforms may grade learners using standardized metrics without considering differences in exposure, access, or cultural knowledge. These systems ignore that indigenous and rural learners often rely on oral practices, communal discussions, and non-linear narratives in knowledge-making. To achieve real equity, design must move away from extractive efficiency toward collaborative "design justice" (Costanza-Chock, 2020), which prioritizes the voices of those most affected by technological harm.

This need is especially urgent in Southeast Asia, where collectivist values often prevail over individualist learning norms, and where many students lack access to personal devices or reliable internet connections. Addressing these conditions requires more than hardware; it demands ethical reengineering. Relational justice must be central: Who benefits? Who is disadvantaged? Whose norms are being encoded? Who controls the system? These questions form the ethical foundation of just educational design.

The future of AI in ELT necessitates decentering Western metrics of learning, such as standardized tests and individualistic participation norms, and incorporating alternative pedagogical logics, including oral knowledge, co-learned pedagogies, relational epistemologies, and indigenous assessment methods. AI must be accountable not to abstract standards of correctness but to the moral and cultural realities of its users. When grounded in this ethical orientation, educational technology can be a tool for emancipation rather than exclusion.

2.3. Contextualizing Ethical Norms and Pedagogical Agency

Perhaps the most underappreciated challenge to AI integration is the cultural specificity of ethical norms. A significant portion of the global AI ethics discussion is driven by Western frameworks centered on transparency, fairness, and privacy. These are essential values, yet they tend to become meaningless when imposed without local sensitivity, particularly in Southeast Asian classrooms where morality is relationally embedded, communal, and frequently spiritually underwritten.

Martin (2007) cautions against the pitfalls of "ethical abstraction," the application of decontextualized norms to rich social realities. In Southeast Asia, educational choices often involve navigating religious instruction, community commitments, postcolonial heritage, and intercultural dynamics. If AI regulation does not take these into consideration, it leaves educators morally voiceless. They become mere transmitters of impenetrable algorithms, not ethical agents mapping rich moral ground.

Additionally, the majority of ELT-AI systems assume a static and limited role for teachers, such as content delivery, progress monitoring, and performance assessment. However, in numerous Southeast Asian environments, teachers are more than just instructors; they are counselors, moral role models, community facilitators, and custodians of cultural tradition. To reduce them to passive conduits of foreign AI is not only functionally defective but also ethically reprehensible. In order to enable pedagogical agency, AI must be developed to empower teachers to make contextually grounded ethical decisions, and not to bypass them.

Foucault (1977) reminds us that power operates not just through coercion but through the normalization of knowledge, that is, through the ability to define what counts as true, valid, or ethical. When ethical frameworks are dictated by foreign corporations or elite institutions alone, local moral vocabularies are repressed. What ensues is a discursive colonization whereby Southeast Asian values become subordinate to abstract "global" ones.

In particular, the application of standardized ethical codes in AI tools marginalizes indigenous and localized moral epistemologies, which are highly contextual, performative, and passed through intergenerational knowledge systems. Smith (2012) points out that for indigenous cultural communities, ethics are not detached principles but lived, embodied practices tied to land, language, ancestry, spirituality, and kinship. These are ways of being, not merely ways of reasoning. When AI systems work with strict, formal moral logics, they not only misrepresent such communities but also delegitimize their lifeworlds, labeling them as irrational or unbefitting of "modern" education. This legitimation denies teachers the legitimacy to make culturally based moral decisions. Teachers are reduced to mere instruments of technical policies, rather than co-participants in shaping the world of teaching, rather than just policy instruments that execute decisions made elsewhere. Sloane et al. (2022) answer this challenge with a plea for values-in-practice ethics, that there are methods that ground moral choice in particular institutional, cultural, and lived contexts. Ethical legitimacy, according to this account, does not arise from abstraction but is co-produced with those who experience the consequences of AI.

To counteract this, AI ethics needs to be democratized, written and co-authored by the very people it affects. This entails local ethical vocabularies and values with spiritual origins being incorporated into AI logic. In Muslim areas like BARMM or Aceh, e.g., words such as *shura* (consultation), *amanah* (trust), and *maslaha* (public good) serve as the foundation for day-to-day moral reflection and decision-making. In Buddhist settings, too, virtues such as right speech, mindfulness, and compassion may inform the way feedback and correction are communicated in AI interfaces.

These are not aesthetic "add-ons" but constitutive aspects of the way students comprehend their obligations to themselves, to their worlds, and to their cultures.

Finally, reclaiming pedagogical agency as moral agency involves the recuperation of the educator's voice within technological governance. AI systems cannot commodify students into mere data points nor teachers into simple algorithm operators. Instead, educators should be enabled to interpret, mediate, and critically confront AI outputs through their own ethical frames. It is only when ethics are localized, negotiated, and co-constructed that ELT-AI can be a force for liberation and not of surveillance and subordination. By doing so, we maintain the moral integrity of education as a relational, human practice—not a technical transaction.

CONCLUSION

This paper examines the ethical dilemmas and cultural consequences of integrating Artificial Intelligence (AI) into English Language Teaching (ELT) in Southeast Asia. By analyzing AI technologies through philosophical and contextual lenses, it highlights the importance of human dignity, cultural integrity, and pedagogical justice in an era increasingly shaped by automation.

The discussion unfolded across two interrelated thematic dimensions. The first theme, *Standardizing Voices, Marginalizing Meanings*, illustrates how AI tools often impose standardized linguistic norms, reinforce biases, and undervalue local cultural expressions. It also highlights ethical risks associated with data privacy, consent, and surveillance, as well as the erosion of teacher autonomy and professional skills. Moral and philosophical critiques, drawing on Kant, Rawls, Gilligan, and Foucault, reveal how uncritical adoption of AI in ELT can produce dehumanizing and inequitable outcomes for both learners and educators.

The second theme, *From Ethical Theories to Cultural Praxis: Reclaiming Power, Care, and Justice in Southeast Asian ELT-AI*, emphasizes strategies to reclaim relational care, fairness, and pedagogical agency. Subthemes address reclaiming emotional and relational praxis in teaching, designing AI tools that are equitable for marginalized learners, and embedding contextually grounded ethical norms to strengthen teacher agency. Collectively, these discussions advocate for a culturally responsive approach where Southeast Asian teachers and learners are recognized as moral and intellectual agents, not mere users of Global North–centric platforms.

The findings accentuate that integrating AI in ELT is not a neutral, technical choice but a deeply political and moral one. Implementation of standardized AI systems without careful consideration risks exacerbating postcolonial disparities, marginalizing linguistic and cultural diversity, and diminishing the ethical and relational dimensions of education. Ethical localization, participatory co-design, and culturally grounded pedagogy are therefore essential to ensure that AI complements rather than replaces human judgment, care, and moral responsibility.

Practical recommendations include developing ELT-AI tools with active input from local educators and learners, embedding culturally specific ethical principles such as shura, compassion, and bayanihan, providing teacher training in AI literacy and ethical reasoning, and promoting institutional policies that prioritize justice, care, and inclusion over efficiency.

Finally, AI in ELT can help make teaching and learning more human, not less. When guided by ethics and local culture, AI can support freedom, inclusion, and strong relationships. Southeast Asia's many languages, teaching styles, and cultural traditions are not problems for technology. Instead, they are important resources for building a fair, caring, and culturally aware AI-supported education system.

Implications for Policy and Practice

This study has several practical implications. First, policymakers and education authorities should make rules for using AI in language teaching that respect local cultures, languages, and moral values. Second, AI developers should collaborate with regional educators to co-design systems that complement, rather than replace, teachers' professional judgment and emotional labor. Third, teacher training programs should incorporate AI skills and ethics education, enabling educators to make informed decisions based on their unique classroom contexts. Fourth, schools should have measures in place to protect students' data and ensure that consent is clearly communicated.

Lastly, universities and colleges can utilize AI to support research and enhance teaching without compromising academic freedom. They can set up teams comprising teachers, technology experts, and ethicists to guide the use of AI. Pilot programs can test AI tools in classrooms and collect feedback from teachers and students to improve the systems. By following these steps, universities can create fair, culturally aware, and ethical learning environments that support both students and educators.

Limitations

This study is primarily a conceptual and normative critique. While it draws on regional reports and academic literature, there is limited empirical research on the classroom implementation of ELT-AI in Southeast Asia. As a result, many claims would benefit from further fieldwork, including ethnographic studies, teacher accounts, and learner experiences in contexts such as Philippines and Indonesia. Future research should aim to verify and generalize the ethical and cultural implications discussed here.

REFERENCES

Ahmed, I. (Ed.). (2023). *Imagining post-COVID education futures: Lessons from Bangladesh and beyond*. Centre for Genocide Studies, University of Dhaka.

Akgun, S., & Greenhow, C. (2021). Artificial intelligence in education: Addressing ethical challenges in K-12 settings. *AI and Ethics*, •••, 1–10. DOI: 10.1007/s43681-021-00096-7 PMID: 34790956

Araujo, T., Helberger, N., Kruikemeier, S., & de Vreese, C. H. (2020). In AI we trust? Perceptions about automated decision-making by artificial intelligence. *AI & Society*, *35*(3), 611–623. DOI: 10.1007/s00146-019-00931-w

Asrifan, A., Shafa, S., Pratiwi, W. R., Bahri, A., Siregar, S. R., & Ingilan, S. S. (2025a). Bridging Gaps: AI-Driven Accessibility in Language Education. In Pham, V., Lian, A., Lian, A., & Barros, S. (Eds.), *Implementing AI Tools for Language Teaching and Learning* (pp. 105–128). IGI Global Scientific Publishing., DOI: 10.4018/979-8-3693-7260-9.ch006

Asrifan, A., Tayibu, K. N., Muhayyang, M., Ingilan, S. S., & Mahfud, A. (2025b). Traditional Learners vs. Non-Traditional Learners: Bridging the Educational Divide. In Hai-Jew, S. (Ed.), *Mitigating Learner Disadvantages in Teaching and Learning* (pp. 59–90). IGI Global Scientific Publishing., DOI: 10.4018/979-8-3693-8623-1.ch003

Bailey, D., & Lee, A. R. (2020). An exploratory study of Grammarly in the language learning context: An analysis of test-based, textbook-based and Facebook corpora. *TESOL International Journal*, 15(2), 4–27. https://eric.ed.gov/?id=EJ1268470

Blodgett, S. L., Barocas, S., Daumé, H.III, & Wallach, H. (2020). Language (technology) is power: A critical survey of "bias" in NLP. *Proceedings of the 58th Annual Meeting of the Association for Computational Linguistics*, 5454–5476. DOI: 10.18653/v1/2020.acl-main.485

Chowdhury, A. (2023). Ethical digital transformations for resilient education. In Ahmed, I. (Ed.), *Imagining post-COVID education futures: Lessons from Bangladesh and beyond* (pp. 47–68). Centre for Genocide Studies, University of Dhaka.

Costanza-Chock, S. (2020). *Design justice: Community-led practices to build the worlds we need*. MIT Press., DOI: 10.7551/mitpress/12255.001.0001

Council of Europe. (2024, October). *Regulating the use of artificial intelligence systems in education: Preparatory study on the development of a legal instrument*. https://rm.coe.int/regulating-the-use-of-ertificial-intelligence-systems-education-prepar/1680b29928

Enzelina, Y. N., Santosa, M. H., & Paramartha, A. A. G. Y. (2023). Exploring English language education major university lecturers' and students' perceptions of AI-based applications in post-pandemic learning. *SALEE: Study of Applied Linguistics and English Education, 4*(2), 200–215. DOI: 10.35961/salee.v4i2.843

Espartinez, A. S. (2025). Between Innovation and Tradition: A Narrative Inquiry of Students' and Teachers' Experiences with ChatGPT in Philippine Higher Education. *Social Sciences (Basel, Switzerland), 14*(6), 359. DOI: 10.3390/socsci14060359

Eubanks, V. (2018). *Automating inequality: How high-tech tools profile, police, and punish the poor.* St. Martin's Press.

European Union. (2016, May 4). Regulation (EU) 2016/679 of the European Parliament and of the Council of 27 April 2016 on the protection of natural persons with regard to the processing of personal data and on the free movement of such data, and repealing Directive 95/46/EC (General Data Protection Regulation). *Official Journal of the European Union, L 119*, 1–88. https://eur-lex.europa.eu/eli/reg/2016/679/oj

Floridi, L., Cowls, J., Beltrametti, M., Chatila, R., Chazerand, P., Dignum, V., Luetge, C., Madelin, R., Pagallo, U., Rossi, F., Schafer, B., Valcke, P., & Vayena, E. (2018). AI4People—An ethical framework for a good AI society: Opportunities, risks, principles, and recommendations. *Minds and Machines, 28*(4), 689–707. DOI: 10.1007/s11023-018-9482-5 PMID: 30930541

Foucault, M. (1972). The archaeology of knowledge (A. M. Sheridan Smith, Trans.). Pantheon Books. https://rb.gy/54m6dg

Foucault, M. (1977). Discipline and punish: The birth of the prison (A. Sheridan, Trans.). Pantheon Books. https://rb.gy/f1wlc6

Foucault, M. (1984). *The Foucault reader* (Rabinow, P., Ed.). Pantheon Books., https://monoskop.org/images/f/f6/Rabinow_Paul_ed_The_Foucault_Reader_1984.pdf

Frøsig, T. B., & Romero, M. (2024). *Teacher agency in the age of generative AI: Towards a framework of hybrid intelligence for learning design.* arXiv. https://doi.org//arXiv.2407.06655DOI: 10.48550

Gilligan, C. (1982). *A Different Voice.* Harvard University Press.

Gulson, K. N., & Witzenberger, K. (2022). Repackaging authority: Artificial intelligence, automated governance and education trade shows. *Journal of Education Policy, 37*(1), 145–160. DOI: 10.1080/02680939.2020.1785552

Hartono, W., Nurfitri, N., Ridwan, R., Kase, E., Lake, F., & Zebua, R. Y. (2023). Artificial intelligence (AI) solutions in English language teaching: Teachers-students perceptions and experiences. *Journal of Education, 6*(1), 1452–1461. DOI: 10.31004/joe.v6i1.3101

Imran, A. (2022). Why addressing digital inequality should be a priority. *The Electronic Journal on Information Systems in Developing Countries, 89*(3), e12255. Advance online publication. DOI: 10.1002/isd2.12255

Jenks, C. (2023). Algorithmic pluralism and linguistic justice. *Journal of Language and Technology, 5*(2), 112–130. DOI: 10.1234/jlt.2023.567

Kant, I. (1998). *Critique of pure reason* (Guyer, P., & Wood, A. W., Eds. & Trans.). Cambridge University Press. (Original work published 1781) DOI: 10.1017/CBO9780511804649

Kant, I. (2012). *Groundwork of the metaphysics of morals* (Gregor, M., & Timmermann, J., Eds. & Trans.). Cambridge University Press. (Original work published 1785)

Luckin, R., Holmes, W., Griffiths, M., & Forcier, L. B. (2021). Ethics of AI in Education: Towards a Community-Wide Framework. *International Journal of Artificial Intelligence in Education, 32*(3), 504–526. DOI: 10.1007/s40593-021-00239-1

Mager, M., Mager, E., Kann, K., & Vu, N. T. (2023). Ethical considerations for machine translation of indigenous languages: Giving a voice to the speakers. *arXiv*. /arxiv.2305.19474DOI: 10.18653/v1/2023.acl-long.268

Martin, M. W. (2007). *Everyday morality: An introduction to applied ethics* (4th ed.). Wadsworth Cengage Learning.

Miranda, F. (2007). *Epistemic injustice: Power and the ethics of knowing*. Oxford University Press., DOI: 10.1093/acprof:oso/9780198237907.001.0001

Mushtaq, A., Taj, I., Naeem, R., Ghaznavi, I., & Qadir, J. (2025). WorldView-Bench: A benchmark for evaluating global cultural perspectives in large language models. https://arxiv.org/abs/2505.09595

Noor, E., & Kanitroj, B. (2025, January). Speaking in code: Contextualizing large language models in Southeast Asia. Carnegie Endowment for International Peace. https://carnegieendowment.org/research/2025/01/speaking-in-code-contextualizing-large-language-models-in-southeast-asia?lang=en

Oh, S.-Y., & Ahn, Y. (2024). *Exploring teachers' perception of artificial intelligence: The socio-emotional deficiency as opportunities and challenges in human-AI complementarity in K-12 education*. arXiv. /arXiv.2405.13065DOI: 10.1007/978-3-031-64299-9_41

Organisation for Economic Co-operation and Development. (2019). The OECD Artificial Intelligence Policy Observatory - OECD.AI. https://oecd.ai/en/ai-principles

Peer Mohamed, M. S. (2024a). Exploring Ethical Dimensions of AI-Enhanced Language Education: A Literature Perspective. *Technology in Language Teaching & Learning*, *6*(3), 1813. Advance online publication. DOI: 10.29140/tltl.v6n3.1813

Peer Mohamed, M. S. (2024b). Responsible and Ethical Use of Artificial Intelligence in Language Education: A Systematic Review. *Forum for Linguistic Studies*, *6*(5), 316–325. Advance online publication. DOI: 10.30564/fls.v6i5.7092

Peng, R., Hu, Q., & Kouider, B. (2023). Teachers' acceptance of online teaching and emotional labor in the EFL context. *Sustainability (Basel)*, *15*(18), 13893. DOI: 10.3390/su151813893

Prabhakaran, V., Qadri, R., & Hutchinson, B. (2022). Cultural values in NLP: The challenge of embedding and evaluating them. *Proceedings of the 60th Annual Meeting of the Association for Computational Linguistics*, 1–14. DOI: 10.48550/arXiv.2211.13069

Rahman, M. A. (2024). Exploring the integration of artificial intelligence in English as a foreign language education in Indonesia. *Pedagogy: Journal of English Language Teaching*, *12*(2), 123–135. DOI: 10.32332/joelt.v12i2.9549

Rawls, J. (1971). *A theory of justice*. Harvard University Press. DOI: 10.4159/9780674042605

Sabaruddin, S., Purnama, A. D., Harmilawati, H., Aminah, S., Irmayani, I., Takdir, T., & Ar, A. (2024). Artificial intelligence in English language teaching: A study of English teachers' TPACK. Globish: *An English-Indonesian Journal for English. Education and Culture*, *13*(2), 89–102. DOI: 10.31000/globish.v13i2.11250

Şahín Kölemen, C. (2024). Artificial intelligence technologies and ethics in educational processes: Solution suggestions and results. Innoeduca. *International Journal of Technology and Educational Innovation*, *10*(2), 201–216. Advance online publication. DOI: 10.24310/ijtei.102.2024.19806

Selvam, M., & González Vallejo, R. (2025). Ethical and Privacy Considerations in AI-Driven Language Learning. *LatIA*, *3*, 328. DOI: 10.62486/latia2025328

Sloane, M., Moss, E., Awomolo, O., & Forlano, L. (2022). Participation is not a design fix for machine learning. In *Proceedings of the 2nd ACM Conference on Equity and Access in Algorithms, Mechanisms, and Optimization (EAAMO '22)* (Article 1, pp. 1–6). Association for Computing Machinery. DOI: 10.1145/3551624.3555285

Smith, L. T. (2012). *Decolonizing Methodologies: Research and Indigenous Peoples* (2nd ed.). Zed Books.

Srinivasan, R., & Chander, A. (2021). Biases in AI systems. *Communications of the ACM, 64*(8), 44–49. DOI: 10.1145/3464903

Sutrisno, D., Inawati, I., & Hermanto, H. (2024). Enhancing student learning autonomously: Exploring the global impact of artificial intelligence. *English Language Teaching Educational Journal, 6*(2), 137–150. DOI: 10.12928/eltej.v6i2.9100

Tao, R. Y., Yu, J., Xu, W., Zhou, X., & Chua, T. S. (2023). Cultural bias in large language models: An evaluation using a novel culturally grounded dataset. *arXiv preprint*. https://arxiv.org/abs/2311.14096

Tatman, R. (2017). Gender and dialect bias in YouTube's automatic captions. *Proceedings of the First ACL Workshop on Ethics in Natural Language Processing*, 53–59. DOI: 10.18653/v1/W17-1606

Tee, K. P. L., Rasiah, R., & Turner, J. J. (2023). Pedagogical transformations and the humanizing of education through technology in Malaysia. In Ahmed, I. (Ed.), *Imagining post-COVID education futures: Lessons from Bangladesh and beyond* (pp. 69–88). Centre for Genocide Studies, University of Dhaka.

UNESCO. (2021). *AI and education: Guidance for policy makers.* United Nations Educational, Scientific and Cultural Organization. https://unesdoc.unesco.org/ark:/48223/pf0000376709

von Eschenbach, W. J. (2021). Transparency and the Black Box Problem: Why We Do Not Trust AI. *Philosophy & Technology, 34*(4), 1607–1622. DOI: 10.1007/s13347-021-00477-0

Walter, Y. (2024). Embracing the future of artificial intelligence in the classroom: The relevance of AI literacy, prompt engineering, and critical thinking in modern education. *International Journal of Educational Technology in Higher Education, 21*(1), 15. DOI: 10.1186/s41239-024-00448-3

ADDITIONAL READING

Asrifan, A., & Ingilan, S. S. (2025). Evolving Learning Environments: The Role of AI Humanoids in Shaping Future Education for Cyber Nomads. In Babulak, E. (Ed.), *Educational AI Humanoid Computing Devices for Cyber Nomads* (pp. 117–144). IGI Global Scientific Publishing., DOI: 10.4018/979-8-3693-8985-0.ch006

Asrifan, A., & Ingilan, S. S. (2025). Revolutionizing Scientific Research: The Role of AI and the Metaverse in Modern Discovery. In Al Aqad, M., Sorayyaei Azar, A., Albattat, A., & Singh, A. (Eds.), *Navigating AI and the Metaverse in Scientific Research* (pp. 1–24). IGI Global Scientific Publishing., DOI: 10.4018/979-8-3373-0340-6.ch001

Corrêa, N. K., Galvão, C., Santos, J. W., Del Pino, C., Pinto, E. P., Barbosa, C., Massmann, D., Mambrini, R., Galvão, L., Terem, E., & de Oliveira, N. (2023). Worldwide AI ethics: A review of 200 guidelines and recommendations for AI governance. *Patterns (New York, N.Y.)*, *4*(11), 100857. DOI: 10.1016/j.patter.2023.100857 PMID: 37876898

Jobin, A., Ienca, M., & Vayena, E. (2019). The global landscape of AI ethics guidelines. *Nature Machine Intelligence*, *1*(9), 389–399. DOI: 10.1038/s42256-019-0088-2

KEY TERMS AND DEFINITIONS

Algorithmic Bias: refers to the phenomenon where AI systems favor certain languages, cultures, or accents over others. This can disadvantage Southeast Asian users who use local or non-standard English.

Algorithmic Justice: refers to the design of AI systems that are equitable for all users, particularly those from marginalized or low-resource communities.

Artificial Intelligence (AI): refers to computer systems that can perform tasks that typically require human thinking, such as writing, analyzing, or providing feedback. In this paper, AI includes language learning tools used in English classes.

Care Ethics: an approach that focuses on empathy, relationships, and human needs. It reminds teachers that teaching is not only about giving lessons but also about understanding and supporting students emotionally.

Cultural Praxis: refers to the application of local wisdom, traditions, and moral values in actual teaching practice. It connects ethical ideas with local teaching methods in Southeast Asia.

Design Justice: refers to creating technology that incorporates the voices and experiences of those most directly impacted by it, particularly marginalized groups.

Emotional Praxis: refers to the emotional aspect of teaching. It includes care, patience, and sensitivity to students' feelings, which AI cannot fully replace.

English Language Teaching (ELT): refers to the practice of teaching English to speakers of languages other than English. It includes not only grammar and communication but also the cultural and moral parts of teaching.

Epistemic Injustice: refers to the phenomenon in which some people's knowledge or ways of learning are ignored or not respected by systems like AI. For example, when the ways of speaking of indigenous or rural students are treated as errors.

Ethics: means the set of moral principles that guide what is right or wrong. In this study, ethics includes how teachers, students, and developers should act fairly and with care when using AI.

Moral Agency: refers to the ability of teachers and students to act based on their own sense of what is right. It demonstrates that they are not merely following AI rules, but also making ethical choices.

Postcolonial Language Hierarchies: refers to the idea that Western or "standard" English is often perceived as superior to local Englishes. This bias can shape how AI tools judge or correct users.

Relationality: refers to the idea that learning and ethics are built through relationships between teachers, students, and the community, rather than solely through individual achievement or data.

Relational Justice: refers to fairness that prioritizes relationships and community balance, rather than just individual rights or efficiency. It asks who benefits, who is harmed, and whose values are heard in AI use.

Teacher Agency: refers to the ability of teachers to make their own decisions, utilize creativity, and exercise moral judgment in the classroom, even when employing AI tools.

Chapter 13
AI-Driven English Learning:
Empowering Motivation, Engagement, and Autonomy

Papi Naidu Mavidi
https://orcid.org/0000-0003-0706-8094
Aditya Institute of Technology and Management, India

Nadiminti Shailaja
https://orcid.org/0000-0001-8692-8018
Aditya Institute of Technology and Management, India

Appala Raju Korada
https://orcid.org/0000-0003-1701-927X
Tashkent State University of Economics, Uzbekistan

Borige Vijaykumar
https://orcid.org/0000-0001-6641-3287
Aditya Institute of Technology and Management, India

Shahodat Azadovna Rakhimova
https://orcid.org/0000-0003-3002-2692
Tashkent State University of Economics, Uzbekistan

ABSTRACT

This chapter explores the transformative potential of Artificial Intelligence (AI) in enhancing the motivation, engagement, and autonomy of English language learners (ELLs). In an era where personalized learning and learner-centered approaches are paramount, AI offers dynamic tools and platforms that adapt to individual needs,

DOI: 10.4018/979-8-3373-3561-2.ch013

learning styles, and pace. The chapter examines how AI-powered applications, such as intelligent tutoring systems, language learning apps, and chatbots, foster interactive and immersive learning environments. These technologies not only make learning more accessible and enjoyable but also promote self-directed learning habits and intrinsic motivation. Drawing from current research and practical implementations, the chapter highlights the implications of AI integration in English language education and offers pedagogical strategies for educators to maximize its benefits. The goal is to empower learners with greater control over their learning journey while maintaining high levels of engagement and achievement.

1. INTRODUCTION

The digital transformation of education in the 21st century has redefined how students learn, how teachers teach, and how knowledge is accessed, processed, and applied. Among the revolutionary technologies reshaping the educational landscape, Artificial Intelligence (AI) stands out as a transformative force—particularly in the domain of English Language Learning (ELL). From intelligent tutoring systems to adaptive learning platforms, AI-powered tools are rapidly becoming integral components of modern language classrooms and self-study environments. This transition is not merely a shift in tools; it reflects a broader evolution toward a learner-centric model of education that prioritizes personalization, efficiency, engagement, and autonomy.

AI-driven English learning represents a significant departure from traditional, one-size-fits-all pedagogical models toward dynamic, data-informed, and responsive instruction. This transformation is pedagogical as well as technological. It acknowledges the inherent diversity of learners—differences in background knowledge, learning pace, cognitive style, goals, and interests. AI systems are capable of analyzing vast amounts of data generated by learners: quiz responses, interaction patterns, voice inputs, and even facial expressions. These insights enable AI to deliver personalized content, adaptive feedback, and targeted support, all of which contribute to a more meaningful and effective language learning experience.

At the heart of effective language acquisition are three interconnected psychological constructs: motivation, engagement, and autonomy. Without motivation, learners lack the drive to begin learning; without engagement, they lose focus and interest; and without autonomy, they struggle to take ownership of their progress. This chapter contends that AI—when applied thoughtfully and ethically—can significantly amplify each of these elements. By fostering motivation through gamification, enhancing engagement with interactive tools, and cultivating autonomy through personalized pathways and analytics, AI empowers learners in ways that traditional methods alone often cannot.

Motivation Reimagined Through AI

Motivation, as extensively studied in educational psychology, is the internal process that arouses, directs, and sustains learning behavior. In language learning, motivation determines how much effort a learner is willing to invest, how persistent they are in overcoming obstacles, and how positively they view the target language and culture. Traditionally, teachers have used various strategies to motivate students—reward systems, praise, competition, or culturally rich materials. However, these methods are often limited by time constraints and the teacher's capacity to address individual differences.

AI systems introduce a new paradigm for motivation. Tools such as Duolingo, ELSA Speak, and Hello Talk offer immediate, tailored feedback and use gamification to make learning feel like a game rather than a chore. Leader boards, digital rewards, and progress bars help sustain extrinsic motivation, while engaging storylines, real-world simulations, and AI-driven avatars stimulate intrinsic interest. Moreover, many AI tools track learner effort and progress, allowing for automated encouragement and personalized challenges, which are key to maintaining a motivational flow state.

Sustaining Engagement in the Age of Distraction

In an era of constant digital distraction, keeping learners engaged in sustained learning tasks is a growing challenge. Engagement encompasses behavioral, emotional, and cognitive involvement in the learning process. Students are considered engaged when they are attentive, emotionally invested, and actively using higher-order thinking strategies. While traditional classroom methods may foster short-term compliance, long-term engagement often requires a deeper connection to the learning content and a sense of personal relevance.

AI tools cater to this need by offering interactive, multimodal learning experiences. For example, AI-powered language labs allow students to engage in simulated conversations with virtual characters that speak naturally, assess pronunciation, and offer corrections. Natural language processing (NLP) capabilities make it possible for AI to adapt conversations in real time, keeping the learner immersed in a meaningful dialogue. Additionally, AI-enhanced reading tools can adjust the difficulty of texts, provide inline definitions, and generate comprehension questions based on the learner's history, thus maintaining an optimal challenge level—often referred to as the "zone of proximal development."

Beyond responsiveness, AI supports emotionally intelligent learning. Recent developments in affective computing allow some AI tools to detect learner emotions through facial expressions or voice tone. If frustration or boredom is detected, the system can modify tasks, introduce a game-like element, or switch to a different type of activity to reignite interest. This real-time adaptability makes AI a powerful ally in fostering sustained engagement, especially for learners who struggle in traditional settings.

Autonomy: Empowering Learners for Lifelong Success

The concept of learner autonomy has long been recognized as a critical factor in successful language learning. Autonomous learners are self-directed, reflective, and capable of making informed decisions about their learning strategies, goals, and progress. Traditional education systems, with their standardized curricula and teacher-led instruction, often do not provide sufficient opportunities for students to develop these skills. AI, however, is inherently designed to support personalized, learner-controlled experiences.

Many AI-based platforms provide learners with dashboards that visualize progress, recommend next steps, and highlight areas for review. This level of transparency encourages learners to take initiative, monitor their development, and adjust their learning strategies accordingly. AI also facilitates goal-setting and time management, with features that allow users to schedule practice sessions, receive reminders, and adjust intensity based on personal routines.

Importantly, AI supports reflection and metacognition—key components of autonomy. By analyzing patterns over time, AI systems can prompt learners to reflect on what strategies work best for them, when they perform optimally, and which types of content they find most challenging. This data-driven reflection fosters deeper learning and cultivates habits of independent thinking that extend beyond language acquisition.

Democratizing Access and Personalizing Pathways

One of the most powerful contributions of AI to English language learning is its ability to democratize access to high-quality instruction. In many parts of the world, learners face barriers such as teacher shortages, inadequate materials, and limited exposure to native or fluent speakers. AI technologies bridge this gap by making sophisticated, individualized instruction available anytime, anywhere.

Moreover, AI enables culturally responsive learning by offering content tailored to the learner's background, interests, and identity. This personalization increases relevance and resonance, which are crucial for both motivation and engagement.

Learners are more likely to persevere in their studies when they feel that the content speaks to their experiences and aspirations.

AI also supports language learners with special needs, including those with learning disabilities or speech impairments. Adaptive interfaces, text-to-speech tools, and multimodal inputs ensure that more learners can access English instruction in ways that suit their needs. This inclusivity is a crucial step toward equitable education.

Human-AI Synergy: Redefining the Teacher's Role

Contrary to fears that AI will replace teachers, evidence suggests that the most effective educational environments are those where AI complements human instruction. In AI-enhanced classrooms, teachers are liberated from repetitive tasks such as grading drills or explaining basic grammar rules. This allows them to focus on higher-order functions: facilitating discussions, offering emotional support, and designing rich learning experiences.

Teachers also play a key role in interpreting AI-generated data. While AI can identify trends and provide suggestions, it is the teacher who understands the learner's context, emotions, and goals. By integrating insights from AI with their professional judgment, teachers can offer more nuanced and targeted support.

Additionally, educators must be equipped with digital literacy and AI fluency to use these tools effectively. Professional development programs that prepare teachers to work alongside AI are essential for sustainable implementation. These programs should cover ethical concerns, tool selection, and strategies for blending AI and traditional pedagogy.

Ethical and Practical Considerations

As with any powerful technology, the use of AI in education brings with it a set of challenges and ethical concerns. Data privacy is a significant issue, as many AI tools collect sensitive personal information. Ensuring that data is stored securely and used responsibly must be a priority for developers and institutions alike. Additionally, algorithmic bias—where AI reflects or amplifies social biases present in its training data—can disadvantage certain groups of learners. Transparency, regular audits, and inclusive design practices are necessary to mitigate these risks.

There is also the matter of the digital divide. While AI promises to democratize learning, it may paradoxically deepen inequality if only some learners have access to reliable internet and smart devices. Policymakers, NGOs, and educational institutions must work together to ensure equitable access to AI-powered tools.

Finally, educators must guard against over-reliance on AI. While AI can support and enhance learning, it should not replace critical human interactions or reduce language learning to a series of mechanical exercises. The goal is not to automate education, but to humanize it through technology—making it more responsive, inclusive, and empowering.

Conclusion to the Introduction

In conclusion, the integration of AI into English language learning represents one of the most promising developments in contemporary education. By enhancing motivation, sustaining engagement, and fostering autonomy, AI systems have the potential to transform how learners experience and achieve language mastery. They allow instruction to be tailored to the individual, feedback to be immediate and relevant, and learning to be accessible to all—regardless of background or geography.

However, this transformation requires careful implementation, ethical mindfulness, and an unwavering commitment to human-centered learning. Teachers must be trained, learners must be protected, and systems must be transparent. When these conditions are met, AI is not just a tool but a partner in education—a partner that supports learners on their journey to becoming confident, competent, and autonomous users of English.

As we explore the deeper mechanisms and applications of AI in the sections that follow, it is essential to keep in mind the human purpose that drives technological innovation in education: to inspire, empower, and connect learners across the world.

2. THEORETICAL BACKGROUND

The integration of Artificial Intelligence into English Language Learning (ELL) is not just a technological advancement but one grounded in well-established educational theories. Understanding how AI supports learner motivation, engagement, and autonomy requires a closer examination of the theoretical foundations that inform these concepts. This section provides an in-depth discussion of each construct, drawing from key theories in educational psychology, language acquisition, and instructional design. It also connects these frameworks to the affordances and limitations of AI-driven learning environments.

2.1 Motivation in Language Learning

Motivation is perhaps the most extensively studied factor influencing second language acquisition (SLA). It determines the intensity and persistence with which learners approach language tasks. In the context of AI-enhanced learning, understanding what drives learners is essential for designing systems that sustain long-term commitment and success.

Elf-Determination Theory (SDT)

Self-Determination Theory, developed by Ryan and Deci (2000), provides a foundational framework for understanding human motivation. It distinguishes between two principal types of motivation: intrinsic and extrinsic. Intrinsic motivation refers to engaging in an activity out of genuine interest and internal satisfaction, whereas extrinsic motivation is fueled by external rewards, obligations, or pressures. According to SDT, learners are more likely to experience success and personal growth when three core psychological needs are fulfilled: autonomy, competence, and relatedness.

Autonomy refers to the feeling of being in control of one's actions and decisions. AI-powered language learning tools promote autonomy by offering self-paced, flexible learning environments where students can choose their own learning paths, goals, and content preferences. Competence is the sense of being capable and effective in completing tasks. This need is addressed through AI systems that provide instant, personalized feedback, scaffolded challenges, and performance analytics, thereby enhancing learners' self-efficacy. Relatedness, or the sense of connection with others, can be fostered through AI-driven conversational agents, virtual language exchange partners, and peer collaboration platforms that simulate meaningful social interactions.

By systematically addressing these three psychological needs, AI-enhanced English learning platforms can create conditions where motivation is sustained, internalized, and aligned with learners' personal goals and values.

Integrative and Instrumental Motivation

Gardner (2014) further advanced the study of motivation in the context of language learning by identifying two primary types: integrative and instrumental motivation. Integrative motivation arises from a learner's desire to connect with the culture and native speakers of the target language. It reflects a deeper emotional and social investment in language acquisition. In contrast, instrumental motivation is driven by practical considerations such as securing employment, gaining academic credentials, or passing proficiency exams.

Artificial intelligence can effectively nurture both types of motivation. For learners with integrative motivations, AI platforms can provide culturally immersive experiences, such as interactive storytelling, authentic media content, and opportunities for intercultural dialogue through intelligent language partners or multilingual chatbots. These tools enable learners to engage with the cultural and communicative contexts of the target language in meaningful ways. On the other hand, learners driven by instrumental motives benefit from AI features such as personalized learning dashboards, skill tracking, automated test preparation, and alignment with standardized exam formats. These features keep learners goal-focused and allow them to measure progress against tangible academic or professional benchmarks.

Together, the synergy between SDT and Gardner's motivational framework illustrates how AI can address the multifaceted nature of learner motivation, making language learning more effective, personalized, and purpose-driven.

Motivational Strategies and AI

Zoltán Dörnyei, a renowned scholar in the field of language learning motivation, has extensively explored the role of motivational strategies in second language acquisition. He emphasized that motivation is not solely an internal trait but can be influenced and sustained through intentional instructional practices and teacher behaviors. Some of the most effective motivational strategies include building learner confidence, setting clear and achievable goals, and introducing variety in tasks to maintain interest and engagement, (Dörnyei, 2001; Dörnyei & Ushioda, 2013).

Artificial Intelligence can effectively implement and enhance these strategies in digital learning environments. For instance, AI-powered language learning platforms can automatically generate positive reinforcement and encouragement through conversational bots, which helps in boosting learners' self-confidence. These systems can also deconstruct complex learning objectives into smaller, achievable milestones, reducing the sense of overwhelm and increasing learners' perceived control over their progress. Additionally, AI-driven algorithms can introduce a diverse array of tasks—ranging from interactive games and quizzes to real-world communication simulations—ensuring that the learning experience remains engaging and stimulating.

Crucially, motivation in AI-enhanced environments is not a fixed attribute but a dynamic construct. These systems continuously monitor and respond to learner behavior, adjusting difficulty levels, content formats, and feedback styles to match individual preferences and needs. In doing so, AI enables the personalization of motivational strategies on a scale previously unattainable in traditional classrooms, helping learners stay motivated and committed throughout their language learning journey.

2.2 Engagement in Learning Environments

Engagement refers to the degree of attention, curiosity, interest, optimism, and passion that learners show during the learning process. It is a multidimensional construct that includes:

Behavioral engagement: participation, effort, and attention.

Emotional engagement: interest, enjoyment, or emotional responses to tasks.

Cognitive engagement: investment in learning, strategic thinking, and deep processing.

Mihaly Csikszentmihalyi's Flow Theory (Csikzentmihalyi & Csikzentmihalyi, 1990) offers a compelling framework for understanding learner engagement, particularly in the context of educational activities. According to the theory, "flow" is a psychological state of deep immersion, concentration, and intrinsic enjoyment, during which learners are so engaged in a task that they lose awareness of time and external distractions. This optimal experience occurs when specific conditions are met: the activity must present a balance between challenge and skill, the goals must be clear, feedback must be immediate, and the learner must feel a sense of control over the process.

Artificial Intelligence (AI) can play a crucial role in facilitating flow in English language learning. Through real-time data collection and analysis, AI systems can continuously assess learner performance, adjusting task complexity to maintain an optimal challenge level. This aligns closely with Vygotsky's (Cole & Scribner, 1978) concept of the *zone of proximal development*, which emphasizes learning that occurs just beyond a learner's current capabilities but within reach with appropriate support. When tasks are too easy, learners tend to become disengaged due to boredom; when tasks are too difficult, they may experience anxiety or frustration. Adaptive AI-powered tools help maintain the delicate balance required to keep learners within the flow channel by offering timely scaffolding, customizing content, and ensuring that each learner is neither overburdened nor under-challenged.

By dynamically calibrating task demands and offering immediate, personalized feedback, AI enhances the likelihood of learners entering and sustaining a state of flow. This, in turn, promotes deeper learning, higher retention, and a more satisfying language acquisition experience.

Technology Engagement Models

Researchers such as Fredricks, Blumenfeld, and Paris (2004) developed comprehensive models to conceptualize student engagement, encompassing behavioral, emotional, and cognitive dimensions. In the context of technology-enhanced learning—especially with the integration of Artificial Intelligence—new and dynamic forms of engagement have emerged. AI-enabled platforms support multimodal interaction through voice, text, video, and gesture, thereby catering to diverse learner preferences and increasing interactivity. Additionally, gamification elements such as points, badges, leaderboards, and virtual environments stimulate motivation and sustained attention. Interactive storytelling further enriches the experience by allowing learners to influence narrative outcomes, fostering deeper cognitive involvement. AI systems can also monitor learner engagement in real time using tools like facial recognition, eye tracking, and speech analysis to detect emotional states such as boredom, confusion, or enthusiasm. This data-driven responsiveness enables the system to adjust content difficulty, pacing, or modality instantly—offering a level of instructional adaptability far beyond what traditional methods can achieve.

Cognitive Load Theory

Developed by John Sweller (2011), Cognitive Load Theory emphasizes that learners possess a limited working memory capacity, and if instructional materials are too complex, disorganized, or overwhelming, it can hinder learning by overloading the cognitive system. Engagement suffers when learners are unable to process information efficiently due to excessive cognitive demand. Artificial Intelligence addresses this challenge through several key mechanisms. First, scaffolded instruction allows content to be broken down into manageable, sequential chunks, making it easier for learners to process and retain information. Second, AI enables content personalization, minimizing extraneous cognitive load by filtering out irrelevant material and focusing on content that matches the learner's current level and goals. Third, just-in-time support systems provide assistance precisely when the learner needs it—whether in the form of hints, definitions, or examples—thereby preventing unnecessary frustration or distraction. Collectively, these AI-driven strategies help maintain cognitive engagement by allowing learners to concentrate on essential content without becoming overwhelmed, thereby optimizing the learning experience.

2.3 Learner Autonomy in Language Acquisition

Autonomy is the capacity to control one's own learning. In language education, this involves setting personal goals, choosing learning strategies, managing time, and evaluating one's own progress. It reflects a shift from teacher-centered instruction to learner-centered experiences.

Holec's Definition of Autonomy

Henri Holec (1981), widely regarded as a pioneer in the field of learner autonomy, defined autonomy as "the ability to take charge of one's own learning." He emphasized that autonomous learners are those who can plan and organize their learning processes, select appropriate strategies and materials, and monitor and evaluate their progress and outcomes. In AI-enhanced learning environments, this vision of autonomy becomes increasingly attainable and practical. Learners are empowered to choose content that aligns with their personal interests or goals—for instance, focusing on vocabulary relevant to job interviews or academic settings. They can also adjust the pacing and sequencing of lessons, allowing for a more flexible and individualized learning experience. Furthermore, AI tools provide detailed performance analytics and real-time feedback, enabling learners to reflect on their progress, identify areas for improvement, and make informed decisions about their next steps. These features collectively foster a sense of ownership and control, reinforcing the core principles of Holec's conceptualization of autonomy in the digital age.

Metacognition and Self-Regulated Learning

Metacognitive awareness—often described as "thinking about one's thinking"—is a crucial component of autonomous learning, as it enables individuals to reflect on their cognitive processes, evaluate their strategies, and make adjustments for more effective outcomes. AI-powered language learning systems actively support the development of metacognitive skills through interactive analytics dashboards that visualize learning trends, highlight strengths and weaknesses, and offer personalized recommendations. These insights encourage learners to become more reflective and strategic, cultivating habits that are essential for lifelong learning. Closely aligned with this is Zimmerman's (Zimmerman, 2013) model of Self-Regulated Learning (SRL), which encompasses key processes such as goal-setting, self-monitoring, and self-evaluation. AI platforms are increasingly embedding SRL frameworks by prompting users to set weekly or daily language goals, track their time investment and progress, and engage in reflection through automated journaling, quizzes, or feedback summaries. These features not only enhance awareness and control over one's learning journey but also scaffold learners gradually toward greater independence and self-direction, reinforcing the core principles of autonomy in AI-mediated educational environments.

Constructivism and Personalized Learning

Rooted in the foundational works of Jean Piaget and Lev Vygotsky, constructivist theories of learning emphasize that knowledge is not passively received but actively constructed by learners through interaction with their environment, experiences, and social contexts. In alignment with this perspective, AI systems offer robust support for constructivist learning by enabling learners to engage with content in dynamic and meaningful ways. For instance, language learners can interact with AI-generated essays by editing, analyzing, or expanding upon them, thereby deepening their understanding and honing critical thinking skills. AI also facilitates social interaction by intelligently matching learners with peers of similar proficiency levels or interests and by supporting group discussions through conversational agents, thus promoting collaborative meaning-making. Moreover, AI platforms can present open-ended tasks—such as developing chatbot scripts or composing dialogues for real-world scenarios—that encourage creativity, problem-solving, and authentic language production. By tailoring instruction to the unique needs, preferences, and progress of each learner, AI fosters agency and self-directed learning, which are central tenets of autonomy within a constructivist framework.

2.4 The Role of Feedback in Learning Theories

Feedback is a cornerstone of effective learning, deeply integrated into most educational theories. AI systems provide instant, targeted, and data-driven feedback that traditional settings may not always achieve.

Behaviorism and Immediate Reinforcement

From a behaviorist perspective, as articulated by B.F. Skinner (1957), learning is viewed as a process shaped by stimulus-response relationships and the reinforcement of desired behaviors. This approach emphasizes observable outcomes, where repetition, feedback, and reinforcement play central roles in shaping learning. AI-powered educational systems are well-suited to incorporate behaviorist principles by offering immediate correction of errors, which helps learners associate correct responses with specific stimuli. These systems also provide reinforcement through mechanisms such as praise from virtual tutors, gamified rewards, or progression indicators that motivate continued effort. Additionally, AI platforms frequently employ repetition and drill-based practices—such as spaced repetition algorithms—to solidify language acquisition through consistent practice over time. Although behaviorist methods have sometimes been criticized for promoting rote learning and lacking depth, modern AI integrates these techniques within more sophisticated instructional frameworks. By combining reinforcement with adaptive feedback, contextual learning, and higher-order tasks, AI achieves a more balanced approach that addresses both foundational skills and deeper cognitive engagement.

Sociocultural Theory and Scaffolding

Vygotsky's Sociocultural Theory highlights the central role of social interaction and cultural context in cognitive development, positing that learning occurs most effectively through collaborative dialogue with more knowledgeable others. A key concept within this framework is scaffolding—temporary, tailored support that enables learners to perform tasks they would not be able to accomplish independently. In AI-enhanced language learning environments, scaffolding is implemented through a variety of intelligent features. For instance, AI systems offer hints, clues, and adaptive difficulty levels that respond to learner performance in real time, ensuring that challenges remain within the learner's zone of proximal development. Step-by-step guidance in writing or speaking tasks allows learners to build skills incrementally, while virtual tutors and AI-based mentors simulate the role of a more knowledgeable peer or instructor. These AI agents act as mediators in the learning process, offering support when needed and gradually reducing assistance as the learner becomes more capable. In doing so, AI systems embody Vygotsky's vision of guided learning, fostering both competence and independence over time.

2.5 Summary: Aligning AI with Pedagogical Theory

The theoretical foundations of motivation, engagement, and autonomy underscore that effective learning extends far beyond the simple transmission of content; it involves crafting educational experiences that connect with learners emotionally, cognitively, and personally. When Artificial Intelligence is designed in alignment with these principles, it holds immense potential to transform language learning. AI can stimulate intrinsic motivation by offering learners relevant, meaningful content and empowering them with a sense of agency in their educational journey. It can sustain engagement through interactive, adaptive learning environments that respond to individual needs and preferences. Moreover, AI fosters autonomy by granting learners control over their learning paths, encouraging reflection through analytics, and personalizing instruction to support independent growth. Yet, it is important to recognize that AI is not inherently pedagogical. If not guided by sound educational theory, AI tools risk becoming reductionist and mechanistic, focusing narrowly on efficiency at the expense of depth and human connection. Therefore, the integration of AI into English language learning must be a collaborative endeavor, drawing on the expertise of educational technologists, linguists, teachers, and psychologists. Only through such interdisciplinary cooperation can AI be leveraged to enhance—not diminish—the deeply human elements of teaching and learning.

Table 1. Motivtion and its impact

Motivation Type	Description	Impact on Learning	Examples	Recommendations
Intrinsic Motivation	Driven by personal interest, enjoyment, or desire to learn	Leads to sustained effort, curiosity, and deeper engagement	Learning English to explore new cultures or pursue personal growth	Encourage self-directed projects, reading for pleasure, and reflective journaling
Extrinsic Motivation	Driven by external rewards or recognition	Helps initiate learning, especially in structured environments	Studying English to pass exams or get a job	Combine extrinsic rewards with meaningful tasks that highlight real-world relevance
Integrative Motivation	Desire to integrate into a community or culture	Promotes authentic communication and cultural understanding	Learning English to interact with global peers or relocate abroad	Create language exchange programs and culturally immersive activities
Instrumental Motivation	Learning for practical or career-oriented reasons	Enhances focus on task completion and skill acquisition	Preparing for job interviews, professional certifications, or academic advancement	Align learning goals with professional interests and career planning tools
Self-Efficacy (Belief in One's Ability)	Confidence in one's ability to learn and use language	Encourages persistence, risk-taking, and experimentation with language use	Feeling capable of speaking in public or writing essays	Provide scaffolded tasks, supportive feedback, and small achievements to build confidence
Anxiety & Fear of Failure	Emotional barriers that hinder motivation	May reduce participation and willingness to practice	Hesitation in speaking or fear of making mistakes	Create a safe learning environment with low-stress assessments and encouraging peer interactions

3. ARTIFICIAL INTELLIGENCE IN EDUCATION

Artificial Intelligence (AI) has emerged as one of the most transformative forces in contemporary education. From automating administrative tasks to personalizing learning experiences, AI technologies are redefining how education is delivered, accessed, and experienced. In the context of English Language Learning (ELL), AI has gone beyond acting as a mere digital tool—it now functions as an interactive tutor, a feedback generator, an evaluator, and even a motivator. To understand its true impact, it is essential to first unpack what AI entails, explore its classifications, trace its evolution in education, and analyze its current role in the language learning ecosystem.

3.1 Defining Artificial Intelligence

At its core, Artificial Intelligence (AI) refers to the creation of computer systems capable of performing tasks that traditionally require human intelligence. These tasks encompass a broad range of cognitive functions, including learning from data through machine learning, recognizing and interpreting human speech, understanding and generating natural language, making informed decisions or personalized recommendations, and interacting with users via voice or text interfaces. In the realm of education, AI holds transformative potential by enabling systems to analyze learner behaviors, adapt instructional content, and respond to student inputs in real time. These capabilities allow for more personalized, responsive, and efficient learning experiences. However, AI in education is not a standalone entity; it is deeply integrated into broader digital ecosystems, such as learning management systems (LMS), mobile learning applications, intelligent tutoring systems, virtual teaching assistants, and even humanoid or robotic educational platforms. These technologies work together to create an interactive and adaptive environment that can support learners in ways previously unattainable through traditional instruction alone.

There are three general levels of AI:

- Artificial Narrow Intelligence (ANI): AI that is designed to perform a specific task, such as grammar correction or pronunciation scoring.
- Artificial General Intelligence (AGI): Hypothetical AI capable of performing any intellectual task that a human can do. It is not yet realized.
- Artificial Superintelligence (ASI): A speculative level of AI that surpasses human intelligence in all domains.

Currently, education relies heavily on ANI, but rapid developments in natural language processing (e.g., GPT-4.5 and beyond), computer vision, and affective computing suggest we are entering a phase of increasingly complex AI capabilities in learning environments.

3.2 Classifications of AI Tools in Education

AI tools in education can be broadly classified into the following categories:

1. Intelligent Tutoring Systems (ITS)

These are AI-based systems that simulate one-on-one tutoring. They analyze student responses, identify misconceptions, and provide tailored instruction or scaffolding. Examples: Carnegie Learning, Squirrel AI, ALEKS.

2. Natural Language Processing (NLP) Tools

Natural Language Processing (NLP) is a branch of Artificial Intelligence that enables machines to understand, interpret, and generate human language in a way that is meaningful and contextually appropriate. In the field of English Language Learning (ELL), NLP serves as the backbone for numerous AI-driven applications that facilitate effective and engaging learning experiences. For instance, chatbots powered by NLP provide learners with real-time conversation practice, simulating authentic dialogues and offering corrective feedback. Essay grading systems utilize NLP to assess grammar, coherence, and vocabulary use, giving instant evaluations that help learners improve their writing skills. Additionally, NLP enables real-time speech transcription, aiding pronunciation practice and listening comprehension. Popular tools such as Grammarly, Write & Improve, and ELSA Speak are practical examples of how NLP is leveraged in ELL. These tools analyze learner input, offer suggestions, and create personalized pathways for language improvement, making NLP a critical component of AI-enhanced language learning environments.

3. Adaptive Learning Platforms

These platforms adjust the content, pace, and level of instruction based on learner performance and preferences. AI algorithms detect patterns in behavior to continuously update learning paths. Examples: DreamBox, Khan Academy (AI-enhanced features), Duolingo.

4. Predictive Analytics and Learning Analytics

AI is used to analyze large datasets to predict student outcomes, identify at-risk learners, and recommend interventions. These tools support both educators and learners in making informed decisions.

5. Virtual and Augmented Reality (VR/AR) with AI

Immersive learning experiences combined with AI provide simulations for real-world language use. Learners can interact with avatars or explore environments using voice commands or AI-generated tasks.

6. AI-Powered Assessment Systems

These tools assess learner performance through automated grading, sentiment analysis, or oral proficiency scoring. Examples include AI-raters in IELTS, PTE, and various speaking apps.

3.3 The Role of Educators in AI-Enhanced Classrooms

One of the most significant transformations brought about by the integration of Artificial Intelligence in education is the evolving role of the teacher. In AI-enhanced learning environments, teachers are no longer viewed solely as transmitters of knowledge; instead, they take on multifaceted roles as facilitators, curators of content, and mentors who guide students through personalized and technology-supported learning journeys. Educators now interpret AI-generated analytics to gain insights into student performance, allowing for more informed and responsive instruction. They also design activities that complement automated processes by fostering meaningful human interaction, such as collaborative projects, discussions, and critical thinking exercises that AI cannot replicate. Beyond academics, teachers play a crucial role in supporting the emotional and social dimensions of learning—areas where empathy and human connection are irreplaceable. Furthermore, in a world increasingly shaped by technology, educators are responsible for teaching digital and AI literacy, ensuring that students understand how to use these tools ethically and effectively. To fulfill these expanded responsibilities, teachers must be provided with the skills and confidence to critically evaluate, select, and integrate AI tools into their pedagogy. This requires ongoing professional development and strong institutional support. Rather than being displaced by AI, empowered educators can leverage it to enhance their teaching and better support diverse learners.

3.4 Future Directions in AI for Education

The future of Artificial Intelligence in education promises to be both dynamic and transformative, driven by a range of emerging trends that are reshaping how learning is designed and delivered. One such development is Explainable AI (XAI), which focuses on making AI systems more transparent and understandable by revealing how decisions are made—an essential feature for building trust among educators and learners. Another key trend is Affective AI, which seeks to interpret students' emotions through cues like facial expressions, tone of voice, or behavioral patterns, enabling systems to adapt learning experiences based on emotional states such as frustration, boredom, or excitement. Multilingual AI is also on the rise, offering real-time translation and cross-cultural communication tools that make education more inclusive and accessible for global learners. Furthermore, the integration of AI with virtual reality is leading to the creation of AI-powered VR classrooms, where immersive environments and intelligent tutors combine to provide highly engaging and personalized instruction. AI is also increasingly being leveraged for teacher support, automating time-consuming administrative tasks such as attendance tracking, assessment analysis, and curriculum recommendations. These advancements not only enhance the efficiency of educational systems but also free up educators to focus more on the human and relational aspects of teaching, making the future of AI in education both promising and profoundly human-centered.

As these innovations unfold, the central goal must remain learner-centered: to empower students, support teachers, and enrich the educational journey.

4. MOTIVATIONAL IMPACT OF AI IN ENGLISH LANGUAGE LEARNING

Motivation is the driving force that initiates, sustains, and directs behavior toward a goal. In the context of English language learning (ELL), motivation influences how long learners persist, how much effort they invest, and how positively they feel about the process. With the rise of AI-enhanced tools, there has been a significant shift in how motivation is cultivated and maintained. Artificial Intelligence provides novel, adaptive, and learner-centered mechanisms that can engage learners emotionally, cognitively, and behaviorally. These mechanisms cater to both intrinsic and extrinsic motivations, creating a dynamic learning environment that fosters curiosity, confidence, and commitment.

4.1 Theoretical Foundations of Motivation in Language Learning

To understand how Artificial Intelligence (AI) enhances learner motivation, it is essential to revisit key theoretical frameworks that explain why learners engage and persist in educational tasks. Self-Determination Theory (Ryan & Deci, 2000) posits that motivation thrives when three basic psychological needs are fulfilled: autonomy (having control over one's actions), competence (feeling capable and effective), and relatedness (feeling connected to others). AI supports these needs by allowing personalized learning paths, offering immediate feedback to build competence, and facilitating social interaction through chatbots and collaborative platforms. Expectancy-Value Theory (Wigfield & Eccles, 2000) asserts that motivation is influenced by a learner's belief in their ability to succeed (expectancy) and the perceived importance or usefulness of the task (value). AI tools address both elements by adapting tasks to learner ability levels and aligning content with personal goals and interests, thereby increasing perceived relevance. Attribution Theory (Weiner, 1985) explains motivation through how learners interpret success and failure—those who attribute outcomes to controllable factors like effort are more likely to stay motivated. AI systems help learners make these constructive attributions by tracking effort and progress over time, reinforcing the link between persistence and improvement. Finally, the ARCS Model of Motivation (Keller, 1987) emphasizes Attention, Relevance, Confidence, and Satisfaction. AI-driven systems excel in capturing attention through gamified and interactive experiences, ensuring relevance through personalized content, building confidence with adaptive feedback, and enhancing satisfaction with progress visualizations and goal attainment features. In sum, AI integrates these motivational principles either explicitly or implicitly through its design, offering engaging, responsive, and psychologically supportive learning environments that promote sustained motivation.

4.2 Gamification and Adaptive Learning for Motivation

One of the most widely adopted motivational strategies in AI-assisted English Language Learning (ELL) platforms is gamification, which involves the integration of game-like elements—such as points, badges, levels, timers, and leaderboards—into non-game educational contexts. These features are designed to make learning more engaging and rewarding, often transforming routine practice into an enjoyable experience. In the AI-enhanced landscape, gamification becomes even more effective through personalization and adaptivity. For instance, Duolingo employs AI algorithms to tailor questions to each learner's proficiency level while maintaining motivation through mechanisms like daily streaks, experience points (XP), timed challenges, and friendly competition via leaderboards. Lingokids, aimed at younger audiences, uses AI-generated avatars and animated feedback to create a dynamic, playful environment that responds directly to a child's actions and progress. Meanwhile, Mondly adapts vocabulary games in real time based on a learner's prior performance and topical interests, ensuring that each session remains relevant and appropriately challenging. The immediate feedback and rewards offered through these systems boost extrinsic motivation by giving learners clear, short-term goals and recognition for their efforts. Over time, these extrinsic motivators can evolve into intrinsic motivation as learners begin to enjoy the learning process itself and associate language acquisition with a sense of fun, mastery, and personal accomplishment. In this way, AI-powered gamification doesn't merely incentivize participation—it builds a motivational structure that sustains long-term engagement.

Adaptive Learning and Zone of Proximal Development (ZPD):

AI ensures that learners receive tasks at the right difficulty level—just beyond their current ability but within reach with effort. This alignment with Vygotsky's ZPD keeps learners motivated by presenting a consistent level of challenge and success.

4.3 Personalized Feedback and Encouragement

Timely and constructive feedback is one of the most powerful motivators in the learning process, especially in language acquisition where confidence and precision are crucial. Unlike traditional resources such as textbooks or static learning modules, AI offers dynamic, personalized, and context-sensitive feedback that adapts to each learner's performance in real time. For instance, writing platforms like Grammarly and Write & Improve not only flag grammatical or structural errors but also provide guidance on tone, clarity, and coherence, often combining corrections with positive reinforcement such as "Well done!" or "Clearer than before!" Similarly, speaking apps like ELSA Speak deliver instant evaluations of pronunciation, intonation, and fluency, complemented by motivational cues like "Excellent progress!" or "You're getting better every day!" These platforms frequently utilize reinforcement learning models, which allow the system to understand which types of feedback—whether detailed correction, praise, or encouragement—are most effective for each user. This adaptability nurtures a sense of competence, one of the three psychological needs in Self-Determination Theory, reinforcing learners' belief in their ability to improve. Beyond correction, some AI-powered tutors employ praise algorithms to simulate empathetic feedback, offering support when learners show signs of frustration or fatigue. For example, if a user struggles repeatedly with a concept, the system might suggest a break, simplify the task, or respond with motivational encouragement like "Don't give up, you're almost there!" These subtle, human-like responses create a psychologically supportive environment that helps sustain both extrinsic and intrinsic motivation, making the learner feel understood, guided, and empowered to persist.

4.4 AI Tutors and Confidence Building

AI-powered conversational agents—such as chatbots and virtual tutors—have revolutionized language learning by providing non-judgmental, always-available speaking partners for learners. These systems play a crucial role in reducing one of the most common barriers in English language learning: communication anxiety. Many learners, particularly beginners or those in non-native environments, feel self-conscious about speaking English in public or making grammatical or pronunciation mistakes in front of peers or teachers. In contrast, AI conversational agents offer a safe, private, and supportive environment for practice, where mistakes are expected and used as learning opportunities rather than points of embarrassment. Key features that make these tools especially powerful include error tolerance, where learners can experiment with language freely; repetition without judgment, allowing unlimited practice on challenging structures or vocabulary without time constraints; and cultural neutrality, ensuring that interactions are inclusive and free from social or cultural bias. These aspects create a space where learners can build fluency and confidence at their own pace. Confidence, in turn, is a foundational component of motivational resilience. As learners experience small wins and positive feedback in a low-stress setting, their willingness to take linguistic risks increases. Over time, this encourages deeper engagement, more ambitious use of language, and a stronger belief in their ability to succeed, all of which fuel sustained motivation and accelerated language development.

4.5 Supporting Goal-Setting and Progress Tracking

Goal-setting is a fundamental aspect of motivation, and AI-enhanced language learning platforms are increasingly leveraging this principle through goal-oriented interfaces that actively engage learners in the process of planning and tracking their progress. These systems typically allow users to set both short- and long-term learning goals, such as mastering a specific number of vocabulary words or committing to a daily practice schedule measured in minutes or sessions. Learners can often customize their study plans to align with personal objectives, making the experience more relevant and meaningful. For instance, platforms like Busuu use AI to analyze learner input and generate personalized study plans that adapt over time. Similarly, Memrise employs spaced repetition algorithms to optimize review schedules based on how well the learner recalls certain items, ensuring that time and effort are focused where they are most needed. These systems typically provide visual progress tracking tools such as graphs, learning streaks, and milestone badges, which offer continuous feedback and reinforce a sense of achievement. This combination of self-directed planning and real-time performance visualization nurtures a strong sense of autonomy and competence, two key pillars of intrinsic motivation. Moreover, the ability to see one's efforts materialize into measurable outcomes fosters a positive reinforcement cycle, where each milestone encourages further practice and deeper engagement with the language learning process.

Table 2. How AI contributes- motivational factor

Motivational Factor	How AI Contributes	Benefits	Challenges	Recommendations
Personalized Feedback	AI provides instant, tailored corrections and suggestions in writing, speaking, and comprehension	Encourages learners to keep trying, builds confidence, and reduces fear of making mistakes	Learners may become dependent on feedback or feel discouraged if mistakes are frequent	Balance automated feedback with positive reinforcement and guide learners to self-reflection
Goal Setting & Achievement Tracking	AI helps set realistic, measurable goals and tracks progress visually	Creates a sense of accomplishment, fosters perseverance, and reinforces commitment	Unrealistic goals or improper tracking can demotivate learners	Offer goal-setting templates and periodic reviews with human mentors for encouragement
Gamified Learning Experiences	Points, badges, streaks, and competitions reward consistent practice	Boosts motivation, makes learning fun, and promotes healthy competition	Extrinsic rewards may overshadow intrinsic motivation or lead to performance pressure	Integrate meaningful tasks and encourage learners to appreciate learning itself
Adaptive Challenges	AI adjusts difficulty levels based on performance, ensuring learners are neither bored nor overwhelmed	Maintains interest, improves problem-solving, and encourages persistence	Some learners may avoid challenging tasks to stay within comfort zones	Design adaptive systems that gently nudge learners towards progressively harder tasks
Accessibility and Convenience	AI-powered tools allow learning anytime, anywhere through mobile apps and online platforms	Supports self-paced learning and accommodates diverse schedules	Lack of discipline or distractions in unstructured environments may hinder progress	Incorporate reminders, schedules, and motivational prompts to encourage regular practice
Supportive Interaction	AI chatbots and virtual tutors provide conversational practice without judgment	Reduces anxiety, builds speaking confidence, and promotes active learning	Lack of emotional understanding may limit depth of interaction	Combine AI interactions with human guidance or community discussions for balanced support

5. ENHANCING LEARNER ENGAGEMENT THROUGH AI

Learner engagement is a multidimensional construct that plays a pivotal role in academic achievement, skill development, and learner satisfaction. In the context of English language learning (ELL), engagement refers to the sustained involvement of learners in listening, speaking, reading, and writing tasks with genuine interest and intellectual investment. Artificial Intelligence (AI) has significantly enhanced the capacity of educators and platforms to promote learner engagement by creating dynamic, responsive, and personalized learning environments. Through intelligent systems that adapt to user input, provide real-time feedback, and simulate real-world communication, AI not only captures learners' attention but also maintains it over extended periods of study.

5.1 Defining Learner Engagement

Engagement in language learning involves three interconnected dimensions: behavioral engagement (active participation in tasks), cognitive engagement (mental investment and strategy use), and emotional engagement (interest and enjoyment). AI enhances all three by personalizing content, pacing, and feedback to suit each learner's needs. Through adaptive tasks, real-time support, and interactive elements, AI fosters deeper focus, sustained effort, and positive emotional connections with the learning process.

5.2 Real-Time Interactivity and Responsiveness

One of AI's most immediate impacts on engagement is its capacity to respond to learners in real time. Unlike traditional systems, which often follow fixed pathways, AI-powered platforms can adapt instantly by adjusting question difficulty, reordering content based on user interaction, and offering immediate corrections. Tools like Quillbot and Write & Improve exemplify this by providing dynamic, personalized feedback during writing tasks, keeping learners actively involved in refining their language use and promoting sustained cognitive and emotional engagement.

5.3 Conversational Agents and Chatbots

Conversational AI, including chatbots and virtual tutors, adds a powerful layer of dialogic engagement in language learning by enabling contextual, interactive communication. These systems use natural language processing to understand learner input, voice capabilities to simulate real-life conversations, and emotional feedback to provide empathy and encouragement. Tools such as Replika, Andy English Bot, and Duolingo's AI Tutor offer safe, judgment-free environments for learners to practice speaking and listening, promoting immersion and sustained engagement through realistic, responsive dialogue.

5.4 Immersive and Multisensory Learning Experiences

AI also powers Augmented Reality (AR) and Virtual Reality (VR) applications that create immersive, multisensory language learning experiences, significantly enhancing both cognitive and emotional engagement. Tools like Mondly VR let learners practice English in realistic scenarios such as airports or restaurants, while platforms like Immerse offer real-time interaction with avatars in virtual classrooms to simulate authentic communication. These environments boost motivation, spark curiosity, and improve retention by transforming passive learning into active, experiential participation.

5.5 Engagement Through Personalization and Customization

AI enables highly personalized language learning by adapting content to individual learner profiles using data such as previous performance, time on task, and personal preferences. This ensures that material remains appropriately challenging—neither too easy nor too difficult—helping learners stay in a state of "flow" (Csikszentmihalyi & Csikszentmihalyi, 1990), where engagement and focus are maximized. For instance, if a learner is interested in sports, an AI system might present idioms through sports-related examples, making lessons more relatable and enjoyable. Such tailored content keeps learners motivated and deeply engaged.

Table 3. AI: Engagement strategy

Engagement Strategy	How AI Enhances It	Benefits	Challenges	Recommendations
Gamification Elements	Points, badges, leaderboards, and streaks motivate learners to stay active	Increases participation, creates a sense of achievement, and encourages consistent practice	May lead to extrinsic motivation only or unhealthy competition	Combine gamification with meaningful learning tasks; focus on intrinsic rewards
Interactive Content	AI generates quizzes, simulations, and real-time exercises tailored to learner's needs	Makes learning more dynamic, reduces monotony, and reinforces concepts	Content relevance may vary; risk of disengagement if not personalized well	Continuously update and diversify content; allow learner feedback to refine interactions
Adaptive Learning Paths	AI adjusts difficulty and topics based on learner progress and preferences	Keeps learners challenged without overwhelming them; sustains attention	Learners may avoid difficult areas, leading to gaps in knowledge	Design adaptive paths that balance reinforcement and challenge; encourage exploration
Multimedia Integration	Videos, animations, and voice-assisted tools enrich learning experiences	Appeals to various learning styles; enhances understanding and retention	Poorly designed media can distract or confuse learners	Ensure high-quality visuals and clear instructions aligned with learning goals

continued on following page

Table 3. Continued

Engagement Strategy	How AI Enhances It	Benefits	Challenges	Recommendations
Collaborative Platforms	AI connects learners through forums, group tasks, and peer feedback systems	Builds community, encourages communication, and promotes shared learning	Miscommunication or lack of moderation may hinder learning	Provide guidelines for constructive interaction and moderate discussions effectively
Emotion Recognition & Feedback	AI analyzes facial expressions or voice tones to tailor learning pace or support	Supports emotional engagement and personalized encouragement	Privacy concerns and technical limitations may arise	Use opt-in systems and ensure data protection; complement with human support
Instant Progress Updates	AI delivers real-time feedback and progress reports	Reinforces learner achievements, builds confidence, and sustains motivation	Too much feedback can overwhelm learners	Present feedback in digestible formats and prioritize key insights

6. FOSTERING LEARNER AUTONOMY THROUGH AI

Learner autonomy refers to the capacity and willingness of learners to take responsibility for their own learning. In English language education, autonomy implies the learner's ability to set goals, select learning strategies, monitor progress, and evaluate outcomes independently. Fostering such autonomy is a key goal in contemporary pedagogy, especially in the context of lifelong learning. With the rise of Artificial Intelligence (AI), opportunities to support, develop, and enhance learner autonomy have expanded significantly.

AI-powered English learning environments provide learners with the tools, feedback, and resources necessary to personalize their education and make informed decisions about their learning process. Unlike traditional classrooms that often rely on teacher-led instruction, AI tools foster a sense of ownership and agency among learners, which is essential for sustainable language development.

6.1 Understanding Learner Autonomy

Learner autonomy, grounded in constructivist and humanistic learning theories, emphasizes the learner's active role in directing their own education. It involves self-direction, self-regulation, goal setting, and reflective practices. While traditional classrooms often struggle to nurture these traits due to rigid structures and limited individual attention, AI offers scalable, personalized tools that support autonomous learning. By enabling learners to plan, monitor, and evaluate their progress with adaptive feedback and goal-oriented features, AI makes the development of autonomy both practical and measurable across diverse educational settings.

6.2 Personalized Learning Paths

AI systems enhance learner autonomy by enabling personalized, self-directed learning paths. By analyzing factors such as proficiency, interests, goals, pace, and past performance, platforms like EdTech Tutor, Duolingo, and Lingvist tailor lessons and suggest next steps. Learners gain the freedom to decide when and how to study, access content aligned with their personal objectives (e.g., business or travel English), and adjust the difficulty and schedule to suit their needs. This dynamic support reduces dependency on constant teacher intervention and fosters greater control over the learning process.

6.3 Goal Setting and Progress Tracking

Autonomous learners thrive when they can set clear goals and monitor their progress effectively. AI supports this by offering features such as customizable goal-setting tools for defining SMART objectives, interactive dashboards that visualize achievements and highlight areas needing improvement, and predictive analytics that anticipate future performance and recommend focus areas. These tools encourage metacognitive awareness and reflective learning. Platforms like Khan Academy and IELTS Prep by Magoosh exemplify how AI-driven analytics empower learners to take charge of their development independently.

6.4 On-Demand Access to Learning Resources

Autonomy is further strengthened through the anytime, anywhere access provided by AI-driven platforms. Features like 24/7 intelligent tutoring systems, mobile apps with offline functionality, and voice-enabled interfaces empower learners to engage with English learning whenever and wherever it suits them. This seamless integration into daily routines—whether during commutes, breaks, or leisure moments—supports self-paced, learner-driven education, making autonomy both practical and sustainable.

6.5 Intelligent Feedback and Error Correction

Constructive feedback is essential for fostering independent learning, and AI delivers it instantly and privately, empowering learners to improve without external pressure. Tools like Grammarly and Write & Improve offer grammar and style suggestions, while speech apps like ELSA Speak evaluate pronunciation and fluency. AI chatbots also provide real-time conversational corrections. This immediate, personalized feedback helps learners self-correct, reduces fear of judgment, and builds confidence in their ability to progress autonomously.

Table 4. AI: Aspect of autonomy

Aspect of Autonomy	How AI Supports It	Benefits	Challenges	Recommendations
Personalized Learning Paths	AI adapts lessons based on learner's pace, preferences, and strengths	Encourages self-directed learning, boosts confidence, prevents frustration	Learners may struggle without guidance; risk of isolation	Provide periodic check-ins with mentors; offer structured learning options alongside flexibility
Goal Setting & Progress Tracking	AI helps set realistic goals and monitor progress through data insights	Empowers learners to take responsibility for their learning journey	Data overload or misinterpretation may lead to confusion	Use intuitive dashboards and provide contextual explanations for data trends
Instant Feedback & Error Correction	AI tools offer immediate suggestions and corrections in writing, pronunciation, and grammar	Helps learners reflect on mistakes and self-correct	Over-reliance on feedback may limit critical thinking	Encourage learners to analyze feedback and explore alternative solutions
Resource Recommendations	AI suggests supplementary materials, videos, and exercises based on learner needs	Enables learners to explore topics independently and at their own pace	Poor-quality resources may mislead or overwhelm learners	Curate resources and ensure content diversity and quality
Flexible Learning Environments	AI-powered platforms allow anytime, anywhere learning	Learners can manage their schedule and learning environment	Distractions and inconsistent study habits	Provide tools for time management and reminders to build disciplined learning routines
Encouraging Reflection	AI prompts learners to assess their learning habits and strategies	Promotes metacognition and deeper engagement with the learning process	Learners may not fully understand how to reflect effectively	Include guided reflection templates and examples to foster meaningful self-assessment

7. CHALLENGES AND ETHICAL CONSIDERATIONS IN AI-DRIVEN ENGLISH LEARNING

While Artificial Intelligence (AI) offers transformative possibilities for English language learning, its integration is not without risks, limitations, and ethical complexities. As AI tools increasingly become embedded in classrooms and self-directed learning environments, stakeholders must grapple with significant concerns related to equity, bias, privacy, dependency, and the very nature of learning itself.

This section explores the key challenges and ethical implications that must be acknowledged and addressed to ensure that AI-enhanced English learning remains inclusive, effective, and aligned with human-centered values.

7.1 Data Privacy and Security

AI systems depend on extensive data collection to personalize instruction and deliver effective feedback. This includes tracking learning behavior, voice inputs, written work, and even emotional cues in some systems. However, such data use raises serious ethical concerns—particularly around consent, security, and transparency. Risks include unauthorized data sharing, unclear privacy terms, and inadequate protection for minors. To address these concerns, developers and educators must ensure transparent data practices, robust consent mechanisms tailored to age groups, and secure storage protocols to protect learner privacy and trust.

7.2 Algorithmic Bias

AI systems, while powerful, can unintentionally reinforce biases if trained on non-representative data. For instance, speech recognition tools may struggle with regional or non-native accents, disadvantaging certain learners. Similarly, recommendation engines might promote narrow cultural content, and automated grading tools may penalize writing styles that deviate from standardized norms. To address these issues, ethical development must include diverse datasets, inclusive design practices, and input from multilingual, multicultural users. Additionally, incorporating human oversight and providing learners the ability to challenge AI decisions ensures fairness and accountability in educational settings.

7.3 Digital Divide and Accessibility

While AI has the potential to democratize English language learning, it can also widen existing disparities. Effective use of AI tools often requires stable internet access, modern digital devices, and foundational digital skills—resources not equally available to all. Learners in rural areas or underserved communities may be left behind, and students with disabilities can face barriers due to inaccessible interfaces. Ethically responsible AI development must prioritize inclusivity by offering offline or low-bandwidth options, integrating accessibility features like text-to-speech and voice navigation, and providing digital literacy training to both learners and educators in marginalized contexts.

7.4 Overreliance on Technology

While AI offers valuable support in English language learning, overreliance on it can undermine critical educational outcomes. Learners may become passive recipients of automated suggestions, potentially limiting their creativity and reducing opportunities for human interaction. AI-driven feedback, though efficient, can be overly prescriptive, discouraging deeper reflection or exploration. To mitigate these risks, ethical implementation should promote human-AI collaboration. This includes encouraging learners to critically engage with AI feedback, integrating peer interaction and teacher support, and ensuring that AI enhances—not replaces—authentic, meaningful learning experiences.

7.5 Ethical Use of Gamification and Nudges

Gamification in AI-powered English learning tools can enhance motivation, but it also raises ethical concerns. Elements like streaks, badges, and point systems may shift learners' focus from genuine language development to superficial rewards. Additionally, AI-driven nudges can exploit psychological vulnerabilities—such as fear of failure or social comparison—leading to compulsive behavior rather than engaged learning. To address this, gamification should be used thoughtfully as a motivational aid rather than a manipulative tool. Learners should have control over gamified features, and design should prioritize intrinsic motivation by emphasizing personal growth, curiosity, and meaningful progress.

8. APPLICATIONS

To better understand how AI transforms English language learning in real-world contexts, it is essential to examine practical implementations across varied educational settings. This section presents case studies and examples from schools, universities, and self-directed learning platforms, highlighting the integration of AI in ways that promote motivation, engagement, and learner autonomy.

These applications demonstrate both the potential and the challenges of using AI in English learning, offering insight into best practices, outcomes, and the evolving roles of teachers and learners.

8.1 Case Study 1: Duolingo – Personalized Learning and Gamification

Duolingo, a leading AI-powered language learning app, utilizes Natural Language Processing, machine learning, and gamification to deliver personalized English instruction to millions of users worldwide. Its adaptive learning paths respond to learner errors, while spaced repetition algorithms reinforce memory retention. Gamified elements such as XP points, streaks, and leaderboards enhance motivation and engagement, and AI-driven chatbots offer conversational practice in low-pressure environments. Duolingo supports learner autonomy by allowing users to control their pace, content sequence, and study times. However, its focus on vocabulary and sentence patterns may limit deeper communicative competence, and the heavy use of external rewards can sometimes shift learners' focus from meaningful learning to point accumulation.

8.2 Case Study 2: Speak – Real-Time Pronunciation and Speaking Practice

Speak is an AI-powered mobile app designed to enhance spoken English proficiency through technologies like Automatic Speech Recognition (ASR) and Natural Language Processing (NLP). It provides real-time feedback on pronunciation, fluency, and tone, using AI avatars to simulate conversational practice. Learners benefit from private, corrective feedback that builds confidence and autonomy, while engaging in realistic scenarios that make learning more meaningful. The app allows flexible, on-demand practice, supporting self-paced improvement. However, it has limitations—ASR may struggle with strong accents or noisy environments, and it cannot fully capture the emotional depth of human interaction.

8.3 Case Study 3: Write & Improve – Automated Writing Feedback

Write & Improve, developed by Cambridge English and iLexIR, is an AI-powered writing tool that provides instant, automated feedback to learners preparing for exams like IELTS and TOEFL. It utilizes AI for essay scoring, grammar and vocabulary correction, and offers iterative suggestions to help learners improve their writing over time. The platform boosts motivation by enabling users to track progress quickly, fosters engagement through revision-based practice, and supports autonomy by reducing reliance on teachers. However, its limitations include occasional misinterpretation of creative writing and feedback that lacks the depth and nuance of human instructors.

8.4 Case Study 4: AI Integration in Indian Higher Education (Pilot Program)

In a pilot program at a public university in India, AI-driven English learning software—powered by ChatGPT—was introduced to support undergraduates from non-English-speaking backgrounds. The tool provided conversational practice, grammar explanations, vocabulary enhancement, and essay structuring support. Students reported increased motivation, feeling less intimidated while practicing with an AI partner, and showed higher engagement by asking more questions and exploring beyond the syllabus. The chatbot also fostered learner autonomy, as students used it independently for exam preparation, interview practice, and creative writing. However, challenges included unequal access to devices, faculty resistance to innovative methods, and the need for training in AI literacy.

8.5 Case Study 5: Virtual Teaching Assistant (VTA) in a Blended Learning Environment

At a private language institute in South Korea, a Virtual Teaching Assistant (VTA) was integrated into a blended English classroom to enhance instruction. The AI system offered personalized vocabulary quizzes, pronunciation drills specifically addressing Korean L1 interference, and custom reading comprehension exercises. Students responded positively, viewing the VTA as a supportive and approachable tool, which increased motivation. Engagement improved as learners used the AI outside of class for additional practice, and autonomy was strengthened through features like native-language explanations. However, initial overreliance on the VTA reduced peer interaction, and instructors required training to effectively balance AI integration with traditional teaching methods.

9. FUTURE DIRECTIONS IN AI AND ENGLISH LANGUAGE EDUCATION

As we look ahead, the integration of Artificial Intelligence in English language education is poised to become more sophisticated, personalized, and inclusive. While current AI applications already show remarkable results in motivating learners, increasing engagement, and fostering autonomy, the next decade will likely bring even deeper transformations across pedagogy, technology, and policy. This section outlines emerging trends, research frontiers, and critical areas for development that will shape the future of AI-enhanced English learning.

9.1 Towards Hyper-Personalized Learning Ecosystems

In the near future, AI tools in English language learning are expected to evolve from basic personalization to deeply adaptive, emotion-aware systems. Rather than relying solely on test scores or behavioral data, these advanced platforms will integrate emotional, cognitive, and physiological inputs—such as facial expressions, heart rate, and eye movement—to customize content, pacing, and feedback in real time. Potential features include emotion-sensitive feedback, personality-adaptive learning paths, voice modulation analysis for speaking practice, and comprehensive learner profiles that capture motivation, learning styles, and progress. These innovations aim to create responsive, human-centric learning experiences that adjust dynamically to both what learners know and how they feel.

9.2 Integration of Augmented Reality (AR) and Virtual Reality (VR)

The convergence of AI with immersive technologies like Augmented Reality (AR) and Virtual Reality (VR) promises transformative opportunities for experiential language learning. In these environments, learners can interact with AI-driven characters in lifelike scenarios—such as ordering food in a virtual café, navigating a job interview, or joining collaborative storytelling adventures. These experiences offer contextualized language practice, deepen emotional engagement, and provide opportunities for authentic cross-cultural communication. By embedding language use in meaningful, realistic contexts, immersive AI-enhanced learning boosts both motivation and long-term retention.

9.3 AI-Powered Assessment of Higher-Order Skills

Traditional language assessments have typically emphasized discrete skills such as grammar accuracy or vocabulary recall. However, the future of assessment is shifting toward AI-powered tools that can evaluate complex, real-world competencies like critical thinking, intercultural communication, collaboration, and creativity in English. Emerging technologies include AI that assesses essay coherence, tone, and argumentation quality; chatbots that simulate culturally nuanced conversations; and machine learning systems that analyze team interactions during collaborative tasks. This evolution supports a move away from rote memorization toward deeper, competency-based language instruction.

9.4 Multilingual AI Models Supporting Translanguaging

Future AI systems will increasingly support multilingualism and translanguaging—the fluid use of multiple languages within communication—allowing English learners to draw on their entire linguistic repertoire rather than being penalized for using their native tongues. This approach reduces cognitive load for bilingual learners, promotes linguistic and cultural diversity, and strengthens connections between English and learners' first languages. While current multilingual models like OpenAI's GPT-4 already demonstrate cross-lingual capabilities, future advancements will enhance contextual code-switching, idiomatic understanding, and culturally sensitive communication, making AI tools more inclusive and adaptive.

9.5 Ethical AI and Data Sovereignty in Language Education

As AI becomes deeply integrated into education, ethical considerations—particularly around privacy, data ownership, and fairness—will take center stage. Future AI models must not only be powerful but also transparent, inclusive, and accountable. Key priorities will include using diverse and representative training data, giving learners control over their personal learning data, minimizing bias in automated assessments, and ensuring AI systems align with local cultures and pedagogical values. To safeguard learners' rights while fostering innovation, both international standards and national policies will need to evolve and enforce ethical, learner-centric governance of educational AI.

Table 5. Adaptive learning systems

Future Direction	Potential Benefits	Challenges	Recommendations
Adaptive Learning Systems	Personalized learning paths, tailored feedback, faster skill acquisition	Over-reliance on technology, data privacy concerns	Combine AI tools with human instructors; ensure ethical use of learner data
AI-powered Chatbots & Virtual Tutors	24/7 learning support, conversational practice, instant corrections	Limited cultural understanding, inability to detect emotional cues	Train chatbots with diverse language inputs; integrate empathy-driven responses
Speech Recognition & Pronunciation Tools	Improved speaking accuracy, real-time feedback, better fluency	Accent bias, software limitations in noisy environments	Use datasets representing diverse accents; enhance noise-filtering algorithms
Learning Analytics & Progress Tracking	Data-driven insights, early identification of learning gaps, personalized suggestions	Data overload, misinterpretation by learners or instructors	Visual dashboards with actionable insights; provide training on how to interpret data
Immersive Learning (AR/VR Integration)	Contextual learning, simulated environments, increased engagement	High cost of hardware, accessibility issues in low-resource areas	Develop affordable AR/VR options; create mobile-friendly solutions for wider reach
Collaborative AI Platforms	Peer learning, community building, shared resources	Potential misuse, difficulty moderating discussions	Establish secure, moderated environments; promote responsible digital citizenship
Ethical AI Governance	Trust-building, fairness, transparency	Regulatory gaps, misuse of AI tools	Implement guidelines for responsible AI use in education; encourage stakeholder participation
Multilingual Support	Accessibility for global learners, easier cross-linguistic learning	Translation inaccuracies, context loss	Use human-in-the-loop approaches for quality control; constantly update datasets

10. CONCLUSION

The integration of Artificial Intelligence (AI) into English language education marks a profound shift in how learners acquire, interact with, and internalize language. Far from being a mere technological add-on, AI is becoming an essential partner in the language learning process—one that reshapes pedagogical practices, learner experiences, and educational outcomes.

At the heart of this transformation lies the potential of AI to empower motivation, engagement, and autonomy—three pillars essential for sustained and meaningful learning.

10.1 AI and Learner Motivation: A New Era of Personalized Encouragement

Motivation has long been a central concern in language education, especially in environments where learners face psychological, social, or linguistic barriers. Through real-time feedback, gamified environments, adaptive challenges, and conversational agents, AI offers learners tailored encouragement and progress tracking.

Unlike static instruction, AI responds to learners' actions, adjusting pace, difficulty, and presentation style. This personalization fuels intrinsic motivation, as learners feel seen, supported, and in control of their development. Extrinsic motivators—like points, badges, and leaderboards—may initiate interest, but deeper, sustained engagement often stems from feeling competent and autonomous.

10.2 AI and Engagement: Making Learning Meaningful and Interactive

Traditional English instruction has often faced challenges with learner disengagement due to its reliance on textbook-driven, uniform approaches. AI tools are transforming this landscape by fostering deeper engagement through multimodal learning experiences that integrate audio, visuals, and interactivity; dynamic content that adapts in real time to learner responses; conversational interfaces such as chatbots and speech recognition for natural communication practice; and contextualized learning scenarios like simulations and real-world tasks tailored to individual interests. This shift makes English learning more personalized, responsive, and meaningful.

By fostering active learning, AI enhances cognitive, emotional, and behavioral engagement. Learners not only consume content but interact with it—posing questions, receiving suggestions, and applying knowledge in simulated or real contexts.

10.3 AI and Autonomy: Empowering the Independent Learner

Autonomous learning is essential for achieving long-term language proficiency, and AI significantly enhances this process by allowing learners to set personal goals, access immediate feedback, engage with resources beyond the classroom, and practice anytime, anywhere in a low-pressure environment that encourages experimentation and self-correction. Rather than replacing educators, AI reshapes their role into that of facilitators and mentors who support students in navigating digital tools, reflecting on progress, and cultivating metacognitive skills. In this partnership, AI provides the scaffolding while teachers and learners collaboratively build a personalized, sustainable learning journey.

10.4 Challenges and Considerations

While the benefits of AI in English learning are substantial, its integration also raises critical concerns related to equity, bias, privacy, and overreliance. Not all learners have equal access to devices or internet infrastructure, potentially widening existing educational gaps. AI models, if not trained on diverse linguistic and cultural data, risk reinforcing stereotypes and marginalizing certain groups. Additionally, the ethical use and protection of student data must be ensured through transparent policies. Finally, excessive dependence on AI can diminish human interaction and collaborative learning. Addressing these challenges requires thoughtful design, inclusive policies, algorithmic transparency, and ongoing teacher training to ensure ethical and equitable AI-enhanced education.

10.5 Vision for the Future

The future of English language education lies in a hybrid model where human teachers and artificial intelligence work together to create flexible, personalized, and inclusive learning environments. Rather than replacing teachers, AI supports them by automating routine tasks, analyzing learning data, and offering adaptive feedback. Learners benefit from AI tutors that respond to their emotions and context, immersive AR scenarios that simulate real-world communication, and platforms that embrace multilingualism and cultural diversity. This collaborative ecosystem redefines language learning—not merely as a set of grammar rules to master, but as a tool for global communication, critical thinking, and authentic human connection.

REFERENCES

Cole, M., & Scribner, S. (1978). *Vygotsky, Lev S.(1978)*. Mind in Society. The Development of Higher Psychological Processes.

Csikszentmihalyi, M., & Csikzentmihaly, M. (1990). *Flow: The psychology of optimal experience* (Vol. 1990). Harper & Row.

Dörnyei, Z. (2001). *Motivational Strategies in the Language Classroom*. Cambridge University Press. DOI: 10.1017/CBO9780511667343

Dörnyei, Z., & Ushioda, E. (2013). *Teaching and Researching Motivation* (2nd ed.). Routledge. DOI: 10.4324/9781315833750

Fredricks, J. A., Blumenfeld, P. C., & Paris, A. H. (2004). School engagement: Potential of the concept, state of the evidence. *Review of Educational Research, 74*(1), 59–109. DOI: 10.3102/00346543074001059

Gardner, R. C. (2014). Attitudes and motivation in second language learning. In *Bilingualism, multiculturalism, and second language learning* (pp. 43–63). Psychology Press.

Holec, H. (1981). Autonomy is the ability to take charge of one's own learning.

Keller, J. M. (1987). Development and use of the ARCS model of instructional design. *Journal of Instructional Development : JID, 10*(3), 2–10. DOI: 10.1007/BF02905780

Ryan, R. M., & Deci, E. L. (2000). Self-determination theory and the facilitation of intrinsic motivation, social development, and well-being. *The American Psychologist, 55*(1), 68–78. DOI: 10.1037/0003-066X.55.1.68 PMID: 11392867

Skinner, B. F. (1957). The experimental analysis of behavior. *American Scientist, 45*(4), 343–371.

Sweller, J. (2011). Cognitive load theory. [). Academic Press.]. *Psychology of Learning and Motivation, 55*, 37–76. DOI: 10.1016/B978-0-12-387691-1.00002-8

Weiner, B. (1985). Attribution theory. In *Human motivation* (pp. 275–326). Springer New York. DOI: 10.1007/978-1-4612-5092-0_7

Wigfield, A., & Eccles, J. S. (2000). Expectancy–value theory of achievement motivation. *Contemporary Educational Psychology, 25*(1), 68–81. DOI: 10.1006/ceps.1999.1015 PMID: 10620382

Zimmerman, B. J. (2013). Theories of self-regulated learning and academic achievement: An overview and analysis. *Self-regulated learning and academic achievement*, 1-36.

ADDITIONAL READING

Al-Azawei, A., Serenelli, F., & Lundqvist, K. (2016). Universal Design for Learning (UDL): A Content Analysis of Peer-Reviewed Journal Papers from 2012 to 2015. *The Journal of Scholarship of Teaching and Learning*, *16*(3), 39–56. DOI: 10.14434/josotl.v16i3.19295

Chen, X., Xie, H., Zou, D., & Hwang, G. J. (2020). Application and Theory-Guided Design of AI-Driven Chatbots in Higher Education: A Systematic Review. *Journal of Educational Technology & Society*, *23*(4), 31–47.

Godwin-Jones, R. (2021). Emerging Technologies: Artificial Intelligence in Language Learning. *Language Learning & Technology*, *25*(1), 1–11.

Graham, S., Hebert, M., & Harris, K. R. (2015). Formative Assessment and Writing: A Meta-Analysis. *Educational Psychologist*, *50*(1), 107–118.

Heffernan, N. T., & Heffernan, C. L. (2014). The ASSISTments Ecosystem: Building a Platform that Brings Scientists and Teachers Together for Minimally Invasive Research on Human Learning and Teaching. *International Journal of Artificial Intelligence in Education*, *24*(4), 470–497. DOI: 10.1007/s40593-014-0024-x

Reeves, T. C., & Lin, L. (2020). Designing Technology-Enhanced Language Learning Environments: Research-Informed Principles and Guidelines. *Journal of Computer Assisted Learning*, *36*(2), 139–153.

Zawacki-Richter, O., Marín, V. I., Bond, M., & Gouverneur, F. (2019). Systematic Review of Research on Artificial Intelligence Applications in Higher Education – Where are the Educators? *International Journal of Educational Technology in Higher Education*, *16*(1), 39. DOI: 10.1186/s41239-019-0171-0

KEY TERMS AND DEFINITIONS

Algorithmic Bias: A tendency in AI systems to produce unfair or inaccurate results due to non-representative training data or flawed design, potentially disadvantaging certain learners.

Artificial Intelligence (AI): Computer systems designed to perform tasks that typically require human intelligence, such as understanding language, recognizing speech, and providing personalized feedback.

Autonomy: The capacity of learners to take control of their own learning by setting goals, selecting strategies, managing time, and reflecting on progress independently.

Data Privacy: The protection of personal information collected during learning activities, including how data is stored, used, and shared, ensuring ethical practices.

Engagement: The degree of attention, interest, and active participation that a learner demonstrates while interacting with learning content or tools, including behavioral, emotional, and cognitive dimensions.

Feedback: Information provided to learners about their performance, which helps guide improvement and enhance learning outcomes.

Gamification: The use of game elements like points, badges, and leaderboards in educational contexts to enhance motivation and participation.

Motivation: The psychological force that initiates, directs, and sustains learning behavior. In language learning, motivation influences persistence, effort, and emotional connection to the learning task.

Natural Language Processing (NLP): A branch of AI that enables computers to understand, interpret, and generate human language in meaningful ways, used for tools like chatbots and grammar checkers.

Personalization: The adaptation of learning content, feedback, and tasks to meet individual learner preferences, pace, and proficiency levels.

Chapter 14
Ethical Considerations and Data Privacy in AI-Driven Learning Environments

S. C. Vetrivel
https://orcid.org/0000-0003-3050-8211
Kongu Engineering College, India

P. Vidhyapriya
https://orcid.org/0000-0002-1421-8743
Kongu Engineering College, India

T. Gunasekar
Kongu Engineering College, India

V. P. Arun
https://orcid.org/0009-0009-1211-2150
JKKN College of Engineering and Technology, India

V. Sabareeshwari
Amrita Vishwa Vidyapeetham, India

ABSTRACT

The integration of Artificial Intelligence (AI) into English language learning and teaching environments has significantly enhanced personalized learning, adaptive content delivery, and student engagement. However, the growing reliance on AI technologies raises critical ethical concerns and data privacy issues that must be systematically addressed. This chapter explores the multifaceted ethical implications

DOI: 10.4018/979-8-3373-3561-2.ch014

involved in AI-driven language education, including algorithmic bias, surveillance, data ownership, informed consent, and the digital divide. It analyzes how AI systems collect, process, and utilize student data, often without transparent mechanisms or user awareness, thereby challenging foundational principles of autonomy and data protection. The chapter also discusses the necessity of safeguarding learners' rights while maintaining pedagogical efficiency, particularly in diverse educational contexts. Special attention is given to the ethical design of AI algorithms, ensuring fairness, accountability, and inclusiveness.

1. INTRODUCTION

1.1 The Rise of AI in English Language Learning (ELL)

The integration of Artificial Intelligence (AI) in English Language Learning (ELL) has rapidly transformed the educational landscape, enabling more personalized, adaptive, and data-driven learning experiences. AI tools—such as Natural Language Processing (NLP), intelligent tutoring systems, chatbots, and voice recognition—have revolutionized how learners interact with language content and instructors. These systems analyze learner data in real-time, adjusting instructional strategies and content delivery to match individual progress, preferences, and proficiency levels. In India, the demand for AI-based English learning platforms has surged in both urban and rural settings, driven by the government's digital literacy initiatives and the increasing popularity of mobile-first learning environments. Startups like Enguru and ConveGenius have begun employing AI to improve pronunciation, vocabulary acquisition, and conversational fluency among students from diverse linguistic backgrounds. These tools not only provide customized feedback but also help bridge the learning gap among students with varying socioeconomic and regional language contexts (Amershi et al., 2019). Moreover, the global shift to online and hybrid classrooms post-COVID-19 has accelerated the adoption of AI in English learning platforms. Tools such as Grammarly, ELSA Speak, and Duolingo use AI to assess grammar, speech clarity, and writing style, supporting learners outside traditional classrooms. Importantly, these technologies are no longer confined to high-resource environments. Low-bandwidth and mobile-optimized solutions are being developed for multilingual users, improving accessibility for learners in underserved areas (Abdullah et al., 2022). As AI continues to evolve, its impact on ELL will likely deepen, reshaping curriculum design, assessment models, and teacher-student interaction. However, while the technological growth is commendable, it also necessitates a parallel focus on ethical considerations and privacy safeguards—a theme explored in the subsequent sections.

1.2 Need for Ethical Awareness in Digital Classrooms

As AI-enhanced tools become integral to English language learning environments, the ethical dimensions of their application are gaining critical attention. The shift from traditional to digital classrooms—driven by AI and big data—raises several concerns about how learner data is collected, analyzed, and used. Ethical awareness in digital classrooms is not merely an adjunct topic; it is foundational for creating safe, inclusive, and respectful learning environments. Issues such as bias in language models, opaque decision-making algorithms, and the potential for invasive surveillance require educators, developers, and institutions to engage with AI responsibly.

Digital classrooms often rely on real-time analytics and user modeling to deliver adaptive content. However, these systems sometimes lack transparency about how decisions are made, leading to potential violations of learner autonomy and informed consent. For example, predictive performance analysis may result in self-fulfilling biases that limit learning opportunities for students incorrectly flagged as "low-performing". Such ethical blind spots necessitate proactive ethical frameworks, where data ownership, algorithmic fairness, and the rights of learners—especially minors—are prioritized (Baker,2019). In India, the National Education Policy (NEP) 2020 emphasizes the use of digital tools but remains relatively silent on AI ethics in learning. This gap becomes more concerning as regional language learners and marginalized communities increasingly access AI-enabled platforms. Without culturally contextual ethical safeguards, digital classrooms may perpetuate inequalities rather than bridge them (Singh & Bose, 2023).

1.3 Data Privacy Concerns in AI-Powered ELL

The proliferation of AI in English Language Learning (ELL) has introduced complex data privacy challenges that are increasingly difficult to ignore. AI-driven ELL platforms routinely collect large volumes of learner data—including voice recordings, writing samples, behavioral analytics, and interaction histories—to deliver personalized instruction. While these capabilities significantly enhance learning outcomes, they also raise critical concerns about the collection, storage, sharing, and potential misuse of sensitive learner information.

A major privacy concern in AI-enabled ELL systems involves the lack of transparency regarding what data is being collected and how it is used. Many platforms utilize third-party services for analytics and cloud storage, often without adequately informing users—especially minors—about potential data sharing with advertisers, developers, or international data centers. This creates vulnerabilities, particularly in jurisdictions like India, where data protection laws such as the recently passed Digital Personal Data Protection (DPDP) Act, 2023 are still evolving and lack clear implementation guidelines in educational contexts .Another layer of complexity arises from the cross-border nature of AI technologies. Multinational ELL platforms like Duolingo or Elsa Speak often process learner data in countries with differing levels of privacy protection, leading to non-compliance risks under global data frameworks like the General Data Protection Regulation (GDPR) (Binns,2018). For instance, speech recognition and NLP tools may retain audio data in global servers for algorithm training, creating long-term privacy exposure without user consent. In light of these developments, educational institutions and developers must incorporate data minimization principles and ensure that privacy is built into AI systems by design. More importantly, learners and educators need to be educated about their rights to access, modify, or erase their data. As AI becomes a fixture in language education, robust privacy safeguards will be key to maintaining trust and integrity in digital learning spaces.

2. ETHICS IN AI-POWERED EDUCATION

2.1 Understanding AI Ethics in Learning Contexts

The integration of Artificial Intelligence into English Language Learning (ELL) environments requires a thorough understanding of educational ethics tailored for intelligent systems. AI ethics in learning contexts refers to a set of moral principles that govern the design, deployment, and usage of AI tools in a way that aligns with educational fairness, learner autonomy, and social responsibility (Brundage et al., 2018). As AI tools increasingly guide personalized instruction, assessment, and feedback in ELL platforms, it becomes imperative to consider ethical issues such as consent, discrimination, misinformation, and learner manipulation.

Ethical considerations in ELL systems must go beyond data protection and delve into value alignment, especially when AI tutors make decisions on curriculum pacing, task difficulty, or corrective feedback (Zuboff 2019). These decisions—although driven by algorithms—carry moral weight as they directly affect learner motivation, confidence, and academic outcomes . For example, if an AI language assistant disproportionately recommends remedial modules to students from a specific linguistic or socio-economic background, it may reinforce systemic biases under the guise of personalization.

Furthermore, AI ethics in education also addresses power asymmetries between technology providers and end-users. Often, learners and educators have limited understanding or control over how AI functions, creating ethical opacity (Crawford 2021). This lack of transparency challenges the foundational principles of trust and informed participation in educational settings (Wang, 2022). Therefore, incorporating ethical guardrails such as explainable AI (XAI), human-in-the-loop (HITL) designs, and ethics-by-design frameworks is essential for sustainable and just AI adoption in ELL systems. India's National Education Policy 2020 and its recent initiatives in AI-for-Education also highlight the importance of aligning technological progress with ethical sensitivity. Ethical guidelines must evolve in parallel with AI capabilities to safeguard the rights, dignity, and intellectual development of all learners, regardless of context or geography.

2.2 Algorithmic Bias and Fairness in Language Tools

The promise of AI in English Language Learning (ELL) lies in its ability to deliver personalized and adaptive learning experiences. However, algorithmic bias presents a critical challenge, particularly in the context of language tools that rely heavily on natural language processing (NLP), machine learning, and large-scale linguistic datasets. Bias in AI models often stems from the skewed nature of training data, where certain accents, dialects, regional vernaculars, or socio-cultural references are underrepresented or misinterpreted.

In the context of ELL, such bias can lead to disproportionate disadvantages for learners from non-dominant linguistic backgrounds (Dignum 2019). For instance, speech recognition systems trained predominantly on American or British English may misclassify Indian or African English pronunciations, thereby affecting feedback accuracy and learner performance evaluations. These inaccuracies, though technical in origin, result in tangible educational disparities that undermine fairness and inclusion.

Moreover, AI systems may carry forward biases in content recommendation and language correction (Ziewitz, 2019). For example, AI grammar tools may flag culturally appropriate idioms or regional usages as errors simply because they deviate from the 'standard' English embedded in training data. This not only marginalizes linguistic diversity but also reinforces normative language hierarchies, which is a serious ethical concern.

To address algorithmic bias, several mitigation strategies are emerging, such as diverse dataset curation, bias audits, and fairness-aware model training. Indian edtech startups working in regional language learning are also beginning to acknowledge these gaps and are moving toward localized NLP development to better represent multilingual learners (Floridi 2019). The National Strategy on Artificial Intelligence by NITI Aayog emphasizes the need for fairness in AI as part of responsible AI development in education. Ensuring fairness in AI-powered language tools thus requires a multidimensional approach—technological, pedagogical, and policy-based. Only through such comprehensive strategies can we create language learning environments that are inclusive, equitable, and free from algorithmic discrimination.

2.3 Transparency and Explainability in AI-Based Learning Systems

Transparency and explainability are foundational to building trust in AI-based English Language Learning (ELL) platforms. As these systems increasingly influence educational decisions—ranging from feedback generation to learner profiling—there is a growing demand for their operations to be understandable and accountable, especially by educators and learners with limited technical knowledge.

Explainable AI (XAI) enables users to comprehend how conclusions, such as a grammar correction or vocabulary suggestion, are derived. In the absence of such clarity, educators may struggle to verify the accuracy of AI recommendations, while learners may blindly accept suggestions that could be linguistically or contextually inappropriate (Gasser & Schmitt 2019). For example, language learning platforms like AI-based writing tutors often give feedback without revealing the reasoning behind grammar rule applications, which may lead to confusion, especially for non-native speakers with unique syntactic patterns.

In India, where multilingualism and diverse linguistic backgrounds are common, explainability becomes even more vital. Many students rely on regional dialects or translanguaging practices, and when these are penalized or misunderstood by opaque AI tools, it reinforces linguistic inequity. Transparent AI can help by highlighting the rules or datasets behind corrections and allowing users to question or override them. Furthermore, explainability is linked to ethical compliance, particularly under India's emerging Personal Data Protection Bill, which supports user rights to understand automated decision-making.

Emerging solutions include the integration of XAI modules into learning dashboards, offering visual indicators for AI-driven feedback, and contextual tips to explain corrections or suggestions (Goodman & Flaxman 2017). Efforts are also being made to train teachers to interpret AI-generated insights critically, rather than accept them at face value. This aligns with global educational guidelines, which advocate for human-centered AI in the classroom, where technology enhances rather than dictates the learning process.

2.4 Ethical Design of AI Tutors and Virtual Assistants

The ethical design of AI tutors and virtual assistants in English Language Learning (ELL) demands a multidisciplinary approach that balances educational effectiveness with student safety, fairness, and autonomy. As these tools grow more sophisticated—mimicking conversational tutors or providing real-time feedback—

they must be developed within ethical frameworks that prevent harm and support learner diversity.

One of the primary concerns in their design is cognitive and emotional alignment with the learner. AI tutors often operate as "black boxes," giving corrections or suggestions without understanding the learner's emotional state, cultural background, or prior knowledge. If improperly designed, this can demotivate students, especially younger learners or those from marginalized communities (Hagendorff .2020). Ethical design should incorporate affective computing features that detect and respond to learner frustration, hesitation, or confusion appropriately . Another significant aspect is the avoidance of over-reliance and digital dependency. AI tutors should be assistive, not authoritative. Ethical AI in education promotes "co-learning," where learners retain agency, rather than passively consuming AI-driven responses. Systems should have built-in boundaries—for instance, nudging learners to reflect on feedback rather than immediately accept it . This promotes metacognitive skills and ensures that students engage critically with language learning processes. From an Indian context, language diversity adds another ethical layer. AI tutors must accommodate multilingual learning and avoid penalizing translanguaging practices common in Indian classrooms. Moreover, voice-based assistants should be trained on accent-inclusive datasets to avoid discriminatory feedback. Ethical design also includes transparent data usage notices, minimal data retention, and inclusive visual/auditory representations that reflect varied learner identities. The future of ethical AI tutors lies in interdisciplinary co-design—bringing together educators, linguists, AI developers, ethicists, and student voices to co-create tools that are pedagogically sound and ethically grounded.

3. DATA PRIVACY IN AI-DRIVEN LEARNING SYSTEMS

3.1 Types of Data Collected in AI-Enhanced ELL Platforms

AI-enhanced English Language Learning (ELL) platforms rely heavily on data to personalize instruction, monitor progress, and adapt content in real-time. However, the variety and sensitivity of the data collected raise important ethical and privacy concerns. These platforms typically gather four broad categories of data: personal identifiers, behavioral interactions, language performance metrics, and device/environmental metadata. Personal identifiers include user name, age, gender, location, and often institutional affiliation (Heaven 2020). This information is essential for account creation and basic personalization, but it can also pose risks if mishandled or stored insecurely. Behavioral data, such as login times, session durations, and navigation patterns, help in understanding user engagement levels and learning habits.

Language performance data—such as voice recordings, grammar errors, vocabulary usage, writing samples, and pronunciation assessments—are particularly sensitive. These data points are often used to train and improve Natural Language Processing (NLP) models, which in turn provide automated feedback to learners. However, if not anonymized, this data could expose learners' linguistic weaknesses or be misused for unintended profiling.Many Indian platforms lack user-friendly data policies in vernacular languages, making it difficult for learners from rural or non-English backgrounds to give informed consent. Therefore, the type and volume of data must be carefully aligned with educational necessity, and minimized wherever possible to uphold user privacy and trust.

3.2 Consent Mechanisms and User Control

In AI-driven English Language Learning (ELL) platforms, user consent and control over data are critical to ensuring ethical deployment and sustaining trust among learners. However, there remains a significant gap between the technical implementation of consent mechanisms and the practical understanding of users, particularly in multilingual and low-digital-literacy environments .Modern ELL platforms utilize click-through agreements, cookie banners, and in-app permission prompts to obtain user consent. Yet, most of these consent forms are presented in complex legal language, often in English, which poses barriers to genuine informed consent among non-native speakers or young learners (Holstein et al., 2019) . A meaningful consent model in ELL must offer clear, accessible, and multilingual explanations of what data is collected, how it will be used, and who will have access to it.

Beyond initial consent, user control over their data is equally crucial. This includes the ability to opt out of data sharing, revoke access, or request deletion of stored data. However, many ELL platforms, especially those operating in India's edtech sector, lack robust data dashboards or granular privacy settings that empower users with such control. Learners often remain unaware of the extent to which their speech, text, and usage patterns are stored and utilized by AI engines for training or commercial reuse.

To bridge this gap, scholars advocate for dynamic consent models—where users are periodically reminded of their data rights and can modify permissions over time. Such approaches not only respect the evolving understanding and maturity of users but also foster a culture of data agency in educational technology. Moreover, involving teachers and institutions in guiding students through consent-related choices, especially in school-based deployments, can further strengthen ethical practices .

3.3 Data Storage, Protection, and Breach Risks

In AI-powered English Language Learning (ELL) systems, the storage, protection, and management of learner data are paramount concerns that require strict adherence to data protection principles. Given the sensitive nature of the data collected, such as speech patterns, learning progress, and behavioral analytics, educational platforms must implement robust data security measures to protect against unauthorized access and data breaches

.The storage infrastructure for ELL platforms often relies on cloud-based services, which offer scalability but also introduce potential risks related to third-party access. Many companies storing data on cloud services face challenges in adhering to regional data protection regulations like the General Data Protection Regulation (GDPR) in Europe or India's Personal Data Protection Bill (PDPB), both of which mandate stringent controls on how personal data is stored, processed, and shared . The lack of data localization or proper encryption often leads to concerns about jurisdictional conflicts and legal compliance, especially in countries with nascent data protection laws like India.

Additionally, the rising number of cyber-attacks targeting educational technology firms has brought to light the risk of data breaches (Jones 2020). A breach can expose a wide range of personally identifiable information (PII), including learners' identities, language proficiency levels, and learning habits, which, if misused, could have detrimental impacts on both individual privacy and institutional trust. For instance, in one study conducted on Indian educational apps, it was found that many platforms were not encrypting speech data, making it vulnerable to interception and misuse.

To mitigate these risks, platforms must adopt end-to-end encryption, two-factor authentication, and regular security audits. Additionally, the principle of data minimization—limiting the collection of sensitive information to what is strictly necessary—should be enforced to reduce exposure. It is also essential for institutions to provide clear policies regarding data retention and deletion: learners should have the ability to request data deletion once their learning journey concludes or when they no longer use the platform.

3.4 Compliance with Global and Local Privacy Regulations

As the deployment of Artificial Intelligence (AI) in English Language Learning (ELL) systems accelerates, the compliance with global and local privacy regulations becomes a significant challenge. These regulations, such as the General Data Protection Regulation (GDPR) in Europe and the Personal Data Protection Bill (PDPB) in India, impose strict rules regarding the collection, processing, and storage of personal data (Koene et al., 2019). For AI-powered ELL platforms, compliance with these regulations is essential for protecting learners' privacy, fostering trust, and ensuring legal conformity.

The GDPR, effective from 2018, mandates that educational technology platforms obtain explicit consent before collecting any personal data. It also grants users the right to access, rectify, and delete their data, reinforcing the data minimization principle, where only the minimum necessary data should be collected for learning purposes. ELL platforms operating within the EU or interacting with EU citizens must also ensure data portability, enabling users to easily transfer their personal data to another provider. Failure to comply with GDPR can result in significant fines, making it critical for AI-powered education tools to integrate features that comply with these requirements.

Similarly, India's PDP Bill (drafted in 2019 and expected to pass into law soon) sets forth similar guidelines, with an emphasis on data localization and user consent. The bill proposes that personal data of Indian citizens be stored within India and requires data handlers to obtain explicit consent before collecting data from minors (Kroll, 2018) . For AI-driven platforms, this means that developers must incorporate privacy by design and ensure that they are fully transparent about how learners' data is being used. The PDPB also emphasizes that sensitive personal data, such as biometric information or speech data, must be handled with extra care and may not be shared without informed consent.

For educational institutions, the compliance journey can be complex, particularly for platforms operating in multiple jurisdictions. Cross-border data flow becomes a significant concern, especially when AI algorithms are trained on large datasets that include data from different countries. The EU-US Privacy Shield and Standard Contractual Clauses (SCCs) are mechanisms that govern international data transfers but need to be carefully evaluated and implemented by AI developers.

Therefore, ELL platforms must design their systems with both GDPR and PDPB principles in mind. Incorporating robust consent management systems, data anonymization techniques, and regular audits will ensure that they remain compliant and reduce the risk of privacy violations. Educational institutions, too, must stay abreast of the evolving legal landscape and adopt institutional policies that align with these regulations.

4. LEARNER-CENTRIC ETHICAL CHALLENGES

4.1 Privacy Concerns for Young Learners and Minors

Privacy concerns for young learners and minors using AI-driven English Language Learning (ELL) platforms are of significant ethical concern. Children are more vulnerable to the misuse of personal data, and their cognitive and emotional development requires extra protections in digital environments. AI-powered systems in education collect vast amounts of data, including interactions, speech patterns, video recordings, and learning behaviors, which can expose minors to privacy risks if not handled appropriately. These risks are particularly critical as minors may not fully understand the implications of their data being collected, shared, or used for purposes beyond their educational needs.

In many jurisdictions, such as the European Union under the GDPR and the Children's Online Privacy Protection Act (COPPA) in the United States, stringent laws require platforms to obtain parental consent before collecting data from minors. However, the situation becomes more complex in countries like India, where regulations around data privacy for children are still in development (Larsson 2020). The Personal Data Protection Bill (PDPB) has proposed specific provisions for the protection of children's data, highlighting the importance of informed consent from parents and guardians before children's data is processed. Additionally, it recommends the creation of child-centric privacy policies that ensure the collection of minimal personal data and its use for educational purposes only.

The lack of proper safeguards can result in the exposure of sensitive information, such as behavioral data, learning difficulties, and biometric information, which may be exploited by malicious entities or lead to discrimination. Therefore, AI systems used by educational platforms should be designed with privacy by design principles that minimize data collection, anonymize sensitive data, and ensure that only those with verified consent can access or process data related to minors.

4.2 Impacts of Surveillance and Monitoring on Learning Behavior

The surveillance and continuous monitoring of students in AI-enhanced ELL platforms raise ethical concerns about the impact on learning behaviors and student autonomy. Many AI-based systems track every action a learner takes—such as time spent on exercises, response accuracy, and interaction patterns—leading to the collection of extensive behavioral data. While this data is typically used to personalize the learning experience, it can also result in significant intrusiveness and loss of privacy for students, especially in virtual classrooms where the boundaries between learning and surveillance can be blurred (Lepri et al., 2018).

The constant tracking of students' behavior may lead to a surveillance culture where learners feel that every action is being watched, potentially hindering their critical thinking and creative expression. This constant monitoring can create feelings of discomfort and anxiety, which could negatively affect the learning process, particularly for young learners or those with certain psychological predispositions.

For instance, if AI tools continuously monitor students' responses, they may adjust their behaviors based on what they believe the system is "expecting," which can compromise the authenticity of learning experiences.

Furthermore, while surveillance can help educators identify students' strengths and weaknesses, there is a risk of over-reliance on AI-driven data that fails to capture the nuances of human learning. For example, AI systems may focus on quantitative metrics like response time or completion rates, which do not always reflect the true learning progress of students. This over-monitoring can also lead to data fatigue and create a toxic learning environment where students feel they are constantly being judged or assessed.

To mitigate these risks, educational platforms should implement ethical guidelines around monitoring. These guidelines should ensure that data collected is used only for educational purposes and that student autonomy is respected (Lu, 2021). It is also essential to educate students and parents about the surveillance practices, allowing them to make informed decisions about their participation in AI-powered learning environments.

4.3 Digital Footprint and the Long-Term Use of Learner Data

In AI-driven English Language Learning (ELL) environments, every user interaction contributes to the creation of a digital footprint—a trail of data that includes browsing history, engagement metrics, performance patterns, keystroke dynamics, and even audio or video recordings. While this data is integral to the personalization and optimization of AI systems, its long-term use poses ethical dilemmas around user privacy, data ownership, and the potential misuse of information.

One major concern is that learners, especially minors, may not be aware of how their digital footprints are stored or used over time. These data trails may persist in cloud systems long after a student discontinues using a platform, leading to indefinite data retention and profiling risks. Such data could be used to make assumptions about learners' abilities, behaviors, or even mental health, affecting future educational or professional opportunities (Marée et al., 2013). Additionally, third-party analytics tools often integrated into ELL platforms may repurpose user data for marketing or research without proper anonymization or consent, which undermines the principles of ethical AI.

In India, the proposed Digital Personal Data Protection (DPDP) Act, 2023 emphasizes the storage limitation principle, which requires data fiduciaries to delete personal data once the purpose is fulfilled or upon withdrawal of consent. However, there is a gap between policy and practice in most EdTech platforms. Ensuring data minimization, purpose limitation, and clear data retention policies are crucial steps toward protecting learners from lifelong digital surveillance (McKeown et al., 2017).

Furthermore, long-term data use raises issues of re-identification risks, where anonymized data can be cross-referenced with other datasets to identify individuals. This undermines claims of privacy protection and highlights the urgent need for privacy-preserving technologies, such as differential privacy and federated learning, to safeguard learner data over time .

4.4 Informed Consent and Autonomy in AI Use

Informed consent is the cornerstone of ethical AI deployment in education. In the context of AI-enhanced ELL platforms, informed consent means that learners (or guardians, in the case of minors) should understand what data is collected, how it is used, and what risks or benefits are associated with its processing. However, in practice, consent mechanisms are often opaque, buried in lengthy terms of service, or designed as click-through agreements with minimal real understanding by users.

True informed consent requires transparency, accessibility, and an understanding of technical implications. Learners should be given control over their data, including the ability to opt in or out of certain data processing functions and to withdraw consent at any time. However, AI systems are typically designed to function optimally with full data access, which raises concerns that denying consent may lead to a compromised learning experience—an ethical paradox that affects learner autonomy.

Autonomy also involves the right to choose whether and how AI is used in learning. For instance, students may prefer human tutoring over AI interaction or may not be comfortable with facial recognition or voice analysis features in language learning tools. Platforms should provide alternative pathways and clearly communicate the implications of using or rejecting AI components. Failure to do so may result in coercion by design, where learners feel forced to accept surveillance or data sharing in order to access educational resources .

In India, where digital literacy varies widely across regions, especially in rural and marginalized communities, informed consent must be contextualized and localized. This includes offering consent forms in regional languages, using visuals or voice-based formats for comprehension, and involving educators in facilitating understanding. Empowering users through data literacy education is essential to support informed decision-making and uphold digital dignity.

5. INSTITUTIONAL AND TEACHER RESPONSIBILITIES

5.1 Role of Educators in Ethical AI Integration

Educators are pivotal in ensuring the ethical deployment of AI tools in English Language Learning (ELL) settings. As the frontline facilitators of AI-enhanced pedagogy, teachers play multiple roles: curators of appropriate technologies, monitors of student data usage, and mediators of ethical understanding within classrooms. However, many educators are not formally trained in the implications of AI, especially regarding privacy, bias, and algorithmic decision-making.

To ethically integrate AI into ELL, educators must first understand how AI algorithms function—what kind of data they rely on, how they adapt based on input, and where bias might occur. Teachers should also be equipped to critically assess AI recommendations rather than adopting them uncritically. For example, predictive writing suggestions or grammar corrections by AI tools may contain cultural biases or reinforce normative language structures that exclude non-native varieties of English.

Additionally, educators have a moral responsibility to create awareness among learners about how their data is used, encourage questioning of AI outputs, and foster a culture of digital agency. They should promote transparency in the classroom by explaining AI tool functionalities and ensuring students understand what is being monitored or stored (Mittelstadt et al., 2016). This is especially vital in India, where digital divides persist, and students may not fully grasp the implications of AI use in their learning environments.

5.2 Policy Guidelines for Safe and Transparent Use of AI Tools

Developing and enforcing policy guidelines is essential to regulate the deployment of AI tools in ELL. Such policies should cover data privacy, algorithmic accountability, informed consent, transparency, equity, and accessibility. Institutions must move beyond ad-hoc adoption of AI platforms to a more structured, policy-driven approach that safeguards learner rights Policy frameworks should mandate regular audits of AI tools to detect and correct biases in language modeling and assessment. Furthermore, guidelines must ensure that learners and teachers are informed about what data is being collected, who has access to it, and how long it will be retained. Institutions should also publish data governance policies that include provisions for data minimization and anonymization. Another critical component of safe AI use is vendor accountability (Miyake 2007). EdTech companies must comply with local and international laws such as India's Digital Personal Data Protection (DPDP) Act, 2023, and the General Data Protection Regulation (GDPR) in the EU. Institutions should require vendors to submit ethical impact assessments before approving AI tools for classroom use.

Furthermore, policies should promote access equity—ensuring that AI tools are accessible across linguistic, socio-economic, and regional boundaries. This is particularly crucial in India, where language diversity and digital disparities can exacerbate educational inequities. To ensure effectiveness, these policies should be co-developed with input from educators, technologists, ethicists, students, and policymakers, fostering a participatory governance model. Transparent policies not only protect learners but also help build institutional trust in AI-enhanced learning environments.

5.3 Professional Development on AI Ethics and Data Security

As AI becomes increasingly embedded in English Language Learning (ELL) platforms, professional development (PD) for teachers and administrators on AI ethics and data security is not just important—it's essential. Most educators, particularly in developing contexts like India, lack formal training in AI's operational logic, ethical pitfalls, and data protection practices. This gap can lead to unintentional misuse of AI tools, risking student privacy and fairness in instruction. Effective PD must go beyond basic digital literacy to include modules on algorithmic bias, data anonymization, informed consent, surveillance risks, and compliance with data regulations such as India's Digital Personal Data Protection (DPDP) Act and global norms like the GDPR (Nelson & Ketelhut 2008). Training must also include hands-on practice with real AI tools, helping educators critically assess features like adaptive feedback, automated grading, and predictive analytics .

Institutions should offer continuous PD opportunities rather than one-time workshops, integrating AI ethics into teacher education curricula and certification programs. Moreover, PD should be contextually relevant—taking into account linguistic diversity, socio-cultural sensitivities, and infrastructure disparities often seen in Indian classrooms. Collaborative learning platforms where educators can share ethical dilemmas, case studies, and mitigation strategies can also enhance long-term understanding. Empowered educators are better equipped to safeguard student data, advocate for ethical AI use, and guide students in responsible technology practices.

5.4 Institutional Frameworks for Ethical Oversight

Institutions bear the overarching responsibility for ensuring that AI tools used in ELL environments align with ethical principles, legal mandates, and educational equity goals. An effective institutional framework should begin with the creation of ethical oversight committees or AI governance boards tasked with reviewing AI tool adoption, ensuring compliance, and resolving ethical dilemmas. These frameworks must include clearly defined policies on data collection, access controls, consent management, algorithmic audits, and accountability structures for breaches or bias incidents. Furthermore, institutions should require ethical impact assessments before any AI tool is implemented—evaluating not just functionality, but implications for learner autonomy and fairness .At the policy level, institutions should also adopt ethics-by-design principles—embedding transparency, explainability, and inclusiveness into their procurement and deployment processes (Neumann & Hood 2009). For example, when adopting grammar correction or pronunciation scoring tools, institutions should ensure these do not disproportionately penalize regional accents or dialectical variations common in multilingual nations like India. A proactive ethical culture also requires regular review cycles, open feedback channels with students and faculty, and mandatory training for administrative staff on AI ethics. Institutions can partner with EdTech providers to co-create customized, ethical AI tools that reflect the needs of diverse learner populations.

In India, the integration of such frameworks can align with broader National Education Policy (NEP) 2020 goals, which stress technological integration with a learner-centered and inclusive approach. Without institutional accountability, even well-intended AI tools can perpetuate inequality, compromise privacy, or erode trust in education.

6. CULTURAL AND CONTEXTUAL SENSITIVITIES

6.1 Cross-Cultural Ethics in Global Language Classrooms

AI-powered English Language Learning (ELL) tools increasingly operate in global and multicultural classrooms, creating the need for cross-cultural ethical considerations. AI systems—trained on predominantly Western linguistic norms—often fail to respect or accommodate the diverse socio-cultural values, idiomatic expressions, and communication styles found in multilingual countries like India, or across South Asia and Africa.

An AI grammar checker, for example, might erroneously flag Indian English expressions such as "do the needful" or "prepone" as incorrect, even though they are contextually accepted and widely used in Indian academia and administration . This raises ethical concerns around cultural erasure, linguistic imperialism, and the reinforcement of one-size-fits-all language standards. Ethical AI design in ELL must prioritize context sensitivity, incorporating datasets from diverse Englishes (e.g., Indian, African, Southeast Asian variants). Moreover, ELL platforms should provide culturally adaptive feedback—where corrections respect the learner's linguistic background instead of imposing native-speaker norms as the default. Educators and developers must also be aware of value-laden cultural assumptions embedded in AI tools, especially in reading comprehension or dialogue-based training modules (Pifarre & Cobos 2010). Topics involving religion, gender roles, family structures, or political references must be handled sensitively, ensuring that AI does not alienate learners from conservative, collectivist, or indigenous cultural contexts.

6.2 Inclusivity and Representation in Language AI Datasets

One of the most critical ethical challenges in AI-driven English education lies in the inclusivity and representation of training data. Most mainstream AI models are trained on English corpora dominated by content from North America, Europe, and Australia. As a result, dialects, accents, and usage patterns from the Global South—especially India, Africa, and Southeast Asia—are grossly underrepresented. This underrepresentation can cause biased outcomes, such as incorrect feedback, pronunciation penalization, or invisibility of regional names, festivals, or real-world references in content generation. In India, this is especially problematic for learners from tribal, rural, or non-Hindi-speaking backgrounds, who may find that AI tools neither understand nor support their local idioms or language interference patterns.

Ethical design of language AI must include dataset diversification strategies—incorporating transcribed speech, text, and examples from Indian English, Nigerian English, Malaysian English, and so on. Additionally, community-based dataset curation involving regional educators and linguists can ensure that AI captures real linguistic richness rather than reinforcing dominant paradigms (Rahwan, 2018). Another important strategy is the implementation of bias audits—regular testing to ensure that tools perform equitably across different socio-linguistic groups. For pronunciation AI, for instance, the system should accurately score speakers with Tamil, Bengali, or Marathi accents without unfairly penalizing them against British or American norms. An inclusive AI doesn't merely correct language; it validates diverse identities, making ELL not only more effective but also more empowering.

6.3 Ethical Concerns in Automated Feedback and Assessment

Automated feedback systems in AI-driven English Language Learning (ELL) offer scalable, real-time responses to grammar, vocabulary, and pronunciation. However, they raise significant ethical concerns, particularly in the areas of fairness, accuracy, and learner autonomy. Most automated scoring algorithms lack the sensitivity to contextual factors such as a learner's linguistic background, learning goals, or cognitive diversity. For instance, a Tamil-speaking learner may produce a grammatically unconventional but communicatively effective sentence. An AI writing tool may still mark it as incorrect due to rigid syntactic expectations, ignoring pragmatic competence. This not only risks demotivating learners but also promotes an overly standardized notion of "correct English."

There's also concern around opaque scoring systems, where learners are given marks or rankings without any meaningful explanation. These black-box models may propagate algorithmic bias, leading to unfair assessments—especially for non-native speakers from underrepresented linguistic groups (Raji & Buolamwini, 2019). Moreover, excessive dependence on AI-generated feedback can reduce learner agency and critical thinking. Students may follow automated suggestions blindly, diminishing their ability to self-edit or understand the rationale behind corrections. This has pedagogical implications, particularly for higher-order language development, such as argumentation and tone. Ethically robust systems must incorporate human-in-the-loop designs, where instructors can review or override AI feedback. Additionally, explanatory feedback—providing learners with justifications and examples—should be prioritized over purely corrective mechanisms.

6.4 Transparency and Explainability in Language AI Systems

Transparency and explainability are central to the ethical deployment of AI in language education. Most AI systems used in ELL—including chatbots, writing assistants, and speech evaluators—function as black boxes. Learners and educators often have little insight into how decisions are made, what data is used, or why certain feedback is provided (Ravindran & Bose, 2023). Lack of transparency raises several concerns. First, it undermines learner trust, especially when feedback is inconsistent or contextually irrelevant. For example, if a sentence like "I have returned back" is flagged without explaining redundancy, the user may not understand the linguistic logic or be able to apply the correction in other contexts. Second, explainability is crucial for accountability (Roschelle 2013). When AI misjudges a learner's answer or pronunciation, both the user and the educator must be able to trace the reasoning path. This is particularly important in high-stakes environments such as IELTS, TOEFL, or national assessments where automated scoring may have real consequences.

From an ethical standpoint, language AI systems should implement explainable AI (XAI) principles: offering justifications for corrections, confidence scores for decisions, and, ideally, visual or textual cues to guide learners. For instance, a writing AI can highlight verb tense errors and provide rule-based explanations or alternate usage examples. Transparency also extends to data sourcing and model limitations. Ethical guidelines must compel developers to disclose whether the AI was trained on native or non-native corpora, the language variants it recognizes, and the potential biases it carries. When learners understand how AI makes decisions, they are more likely to engage critically, question outcomes, and grow as autonomous language users.

7. CASE STUDIES AND CURRENT PRACTICES

7.1 Ethical AI Implementation in Indian ELL EdTech

The Indian EdTech ecosystem has witnessed a surge in AI-powered English Language Learning (ELL) platforms, particularly post-pandemic. Among the most notable examples are EnglishBolo, Hello English, and Enguru, which integrate AI to personalize instruction, generate feedback, and automate assessments. These platforms are increasingly integrating ethical frameworks to address issues of privacy, fairness, and learner autonomy, though challenges persist.

EnglishBolo, developed through a partnership between IL&FS and the British Council, demonstrates a responsible AI approach by limiting data collection to essential learner performance metrics, using anonymized IDs, and offering clear user consent mechanisms. The platform refrains from storing voice data permanently and allows users to opt-out of specific data uses, aligning partially with India's proposed Digital Personal Data Protection (DPDP) Act. Hello English, a popular mobile app with over 50 million users, uses Natural Language Processing (NLP) and predictive learning algorithms to tailor lessons based on learner profiles. The app developers have increasingly moved toward ethical personalization, ensuring that adaptive learning doesn't reinforce linguistic stereotypes or restrict content diversity. They introduced a transparency panel in 2023 explaining why certain grammar or vocabulary suggestions are made, enhancing learner trust and agency .

However, ethical blind spots remain. Many platforms use freemium models that rely heavily on passive data collection, behavioral tracking, and recommendation engines. In some cases, users—particularly children—may not fully comprehend how their data is being processed, highlighting the need for child-specific privacy frameworks.

In response to these concerns, several Indian startups have begun incorporating third-party audits, explainable AI models, and teacher-in-the-loop mechanisms (Roschelle et al., 2011). Enguru, for instance, includes live tutors to complement AI feedback, balancing algorithmic support with human pedagogical judgment. It also flags confidence scores alongside automated corrections, encouraging learners to make independent decisions.

Furthermore, initiatives like the AI in Education Guidelines by CBSE (2022) and NEP 2020's digital ethics focus have prompted EdTech firms to rethink ethical AI design. The industry is gradually shifting toward a learner-centric AI framework—emphasizing fairness, accountability, inclusivity, and transparency (FAIR principles).

7.2 Global Examples

The integration of Artificial Intelligence in English Language Learning (ELL) tools like Duolingo, Grammarly, and Edmodo has revolutionized how learners engage with language content globally. Each platform exemplifies distinct ethical practices and challenges associated with AI in education, especially concerning personalization, data privacy, and algorithmic accountability. Duolingo, one of the most widely used language apps, employs AI-driven gamification, adaptive learning algorithms, and behavioral analytics. The company introduced a transparency report in 2022 outlining how learner data is used to train its machine learning models for personalized content delivery (Roschelle et al., 2010). However, ethical concerns have emerged around data retention and the extent of user profiling, especially among minors . Duolingo has responded by adopting Federated Learning models in some of its testing features, reducing centralized data dependency and enhancing privacy.

Grammarly, which utilizes NLP and deep learning to provide grammar and stylistic feedback, has made strides in explainable AI. In 2023, the platform launched an "Insights" feature explaining the rationale behind AI-suggested corrections, helping users understand rather than blindly follow feedback. Despite these steps, critiques persist over potential algorithmic bias in tone detection—where non-native English expressions are sometimes mischaracterized as impolite or incorrect. Grammarly's developers have since expanded their training datasets to include more diverse linguistic inputs to address this issue.

Edmodo, a social learning network, has integrated AI to support moderation, assignment feedback, and classroom analytics. While it offers valuable teacher dashboards, studies have shown that Edmodo's earlier versions lacked robust consent protocols and clear data-sharing disclosures, especially in regions without strong privacy laws. In response, Edmodo updated its policies in 2022 to be GDPR and FERPA compliant, incorporating clearer opt-in mechanisms and more granular data access controls.

These platforms collectively underscore the importance of integrating ethics-by-design in AI tools. Best practices include:

- **Contextual transparency** (explaining recommendations),
- **Inclusive data practices** (avoiding bias through diverse training data), and
- **User-centric privacy controls** (e.g., data portability and deletion requests).

Though progress has been made, these examples highlight that user trust in AI-enhanced ELL hinges on ongoing commitment to ethical governance, particularly when scaling across global and multilingual audiences.

7.3 Lessons from Policy Failures and Data Misuse

AI-powered English Language Learning (ELL) platforms have occasionally faced significant setbacks due to insufficient data governance, lack of ethical oversight, and opaque privacy policies. Lessons from these failures stress the importance of regulatory compliance, transparent data practices, and ethical safeguards.

One prominent example is the 2019 Edmodo data breach, which exposed sensitive student and teacher information affecting over 77 million users. The breach, attributed to weak encryption and absence of role-based access controls, illustrated how educational platforms are high-value targets for cyber attacks (Russell 2019). Although Edmodo later improved its privacy protocols, this event highlighted the cost of delayed compliance with standards like GDPR and the absence of early-stage privacy-by-design thinking. In India, the case of DIKSHA (Digital Infrastructure for Knowledge Sharing)—a government-run e-learning platform—showed ethical gaps when user data was shared with third-party analytics tools without adequate consent. An audit conducted in 2022 by the Internet Freedom Foundation revealed that students, especially minors, were unaware of how their interaction data was being processed or monetized. This instance emphasized the critical need for informed consent mechanisms and child-specific data protection norms.

Another relevant case involved AI chatbots integrated into LMS platforms, where predictive models flagged students for low engagement without adequate explainability or recourse. In several US-based pilot schools, flagged students reported stigmatization and biased assessments, which were later traced to algorithmic errors stemming from underrepresented language patterns in training data.

These failures suggest key preventive strategies:

- Embedding continuous audit trails in AI systems,
- Enforcing user education and feedback loops, and
- Strengthening regional legislation such as India's Digital Personal Data Protection Act, 2023, in alignment with global standards.

7.4 Evaluation of OpenAI and Google's AI Ethics Policies

Major AI developers like OpenAI and Google play a pivotal role in shaping the ethical frameworks adopted across ELL tools. Their policies directly influence how educational institutions and developers incorporate AI responsibly.

OpenAI, the creator of ChatGPT, emphasizes a human-in-the-loop approach, transparency, and responsible use in educational contexts. In 2023, it updated its Usage Policies to explicitly restrict the use of its models in scenarios involving deceptive practices, unauthorized surveillance, or profiling of minors (Santos-Martin, et al., 2012). Moreover, OpenAI's commitment to model explainability and bias reduction through fine-tuning has enabled safer use in ELL environments. However, critiques remain about the opacity in dataset origins and the risk of hallucinations in sensitive educational contexts.

Google's AI principles, launched in 2018 and periodically revised, focus on safety, fairness, privacy, and accountability. In 2022, Google expanded its Know Your Data tool to help developers evaluate bias in datasets used in AI-powered applications like Google Classroom and Socratic. Google also introduced differential privacy mechanisms in some of its educational tools, enhancing anonymization without losing analytical value. Google's AI ethics enforcement still lacks local contextual sensitivity, particularly in multilingual education ecosystems in South Asia (Sao Pedro et al., 2014). Despite good intentions, both organizations must move from principle-based ethics to enforceable accountability mechanisms, ensuring that ethical standards are auditable, contextual, and globally adaptable.

8. EMERGING TRENDS AND FUTURE OUTLOOK

8.1 Federated Learning and Privacy-Preserving AI

The shift toward federated learning (FL) has marked a significant leap in addressing privacy concerns in AI-powered English Language Learning (ELL). FL enables model training across decentralized devices without transferring raw data to a central server, thus minimizing privacy risks and enhancing data sovereignty (Sclater 2017). In India, the IIT Madras-led "Project FLAME" piloted a federated learning model integrated into English learning apps targeting rural schoolchildren. This setup maintained user privacy while allowing language personalization using only edge data. Internationally, Google's GBoard keyboard—powered by FL—demonstrated success in training language models without accessing user messages, making it a relevant case for ELL platforms. Federated learning not only strengthens compliance with privacy legislation like the EU's GDPR or India's Digital Personal Data Protection Act (2023) but also fosters equity in data representation, as models learn from diverse linguistic users without centralized bias.

8.2 Transparent AI: Designing Ethical Dashboards and Audit Trails

Transparency in AI systems is critical for trust, especially in educational environments. The use of ethical dashboards and automated audit trails allows stakeholders-including learners, educators, and regulators- to track how AI models make decisions, especially in assessments, feedback, and content recommendations. Leading platforms like Coursera and ELSA Speak have incorporated AI explainability layers, allowing users to see how pronunciation scores or grammar corrections are derived. These visual dashboards enhance user agency and reduce algorithmic opacity.

In India, efforts by the Centre for Internet and Society (CIS) have promoted the design of localized explainable AI models for edtech, especially in multilingual contexts. Ethical dashboards not only facilitate algorithmic accountability but also help identify bias, drift, and misuse in real-time, creating a feedback-rich loop that improves both model and pedagogy .

8.3 Evolution of Global Ethical Standards for AI in Education

International frameworks for AI ethics in education are rapidly evolving to address rising concerns of surveillance, discrimination, and dehumanization. UNESCO's 2021 "Recommendation on the Ethics of Artificial Intelligence" has provided a landmark guideline focusing on inclusion, transparency, and data governance in education.

Parallelly, the IEEE's Ethically Aligned Design for Education Systems promotes standards that ensure learner-centric AI, emphasizing fairness, safety, and consent. In India, NITI Aayog's discussion paper on "Responsible AI for All" calls for context-specific, culturally sensitive ethical protocols for deploying AI in learning environments (NITI Aayog, 2021).

As more countries adopt AI literacy and ethics education as curricular goals, the global trend is moving toward standardization of ethical benchmarks, allowing for cross-border edtech collaborations and universal learner protections.

8.4 Toward Human-Centered, Privacy-Respecting Language Learning

Future ELL systems must prioritize human-centric design, where AI supports rather than replaces educators, and privacy-by-default becomes a core architecture principle. This includes:

- Real-time consent layers,
- Adaptive difficulty without intrusive profiling,
- Culturally sensitive content generation, and
- Built-in mechanisms for user feedback and redressal.

Startups in India such as OckyPocky and Multibhashi have begun integrating age-appropriate nudges, anonymized feedback loops, and gender-neutral avatars to make language learning both ethical and engaging .

Globally, researchers are exploring emotion-aware AI tutors that adjust pace and complexity based on learner sentiment while ensuring empathy and fairness (Shaw 2013). The future of ELL lies not just in technological advancement, but in embedding values of dignity, agency, and contextual fairness within every layer of design and delivery.

9. CONCLUSION

AI-powered English Language Learning (ELL) systems are rapidly evolving, bringing transformative potential to global education while raising critical ethical concerns. As these technologies become increasingly integrated into mainstream learning platforms, the need to balance innovation with privacy, fairness, transparency, and inclusivity becomes paramount. Emerging trends such as federated learning, ethical dashboards, and global ethical frameworks are reshaping the landscape toward more responsible AI deployment. The future of ELL lies not just in technical sophistication but in designing systems that respect learner autonomy, safeguard data, and uphold human values—ensuring that the benefits of AI are equitably distributed across diverse linguistic and cultural contexts.

REFERENCES

Amershi, S., Weld, D., Vorvoreanu, M., Fourney, A., Nushi, B., Collisson, P., & Horvitz, E. (2019). Guidelines for human-AI interaction. *Proceedings of the ACM Conference on Human Factors in Computing Systems*, 1-13.

Baker, R. S. (2019). Challenges for the future of educational data mining: The Baker learning analytics prizes. *Journal of Educational Data Mining*, *11*(1), 1–17.

Binns, R. (2018). Fairness in machine learning: Lessons from political philosophy. *Proceedings of the Conference on Fairness, Accountability, and Transparency*, 149-159.

Brundage, M., Avin, S., Clark, J., Toner, H., Eckersley, P., Garfinkel, B., . . . Amodei, D. (2018). The malicious use of artificial intelligence: Forecasting, prevention, and mitigation. arXiv preprint arXiv:1802.07228.

Crawford, K. (2021). *Atlas of AI: Power, Politics, and the Planetary Costs of Artificial Intelligence*. Yale University Press.

Dignum, V. (2019). *Responsible Artificial Intelligence: How to Develop and Use AI in a Responsible Way*. Springer. DOI: 10.1007/978-3-030-30371-6

Floridi, L. (2019). Establishing the rules for building trustworthy AI. *Nature Machine Intelligence*, *1*(6), 261–262. DOI: 10.1038/s42256-019-0055-y

Gasser, U., & Schmitt, C. (2019). AI governance: A research agenda. SSRN Electronic Journal, 12(3), 1-15.

Goodman, B., & Flaxman, S. (2017). European Union regulations on algorithmic decision-making and a "right to explanation.". *AI Magazine*, *38*(3), 50–57. DOI: 10.1609/aimag.v38i3.2741

Hagendorff, T. (2020). The ethics of AI ethics: An evaluation of guidelines. *Minds and Machines*, *30*(1), 99–120. DOI: 10.1007/s11023-020-09517-8

Heaven, W. D. (2020). AI-powered education tools raise concerns over student data privacy. *MIT Technology Review*, *123*(4), 45–50.

Holstein, K., Wortman Vaughan, J., Daumé, H., Dudik, M., & Wallach, H. (2019). Improving fairness in machine learning systems: What do industry practitioners need? *Proceedings of the Conference on Fairness, Accountability, and Transparency*, 563-573. DOI: 10.1145/3290605.3300830

Jones, K. M. (2020). Data ethics and student privacy: The risks of AI surveillance in education. *Ethics and Information Technology*, *22*(1), 31–44.

Koene, A., Perez, E., & Carter, C. J. (2019). A governance framework for AI in education. *AI & Society*, *34*(4), 765–777.

Kroll, J. A. (2018). The fallacy of inscrutability. *Proceedings of the ACM Conference on Fairness, Accountability, and Transparency*, 369-378.

Larsson, S. (2020). AI transparency: A matter of human rights. *AI & Society*, *35*(2), 341–349.

Lepri, B., Oliver, N., Letouzé, E., Pentland, A. S., & Vinck, P. (2018). Fair, transparent, and accountable algorithmic decision-making processes. *Philosophy & Technology*, *31*(4), 611–627. DOI: 10.1007/s13347-017-0279-x

Loke, S. K., Al-Sallami, H. S., Wright, D. F., McDonald, J., Jadhav, S., & Duffull, S. B. (2012). Challenges in integrating a complex systems computer simulation in class: An educational design research. *Australasian Journal of Educational Technology*, *28*(4).

Lu, L. (2021). Ethical AI in education: Challenges and policy implications. *Journal of Ethics and Education*, *15*(1), 21–36.

Marée, T. J., van Bruggen, J. M., & Jochems, W. M. (2013). Effective self-regulated science learning through multimedia-enriched skeleton concept maps. *Research in Science & Technological Education*, *31*(1), 16–30. DOI: 10.1080/02635143.2013.782283

McKeown, J., Hmelo-Silver, C. E., Jeong, H., Hartley, K., Faulkner, R., & Emmanuel, N. (2017). A meta-synthesis of CSCL literature in STEM education. In Smith, B. K., Borge, M., Mercier, E., & Lim, K.-Y. (Eds.), *Proceedings of CSCL 2017*. Philadelphia, PA: International Society of the Learning Sciences.

Mittelstadt, B. D., Allo, P., Taddeo, M., Wachter, S., & Floridi, L. (2016). The ethics of algorithms: Mapping the debate. *Big Data & Society*, *3*(2), 2053951716679679. DOI: 10.1177/2053951716679679

Miyake, N. (2007). Computer supported collaborative learning. In Andrews, R., & Haythornwaite, C. (Eds.), *Sage handbook of E-learning research* (pp. 248–266). Sage. DOI: 10.4135/9781848607859.n11

Nelson, B. C., & Ketelhut, D. J. (2008). Exploring embedded guidance and self-efficacy in educational multi-user virtual environments. *International Journal of Computer-Supported Collaborative Learning*, *3*(4), 413–427. DOI: 10.1007/s11412-008-9049-1

Neumann, D. L., & Hood, M. (2009). The effects of using a wiki on student engagement and learning of report writing skills in a university statistics course. *Australasian Journal of Educational Technology, 25*(3), 382–398. DOI: 10.14742/ajet.1141

Pifarre, M., & Cobos, R. (2010). Promoting metacognitive skills through peer scaffolding in a CSCL environment. *International Journal of Computer-Supported Collaborative Learning, 5*(2), 237–253. DOI: 10.1007/s11412-010-9084-6

Rahwan, I. (2018). Society-in-the-loop: Programming AI for social norms. *Ethics and Information Technology, 20*(1), 5–14. DOI: 10.1007/s10676-017-9430-8

Raji, I. D., & Buolamwini, J. (2019). Actionable auditing: Investigating the impact of publicly naming biased performance results of commercial AI products. Proceedings of the AAAI/ACM Conference on AI Ethics and Society, 429-435.

Roschelle, J. (2013). Special issue on CSCL [Discussion]. *Educational Psychologist, 48*(1), 67–70. DOI: 10.1080/00461520.2012.749445

Roschelle, J., Bakia, M., Toyama, Y., & Patton, C. (2011). Eight issues for learning scientists about education and the economy. *Journal of the Learning Sciences, 20*(1), 3–49. DOI: 10.1080/10508406.2011.528318

Roschelle, J., Rafanan, K., Estrella, G., Nussbaum, M., & Claro, S. (2010). From handheld collaborative tool to effective classroom module: Embedding CSCL in a broader design framework. *Computers & Education, 55*(3), 1018–1026. DOI: 10.1016/j.compedu.2010.04.012

Russell, S. (2019). *Human Compatible: Artificial Intelligence and the Problem of Control.* Viking.

Santos-Martin, D., Alonso-Martínez, J., Carrasco, J. E. G., & Arnaltes, S. (2012). Problem-based learning in wind energy using virtual and real setups. *IEEE Transactions on Education, 55*(1), 126–134. DOI: 10.1109/TE.2011.2151195

Sao Pedro, M., Baker, R. S., & Rodrigo, M. M. T. (2014). Carelessness and affect in an intelligent tutoring system for mathematics. *International Journal of Artificial Intelligence in Education, 24*(2), 189–210. DOI: 10.1007/s40593-014-0015-y

Sclater, N. (2017). Learning analytics and privacy: A proposed model for data governance. *International Review of Research in Open and Distance Learning, 18*(5), 25–40.

Shaw, R. S. (2013). The relationships among group size, participation, and performance of programming language learning supported with online forums. *Computers & Education, 62*, 196–207. DOI: 10.1016/j.compedu.2012.11.001

Ziewitz, M. (2019). Rethinking algorithmic accountability. *Information Communication and Society*, *22*(7), 944–961.

Zuboff, S. (2019). *The age of surveillance capitalism: The fight for a human future at the new frontier of power*. PublicAffairs.

KEY TERMS AND DEFINITIONS

Accountability in AI: The obligation of institutions, developers, and educators to take responsibility for the outcomes and impacts of AI systems deployed in learning environments.

AI-Driven Learning Environments: Educational systems or platforms that integrate artificial intelligence to personalize instruction, automate assessment, provide adaptive feedback, or support decision-making related to teaching and learning.

Algorithmic Bias: Systematic and unfair discrimination resulting from the design or training of AI algorithms, often caused by imbalanced datasets or flawed modelling assumptions.

Anonymization: A data-processing technique that removes identifying information from datasets so that individuals cannot be reconstructed or re-identified.

Artificial Intelligence (AI): The field of computer science that develops systems capable of performing tasks that normally require human intelligence—such as reasoning, pattern recognition, decision-making, and language understanding—by using algorithms and data-driven models.

Automated Decision-Making: The use of AI systems to make or support decisions without direct human involvement, such as grading, recommendations, or adaptive pathway selection.

Cybersecurity in Education: The set of practices and technologies used to protect educational data systems from cyber threats, unauthorized access, malware, and breaches.

Data Governance: A structured framework of policies, procedures, and standards that regulate how educational data is collected, managed, stored, shared, and protected.

Data Minimization: A privacy principle requiring that only the data strictly necessary for a specific educational purpose be collected and retained.

Data Privacy: The protection of personal information from unauthorized access, use, disclosure, or modification, ensuring that individuals maintain control over how their data is collected and processed.

Data Protection: The legal, technical, and administrative measures implemented to safeguard personal information from misuse, loss, or security breaches.

Digital Footprint: The trail of data generated by learners through their interactions with digital platforms, including logs, usage statistics, and behavioural patterns.

Educational Data Mining (EDM): A research area focused on applying data-mining techniques to educational datasets to identify patterns and insights that can inform teaching and learning.

Ethical Considerations: The moral principles and value-based judgments that guide responsible development and use of AI technologies, including fairness, accountability, transparency, and respect for learner autonomy.

Federated Learning: A decentralized machine-learning approach in which AI models are trained locally on individual devices or servers, ensuring that raw data remains private and is not centralized.

Informed Consent: A process by which learners are clearly informed about what data is collected, how it is used, and what rights they hold—after which they voluntarily agree to participate.

Learning Analytics: The systematic collection, measurement, and analysis of learner data to understand learning processes, improve instruction, and support educational decision-making.

Personal Data (or Personally Identifiable Information – PII): Any information that can identify an individual directly or indirectly, including names, IDs, contact details, behavioural data, or digital traces generated during learning activities.

Surveillance Technologies in Education: Digital tools that monitor, track, or record student activities—such as proctoring software, behavioural analytics, or real-time monitoring systems.

Transparency in AI: The clarity with which an AI system's functions, decision-making processes, data usage, and limitations are communicated to educators, learners, and stakeholders.

Chapter 15
The Ethics of AI in English Language Teaching:
Balancing Innovation With Learner Rights

Vivit Rosmayanti
https://orcid.org/0000-0002-3648-9878
Universitas Negeri Makassar, Indonesia

ABSTRACT

The chapter explores the ethical implications of Artificial Intelligence (AI) in English Language Teaching, highlighting the need to balance innovation with safeguarding autonomy, privacy, and fairness to learners. AI technologies like intelligent tutoring systems and adaptive learning platforms can improve language instruction, but concerns over data privacy, security, transparency, and the balance between autonomy and AI's role are also discussed. The article proposes a framework for balancing AI's role with learners' rights protection, emphasizing transparency, accountability, and justice. It calls for further studies on the ethical environment surrounding AI use in education and the development of comprehensive frameworks for its ethical integration.

INTRODUCTION

The adoption of artificial intelligence (AI) for English Language Teaching (ELT) is indicative of a change in pedagogical practices, illustrating a remarkable evolution in the field of education. The implementation of AI technologies is rapidly

DOI: 10.4018/979-8-3373-3561-2.ch015

increasing for the purposes of improving teaching methods and customizing learning pathways for students. In the case of ELT, tools such as chatbots, automated essay scoring, and other intelligent tutoring systems can nurture and improve learner engagement, retention, and outcomes concerning language learning (Seo et al., 2021; Almelhes, 2023; Magtoto et al., 2024). Research shows that the use of AI tools leads to higher AI-human interactions among students and teachers, which is likely to foster greater trust and acceptance of AI systems in educational settings (Seo et al., 2021; Magtoto et al., 2024).

It is important to examine the ethics of AI education technology as it becomes more commonplace in the classroom. Chen & Liu (2024) suggest that the ethics of AI education technology include privacy concerns, data protection, algorithm bias, and the growing disregard of AI equity on learners' rights and educational fairness. Guided by Wang'ang'a's (2024) and Berendt et al.'s (2020) work, the data privacy and privacy tradeoff AI systems present new issues about learner autonomy and educational freedom. In their review of literature on policies governing the use of educational technologies, ethics and human rights served as foundational anchors to policies AIs need to function without creating a threat to humanity's basic needs, like quality education (Wang'ang; Berendt et al., 2020; Chen & Liu, 2024). Emphasize the dangerous reliance on automated technologies and the corresponding learner indignity, lack of protection, and loss of privacy, as strong morality will shield innovative practices that require learners to be treated as more than cyborgs.

The primary focus of this chapter is to address the ethical concerns on the deployment of AI in English Language Teaching (ELT) systems, which attempts to find an equilibrium between technological advancements and the protection of learners' rights. The next parts will analyze the most proprietary concerns in relation to the use of AI concerning teaching and learning responsibilities, learner Agency, and the possible AI-induced educational inequality (Berendt et al. 2020; Nasir et al. 2024; Chen & Liu, 2024). The chapter will also analyze some competing ethical theories and propose practical solutions for educators and policymakers who want to use AI of its advantages and mitigate the disadvantages of its use. The focus of this multidisciplinary study is to advocate policies that consider the profound and multilayered impact of artificial intelligence on the education of English language learners while ensuring that learners' rights are respected and protected in the context of relentless shifts in technology (Chen & Liu, 2024; Popova & Gorokhova, 2021).

To conclude, the application of AI in English language teaching comes with wonderful opportunities accompanied by troubling ethical dilemmas. As the area of education continues to develop with such technologies, a thorough analysis of the ethics involved is critical to ensure that advancement does not infringe upon basic learner rights. The following discussion will illustrate how teachers can address dilemmas along these lines while protecting education as a beneficial domain for all learners, actively harnessing and integrating new technological enhancements without sacrificing moral principles.

THE ROLE OF AI IN ENGLISH LANGUAGE TEACHING

AI's purpose is to replicate human mental activities like memorizing, comprehending, problem-solving, decision-making, and more (Wang, 2024; Anggraini & Faisal 2024). Its application in English Language Teaching involves smart tutoring systems, adaptive learning platforms, chatbots, and a few others. Through real-time data execution analysis, intelligent tutoring systems give learners personalized pedagogical support and develop individualized pathways (Anggraini & Faisal, 2024). Chatbots, in addition, create enhanced opportunities for streamlined language practice by providing off-the-clock help and interaction outside conventional schooling hours (Fitria, 2021; Huang et al., 2021). Lastly, from lecture engagement levels to course material retention, adaptive learning encourages students to perform better (Chen et al., 2020; Huang et al., 2021).

The integration of AI technologies in ELT is promoted with information on their efficiency and advantages for the overall learning and teaching experience. AI in particular aids in creating personalized learning and teaching experiences that improve engagement with the lesson and address particular needs of the learners in a classroom, which is critically important in a multi skilled classroom where there are students with various levels of proficiency (Anggraini & Faisal, 2024; Fitria, 2021; Yin et al., 2022). The immediate reception of feedback, an indisputable asset of AI utilizing learning aids, provides opportunities for a learner to receive useful corrections and suggestions immediately, thus enabling students to improve their language skills in real time instead of during set evaluations which can lead to postponements (Wang, 2024; Chen et al., 2020). In addition, these systems can achieve exponential educational outreach, which allows more learners to gain access to quality materials and instructions at the same time, which helps meet the ever-increasing demand for the teaching of the English language across the world (Akbarani, 2024; Idham et al., 2024). Moreover, this scalability aids the instructors in attending to bigger classes while retaining educational standards, which helps optimize the use of available resources (Barzani et al., 2021; Yin et al., 2022).

Recent developments and trends in the innovations of AI in language education suggest continuous advancement from the cutting-edge technologies of the present time. The development of conversational AI, particularly sophisticated chatbots like ChatGPT, has motivated language learning through life-like interactive practice sims that offer context-rich interactions with students (Fitria, 2021; Idham et al., 2024; Wu, 2024). In addition, the capabilities of AI tools have recently been improved due to advancements in natural language processing and machine learning, allowing them to more accurately evaluate and instruct learners (Fitria, 2021; Men, 2024). Innovative AI applications such as gamification and other immersive experience learning tools, including virtual reality, promise a high degree of student engagement as well as motivation (Tiwari, 2024; Sun, 2023; Li, 2022). Collectively, these innovations demonstrate the increasing importance of AI as a powerful instrument in English language teaching (ELT) and an emerging shift toward novel approaches in language education along with redefined pedagogical frameworks.

The rapid integration of AI technologies in English Language Teaching (ELT) disorders the existing methodologies and, at the same time, welcomes an era of tailored education and its easier access on an unprecedented level. Harnessing the power of AI strengthens the capacity of educators to optimize learning settings in ways that support self-directed individualized learning and different learner educational requirements. In this landscape of never-ending technological opportunities, actors in the field need to balance such advancements with appropriate concerns, which means the application of AI technologies in ELT must focus on human rights, educational justice, and social equity principles.

ETHICAL CONSIDERATIONS IN AI-DRIVEN LANGUAGE EDUCATION

Data Privacy and Security

The application of Artificial Intelligence Technologies (AI) in English Language Teaching (ELT) raises ethical concerns, especially around matters of privacy and security. The focus of this debate is learner data collection, usage, and retention, which significantly impact learner experiences and outcomes. Many AI applications in ELT, like intelligent tutoring systems or adaptive learning systems, require vast quantities of educational and demographic data to optimize learning experiences. Idham et al. (2024); Gyawali and Mehandroo (2022) note that students' personal and performance data are necessary for the systems to be functional and thus have a great bearing on system performance. Because these systems need information in order to function, questions regarding consent, ownership, and access are increasingly relevant. The information restricted to students' educational preferences and behavioral patterns, as well as identifiable details related to test results, engenders concern regarding privacy and, thus, sensitive information protection protocols.

George and Wooden (2023) and Igbokwe (2024) suggest the need for data protection protocols to safeguard students' sensitive documents.

In addition, there is a significant threat, mostly related to a potential data breach and its inappropriate use, which might negatively impact the educational goals for integrating AI. Data breaches can compromise sensitive information and make it accessible to malicious actors. This can result in learners suffering from identity theft and reputational harm (Igbokwe, 2024; Lee et al., 2024). Besides, such information can be misused to shape the experiences of learners or to deepen pre-existing gaps and biases, which might undermine the fair distribution of education (Idham et al., 2024; Halat et al., 2024). Achieving best practices in the management of learner information requires the application of learner information protection protocols and strong encryption techniques, as well as limited access and auditing of data usage to mitigate risk (Igbokwe, 2024; George & Wooden, 2023). Also, institutions need to adopt policies that clearly define the ethical terms and conditions regarding data protection and user confidentiality to promote openness and confidence among learners and other stakeholders (Binta et al., 2023; Asirit & Hua, 2023).

How to take advantage of the potential of AI technology while protecting the privacy of the learners raises ethical dilemmas. As AI technologies advance, educators and developers must ensure that implemented systems improve learning while not violating students' privacy (Tiwari, 2024; Lee et al., 2024). Ethical approaches dealing with issues of consent and data protection are central to this discussion. This means informing learners about the data collection processes and how the data will be used, and allowing learners to withdraw from data collection (George & Wooden, 2023; Siau & Wang, 2020). Furthermore, AI system developers should strive to anonymize data to the greatest extent possible to reduce exposure to misuse while still enabling the system to deliver tailored learning assistance (Tran & Nguyen, 2020; Xi, 2024).

The integration of AI technologies into ELT can be more effectively unlocked if educators resolve the concerns regarding ethics, especially data privacy and security, ensuring that the fundamental rights of learners are preserved. The continuing discussions among educators, policymakers, and technology designers will form an ethical governance policy on learner privacy and the application of AI technologies (Siau & Wang, 2020; Xi, 2024). Adherence to ethical principles in AI-based language teaching will create a better learning environment and guarantee that technology is utilized for empowerment, and not as a risk, in education.

Transparency and Accountability

The integration of Artificial Intelligence (AI) in English Language Teaching comes with its own set of ethical challenges, especially questions of transparency and accountability within AI systems. These aspects are critical in preserving the trust that a community of educational stakeholders, teachers, and learners may have. AI transparency is the degree of clarity with which these systems operate as regards a given system's decisions. Such understanding is necessary for users to know how decisions and recommendations are made, and so that stakeholders can meaningfully interact with AI technologies (Chaudhry et al., 2022). In the general AI technology context, and in particular the ELT context, transparency permits decisions made by the AI to be challenged by educators and learners, which is crucial for a meaningful collaboration aimed at effectively using AI to improve learning and teaching results. Developing mechanisms for transparency can help solve AI's "black box" problem, where users do not have access to the information and reasoning systems used to make decisions (Chaudhry et al., 2022; Arrieta et al., 2020).

Responsibility falls on the developers of AI educational tools for erroneous biases and blame, all pointing toward AI designers, educators, and institutional leaders. D'Souza et al. (2024) claim stakeholders, in this case decision makers, must have a defined structure on ascribed domains and active procedures on voluntary help toward mitigating the impact of AI mistakes on image distortion. Constraining these measures fosters a culture of responsibility aimed toward a broad spectrum, initiating from proactive bias combat, error rectification, and upholding ethical standards in AI education tools Igbokwe, 2024). D'Souza et al. (2024) assert institutional stakeholders need to acknowledge their burdens regarding to expectations of probes that prospective users will impose on usefulness, trust, transparency, and the limits of AI systems. Responsibility in the application of AI technologies deepens when one considers the biases that such systems may embed. Since these systems depend on prior data for training, biases that exist in the data are likely to produce adverse outcomes in decision making. It is therefore important for algorithm developers and educators to evaluate and comprehend the biases these algorithms are likely to impose together (Anuyahong et al., 2023; Igbokwe, 2024). This implies the need for sustained vigilance, periodic reviews, and user-driven reporting systems that address the efficacy of the system (Arrieta et al., 2020). Moreover, solving these problems goes beyond the technical realm. It also requires an institutional framework embedded within the AI developmental and operational architecture focused on diversity, equity, and inclusion (Igbokwe, 2024; Anuyahong et al., 2023).

The use of AI tools for teaching and assessing students has escalated, heightening the demand for responsibility and the transparency of information. Technology must serve pedagogy through lending its capabilities, but any technology used must possess ethical norms respecting the rights of the learner (Anuyahong et al., 2023; Igbokwe, 2024). Institutions need to adopt comprehensive policies that ensure the comprehension of the workings of AI systems and create safe environments where educators and learners are encouraged to interact with the tools (Anuyahong et al, 2023). These capabilities foster trust among users, which is essential for the integration of AI into education systems where it is seen as a supportive tool rather than a problematic one.

In a nutshell, the attention given to issues of ethics concerning the reasoning of AI technology in language education is important for the construction, deployment, and ecosystem surrounding the use of these technologies. While the dynamics of education change with AI technologies, ensuring a reliable understanding of such systems will alter their reliability, acceptance, and overall effectiveness. By preemptively resolving these matters, a vision can be made possible wherein AI technology provides educational support while actively protecting the interests of learners.

Autonomy and Learner Rights

The introduction of AI to English Language Teaching (ELT) has generated deeper considerations of autonomy and learner rights. What stands out the most is the attempt to strike a balance between AI's contribution to autonomy and the concerns of dependency on technology. Autonomy in education is primarily centered around the ability of the learner to make decisions, manage themselves, and control the learning processes (Saeed, 2021; Pitychoutis, 2024). Learning autonomy is amplified by AI in the personalized learning experiences it offers, which address specific needs (Huang et al., 2024). On the other hand, the provision of AI tools like adaptive learning programs and chatbots raises concerns of over-reliance on these technologies, which could lead to a reduced capacity for critical thought and independent action in the learning process (Saeed, 2021; Song & Song, 2023).

The chronic dependency on AI resources can be counterproductive in that it diminishes the sense of ownership and agency in one's learning path. Educational instructors should aim for a middle ground where AI facilitates learning, but does not act as a disabling prop that prevents the development of self-directed learning and analytic skills. In this regard, technology should enhance, not substitute, the important didactic interaction between the teacher and the learners (Saeed, 2021; Pitychoutis, 2024). Studies suggest that in certain cases, the use of AI makes some educational tasks easier, but autonomy and independence that AI is not capable of providing are fundamentally a human construct (Minh, 2024; Ghobain & Zughaibi, 2021). Hence, an effective educational AI-centered paradigm must be built where students are free to use AI when working on tasks, but the tasks themselves require active participation to shape a thoughtful and responsible independent learner.

Accompanying this, learners have basic rights concerning their information, which must be protected in this AI era. The collection, storage, and use of a learner's information by AI systems require ethics in terms of privacy and consent (Al-musharraf, 2020). Students should be informed about what information is collected from them, for what purposes, and with whom this information is shared. Protecting individual autonomy through informed consent enhances ethical parameters and empowers learners to control their participation and discretion over technology use (Almusharraf, 2020). Educational institutions need to implement strong frameworks that safeguard the rights of learners by allowing them control over their consent and the ability to withdraw from data collection processes at their discretion.

Moreover, ethically acting requires constant interactions with educators, learners, and AI technology creators on the possible consequences of data usage and automation on the self-direction of the learner. Giving learners the ability to express their grievances regarding data privacy practices enhances their trust in the AI tools while strengthening their control over their educational journey. It is necessary to build clear policies regarding data stewardship and inform students of their responsibilities and the power they hold in this context (Kruk & Kałużna, 2024; Tajik, 2025).

Finally, there is great potential for AI to transform learning; however, it is essential to strike a balance between AI technology, the autonomy of the learner, and their rights. Fostering independent learning while protecting personal data will promote an ethical use of AI in education. As technology progresses, the education framework should focus on the rights and autonomy of the learners in order to develop responsive, responsible, and ready citizens.

Bias and Fairness

The ethical implications of incorporating Artificial Intelligence (AI) into English Language Teaching (ELT) focus more on issues of bias and equity. The pre-existing biases of AI systems can profoundly impact learners' language acquisition skills. Because AI-based systems are trained utilizing data containing societal prejudices, they reflect societal discrimination, resulting in outputs that disadvantage certain learners (Choi, 2022). Take, for example, language models that prioritize content from dominant dialects or cultural contexts. Such models may provide tailored instructional content that reinforces learning for native speakers but disenfranchises learners from diverse linguistic or cultural contexts (Cohen et al., 2024). These biases can permeate every facet of education, such as learner recommendations, learning materials, and even tests, which all could create an unlevel playing field (Nghi & Nguyen, 2024; Cohen et al., 2024).

These biases can be mitigated to promote equality in education, as institutions need to proactively resolve inequalities in access to AI-enabled tools, which perpetuate inequities arising from algorithmic bias (Baker & Hawn, 2021; Mohamed, 2024). This includes undertaking sophisticated auditing to address bias in AI systems, especially where such systems shape or influence the views and experiences of learners (Escalante et al., 2023; Mohamed, 2024). AI can be made more equitable and inclusive if builders and educators employ diverse datasets that authentically capture varying experiences of language and culture (Alrayes et al., 2024; Kanont et al., 2024). In addition, bias in AI systems can also be addressed through self-correction when learners actively give feedback about their experiences using AI tools (Baker & Hawn, 2021; Escalante et al., 2023).

The primary focus of AI when integrated into English Language Teaching, or ELT, should remain on augmenting language experiences fairly and inclusively. This includes not only addressing biases but also providing AI tools and access to resources equitably across different socioeconomic classes. No learner, regardless of their background, should be excluded from the advantages of AI-enabled language learning (Cohen et al., 2024; Baker & Hawn, 2021). Teachers need to be trained to identify biases in AI systems and instructional methods that bias AI claims. This dual purpose both advances AI technology and allows educators to design educational settings that embrace inclusivity and equity to enhance respect for all learners.

Furthermore, institutions should think about creating policies that specifically deal with the issues of bias and fairness in AI use. Policies should state the educator, developer, and administrator's roles in the responsible use of AI concerning the educational rights of the learners towards equity in education (Escalante et al., 2023; Wei, 2023). Including all relevant stakeholders, such as the learners, teachers, and AI designers, is necessary in order to ensure that the application of AI in education is useful, relevant to the context, and free from bias (Mohamed, 2024; AlAfnan, 2024).

In conclusion, even though AI might change the face of English Language Teaching through personalization of learning experiences and adaptive models, educators must address the challenges of bias and equitable resource allocation to educational opportunities. With a commitment to equity in the design and utilization of AI systems, all stakeholders can promote educational frameworks that authentically assist every learner in mastering the English language.

BALANCING INNOVATION WITH LEARNER RIGHTS

The swift development of Artificial Intelligence (AI) technologies in English Language Teaching (ELT) poses a distinct challenge of the need to encourage creativity and at the same time protect learners' rights. The concern becomes even more serious when educational institutions set their sights on adopting new technologies, as this could mean placing innovation at the expense of learner rights. Cleavages between the ethical frameworks and the pe- vontade social needs in educational institutions are defined, focusing on neglecting the fundamental principles of social justice, privacy, and academic honesty (AlAli & Wardat, 2024; Holmes et al., 2021). This situation indicates the lack of balanced policies and laws that enable educational technologies to empower the learners without trampling on their citizenship rights.

One important ethical issue is the dependence on AI systems that could take over language teaching and even instructors. AI can provide some scaling solutions to cumulative problems, as well as personalized solutions. However, removing the human element in language education has serious implications in terms of the social and emotional supportive case. (Barrett & Pack, 2023; Starčič et al., 2021). The danger is greatest in the very delicate areas, such as motivation, emotional sensing, and, in general, providing motivational support and communication skills. (PAN, 2024; Rosmayanti, 2025). This is also very important in language learning through personal interaction because language education will fail if not, personal interaction is not incorporated. For that reason, it is first of all important to study models in which AI serves as a supplement to human faculties rather than fully substituting them, in which the fundamental role of the teachers is preserved. (Starčič et al., 2021; Agarwal et al., 2024).

To address these ethical challenges, appropriate policies regarding the use of AI in educational contexts need to be crafted, considering the learners' individual personal, social, and cultural dimensions. This calls for attention to the learners and embracing a broader scope, such as tailoring technology to improve learning and fostering inclusiveness and cultural sensitivity (Agarwal et al., 2024; Ibrahim et al., 2024). As part of our AI integration policies, educators and institutions should consult different community members, including students, parents, and education practitioners, to ensure that the policies incorporate all societal values and concerns. If educational institutions integrate ethics in the design and implementation of AI systems, they will be able to avert the consequences of tech-centric prejudices and biases focused on unequal access to education resources (AlAli & Wardat, 2024; Holmes et al., 2021).

Stakeholder responsibility is important in relation to managing the ethical issues that AI brings up in the context of education. Classroom-related issues are work that educators need to address and understand. Ethical teaching practice revolves around understanding and with other technologies concerning equipping oneself with the knowledge to ethically address the skills needed with the concerns that arise (Agarwal et al., 2024; Ibrahim et al., 2024). Concerns that teachers must demonstrate ethical AI practices include guiding students around the dangers offered by technology, such as academic fraud and data privacy concerns (Barrett & Pack, 2023; Wirzal et al., 2024).

Policymakers have a great deal of control in governing the use of AI in learning situations. Regulations must be flexible so that the application of AI technology is within ethical boundaries, protecting the rights of the learners while fostering growth (Karimi & Khawaja, 2023; Dwivedi et al., 2021). Data protection, the avoidance of bias, and AI resources for all from education must be governed by policies set to allow for the proper use of AI in teaching and learning processes. All must provide these materials to support understanding the ethics for all stakeholders using (Karimi & Khawaja, 2023; Wirzal et al., 2024; Asrifan et al., 2025).

In addition, the ethical design and implementation of technologies rest firmly on the shoulders of AI developers. As mentioned (Balta, 2023; Eden et al., 2024), all educators need to be aware of the cultural sensitivity issues, intelligence erasure, and issues pertinent to transparency in educational technology AI solutions. Consideration of diverse datasets, along with the incorporation of ethical principles during the development phase, will mitigate the biases AI educational technologies carry concerning various experiences and learners (Balta, 2023). There is scope for synergy between AI developers, educators, and policymakers such that the development of AI technologies is done ethically and equitably for the purpose of education (Kasztelnik, 2024; Leddy & Creanor, 2024).

To sum up, responsiveness towards protecting the rights of the learners while seeking innovation in education technologies requires all the stakeholders to act together purposefully. Operating within ethical boundaries, managing the risks brought by AI, and taking joint responsibility among educators at different levels of policy making and developing AI technologies will permit the education systems to use AI advancements in learning enhancements devoid of compromising the foundational rights and values of the learners. The changed opportunity that comes with AI is the ability to improve the quality of education while assuring the dignity and rights.

BEST PRACTICES FOR ETHICAL AI IMPLEMENTATION

The successful implementation of AI within the English Language Teaching (ELT) framework is predicated upon the formulation of identified best practices that safeguard and enhance the learner's welfare and rights. Fostering educational enhancements through AI technologies requires an understanding of the holistic needs of the learner; as such, these tools must address usability, accessibility, and cultural sensitivity to enable students to feel safe and empowered to interact with (Lin et al. 2024; Holmes et al. 2021). Striking a balance between learners' rights and innovations ensures that educational technologies aid in language exploration and engagement in manners appropriate to the learners' experiences and identities. Such an emphasis on learner-informed AI design provides a base for ethical considerations in AI applications bounded by inclusivity (Ayling & Chapman, 2021; Rosmayanti et al., 2022).

It is a fundamental best practice to include ethical considerations when developing AI-powered language educational tools. The design of AI systems should be guided by holistic frameworks that include aspects of equity, justice, and responsibility (Holmes et al., 2021; Upadhyay et al., 2023). Derived from diverse disciplines, ethics must be considered at all levels of product development so that biases are actively addressed from the earliest stages (Upadhyay et al., 2023). The ethical focus must not only pertain to how AI systems operate, but also to how these systems interface with training data, including what is deemed appropriate data, and the algorithms crafted to process said data (Ayling & Chapman, 2021). Such frameworks could enhance the collaboration of educators, AI designers, legal and ethical scholars, as well as policymakers, to foster a shared vision of responsible AI adoption in the educational environment (Holmes et al., 2021; PAN, 2024).

As stated, informed consent and disclosure of information are key components of ethical AI use in education. Students must understand the processes of data collection, data usage, and data retention to cultivate an atmosphere of trust and participation (Tiwari, 2024). Tools powered with AI should provide users with explanations regarding the management of data and allow participants to make informed decisions relating to the repercussions of their actions, including the ability to reclaim control over their personal information (Tiwari, 2024; Kemell et al., 2022). Functional transparency of the platform not only supports the learners but also enables them to make reasoned decisions regarding the use of technology (Leddy & Creanor, 2024).

Another high-priority practice is logging and verifying the fairness and correctness of AI systems. Continuous monitoring of AI systems is crucial for identifying and addressing any emerging biases or inaccuracies over time (Strümke, 2021). Conducting regular audits helps ensure that ethical standards are met and enhances the trustworthiness of AI language education tools. Creating avenues for feedback from participants allows institutions to evaluate the influence of AI on learners' academic performance and engagement, leading to iterative improvements based on evidence (PAN, 2024; Kristiawan et al., 2024).

Furthermore, as far as the use of AI in teaching languages goes, the training of teachers revolves around its ethical considerations. There is a need to prepare teachers by understanding the ethical ramifications and making use of AI systems in the classroom. Such programs need to ensure that teachers are capable of controlling AI utilization, while providing appropriate direction to students and applying technology appropriately (Tiwari, 2024). Such programs should also provide educators with training on how to make ethical choices, including how to constructively deal with instructional AI-use ethical issues so that all learners benefit from supportive and equity-inclusive environments (Tiwari, 2024; Mai et al., 2024).

Best practices for the responsible use of AI in English Language Teaching must be implemented to cultivate positive and inclusive learning environments. Stakeholders can balance the integration of AI with the protection of student rights by prioritizing learner wellbeing, including ethical frameworks, enhancing transparency and informed consent, monitoring, and providing ongoing supervision of AI system checks. Educator training initiatives must adapt commensurately with technology to prepare instructors as ethically responsible guardians where language teaching and technology converge. Such efforts will enable the application of AI to transform ELT while observing critical ethical standards.

CASE STUDIES OF ETHICAL AI IMPLEMENTATION IN ELT

The use of Artificial Intelligence (AI) in English Language Teaching (ELT) has encouraged numerous case studies documenting the fruitful and intricately challenging applications of ethical AI in education. A remarkable instance is the adaptation of AI systems like personalized learning platforms, which optimize content based on specific requirements of individual learners in a sophisticated manner, minded towards student engagement and their rights (Gutiérrez, 2023). These systems aim at the learner's well-being through providing appropriate feedback and learning materials tailored to their preferences and learning styles (Tiwari, 2024). Such successful implementations reinforce the rationale behind the importance of the integration of AI with principles of education — tools serve not only the teaching and learning goals but also perpetuate inclusiveness and fairness (Ulum, 2024).

On the other hand, there are examples of lost opportunities that instruct us on the ethical use of AI in education. An example is the implementation of AI-based grading systems, which have been criticized for fairness issues. Many systems have been blasted for generating outcomes that are overly punitive for some marginalized populations (Xue, 2024). This underscores the need for monitoring and evaluation of AI systems long after the initial implementation in order to make certain that such tools serve the educational purposes of the learners' rights and wider educational aspirations (Sharanesha et al., 2025). These lessons highlight the lack of engagement with stakeholders during the design and implementation processes, as well as the need for openness regarding the operational logic of the AI systems and how decisions are made (Eslit, 2023).

International views on the use of AI technologies in teaching and learning indicate varying cultures and legal frameworks concerning learners' rights and AI in different parts of the world. For example, in some jurisdictions, known data protection laws require obtaining explicit permission to collect and process data, which influences the way in which educational institutions use AI technologies (Sharanesha et al., 2025). On the other hand, some areas may focus more on the speed of adopting new technologies, sometimes lacking sufficient ethical examination, which can lead to uneven burdens and benefits of AI on learners (Gutiérrez, 2023). Cultural factors also come into play since educators and educational planners face diverse societal attitudes toward the use of technology, privacy, and AI in education. For example, the impact of collectivist vs individualistic cultures may determine how AI is integrated into the educational setting (Lee & Joshi, 2020).

Moreover, the integration of AI within language education can be promoted or challenged by distinctive policies within different regions. Countries that prioritize educational technology and actively invest in teacher training focused on AI have realized enhanced language learning experiences, with their benefits positively being manifested (Ulum, 2024). In contrast, regions where there is inadequate funding and untrained staff may enhance AI implementation, yet their potential remains unmet alongside heightened educational inequities (Xue, 2024). This imbalance exists in conjunction with the varying legal AI frameworks, where laws controlling data, algorithm-based accountability, as well as intellectual property legislation pose either opportunities or limitations to the institution's efforts to responsibly leverage artificial intelligence technologies in education (Tiwari, 2024).

The case studies discussed epitomize the spectrum of possibilities regarding the ethical application of AI in ELT with a particular focus on the essential gaps of ethics, participatory culture, and underpinning sociocultural dynamics. With the rapid advancements in AI, these real-life examples will assist educational institutions to effectively utilize AI in language education while continually protecting the rights of the learners from different sociocultural contexts.

CONCLUSION

The use of Artificial Intelligence (AI) technologies in English Language Teaching (ELT) are both an educative improvement paradigm shift and a potential danger in the form of infringing upon ethical boundaries relating to the rights of the learners. The amalgamation of AI with the educational sector creates several pertinent concerns on the now popular issues of equity, autonomy, and justice which need to be answered before the appropriate use of such technologies is made. Foremost, the application of AI should focus ethical aspects concerning social responsibility directed to the wellbeing and rights of the learners while advancing towards innovation and technological development.

Carefully thought-out methodologies in the integration of AI tools into language classes are already yielding fruit. Tailor-made AI systems strategically employed, for example, AI-powered teaching assistants designed to enhance interactions with the learners at their various stages of learning have proven to improve outcomes at an unprecedented level (PAN, 2024). Additionally, the catastrophically wrong examples, such as grade-aiding algorithms that perpetuate bigotry or content recommending systems perpetuating falsehoods, underscore the need for vigilant scrutiny on the application of such systems to level the unjust paradigms being employed towards learners (Seo et al., 2021).

Around the world, differing societal and legal factors related to learner rights, as well as the application of AI technologies, further hinder the implementation of these technologies. Some jurisdictions have specific laws regarding information privacy, emerging technologies, business ethics, and even pedagogy, which affect the application of AI within educational settings (Choi et al., 2024; Bearman et al., 2022). These differences highlight the need for context-sensitive responses to AI in education that consider the socio-economic, political, and ethical frameworks that govern educational culture and architecture (Sanusi & Olaleye, 2022).

In order to achieve inclusivity as well as a morally correct use of AI in ELT, it is important that all stakeholders, educators, policy makers, and AI developers work together toward the development of policies that emphasize fairness, elucidation, and responsibility. There is a need for proper training and resources for educators to ethically navigate the complexities of AI integration in the classroom and make decisions that advocate for and preserve learner rights (Holmes et al., 2021; Balta, 2023). As for the policymakers, more focus needs to be paid toward the creation of regulations that midwife bias and AI technologies discrimination so that all the students will benefit from the use of AI in education. They should ensure an environment where learners are able to reach their full potential. Last but not least, AI developers have the duty of ensuring that technology is designed and implemented ethically so that educational outcomes developed are within ethical boundaries and prioritize learner welfare over profit (Balta, 2023).

To summarize, the responsible use of Artificial Intelligence in English Language Teaching comes with both unprecedented opportunities and formidable challenges. As educators and stakeholders work to leverage the AI revolution, protecting the rights of learners and addressing ethical concerns should be fundamental throughout this endeavor. As the implementation of AI is approached from an ethical perspective, equitable and meaningful learning experiences can be developed with the dignity, autonomy, and rights of all learners taken into consideration, making it possible to envision a future where technology and education converge to provide real learning opportunities.

REFERENCES

Agarwal, B., Urlings, C., Lankveld, G., & Klemke, R. (2024). Identifying the ethical values and norms of artificial intelligence in education: a systematic literature review. DOI: 10.35542/osf.io/e7t3f

Akbarani, R. (2024). Use of artificial intelligence in english language teaching. *International Journal of English Learning and Applied Linguistics (Ijelal)*, *4*(1), 14–23. DOI: 10.21111/ijelal.v4i1.10756

AlAfnan, M. (2024). Artificial intelligence and language: Bridging arabic and english with technology. *Journal of Ecohumanism*, *3*(8). Advance online publication. DOI: 10.62754/joe.v3i8.4961

AlAli, R., & Wardat, Y. (2024). Opportunities and challenges of integrating generative artificial intelligence in education. *International Journal of Religion*, *5*(7), 784–793. DOI: 10.61707/8y29gv34

Almelhes, S. (2023). A review of artificial intelligence adoption in second-language learning. *Theory and Practice in Language Studies*, *13*(5), 1259–1269. DOI: 10.17507/tpls.1305.21

Almusharraf, N. (2020). Teachers' perspectives on promoting learner autonomy for vocabulary development: A case study. *Cogent Education*, *7*(1), 1823154. Advance online publication. DOI: 10.1080/2331186X.2020.1823154

Alrayes, A., Henari, T., & Ahmed, D. (2024). Chatgpt in education – understanding the bahraini academics perspective. *Electronic Journal of e-Learning*, *22*(2), 112–134. DOI: 10.34190/ejel.22.2.3250

Anggraini, A., & Faisal, F. (2024). The use of artificial intelligence based technology in english language teaching. *Golden Ratio of Data in Summary*, *4*(2), 950–957. DOI: 10.52970/grdis.v4i2.749

Anuyahong, B., Rattanapong, C., & Patcha, I. (2023). Analyzing the impact of artificial intelligence in personalized learning and adaptive assessment in higher education. *International Journal of Innovation and Scientific Research*, *X*(IV), 88–93. DOI: 10.51244/IJRSI.2023.10412

Arrieta, A., Díaz-Rodríguez, N., Ser, J., Bennetot, A., Tabik, S., Barbado, A., & Herrera, F. (2020). Explainable artificial intelligence (xai): Concepts, taxonomies, opportunities and challenges toward responsible ai. *Information Fusion*, *58*, 82–115. DOI: 10.1016/j.inffus.2019.12.012

Asirit, L., & Hua, J. (2023). Converging perspectives: Assessing ai readiness and utilization in philippine higher education. *Polaris Global Journal of Scholarly Research and Trends*, *2*(3), 1–50. DOI: 10.58429/pgjsrt.v2n3a152

Asrifan, A., Dewi, A. C., Rosmayanti, V., Saodi, S., Kaddas, B., & Mulyadi, M. (2025). Avatars of Academia: Exploring Virtual Collaboration's Tapestry. In Burris-Melville, T., & Burris, S. (Eds.), *Developing Effective and High-Performing Teams in Higher Education* (pp. 285–312). IGI Global Scientific Publishing., DOI: 10.4018/979-8-3693-3852-0.ch010

Ayling, J., & Chapman, A. (2021). Putting ai ethics to work: Are the tools fit for purpose? *AI and Ethics*, *2*(3), 405–429. DOI: 10.1007/s43681-021-00084-x

Baker, R., & Hawn, A. (2021). Algorithmic bias in education. DOI: 10.35542/osf.io/pbmvz

Balta, N. (2023). Ethical considerations in using ai in educational research., 2(1), 14205. DOI: 10.51853/jorids/14205

Barrett, A., & Pack, A. (2023). Not quite eye to a.i.: Student and teacher perspectives on the use of generative artificial intelligence in the writing process. *International Journal of Educational Technology in Higher Education*, *20*(1), 59. Advance online publication. DOI: 10.1186/s41239-023-00427-0

Barzani, S., Aslam, M., & Aslam, T. (2021). The role of technology in ell classes in turkish republic of northern cyprus. *International Journal of Language Education*, *5*(2), 30. DOI: 10.26858/ijole.v5i2.14109

Bearman, M., Ryan, J., & Ajjawi, R. (2022). Discourses of artificial intelligence in higher education: A critical literature review. *Higher Education*, *86*(2), 369–385. DOI: 10.1007/s10734-022-00937-2

Berendt, B., Littlejohn, A., & Blakemore, M. (2020). Ai in education: Learner choice and fundamental rights. *Learning, Media and Technology*, *45*(3), 312–324. DOI: 10.1080/17439884.2020.1786399

Chaudhry, M., Cukurova, M., & Luckin, R. (2022). A transparency index framework for ai in education. DOI: 10.1007/978-3-031-11647-6_33

Chen, H., & Liu, Z. (2024). Educational applications of chatgpt: Ethical challenges and countermeasures. *English Language Teaching and Linguistics Studies*, *6*(3), 100. DOI: 10.22158/eltls.v6n3p100

Chen, L., Chen, P., & Lin, Z. (2020). Artificial intelligence in education: A review. *IEEE Access : Practical Innovations, Open Solutions*, *8*, 75264–75278. DOI: 10.1109/ACCESS.2020.2988510

Choi, J., Yang, E., & Goo, E. (2024). The effects of an ethics education program on artificial intelligence among middle school students: Analysis of perception and attitude changes. *Applied Sciences (Basel, Switzerland)*, *14*(4), 1588. DOI: 10.3390/app14041588

Choi, L. (2022). Interrogating structural bias in language technology: Focusing on the case of voice chatbots in south korea. *Sustainability (Basel)*, *14*(20), 13177. DOI: 10.3390/su142013177

Cohen, S., Mompelat, L., Mann, A., & Connors, L. (2024). The linguistic leap: Understanding, evaluating, and integrating ai in language education. *Tydskrif vir Taalonderrig*, *4*(2), 23–31. DOI: 10.54475/jlt.2024.012

D'Souza, R., Mathew, M., Mishra, V., & Surapaneni, K. (2024). Twelve tips for addressing ethical concerns in the implementation of artificial intelligence in medical education. *Medical Education Online*, *29*(1), 2330250. Advance online publication. DOI: 10.1080/10872981.2024.2330250 PMID: 38566608

Dwivedi, Y., Hughes, L., Ismagilova, E., Aarts, G., Coombs, C., Crick, T., Duan, Y., Dwivedi, R., Edwards, J., Eirug, A., Galanos, V., Ilavarasan, P. V., Janssen, M., Jones, P., Kar, A. K., Kizgin, H., Kronemann, B., Lal, B., Lucini, B., & Williams, M. (2021). Artificial intelligence (ai): Multidisciplinary perspectives on emerging challenges, opportunities, and agenda for research, practice and policy. *International Journal of Information Management*, *57*, 101994. DOI: 10.1016/j.ijinfomgt.2019.08.002

Eden, C., Chisom, O., & Adeniyi, I. (2024). Integrating ai in education: opportunities, challenges, and ethical considerations. Magna Scientia Advanced Research and Reviews, 10(2), 006-013. DOI: 10.30574/msarr.2024.10.2.0039

Escalante, J., Pack, A., & Barrett, A. (2023). Ai-generated feedback on writing: Insights into efficacy and enl student preference. *International Journal of Educational Technology in Higher Education*, *20*(1), 57. Advance online publication. DOI: 10.1186/s41239-023-00425-2

Eslit, E. (2023). Revitalizing english language teaching (elt): unveiling evolving pedagogies and ai-driven dynamics in the post-pandemic era. DOI: 10.20944/preprints202308.1774.v1

Fitria, T. (2021). The use technology based on artificial intelligence in english teaching and learning). *Elt Echo the Journal of English Language Teaching in Foreign Language Context*, *6*(2). Advance online publication. DOI: 10.24235/eltecho.v6i2.9299

George, B., & Wooden, O. (2023). Managing the strategic transformation of higher education through artificial intelligence. *Administrative Sciences*, *13*(9), 196. DOI: 10.3390/admsci13090196

Ghobain, E., & Zughaibi, A. (2021). Examining saudi efl university students' readiness for online learning at the onset of covid-19 pandemic. *Arab World English Journal*, *7*(1), 3–21. DOI: 10.24093/awej/call7.1

Gutiérrez, L. (2023). Artificial intelligence in language education: Navigating the potential and challenges of chatbots and nlp. *RSELTL*, *1*(3), 180–191. DOI: 10.62583/rseltl.v1i3.44

Gyawali, Y., & Mehandroo, M. (2022). Artificial intelligence in english language teaching: Navigating the future with emerging perspectives. *Journal of Language and Linguistics in Society*, (26), 21–27. DOI: 10.55529/jlls.26.21.27

Halat, D., Shami, R., Daud, A., Sami, W., Soltani, A., & Malki, A. (2024). Artificial intelligence readiness, perceptions, and educational needs among dental students: A cross-sectional study. *Clinical and Experimental Dental Research*, *10*(4), e925. Advance online publication. DOI: 10.1002/cre2.925 PMID: 38970241

Holmes, W., Porayska-Pomsta, K., Holstein, K., Sutherland, E., Baker, T., Shum, S., Santos, O. C., Rodrigo, M. T., Cukurova, M., Bittencourt, I. I., & Koedinger, K. (2021). Ethics of ai in education: Towards a community-wide framework. *International Journal of Artificial Intelligence in Education*, *32*(3), 504–526. DOI: 10.1007/s40593-021-00239-1

Huang, F., Wang, Y., & Zhang, H. (2024). Modelling generative ai acceptance, perceived teachers' enthusiasm and self-efficacy to english as a foreign language learners' well-being in the digital era. *European Journal of Education*, *59*(4), e12770. Advance online publication. DOI: 10.1111/ejed.12770

Huang, W., Hew, K., & Fryer, L. (2021). Chatbots for language learning—Are they really useful? a systematic review of chatbot-supported language learning. *Journal of Computer Assisted Learning*, *38*(1), 237–257. DOI: 10.1111/jcal.12610

Ibrahim, A., Taura, A., Iliyasu, A., Shogbesan, Y., & Lukman, S. (2024). Artificial intelligence (ai): Perception and utilization of ai technologies in educational assessment in nigerian universities. *Edukasiana Jurnal Inovasi Pendidikan*, *3*(3), 367–380. DOI: 10.56916/ejip.v3i3.763

Idham, A., Rauf, W., & Rajab, A. (2024). Navigating the transformative impact of artificial intelligence on english language teaching: Exploring challenges and opportunities. *JES*, *4*(1), 8–14. DOI: 10.56185/jes.v4i1.620

Igbokwe, I. (2024). Artificial intelligence in educational leadership: Risks and responsibilities. *EJAHSS*, *1*(6), 3–10. DOI: 10.59324/ejahss.2024.1(6).01

Kanont, K., Pingmuang, P., Simasathien, T., Wisnuwong, S., Wiwatsiripong, B., Poonpirome, K., Songkram, N., & Khlaisang, J. (2024). Generative-ai, a learning assistant? factors influencing higher-ed students' technology acceptance. *Electronic Journal of e-Learning*, *22*(6), 18–33. DOI: 10.34190/ejel.22.6.3196

Karimi, H., & Khawaja, S. (2023). The impact of artificial intelligence on higher education in england. *Creative Education*, *14*(12), 2405–2415. DOI: 10.4236/ce.2023.1412154

Kasztelnik, K. (2024). Artificial intelligence-assisted curriculum development: Innovations in designing educational content for the 21st century learner. *Journal of Higher Education Theory and Practice*, *24*(11). Advance online publication. DOI: 10.33423/jhetp.v24i11.7367

Kemell, K., Vakkuri, V., & Halme, E. (2022). Utilizing user stories to bring ai ethics into practice in software engineering., 553-558. DOI: 10.1007/978-3-031-21388-5_41

Kristiawan, D., Bashar, K., & Pradana, D. (2024). Artificial intelligence in english language learning: A systematic review of ai tools, applications, and pedagogical outcomes. *The Art of Teaching English as a Foreign Language*, *5*(2), 207–218. DOI: 10.36663/tatefl.v5i2.912

Kruk, M., & Kałużna, A. (2024). Investigating the role of ai tools in enhancing translation skills, emotional experiences, and motivation in l2 learning. *European Journal of Education*, *60*(1), e12859. Advance online publication. DOI: 10.1111/ejed.12859

Leddy, M., & Creanor, N. (2024). Exploring how education can leverage artificial intelligence for social good. *European Conference on Innovation and Entrepreneurship*, 19(1), 1041-1048. DOI: 10.34190/ecie.19.1.2906

Lee, J., Hong, M., & Cho, J. (2024). Development of a content framework of artificial intelligence integrated education considering ethical factors. *International Journal on Advanced Science, Engineering and Information Technology*, *14*(1), 205–213. DOI: 10.18517/ijaseit.14.1.19558

Lee, K., & Joshi, K. (2020). Understanding the role of cultural context and user interaction in artificial intelligence based systems. *Journal of Global Information Technology Management*, *23*(3), 171–175. DOI: 10.1080/1097198X.2020.1794131

Li, Y. (2022). Teaching mode of oral english in the age of artificial intelligence. *Frontiers in Psychology*, *13*, 953482. Advance online publication. DOI: 10.3389/fpsyg.2022.953482 PMID: 35936279

Lin, M., Liu, A., Poitras, E., Chang, M., & Chang, D. (2024). An exploratory study on the efficacy and inclusivity of ai technologies in diverse learning environments. *Sustainability (Basel)*, *16*(20), 8992. DOI: 10.3390/su16208992

Magtoto, G., Bagnol, F., & Abunda, R. (2024). Chatgpt — A threat or an aid in teaching and learning. *IJODeL*, *9*(2). Advance online publication. DOI: 10.58887/ijodel.v9i2.250

Mai, W., Ambashe, M., & Ohueri, C. (2024). Artificial intelligence ethics best practices model for financial decision-making in chinese financial institutions. *International Journal of Information Technologies and Systems Approach*, *17*(1), 1–18. DOI: 10.4018/IJITSA.337388

Men, Q. (2024). Exploration of the application of artificial intelligence in high school english speaking teaching. *Communications in Humanities Research*, *35*(1), 133–137. DOI: 10.54254/2753-7064/35/20240035

Minh, A. (2024). Leveraging chatgpt for enhancing english writing skills and critical thinking in university freshmen. Journal of Knowledge Learning and Science Technology Issn 2959-6386 (Online), 3(2), 51-62. DOI: 10.60087/jklst.vol3.n2.p62

Mohamed, M. (2024). Exploring ethical dimensions of ai-enhanced language education: A literature perspective. *Technology in Language Teaching & Learning*, *6*(3), 1813. DOI: 10.29140/tltl.v6n3.1813

Nasir, M., Hasan, M., Adlim, A., & Syukri, M. (2024). Utilizing artificial intelligence in education to enhance teaching effectiveness. *Proceedings of ICE*, *2*(1), 280–285. DOI: 10.32672/pice.v2i1.1367

Nghi, T., & Nguyen, T. (2024). Transforming language acquisition: advanced artificial intelligence approaches for second language education in asia. DOI: 10.21203/rs.3.rs-4182646/v1

Pan, J.PAN. (2024). Ai-driven english language learning program and academic writing integrity in the era of intelligent interface. *English Language Teaching and Linguistics Studies*, *6*(4), 120. DOI: 10.22158/eltls.v6n4p120

Pitychoutis, K. (2024). Harnessing ai chatbots for efl essay writing: a paradigm shift in language pedagogy. DOI: 10.31235/osf.io/xrvth

Popova, A., & Gorokhova, S. (2021). Digital technologies and artificial intelligence technologies in education. *European Journal of Contemporary Education, 10*(2). Advance online publication. DOI: 10.13187/ejced.2021.2.285

Rosmayanti, V. (2025). Eco-Linguistics and Digital Learning: Integrating Environmental Awareness in Language Education. In *Nexus of Environmental Quality and Technology Innovation* (pp. 71-96). IGI Global Scientific Publishing. DOI: 10.4018/979-8-3373-1822-6.ch004

Rosmayanti, V., Noni, N., & Patak, A. A. (2022). Students' Acceptance of Technology Use in Learning English Pharmacy. *International Journal of Language Education, 6*(3), 314–331. DOI: 10.26858/ijole.v6i3.24144

Saeed, M. (2021). Learner autonomy: Learners' perceptions on strategies to achieve autonomy in an efl classroom. *International Journal of Linguistics Literature and Translation, 4*(3), 150–158. DOI: 10.32996/ijllt.2021.4.3.17

Sanusi, I. and Olaleye, S. (2022). An insight into cultural competence and ethics in k-12 artificial intelligence education., 790-794. DOI: 10.1109/EDUCON52537.2022.9766818

Seo, K., Tang, J., Roll, I., Fels, S., & Yoon, D. (2021). The impact of artificial intelligence on learner–instructor interaction in online learning. *International Journal of Educational Technology in Higher Education, 18*(1), 54. Advance online publication. DOI: 10.1186/s41239-021-00292-9 PMID: 34778540

Sharanesha, R., Alqarni, A., Alagla, M., Ghwainem, A., Abushạnan, A., Alazmah, A., & Alghamdi, S. (2025). Perceptions and utilization of artificial intelligence in manuscript writing: a cross-sectional survey in health care academics. DOI: 10.21203/rs.3.rs-5518955/v1

Siau, K., & Wang, W. (2020). Artificial intelligence (ai) ethics. *Journal of Database Management, 31*(2), 74–87. DOI: 10.4018/JDM.2020040105

Song, C., & Song, Y. (2023). Enhancing academic writing skills and motivation: Assessing the efficacy of chatgpt in ai-assisted language learning for efl students. *Frontiers in Psychology, 14*, 1260843. Advance online publication. DOI: 10.3389/fpsyg.2023.1260843 PMID: 38162975

Starčič, A., Bratko, I., & Rosanda, V. (2021). Pre-service teachers' concerns about social robots in the classroom: A model for development. *Education & Self Development, 16*(2), 60–87. DOI: 10.26907/esd.16.2.05

Strümke, I. (2021). The social dilemma in artificial intelligence development and why we have to solve it. https://doi.org//arxiv.2107.12977DOI: 10.48550

Sun, M. (2023). Exploring the opportunities and challenges of ai technology in college english teaching., 1532-1541. DOI: 10.2991/978-2-38476-126-5_171

Tajik, A. (2025). Exploring the role of ai-driven dynamic writing platforms in improving efl learners' writing skills and fostering their motivation. DOI: 10.21203/rs.3.rs-5788599/v1

Tiwari, H. (2024). Artificial intelligence in the classroom: Revolutionizing english language teaching. [Jet Li]. *Journal of English Teaching and Linguistics Studies*, *6*(1), 42–59. DOI: 10.55215/jetli.v6i1.9757

Tran, D., & Nguyen, H. (2020). Efl teachers' beliefs and practices of teaching pronunciation in a vietnamese setting. *Universal Journal of Educational Research*, *8*(12), 7022–7035. DOI: 10.13189/ujer.2020.081270

Ulum, Ö. (2024). Unveiling the layers: Analyzing chatgpt implementations in turkish state universities. *BEDU*, *5*(1), 114–134. DOI: 10.29329/bedu.2024.651.7

Upadhyay, U., Gradišek, A., Iqbal, U., Dhar, E., Li, Y., & Syed-Abdul, S. (2023). Call for the responsible artificial intelligence in the healthcare. *BMJ Health & Care Informatics*, *30*(1), e100920. DOI: 10.1136/bmjhci-2023-100920 PMID: 38135293

Wang, D. (2024). Design of college english teaching model under the background of artificial intelligence + big data. *Advances in Educational Technology and Psychology*, *8*(2). Advance online publication. DOI: 10.23977/aetp.2024.080202

Wang'ang'a, A. (2024). Consequences of artificial intelligence on teaching and learning in higher education in kenya: Literature review. *East African Journal of Education Studies*, *7*(1), 202–215. DOI: 10.37284/eajes.7.1.1718

Wei, L. (2023). Artificial intelligence in language instruction: Impact on english learning achievement, l2 motivation, and self-regulated learning. *Frontiers in Psychology*, *14*, 1261955. Advance online publication. DOI: 10.3389/fpsyg.2023.1261955 PMID: 38023040

Wirzal, M., Nordin, N., Halim, N., & Bustam, M. (2024). Generative ai in science education: A learning revolution or a threat to academic integrity? a bibliometric analysis. *Jurnal Penelitian Dan Pengkajian Ilmu Pendidikan E-Saintika*, *8*(3), 319–351. DOI: 10.36312/e-saintika.v8i3.2127

Wu, Y. (2024). Study on the impact of utilizing chatgpt and other ai tools for feedback in eap writing classrooms on the discursive writing performance of english major students. *TSSEHR*, *4*, 143–150. DOI: 10.62051/4se95x52

Xi, L. (2024). Research on the english writing teaching model in the ai era. *MMSE*, *6*(3), 111. DOI: 10.22158/mmse.v6n3p111

Xue, F. (2024). Ai integration in creative industries: Challenges and opportunities. *Applied and Computational Engineering*, *104*(1), 21–27. DOI: 10.54254/2755-2721/104/20240906

Yin, H., Khan, S., Alharbi, A., & Nazir, S. (2022). Assessing english teaching linguistic and artificial intelligence for efficient learning using analytical hierarchy process and technique for order of preference by similarity to ideal solution. *Journal of Software (Malden, MA)*. Advance online publication. DOI: 10.1002/smr.2462

Zhao, X. (2022). Leveraging artificial intelligence (ai) technology for english writing: Introducing wordtune as a digital writing assistant for efl writers. *RELC Journal*, *54*(3), 890–894. DOI: 10.1177/00336882221094089

KEY TERMS AND DEFINITIONS

Algorithmic Bias: This happens when AI-generated results are skewed in a systematic way because the training data is unbalanced, incomplete, or biased. This gives some groups of learners unfair advantages or disadvantages.

Data Privacy: The ethical and legal obligation to protect personal information gathered by AI systems to prevent the misuse of learners' identity, behavior, and performance data.

Explainable AI (XAI): A type of AI that makes system processes, decisions, and outputs easier for users to understand, which builds trust and transparency.

Learner Autonomy: The ability of students to make their own decisions about how to learn and what strategies to use, which AI-based educational tools can help or hurt.

Personalized Learning: An instructional method in which AI customizes content, pacing, and feedback to meet the specific needs and capabilities of learners, thereby enhancing language development.

Predictive Analytics: The AI-powered process of looking at learner data to guess how they will do in the future, figure out what they need to learn, and suggest ways to teach them.

Transparency: The degree to which an AI system openly communicates how it collects data, functions, and produces outcomes, enabling users to understand and evaluate its operations.

User Consent: The informed and voluntary agreement provided by learners before their data is collected or processed by AI systems, ensuring respect for personal autonomy and rights.

Chapter 16

A Chronological Investigation of Free Online and Artificial Intelligence Translation Services:

Telescoping Sixteen Years of the Product Accuracy Progress

Hussein Ali Habtoor
https://orcid.org/0000-0002-5146-0774
Department of English, College of Education, Shabwah University, Yemen

ABSTRACT

This paper aims to investigate chronologically the progress of online Machine Translation (MT) services and the accuracy of the products of such translations verses Artificial Intelligence (AI) translation. The descriptive comparative approach has been used to do the chronological linguistic analysis of the texts and four raters asked to judge the Target Texts. The text that has been assigned for translation task in this paper has been translated by Google Translation, World Lingo and Reverso services in 2009, and then translated again by the same services in 2025. Another translation for the same texts is done in 2025 by DeepL as an AI translation service. The results show a very big gap in the product quality over these sixteen years of progress at all levels of language and, more specifically, at the semantic level with a wide-ranging development in such online services in translating Arabic-English texts, but compared to AI services they remain lagging behind in several matters at different linguistic and cultural-bound linguistic matters.

DOI: 10.4018/979-8-3373-3561-2.ch016

INTRODUCTION

Machine translation (MT) has been considered as common practice in recent times of translation activities. In tracing the history of MT, it is relatively new if compared to the long history of the practice of human translation that lasted for several ages parallel to the development of human history. Due to the urgent need for fast translation, a great deal of translation of science, technology and medicine is handled since the early beginnings of MT services and "systems for automatic translation have been under development for 50 years – in fact, ever since the electronic computer was invented in the 1940s there has been research on their application for translating languages" (Hutchins 1986). To begin with, the definition of "Automatic Translation, or Machine Translation (MT) as it is generally known— the attempt to automate all, or part of the process of translating from one human language to another." (Arnold, et al., 1994 p.1), which enabled enormous amount of translation to be performed on day-to-day bases human activities. The rapid rhythm of life demands faster and parallel action in regular human responsibilities, where time is too short and tasks are totally huge. Translation is, no doubt, in the heart of such an activity executed around the clock. The immense literature being rendered across the globe language pairs requires faster and accurate tools to handle these bulky tasks that may go beyond human capacity to be done manually and yet cope with the time commitments.

The beginnings of MT services online are undoubtedly modest and time-consuming, compared to what is experienced today. To trace the developments of MT, this apparently reflects the hardship that developers of such machine passed through. Tracing the historical development of MT leads to the modest beginnings of such activity through mechanical dictionaries in the 17th century that were used as a tool to overcome the language barriers.it was only recently when in the 20th century with some modest trials in both France and Russia through word equivalents between languages Hutchins (1995), but these trials remain open for more initiated advancements. It is from 1950s till 1980s that Rule Based Machine Translation (RBMT) had been introduced and IBM pioneering this activity by translating Russian into English at the sentence level (Zughoul, and Abu-alshaar 2005).

More recently, that is in the mid of 1990s, a revolutionised steps have been witnessed by the Internet being introduced to our lives and ultimately into the development of MT. Offline machine translation has been developed in the initial phase with specially designed software products that cater for web pages electronic mail messages. After that, several online MT service providers started to offer Internet -based online translation services intended at helping on-demand translation. This sort of commotion was initiated at first by Systran; however, broader acceptance did not materialize until CompuServe launched a trial service utilizing the Transcend system in 1995. Shortly thereafter, the now widely recognized service Babelfish emerged on the AltaVista platform, providing versions of Systran to facilitate translations between French, German, and Spanish, as well as English (and subsequently numerous other language pairs). This expansion was flourished by an overabundance of additional online services (most of which are provided freely), including Softissimo with its online versions of the Reverso systems, LogoMedia with its online offerings of LogoVista, and PARS. Certain services afford post-editing by human translators (revisers) for an extra payment; however, in the mainstream of occurrences, the delivered outcomes remain intact. (Hutchins, 2010).

MT is ever developing field of both theory and practice that has witnessed a series of advancements over history which have led subsequently to the appearance of approaches that account for the craft to cope with time changes and developments in the present highly technological dependent world. A thorough but brief chronological account on the topic has been reported in a nutshell by Mercan, Akgün, Odacioglu, (Mercan et al., 2024). We give an outline of that as noted below:

1. Rule-based Machine Translation (1950s-1980s)
2. Transfer-based Machine Translation (1980s-1990s)
3. Interlingual Machine Translation (1990s)
4. Corpus-based Machine Translation (1990s)
5. Example-based Machine Translation (1990s-2000s)
6. Statistical Machine Translation (2000s-2010s)
7. Neural Machine Translation (2010s-present)
8. Hybrid Machine Translation (present)

Statement of the Problem

This paper focuses on investigating the translation accuracy of three machine translation software services viz., *Google Translate (GT), World Lingo (WL) and Reverso (RV)* and comparing their TTs with AI translations done by *DeepL* free online service. The data collected in 2009 is an Arabic text translated at that time using these services and it is translated again by the same services for comparative purposes in 2025, while the *DeepL* translation is done in 2025 for the same purpose. While machine translation has made significant advancements, it still faces many problematic issues. Some common issues are: The failure to account for transferring the accurate meaning of idioms and fixed expressions, reformulation of structures into the TL, syntactic peculiarities of both SL and TL, specific expressions, word order, proper punctuation of the product such as full stops and commas, and also the lack of context understanding in varied products of these free online services. Of course, some of these problems in MT no longer constitute a problematic confrontation for the clients and native speakers in terms of legibility due to new developments and updates in MT in recent years.

The early translations of *Google Translate, Lingo and Reverso* when they were first launched, included so many errors related to the syntax, lexicon and meaning of the target language, as noted above. However, these three machine translation software have been subjected to never-ending attempts to improve their translation quality. To the best of the researchers' knowledge, no previous study has investigated the improvement of these software's translations from Arabic into English. Thus, there is a gap in the literature and this study is hoped to abridge. This paper as an academic attempt to offer an insight of such problem and try to be of good use by researchers interested in MT and programming developers of such free software services who are in charge of quality improvements in the outcomes of these MT tools in addition to the learners of translation who are concerned about online MT research. This research is expected to bridge a gap in the literature so as to benefit a large number of audiences like translators, translation studies scholars, students, teachers and materials developers and syllabus designers.

Significance and Limitations of the Study

There is an excessive increase and interest in labour market for free online machine translation. These services are very popular world-wide nowadays and the translation transactions executed on daily bases are tremendous involving various language pairs of such activity. Arabic English and English Arabic pairs of translation have attracted the attention of scholars for both product quality and quantity. As this study attempts to figure out the quality of the product of these free services, it is essential to focus tremendous demand for this type of translation that highlighted the scarcity of well-qualified translators and the zero-costs of these services.

The significance of this study lies in its importance and benefit for teachers, researchers, programming developers and students of translations. Those who are interested in computational linguistics in general and MT in particular will find it useful as well.

The current study focuses only on three MT software, namely, *Google Translate, Lingo* and *Reverso*. Furthermore, it will focus only on Arabic-English translations within a specific period, i.e. (2009-2025).

Research Questions

The current study aims at answering the following research questions

1. What are the translation errors in in the early versions of Arabic-English translations of Google Translate, World lingo and Reverso?
2. What are the translation errors in the latest versions of Arabic-English translations of Google Translate, Lingo and Reverso?
3. To what extent have Google Translate, World lingo and Reverso succeeded in developing their recent translations?

LITERATURE REVIEW

MT has been tackled thoroughly by various scholars all over the world contributing to its grounding of theoretical bases and it has made significant development over years of its history. There are abundance of studies evaluating the performance of MT (Hutchins, 2001; Hutchins & Somers, 1992). As noted above, MT has been tackled by many research scholars, but from various perspectives over time due to its fast and wide spread utilization in human lives. Nevertheless, in Arabic MT context, there are several studies that have been carried out either in translation from Arabic to English or English to Arabic. These works may include, but not limited to (; Ali, 2020; Almahasees, 2021; Ameur et al., 2020; At-tall, 2019; Banimelhem & Amayreh, 2023; Zakraoui, Saleh, Al-Maadeed & Alja'am 2020; Zakraoui, Saleh, Al-Maadeed & Alja'am, 2021).

In the following paragraphs, a brief survey of literature is to be accounted for so as to give a clear vision of such field of knowledge that has influenced our lives for its effectiveness and very rapid achievements, i.e., a big amount of source language will be accomplished into another target language within a blink of eye. This survey will give a background to online MT evaluation in general and the focus will be on Arabic to English and vice versa, but in a nutshell of chronological viewpoint of some of the works noted above and others, of course.

One of the earliest studies is that of Aiken, Ghosh, Wee and Vanjani (2009), who examined the accuracy of online MT services and their costly charges and their effective support for translation field. Focusing on German to English and Spanish to English, they found that superiority of Google over the other three free online machines. They also did not neglect the perfection of such services which is far reaching but to understand the outcomes remains so high.

Brazill, Masters, and Munday (2016) on the other hand, investigated human versus machine translation accuracy in Chinese-to-English between moderate to higher-level human translators and frequently employed free of charge accessible MT tools, they discovered that native Chinese speakers with this lower level of English proficiency were absolutely better at translating structures from Chinese to English. These individuals with at least a reasonable level of exposure to a foreign language made far fewer translation errors, taking into account intangible linguistic variants, situation, and unpredictable meaning related to the language and culture of diverse groups.

Regrading Arabic, Almahasees (2017) evaluated Google and Microsoft machine translation tools online in translating poetical texts through BLEU metrics. The result of his study revealed that Google translate attains better outcomes than Microsoft Bing in comparison to human referenced translation. However, MT needs further improvement to make its quality closer to that of human products of translation.

Another study on Arabic-English MT, focusing on Google Translate, was carried out by Elkaffash (2020). It was from neural machine translation perspective, examining the academic genre in translating between Arabic and English pairs. It showed that the model used for evaluation is vigorous and effective. The error analysis offered a closer insight on the grammatical errors pertaining to both locating the errors within the engine's translation process and its deficiency in analysing language or the translation process itself.

Sabtan and Hussein (2021) attempted to address the gap of evaluating the MT output for the standard varieties of Arabic through presenting an evaluation of the performance of MT output for vernacular or colloquial Arabic in the social media domain. They found that several translation problems have been detected for Google Translate production such as incorrect equivalents, inappropriate additions and omissions, and transliteration for out-of-vocabulary words, which are mostly due to the literal translation of the Arabic vernacular sentences into English.

Almahasees and Mahmoud (2022) investigated how neural machine translation powering Google Translate in performing content translations of images and texts freely and how accurately this translation product is through 'linguistic error analysis', with a special focus on Arabic and English without human aid editing. They have come up with results reflecting errors all linguistic levels. Ultimately, Human intervention in such translation is inevitable.

Shormani (2024) investigated artificial intelligence (AI) contribution to translation industry (ACTI) research, synthesizing it over forty-five years using scientometric and thematic types of analysis. He was focusing on cluster, subject categories, keywords, burstness, centrality and research centres as for the former. He added that, the more AI develops, the better machine translation will be, integrating Neural Networking Algorithms and (Deep) Language Learning Models like ChatGPT whose translation output has developed considerably.

More recently, Matviienko, L. Khomenko, L. Denysovets, I., Horodenska, K., Nikolashyna, T. Pavlova, I (2024) focused on discovering the efficiency and accurateness of the translation, noticing the strengths and weaknesses of three common online translators: Google Translate, DeepL and Microsoft Translator. The study revealed that each of these machine translators has its own merits and demerits, and the choice hinges on the precise needs of the operator. To ensure accuracy and effectiveness, continuous updating and improvement are essential according to these scholars.

METHODS AND PROCEDURES

The data for this paper have been collected from Aljazeera.net and. An Arabic source text (ST) has been designated from Aljazeera website. It is of political genre in nature and related to Arabic backgrounds. It of 113 words length, as indicated above the text below in the Analysis section. It is selected randomly from that website in 2009 and assigned for translation in the Arabic into English and pairs using Reverso, World Lingo and Google translate free online translation services.

The comparative descriptive approach has been used to conduct this research so as to handle the research problem related to the linguistic variation and translation quality of the translation systems outputs. To tackle the changes these systems experienced over sixteen years of development, that have eventually influenced the output credibility the customers have witnessed over this long period, Costa's et al (2015) taxonomy was adopted to check the errors committed by these online translation services, (see figure no. 1 below). It tracked how these errors have either been retained or taken over with machine improvement over time. Evaluating accuracy, as stated by Saldanha and O'Brien (2014), "allows us to measure the impact and effect of different variables on the translation product and process and to subsequently change our techniques, training, or tools in order to better meet quality requirements" (p. 96), is the main focus of the study along with other important related issues such as comprehensibility, readability and fluency.

Figure 1. Costa's et al Taxonomy (A framework of MT online Services Error Analysis)

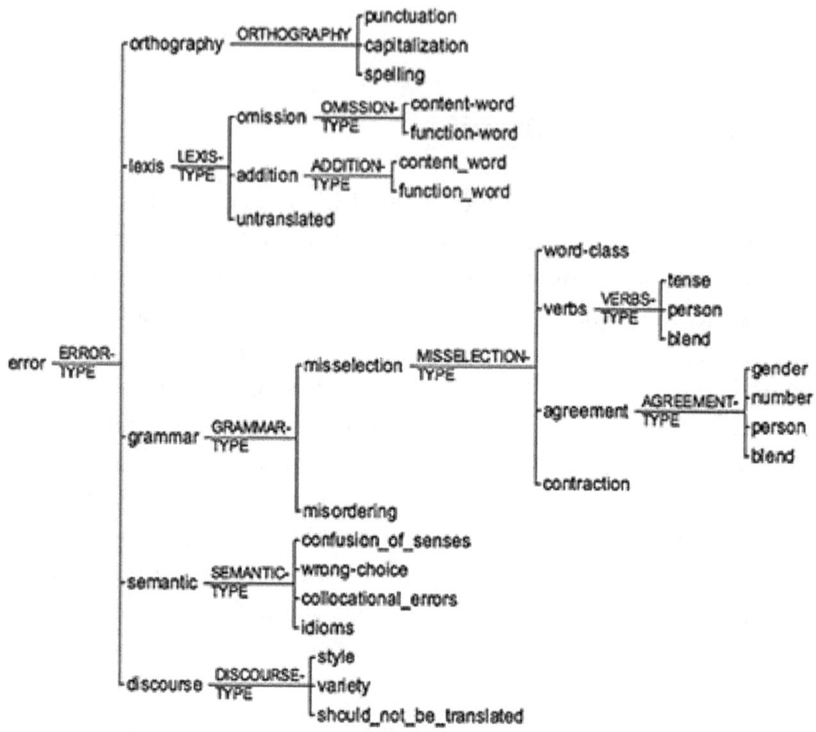

Source: Costa et al., 2015, p. 139.

DISCUSSION OF FINDINGS

In this section a detailed account of findings is to be reported so as to give a thorough idea to answer the inquiries postulated above and to attain the outcomes this paper has investigated. We will begin with the assigned text and present its translations of both 2009 and 2025 in two columns of one table so as to make it a reader- friendly table and easier to compare. AI translation is to be put after the three translations as a reference translation against which all the translations will be checked.

Arabic to English Translations

An Arabic source text has been assigned to this task of online free translation. It is taken from aljazeera.net, as noted earlier, and it is of political register as being an item of news of the day in this website. This text is 113 words length.

Arabic Source Text (113 words)

لم تغب الخلافات العربية بشكل كامل عن قمة الدوحة التي خيمت عليها -في رأي مراقبين- أجواء المصالحة، في وقت تضمنت كلمات الزعماء رسائل ضمنية في أكثر من اتجاه. وفي هذا السياق رأى محللون أن غياب الرئيس المصري حسني مبارك عن حضور القمة أعطى انطباعا بأن العرب قد سلموا ملف القضية الفلسطينية إلى الجانب المصري. الناطق الرسمي باسم الخارجية المصرية السفير حسام زكي لم ينف تلك المقولة، وقال إن الملف أصلا في أيادي مصر و "هي تشرف عليه وليس هناك جديد في ذلك". وردا على سؤال بشأن صحة أنباء ترددت في أروقة المؤتمر عن تشدد مصر في إجراء مصالحة مع الدولة الرئيسة للمؤتمر في دورته الحالية، قال زكي "لا أحبذ التعليق على هذه الأنباء".(الجزيرة نت 31-3-2009) http://www.aljazeera.net/NR/exeres/E20D4A94-6190-422F-AA4D-439DDA66C6DF.htm

Table 1. Target Text 1-A, (By Reverso)

Reverso	2009 translation	2025 translation
	We have not forgotten Arab disagreements fully on the Doha summit overshadowed by - in the view of observers - the atmosphere of reconciliation, at the time included the words of the leaders messages implicit in more than one direction. In this context, analysts said the absence of the Egyptian President Hosni Mubarak to attend the summit gave the impression that the Arabs have handed over the file of the Palestinian issue to the Egyptian side. The foreign ministry spokesman Egyptian ambassador Hossam Zaki did not deny that statement, he said that the dossier already in the hands of Egypt and "is supervised by there is not new in it". In response to a question on the health news in the corridors of the Conference on stresses Egypt of a reconciliation with the State the Chairperson of the Conference in its current session, Zaki said "does not in favour of the commentary to this news"	Arab disagreements did not completely lose sight of the Doha Summit, which, in the view of observers, was overshadowed by an atmosphere of reconciliation, at a time when the leaders' words contained implicit messages in more than one direction. In this context, analysts felt that Egyptian President Hosni Mubarak's absence from the summit gave the impression that Arabs had handed over the file of the Palestinian issue to the Egyptian side. The official spokesman for Egyptian Foreign Affairs, Ambassador Husam Zaki, did not deny this statement and said that the file was originally in Egypt's hands and "it is supervised and there is nothing new in it." In response to a question about the veracity of reports in the corridors of the Conference about Egypt's tightening reconciliation with the President of the Conference at its current session, Zaki said, "I do not favour commenting on this news."

Reverso Translation Analysis

To compare the two texts and make changes over time accentuated enough to ensure the accuracy of the translation, we may have a closer look in a level-wise linguistic analysis. It is obviously realised the good level of language progress attained in reverso translation of 2025, compared to 2009 translation, as it is shown in table (1) above. As for the linguistic errors committed by Reverso in 2009, the orthographical level; including punctuation, capitalization and spelling, does not seem to have much errors that constitute vital seriousness to the texts' ineligibility in both products of Reverso. The noun phrase '*leaders messages*' is to be written with apostrophe as: (*leaders' messages*). Another error is related to punctuation, where commas are supposed to supply a good support to meaning, where a string of words that have to be separated as a noun phrase such as the sentence in italics below:

- *The foreign ministry spokesman Egyptian ambassador Hossam Zaki did not deny that statement, he said that the dossier already in the hands of Egypt and "is supervised by there is not new in it".*

Lexically, both of these translations have, to some extent, utilized a closer vocabulary almost with some variation. Expressions focusing on political and diplomatic terms related to an Arab summit, disagreements, reconciliation, and the Palestinian issue are utilised. The differences are minor and seldomly constitute a serious mistake. Word choice can be tackled as illustrating the variation in: *We have not forgotten Arab disagreements fully* (2009) vs. *Arab disagreements did not completely lose sight of* (2025). Both of them convey the idea that disagreements were still present, but 2025's wording is somewhat more idiomatic and a bit acceptable than the other. Generally, these two sentences did not convey the intended meaning in the target text in Arabic. The normal translation might be performed by DeepL AI translation in table (4) below, which looks closer to human translation for such statement as it is noted here: *Arab disagreements were not entirely absent from the Doha summit. "We have not forgotten*" is an addition that is to be considered lexically an error of adding both functional and content words in the target text, which are not necessarily needed at all.

Another observation may be in the following two sentences: "*overshadowed by - in the view of observers - the atmosphere of reconciliation at the time included the words of the leaders messages implicit in more than one direction.* " (2009) vs. "*overshadowed by an atmosphere of reconciliation, at a time when the leaders' words contained implicit messages in more than one direction*" (2025). The second text fits in the idea about implicit messages more efficiently into the portrayal of the summit's atmosphere. Ther are some grammatical mistakes in translation in the first sentence including miss-selection and miss-ordering. 2025 Reverso translation is more concise and grammatically precise. The past perfect is used in 2025's translation as in the sentence "gave the impression that Arabs had handed over the file of the Palestinian issue to the Egyptian side" and this emphasises the action completion rather than focusing on the result as done in 2009's translation of the sentence using "*Arabs have handed over...*". Using the demonstratives '*that*' and '*that*' by these two translations, respectively, gives an indication of improving the quality of translation and moving from literal translation to more communicative one. The sentence translated into: *"The foreign ministry spokesman Egyptian ambassador Hossam Zaki"* vs. "*The official spokesman for Egyptian Foreign Affairs, Ambassador Husam Zaki" by* Reverso (2009) and (2025) service, respectively, have got some differences in formality, while the former is less formal the latter is more formal by providing a clearer title ("*official spokesman for Egyptian Foreign Affairs*").

Generally, and as far as grammar is concerned, 2025 translation is far better more than that of 2009, in many respects. They are more formal with better flow of language reflected in adding some sort of a tone of time in using demonstratives such as '*this*' in direct quotes in the text, for instance. Furthermore, 2025's translation is unquestionably clearer and syntactically more accurate while 2009's translation phrasing is obstinate and less accurate. 2025's translation provides a more natural phrasing of the quote. It largely exhibits better lexical accuracy and evades the slightly difficult or grammatically improper wording present in 2009's translation.

Syntactically speaking, 2025's translation demonstrates more grammatically sound and fluent sentence structures; while 2009's target text contains several instances of awkward wording and less conventional syntax. For instance, the opening sentence of that text is less smoothly constructed than 2025's. Thus, the phrase "*at the time included the words of the leaders messages implicit*" (2009) is grammatically clumsy compared to "*at a time when the leaders' words contained implicit messages*" (2025). Word Order, on the other hand, in both target texts generally follow standard English word order, but the bulky wording in 2009's translation sometimes makes the intended relationships between words less clear.

As for Cohesion and Coherence, the target text of 2025 achieved better attainment through clearer sentence structures and more logical flow of information. The connections between ideas are more easily followed in the latest version of translation. In the earlier version of translation, syntactic issues occasionally interrupt the smooth flow of the narrative.

Regarding the semantic level, both of the target texts attain the same fundamental information about the Doha summit, the presence of underlying Arab disagreements despite an atmosphere of reconciliation, the perceived handing over of the Palestinian issue to Egypt due to Mubarak's absence, and the Egyptian spokesman's responses regarding these matters and reconciliation rumours. Clarity and Readability also seem to be significantly clearer and easier to read and understand in 2025's version due to its more grammatically correct and fluent language. 2009 text's syntactic awkwardness and less precise word choices can hinder comprehension. In the same way, formality and tone, 2025's text adopts a slightly more formal and professional tone through its more precise language and standard grammatical structures. Target text of 2009 feels slightly less polished.

As an overall impression, Reverso's targe text of 2025 is likely to be perceived as more trustworthy and convincing due to its clearer and more standard use of English. The message is conveyed more successfully without the grammatical stumbling blocks present in the previous version of the translation.

To sum up, while both texts discuss the same events and issues, 2025's text exhibits a marked improvement in grammatical correctness, syntactic fluency, and lexical precision compared to 2009's text. The target text of Reverso 2009 suffers from several instances of obstinate and intricate phrasing that hamper clearness and legibility. Target text of 2025 presents the information in a more refined, qualified, and effortlessly comprehensible style.

World Lingo Translation Analysis

Following the same procedure in analysing Reverso product of translation, World Lingo translation is going to be tackled. A closer look at the language of the two target texts at all linguistic levels will give us a very precise idea about the level of each translation and the progress World Lingo has accomplished over sixteen years of research and improvement of software concerned with translation. Let's compare them at the orthographical, lexical, syntactical, and semantic levels and investigate the errors committed in the process of translation of this political text from Arabic into English.

At the orthographical level, and as revealed in table (2) below, there are some orthographical problems with World Lingo's 2009 translation that made the text less acceptable and even, to some extent, unintelligible. The comma is supposed to separate the adverbial at the beginning of a sentence from the rest of the components of that sentence such as this; "*in this context analysts saw that the absence of President Egyptian Hosni Mubarak …*", and even the proper name *Husni Mubarak* is to be separated from the rest of the sentence components with two commas. The use of dashes and quotation marks also looks unpredictable in the earlier version of translation.

World Lingo's 2009 translation, table (2), has much more problems. At the lexical level, for instance, we can see that the word (قمة) has been translated as (top), which is a literal translation and it is incorrect as well, but in the second translation as in table (2), this word is translated as (summit), which is an acceptable and correct equivalence. Moreover, the use of "[ynf]" is unclear and doesn't follow typical English morphology, rather it is left untranslated and a transliteration of the word is given. The word (باسم) also has been translated wrongly in the first one as (smiling) and the word (الخارجية) (Foreign Affairs) also translated as (externality). All of these two words are not correct and give a bad lexical choice. In the second translation of World Lingo, we find that they are translated as in the following phrase: "*The official spokesman for Egyptian Foreign Affairs*". This reflects the development of these free online services of World Lingo as a translation machine. The word (العرب) translated as (Arabic) instead of Arabs, while it is translated correctly in the second translation as (Arabs). These are examples of how translation was handled in both two trials of World Lingo.

There are some other problems at the lexical level. As can be seen in the target text of (2009), it contains several words that are either misspelled, transliterated inappropriately, or appear to be direct Arabic words not fully integrated into English. Examples include: "*top of Doha which camped on her*," a translation for "*leader words*," "*implicit letters*," "*folder*," "*externality*," "*pure sword*", [*ynf*]," "*superviz-es*," "*Incoming on question*," "*galleries of the conference*," "*insisting strictness*," "*head for the conference in his cycle*," and "*Al-Anba*.", while (2025) translation uses standard English vocabulary all over the text. Phrases like "*Doha summit*," "*observers*," "*setting of reconciliation*," "*Lords' words*," "*implicit messages*," "*case file*," "*foreign official*," "*did not deny that statement*," "*in response to a question*," "*validity of news*," and "*frequented throughout the conference*" are all common English expressions and they do not constitute any trouble to the native language reader at all. In fact, these expressions and words have got some other semantic problems in the first translation, which have been avoided in the latest version of 2025 as evidence of the detected improvement World Lingo has experienced over these sixteen years of research and implementation.

At the structural or syntactic level, we find that a very long sentence in English has been given to the Arabic equivalent. This long English sentence is:

The Arabic disagreements thoroughly about top of Doha which camped on her - in opinion of observed - atmospheres of the reconciliation, at the time leader words included implicit letters in more than direction.

The Arabic equivalence is:

لم تغب الخلافات العربية بشكل كامل عن قمة الدوحة التي خيمت عليها - في رأي المراقبين - أجواء المصالحة، في وقت تضمنت كلمات الزعماء رسائل ضمنية في أكثر من اتجاه.

The translation has some syntactic problems like, for example, (في رأي المراقبين) has been translated in the first translation as (in opinion of observed), which is incorrect and unacceptable translation at all, but in the second one it is (in the view of observers), which is acceptable and correct and this makes us confident that the second is better and there is some improvement. Furthermore, World Lingo's 2009 translation exhibits significant issues with English sentence structure. Word order is often inappropriate, making grammatically defective and hard-to-grasp sentences. Examples include: "*The Arabic disagreements thoroughly about top of Doha which camped on her - in opinion of observed - atmospheres of the reconciliation...*" and "*The official spokesman the smiling externality the Egyptian ambassador pure sword **[ynf]** that stated, and said indeed the folder originally in hands of insisting and 'she **supervizes** on him and not there new at that*". Whereas 2025's product follows normal English sentence structure with clear subjects, verbs, and objects. Phrases and clauses are assembled logically, making the text intelligible. For example: "*Arabic disagreements have not completely missed the Doha summit, which, in the opinion of observers, was a setting of reconciliation...*" and "*The official spokesperson for the Egyptian foreign official, Ambassador Hussam Zaki, did not deny that statement.*"

Semantic level also has many problems in the (2009) translation of World Lingo. In the first translation, the phrase (السفير حسام زكي), has been translated as: (Egyptian ambassador <u>pure sword</u>). With back translation into Arabic the phrase will be (السيف النقي). This shows how World Lingo in 2009 produced such expressions and words with very wrong semantic equivalence that may be misunderstood by the reader of the target text. Words like (حسام and زكي) are mistranslated semantically, because they are polysemous words and have very many meanings. As proper nouns, they should be Zaki and Husam. World Lingo gave different translations for Husam as another name of Arabic word (Sword) and Zaki for (Pure). In the same way, "*top of Doha which camped on her*," is a bad translation for (قمة الدوحة التي خيّمت عليها), which is semantically un acceptable, because the Arabic word (خيّم) is a polysemous word that has more than one meaning. In 2025 translation of World Lingo, we found that they have been translated properly as (Ambassador Husam Zaki), for the former and (was a setting of), for the later. Another example is "*implicit letters,*", which is supposed to be '*implicit messages*', because this word is also of a polysemous nature in the target language, viz., English, in which the words '*letter*' and '*message*' have only one equivalent in Arabic. Anyway, in 2025 World Lingo's translation we found that the proper equivalent has been opted for. This also reflects, to some extent, the degree of improvement in the product of this machine translation after fifteen years of development.

Furthermore, and as a semantic matter, owing to the lexical, morphological, and syntactical errors, the meaning of World Lingo's 2009 translation is normally ambiguous and hard to comprehend. While the general topic appears to be associated to Arabic differences, a summit in Doha, Egypt's role in the Palestinian problem, and news immediate to the conference, the specific details and nuances are lost in the grammatical inaccuracies. As has been discussed above, the phrase "pure sword and [ynf]" are particularly semantically vague. While the latest version of 2025 conveys a clear and comprehensible sense. It discusses the Arab disagreements in the situation of the Doha summit, observers' views on it as a reconciliation setting, implicit messages from leaders, the significance of Hosni Mubarak's absence, Egypt's constant participation in the Palestinian issue as specified by its spokesperson, and the spokesperson's unwillingness to remark on news about Egypt's firm reconciliation stance.

Finally, the latest version of translation by World Lingo is, to some extent, a well-formed English target text that successfully conveys clear account on a political situation. The earlier version of 2009 target text, on the other hand, suffers from significant linguistic errors at all levels, making it difficult to understand and interpret accurately, and it constitutes a big problem for the English native speakers. It looks a poor translation, possibly lacks accuracy of a software that is not proficient enough to produce normal equivalent in English texts.

Table 2. Target Text 1- B (World Lingo)

World Lingo	2009 translation	2025 translation
	The Arabic disagreements thoroughly about top of Doha which camped on her - in opinion of observed - atmospheres of the reconciliation, at the time leader words included implicit letters in more than direction. In this context analysts saw that absence of President Egyptian Hosni Mubarak about attendance the top gave impression that Arabic Palestinian folder the case to the Egyptian side hand over. The official spokesman the smiling externality the Egyptian ambassador pure sword [ynf] that stated, and said indeed the folder originally in hands of insisting and " she supervizes on him and not there new at that ". Incoming on question concerning health of news hesitated in galleries of the conference about insisting strictness in measure of reconciliation with the state the current head for the conference in his cycle, Zaki said "the commentary on this Al-Anba does not favor".	Arabic disagreements have not completely missed the Doha summit, which, in the opinion of observers, was a setting of reconciliation, at a time when the Lords' words included implicit messages in more than one direction. In this context, analysts saw that the absence of the Egyptian President Hosni Mubarak from attending the summit gave the impression that the Arabs had handed over the Palestinian case file to the Egyptian side. The official spokesperson for the Egyptian foreign official, Ambassador Hussam Zaki, did not deny that statement. He said that the file was originally in the hands of Egypt and that "she supervises it and there is no new thing in that." In response to a question about the validity of news that was frequented throughout the conference about Egypt's strict reconciliation with the main state of the conference in its current session, Zaki said, "I don't like commenting on this news."

Google Translation Analysis

At the orthographical level, and compared to the two counterparts of MT used in this study, Google Translate product of 2009 seems to have no errors as well as the other text of 2025. As for the lexical level, 2009's target text seems to have fewer problematic structures than the previous two have exhibited. As for the word choice, Google Translate text of 2009 encompasses some less common or even slightly obstinate word choices and phrasing, (see table 3 below). Here are some illustrations as in the following structures: "*would not have been lost completely*" (instead of "*were not entirely absent*"), "*overshadowed by - in the view of observers - an atmosphere,*" "*in the words of the leaders included the messages implicit,*" "*had been handed the case file to the Palestinian side of Egypt,*" "*'is sponsored by and there is the new',*" "*on health had been reported,*" and "*stresses in the conduct of Egypt's reconciliation.*" On the other hand, Google Translate text produced in 2025 utilised more accepted and standard English vocabulary and phrasing. For instance, we give these Example sentences and structures to show the difference chronologically manifested in the service offered by Google online: "*Were not entirely absent,*" "*observers believe was overshadowed,*" "*the leaders' speeches contained implicit messages,*" "*had handed over the Palestinian issue to the Egyptian side,*" "*'it is supervising it, and there is nothing new in that',*" "*reports circulating within the conference halls,*" and "*Egypt's insistence on reconciling.*"

Additionally, the earlier version of Google Translate demonstrations a few examples of probable morphological issues or uncommon forms. For example, "*'is sponsored by'*" might be regarded somewhat less formal than "*is supervised by.*" The absence of a clear subject for "*is sponsored*" also adds to a grammatical vagueness, whereas the 2025 version of Google Translate utilised standard English morphological forms constantly. Furthermore, Verb conjugations, pluralization, and possessives are all correctly applied.

At the syntactical Level, 2009 translation by Google Translate displays some awkward and less fluent sentence structures. The phrase "*which was overshadowed by - in the view of observers - an atmosphere*" interrupts the flow. The sentence "*In this context, analysts felt that the absence of Egyptian President Hosni Mubarak, the summit gave the impression that the Arabs had been handed the case file to the Palestinian side of Egypt*" has a somewhat complicated structure and a possible missing "from" after Mubarak. The direct quote "*'is sponsored by and there is the new'*" lacks an obvious subject. 2025 translation, on the other hand, reflects reader-friendly and more grammatically accurate sentence structures. Phrases and clauses are connected logically, making the text easier to read and comprehend. For example, "*which observers believe was overshadowed by an atmosphere of reconciliation*" flows more naturally. The sentence about Mubarak's absence is also more clearly constructed.

At the semantic level the earlier version of 2009 by Google Translate is generally comprehensible, the obstinate wording and grammatical discrepancies can to some extent hamper comprehension and may lead to inconsequential uncertainties. For instance, the exact tone of "*'is sponsored by and there is the new'*" is a bit less clear than 2025's version. Google's 2025 version communicates the meaning clearly and efficiently. The more natural language and improved sentence structure ensure that the proposed message about the Arab disagreements, the Doha summit, Mubarak's absence, Egypt's role in the Palestinian issue, and the spokesperson's comments is easily understood.

In Summary, the latest version of 2025 reveals an advanced level of fluency and grammatical correctness in English compared to the earlier version of 2009. While that text of 2009 rendered by Google Translate is still understandable, it contains several instances of difficult phrasing, less common word choices, and somewhat faulty sentence structures that make it less refined and possibly open to minor misapprehensions. The latest version of the target text presents the same information in a stronger, briefer, and grammatically comprehensive style.

Table 3. Target Text 1- C, (Google Translate)

Google Translate	2009 translation	2025 translation
	Arab differences would not have been lost completely from the Doha summit, which was overshadowed by - in the view of observers - an atmosphere of reconciliation, in the words of the leaders included the messages implicit in more than one direction. In this context, analysts felt that the absence of Egyptian President Hosni Mubarak, the summit gave the impression that the Arabs had been handed the case file to the Palestinian side of Egypt. Spokesman for the Egyptian Foreign Ministry, Ambassador Hossam Zaki did not deny that assertion, saying that the file already in the hands of Egypt, 'is sponsored by and there is the new'. In response to a question on health had been reported in the corridors of the Conference on the stresses in the conduct of Egypt's reconciliation with the State President of the Conference at its current session, Zaki said 'do not like to comment on the news'	Arab differences were not entirely absent from the Doha summit, which observers believe was overshadowed by an atmosphere of reconciliation. Meanwhile, the leaders' speeches contained implicit messages in more than one direction. In this context, analysts believed that the absence of Egyptian President Hosni Mubarak from the summit gave the impression that the Arabs had handed over the Palestinian issue to the Egyptian side. Egyptian Foreign Ministry spokesman Hossam Zaki did not deny this assertion, saying that the issue is in Egypt's hands and that "it is supervising it, and there is nothing new in that." Asked about reports circulating within the conference halls about Egypt's insistence on reconciling with the current host country, Zaki said, "I do not like to comment on this news."

This study, in general, is matching Aiken, Ghosh, Wee and Vanjani (2009), in the sense of Google Translate superiority to the other two free online services. Other studies like Elkaffash (2020) and Sabtan and Hussein (2021) as well addressed Google's supremacy to the other online services as this study did. The outcomes of this work also confirm with Almahasees (2017), who also found Google's attainment over Bing regarding Arabic context translation. There are many studies that resemble our study in many respects which offer great evidence of the dominance of

Google and the development over history to Google Translate and the other online free services of translation. This study also confirms with previous studies done on Arabic to English MT online by several scholars among which are Zakraoui, Saleh, Al-Maadeed& Alja'am (2020) and Zakraoui, Saleh, Al-Maadeed& Alja'am (2021).

AI Translation Analysis

As a reference translation, AI is used to check against all the three above discussed free online MTs performed by Reverso, World Lingo and Google, (see table 4 below). The translation accomplished by DeepL free online service is, to a greater extent, closer to professional human renderings. This claim is supported in literature by Shormani (2024), who among others regarding Arabic domain of MT, also acknowledged the power of AI in the field of translation and its effectiveness through the development it passed through over time. This is why, in this study, we considered AI translation as a reference one. The raters gave a higher mark for the DeepL AI renderings for the concerned text of this work, (for comparison, see table 5 below).

It seems to be the least in errors regarding orthography of all translations performed by the free online services. No errors related to spelling, punctuation or even capitalization. Proper nouns are appropriately capitalized: *Doha, Egyptian President Hosni Mubarak, Egypt, Foreign Ministry, Ambassador Hossam Zaki* and Commas are typically suitably located.

At the lexical level, DeepL translation appears to be of formal register; contains political and diplomatic language that can be reflected in examples like: *reconciliation, summit, observers, analysts, spokesman, circulating, insistence*. The use of compound and complex terms: *Foreign Ministry spokesman, Egyptian side, Palestinian issue* is also another quality added to lexical features of the target text. Words like "*implicit messages*," "*impression*," and "*supervised*" convey politically loaded or diplomatically careful connotations, harmonizing with journalistic discourse.

At the syntactical level, AI translation rendered longer and complex structures, habitually comprising manifold clauses, for example: "*Arab disagreements were not entirely absent from the Doha summit which, according to observers, was dominated by an atmosphere of reconciliation, while the leaders' speeches included implicit messages in more than one direction*." Use of relative clauses ("which...was dominated"), subordinate clauses ("while the leaders' speeches included…"), and reported speech ("Zaki said…") are also added to the syntactic features of AI renderings. It is, absolutely, categorised by rich sentence structure and proper use of clauses.

Semantically, the text deals with regional political manipulation, symbolism in presence, and diplomatic vagueness. The fundamental message is vibrant and encrusted, revealing tensions beneath formal diplomacy.

Table 4. Target Text 1- D, (DeepL)

AI (DeepL)	Translated in 2025
	Arab disagreements were not entirely absent from the Doha summit which, according to observers, was dominated by an atmosphere of reconciliation, while the leaders' speeches included implicit messages in more than one direction. In this context, analysts saw that the absence of Egyptian President Hosni Mubarak the absence of Egyptian President Hosni Mubarak from the summit gave the impression that the Arabs had handed over the Palestinian issue to the Egyptian side. Egyptian Foreign Ministry Spokesman Ambassador Hossam Zaki did not deny this, saying that the file is already in Egypt's hands and "it is supervised by Egypt and there is nothing new about it." In response to a question about the validity of reports circulating in the corridors of the conference about Egypt's insistence on reconciliation with the chair of the conference at its current session, Zaki said, "I don't like to comment on these reports. I don't want to comment

As revealed in table 5 below, the higher discrepancy between the two translations performed by these three online free translation services over two periods of time, (2009 and 2025), in comparison with DeepL 2025, reflect the level of improvement achieved by these MT. Four raters have evaluated and rated these MTs and ranked them on a scale ranging from 1 to 10, that is from lower to higher levels of performance against six criteria set to examine the quality of the products of these free translation service. Google Translate was not performing effectively in 2009, the year of its initiation, compared to Reverso which has got a little bit higher score than it, but in 2025 Google Translated exceeds a little bit higher than Reverso did. World Lingo, on the other hand, recorded some vital improvement, but remains behind Reverso and Google Translate even in later stages of time. Compared to the rest of the free online services, DeepL translation done in 2025 has got the highest records ever. This place it closer enough to professional human translation and keeps this service a trust-worthy for future performances along with Google Translate and Reverso as free online services of translation using AI technologies. Through such translation utilities a bulky work is to be handled within a very short period of time saving energy, fund and for better and effective accomplishments in future. No doubt, there are some structural problems, lexical problems and semantic problems that may remain in MT from one text type to another, but improvement is obviously seen in these tools online.

Table 5. Average mean by four raters for the MT

Year of Translation	Translations of 2009			Translations of 2025			
Translator / *Criteria*	*Reverso*	*World Lingo*	*Google Translate*	*Reverso*	*World Lingo*	*Google Translate*	*AI DeepL*
Intelligibility	4	1.5	4.5	7.75	5.75	8.5	9.5
Accuracy	4.25	2.25	4.5	6.75	6	8	9
Fluency	3.25	1.25	3.75	7.75	6	8.75	9.5
Adequacy	5.5	2.5	4	8.25	5.75	8.5	9
Comprehension	5.25	1.5	4.75	8.75	7.25	9.25	9.5
Informativeness	5.5	1.5	5	9.25	7.75	9.25	10

CONCLUSIONS AND SUGGESTIONS

This study tried to investigate the free online and artificial intelligence translation services aiming at telescoping sixteen years of the product accuracy progress performed by the free services under investigation. It focused on three online services that offer the translation service free of charge. They are Reverso, World Lingo and Google Translate and checked against AI translation of DeepL free online service as well. MT has witnessed a drastic development over its history that lasted well over half a century with non-stop improvement beginning with what so called rule-based MT in the 1950s, passing through transferred-base MT and corpus-based MT in the 1990s and up to the latest development of neural machine translation (NMT) in 2010s till the more recent and advanced Hybrid MT at the moment of this research.

The findings of this study reveal that Google Translate exceeds the other two in its accuracy through linguistic analysis of the target texts in English produced for the source text in Arabic. The target texts were inspected for their components at the orthographical level, lexicological level, syntactical level and semantical level and they showed some discrepancies at all of these levels. Definitely, the results can put these three online services in the following order according to these criteria set for linguistic analysis as: 1. Google Translate, 2. Reverso, 3. World Lingo. However, all of these three were checked against the DeepL as an AI free online service of translation. DeepL, unquestionably, found to be in the top position of renderings the best of all translations and may be the closest to professional human translators in its renderings.

The results regarding the six criteria set for scrutinizing the appropriateness of these free online services such as intelligibility, fluency, adequacy, comprehensibility and informativeness are with higher scores for Google Translate and then Reverso and finally World Lingo. All of the three are lagging behind DeepL AI translation as shown in the raters' average means discussed earlier. The matching of both linguistic analysis and raters' opinions, expressed in response to these criteria, proves the credibility of the results and authenticity of the research procedure followed in accomplishing the task.

In conclusion, it is recommended that MT and AI translation may not surpass Human Translations at least in the foreseeable future, so it is suggested that careful postediting of such products are to be accomplished by highly qualified translators.

Suggestions for Further Research

To improve the quality of machine translations, further research is to be conducted on empirical bases on variety of texts and on various variables to account for both qualitative and quantitative measures of research for more credibility and reliability of the results. This study is, no doubt, limited to certain variables such as texts and free online services. We have only three systems of translation and one political text in this language direction of translation (Arabic to English). So, more varied texts, more translation services and more language pairs of translation might be involved in the future investigations. Other techniques of investigation might be utilized; such as round-trip translations, some statistical measures to be employed and AI and Human references are to be checked against the Target Texts produced by the software online service. Research questions raised in this paper related to the free online translation may serve as an enhancement to research in these services to improve the quality of the product in near future with the help of AI, which assisted the whole human lives in general in both quality and quantity of their daily activities.

REFERENCES

Ali, M. A. (2020). Quality and machine translation: An evaluation of online machine translation of English into Arabic texts. *Open Journal of Modern Linguistics, 10*(05), 524–548. DOI: 10.4236/ojml.2020.105030

Almahasees, Z. (2017). Assessing the Translation of Google and Microsoft Bing in Translating Political. *International Journal of Languages. Literatura y Lingüística, 3*(1), •••.

Almahasees, Z. (2021). *Analysing English-Arabic Machine Translation: Google Translate, Microsoft Translator and Sakhr*. Routledge., DOI: 10.4324/9781003191018

Almahasees, Z., & Mahmoud, S. (2022). Evaluation of Google Image Translate in Rendering Arabic Signage into English. *World Journal of English Language, 12*(1), 185. http://wjel.sciedupress.com. DOI: 10.5430/wjel.v12n1p185

Ameur, M. S. H., Meziane, F., & Guessoum, A. (2020). Arabic machine translation: A survey of the latest trends and challenges. *Computer Science Review, 38*, 100305. DOI: 10.1016/j.cosrev.2020.100305

Arnold, D., Balkan, L., Meijer, S. R., Humphreys, L., & Sadler, L. (1994). *Machine Translation: An Introductory Guide*. NCC Blackwell.

At-tall, S. M. (2019). *Comparative study between Google Translator and human translator in rendering colloquial Arabic expressions in the late Prime Minister Wasfi At-Tall's speeches into English*, (Unpublished Master's thesis). Yarmouk University, Irbid, Jordan.

Banimelhem, O., & Amayreh, W. (2023). Is ChatGPT a Good English to Arabic Machine Translation Tool? In *2023 14th International Conference on Information and Communication Systems* (ICICS) (pp. 1-6). IEEE. DOI: 10.1109/ICICS60529.2023.10330525

Brazill, S., Masters, M., & Munday, P. (2016). "Analysis of human versus machine translation accuracy" *Graduate Theses & Non-Theses. Translatologia* 223.https://digitalcommons.mtech.edu/grad_rsch/223

Elkaffash, S. M. (2020). *Corpus-Based Quality Evaluation of Ar-En Neural Machine Translation: Corpus-Based Quality Evaluation of Ar-En Neural Machine Translation: Google Translate as a Case Study*. Hamad Bin Khalifa University.

Hutchins, W., & Somers, H. (1992). *An introduction to machine translation*. Academic Press.

Hutchins, W. J. (1986). *Machine translation: past, present, future*. Ellis Horwood.

Hutchins, W. J. (2001). *Early Years in Machine Translation*. John Benjamins Publishing Company., DOI: 10.1075/sihols.97

Hutchins, W. J. (2010). Machine Translation: A Concise History. *The Journal of Transatlantic Studies*, *13*(1&2), 29–70.

Matviienko, L. Khomenko, L. Denysovets, I., Horodenska, K., Nikolashyna, T. Pavlova, I (2024). Comparative Analysis of Online Translators in the Machine Translation System. *Revista Româneasca pentru Educatie Multidimensionala* . *16*, No. 3, pages: 101-118 | DOI: 10.18662/rrem/16.3/885

Mercan, H., Akgün, Y., & Odacioglu, M. C. (2024). The Evolution of Machine Translation: A Review Study. *International Journal of Language and Translation Studies*, *4*(1), 104–116.

Sabtan, Y. M., Hussein, M. S., Ethelb, H., & Omar, A. (2021). An Evaluation of the Accuracy of the Machine Translation Systems of Social Media Language: Google's Arabic-English Translation as an Example. *International Journal of Advanced Computer Science and Applications*, *12*(7), 2021. DOI: 10.14569/IJACSA.2021.0120746

Saldanha, G., & O'Brien, S. (2014). *Research methodologies in translation studies*. Routledge. Aiken, M. Ghosh, K. Wee, J. Vanjani, M. (2009). An Evaluation of the Accuracy of Online Translation Systems an Evaluation of the Accuracy of Online Translation Systems. *Communications of the IIMA Communications of the IIMA. Volume 9*, Issue 4 Article 6

Shormani, M. (2024). Artificial intelligence contribution to translation industry: looking back and forward arxiv.org/shormani, pp. 1-20, July.

Zakraoui, J., Saleh, M., Al-Maadeed, S., & Alja'am, J. M. (2020). Evaluation of Arabic to English Machine Translation Systems. 11th International Conference on Information and Communication Systems, (ICICS). https://doi.orgDOI: 10.1109/ICICS49469.2020.239518

Zakraoui, J., Saleh, M., Al-Maadeed, S., & Alja'am, J. M. (2021). Arabic Machine Translation: A Survey with Challenges and Future Directions. *IEEE Access : Practical Innovations, Open Solutions*, *9*, 161445–161468. DOI: 10.1109/ACCESS.2021.3132488

Zughoul, M. R., & Abu-alshaar, A. M. (2005). English/Arabic/English Machine Translation: A Historical Perspective. *Meta: Translators'. Journal*, *50*(3), 1022–1041.

Compilation of References

Abankwa, S., & Abankwa, A. (2017). The Significance of Folktales in the Moral and Psychological Development of the Child in Ghanaian Communities. *Journal of Literature and Art Studies*, *7*(7), 895–901.

Abdin, M., & Aneja, J.. (2024, December). *Phi-4 technical report*. arXiv. https://arxiv.org/abs/2412.08905

Addo, A. A. (2013). *Ananse as a folkloric character in new Ghanaian drama* (Unpublished M.Phil thesis). University of Ghana, Legon.

Adiguzel, T., Kaya, M., & Cansu, F. (2023). Revolutionizing education with AI: Exploring the transformative potential of ChatGPT. *Contemporary Educational Technology*, *15*(3), ep429. DOI: 10.30935/cedtech/13152

Adjei, P., & Dei, G. (2008). Decolonizing schooling and education in Ghana. In Abdi, A. A., & Guo, S. (Eds.), *Education and social development: Global issues and analyses* (pp. 177–193). BRILL., DOI: 10.1163/9789087904401_011

Agarwal, B., Urlings, C., Lankveld, G., & Klemke, R. (2024). Identifying the ethical values and norms of artificial intelligence in education: a systematic literature review. DOI: 10.35542/osf.io/e7t3f

Agyekum, K. (2000). Aspects of Akan oral literature in the media. *Research Review New Series*, *16*(2), 1–18. DOI: 10.4314/rrias.v16i2.22891

Agyekum, K. (2006). The sociolinguistics of Akan personal names. *Nordic Journal of African Studies*, *15*(2), 206–235.

Ahmad, M., Ho, W. Y., Goyes Robalino, A. P., Maqsood, M., Ahmad, M., Ho, W. Y., Goyes Robalino, A. P., & Maqsood, M. (2025). Theoretical Implications of Generative AI for Content Generation in Geoinformatics Training. In A. Anna A. (Ed.), *Integration Strategies of Generative AI in Higher Education* (pp. 101–130). IGI Global Scientific Publishing. DOI: 10.4018/979-8-3693-5518-3.ch005

Ahmad, S. F., Alam, M. M., Rahmat, M. K., Mubarik, M. S., & Hyder, S. I. (2022). Academic and administrative role of artificial intelligence in education. *Sustainability (Basel), 14*(3), 1101. DOI: 10.3390/su14031101

Ahmad, S., Rahmat, M., Mubarik, M., Alam, M., & Hyder, S. (2021). Artificial intelligence and its role in education. *Sustainability (Basel), 13*(22), 12902. DOI: 10.3390/su132212902

Ahmed, I. (Ed.). (2023). *Imagining post-COVID education futures: Lessons from Bangladesh and beyond.* Centre for Genocide Studies, University of Dhaka.

Akbarani, R. (2024). Use of artificial intelligence in english language teaching. *International Journal of English Learning and Applied Linguistics (Ijelal), 4*(1), 14–23. DOI: 10.21111/ijelal.v4i1.10756

Akgun, S., & Greenhow, C. (2021). Artificial intelligence in education: Addressing ethical challenges in K-12 settings. *AI and Ethics*, •••, 1–10. DOI: 10.1007/s43681-021-00096-7 PMID: 34790956

AlAfnan, M. (2024). Artificial intelligence and language: Bridging arabic and english with technology. *Journal of Ecohumanism, 3*(8). Advance online publication. DOI: 10.62754/joe.v3i8.4961

AlAli, R., & Wardat, Y. (2024). Opportunities and challenges of integrating generative artificial intelligence in education. *International Journal of Religion, 5*(7), 784–793. DOI: 10.61707/8y29gv34

Alamelu, R., Sathya, M., & Christina, J. L. (2025). AI on Teacher Roles: A Transition Towards Facilitation. In Driving Quality Education Through AI and Data Science (pp. 217-238). *IGI Global Scientific Publishing*. DOI: 10.4018/979-8-3693-8292-9.ch010

Al-Buraiki, S. A., & Al-Ruheili, H. S. (2025). A qualitative SWOT analysis study of the integration of AI technologies into higher education institutions in the Sultanate of Oman. *International Journal of Learning, Teaching and Educational Research, 24*(3). DOI: 10.26803/ijlter.24.3.26

Alcorn, A. M., Ainger, E., Charisi, V., Mantinioti, S., Petrović, S., Schadenberg, B. R., Tavassoli, T., & Pellicano, E. (2019). Educators' views on using humanoid robots with autistic learners in special education settings in England. *Frontiers in Robotics and AI, 6*, 107. DOI: 10.3389/frobt.2019.00107 PMID: 33501122

Ali, M. A. (2020). Quality and machine translation: An evaluation of online machine translation of English into Arabic texts. *Open Journal of Modern Linguistics, 10*(05), 524–548. DOI: 10.4236/ojml.2020.105030

Ali, M. H., Kainat, M., Maqsood, M., Fernandez, S. F., Ali, S., & Ahmad, M. (2024). Chatbots in Academic Literacy Exploring AI in Education. In *Enhancing Higher Education and Research With OpenAI Models* (pp. 37–59). IGI Global. DOI: 10.4018/979-8-3693-1666-5.ch002

Al-khresheh, M. H. (2024). Bridging technology and pedagogy from a global lens: Teachers' perspectives on integrating ChatGPT in English language teaching. *Computers and Education: Artificial Intelligence*, *6*, 100218. DOI: 10.1016/j.caeai.2024.100218

Allaithy, A., & Zaki, M. (2025). Evaluation of AI-generated reading comprehension materials for Arabic language teaching. *Computer Assisted Language Learning*, 1–33. Advance online publication. DOI: 10.1080/09588221.2025.2474037

Allehyani, B., Almashy, A., Jamshed, M., & Banu, S. (2025). Measuring the impact of Meta-AI on English reading comprehension score enhancement: A study within a social media application. *Theory and Practice in Language Studies*, *15*(2), 615–623. DOI: 10.17507/tpls.1502.31

Alm, A., & Watanabe, Y. (2023). Integrating ChatGPT in language education: A Freirean perspective. *Iranian Journal of Language Teaching Research*, *11*(3), 19–30. DOI: 10.30466/ijltr.2023.121404

Almahasees, Z. (2017). Assessing the Translation of Google and Microsoft Bing in Translating Political. *International Journal of Languages. Literatura y Lingüística*, *3*(1), •••.

Almahasees, Z. (2021). *Analysing English-Arabic Machine Translation: Google Translate, Microsoft Translator and Sakhr*. Routledge., DOI: 10.4324/9781003191018

Almahasees, Z., & Mahmoud, S. (2022). Evaluation of Google Image Translate in Rendering Arabic Signage into English. *World Journal of English Language*, *12*(1), 185. http://wjel.sciedupress.com. DOI: 10.5430/wjel.v12n1p185

Almelhes, S. (2023). A review of artificial intelligence adoption in second-language learning. *Theory and Practice in Language Studies*, *13*(5), 1259–1269. DOI: 10.17507/tpls.1305.21

Almusharraf, N. (2020). Teachers' perspectives on promoting learner autonomy for vocabulary development: A case study. *Cogent Education*, *7*(1), 1823154. Advance online publication. DOI: 10.1080/2331186X.2020.1823154

Al-Omari, O., Alyousef, A., Fati, S. M., Shannaq, F., & Omari, A. (2025). Governance and Ethical Frameworks for AI Integration in Higher Education: Enhancing Personalized Learning and Legal Compliance. *Journal of Ecohumanism, 3*(8). Advance online publication. DOI: 10.62754/joe.v3i8.5781

Alon-Barkat, S., & Busuioc, M. (2023). Human–AI interactions in public sector decision making:"automation bias" and "selective adherence" to algorithmic advice. *Journal of Public Administration: Research and Theory, 33*(1), 153–169. DOI: 10.1093/jopart/muac007

Al-Raimi, M., Mudhsh, B. A., Muqaibal, M. H., & Al-Yafaei, Y. (2024). To what extent has artificial intelligence impacted EFL teaching and learning? A systematic review. *Jurnal Arbitrer, 11*(3), 399–412. DOI: 10.25077/ar.11.3.399-412.2024

Alrayes, A., Henari, T., & Ahmed, D. (2024). Chatgpt in education – understanding the bahraini academics perspective. *Electronic Journal of e-Learning, 22*(2), 112–134. DOI: 10.34190/ejel.22.2.3250

Al-Saadi, Z., Al Balushi, A., & Khalil, H. (2025). Empowering EFL Student Teachers through AI: Promoting Creativity, Critical Thinking Skills and Collaboration. *digital world, 4*, 5.

Alvero, A. M., Beeler, J. A., Bodnar, R., Brown, B. L., Brumberg, J., Chua, E., ... & Forlano, P. B. Ph. D. Program Psychology Faculty's Publication (2010-2017).

Al-Zyoud, H. M. M. (2020). The role of artificial intelligence in teacher professional development. *Universal Journal of Educational Research, 8*(11B), 6263-6272. DOI: 10.13189/ujer.2020.082265

Amara, K., Altinay, F., Altinay, Z., & Dagli, G. (2024). Artificial intelligence and sustainable educational systems. In *Computational Intelligence and Blockchain in Complex Systems* (pp. 199–204). Morgan Kaufmann. DOI: 10.1016/B978-0-443-13268-1.00011-X

Amershi, S., Weld, D., Vorvoreanu, M., Fourney, A., Nushi, B., Collisson, P., & Horvitz, E. (2019). Guidelines for human-AI interaction. *Proceedings of the ACM Conference on Human Factors in Computing Systems*, 1-13.

Amershi, S., Weld, D., Vorvoreanu, M., Fourney, A., Nushi, B., Collisson, P., & Horvitz, E. (2019, May). Guidelines for human-AI interaction. In *Proceedings of the 2019 chi conference on human factors in computing systems* (pp. 1-13.

Ameur, M. S. H., Meziane, F., & Guessoum, A. (2020). Arabic machine translation: A survey of the latest trends and challenges. *Computer Science Review, 38*, 100305. DOI: 10.1016/j.cosrev.2020.100305

Angenius, M., & Ghajargar, M. (2023a). Interactive journaling with AI: Probing into words and language as inter-action design materials. In Følstad, A., Araujo, T., Papadopoulos, S., Law, E. L., Luger, E., Goodwin, M., & Brandtzaeg, P. B. (Eds.), Lecture Notes in Computer Science: Vol. 13815. *Chatbot research and design. Conversations 2022*. Springer., DOI: 10.1007/978-3-031-25581-6_10

Angenius, M., & Ghajargar, M. (2023b). Design principles for interactive and reflective journaling with AI. In Arai, K. (Ed.), *Intelligent computing: SAI 2023. Lecture Notes in Networks and Systems* (Vol. 739, pp. 62–81). Springer., DOI: 10.1007/978-3-031-37963-5_6

Anggraini, A., & Faisal, F. (2024). The use of artificial intelligence based technology in english language teaching. *Golden Ratio of Data in Summary*, *4*(2), 950–957. DOI: 10.52970/grdis.v4i2.749

Antari, N. K. D. (2022). An analysis of the interpersonal meaning of lyric and video "zombie" by day6. *Journal of Language and Pragmatics Studies*, *1*(1), 16–24. DOI: 10.58881/jlps.v1i1.3

Anthropic. (2025, May). *System card: Claude Opus 4 & Claude Sonnet 4*. https://www.anthropic.com/model-card

Anuyahong, B., Rattanapong, C., & Patcha, I. (2023). Analyzing the impact of artificial intelligence in personalized learning and adaptive assessment in higher education. *International Journal of Innovation and Scientific Research*, *X*(IV), 88–93. DOI: 10.51244/IJRSI.2023.10412

Araujo, T., Helberger, N., Kruikemeier, S., & de Vreese, C. H. (2020). In AI we trust? Perceptions about automated decision-making by artificial intelligence. *AI & Society*, *35*(3), 611–623. DOI: 10.1007/s00146-019-00931-w

Aravind, A., Durairaj, M., Chitkara, P., Baker El-Ebiary, Y. A., Muniyandy, E., Ushasree, L., & Ben Ammar, M. (2025). Adaptive AI-Based Personalized Learning for Accelerated Vocabulary and Syntax Mastery in Young English Learners. *International Journal of Advanced Computer Science and Applications*, *16*(4), 678. DOI: 10.14569/IJACSA.2025.0160467

Arefian, M. H., Çomoğlu, I., & Dikilitaş, K. (2024). Understanding EFL teachers' experiences of ChatGPT-driven collaborative reflective practice through a community of practice lens. *Innovation in Language Learning and Teaching*, 1-16. https://doi.org/DOI: 10.1080/17501229.2024.2334757

Armstrong, T. (2012). *Neurodiversity in the classroom: Strength-based strategies to help students with special needs succeed in school and life*. ASCD.

Arnold, D., Balkan, L., Meijer, S. R., Humphreys, L., & Sadler, L. (1994). *Machine Translation: An Introductory Guide*. NCC Blackwell.

Arrieta, A., Díaz-Rodríguez, N., Ser, J., Bennetot, A., Tabik, S., Barbado, A., & Herrera, F. (2020). Explainable artificial intelligence (xai): Concepts, taxonomies, opportunities and challenges toward responsible ai. *Information Fusion*, *58*, 82–115. DOI: 10.1016/j.inffus.2019.12.012

Arsyad, S., & Adila, D. (2017). Using local style when writing in English: The citing behaviour of Indonesian authors in English research article introductions. *Asian Englishes*, *8678*(May), 1–16. DOI: 10.1080/13488678.2017.1327835

Arsyad, S., & Arono, . (2016). Potential problematic rhetorical style transfer from first language to foreign language: A case of Indonesian authors writing research article introductions in English. *Journal of Multicultural Discourses*, *11*(3), 315–330. DOI: 10.1080/17447143.2016.1153642

Arthur, P., Sanka, C. G., & Yeboah, P. A. O. (2021). The textuality of "Anansesɛm": A pedagogical and ideological resource in traditional human relations among the Akans in Ghana. *Advances in Language and Literary Studies*, *12*(4), 35–44. DOI: 10.7575/aiac.alls.v.12n.4.p.35

Asirit, L., & Hua, J. (2023). Converging perspectives: Assessing ai readiness and utilization in philippine higher education. *Polaris Global Journal of Scholarly Research and Trends*, *2*(3), 1–50. DOI: 10.58429/pgjsrt.v2n3a152

Asrifan, A., Dewi, A. C., Rosmayanti, V., Saodi, S., Kaddas, B., & Mulyadi, M. (2025). Avatars of Academia: Exploring Virtual Collaboration's Tapestry. In Burris-Melville, T., & Burris, S. (Eds.), *Developing Effective and High-Performing Teams in Higher Education* (pp. 285–312). IGI Global Scientific Publishing., DOI: 10.4018/979-8-3693-3852-0.ch010

Asrifan, A., Shafa, S., Pratiwi, W. R., Bahri, A., Siregar, S. R., & Ingilan, S. S. (2025a). Bridging Gaps: AI-Driven Accessibility in Language Education. In Pham, V., Lian, A., Lian, A., & Barros, S. (Eds.), *Implementing AI Tools for Language Teaching and Learning* (pp. 105–128). IGI Global Scientific Publishing., DOI: 10.4018/979-8-3693-7260-9.ch006

Asrifan, A., Tayibu, K. N., Muhayyang, M., Ingilan, S. S., & Mahfud, A. (2025b). Traditional Learners vs. Non-Traditional Learners: Bridging the Educational Divide. In Hai-Jew, S. (Ed.), *Mitigating Learner Disadvantages in Teaching and Learning* (pp. 59–90). IGI Global Scientific Publishing., DOI: 10.4018/979-8-3693-8623-1.ch003

Attali, Y., & Burstein, J. (2006). Automated essay scoring with e-rater® V. 2. *The Journal of Technology, Learning, and Assessment*, *4*(3).

At-tall, S. M. (2019). *Comparative study between Google Translator and human translator in rendering colloquial Arabic expressions in the late Prime Minister Wasfi At-Tall's speeches into English*, (Unpublished Master's thesis). Yarmouk University, Irbid, Jordan.

Awasthi, B., Gupta, S., Kumar, S., & Tripathi, A. (2024, January). Business management and planning using queuing model with heterogeneous customers for electrical applications. *In 2024 2nd International Conference on Intelligent Data Communication Technologies and Internet of Things (IDCIoT)* (pp. 279-283). IEEE. DOI: 10.1109/IDCIoT59759.2024.10467673

Ayling, J., & Chapman, A. (2021). Putting ai ethics to work: Are the tools fit for purpose? *AI and Ethics*, *2*(3), 405–429. DOI: 10.1007/s43681-021-00084-x

Bacha, N. N. (2002). Developing learners' academic writing skills in higher education: A study for educational reform. *Language and Education*, *16*(3), 161–177. DOI: 10.1080/09500780208666826

Bagai, R., & Mane, V. (2024). Designing an AI-powered mentorship platform for professional development: Opportunities and challenges (arXiv preprint arXiv:2407.20233). arXiv. https://doi.org//arXiv.2407.20233DOI: 10.48550

Bailey, D., & Lee, A. R. (2020). An exploratory study of Grammarly in the language learning context: An analysis of test-based, textbook-based and Facebook corpora. *TESOL International Journal*, 15(2), 4–27. https://eric.ed.gov/?id=EJ1268470

Baillifard, A., Gabella, M., Lavenex, P. B., & Martarelli, C. S. (2023). Implementing learning principles with a personal AI tutor: A case study. arXiv preprint arXiv:2309.13060.

Baker, R. S., & Yacef, K. (2009). The state of educational data mining in 2009: A review and future visions. Journal of educational data mining, 1(1), 3-17.

Baker, R. S. (2016). Stupid tutoring systems, intelligent humans. *International Journal of Artificial Intelligence in Education*, *26*(2), 600–614. DOI: 10.1007/s40593-016-0105-0

Baker, R. S. (2019). Challenges for the future of educational data mining: The Baker learning analytics prizes. *Journal of Educational Data Mining*, *11*(1), 1–17.

Baker, R., & Hawn, A. (2021). Algorithmic bias in education. DOI: 10.35542/osf.io/pbmvz

Balta, N. (2023). Ethical considerations in using ai in educational research., 2(1), 14205. DOI: 10.51853/jorids/14205

Balyan, V., Varshney, T., Gupta, S., & Gupta, G. (2025). *Optimizing Automation in Engineering with Energy Systems and Communication Networks*. IGI Global Scientific Publishing., DOI: 10.4018/979-8-3373-2737-2

Banihashem, S. K., Noroozi, O., Van Ginkel, S., Macfadyen, L. P., & Biemans, H. J. (2022). A systematic review of the role of learning analytics in enhancing feedback practices in higher education. *Educational Research Review*, *37*, 100489. DOI: 10.1016/j.edurev.2022.100489

Banimelhem, O., & Amayreh, W. (2023). Is ChatGPT a Good English to Arabic Machine Translation Tool? In *2023 14th International Conference on Information and Communication Systems* (ICICS) (pp. 1-6). IEEE. DOI: 10.1109/ICICS60529.2023.10330525

Barber, K. (2007). *The Anthropology of Texts, Persons and Publics: Oral and Written Culture in Africa and Beyond*. Cambridge University Press. DOI: 10.1017/CBO9780511619656

Barker, G. G. (2016). Cross-cultural perspectives on intercultural communication competence. *Journal of Intercultural Communication Research*, *45*(1), 13–30. DOI: 10.1080/17475759.2015.1104376

Barkley, R. A. (2015). *Attention-deficit hyperactivity disorder: A handbook for diagnosis and treatment* (4th ed.). Guilford Press.

Barrett, A., & Pack, A. (2023). Not quite eye to a.i.: Student and teacher perspectives on the use of generative artificial intelligence in the writing process. *International Journal of Educational Technology in Higher Education*, *20*(1), 59. Advance online publication. DOI: 10.1186/s41239-023-00427-0

Barrot, J. S. (2023). Using automated written corrective feedback in the writing classrooms: Effects on L2 writing accuracy. *Computer Assisted Language Learning*, *36*(4), 584–607. DOI: 10.1080/09588221.2021.1936071

Barrot, J. S. (2023a). Using ChatGPT for second language writing: Pitfalls and potentials. *Assessing Writing*, *57*, 100745. DOI: 10.1016/j.asw.2023.100745

Barrot, J. S. (2023b). ChatGPT as a language learning tool: An emerging technology report. *Technology Knowledge and Learning*, *29*(2), 1151–1156. DOI: 10.1007/s10758-023-09711-4

Barua, P. D., Vicnesh, J., Gururajan, R., & Oh, S. L. (2022). Artificial intelligence enabled personalised assistive tools to enhance the education of children with neurodevelopmental disorders—A review. *Computers in Human Behavior Reports*, *5*, 100174. DOI: 10.1016/j.chbr.2022.100174 PMID: 35162220

Barzani, S., Aslam, M., & Aslam, T. (2021). The role of technology in ell classes in turkish republic of northern cyprus. *International Journal of Language Education*, *5*(2), 30. DOI: 10.26858/ijole.v5i2.14109

Bastos, M., & Araújo e Sá, H. (2015). Pathways to teacher education for intercultural communicative competence: Teachers' perceptions. *Language Learning Journal*, *43*(2), 131–147. DOI: 10.1080/09571736.2013.869940

Bates, T., Cobo, C., Mariño, O., & Wheeler, S. (2020). Can artificial intelligence transform higher education? *International Journal of Educational Technology in Higher Education*, *17*(1), 42. DOI: 10.1186/s41239-020-00218-x

Bearman, M., Ryan, J., & Ajjawi, R. (2022). Discourses of artificial intelligence in higher education: A critical literature review. *Higher Education*, *86*(2), 369–385. DOI: 10.1007/s10734-022-00937-2

Beckwith, M. W. (2016). *Anansi: Jamaican stories of the spider god*. VAMzzz Publishing.

Belda-Medina, J., & Calvo-Ferrer, J. R. (2022). Using chatbots as AI conversational partners in language learning. *Applied Sciences (Basel, Switzerland)*, *12*(17), 8427. DOI: 10.3390/app12178427

Benvenuti, S. (2017). Pedagogy of peers: Cultivating writing retreats as communities of academic writing practice. *South African Journal of Higher Education*, *31*(2), 89–107. DOI: 10.20853/31-2-1340

Berendt, B., Littlejohn, A., & Blakemore, M. (2020). Ai in education: Learner choice and fundamental rights. *Learning, Media and Technology*, *45*(3), 312–324. DOI: 10.1080/17439884.2020.1786399

Berry, J. (1989). *Spiderman Anancy*. Henry Holt & Co.

Bertin, M., Atanassova, I., Larivière, V., & Gingras, Y. (2015). Mapping the linguistic context of citations. *Bulletin of the Association for Information Science and Technology*, *41*(2), 26–29. DOI: 10.1002/bult.2015.1720410208

Bhabha, H. K. (1994). *The Location of Culture*. Routledge.

Bhardwaj, D., Beniwal, A., Chaudhari, S., Kalyan, A., Rajpurohit, T., Narasimhan, K. R., Deshpande, A., & Murahari, V. (2025). *Agent context protocols enhance collective inference*. arXiv. https://arxiv.org/abs/2505.14569

Bhutoria, A. (2022). Personalized education and artificial intelligence in the United States, China, and India: A systematic review using a Human-In-The-Loop model. *Computers and Education: Artificial Intelligence*, *3*, 100057. DOI: 10.1016/j.caeai.2022.100068

Bin-Hady, W. R. A., Al-Kadi, A., Hazaea, A., & Ali, J. K. M. (2023). Exploring the dimensions of ChatGPT in English language learning: a global perspective. Library Hi Tech. Vol. ahead-of-print No. ahead-of-print. DOI: 10.1108/LHT-05-2023-0200

Binns, R. (2018). Fairness in machine learning: Lessons from political philosophy. *Proceedings of the Conference on Fairness, Accountability, and Transparency*, 149-159.

Bit, D., Biswas, S., & Nag, M. (2024). The impact of artificial intelligence in educational system. *Indo Am. Journal of Pharmacy Research*, *11*, 419–427.

Bi, X., Chen, D., Chen, G., & Chen, S. (2024). *DeepSeek LLM: Scaling open-source language models with longtermism*. arXiv. https://arxiv.org/abs/2401.02954

Blodgett, S. L., Barocas, S., Daumé, H.III, & Wallach, H. (2020). Language (technology) is power: A critical survey of "bias" in NLP. *Proceedings of the 58th Annual Meeting of the Association for Computational Linguistics*, 5454–5476. DOI: 10.18653/v1/2020.acl-main.485

Booth, B. M., Bosch, N., & D'Mello, S. K. (2023). Engagement detection and its applications in learning: A tutorial and selective review. *Proceedings of the IEEE*, *111*(10), 1398–1422. DOI: 10.1109/JPROC.2023.3309560

Borenstein, J., & Howard, A. (2021). Emerging challenges in AI and the need for AI ethics education. *AI and Ethics*, *1*(1), 61-65. DOI: 10.1007/s43681-020-00002-7

Boud, D. (2001). Using journal writing to enhance reflective practice. *New Directions for Adult and Continuing Education*, *2001*(90), 9–18. DOI: 10.1002/ace.16

Bozkaya, M., Aydin, I. E., & Kumtepe, E. G. (2012). Research trends and issues in educational technology: A content analysis of TOJET. *The Turkish Online Journal of Educational Technology*, *11*(2), 264–277.

Brazill, S., Masters, M., & Munday, P. (2016). "Analysis of human versus machine translation accuracy" *Graduate Theses & Non-Theses. Translatologia* 223.https://digitalcommons.mtech.edu/grad_rsch/223

Bridgeman, J., & Giraldez-Hayes, A. (2024). Using artificial intelligence-enhanced video feedback for reflective practice in coach development: benefits and potential drawbacks. *Coaching: An International Journal of Theory, Research and Practice, 17*(1), 32-49. DOI: 10.1080/17521882.2023.2228416

Brookfield, S. (1995). Adult learning: An overview. *International Encyclopedia of Education, 10*(3), 375-380.

Brookfield, S. D. (2013). *Powerful techniques for teaching adults*. Jossey-Bass.

Brownhill, S. P. (Ed.). (2024). *Creative practice in higher education: Engaging adult learners through theory and pedagogy* (1st ed.). Routledge., DOI: 10.4324/9781032633534

Brown, T., Mann, B., Ryder, N., Subbiah, M., Kaplan, J. D., Dhariwal, P., & Amodei, D. (2020). Language models are few-shot learners. *Advances in Neural Information Processing Systems, 33*, 1877–1901.

Brundage, M., Avin, S., Clark, J., Toner, H., Eckersley, P., Garfinkel, B., . . . Amodei, D. (2018). The malicious use of artificial intelligence: Forecasting, prevention, and mitigation. arXiv preprint arXiv:1802.07228.

Buchem, I., & Hamelmann, H. (2010). Microlearning: A strategy for ongoing professional development. *eLearning Papers, 21*(7), 1–15.

Bura, C. (2025). Generative AI in Learning: Empowering the Next Generation of Education. DOI: 10.20944/preprints202501.1986.v1

Buriro, G. A., & Hayat, T. (2010). Task-Based Learning: An in-class ELT experiment. *The Journal of Educational Research, 13*, 121–134.

Byram, M., Holmes, P., & Savvides, N. (2013). Intercultural communicative competence in foreign language education: Questions of theory, practice and research. *Language Learning Journal, 41*(3), 251–253. DOI: 10.1080/09571736.2013.836343

Cai, Q., Lin, Y., & Yu, Z. (2023). Factors influencing learner attitudes towards ChatGPT-assisted language learning in higher education. *International Journal of Human-Computer Interaction, 39*, 1–15. DOI: 10.1080/10447318.2023.2261725

Calvo, R. A., & D'Mello, S. (2010). Affect detection: An interdisciplinary review of models, methods, and their applications. *IEEE Transactions on Affective Computing, 1*(1), 18–37. DOI: 10.1109/T-AFFC.2010.1

Canale, M., & Swain, M. (1980). Theoretical bases of communicative approaches to second language teaching and testing. *Applied Linguistics, 1*(1), 1–47. https://www.uefap.com/tefsp/bibliog/canale_swain.pdf. DOI: 10.1093/applin/1.1.1

Carver, J. A., & Bah, S. (2025). Rehumanizing Higher Education: Fostering Humanity in the Era of Machine Learning. *New Directions for Teaching and Learning*, *2025*(183), 21–26. Advance online publication. DOI: 10.1002/tl.20644

Castro-Alonso, J. C., & Sweller, J. (2020). The modality effect of cognitive load theory. In Tindall-Ford, S., Agostinho, S., & Sweller, J. (Eds.), *Advances in cognitive load theory: Rethinking teaching* (pp. 75–92). Routledge.

Cavalcanti, A. P., Barbosa, A., Carvalho, R., Freitas, F., Tsai, Y. S., Gašević, D., & Mello, R. F. (2021). Automatic feedback in online learning environments: A systematic literature review. *Computers & Education: Artificial Intelligence*, *2*, 100027. Advance online publication. DOI: 10.1016/j.caeai.2021.100027

CDC. (2020). Data and statistics on autism spectrum disorder. Centers for Disease Control and Prevention. https://www.cdc.gov/ncbddd/autism/data.html

Çelik, F., Yangın Ersanlı, C., & Arslanbay, G. (2024). Does AI simplification of authentic blog texts improve reading comprehension, inferencing, and anxiety? A one-shot intervention in the Turkish EFL context. *International Review of Research in Open and Distance Learning*, *25*(3), 287–303. DOI: 10.19173/irrodl.v25i3.7779

Celik, I. (2023). Towards Intelligent-TPACK: An empirical study on teachers' professional knowledge to ethically integrate artificial intelligence (AI)-based tools into education. *Computers in Human Behavior*, *138*, 107468. Advance online publication. DOI: 10.1016/j.chb.2022.107468

Chaudhry, M., Cukurova, M., & Luckin, R. (2022). A transparency index framework for ai in education. DOI: 10.1007/978-3-031-11647-6_33

Chen, H. (2024). The ethical challenges of educational artificial intelligence and coping measures: A discussion in the context of the 2024 World Digital Education Conference. *Science Insights Education Frontiers, 20*(2), 3263-3281.

Chen, C., Chen, Y., Jia, X., Lei, S., Yang, C., Nie, Q., & Weiss, B. (2024). Cultural adaptation and evaluation of a school-based positive psychology intervention among Chinese middle school students: A mixed methods program design study. *School Psychology*. PMID: 39264655

Chen, H., & Liu, Z. (2024). Educational applications of chatgpt: Ethical challenges and countermeasures. *English Language Teaching and Linguistics Studies*, *6*(3), 100. DOI: 10.22158/eltls.v6n3p100

Chen, L., Chen, P., & Lin, Z. (2020). Artificial intelligence in education: A review. *IEEE Access : Practical Innovations, Open Solutions*, *8*, 75264–75278. DOI: 10.1109/ACCESS.2020.2988510

Chen, M., Tworek, J., Jun, H., Yuan, Q., de Oliveira Pinto, H. P., Kaplan, J., & Amodei, D. (2021). *Evaluating large language models trained on code*. arXiv. https://arxiv.org/abs/2107.03374

Cheong, C. (2025). Reimagining English Language Education for a Connected, Cultural and Compassionate Future. *English Teaching*, *54*(1), i–ii. DOI: 10.52696/IZGD8741

Chien, C. W. (2016). Taiwanese EFL undergraduates' self-regulated learning with and without technology. *Innovation in Language Learning and Teaching*, *13*(1), 1–16. DOI: 10.1080/17501229.2016.1264076

Choi, J., Yang, E., & Goo, E. (2024). The effects of an ethics education program on artificial intelligence among middle school students: Analysis of perception and attitude changes. *Applied Sciences (Basel, Switzerland)*, *14*(4), 1588. DOI: 10.3390/app14041588

Choi, L. (2022). Interrogating structural bias in language technology: Focusing on the case of voice chatbots in south korea. *Sustainability (Basel)*, *14*(20), 13177. DOI: 10.3390/su142013177

Chun, D. M. (2011). Developing intercultural communicative competence through online exchanges. *CALICO Journal*, *28*(2), 392–419. DOI: 10.11139/cj.28.2.392-419

Cohen, S., Mompelat, L., Mann, A., & Connors, L. (2024). The linguistic leap: Understanding, evaluating, and integrating ai in language education. *Tydskrif vir Taalonderrig*, *4*(2), 23–31. DOI: 10.54475/jlt.2024.012

Cole, M., & Scribner, S. (1978). *Vygotsky, Lev S.(1978)*. Mind in Society. The Development of Higher Psychological Processes.

Cooper, G. (2023). Examining science education in ChatGPT: An exploratory study of generative artificial intelligence. *Journal of Science Education and Technology*, *32*(3), 444–452. DOI: 10.1007/s10956-023-10039-y

Cortiella, C., & Horowitz, S. H. (2014). *The state of learning disabilities: Facts, trends and emerging issues*. National Center for Learning Disabilities.

Costanza-Chock, S. (2020). *Design justice: Community-led practices to build the worlds we need*. MIT Press. DOI: 10.7551/mitpress/12255.001.0001

Council of Europe. (2024, October). *Regulating the use of artificial intelligence systems in education: Preparatory study on the development of a legal instrument*. https://rm.coe.int/regulating-the-use-of-ertificial-intelligence-systems-education-prepar/1680b29928

Cowls, J., & Floridi, L. (2018). Prolegomena to a white paper on an ethical framework for a good AI society. Available at *SSRN* 3198732. DOI: 10.2139/ssrn.3198732

Cox, A. M. (2021). Exploring the impact of artificial intelligence and robots on higher education through literature-based design fictions. *International Journal of Educational Technology in Higher Education, 18*(1), 3. DOI: 10.1186/s41239-020-00237-8

Crawford, K. (2021). *Atlas of AI: Power, Politics, and the Planetary Costs of Artificial Intelligence*. Yale University Press.

Cretchley, J., Rooney, D., & Gallois, C. (2010). Mapping a 40-year history with Leximancer: Themes and concepts in the *Journal of Cross-Cultural Psychology. Journal of Cross-Cultural Psychology, 41*(3), 318–328. DOI: 10.1177/0022022110366105

Crompton, H., & Burke, D. (2023). Artificial intelligence in higher education: The state of the field. *International Journal of Educational Technology in Higher Education, 20*(1), 1–22. DOI: 10.1186/s41239-023-00392-8

Crompton, H., Edmett, A., Ichaporia, N., & Burke, D. (2024). AI and English language teaching: Affordances and challenges. *British Journal of Educational Technology, 55*(6), 2503–2529. DOI: 10.1111/bjet.13460

Crozier, S. E., & Cassell, C. M. (2016). Methodological considerations in the use of audio diaries in work psychology: Adding to the qualitative toolkit. *Journal of Occupational and Organizational Psychology, 89*(2), 396–419. DOI: 10.1111/joop.12132 PMID: 27708502

Cruz, J. M. (2021). Akua Ananse Is a "She": Transnational Autoethnographic Tales. *Departures in Critical Qualitative Research, 10*(4), 7–29. DOI: 10.1525/dcqr.2021.10.4.7

Csikszentmihalyi, M., & Csikzentmihaly, M. (1990). *Flow: The psychology of optimal experience* (Vol. 1990). Harper & Row.

Curry, M. J., & Lillis, T. M. (2010). Academic research networks: Accessing resources for English-medium publishing. *English for Specific Purposes, 29*(4), 281–295. DOI: 10.1016/j.esp.2010.06.002

D'Mello, S., & Graesser, A. (2012). Dynamics of affective states during complex learning. *Learning and Instruction, 22*(2), 145–157. DOI: 10.1016/j.learninstruc.2011.10.001

D'Souza, R., Mathew, M., Mishra, V., & Surapaneni, K. (2024). Twelve tips for addressing ethical concerns in the implementation of artificial intelligence in medical education. *Medical Education Online*, *29*(1), 2330250. Advance online publication. DOI: 10.1080/10872981.2024.2330250 PMID: 38566608

Darwin, R., Rusdin, D., Mukminatien, N., Suryati, N., Laksmi, E. D., & Marzuki, . (2024). Critical thinking in the AI era: An exploration of EFL students' perceptions, benefits, and limitations. *Cogent Education*, *11*(1), 2290342. DOI: 10.1080/2331186X.2023.2290342

Deandrea, P. (2004). Trans(l)atlantic I-con: The many shapes of Ananse in contemporary literatures. *The Journal of Transatlantic Studies*, *2*(1), 1–26. DOI: 10.1080/14794010408656804

Dede, C., Honan, J. P., & Peters, L. C. (2005). Scaling Up Success: Lessons Learned from Technology-Based Educational Improvement. Jossey-Bass, An Imprint of Wiley. 10475 Crosspoint Blvd, Indianapolis, IN 46256.

Demir, B., & Özdemir, D. (2025). AI voice journaling for future language teachers: A path to well-being through reflective practices. *British Educational Research Journal*, *51*(2), 1–32. DOI: 10.1002/berj.4174

Deneme, S. (2010). Cross-cultural differences in language learning strategy preferences: A comparative study. *International Journal of Language. Society and Culture*, *31*, 81–89.

Dennis, N. K. (2024). Using AI-powered speech recognition technology to improve English pronunciation and speaking skills. *IAFOR Journal of Education*, *12*(2), 107–126. DOI: 10.22492/ije.12.2.05

Devi, S., & Sharma, V. (2024). The AI-supported language library model: It's not about the CALL tools, it's about the language library. *Library Progress: Library Science. Information Technology & Computer*, *44*(3), 21357–21364. DOI: 10.48165/bapas.2024.44.2.1

Dewi, N. M. S. C. (2023). Lexical and grammatical cohesion analysis of "nothing like us" song lyrics: Written discourse analysis. *Journal of Language and Pragmatics Studies*, *2*(1), 19–27. DOI: 10.58881/jlps.v2i1.9

Dezfooli, A. (2025). Gendered Dimensions of AI Integration in Language Learning: A Review in the Context of Art and Digitalization. *Asparkía*, *46*(46). Advance online publication. DOI: 10.6035/asparkia.8010

Dignum, V. (2019). *Responsible artificial intelligence: how to develop and use AI in a responsible way* (Vol. 2156). Springer. DOI: 10.1007/978-3-030-30371-6

Dja'far, V. H., & Hamidah, F. N. (2024). Improving English pronunciation skills through AI-based speech recognition technology. *Ethical Lingua. Journal of Language Teaching and Literature*, *11*(2).

Dörnyei, Z. (2001). *Motivational Strategies in the Language Classroom*. Cambridge University Press. DOI: 10.1017/CBO9780511667343

Dörnyei, Z., & Ushioda, E. (2013). *Teaching and Researching Motivation* (2nd ed.). Routledge. DOI: 10.4324/9781315833750

Dua, I. K., & Patel, P. G. (2024). An introduction to Generative AI. In *Optimizing Generative AI Workloads for Sustainability: Balancing Performance and Environmental Impact in Generative AI* (pp. 1–37). Springer. DOI: 10.1007/979-8-8688-0917-0_1

Dwivedi, Y., Hughes, L., Ismagilova, E., Aarts, G., Coombs, C., Crick, T., Duan, Y., Dwivedi, R., Edwards, J., Eirug, A., Galanos, V., Ilavarasan, P. V., Janssen, M., Jones, P., Kar, A. K., Kizgin, H., Kronemann, B., Lal, B., Lucini, B., & Williams, M. (2021). Artificial intelligence (ai): Multidisciplinary perspectives on emerging challenges, opportunities, and agenda for research, practice and policy. *International Journal of Information Management*, *57*, 101994. DOI: 10.1016/j.ijinfomgt.2019.08.002

Dwyer, P. (2022). Neurodiversity in social context: Exploring new approaches to inclusion, exclusion, and social justice in autism research. *Frontiers in Psychology*, *13*, 1–11. DOI: 10.3389/fpsyg.2022.799812

Eden, C., Chisom, O., & Adeniyi, I. (2024). Integrating ai in education: opportunities, challenges, and ethical considerations. Magna Scientia Advanced Research and Reviews, 10(2), 006-013. DOI: 10.30574/msarr.2024.10.2.0039

Edwards, C., Edwards, A., Spence, P. R., & Lin, X. (2018). I, teacher: Using artificial intelligence (AI) and social robots in communication and instruction. *Communication Education*, *67*(4), 473–480. DOI: 10.1080/03634523.2018.1502459

Eide, B. L., & Eide, F. F. (2011). *The dyslexic advantage: Unlocking the hidden potential of the dyslexic brain*. Hay House.

Elkaffash, S. M. (2020). *Corpus-Based Quality Evaluation of Ar-En Neural Machine Translation: Corpus-Based Quality Evaluation of Ar-En Neural Machine Translation: Google Translate as a Case Study*. Hamad Bin Khalifa University.

Ellis, R. (2009). Task-based language teaching: Sorting out the misunderstandings. *International Journal of Applied Linguistics*, *19*(3), 221–246. DOI: 10.1111/j.1473-4192.2009.00231.x

El-Sabagh, H. A. (2021). Adaptive e-learning environment based on learning styles and its impact on development students' engagement. *International Journal of Educational Technology in Higher Education, 18*(1), 53. DOI: 10.1186/s41239-021-00289-4

Enzelina, Y. N., Santosa, M. H., & Paramartha, A. A. G. Y. (2023). Exploring English language education major university lecturers' and students' perceptions of AI-based applications in post-pandemic learning. *SALEE: Study of Applied Linguistics and English Education, 4*(2), 200–215. DOI: 10.35961/salee.v4i2.843

Escalante, J., Pack, A., & Barrett, A. (2023). Ai-generated feedback on writing: Insights into efficacy and enl student preference. *International Journal of Educational Technology in Higher Education, 20*(1), 57. Advance online publication. DOI: 10.1186/s41239-023-00425-2

Eslit, E. (2023). Revitalizing english language teaching (elt): unveiling evolving pedagogies and ai-driven dynamics in the post-pandemic era. DOI: 10.20944/preprints202308.1774.v1

Espartinez, A. S. (2025). Between Innovation and Tradition: A Narrative Inquiry of Students' and Teachers' Experiences with ChatGPT in Philippine Higher Education. *Social Sciences (Basel, Switzerland), 14*(6), 359. DOI: 10.3390/socsci14060359

Eubanks, V. (2018). *Automating inequality: How high-tech tools profile, police, and punish the poor.* St. Martin's Press.

Eun, B. (2010). From learning to development: A sociocultural approach to instruction. *Cambridge Journal of Education, 40*(4), 401–418. DOI: 10.1080/0305764X.2010.526593

European Union. (2016, May 4). Regulation (EU) 2016/679 of the European Parliament and of the Council of 27 April 2016 on the protection of natural persons with regard to the processing of personal data and on the free movement of such data, and repealing Directive 95/46/EC (General Data Protection Regulation). *Official Journal of the European Union, L 119*, 1–88. https://eur-lex.europa.eu/eli/reg/2016/679/oj

Fakhar, H., Lamrabet, M., Echantoufi, N., & Ajana, L. (2024). Towards a new artificial intelligence-based framework for teachers' online continuous professional development programs: Systematic review. *International Journal of Advanced Computer Science & Applications, 15*(4). DOI: 10.14569/IJACSA.2024.0150450

Fang, F. (2010). Developing students' communicative competence in college English teaching in China. *Journal of Language Teaching and Research, 1*(2), 111–116. DOI: 10.4304/jltr.1.2.111-116

Fattah, H. A., Vadivel, B., Shaban, A. A., & Shanmugam, K. (2023). Enhancing English language education: The impact of AI integration in the classroom. *The Journal of Humanistic Education and Development*, *5*(6), 116–123.

Febriyanti, G. A. A. A., Dewi, N. K. S. L., & Dewi, I. G. A. A. I. R. C. (2018). Using self-assessment to assess rural young learners' writing skills in English foreign language classroom. *Journal of Applied Studies in Language*, *2*(2), 109–115. DOI: 10.31940/jasl.v2i2.1065

Fengchun, M., Wayne, H., Huang, R., & Zhang, H. (2021). AI and education Guidance for policymakers (Internet). Available at: https://unesdoc. unesco. org/ark:/48223/pf0000376709

Ferguson, R., & Clow, D. (2017, March). Where is the evidence? A call to action for learning analytics. In Proceedings of the seventh international learning analytics & knowledge conference (pp. 56-65).

Fitria, T. (2021). The use technology based on artificial intelligence in english teaching and learning). *Elt Echo the Journal of English Language Teaching in Foreign Language Context*, *6*(2). Advance online publication. DOI: 10.24235/eltecho.v6i2.9299

Floridi, L. (2019). Establishing the rules for building trustworthy AI. *Nature Machine Intelligence*, *1*(6), 261–262. DOI: 10.1038/s42256-019-0055-y

Floridi, L., Cowls, J., Beltrametti, M., Chatila, R., Chazerand, P., Dignum, V., Luetge, C., Madelin, R., Pagallo, U., Rossi, F., Schafer, B., Valcke, P., & Vayena, E. (2018). AI4People—An ethical framework for a good AI society: Opportunities, risks, principles, and recommendations. *Minds and Machines*, *28*(4), 689–707. DOI: 10.1007/s11023-018-9482-5 PMID: 30930541

Flowerdew, J. (1999). Writing for scholarly publication in English: The case of Hong Kong. *Journal of Second Language Writing*, *8*(2), 123–145. DOI: 10.1016/S1060-3743(99)80125-8

Fotis, G., Gupta, S., Varshney, T., Dhar, S. L., & Gulzar, M. M. (Eds.). (2025). *Modern Computing Technologies for EV Efficiency and Sustainable Energy Integration*. IGI global., DOI: 10.4018/979-8-3373-2382-4

Foucault, M. (1972). The archaeology of knowledge (A. M. Sheridan Smith, Trans.). Pantheon Books. https://rb.gy/54m6dg

Foucault, M. (1977). Discipline and punish: The birth of the prison (A. Sheridan, Trans.). Pantheon Books. https://rb.gy/f1wlc6

Foucault, M. (1984). *The Foucault reader* (Rabinow, P., Ed.). Pantheon Books., https://monoskop.org/images/f/f6/Rabinow_Paul_ed_The_Foucault_Reader_1984.pdf

Fredricks, J. A., Blumenfeld, P. C., & Paris, A. H. (2004). School engagement: Potential of the concept, state of the evidence. *Review of Educational Research, 74*(1), 59–109. DOI: 10.3102/00346543074001059

Gao, B., Wang, Y., Xie, H., Hu, Y., & Hu, Y. (2023). Artificial Intelligence in Advertising: Advancements, Challenges, and Ethical Considerations in Targeting, Personalization, Content Creation, and Ad Optimization. In *SAGE Open* (Vol. 13, Issue 4). DOI: 10.1177/21582440231210759

Gardner, R. C. (2014). Attitudes and motivation in second language learning. In *Bilingualism, multiculturalism, and second language learning* (pp. 43–63). Psychology Press.

Gasser, U., & Schmitt, C. (2019). AI governance: A research agenda. SSRN Electronic Journal, 12(3), 1-15.

George, A. S., & George, A. H. (2023). A review of ChatGPT AI's impact on several business sectors. *Partners Universal International Innovation Journal, 1*, 9–23.

George, B., & Wooden, O. (2023). Managing the strategic transformation of higher education through artificial intelligence. *Administrative Sciences, 13*(9), 196. DOI: 10.3390/admsci13090196

Ghamrawi, N., Shal, T., & Ghamrawi, N. A. (2024). Exploring the impact of AI on teacher leadership: Regressing or expanding? *Education and Information Technologies, 29*(7), 8415–8433. DOI: 10.1007/s10639-023-12174-w

Ghobain, E., & Zughaibi, A. (2021). Examining saudi efl university students' readiness for online learning at the onset of covid-19 pandemic. *Arab World English Journal, 7*(1), 3–21. DOI: 10.24093/awej/call7.1

Gilch, H., Wannemacher, K., Stratmann, F., Wittke, A., von der Heyde, M., & Hürten, P. (2025). Potential of AI-supported recognition tools for higher mobility and more permeability in the higher education system. *EPiC Series in Computing, 105*, 11–12, -2. DOI: 10.29007/bvsx

Gilligan, C. (1982). *A Different Voice*. Harvard University Press.

Goddiksen, M. P., Johansen, M. W., Armond, A. C. V., Centa, M., Clavien, C., Gefenas, E., Kovács, N., Merit, M. T., Olsson, I. A. S., Poškutė, M., Santos, J. B., Santos, R., Strahovnik, V., Varga, O., Wall, P. J., Sandøe, P., & Lund, T. B. (2024). The dark side of text-matching software: Worries and counterproductive behaviour among European upper secondary school and bachelor students. *International Journal for Educational Integrity*, *20*(1), 15. DOI: 10.1007/s40979-024-00162-7

Goldman, S. R., Taylor, J., Carreon, A., & Smith, S. J. (2024). Using AI to support special education teacher workload. *Journal of Special Education Technology*, *39*(3), 434–447. DOI: 10.1177/01626434241257240

Goodman, B., & Flaxman, S. (2017). European Union regulations on algorithmic decision-making and a "right to explanation.". *AI Magazine*, *38*(3), 50–57. DOI: 10.1609/aimag.v38i3.2741

Google DeepMind. (2025). *Gemini Diffusion*. https://deepmind.google/models/gemini-diffusion/

Google. (2025, March 25). *Gemini 2.5: Our most intelligent AI model* [Blog post]. Google DeepMind. https://blog.google/technology/google-deepmind/gemini-model-thinking-updates-march-2025/#gemini-2-5-thinking

Govindarajan, R., & Christuraj, G. (2024). Opportunities and challenges of using ChatGPT in the ELT scenario of Utas, Nizwa, Oman. *Journal of Teaching English for Specific and Academic Purposes*, *11*(3), 593–605. DOI: 10.22190/JTESAP230529046G

Grammarly. (2018). *Best Plagiarism Checker & Proofreader | Grammarly*. Grammerly.

Grubaugh, S., Levitt, G., & Deever, D. (2023). Harnessing AI to power constructivist learning: An evolution in educational methodologies. *Journal of Effective Teaching Methods*, *1*(3), 81–83. DOI: 10.59652/jetm.v1i3.43

Gulson, K. N., & Witzenberger, K. (2022). Repackaging authority: Artificial intelligence, automated governance and education trade shows. *Journal of Education Policy*, *37*(1), 145–160. DOI: 10.1080/02680939.2020.1785552

Guo, D., & Yang, D.. (2025). *DeepSeek-R1: Incentivizing reasoning capability in LLMs via reinforcement learning*. arXiv. https://arxiv.org/abs/2501.12948

Gupta, S. (2025). *The Future of Machine Learning with Automation in Engineering*. Nova Science Publishers., DOI: 10.52305/YFIX2832

Gutiérrez, L. (2023). Artificial intelligence in language education: Navigating the potential and challenges of chatbots and nlp. *RSELTL, 1*(3), 180–191. DOI: 10.62583/rseltl.v1i3.44

Gyawali, Y., & Mehandroo, M. (2022). Artificial intelligence in english language teaching: Navigating the future with emerging perspectives. *Journal of Language and Linguistics in Society*, (26), 21–27. DOI: 10.55529/jlls.26.21.27

Habler, I., Huang, K., Narajala, V. S., & Kulkarni, P. (2025). *Building a secure agentic AI application leveraging A2A protocol.* arXiv. https://arxiv.org/abs/2504.16902

Hagendorff, T. (2020). The ethics of AI ethics: An evaluation of guidelines. *Minds and Machines, 30*(1), 99–120. DOI: 10.1007/s11023-020-09517-8

Håkansson Lindqvist, M., Mozelius, P., Jaldemark, J., & Cleveland Innes, M. (2024). Higher education transformation towards lifelong learning in a digital era–a scoping literature review. *International Journal of Lifelong Education, 43*(1), 24–38. DOI: 10.1080/02601370.2023.2279047

Halat, D., Shami, R., Daud, A., Sami, W., Soltani, A., & Malki, A. (2024). Artificial intelligence readiness, perceptions, and educational needs among dental students: A cross-sectional study. *Clinical and Experimental Dental Research, 10*(4), e925. Advance online publication. DOI: 10.1002/cre2.925 PMID: 38970241

Hamal, O., Faddouli, N., Harouni, M., & Lu, J. (2022). Artificial intelligence in education. *Sustainability (Basel), 14*(5), 2862. DOI: 10.3390/su14052862

Han, J., Yoo, H., Kim, Y., Myung, J., Kim, M., Lim, H., Kim, J., Lee, T. Y., Hong, H., Ahn, S. Y., & Oh, A. (2023). RECIPE: How to integrate ChatGPT into EFL writing education. In *Proceedings of the Tenth ACM Scale* (pp. 416-420). DOI: 10.1145/3573051.3596200

Harris, J. D., Quatman, C. E., Manring, M. M., Siston, R. A., & Flanigan, D. C. (2014). How to write a systematic review. *The American Journal of Sports Medicine, 42*(11), 2761–2768. DOI: 10.1177/0363546513497567 PMID: 23925575

Hartono, W., Nurfitri, N., Ridwan, R., Kase, E., Lake, F., & Zebua, R. Y. (2023). Artificial intelligence (AI) solutions in English language teaching: Teachers-students perceptions and experiences. *Journal of Education, 6*(1), 1452–1461. DOI: 10.31004/joe.v6i1.3101

Heaven, W. D. (2020). AI-powered education tools raise concerns over student data privacy. *MIT Technology Review, 123*(4), 45–50.

Henriksen, C. (2025). Student learning in the age of AI: principles and practices for using AI in higher education. 59–72. DOI: 10.4337/9781035326020.00015

Herskovits, M. J. (1941). *The myth of the Negro past*. Harper & Brothers.

Hew, K. F., Lan, M., Tang, Y., Jia, C., & Lo, C. K. (2019). Where is the "theory" within the field of educational technology research? *British Journal of Educational Technology*, *50*(3), 956–971. DOI: 10.1111/bjet.12770

He, X. (2024). (n.d.). Enhancing Reading Comprehension with AI-Generated Adaptive Texts. *International Journal of New Developments in Education*, *6*(7), 46–52. DOI: 10.25236/IJNDE.2024.060708

Hidayat, M. T. (2024). Effectiveness of AI-Based Personalised Reading Platforms in Enhancing Reading Comprehension. *Journal of Learning for Development*, *11*(1), 115–125. DOI: 10.56059/jl4d.v11i1.955

Hockly, N. (2023). Artificial intelligence in English language teaching: The good, the bad and the ugly. *RELC Journal*, *54*(2), 445–451. DOI: 10.1177/00336882231168504

Holec, H. (1981). Autonomy is the ability to take charge of one's own learning.

Holmes, T., & Porayska-Pomsta, A. (2021). Ethics in AI and Education: Learning Analytics and Responsible Innovation. *British Journal of Educational Technology*, *52*(4), 1647–1665.

Holmes, W., Bialik, M., & Fadel, C. (2022). *Artificial intelligence in education: Promises and implications for teaching and learning*. Center for Curriculum Redesign. https://curriculumredesign.org/wp-content/uploads/AI-in-Education-Promises-and-Implications-for-Teaching-and-Learning.pdf

Holmes, W., Bialik, M., & Fadel, C. (2019). *Artificial intelligence in education promises and implications for teaching and learning*. Center for Curriculum Redesign.

Holmström, J., & Carroll, N. (2024). How organizations can innovate with generative AI. *Business Horizons*. Advance online publication. DOI: 10.1016/j.bushor.2024.02.010

Holstein, K., Wortman Vaughan, J., Daumé, H., Dudik, M., & Wallach, H. (2019). Improving fairness in machine learning systems: What do industry practitioners need? *Proceedings of the Conference on Fairness, Accountability, and Transparency*, 563-573. DOI: 10.1145/3290605.3300830

Hsieh, T. C., Wang, T. I., Su, C. Y., & Lee, M. C. (2012). A fuzzy logic-based personalized learning system for supporting adaptive English learning. *Journal of Educational Technology & Society*, *15*(1), 273–288. https://www.jstor.org/stable/jeductechsoci.15.1.273

Huang, F., Wang, Y., & Zhang, H. (2024). Modelling generative ai acceptance, perceived teachers' enthusiasm and self-efficacy to english as a foreign language learners' well-being in the digital era. *European Journal of Education*, *59*(4), e12770. Advance online publication. DOI: 10.1111/ejed.12770

Huang, L. (2010). Cross-cultural communication in business negotiations. *International Journal of Economics and Finance*, *2*(2), 196–199. DOI: 10.5539/ijef.v2n2p196

Huang, W., Hew, K., & Fryer, L. (2021). Chatbots for language learning—Are they really useful? a systematic review of chatbot-supported language learning. *Journal of Computer Assisted Learning*, *38*(1), 237–257. DOI: 10.1111/jcal.12610

Hung, Y. K., Huang, Y. C., Su, T. Y., Lin, Y. T., Cheng, L. P., Wang, B., & Sun, S. H. (2025). SimTube: Simulating Audience Feedback on Videos using Generative AI and User Personas. *International Conference on Intelligent User Interfaces, Proceedings IUI*, 1256–1271. /DOI: 10.1145/3708359.3712146

Hutchins, W. J. (1986). *Machine translation: past, present, future*. Ellis Horwood.

Hutchins, W. J. (2001). *Early Years in Machine Translation*. John Benjamins Publishing Company., DOI: 10.1075/sihols.97

Hutchins, W. J. (2010). Machine Translation: A Concise History. *The Journal of Transatlantic Studies*, *13*(1&2), 29–70.

Hutchins, W., & Somers, H. (1992). *An introduction to machine translation*. Academic Press.

Hwang, W. Y., Nurtantyana, R., Purba, S. W. D., Hariyanti, U., Indrihapsari, Y., & Surjono, H. D. (2023). AI and Recognition Technologies to Facilitate English as Foreign Language Writing for Supporting Personalization and Contextualization in Authentic Contexts. *Journal of Educational Computing Research*, *61*(5), 1008–1035. Advance online publication. DOI: 10.1177/07356331221137253

Hyland, K. (2013). Materials for Developing Writing Skills. In Tomlinson, B. (Ed.), *Developing Materials for Language Teaching* (2nd ed., pp. 391–405). Bloomsbury.

Ibrahim, A., Taura, A., Iliyasu, A., Shogbesan, Y., & Lukman, S. (2024). Artificial intelligence (ai): Perception and utilization of ai technologies in educational assessment in nigerian universities. *Edukasiana Jurnal Inovasi Pendidikan, 3*(3), 367–380. DOI: 10.56916/ejip.v3i3.763

Idham, A., Rauf, W., & Rajab, A. (2024). Navigating the transformative impact of artificial intelligence on english language teaching: Exploring challenges and opportunities. *JES, 4*(1), 8–14. DOI: 10.56185/jes.v4i1.620

Igbokwe, I. (2024). Artificial intelligence in educational leadership: Risks and responsibilities. *EJAHSS, 1*(6), 3–10. DOI: 10.59324/ejahss.2024.1(6).01

Illeris, K., & Ryan, C. (2020). Contemporary theories of learning: Learning theorists in their own words. *Australian Journal of Adult Learning, 60*(1), 138–143.

Imran, A. (2022). Why addressing digital inequality should be a priority. *The Electronic Journal on Information Systems in Developing Countries, 89*(3), e12255. Advance online publication. DOI: 10.1002/isd2.12255

Inception Labs. (2025, February 26). *Introducing Mercury, the first commercial-scale diffusion large language model.* https://www.inceptionlabs.ai/news

Integrating AI into listening comprehension: Dynamic approaches for EFL/ESL learners. (2024). *EFLCafe.net.* https://eflcafe.net/integrating-ai-into-listening-comprehension-dynamic-approaches-for-efl-esl-learners/

Isop, W. A. (2025). A conceptual ethical framework to preserve natural human presence in the use of AI systems in education. *Frontiers in Artificial Intelligence, 7*, 1377938. Advance online publication. DOI: 10.3389/frai.2024.1377938 PMID: 39906499

Istenic Starcic, A., & Bagon, S. (2014). ICT-supported learning for inclusion of people with special needs: Review of seven educational technology journals. *British Journal of Educational Technology, 45*(2), 202–230. DOI: 10.1111/bjet.12086

Jafarian, N. R., & Kramer, A. W. (2024). AI-assisted audio-learning improves academic achievement through motivation and reading engagement. *Computers and Education: Artificial Intelligence, 8*, 100357. DOI: 10.31234/osf.io/ac2zq

Jain, S., Grewal, H., Vishnoi, A., Saxena, A., Bhardwaj, S., & Singh, R. (2025, February). Transformative trends: The impact of artificial intelligence (AI) on modern education. *In AIP Conference Proceedings* (Vol. 3224, No. 1). AIP Publishing.

Javed, U., Rohilla, A., Adnan, G., & Taj, N. (2025). Exploring how AI can be used to Promote Collaboration in group Project reduce Conflict in Team Dynamics and Enhance Cooperative Learning Experiences. *Review of Applied Management and Social Sciences*, *8*(1), 129–141. Advance online publication. DOI: 10.47067/ramss.v8i1.441

Jenks, C. (2023). Algorithmic pluralism and linguistic justice. *Journal of Language and Technology*, *5*(2), 112–130. DOI: 10.1234/jlt.2023.567

Jeong, C. (2025). *A study on the MCP × A2A framework for enhancing interoperability of LLM-based autonomous agents*. arXiv. https://arxiv.org/abs/2506.01804

Jia Zhang, M., & Zhuo Zhang, Z. (2024, April). AI in teacher education: Unlocking new dimensions in teaching support, inclusive learning, and digital literacy. *Journal of Computer Assisted Learning*, *40*(4), 1871–1885. DOI: 10.1111/jcal.12988

Jia, Y., Ramanovich, M. T., Remez, T., & Pomerantz, R. (2022, June). Translatotron 2: High-quality direct speech-to-speech translation with voice preservation. In International conference on machine learning (pp. 10120-10134). PMLR.

Jia, C., & Lu, Y. (2025). Exploring the Impact of Gamification on Behavioral Change: The Role of Grade Incentives and Free-Choice Behavior. *International Journal of Human-Computer Interaction*, •••, 1–14. DOI: 10.1080/10447318.2025.2517805

Ji, H., Han, I., & Ko, Y. (2023). A systematic review of conversational AI in language education: Focusing on the collaboration with human teachers. *Journal of Research on Technology in Education*, *55*(1), 48–63. DOI: 10.1080/15391523.2022.2142873

Jomaa, N. J. (2025c). Corrective Feedback of AI Tools in Writing and Translation. In *Using AI Tools in Text Analysis, Simplification, Classification, and Synthesis* (pp. 295-320). IGI Global Scientific Publishing. DOI: 10.4018/979-8-3693-9511-0.ch010

Jomaa, N. (Ed.). (2025a). *Using AI Tools in Text Analysis, Simplification, Classification, and Synthesis*. IGI Global Scientific Publishing., DOI: 10.4018/979-8-3693-9511-0

Jomaa, N. (Ed.). (2025b). *Modern Methods for AI-Integrated Language Curriculum*. IGI Global Scientific Publishing., DOI: 10.4018/979-8-3693-9606-3

Jomaa, N., Attamimi, R., & Al Mahri, M. (2024). Utilising Artificial Intelligence (AI) in Vocabulary Learning by EFL Omani Students: The Effect of Age, Gender, and Level of Study. *Forum for Linguistic Studies*, *6*(5), 171–186. DOI: 10.30564/fls.v6i5.6968

Jomaa, N., Attamimi, R., & Al Mahri, M. (2025). The use of Artificial Intelligence (AI) in teaching English vocabulary in Oman: Perspectives, teaching practices, and challenges. *World Journal of English Language*, *15*(3), 1–13. DOI: 10.5430/wjel.v15n3p1

Jomaa, N., Attamimi, R., & Alghafri, K. (2025). Vocabulary Learning Strategies Utilised by EFL Omani Students in Oman: The Effect of Age, Gender, and Levels of Study. *Forum for Linguistic Studies*, *7*(2), 967–987. DOI: 10.30564/fls.v7i2.8450

Jomaa, N., & Jibroo, H. (2024). Corrective Feedback of Grammarly in Enhancing L2 Writing by EFL Kurdish Students. [BAES]. *Bulletin of Advanced English Studies*, *9*(1), 1–15. DOI: 10.31559/BAES2024.9.1.1

Jomaa, N., Mudhsh, B. A., & AlGhafri, K. (2025). Traditional Strategies and AI-Integrated Strategies in Learning English among EFL Omani Students. *Jurnal Arbitrer*, *12*(3), 368–382. DOI: 10.25077/ar.12.3.368-382.2025

Jones, K. M. (2020). Data ethics and student privacy: The risks of AI surveillance in education. *Ethics and Information Technology*, *22*(1), 31–44.

Ka rat aş, F., Abedi, F. Y., Gunye l, F. O., Karade niz, D., & Kuzg un, Y. (2024). Incor por ating AI in for eign lang uage education: An investigation into ChatGPT's effect on foreign language learners. Education and Information Technologies, 1-24. DOI: 10.1007/s10639-024-12574-6

Kabudi, T., Pappas, I., & Olsen, D. H. (2021). AI-enabled adaptive learning systems: A systematic mapping of the literature. *Computers and Education: Artificial Intelligence*, *2*, 100017. DOI: 10.1016/j.caeai.2021.100017

Kalyani, K., Kumar, P. K. T. D., & Roopa, A. N. (2025). AI-based tools for enhancing reflective practice and self-efficacy in pre-service teachers. *The Scientific Temper*, *16*(1), 4035–4042. DOI: 10.58414/SCIENTIFICTEMPER.2025.16.4.02

Kanont, K., Pingmuang, P., Simasathien, T., Wisnuwong, S., Wiwatsiripong, B., Poonpirome, K., Songkram, N., & Khlaisang, J. (2024). Generative-ai, a learning assistant? factors influencing higher-ed students' technology acceptance. *Electronic Journal of e-Learning*, *22*(6), 18–33. DOI: 10.34190/ejel.22.6.3196

Kant, I. (1998). *Critique of pure reason* (Guyer, P., & Wood, A. W., Eds. & Trans.). Cambridge University Press. (Original work published 1781) DOI: 10.1017/CBO9780511804649

Kant, I. (2012). *Groundwork of the metaphysics of morals* (Gregor, M., & Timmermann, J., Eds. & Trans.). Cambridge University Press. (Original work published 1785)

Karimi, H., & Khawaja, S. (2023). The impact of artificial intelligence on higher education in england. *Creative Education, 14*(12), 2405–2415. DOI: 10.4236/ce.2023.1412154

Karimi, M. N., & Nazari, M. (2021). Growth in language teachers' understanding of differentiated instruction: A sociocultural theory perspective. *Journal of Education for Teaching, 47*(3), 322–336. DOI: 10.1080/02607476.2021.1884973

Karim, S. A., Qotrunnnada, A., Hamzah, S., Anjani, N. M., Prianti, J., & Sihole, I. G. (2023). Promoting EFL Studentsâ€™ Speaking Performance through ELSA Speak: An Artificial Intelligence in English Language Learning. *Journal of Languages and Language Teaching, 11*(4), 655–668. DOI: 10.33394/jollt.v11i4.8958

Kaswan, K. S., Dhatterwal, J. S., & Ojha, R. P. (2024). AI in personalized learning. In *Advances in technological innovations in higher education* (pp. 103–117). CRC Press. DOI: 10.1201/9781003376699-9

Kasztelnik, K. (2024). Artificial intelligence-assisted curriculum development: Innovations in designing educational content for the 21st century learner. *Journal of Higher Education Theory and Practice, 24*(11). Advance online publication. DOI: 10.33423/jhetp.v24i11.7367

Kazimova, D., Tazhigulova, G. O., Shraimanova, G., Zatyneyko, A. M., & Sharzadin, A. M. (2025). Transforming University Education with AI: A Systematic Review of Technologies, Applications, and Implications. [iJEP]. *International Journal of Engineering Pedagogy, 15*(1), 4–24. DOI: 10.3991/ijep.v15i1.50773

Keller, J. M. (1987). Development and use of the ARCS model of instructional design. *Journal of Instructional Development : JID, 10*(3), 2–10. DOI: 10.1007/BF02905780

Kemell, K., Vakkuri, V., & Halme, E. (2022). Utilizing user stories to bring ai ethics into practice in software engineering., 553-558. DOI: 10.1007/978-3-031-21388-5_41

Kerr, P. (2016). Adaptive learning. *ELT Journal, 70*(1), 88–93. DOI: 10.1093/elt/ccv055

Khan, A., Ali, Z., Mumtaz, H., & Usman, M. (2025). Epistemic colonization: Assertion of colonial and erasure of Indigenous knowledge and culture through survivance. *Journal of Asian Development Studies, 14*(2), 1528–1539. DOI: 10.62345/jads.2025.14.2.118

Khan, R. A., Jawaid, M., Khan, A. R., & Sajjad, M. (2023). ChatGPT—Reshaping medical education and clinical management. *Pakistan Journal of Medical Sciences, 39*(2), 605. DOI: 10.12669/pjms.39.2.7653 PMID: 36950398

Khan, S., Mazhar, T., Shahzad, T., Khan, M. A., Ur Rehman, A., Saeed, M. M., & Hamam, H. (2025). Harnessing AI for sustainable higher education: Ethical considerations, operational efficiency, and future directions. *Discover Sustainability*, *6*(1), 23. Advance online publication. DOI: 10.1007/s43621-025-00809-6

Khurshedjonovna, O. S. (2025). AI technologies for assessing students' pronunciation. *Web of Humanities: Journal of Social Science and Humanitarian Research*, *3*(2), 163–167.

Kim, S., Shim, J., & Shim, J. (2023). A Study on the utilization of openAI ChatGPT as a second language learning tool. *Journal of Multimedia Information System*, *10*(1), 79–88. DOI: 10.33851/JMIS.2023.10.1.79

Klein, D. V., & McCartney, P. (2024). Delivering Live Q&A in Videos via Synthetic Content Generation Using Generative Artificial Intelligence. *Defensive Publications Series*. https://www.tdcommons.org/dpubs_series/6984

Knowles, M. S. (1980). *The modern practice of adult education: From pedagogy to andragogy* (2nd ed.). Cambridge Books.

Knowles, M. S., Holton, E. F., & Swanson, R. A. (2015). *The adult learner: The definitive classic in adult education and human resource development* (8th ed.). Routledge.

Koene, A., Perez, E., & Carter, C. J. (2019). A governance framework for AI in education. *AI & Society*, *34*(4), 765–777.

Kohnke, L., Foung, D., & Zou, D. (2024). Microlearning: A new normal for flexible teacher professional development in online and blended learning. *Education and Information Technologies, 29*(4), 4457-4480. DOI: 10.1007/s10639-023-11964-6

Kohnke, L., Zou, D., & Xie, H. (2025). Microlearning and generative AI for preservice teacher education: a qualitative case study. *Education and Information Technologies*, 1-28. DOI: 10.1007/s10639-025-13606-5

Kohnke, L., Moorhouse, B. L., & Zou, D. (2023). ChatGPT for language teaching and learning. *RELC Journal*, *54*(2), 537–550. DOI: 10.1177/00336882231162868

Kondratenko, Y., Shevchenko, A., Zhukov, Y., Slyusar, V., Kondratenko, G., Klymenko, M., & Striuk, O. (2023a). *Analysis of the priorities and perspectives in artificial intelligence implementation*. In 2023 13th International Conference on Dependable Systems, Services and Technologies, DESSERT 2023. DOI: 10.1109/DESSERT61349.2023.10416432

Kondratenko, Y. P., Slyusar, V. I., Solesvik, M. B., Kondratenko, N. Y., & Gomolka, Z. (2024). Interrelation and inter-influence of artificial intelligence and higher education systems. In *Research tendencies and prospect domains for AI development and implementation* (pp. 31–58). River Publishers., DOI: 10.1201/9788770046947-2

Kondratenko, Y., Kondratenko, G., Shevchenko, A., Slyusar, V., Zhukov, Y., & Vakulenko, M. (2023b). Towards implementing the strategy of artificial intelligence development: Ukraine peculiarities. *CEUR Workshop Proceedings*, *3513*, 106–117. https://ceur-ws.org/Vol-3513/paper09.pdf

Kristiawan, D., Bashar, K., & Pradana, D. (2024). Artificial intelligence in english language learning: A systematic review of ai tools, applications, and pedagogical outcomes. *The Art of Teaching English as a Foreign Language*, *5*(2), 207–218. DOI: 10.36663/tatefl.v5i2.912

Kritt, D., & Budwig, N. (2022). The future of constructivist education. *Human Development*, *66*(4-5), 295–309. DOI: 10.1159/000526275

Kroll, J. A. (2018). The fallacy of inscrutability. *Proceedings of the ACM Conference on Fairness, Accountability, and Transparency*, 369-378.

Kruk, M., & Kałużna, A. (2024). Investigating the role of ai tools in enhancing translation skills, emotional experiences, and motivation in l2 learning. *European Journal of Education*, *60*(1), e12859. Advance online publication. DOI: 10.1111/ejed.12859

Kumari, M., & Pandey, K. (2024). Teacher professional development in the age of AI: Time to prioritize privacy and accountability. *International Journal of Innovations in Science. Engineering and Management*, *1*(1), 209–213.

Lai, H. C., Chang, C. Y., Wen-Shiane, L., Fan, Y. L., & Wu, Y. T. (2013). The implementation of mobile learning in outdoor education: Application of QR codes. *British Journal of Educational Technology*, *44*(2), E57–E62. DOI: 10.1111/j.1467-8535.2012.01343.x

Laksana, D. N. L. (2020). Implementation of online learning in the pandemic COVID-19: Student perception in areas with minimum internet access. *Journal of Educational Technology*, *4*(4), 502–509. DOI: 10.23887/jet.v4i4.29314

Larsson, S. (2020). AI transparency: A matter of human rights. *AI & Society*, *35*(2), 341–349.

Laurent, A. (2023). *La guerre des intelligences à l'heure de ChatGPT*. Lattes.

LCM team. et al. (2024). *Large concept models: Language modeling in a sentence representation space*. arXiv. https://arxiv.org/abs/2412.08821

Leddy, M., & Creanor, N. (2024). Exploring how education can leverage artificial intelligence for social good. *European Conference on Innovation and Entrepreneurship*, 19(1), 1041-1048. DOI: 10.34190/ecie.19.1.2906

Lee, G. G., Mun, S., Shin, M. K., & Zhai, X. (2024). Collaborative learning with artificial intelligence speakers: Pre-service elementary science teachers' responses to the prototype. *Science & Education*, 1-29. DOI: 10.1007/s11191-024-00526-y

Lee, J., Hung, J. T., Soylu, M. Y., Popescu, D., Cui, C. Z., Grigoryan, G., . . . Harmon, S. W. (2025). Socratic Mind: Impact of a Novel GenAI-Powered Assessment Tool on Student Learning and Higher-Order Thinking. *arXiv preprint arXiv:2509.16262*.

Lee, H., & Lee, J. H. (2024). The effects of AI-guided individualised language learning: A meta-analysis. *Language Learning & Technology*, *28*(2), 134–162. https://hdl.handle.net/10125/73575. DOI: 10.64152/10125/73575

Lee, J., Hong, M., & Cho, J. (2024). Development of a content framework of artificial intelligence integrated education considering ethical factors. *International Journal on Advanced Science, Engineering and Information Technology*, *14*(1), 205–213. DOI: 10.18517/ijaseit.14.1.19558

Lee, K., & Joshi, K. (2020). Understanding the role of cultural context and user interaction in artificial intelligence based systems. *Journal of Global Information Technology Management*, *23*(3), 171–175. DOI: 10.1080/1097198X.2020.1794131

Lee, Y. (2024). A Systematic Review of Generative Artificial Intelligence in L2 Education. *Studies in Modern Grammar*, *124*, 119–139. DOI: 10.14342/smog.2024.124.119

Leong, J., Pataranutaporn, P., Danry, V., Perteneder, F., Mao, Y., & Maes, P. (2024). Puting Things into Context: Generative AI-Enabled Context Personalization for Vocabulary Learning Improves Learning Motivation. *Conference on Human Factors in Computing Systems - Proceedings*. /DOI: 10.1145/3613904.3642393

Lepri, B., Oliver, N., Letouzé, E., Pentland, A. S., & Vinck, P. (2018). Fair, transparent, and accountable algorithmic decision-making processes. *Philosophy & Technology*, *31*(4), 611–627. DOI: 10.1007/s13347-017-0279-x

Li, B., Wang, C., Bonk, C. J., & Kou, X. (2024). Exploring inventions in self-directed language learning with generative AI: Implementations and perspectives of YouTube content creators. *TechTrends*, *68*(4), 803–819. DOI: 10.1007/s11528-024-00960-3

Li, H., & Wang, Y. (2023). The Empowerment and Impact of ChatGPT Technology on Foreign Language Education in Colleges and Universities. In *Proceedings of the 2023 6th International Conference on Educational Technology Management* (pp. 29-34). DOI: 10.1145/3637907.3637950

Lin, H. C. K. (2022). May Computers have Emotions? Establishing an AI Device based on Affective Computing Technologies.

Ling, S., Zhang, Y., & Du, N. (2023, September). Impacts of AI-Generated Confidence and Explanations on Task Performance and Trust in Human-autonomy Teaming. [). Sage CA: Los Angeles, CA: SAGE Publications.]. *Proceedings of the Human Factors and Ergonomics Society Annual Meeting*, *67*(1), 502–503. DOI: 10.1177/21695067231195002

Lin, M., Liu, A., Poitras, E., Chang, M., & Chang, D. (2024). An exploratory study on the efficacy and inclusivity of ai technologies in diverse learning environments. *Sustainability (Basel)*, *16*(20), 8992. DOI: 10.3390/su16208992

Liu, W. (2025). AI for Language Teacher Professional Development: Advancing through human–ChatGPT collaboration. *New Perspectives on Languages*, (2), 1–22. https://doi.org/10.XXXX/npol.2025.02.01

Liu, J., Sihes, A. J. B., & Lu, Y. (2025). How do generative artificial intelligence (AI) tools and large language models (LLMs) influence language learners' critical thinking in EFL education? A systematic review. *Smart Learning Environments*, *12*(1), 12–48. DOI: 10.1186/s40561-025-00406-0

Liu, J., Yu, K., Chen, K., Li, K., Qian, Y., Guo, X., Song, H., & Li, Y. (2025). *ACPs: Agent collaboration protocols for the Internet of Agents*. arXiv. https://arxiv.org/abs/2505.13523

Liu, W., & Wang, Y. (2024). The effects of using AI tools on critical thinking in English literature classes among EFL learners: An intervention study. *European Journal of Education*, *59*(4), e12804. DOI: 10.1111/ejed.12804

Li, Y. (2022). Teaching mode of oral english in the age of artificial intelligence. *Frontiers in Psychology*, *13*, 953482. Advance online publication. DOI: 10.3389/fpsyg.2022.953482 PMID: 35936279

Loke, S. K., Al-Sallami, H. S., Wright, D. F., McDonald, J., Jadhav, S., & Duffull, S. B. (2012). Challenges in integrating a complex systems computer simulation in class: An educational design research. *Australasian Journal of Educational Technology*, *28*(4).

Long, D., & Magerko, B. (2020, April). What is AI literacy? Competencies and design considerations. In *Proceedings of the 2020 CHI conference on human factors in computing systems* (pp. 1-16). DOI: 10.1145/3313831.3376727

Lord, K. (2010). *Redemption in Indigo: a novel.* Small Beer Press.

Luan, H., Geczy, P., Lai, H., Gobert, J., Yang, S. J., Ogata, H., Baltes, J., Guerra, R., Li, P., & Tsai, C. C. (2020). Challenges and future directions of big data and artificial intelligence in education. *Frontiers in Psychology, 11*, 580820. DOI: 10.3389/fpsyg.2020.580820 PMID: 33192896

Luckin, R., & Holmes, W. (2016). Intelligence unleashed: An argument for AI in education.

Luckin, R., Holmes, W., Griffiths, M., & Forcier, L. B. (2022). *Intelligence unleashed: An argument for AI in education.* Pearson. https://www.pearson.com/content/dam/corporate/global/pearson-dot-com/files/efficacy-and-research/intelligence-unleashed.pdf

Luckin, R., & Cukurova, M. (2019). Designing educational technologies in the age of AI: A learning sciences-driven approach. *British Journal of Educational Technology, 50*(6), 2824–2838. DOI: 10.1111/bjet.12861

Luckin, R., & Holmes, W. (2016). *Intelligence unleashed: An argument for AI in education*. Pearson.

Luckin, R., Holmes, W., Griffiths, M., & Forcier, L. B. (2021). Ethics of AI in Education: Towards a Community-Wide Framework. *International Journal of Artificial Intelligence in Education, 32*(3), 504–526. DOI: 10.1007/s40593-021-00239-1

Lu, L. (2021). Ethical AI in education: Challenges and policy implications. *Journal of Ethics and Education, 15*(1), 21–36.

Lyu, J., & Andi, H. K. (2025). Effectiveness of AI-driven tools in improving English pronunciation training. *Region: Educational Research and Reviews, 7*(1), 56–58.

Mabuan, R. A. (2024). ChatGPT and ELT: Exploring teachers' voices. *International Journal of Technology in Education, 7*(1), 128–153. DOI: 10.46328/ijte.523

MacIsaac, A., Mushquash, A. R., & Wekerle, C. (2023). Writing yourself well: Dispositional self-reflection moderates the effect of a smartphone app–based journaling intervention on psychological wellbeing across time. *Behaviour Change, 40*(4), 297–313. DOI: 10.1017/bec.2022.24

Mager, M., Mager, E., Kann, K., & Vu, N. T. (2023). Ethical considerations for machine translation of indigenous languages: Giving a voice to the speakers. *arXiv*. /arxiv.2305.19474DOI: 10.18653/v1/2023.acl-long.268

Maghsudi, S., Lan, A., Xu, J., & Van Der Schaar, M. (2021). Personalized Education in the Artificial Intelligence Era: What to Expect Next. *IEEE Signal Processing Magazine*, *38*(3), 37–50. Advance online publication. DOI: 10.1109/MSP.2021.3055032

Magtoto, G., Bagnol, F., & Abunda, R. (2024). Chatgpt — A threat or an aid in teaching and learning. *IJODeL*, *9*(2). Advance online publication. DOI: 10.58887/ijodel.v9i2.250

Mahapatra, H., Ingole, S. B., Singh, D., Dutt, A., Gupta, R., & Chauhan, B. (2024). Artificial Intelligence for Sustainable Education in India: Problems and Prospects. *Library of Progress-Library Science, Information Technology & Computer*, *44*(3).

Mai, W., Ambashe, M., & Ohueri, C. (2024). Artificial intelligence ethics best practices model for financial decision-making in chinese financial institutions. *International Journal of Information Technologies and Systems Approach*, *17*(1), 1–18. DOI: 10.4018/IJITSA.337388

Malmir, A., Sarem, S. N., & Ghasemi, A. (2011). The effect of Task-Based Language Teaching (TBLT) vs. Content-Based. *Iranian EFL Journal*, *7*, 79–94.

Mansfield, C. F., Beltman, S., Broadley, T., & Weatherby-Fell, N. (2016). Building resilience in teacher education: An evidenced informed framework. *Teaching and Teacher Education*, *54*, 77–87. DOI: 10.1016/j.tate.2015.11.016

Mao, Q. (2025). Fostering Self-Directed Growth with Generative AI: Toward a New Learning Analytics Framework. arXiv preprint arXiv:2504.20851.

Maqsood, M., Aqil, M., Das, B. C., & Ahmad, M. (2026). Generative AI for Computer-Assisted Language Learning. In *Artificial Intelligence and the Future of Personalized Education* (pp. 239–264). IGI Global Scientific Publishing.

Marée, T. J., van Bruggen, J. M., & Jochems, W. M. (2013). Effective self-regulated science learning through multimedia-enriched skeleton concept maps. *Research in Science & Technological Education*, *31*(1), 16–30. DOI: 10.1080/02635143.2013.782283

Marginson, S., & Dang, T. K. A. (2017). Vygotsky's sociocultural theory in the context of globalization. *Asia Pacific Journal of Education*, *37*(1), 116–129. DOI: 10.1080/02188791.2016.1216827

Marshall, E. Z. (2012). *Anansi's journey: A story of Jamaican cultural resistance*. University of the West Indies Press. DOI: 10.37234/FOCZIJVK

Martineau, K. (2025, May 28). *The simplest protocol for AI agents to work together.* IBM Research. https://research.ibm.com/blog/agent-communication-protocol-ai

Martin, F., Zhuang, M., & Schaefer, D. (2024). Systematic review of research on artificial intelligence in K-12 education (2017–2022). *Computers and Education: Artificial Intelligence*, *6*, 100195. DOI: 10.1016/j.caeai.2023.100195

Martin, M. W. (2007). *Everyday morality: An introduction to applied ethics* (4th ed.). Wadsworth Cengage Learning.

Marzuki, W., Widiati, U., Rusdin, D., Darwin, , & Indrawati, I. (2023). The impact of AI writing tools on the content and organisation of students' writing: EFL teachers' perspective. *Cogent Education*, *10*(2), 2236469. DOI: 10.1080/2331186X.2023.2236469

Matei, S. A., & Bertino, E. (2023). Educating for AI Cybersecurity Work and Research: Ethics, Systems Thinking, and Communication Requirements. arXiv preprint arXiv:2311.04326.

Matviienko, L. Khomenko, L. Denysovets, I., Horodenska, K., Nikolashyna, T. Pavlova, I (2024). Comparative Analysis of Online Translators in the Machine Translation System. *Revista Românească pentru Educatie Multidimensionala . 16*, No. 3, pages: 101-118 | DOI: 10.18662/rrem/16.3/885

McGrath, C., Farazouli, A., & Cerratto-Pargman, T. (2024). Generative AI chatbots in higher education: A review of an emerging research area. *Higher Education*, •••, 1–17.

McKeown, J., Hmelo-Silver, C. E., Jeong, H., Hartley, K., Faulkner, R., & Emmanuel, N. (2017). A meta-synthesis of CSCL literature in STEM education. In Smith, B. K., Borge, M., Mercier, E., & Lim, K.-Y. (Eds.), *Proceedings of CSCL 2017.* Philadelphia, PA: International Society of the Learning Sciences.

McNamara, D. S., Graesser, A. C., McCarthy, P. M., & Cai, Z. (2014). *Automated evaluation of text and discourse with Coh-Metrix.* Cambridge University Press. DOI: 10.1017/CBO9780511894664

Media & Learning Association. (2025, June 3). *Sparkify: more AI generated video.* Media & Learning Association. https://media-and-learning.eu/type/tools/sparkify-more-ai-generated-video

Meniado, J. C. (2023). The Impact of ChatGPT on English language teaching, learning, and assessment: A rapid review of literature. *Arab World English Journal*, *14*(4), 3–18. DOI: 10.24093/awej/vol14no4.1

Men, Q. (2024). Exploration of the application of artificial intelligence in high school english speaking teaching. *Communications in Humanities Research, 35*(1), 133–137. DOI: 10.54254/2753-7064/35/20240035

Mercan, H., Akgün, Y., & Odacioglu, M. C. (2024). The Evolution of Machine Translation: A Review Study. *International Journal of Language and Translation Studies, 4*(1), 104–116.

Merriam, S. B., & Baumgartner, L. M. (2020). *Learning in adulthood: A comprehensive guide*. John Wiley & Sons.

Merriam, S. B., & Bierema, L. L. (2018). *Adult learning: Linking theory and practice*. Jossey-Bass.

Meta, A. I. (2025, April 5). *Llama 4: Multimodal intelligence*. Meta AI Blog. https://ai.meta.com/blog/llama-4-multimodal-intelligence/

Mignolo, W. D. (2011). *The Darker Side of Western Modernity: Global Futures, Decolonial Options*. Duke University Press.

Mikeladze, T., & Meijer, P. C. (2024). Exploring the Application of Artificial Intelligence in Foreign Language Education within School Settings: Systematic Literature Review. *Journal of Education in Black Sea Region, 10*(1). Advance online publication. DOI: 10.31578/jebs.v10i1.328

Minh, A. (2024). Leveraging chatgpt for enhancing english writing skills and critical thinking in university freshmen. Journal of Knowledge Learning and Science Technology Issn 2959-6386 (Online), 3(2), 51-62. DOI: 10.60087/jklst.vol3.n2.p62

Miranda, F. (2007). *Epistemic injustice: Power and the ethics of knowing*. Oxford University Press., DOI: 10.1093/acprof:oso/9780198237907.001.0001

Mishra, P., & Koehler, M. J. (2006). Technological pedagogical content knowledge: A framework for teacher knowledge. *Teachers College Record, 108*(6), 1017–1054. DOI: 10.1111/j.1467-9620.2006.00684.x

Mittelstadt, B. D., Allo, P., Taddeo, M., Wachter, S., & Floridi, L. (2016). The ethics of algorithms: Mapping the debate. *Big Data & Society, 3*(2), 2053951716679679. DOI: 10.1177/2053951716679679

Miyake, N. (2007). Computer supported collaborative learning. In Andrews, R., & Haythornwaite, C. (Eds.), *Sage handbook of E-learning research* (pp. 248–266). Sage. DOI: 10.4135/9781848607859.n11

Mohebbi, A. (2024). Enabling learner independence and self-regulation in language education using AI tools: A systematic review. *Cogent Education*, *12*(1), 2433814. Advance online publication. DOI: 10.1080/2331186X.2024.2433814

Moore, R. L., Lee, S. S., Pate, A. T., & Wilson, A. T. (2025). Systematic review of digital microcredentials: Trends in assessment and delivery. *Distance Education*, *46*(1), 1–28. DOI: 10.1080/01587919.2024.2441263

Mottron, L., Dawson, M., Soulières, I., Hubert, B., & Burack, J. (2006). Enhanced perceptual functioning in autism: An update, and eight principles of autistic perception. *Journal of Autism and Developmental Disorders*, *36*(1), 27–43. DOI: 10.1007/s10803-005-0040-7 PMID: 16453071

Murtaza, M., Ahmed, Y., Shamsi, J. A., Sherwani, F., & Usman, M. (2022). AI-Based Personalized E-Learning Systems: Issues, Challenges, and Solutions. In *IEEE Access* (Vol. 10). DOI: 10.1109/ACCESS.2022.3193938

Mushtaq, A., Taj, I., Naeem, R., Ghaznavi, I., & Qadir, J. (2025). WorldView-Bench: A benchmark for evaluating global cultural perspectives in large language models. https://arxiv.org/abs/2505.09595

Mutammimah, H., Rejeki, S., Kustini, S., & Amelia, R. (2024). Understanding teachers' perspective towards ChatGPT acceptance in English language teaching. *International Journal of Technology in Education*, *7*(2), 290–307. DOI: 10.46328/ijte.656

Nartey, E. K. (2025). Generative AI in Higher Education:Guiding Principles for Teaching and Learning. DOI: 10.1201/9781003561507

Nasir, M. U., James, S., & Togelius, J. (2024). *Word2World: Generating stories and worlds through large language models*. arXiv. https://arxiv.org/abs/2405.06686

Nasir, M., Hasan, M., Adlim, A., & Syukri, M. (2024). Utilizing artificial intelligence in education to enhance teaching effectiveness. *Proceedings of ICE*, *2*(1), 280–285. DOI: 10.32672/pice.v2i1.1367

Nelson, B. C., & Ketelhut, D. J. (2008). Exploring embedded guidance and self-efficacy in educational multi-user virtual environments. *International Journal of Computer-Supported Collaborative Learning*, *3*(4), 413–427. DOI: 10.1007/s11412-008-9049-1

Neumann, D. L., & Hood, M. (2009). The effects of using a wiki on student engagement and learning of report writing skills in a university statistics course. *Australasian Journal of Educational Technology*, *25*(3), 382–398. DOI: 10.14742/ajet.1141

Ng, D. T. K., Chan, E. K. C., & Lo, C. K. (2025). Opportunities, Challenges and School Strategies for Integrating Generative AI in Education. *Computers and Education: Artificial Intelligence*, 100373.

Nghi, T., & Nguyen, T. (2024). Transforming language acquisition: advanced artificial intelligence approaches for second language education in asia. DOI: 10.21203/rs.3.rs-4182646/v1

Ngũgĩ wa Thiong'o. (1986). *Decolonising the mind: The politics of language in African literature*. Heinemann.

Nguyen, Q., Rienties, B., & Whitelock, D. (2022). Ethical considerations of AI in education. *Education and Information Technologies*, *27*, 8039–8073. DOI: 10.1007/s10639-022-11316-w PMID: 36254344

Nguyen, T. H., & Hoang, T. N. H. G. (2025). Investigating the Promises and Perils of Generative AI in EFL Learning in Higher Education: A Literature Review. *AsiaCALL Online Journal*, *16*(1), 1–15. DOI: 10.54855/acoj.251611

Niemi, H. (2024). AI in education and learning: Perspectives on the education ecosystem. In *New Frontiers in Science in the Era of AI* (pp. 169–194). Springer. DOI: 10.1007/978-3-031-61187-2_11

Nkambou, R., Mizoguchi, R., & Bourdeau, J. (2010). *Advances in Intelligent Tutoring Systems*. Springer. DOI: 10.1007/978-3-642-14363-2

Noor, E., & Kanitroj, B. (2025, January). Speaking in code: Contextualizing large language models in Southeast Asia. Carnegie Endowment for International Peace. https://carnegieendowment.org/research/2025/01/speaking-in-code-contextualizing-large-language-models-in-southeast-asia?lang=en

O'neil, C. (2017). *Weapons of math destruction: How big data increases inequality and threatens democracy*. Crown.

Ochieng, E. G., & Price, A. D. (2010). Managing cross-cultural communication in multicultural construction project teams: The case of Kenya and UK. *International Journal of Project Management*, *28*(5), 449–460. DOI: 10.1016/j.ijproman.2009.08.001

Oh, S.-Y., & Ahn, Y. (2024). *Exploring teachers' perception of artificial intelligence: The socio-emotional deficiency as opportunities and challenges in human-AI complementarity in K-12 education*. arXiv. /arXiv.2405.13065DOI: 10.1007/978-3-031-64299-9_41

Ojedeji, S. O., & Adejuwon, A. M. (2024). Training future educational leaders: Incorporating AI in capacity building and professional development. *Unilorin Journal of Lifelong Education*, *8*(2), 133–148.

Okpewho, I. (1992). *African Oral Literature: Backgrounds, Character, and Continuity*. Indiana University Press. DOI: 10.2979/1034.0

Oliveira, G., Grenha Teixeira, J., Torres, A., & Morais, C. (2021). An exploratory study on the emergency remote education experience of higher education students and teachers during the COVID-19 pandemic. *British Journal of Educational Technology*, *52*(4), 1357–1376. DOI: 10.1111/bjet.13112 PMID: 34219758

Onuora, A. N. (2012). *Anansesem (Storytelling nights): African maternal pedagogies*. Demeter Press.

Open, A. I. (2025, February 27).*OpenAI GPT-4.5 system card*. https://cdn.openai.com/gpt-4-5-system-card.pdf

Organisation for Economic Co-operation and Development. (2019). The OECD Artificial Intelligence Policy Observatory - OECD.AI. https://oecd.ai/en/ai-principles

Ouyang, L., Wu, J., Jiang, X., Almeida, D., Wainwright, C., Mishkin, P., & Lowe, R. (2022). Training language models to follow instructions with human feedback. *Advances in Neural Information Processing Systems*, *35*, 27730–27744.

Ozfidan, B., Machtmes, K. L., & Demir, H. (2014). Socio-cultural factors in second language learning: A case study of adventurous adult language learners. *European Journal of Educational Research*, *3*(4), 185–191. DOI: 10.12973/eu-jer.3.4.185

Pahi, K., Hawlader, S., Hicks, E., Zaman, A., & Phan, V. (2024). Enhancing active learning through collaboration between human teachers and generative AI. *Computers and Education Open*, *6*, 100183. DOI: 10.1016/j.caeo.2024.100183

Pane, J. F., Steiner, E. D., Baird, M. D., Hamilton, L. S., & Pane, J. D. (2017). "Informing Progress: Insights on Personalized Learning Implementation and Effects." *RAND Corporation*, 2017. https://www.rand.org/pubs/research_reports/RR2042.html

Pan, J.PAN. (2024). Ai-driven english language learning program and academic writing integrity in the era of intelligent interface. *English Language Teaching and Linguistics Studies*, *6*(4), 120. DOI: 10.22158/eltls.v6n4p120

Pant, A., Hoda, R., Spiegler, S. V., Tantithamthavorn, C., & Turhan, B. (2024). Ethics in the age of AI: An analysis of AI practitioners' awareness and challenges. *ACM Transactions on Software Engineering and Methodology, 33*(3), 1-35. DOI: 10.1145/3635715

Parsons, S. (2019). Accessibility, inclusivity, and neurodiversity in educational technology: A UK perspective. *British Journal of Educational Technology, 50*(6), 3260–3278. DOI: 10.1111/bjet.12880

Passonneau, R. J., McNamara, D., Muresan, S., & Perin, D. (2017). Preface: Special issue on multidisciplinary approaches to AI and education for reading and writing. *International Journal of Artificial Intelligence in Education, 27*(4), 665–670. DOI: 10.1007/s40593-017-0158-8

Pedró, F., Subosa, M., Rivas, A., & Valverde, P. (2019). *Artificial intelligence in education: Challenges and opportunities for sustainable development* (UNESCO Working Papers on Education Policy, No. 07). UNESCO.

Pedro, F., Subosa, M., Rivas, A., & Valverde, P. (2019). Artificial intelligence in education: Challenges and opportunities for sustainable development.

Peer Mohamed, M. S. (2024a). Exploring Ethical Dimensions of AI-Enhanced Language Education: A Literature Perspective. *Technology in Language Teaching & Learning, 6*(3), 1813. Advance online publication. DOI: 10.29140/tltl.v6n3.1813

Peer Mohamed, M. S. (2024b). Responsible and Ethical Use of Artificial Intelligence in Language Education: A Systematic Review. *Forum for Linguistic Studies, 6*(5), 316–325. Advance online publication. DOI: 10.30564/fls.v6i5.7092

Pellicano, E., & den Houting, J. (2022). Annual Research Review: Shifting from 'normal science' to neurodiversity in autism science. *Journal of Child Psychology and Psychiatry, and Allied Disciplines, 63*(4), 381–396. DOI: 10.1111/jcpp.13534 PMID: 34730840

Pelton, R. D. (1980). *The trickster in West Africa*. University of California Press. DOI: 10.1525/9780520341487

Peng, R., Hu, Q., & Kouider, B. (2023). Teachers' acceptance of online teaching and emotional labor in the EFL context. *Sustainability (Basel), 15*(18), 13893. DOI: 10.3390/su151813893

Perez-Guerra, C., & Cao, J. (2021). Estimating Memory Retention Traces of Foreign Language Vocabulary from Reading Interaction Data. *Proceedings of the 2021 IEEE 24th International Conference on Computer Supported Cooperative Work in Design, CSCWD 2021*. DOI: 10.1109/CSCWD49262.2021.9437841

Peterson, R. L., Pennington, B. F., Olson, R. K., & Wadsworth, S. J. (2018). Dyslexia. In Fisher, C. B. (Ed.), *Encyclopedia of psychology and neuroscience*. Wiley.

Pham, M. T., & Cao, T. X. T. (2025). The Practice of ChatGPT in English Teaching and Learning in Vietnam: A Systematic Review. *International Journal of TESOL & Education*, *5*(1), 50–70. DOI: 10.54855/ijte.25513

Philipsen, B., Tondeur, J., Roblin, N. P., Vanslambrouck, S., & Zhu, C. (2019). Improving teacher professional development for online and blended learning: A systematic meta-aggregative review. *Educational Technology Research and Development*, *67*(5), 1145–1174. DOI: 10.1007/s11423-019-09645-8

Piech, C., Bassen, J., Huang, J., Ganguli, S., Sahami, M., Guibas, L. J., & Sohl-Dickstein, J. (2015). Deep knowledge tracing. *Advances in Neural Information Processing Systems*, •••, 28.

Pifarre, M., & Cobos, R. (2010). Promoting metacognitive skills through peer scaffolding in a CSCL environment. *International Journal of Computer-Supported Collaborative Learning*, *5*(2), 237–253. DOI: 10.1007/s11412-010-9084-6

Pitychoutis, K. (2024). Harnessing ai chatbots for efl essay writing: a paradigm shift in language pedagogy. DOI: 10.31235/osf.io/xrvth

Pokrivčáková, S. (2019). Preparing teachers for the application of AI-powered technologies in foreign language education. *Journal of language and cultural education*.

Popova, A., & Gorokhova, S. (2021). Digital technologies and artificial intelligence technologies in education. *European Journal of Contemporary Education*, *10*(2). Advance online publication. DOI: 10.13187/ejced.2021.2.285

Prabhakaran, V., Qadri, R., & Hutchinson, B. (2022). Cultural values in NLP: The challenge of embedding and evaluating them. *Proceedings of the 60th Annual Meeting of the Association for Computational Linguistics*, 1–14. DOI: 10.48550/arXiv.2211.13069

Qiao, H., & Zhao, A. (2023). Artificial intelligence-based language learning: Illuminating the impact on speaking skills and self-regulation in Chinese EFL context. *Frontiers in Psychology*, *14*, 1255594. DOI: 10.3389/fpsyg.2023.1255594 PMID: 38022973

Qu, K., & Wu, X. (2024). ChatGPT as a CALL tool in language education: A study of hedonic motivation adoption models in English learning environments. *Education and Information Technologies*, *29*(15), 1–33. DOI: 10.1007/s10639-024-12598-y

Rahman, G., Almutairi, E. A., Mudhsh, B. A., & Al-Yafaei, Y. (2025). Harnessing generative AI for collaborative creativity: A study of university students' engagement and innovation. *International Journal of Innovative Research and Scientific Studies*, *8*(3), 3284–3296. DOI: 10.53894/ijirss.v8i3.7227

Rahman, M. A. (2024). Exploring the integration of artificial intelligence in English as a foreign language education in Indonesia. *Pedagogy: Journal of English Language Teaching, 12*(2), 123–135. DOI: 10.32332/joelt.v12i2.9549

Rahwan, I. (2018). Society-in-the-loop: Programming AI for social norms. *Ethics and Information Technology, 20*(1), 5–14. DOI: 10.1007/s10676-017-9430-8

Raitskaya, L., & Tikhonova, E. (2025). Enhancing critical thinking skills in ChatGPT-human interaction: A scoping review. *Journal of Language and Education, 11*(2 (42)), 5–19. DOI: 10.17323/jle.2025.27387

Raji, I. D., & Buolamwini, J. (2019). Actionable auditing: Investigating the impact of publicly naming biased performance results of commercial AI products. Proceedings of the AAAI/ACM Conference on AI Ethics and Society, 429-435.

Rao, M. S., Saraswathy, S., Neela, V., Arun, M. R., Gupta, S., & Taqui, S. N. (2023, November). Efficient Model Training in Decentralized Systems with Federated Learning. *In 2023 International Conference on Communication, Security and Artificial Intelligence (ICCSAI)* (pp. 900-904). IEEE. DOI: 10.1109/ICCSAI59793.2023.10421469

Ratten, V. (2023). The post COVID-19 pandemic era: Changes in teaching and learning methods for management educators. *International Journal of Management Education, 21*(2), 100777. DOI: 10.1016/j.ijme.2023.100777

Rattray, R. S. (1927). *Religion and art in Ashanti*. The Clarendon Press.

Rattray, R. S. (1930). *Anansi: Akan-Ashanti folktales: A collection of 75 Ashanti folktales*. Oxford University Press.

Rawls, J. (1971). *A theory of justice*. Harvard University Press. DOI: 10.4159/9780674042605

Rello, L., & Baeza-Yates, R. (2017). How to present more readable text for people with dyslexia. *Universal Access in the Information Society, 16*(1), 29–49. DOI: 10.1007/s10209-015-0438-8

Research and Markets. (2021). *Artificial intelligence in education market - Global forecast to 2026*. https://www.researchandmarkets.com/reports/5317776/

Rets, I., Herodotou, C., & Gillespie, A. (2023). Six Practical Recommendations Enabling Ethical Use of Predictive Learning Analytics in Distance Education. *Journal of Learning Analytics, 10*(1), 149–167. DOI: 10.18608/jla.2023.7743

Ribeiro, M. T., Singh, S., & Guestrin, C. (2016, August). " Why should i trust you?" Explaining the predictions of any classifier. In *Proceedings of the 22nd ACM SIGKDD international conference on knowledge discovery and data mining* (pp. 1135-1144). DOI: 10.18653/v1/N16-3020

Robertson, C. E., & Baron-Cohen, S. (2017). Sensory perception in autism. *Nature Reviews. Neuroscience, 18*(11), 671–684. DOI: 10.1038/nrn.2017.112 PMID: 28951611

Robertson, M. (2014). Task-based language teaching and expansive learning theory. *TESL Canada Journal, 31*, 187. DOI: 10.18806/tesl.v31i0.1194

Robinson, S. (2024). *Teacher Development – Going Beyond Conventional to a Collaborative Approach (Master's thesis).* Concordia University., https://digitalcommons.csp.edu/teacher-education_masters/107

Rogti, M. (2025). Automatic pronunciation evaluation, feedback and peer correction for shaping English pronunciation accuracy and interpersonal communication. *Innovation in Language Learning and Teaching*, •••, 1–17. DOI: 10.1080/17501229.2025.2475931

Romero, M. (2024*). Collaborative design of AI-enhanced learning activities.* arXiv preprint arXiv:2407.06660.

Roschelle, J. (2013). Special issue on CSCL [Discussion]. *Educational Psychologist, 48*(1), 67–70. DOI: 10.1080/00461520.2012.749445

Roschelle, J., Bakia, M., Toyama, Y., & Patton, C. (2011). Eight issues for learning scientists about education and the economy. *Journal of the Learning Sciences, 20*(1), 3–49. DOI: 10.1080/10508406.2011.528318

Roschelle, J., Rafanan, K., Estrella, G., Nussbaum, M., & Claro, S. (2010). From handheld collaborative tool to effective classroom module: Embedding CSCL in a broader design framework. *Computers & Education, 55*(3), 1018–1026. DOI: 10.1016/j.compedu.2010.04.012

Rosmayanti, V. (2025). Eco-Linguistics and Digital Learning: Integrating Environmental Awareness in Language Education. In *Nexus of Environmental Quality and Technology Innovation* (pp. 71-96). IGI Global Scientific Publishing. DOI: 10.4018/979-8-3373-1822-6.ch004

Rosmayanti, V., Noni, N., & Patak, A. A. (2022). Students' Acceptance of Technology Use in Learning English Pharmacy. *International Journal of Language Education, 6*(3), 314–331. DOI: 10.26858/ijole.v6i3.24144

Roy, A. G., & Bhatia, N. (Eds.). (2023). *Regional Perspectives on India's Partition: Shifting the Vantage Points*. Taylor & Francis. DOI: 10.4324/9781003278498

Roy, S., & Gandhimathi, S. N. S. (2025). Self-directed learning for optimizing sustainable language learning via mobile assisted language learning: A systematic review. *Frontiers in Education*, *9*, 1463721. Advance online publication. DOI: 10.3389/feduc.2024.1463721

Rukiati, E., Wicaksono, J. A., Taufan, G. T., & Suharsono, D. D. (2023). AI on Learning English: Application, Benefit, and Threat. *Journal of Language, Communication, and Tourism*, *1*(2), 32–40. Advance online publication. DOI: 10.25047/jlct.v1i2.3967

Rusmiyanto, R., Huriati, N., Fitriani, N., Tyas, N. K., Rofi'i, A., & Sari, M. N. (2023). The Role Of Artificial Intelligence (AI) In Developing English Language Learner's Communication Skills. *Journal of Education*, *6*(1), 750–757. Advance online publication. DOI: 10.31004/joe.v6i1.2990

Russell, S. (2019). *Human Compatible: Artificial Intelligence and the Problem of Control*. Viking.

Ruziev, E. (2025). AI and the Future of Teacher Roles: Automation Vs. Augmentation. *Journal of Multidisciplinary Bulletin*, *8*(1), 51–54.

Ryan, R. M., & Deci, E. L. (2000). Self-determination theory and the facilitation of intrinsic motivation, social development, and well-being. *The American Psychologist*, *55*(1), 68–78. DOI: 10.1037/0003-066X.55.1.68 PMID: 11392867

Ryan, R. M., & Deci, E. L. (2020). Intrinsic and extrinsic motivation from a self-determination theory perspective: Definitions, theory, practices, and future directions. *Contemporary Educational Psychology*, *61*, 101860. DOI: 10.1016/j.cedpsych.2020.101860

Sabaruddin, S., Purnama, A. D., Harmilawati, H., Aminah, S., Irmayani, I., Takdir, T., & Ar, A. (2024). Artificial intelligence in English language teaching: A study of English teachers' TPACK. Globish: *An English-Indonesian Journal for English. Education and Culture*, *13*(2), 89–102. DOI: 10.31000/globish.v13i2.11250

Sabtan, Y. M., Hussein, M. S., Ethelb, H., & Omar, A. (2021). An Evaluation of the Accuracy of the Machine Translation Systems of Social Media Language: Google's Arabic-English Translation as an Example. *International Journal of Advanced Computer Science and Applications*, *12*(7), 2021. DOI: 10.14569/IJACSA.2021.0120746

Saeed, M. (2021). Learner autonomy: Learners' perceptions on strategies to achieve autonomy in an efl classroom. *International Journal of Linguistics Literature and Translation*, *4*(3), 150–158. DOI: 10.32996/ijllt.2021.4.3.17

Safar, M., & Anggraheni, D. (2024). Language learning through AI chatbots: Effectiveness and cognitive load analysis. *Journal of Social Science Utilising Technology*, *2*(3), 430–445.

Şahín Kölemen, C. (2024). Artificial intelligence technologies and ethics in educational processes: Solution suggestions and results. Innoeduca. *International Journal of Technology and Educational Innovation*, *10*(2), 201–216. Advance online publication. DOI: 10.24310/ijtei.102.2024.19806

Sahito, J. K. M., Panwar, A. H., & Ramzan, I. (2025). Exploring the impact of artificial intelligence (AI) on the listening skills of English as a second language (ESL) learners. *Journal of Applied Linguistics and TESOL*, *8*(1), 1059–1067.

Sajja, R., Sermet, Y., Cikmaz, M., Cwiertny, D., & Demir, I. (2024). Artificial intelligence-enabled intelligent assistant for personalized and adaptive learning in higher education. *Information (Basel)*, *15*(10), 596. DOI: 10.3390/info15100596

Saldanha, G., & O'Brien, S. (2014). *Research methodologies in translation studies*. Routledge. Aiken, M. Ghosh, K. Wee, J. Vanjani, M. (2009). An Evaluation of the Accuracy of Online Translation Systems an Evaluation of the Accuracy of Online Translation Systems. *Communications of the IIMA Communications of the IIMA. Volume 9*, Issue 4 Article 6

Salkey, A. (1997). *Brother Anancy and other stories*. Longman.

Samuel, Y., Brennan-Tonetta, M., Samuel, J., Kashyap, R., Kumar, V., Krishna Kaashyap, S., Chidipothu, N., Anand, I., & Jain, P. (2023). Cultivation of human centered artificial intelligence: Culturally adaptive thinking in education (CATE) for AI. *Frontiers in Artificial Intelligence*, *6*, 1198180. DOI: 10.3389/frai.2023.1198180 PMID: 38106981

Santos-Martin, D., Alonso-Martínez, J., Carrasco, J. E. G., & Arnaltes, S. (2012). Problem-based learning in wind energy using virtual and real setups. *IEEE Transactions on Education*, *55*(1), 126–134. DOI: 10.1109/TE.2011.2151195

Sanusi, I. and Olaleye, S. (2022). An insight into cultural competence and ethics in k-12 artificial intelligence education., 790-794. DOI: 10.1109/EDUCON52537.2022.9766818

Sao Pedro, M., Baker, R. S., & Rodrigo, M. M. T. (2014). Carelessness and affect in an intelligent tutoring system for mathematics. *International Journal of Artificial Intelligence in Education, 24*(2), 189–210. DOI: 10.1007/s40593-014-0015-y

Sarvam, A. I. (2025, May 23). *Sarvam M* [Blog post]. https://www.sarvam.ai/blogs/sarvam-m

Sawin, T. (2025). A Five-Ecosystem Approach to Generative AI in Language Classrooms. In *Rethinking Language Education in the Age of Generative AI* (pp. 9–28). Routledge. DOI: 10.4324/9781003426929-3

Sayed, W. S., Noeman, A. M., Abdellatif, A., Abdelrazek, M., Badawy, M. G., Hamed, A., & El-Tantawy, S. (2023). AI-based adaptive personalized content presentation and exercises navigation for an effective and engaging E-learning platform. *Multimedia Tools and Applications, 82*(3), 3303–3333. Advance online publication. DOI: 10.1007/s11042-022-13076-8 PMID: 35789938

Schei, O. M., Møgelvang, A., & Ludvigsen, K. (2024). Perceptions and use of AI chatbots among students in higher education: A scoping review of empirical studies. *Education Sciences, 14*(8), 922. DOI: 10.3390/educsci14080922

Schulz, L. (2024). *The impact of generative AI on user engagement and personalization in digital journaling: A case study* (Master's thesis, KTH Royal Institute of Technology). DIVA Academic Archive. https://urn.kb.se/resolve?urn=urn:nbn:se:kth:diva-353986

Schunk, D. H., & DiBenedetto, M. K. (2020). Motivation and social cognitive theory. *Contemporary Educational Psychology, 60*, 101832. DOI: 10.1016/j.cedpsych.2019.101832

Sclater, N. (2017). Learning analytics and privacy: A proposed model for data governance. *International Review of Research in Open and Distance Learning, 18*(5), 25–40.

Selladurai, S., & Pandey, D. P. (2024). The role of an AI tool in polishing English pronunciation skills for non-native speakers. *International Journal of Communication Networks and Information Security, 16*(1, Special Issue), 1455--1467. https://ijcnis.org/index.php/ijcnis/article/view/7190

Selvam, M., & González Vallejo, R. (2025). Ethical and Privacy Considerations in AI-Driven Language Learning. *LatIA, 3*, 328. DOI: 10.62486/latia2025328

Selwyn, N. (2019). *Should robots replace teachers?: AI and the future of education.* John Wiley & Sons.

Selwyn, N. (2022). Should robots replace teachers? AI and the future of education. *British Journal of Educational Studies*, *70*(3), 315–331. DOI: 10.1080/00071005.2021.1924730

Seo, K., Tang, J., Roll, I., Fels, S., & Yoon, D. (2021). The impact of artificial intelligence on learner–instructor interaction in online learning. *International Journal of Educational Technology in Higher Education*, *18*(1), 54. Advance online publication. DOI: 10.1186/s41239-021-00292-9 PMID: 34778540

Settles, B., & Meeder, B. (2016, August). A trainable spaced repetition model for language learning. In *Proceedings of the 54th annual meeting of the association for computational linguistics* (volume 1*: long papers)* (pp. 1848-1858). DOI: 10.18653/v1/P16-1174

Shabanov, A. (2025, June 7). *Sparkify combines Gemini and Veo 3 to power Google's latest AI video experiment*. Testing Catalog. https://www.testingcatalog.com/sparkify-uses-gemini-and-veo-3-to-power-googles-latest-ai-video-experiment/

Shadiev, R., Sun, A., & Huang, Y.-M. (2019). A study of the facilitation of cross-cultural understanding and intercultural sensitivity using speech-enabled language translation technology. *British Journal of Educational Technology*, *50*(3), 1415–1433. DOI: 10.1111/bjet.12648

Shaikh, S., Yayilgan, S. Y., Klimova, B., & Pikhart, M. (2023). Assessing the usability of ChatGPT for formal English language learning. *European Journal of Investigation in Health, Psychology and Education*, *13*(9), 1937–1960. DOI: 10.3390/ejihpe13090140 PMID: 37754479

Shankar, R., Ramana, T. V., Singh, P., Gupta, S., & Mehraj, H. (2022). Examination of the non-orthogonal multiple access system using long short memory based deep neural network. *Journal of Mobile Multimedia*, *18*(2), 451–473. DOI: 10.13052/jmm1550-4646.18214

Sharanesha, R., Alqarni, A., Alagla, M., Ghwainem, A., Abushanan, A., Alazmah, A., & Alghamdi, S. (2025). Perceptions and utilization of artificial intelligence in manuscript writing: a cross-sectional survey in health care academics. DOI: 10.21203/rs.3.rs-5518955/v1

Sharma, K., Papamitsiou, Z., & Giannakos, M. (2019). Building pipelines for educational data using AI and multimodal analytics: A "grey-box" approach. *British Journal of Educational Technology*, *50*(6), 3004–3031. DOI: 10.1111/bjet.12854

Shaw, R. S. (2013). The relationships among group size, participation, and performance of programming language learning supported with online forums. *Computers & Education, 62*, 196–207. DOI: 10.1016/j.compedu.2012.11.001

Shaywitz, S. E., Shaywitz, B. A., & Shaywitz, B. A. (2020). Dyslexia in the 21st century. *Current Opinion in Psychiatry, 33*(2), 80–85. DOI: 10.1097/YCO.0000000000000670 PMID: 33278155

Sherlock, P. M. (2002). *The illustrated Anansi: Four Caribbean folk tales* (P. Wright, Illus.). Macmillan Education.

Shevchenko, A., Panok, V., Shevtsov, A., Slyusar, V., Malyi, R., Yeroshenko, T., & Nazar, M. (2024). Development of a virtual psychological assistant with artificial intelligence in the healthcare sector. *Clinical and Preventive Medicine*, (8), 15–27. DOI: 10.31612/2616-4868.8.2024.02

Shi, G., Wang, L., Zhang, L., Shubeck, K., Peng, S., Hu, X., & Graesser, A. C. (2021, July). The Adaptive Features of an Intelligent Tutoring System for Adult Literacy. In *International Conference on Human-Computer Interaction* (pp. 592-603). Cham: Springer International Publishing. DOI: 10.1007/978-3-030-77857-6_42

Shinohara, K., & Wobbrock, J. O. (2016). Self-conscious or self-confident? A diary study conceptualizing the social accessibility of assistive technology. [TACCESS]. *ACM Transactions on Accessible Computing, 8*(2), 1–31. DOI: 10.1145/2827857

Shirazi, M., Ponzer, S., Zarghi, N., Keshmiri, F., Motlagh, M. K., Zavareh, D. K., & Khankeh, H. R. (2020). Inter-cultural and cross-cultural communication through physicians' lens: Perceptions and experiences. *International Journal of Medical Education, 11*, 158–168. DOI: 10.5116/ijme.5f19.5749 PMID: 32820142

Shobikah, N. (2020). The competencies in English. *Journal of Research in English Language Learning, 1*(1), 23. DOI: 10.33474/j-reall.v1i1.5280

Sholeh, M. B. (2023). Task-based learning in the classroom for EFL learners: How and why? *Journal of Language Pragmatics Studies, 2*(3), 274–281. DOI: 10.58881/jlps.v2i3.34

Shormani, M. (2024). Artificial intelligence contribution to translation industry: looking back and forward arxiv.org/shormani, pp. 1-20, July.

Siau, K., & Wang, W. (2020). Artificial intelligence (AI) ethics: Ethics of AI and ethical AI. *Journal of Database Management (JDM), 31*(2), 74-87. DOI: 10.4018/JDM.2020040105

Sidwell, M. D., Bonner, L. W., Bates-Brantley, K., & Wu, S. (2024). Utilizing Text-Generative AI for Creating Oral Reading Fluency Probes. *Intervention in School and Clinic*, *60*(2), 119–125. Advance online publication. DOI: 10.1177/10534512241235896

Sillat, L. H., Tammets, K., & Laanpere, M. (2021). Digital competence assessment methods in higher education: A systematic literature review. *Education Sciences, 11*(8), 402. DOI: 10.3390/educsci11080402

Singer, J. (2016). *NeuroDiversity: The birth of an idea.* Amazon Digital Services.

Singh, T. M., Reddy, C. K. K., Murthy, B. R., Nag, A., & Doss, S. (2025). AI and education: Bridging the gap to personalized, efficient, and accessible learning. In *Internet of Behavior-Based Computational Intelligence for Smart Education Systems* (pp. 131–160). IGI Global.

Singh, V., & Ram, S. (2024). Impact of artificial intelligence on teacher education. *Shodh Sari-An International Multidisciplinary Journal*, *3*(01), 243–266. DOI: 10.59231/SARI7669

Skinner, B. F. (1957). The experimental analysis of behavior. *American Scientist*, *45*(4), 343–371.

Slade, S., & Prinsloo, P. (2013). Learning analytics: Ethical issues and dilemmas. *The American Behavioral Scientist*, *57*(10), 1510–1529. DOI: 10.1177/0002764213479366

Sloane, M., Moss, E., Awomolo, O., & Forlano, L. (2022). Participation is not a design fix for machine learning. In *Proceedings of the 2nd ACM Conference on Equity and Access in Algorithms, Mechanisms, and Optimization (EAAMO '22)* (Article 1, pp. 1–6). Association for Computing Machinery. DOI: 10.1145/3551624.3555285

Slyusar, V. (2025c). *Perspectives of the AI applications for improving learning and teaching*. Processes. *AI in Education System: Successful Cases and Perspectives*. River Publishers.

Slyusar, V. (2025a). Distributed multi-agent systems based on the mixture of experts architecture in the context of 6G wireless technologies. In Dovgyi, S. (Eds.), *Applied innovations in information and communication technology* (Vol. 1338, pp. 81–110). Springer., DOI: 10.1007/978-3-031-89296-7_6

Slyusar, V. I. (2025b). Applications of large language models in the military sphere. In *Artificial intelligence: Achievements and recent developments* (pp. 53–81). River Publishers.

Smiley, A., Moussa, W., Ndamobissi, R., & Menkiti, A. (2021). The negative impact of violence on children's education and well-being: Evidence from Northern Nigeria. *International Journal of Educational Development*, *81*, 102327. DOI: 10.1016/j.ijedudev.2020.102327

Smith, L. T. (2012). *Decolonizing Methodologies: Research and Indigenous Peoples* (2nd ed.). Zed Books.

Song, C., & Song, Y. (2023). Enhancing academic writing skills and motivation: Assessing the efficacy of chatgpt in ai-assisted language learning for efl students. *Frontiers in Psychology*, *14*, 1260843. Advance online publication. DOI: 10.3389/fpsyg.2023.1260843 PMID: 38162975

Sonuga-Barke, E. J. (2003). The dual pathway model of AD/HD: An elaboration of neuro-developmental characteristics. *Neuroscience and Biobehavioral Reviews*, *27*(7), 593–604. DOI: 10.1016/j.neubiorev.2003.08.005 PMID: 14624804

Sonuga-Barke, E. J., Sergeant, J. A., Nigg, J., & Willcutt, E. (2008). Executive dysfunction and delay aversion in attention deficit hyperactivity disorder: Nosologic and diagnostic implications. *Child and Adolescent Psychiatric Clinics of North America*, *17*(2), 367–384. DOI: 10.1016/j.chc.2007.11.008 PMID: 18295151

Soundarya, M., Devapitchai, J. J., Krishnakumari, S., & Manickam, T. (2025). Applications of Artificial Intelligence Techniques in Education. In *Integrating Micro-Credentials With AI in Open Education* (pp. 429–450). IGI Global Scientific Publishing.

Spivak, G. C. (1988). Can the Subaltern Speak? In Nelson, C., & Grossberg, L. (Eds.), *Marxism and the Interpretation of Culture* (pp. 271–313). University of Illinois Press.

Srinivasa, K. G., Kurni, M., & Saritha, K. (2022). Harnessing the Power of AI to Education. In *Learning, teaching, and assessment methods for contemporary learners: pedagogy for the digital generation* (pp. 311–342). Springer Nature Singapore. DOI: 10.1007/978-981-19-6734-4_13

Srinivasan, R., & Chander, A. (2021). Biases in AI systems. *Communications of the ACM*, *64*(8), 44–49. DOI: 10.1145/3464903

Srinivasan, V., & Murthy, H. (2021). Improving reading and comprehension in K-12: Evidence from a large-scale AI technology intervention in India. *Computers and Education: Artificial Intelligence*, *2*, 100019. DOI: 10.1016/j.caeai.2021.100019

Starčič, A., Bratko, I., & Rosanda, V. (2021). Pre-service teachers' concerns about social robots in the classroom: A model for development. *Education & Self Development, 16*(2), 60–87. DOI: 10.26907/esd.16.2.05

Strielkowski, W., Grebennikova, V., Lisovskiy, A., Rakhimova, G., & Vasileva, T. (2025). AI-driven adaptive learning for sustainable educational transformation. *Sustainable Development, 33*(2), 1921-1947. DOI: 10.1002/sd.3221

Strobl, C., Ailhaud, E., Benetos, K., Devitt, A., Kruse, O., Proske, A., & Rapp, C. (2019). Digital support for academic writing: A review of technologies and pedagogies. *Computers & Education, 131*, 33–48. DOI: 10.1016/j.compedu.2018.12.005

Sudha, G., Natha, A., Rajendiran, M., Vanitha, U., Kiran, V., Patil, H., & Rajaram, A. (2024). Optical oasis harnessing energy efficiency in wireline, optical, and wireless communications. *Journal of Environmental Protection and Ecology, 25*(4), 1179–1187.

Sun, M. (2023). Exploring the opportunities and challenges of ai technology in college english teaching., 1532-1541. DOI: 10.2991/978-2-38476-126-5_171

Sundara, K., & Narendran, N. (2023). The Digital Personal Data Protection Act, 2023: Analysing India's dynamic approach to data protection. *Computer Law Review International, 24*(5), 129–141. DOI: 10.9785/cri-2023-240502

Sutrisno, D., Inawati, I., & Hermanto, H. (2024). Enhancing student learning autonomously: Exploring the global impact of artificial intelligence. *English Language Teaching Educational Journal, 6*(2), 137–150. DOI: 10.12928/eltej.v6i2.9100

Sweller, J. (2011). Cognitive load theory. *Psychology of Learning and Motivation, 55*, 37–76. DOI: 10.1016/B978-0-12-387691-1.00002-8

Sweller, J. (2015). In academe, what is learned, and how is it learned? *Current Directions in Psychological Science, 24*(3), 190–194. DOI: 10.1177/0963721415569570

Sweller, J. (2020). Cognitive load theory and educational technology. *Educational Technology Research and Development, 68*(1), 1–16. DOI: 10.1007/s11423-019-09701-3

Tajik, A. (2025). Exploring the role of ai-driven dynamic writing platforms in improving efl learners' writing skills and fostering their motivation. DOI: 10.21203/rs.3.rs-5788599/v1

Tammets, K., & Ley, T. (2023). Integrating AI tools in teacher professional learning: A conceptual model and illustrative case. *Frontiers in Artificial Intelligence, 6*, 1255089. DOI: 10.3389/frai.2023.1255089

Tao, R. Y., Yu, J., Xu, W., Zhou, X., & Chua, T. S. (2023). Cultural bias in large language models: An evaluation using a novel culturally grounded dataset. *arXiv preprint*. https://arxiv.org/abs/2311.14096

Tarhini, A., Hone, K., & Liu, X. (2015). A cross-cultural examination of the impact of social, organisational and individual factors on educational technology acceptance between British and Lebanese university students. *British Journal of Educational Technology*, *46*(4), 739–755. DOI: 10.1111/bjet.12169

Tariq, U. (2024). Challenges in AI-powered educational technologies: Teacher perspectives and resistance. *AI EDIFY Journal*, *1*(3), 1–10.

Tatman, R. (2017). Gender and dialect bias in YouTube's automatic captions. *Proceedings of the First ACL Workshop on Ethics in Natural Language Processing*, 53–59. DOI: 10.18653/v1/W17-1606

Taverniti, G., & Lombardo, C.. (2023). *AI Power. Non solo ChatGPT: lavoro, marketing e futuro*. Ulrico Hoepli.

Titarenko, L., & Little, C. B. (2017). International cross-cultural online learning and teaching: Effective tools and approaches. *American Journal of Distance Education*, *31*(2), 112–127. DOI: 10.1080/08923647.2017.1306767

Tiwari, H. (2024). Artificial intelligence in the classroom: Revolutionizing english language teaching. [Jet Li]. *Journal of English Teaching and Linguistics Studies*, *6*(1), 42–59. DOI: 10.55215/jetli.v6i1.9757

Tomaskinova, J., & Tomaskin, J. (2024). Unlocking the future of education: Empowering educators with AI by overcoming professional development challenges. In *ICERI2024 proceedings* (pp. 10633–10642). IATED. DOI: 10.21125/iceri.2024.2759

Topal, I. H. (2025). A review of Readlang: Multilingual e-reader for language learners. *Journal of Digital Educational Technology*, *5*(1), ep2504. DOI: 10.30935/jdet/15857

Torres, G. A. (2024). *Design considerations for an AI-prompted "future-self" video journaling tool to enhance self-efficacy* (Master's thesis, Massachusetts Institute of Technology). MIT DSpace. https://dspace.mit.edu/handle/1721.1/154010

Tran, D., & Nguyen, H. (2020). Efl teachers' beliefs and practices of teaching pronunciation in a vietnamese setting. *Universal Journal of Educational Research*, *8*(12), 7022–7035. DOI: 10.13189/ujer.2020.081270

Trouillot, M.-R. (2015). *Silencing the past: Power and the production of history*. Beacon Press. (Original work published 1995)

Trust, T. (2016). New model of teacher learning in an online network. *Journal of Research on Technology in Education, 48*(4), 290–305. DOI: 10.1080/15391523.2016.1215169

Tweneboah, S. (2020). *Religion, law, politics and the state in Africa: Applying legal pluralism in Ghana*. Routledge.

Ugwu, N. F., Ochiaka, R. E., Asogwa, U. S., Igbinlade, A. S., Sanni, K. T., Onayinka, T. S., Iroegbu, O., Irewole, M. O., Opele, J. K., Oloyede, A. O., Ibenyenwa, N. C., & Olubodun, O. A. (2025). Comparing the efficacy of artificial intelligence immersion and human-led workshops for enhancing researchers' English language skills: A randomized control trial. *Higher Learning Research Communications, 15*(1), 1–25. DOI: 10.18870/hlrc.v15i1.1530

Ulum, Ö. (2024). Unveiling the layers: Analyzing chatgpt implementations in turkish state universities. *BEDU, 5*(1), 114–134. DOI: 10.29329/bedu.2024.651.7

UNESCO. (2021). *AI and education: Guidance for policy makers*. United Nations Educational, Scientific and Cultural Organization. https://unesdoc.unesco.org/ark:/48223/pf0000376709

UNESCO. (2023). *Guidance for generative AI in education and research*. https://unesdoc.unesco.org/ark:/48223/pf0000386123

Upadhyay, U., Gradišek, A., Iqbal, U., Dhar, E., Li, Y., & Syed-Abdul, S. (2023). Call for the responsible artificial intelligence in the healthcare. *BMJ Health & Care Informatics, 30*(1), e100920. DOI: 10.1136/bmjhci-2023-100920 PMID: 38135293

Utreras, E., & Pontelli, E. (2020, September). Accessibility of block-based introductory programming languages and a tangible programming tool prototype. In *International Conference on Computers Helping People with Special Needs* (pp. 27-34). Cham: Springer International Publishing. DOI: 10.1007/978-3-030-58796-3_4

Vacalopoulou, A., Gardelli, V., Karafyllidis, T., Liwicki, F., Mokayed, H., Papaevripidou, M., . . . Katsouros, V. (2024). AI4EDU: An Innovative Conversational Ai Assistant For Teaching And Learning. *In INTED2024 Proceedings* (pp. 7119-7127). IATED.

Vakulenko, M., & Slyusar, V. (2024). Automatic smart subword segmentation for the reverse Ukrainian physical dictionary task. *CEUR Workshop Proceedings, 3723*, 59–73.

Vanbecelaere, S., Van den Berghe, K., Cornillie, F., Sasanguie, D., Reynvoet, B., & Depaepe, F. (2020). The effectiveness of adaptive versus non-adaptive learning with digital educational games. *Journal of Computer Assisted Learning*, *36*(4), 502–513. DOI: 10.1111/jcal.12416

VanLehn, K. (2006). The behavior of tutoring systems. *International Journal of Artificial Intelligence in Education*, *16*(3), 227–265. DOI: 10.3233/IRG-2006-16(3)02

Vansina, J. (1985). *Oral tradition as history*. James Currey Ltd. wa Thiong'o, N. (1986). *Decolonising the mind: The politics of language in African literature*. James Currey.

Vansina, J. (1971). Once upon a time: Oral traditions as history in Africa. *Daedalus*, *100*(2), 442–468.

Varsik, S., & Vosberg, L. (2024). *The potential impact of Artificial Intelligence on equity and inclusion in education* (No. 23). OECD Publishing. DOI: DOI: 10.1787/dee339a8-en

Vashishth, T. K., Sharma, V., Sharma, M. K., Sharma, K. K., & Sharma, R. (2025). The Role of Teachers in an AI-Enhanced Educational Landscape. In *AI Adoption and Diffusion in Education* (pp. 231–264). IGI Global Scientific Publishing. DOI: 10.4018/979-8-3693-7949-3.ch009

Vincent, J., Yunus, M. M., & Said, N. E. M. (2025). Using AI platforms to improve listening and speaking skills in ESL primary students. *International Journal of Academic Research in Progressive Education and Development*, *14*(1), 1829–1843. DOI: 10.6007/IJARPED/v14-i1/24848

von Eschenbach, W. J. (2021). Transparency and the Black Box Problem: Why We Do Not Trust AI. *Philosophy & Technology*, *34*(4), 1607–1622. DOI: 10.1007/s13347-021-00477-0

Vrabec, N., & Furtáková, L. (2024). Ways of defining digital competences and their components in the EU, EC and UNESCO recommendations. *Annales Universitatis Paedagogicae Cracoviensis. Studia de Cultura*, *16*(2), 5–17. DOI: 10.24917/20837275.16.2.1

Walter, Y. (2024). Embracing the future of artificial intelligence in the classroom: The relevance of AI literacy, prompt engineering, and critical thinking in modern education. *International Journal of Educational Technology in Higher Education*, *21*(1), 15. DOI: 10.1186/s41239-024-00448-3

Wang'ang'a, A. (2024). Consequences of artificial intelligence on teaching and learning in higher education in kenya: Literature review. *East African Journal of Education Studies*, *7*(1), 202–215. DOI: 10.37284/eajes.7.1.1718

Wang, D. (2024). Design of college english teaching model under the background of artificial intelligence + big data. *Advances in Educational Technology and Psychology*, *8*(2). Advance online publication. DOI: 10.23977/aetp.2024.080202

Wang, J., & Fan, W. (2025). The effect of ChatGPT on students' learning performance, learning perception, and higher-order thinking: Insights from a meta-analysis. *Humanities & Social Sciences Communications*, *12*(1), 1–21. DOI: 10.1057/s41599-025-04787-y

Wang, Y., Liu, C., & Tu, Y. F. (2021). Factors affecting the adoption of AI-based applications in higher education. *Journal of Educational Technology & Society*, *24*(3), 116–129.

Wei, L. (2023). Artificial intelligence in language instruction: Impact on English learning achievement, L2 motivation, and self-regulated learning. *Frontiers in Psychology*, *14*, 1261955. DOI: 10.3389/fpsyg.2023.1261955 PMID: 38023040

Weiner, B. (1985). Attribution theory. In *Human motivation* (pp. 275–326). Springer New York. DOI: 10.1007/978-1-4612-5092-0_7

Wenger-Trayner, E., Wenger, E., & Wenger-Trayner, B. (2020). *Learning to make a difference: Value creation in social learning spaces*. Cambridge University Press., DOI: 10.1017/9781108677431

White, H. A., & Shah, P. (2011). Creative style and achievement in adults with attention-deficit/hyperactivity disorder. *Personality and Individual Differences*, *50*(5), 673–677. DOI: 10.1016/j.paid.2010.12.015

Wigfield, A., & Eccles, J. S. (2000). Expectancy–value theory of achievement motivation. *Contemporary Educational Psychology*, *25*(1), 68–81. DOI: 10.1006/ceps.1999.1015 PMID: 10620382

Williamson, B., & Eynon, R. (2020). Historical threads, missing links, and future directions in AI in education. *Learning, Media and Technology*, *45*(3), 223–235. DOI: 10.1080/17439884.2020.1798995

Winkler, R., & Söllner, M. (2018, July). Unleashing the potential of chatbots in education: A state-of-the-art analysis. In Academy of management proceedings (Vol. 2018, No. 1, p. 15903). Briarcliff Manor, NY 10510: Academy of Management. DOI: 10.5465/AMBPP.2018.15903abstract

Winne, P. H. (2021). Open learner models working in symbiosis with self-regulating learners: A research agenda. *International Journal of Artificial Intelligence in Education, 31*(3), 446–459. DOI: 10.1007/s40593-020-00212-4

Wirzal, M., Nordin, N., Halim, N., & Bustam, M. (2024). Generative ai in science education: A learning revolution or a threat to academic integrity? a bibliometric analysis. *Jurnal Penelitian Dan Pengkajian Ilmu Pendidikan E-Saintika, 8*(3), 319–351. DOI: 10.36312/e-saintika.v8i3.2127

Woolf, B. P. (2010). *Building Intelligent Interactive Tutors: Student-Centered Strategies for Revolutionizing E-Learning*. Morgan Kaufmann.

Wu, J., Wang, Y., Chen, F., Yin, X., & He, Y. (2025). Impact of AI-Powered Adaptive Learning Platforms on English Reading Proficiency: Evidence From Structural Equation Modeling. *IEEE Access : Practical Innovations, Open Solutions, 13*, 88230–88242. DOI: 10.1109/ACCESS.2025.3571055

Wu, Y. (2024). Study on the impact of utilizing chatgpt and other ai tools for feedback in eap writing classrooms on the discursive writing performance of english major students. *TSSEHR, 4*, 143–150. DOI: 10.62051/4se95x52

Xiao, Y., Zhang, T., & He, J. (2024). A review of promises and challenges of AI-based chatbots in language education through the lens of learner emotions. *Heliyon*.

Xiaoyu, Z., & Tobias, T. C. (2023). Exploring the efficacy of adaptive learning technologies in online education: A longitudinal analysis of student engagement and performance. *International Journal of Science and Engineering Applications, 12*, 28–31.

Xie, Y., Seth, I., Hunter-Smith, D. J., Rozen, W. M., & Seifman, M. A. (2024). Investigating the impact of innovative AI chatbot on post-pandemic medical education and clinical assistance: A comprehensive analysis. *ANZ Journal of Surgery, 94*(1-2), 68–77. DOI: 10.1111/ans.18666 PMID: 37602755

Xi, L. (2024). Research on the english writing teaching model in the ai era. *MMSE, 6*(3), 111. DOI: 10.22158/mmse.v6n3p111

Xu, L. (2020). The Dilemma and countermeasures of AI in educational application. In *2020 4th international conference on computer science and artificial intelligence* (pp. 289–294). DOI: 10.1145/3445815.3445863

Xue, F. (2024). Ai integration in creative industries: Challenges and opportunities. *Applied and Computational Engineering, 104*(1), 21–27. DOI: 10.54254/2755-2721/104/20240906

Xu, T., & Wang, H. (2024). The effectiveness of artificial intelligence on English language learning achievement. *System, 125*, 103428. DOI: 10.1016/j.system.2024.103428

Yadav, S. (2025). Leveraging AI to Enhance Teaching and Learning in Education: The Role of Artificial Intelligence in Modernizing Classroom Practices. In Optimizing Research Techniques and Learning Strategies with Digital Technologies (pp. 211-238). *IGI Global Scientific Publishing.*

Yadav, R., Huzooree, G., Yadav, M., & Gangodawilage, D. S. K. (2025). Generative AI for Personalized Learning Content Creation. In *Transformative AI Practices for Personalized Learning Strategies* (pp. 107–130). IGI Global Scientific Publishing. DOI: 10.4018/979-8-3693-8744-3.ch005

Yang, Y. F., Tseng, C. C., & Lai, S. C. (2024). Enhancing teachers' self-efficacy beliefs in AI-based technology integration into English speaking teaching through a professional development program. *Teaching and Teacher Education, 144*, 104582. DOI: 10.1016/j.tate.2024.104582

Yankah, K. (1995). *Speaking for the Chief: Okyeame and the Politics of Akan Oratory*. Indiana University Press. DOI: 10.2979/3032.0

Ye, L., Ismail, H. H., & Aziz, A. A. (2025). Bridging the AI gap: A needs analysis of Chinese pre-service EFL teachers in developing intelligent-technological pedagogical content knowledge. [AWEJ]. *Arab World English Journal, 16*(1), 59–80. DOI: 10.24093/awej/AI.4

Yesilyurt, Y. E. (2023). AI-enabled assessment and feedback mechanisms for language learning: Transforming pedagogy and learner experience. In *Transforming the language teaching experience in the age of AI* (pp. 25–43). IGI Global. DOI: 10.4018/978-1-6684-9893-4.ch002

Yeung, C., Yu, J., Cheung, K. C., Wong, T. W., Chan, C. M., Wong, K. C., & Fujii, K. (2025). A Zero-Shot LLM Framework for Automatic Assignment Grading in Higher Education. arXiv preprint arXiv:2501.14305.

Yingsoon, G. Y., Zhang, S., & Chua, N. A. (2025). Empowering educators in the era of next-generation AI: Redefining the teacher's role in an AI-enhanced learning environment. In Tan, S., & Lim, R. (Eds.), *Teachers' roles and perspectives on AI integration in schools* (pp. 1–30). IGI Global Scientific Publishing., DOI: 10.4018/978-1-6684-9999-0.ch001

Yin, H., Khan, S., Alharbi, A., & Nazir, S. (2022). Assessing english teaching linguistic and artificial intelligence for efficient learning using analytical hierarchy process and technique for order of preference by similarity to ideal solution. *Journal of Software (Malden, MA)*. Advance online publication. DOI: 10.1002/smr.2462

Yin, X., & Dou, K. (2025). An AI-assisted critical thinking intervention to enhance undergraduate EFL learners' writing proficiency. *Studies in Educational Evaluation*, *86*, 101480. DOI: 10.1016/j.stueduc.2025.101480

Yu, P., Shen, D., Meng, S., Lee, J., Yin, W., Cui, A. Y., Xu, Z., Zhu, Y., Shi, X., Li, M., & Smola, A. (2025). *RPGBENCH: Evaluating large language models as role-playing game engines*. arXiv. https://arxiv.org/abs/2502.00595

Yunjiu, L., Wei, W., & Zheng, Y. (2022). Artificial Intelligence-Generated and Human Expert-Designed Vocabulary Tests: A Comparative Study. *SAGE Open*, *12*(1), 21582440221082130. Advance online publication. DOI: 10.1177/21582440221082130

Zakaria, N. Y. K., Hashim, H., & Jamaludin, K. J. (2025). Exploring the impact of AI on critical thinking development in ESL: A systematic literature review. *Arab World English Journal (AWEJ) Special Issue on Artificial Intelligence*, 330-347.

Zakraoui, J., Saleh, M., Al-Maadeed, S., & Alja'am, J. M. (2020). Evaluation of Arabic to English Machine Translation Systems. 11th International Conference on Information and Communication Systems, (ICICS). https://doi.orgDOI: 10.1109/ICICS49469.2020.239518

Zakraoui, J., Saleh, M., Al-Maadeed, S., & Alja'am, J. M. (2021). Arabic Machine Translation: A Survey with Challenges and Future Directions. *IEEE Access : Practical Innovations, Open Solutions*, *9*, 161445–161468. DOI: 10.1109/ACCESS.2021.3132488

Zaugg, T. (2024). Embracing Innovation in Education: Investigating the Use and Impact of Artificial Intelligent Assistants Among Preservice Teachers.

Zawacki-Richter, O., Marín, V. I., Bond, M., & Gouverneur, F. (2019). Systematic review of research on artificial intelligence applications in higher education–where are the educators?. *International Journal of Educational Technology in Higher Education, 16*(1), 1-27. DOI: 10.1186/s41239-019-0171-0

Zawacki-Richter, O., Sari, B. C., & Bai, J. Y. H. (2025). Towards reproducible systematic reviews in Open, Distance, and Digital Education—An umbrella mapping review. *Review of Education*, *13*(1), e70031. Advance online publication. DOI: 10.1002/rev3.70031

Zeide, E. (2019). Artificial intelligence in higher education: Applications, promise and perils, and ethical questions. *EDUCAUSE Review*, *54*(3), 31–39.

Zhang, K., & Aslan, A. B. (2021). AI technologies for education: Recent research & future directions. Computers and education. *Artificial Intelligence*, *2*, 100025.

Zhao, Y. (2024). The exploration of artificial intelligence in pronunciation teaching. In *Proceedings of the 1st International Conference on Data Science and Engineering* -- Volume 1*: ICDSE* (pp. 127--131). SciTePress. DOI: 10.5220/0012829100004547

Zhao, W., Popkewitz, T. S., & Autio, T. (Eds.). (2023). *Epistemic colonialism and the transfer of curriculum knowledge across borders: Applying a historical lens to contest unilateral logics*. Routledge.

Zhao, X. (2022). Leveraging artificial intelligence (ai) technology for english writing: Introducing wordtune as a digital writing assistant for efl writers. *RELC Journal*, *54*(3), 890–894. DOI: 10.1177/00336882221094089

Ziewitz, M. (2019). Rethinking algorithmic accountability. *Information Communication and Society*, *22*(7), 944–961.

Zimmerman, B. J. (2013). Theories of self-regulated learning and academic achievement: An overview and analysis. *Self-regulated learning and academic achievement*, 1-36.

Zimmerman, T. (2023). Fiction as a Spider's Web? Ananse and Gender in Karen Lord's Speculative Folktale *Redemption in Indigo*. In Ferly, O., & Zimmerman, T. (Eds.), *Chronotropics: Caribbean Women Writing Spacetime* (pp. 271–289). Palgrave Macmillan. DOI: 10.1007/978-3-031-32111-5_15

Zou, B., Du, Y., Wang, Z., Chen, J., & Zhang, W. (2023). An investigation into artificial intelligence speech evaluation programs with automatic feedback for developing EFL learners' speaking skills. *SAGE Open*, *13*(3), 21582440231193818. DOI: 10.1177/21582440231193818

Zuboff, S. (2019). *The age of surveillance capitalism: The fight for a human future at the new frontier of power*. PublicAffairs.

Zughoul, M. R., & Abu-alshaar, A. M. (2005). English/Arabic/English Machine Translation: A Historical Perspective. *Meta: Translators'. Journal*, *50*(3), 1022–1041.

About the Contributors

Yasir Al-Yafaei holds a PhD in Education from the University of Exeter, UK. He is currently the Deputy of the Assistant Vice Chancellor for Postgraduate Studies Scientific Research and Innovation at the University of Technology and Applied Sciences, Salalah. His research interests include English language teaching, technology-enhanced language learning, critical thinking skills, and the role of culture in foreign language education.

Nayef J. Jomaa is an assistant professor in Applied Linguistics at the University of Technology and Applied Sciences-Salalah, Sultanate of Oman. He has several years of teaching experience in Syria, Saudi Arabia, Malaysia, and Turkey. His research interests focus on L2 writing, academic writing, genre analysis, and Systemic Functional Linguistics (Functional Grammar), AI in language learning and teaching.

Rais Ahmed Attamimi is a Senior Lecturer in Applied Linguistics at the University of Technology and Applied Sciences in Salalah, Sultanate of Oman. He holds a PhD in Applied Linguistics from the Malaysian University of Science (USM) and has nearly two decades of experience in linguistics education, research, translation, proofreading, and editing. His research interests include sociolinguistics, psycholinguistics, language identity, motivation, and academic literacies, with a focus on integrating theoretical knowledge into practical applications.

***

Senthil Kumar A is a dedicated academic professional in the Department of Computer Science with Data Analytics at Sri Ramakrishna College of Arts and Science. With a strong foundation in data-driven technologies and a passion for teaching, he specializes in areas such as data analytics, machine learning, and programming. SenthilKumar is known for his student-centered approach, integrating real-world applications and analytics tools to enhance classroom learning. His commitment to academic excellence and continuous learning contributes to the development of future-ready graduates in the evolving field of computer science and data analytics.

Munir Ahmad is a seasoned professional in the realm of Spatial Data Infrastructure (SDI), Geo-Information Productions, Information Systems, and Information Governance, boasting over 25 years of dedicated experience in the field. With a PhD in Computer Science, Dr. Ahmad's expertise spans Spatial Data Production, Management, Processing, Analysis, Visualization, and Quality Control. Throughout his career, Dr. Ahmad has been deeply involved in the development and deployment of SDI systems specially in the context of Pakistan, leveraging his proficiency in Spatial Database Design, Web, Mobile & Desktop GIS, and Geo Web Services Architecture. His contributions to Volunteered Geographic Information (VGI) and Open Source Geoportal & Metadata Portal have significantly enriched the geospatial community. As a trainer and researcher, Dr. Ahmad has authored over 50 publications, advancing the industry's knowledge base and fostering innovation in Geo-Tech, Data Governance, and Information Infrastructure, and Emerging Technologies. His commitment to Research and Development (R&D) is evident in his role as a dedicated educator and mentor in the field.

Sheikha Al-Buraiki is an educator with a BA and MA from Sultan Qaboos University, and a PhD from the United Arab Emirates University. She has over 20 years of experience in teaching English as a Foreign Language (EFL). She is currently an assistant professor at Sohar University in the Sultanate of Oman. Her research interests include second language teaching and teacher education.

Andi Asrifan, S.Pd, M.Pd, a distinguished figure in the realm of education, particularly in English Language Education, has made significant contributions through his extensive research, teaching, and leadership roles. As the Head of the Institute for Cooperation and International Affairs at Universitas Muhammadiyah Sidenreng Rappang and now a lecturer in Universitas Negeri Makassar (UNM), Dr. Asrifan's academic journey is marked by a rich tapestry of achievements, including a Doctor of Education in English Language Education. His work spans various facets of education, language, and technology, reflecting the diverse topics covered in his publications and research endeavors. These include, but are not limited to, 563 the impact of the COVID-19 pandemic on educational practices, methodologies in English as a Foreign Language (EFL) classrooms, and the integration of technology in teaching and learning processes. Dr. Asrifan's commitment to advancing educational standards and practices is further evidenced by his active participation in international conferences, webinars, and workshops across countries like India, the Philippines, and Pakistan. These events, organized by various institutions and associations, underscore his role as a global educator and thought leader. His dedication to professional development is also highlighted through his involvement in numerous courses and certifications in personal branding, public speaking, and literacy teaching. Moreover, Dr. Asrifan's leadership extends beyond academia into organizational and educational development, where he has served in various capacities, including as an external examiner for Ph.D. dissertations and a reviewer for scientific journals. His accolades, memberships in professional organizations, and roles as an ambassador for international associations speak volumes of his influence and commitment to fostering educational excellence and sustainable development goals globally.

Omdev Dahiya is working as an Assistant Professor in the School of Computer Science & Engineering, Lovely Professional University, Phagwara, Punjab, India. He holds a Ph.D. in Computer Science & Engineering from Maharshi Dayanand University, Rohtak, Haryana, India. With over 5 years of experience in teaching and research within the field of Computer Science & Engineering, he has published over 45 research articles indexed in Scopus and Web of Science databases. Additionally, he has supervised numerous UG/PG students and is currently overseeing the work of two Ph.D. scholars, with one already awarded their Ph.D. He has been a session chair and technical program committee member at various national and international conferences. He also serves as a potential reviewer for several international journals, including IEEE ACCESS, Heliyon, Recent Advances in Electrical & Electronic Engineering, and Social Sciences & Humanities Open. He is currently working in various domains of computer engineering which includes Data Mining, Learning Analytics, Cloud Computing, and soft computing approaches involving advanced AI/ML techniques.

Viji Gripsy J. is an Associate Professor in the Department of Computer Science with Cognitive Systems at PSGR Krishnammal College for Women, Coimbatore. She earned her Ph.D. in Computer Science from Bharathiar University in 2015 and completed a postdoctoral fellowship at Srinivas University in 2024. With over a decade of academic experience, her research focuses on mobile ad-hoc networks, wireless sensor networks, cybersecurity, and AI-driven healthcare systems. Dr. Gripsy has authored more than 60 publications, including journal articles, conference papers, and book chapters, and holds an h-index of 6 with over 100 citations. Her notable projects include developing Tamil speech-enabled mobile interfaces for children with learning disabilities, funded by the Indian Council of Social Science Research and GRG Trust. She actively contributes to academic governance, serving on Boards of Studies for multiple institutions, and is recognized in the AD Scientific Index 2025 for her contributions to mobile ad-hoc and wireless sensor networks.

Sandeep Gupta is presently working as an Associate Professor at Graphic Era (Deemed to be University), Dehradun (India). He has a total of 15 years of experience. His areas of interest in research are the application of artificial intelligence to power system control design, FACTS devices, renewable energy, power electronics, and stability of power systems with machine learning. He is a member of numerous professional organizations, including IE, IRED, IDES, IAENG, IAER, and the Society of Professional Engineers. He has been the author or co-author of more than 130 papers published in international journals and presented at different national and international conferences. He is currently guiding the research scholars under Machine Learning, Control & Power Systems, Wireless Technology, and the Internet of Things.

Sajed S. Ingilan is an Associate Professor V and AB English Language Program Head at the University of Southeastern Philippines (USeP), where he teaches linguistics and Mindanao studies. He is the Chief Editor of the Southeastern Philippines Journal of Research and Development, a Q2 Scopus-indexed journal. Educated at USeP and University of the Philippines Diliman, he is a certified writer and editor by the National Book Development Board-Philippines and associate member of the National Research Council of the Philippines. To give voice to what has been silenced in the discourse of the majority, he has been involved with government-funded research and extension projects about and for the indigenous cultural communities, which he has presented in onsite fora in the United States of America, Malaysia, Thailand, Taiwan, Vietnam, Indonesia, and the Philippines and published in Scopus and Web of Science-indexed journals and books.

SindhuK. is a dedicated faculty member in the Department of Information Technology at Sri Ramakrishna Engineering College, Coimbatore. With a strong academic background and a passion for teaching, she specializes in areas related to software development, data analytics, and emerging technologies in IT. Ms. Sindhu is committed to fostering innovation and critical thinking among her students, guiding them toward academic excellence and practical expertise. She actively participates in research, workshops, and technical events, contributing to the advancement of both the department and the institution.

Sandeep Kanaujia is pursuing his PhD from United University Rawatpur Jhalwa, Prayagraj, India. He is the assistant Professor in United Group of Institution and teaching in various department of engineering since 2011. He has published over many papers in reputed journals and conference and chapters also .He has many numbers of National and international Patent design, copyrights and grants. Attended many Conferences, Workshops and Seminar. Work as Reviewer and organiser for many conferences. Received best paper award as well as key note speaker.

Khalefa Kheder is a PhD candidate specialised in Applied Linguistics. He has several studies on SLA and vocabulary learning.

Appala Raju Korada is an Associate Professor of English in the Department of Foreign Languages Education at Tashkent State University of Economics, Tashkent, Uzbekistan. Dr. Raju holds an M.A., PGDL, and Ph.D. in English, along with PGCTE and PGDTE qualifications from the English and Foreign Languages University, Hyderabad. An accomplished academic, he has participated in numerous workshops, presented papers at national and international conferences, and published 16 research papers in reputed journals. He has also edited a book and continues to contribute actively to the field of English studies. He previously served at Andhra University, Visakhapatnam, Andhra Pradesh, and gained international teaching experience at Jazan University in the Kingdom of Saudi Arabia. His academic interests span World Literature, English Language Teaching (ELT), and Action Research. Known for his commitment to teaching, research, and community engagement, he is highly respected by both students and colleagues.

L. Sheeba Lakshamana is an Assistant Professor in the Department of BCA at PSGR Krishnammal College for Women, Coimbatore. She holds a Ph.D. in Computer Science from Bharathiar University, with research focused on enhancing intrusion detection systems for wireless sensor networks. With over a decade of teaching experience, her areas of expertise include networking, wireless sensor networks, and cybersecurity. She has authored several research papers, holds a patent related to lung cancer detection using intelligent image pattern recognition, and has been part of projects funded by the GRG Trust. Dr. Sheeba also contributes to academic administration, serving as the Eco-watch Club Coordinator and NAAC Criteria III Coordinator, and is actively involved in professional bodies such as The Indian Science Congress Association.

Papi Naidu Mavidi is currently working as Assco. Professor of English in the Department of English at Aditya Institute of Technology and Management, Tekkali, Andhra Pradesh. He completed MA in English Language and Literature from Andhra University M.Phil&Ph.D from Acharya Nagarjuna University. He also got qualified APSET. His interested research areas are Indian Writing in English, English Language Teaching and Black Literature. He has passion for creative reading and writing. He has been training thousands of students in terms of academic English as well as communicative English for many years. He has published 26 research papers and 3 book chapters in international journals. He is also one of the authors for the text books prepared for B.Tech students entitled “Preparing for the Future” and “Studying for the Success”(2013).His area of research interest is English language teaching and Indian writing in English.

Brindha NV serves as an esteemed faculty member in the Department of Computer Applications at PSGR Krishnammal College for Women, Coimbatore. With a solid foundation in computer science and a passion for academic excellence, she has actively contributed to teaching, research, and student development. Her areas of expertise include artificial intelligence, data mining, and programming methodologies. Dr. Brindha is known for her engaging teaching style, mentorship, and involvement in organizing academic events and skill development programs. Her dedication to nurturing innovation and critical thinking makes her a valuable asset to the institution.

Vidhya Priya P. is a dedicated academician with a strong foundation in both computer science and business management. She holds an MBA from Avinashilingam Deemed University, Coimbatore, and earned her Ph.D. from Bharathiar University, Coimbatore, in 2010. Before transitioning to academia, she gained valuable industry experience working with a textile firm for over three years. In 2000, she joined Kongu Engineering College, where she has since built an illustrious career in research and teaching. With over 24 years of academic experience, Dr. Vidhya Priya's research interests lie in corporate finance, corporate governance, and behavioral finance. She has published 57 research papers in reputed national and international journals, including Scopus-indexed publications. Throughout her career, she has actively engaged with the academic community by attending numerous Faculty Development Programs (FDPs) at leading B-Schools, including IIM Bangalore, IIT Madras, Pondicherry University, and Mangalore University. Dr. Vidhya Priya has also presented papers at 30 national and international conferences and has organized multiple conferences, seminars, FDPs, workshops, and training programs. She has successfully completed two ICSSR-sponsored projects focused on start-up entrepreneurship and the Stand-Up India Scheme for entrepreneurs.

Ashish Kumar Pandey is a Assistant Professor in the Department of Civil Engineering at United College of Engineering and Research, Prayagraj, India. He holds a B.Tech and M.Tech in Civil Engineering. His current research focuses on sustainable pavement materials, cool pavement technology, and recycled waste utilization in concrete. He has published several papers in peer-reviewed journals and conferences.

Shahodat Rakhimova began her career as an English language teacher at Urgench State University in 1998 and later joined TSUE, where she steadily progressed from teacher to senior teacher, department head, and eventually departmental leader. She also served as the Director of the "Ma'mun Educational Centre" from 2017 to 2020, strengthening her expertise in educational management. Dr. Rakhimova holds bachelor's and master's degrees in English and German philology, along with a bachelor's degree in World Economy and International Economic Relations. She is currently a PhD student at the Research Institute named after Q. Niyozi. Her academic contributions include research articles, conference presentations, and publications in national and international journals. Recognized for her service, she has been honored with the Medal of the President of Uzbekistan and a Diploma from the Ministry of Higher Education, Science and Innovations. She is an active member of ELT@I and currently leads the Attestation Committee at TSUE.

Francis N. Reginio is an academic and social advocate specializing in policy analysis, human capital development, and community empowerment. He serves as Head of the Institute of Languages and Creative Arts at the University of Southeastern Philippines and Managing Editor of the Southeastern Philippines Journal for Research and Development (SPJRD), a Scopus-indexed journal. His research focuses on inequality, displacement, and Indigenous Peoples in conflict-affected Mindanao. He has contributed to policy reforms, government-funded projects, and extension programs, including Pangandoy, a community-based education approach for the Bagobo-Tagabawa, promoting cultural preservation, peacebuilding, and sustainable development.

Vivit Rosmayanti, S.Pd.I., M.Pd was born in Botta on June 26, 1987. She has over 10 years of experience teaching at the University. She obtained a bachelor's degree in English Education from Alauddin State Islamic University. She completed her master's and doctoral degrees in English Education from Makassar State University. She is currently a lecturer in the Post Graduate Program, Department of English Education at Makassar State University, South Sulawesi, Indonesia. She is also actively writing research articles to be published in nationally and internationally accredited journals. She has written in some chapter books, monographs, and reference books. She is interested in teaching methods for teaching English. Her research interests include language teaching methodology, ICT instruction, and ESP teaching. She can be contacted at email: rosmayantivivit@gmail.com

Kamalam KS is a dedicated Assistant Professor in the Department of Computer Applications at PSGR Krishnammal College for Women, Coimbatore. With a strong academic background and a passion for teaching, she has made significant contributions to the field of computer science through research, publications, and academic guidance. Her areas of interest include data analytics, machine learning, and cloud computing. Dr. Kamalam is known for her commitment to student-centered learning and active participation in departmental activities, workshops, and curriculum development. Her blend of academic rigor and practical insight continues to inspire and empower young women in the tech domain.

VetrivelSC is a faculty member in the Department of Management Studies, Kongu Engineering College (Autonomous), Perundurai, Erode Dt. Having experience in Industry 20 years and Teaching 16 years. Awarded with Doctoral Degree in Management Sciences in Anna University, Chennai. He has organized various workshops and Faculty Development Programmes. He is actively involved in research and consultancy works. He acted as a resource person to FDPs & MDPs to various industries like, SPB ltd, Tamilnadu Police, DIET, Rotary school and many. His areas of interest include Entrepreneurship, Business Law, Marketing and Case writing. Articles published more than 100 International and National Journals. Presented papers in more than 30 National and International conferences including IIM Bangalore, IIM Kozhikode, IIM Kashipur and IIM Indore. He was a Chief Co-ordinator of Entrepreneurship and Management Development Centre (EMDC) of Kongu Engineering College, he was instrumental in organizing various Awareness Camps, FDP, and TEDPs to aspiring entrepreneurs which was funded by NSTEDB – DST/GoI

Satya Prakash Singh has been working in the field of electronics as an Assistant Professor for more than 17 years. A research enthusiast in the area of the fundamentals of electronics, communication and antenna design and simulation for modern communication technology.

Vadym Slyusar is a Doctor of Sciences, Professor, and Honored Worker of Science and Technology of Ukraine He is the author of over 1,030 publications, including 72 copyright certificates and patents (www .slyusar .kiev .ua). As a scientific advisor and supervisor, he has guided 17 Candidates of Sciences and PhD and 2 Doctors of Sciences, cultivating the next generation of researchers in critical technological domains. Prof. Slyusar introduced novel matrix operations that are now widely applied in AI and statistical data processing. His contributions have led to new research directions in data transmission, as well as technological advancements in both hardware and software, including augmented and mixed reality systems. He demonstrated ability to identify emerging trends ahead of their time and transform abstract concepts into implementable and efficient solutions.

Ravi Srivastava has been working in the field of electronics as Assistant Professor for more than 14 years. A research enthusiast in the area of communication, integrated circuits & digital design suitable for modern communication technology.

Guna Sekar T., currently working as Associate Professor in the Department of Electrical and Electronics Engineering, Kongu Engineering College, Erode, Tamilnadu, India. He completed his Bachelor Degree in Electrical and Electronics Engineering, Bharathiar University, Coimbatore during 2004 and Master Degree in Power Systems Engineering, Anna University, Chennai during 2007. He also completed his PhD in Anna University, Chennai during 2014. He has published more than 45 papers in various International Journals and Conferences. His area of interest includes, Power Systems, Machines, Networks, Power Quality and Medical Analysis. Four research scholars have completed their PhD and three scholars are currently pursuing PhD under his guidance. He also has an industrial experience of two years. He received various awards in state and national level. He also acted as resource person in various institutes.

Pradeep Kumar Tiwari is working as Assistant Professor in United college of Engineering and Research, Prayagraj. He has over 18 years of experience in academics. He has published many papers in the field of Electrical and Electronics Engineering. His area of interest is the application of Electrical engineering towards renewable and sustainable energy systems.

SabareeshwariV. currently serves as Assistant Professor in Department of Soil Science, Amrita School of Agricultural Sciences, Coimbatore. Having more than 5 years of research experience and more than 2 years of teaching experience. She got 7 awards in the field of agriculture. Her field of expertise are soil genesis, soil pedological studies as well as soil fertility mapping using advanced software like Arc GIS. She had published 22 research papers and more than 10 book chapters and books in high- impact reputed journals. She has actively participated and presented her papers in more than 20 conferences and seminars. She not only restrict her contribution only in the academic and research part, she had extension experience at farm level (lab to land) with varied crop research

BorigeVijaykumar is an experienced educator specializing in English Language Teaching, with over twelve years of dedicated classroom experience. His teaching philosophy centers on interactive and learner-centered approaches that encourage students to think critically and communicate confidently. Mr. Borige has authored and co-authored research papers focusing on Vocabulary Development and Activity-Based Learning, contributing valuable insights to the field of English Language Teaching. His scholarly work reflects a commitment to improving language pedagogy through practical, evidence-based strategies that enhance student engagement and retention. In addition to teaching, he actively participates in professional development programs and academic discussions, continuously integrating new methods to meet the evolving needs of learners. Committed to bridging theory and practice, Mr. Borige strives to create a dynamic learning environment that supports both student growth and educator collaboration.

ArunV.P. is a driven and accomplished professional with a diverse educational background and extensive hands-on experience across various industries. Graduating with honors, Arun earned his Master of Business Administration (M.B.A) with a specialization in Human Resources and Marketing from the renowned Sona School of Management in Salem in 2018, where he excelled academically with an impressive 8.3 Cumulative Grade Point Average (CGPA).Throughout his academic journey, Arun displayed an unwavering commitment to learning and personal growth, actively seeking opportunities to expand his knowledge and skills beyond the confines of traditional education. He sought practical experiences to complement his theoretical understanding, such as a 45-day summer internship focused on conducting a feasibility study for R-Doc Sustainability in the market. Additionally, Arun broadened his horizons through a 7-day industrial visit to Malaysia and Singapore, immersing himself in diverse cultural and professional environments. Arun's academic pursuits were further enriched by his involvement in hands-on projects, including a comprehensive study on Employee Job Satisfaction at Roots Cast Private Limited. His professional trajectory includes serving as a Growth Officer at Parle Agro Private Limited, where he played a crucial role in driving sales growth and market expansion. Arun is a dedicated professional, currently employed at JKKN Engineering College in the Management Studies Department. He holds expertise in his field and has contributed significantly to academia through the publication of two journal articles. Arun's work focuses on advancing knowledge and understanding in management studies, making valuable contributions to the academic community.

Index

A

C

D

E

G

H

I

L

M

N

O

P

R

www.ingramcontent.com/pod-product-compliance
Lightning Source LLC
LaVergne TN
LVHW081318300926
849161LV00008B/1806